AUGUSTO MIJARES

THE
LIBERATOR

English version by Dr. John Fisher
University of Liverpool

Prologue by Dr. Pedro Grases

**"The title of Liberator
is greater than any received by human pride."**
Bolívar to Páez, March 6, 1826.

**"The title of Liberator is the greatest of all,
and for this reason I will not demean myself by accepting a throne."**
Bolívar to Santander, September 19, 1826.

●

NORTH AMERICAN ASSOCIATION OF VENEZUELA
CARACAS, 1983

Legal Registry lf 83-0698

TABLE OF CONTENTS

PREFACE

The Bicentennial of the birth of Simón Bolívar is an event to which the North American Association of Venezuela wishes to make a unique contribution through the publication in English of the outstanding biography of Bolívar, "El Libertador," by Augusto Mijares (1897-1979).

We wish to express our gratitude to the Mendoza Foundation for its generous permission to use the unpublished translation commissioned by Don Eugenio Mendoza upon which this edition is based and to Dr. Pedro Grases for coordinating the project. Particular thanks are given to Andrés Duarte Vivas, who provided the crucial initiative. Special thanks also are given to Elizabeth Tylor and Calista Moon for their work on the translation and proofreading. And, of course, our thanks are given to the North American Association staff who provided administrative backup to all phases of the project.

Eight hundred copies of this edition are being donated to the President, Dr. Luis Herrera Campíns, who will distribute these books throughout the English-speaking world. Further distribution is also being made by those private contributors listed on the previous pages, to whom we express our deep appreciation. Finally, the North American Association has a limited number of books available.

We believe an important service is being rendered to English readers with this publication of the life of Simón Bolívar. As a leader of South American independence, Bolívar deserves to be much better known in the English-speaking world. We hope you will enjoy reading about one of the world's outstanding leaders.

JAMES F. WOOD, *President*
North American Association of Venezuela

Caracas, November 15, 1983

PROLOGUE

Don Augusto Mijares (1897-1979) was born in Villa de Cura, Venezuela on November 12, 1897 to a prominent family. He studied political science at Venezuelan Central University in Caracas, but for various reasons did not finish this career, and upon graduating from the National Pedagogic Institute in Caracas, became a teacher.

He first taught in high schools and the Pedagogic Institute, and later at Central University, founding the Faculty of Philosophy and Letters (now Humanities and Education). The University conferred upon him the degree of Doctor Honoris Causa.

Apart from teaching positions, he held the post of Director of the National Archives for two terms, and became Minister of Education in 1949. Also during his career he held two posts in the Venezuelan diplomatic service, as Chargé d'Affaires in Mexico and Ambassador to Spain. He was the foremost member of the Academies of History, Language, and Political Science. The National Prize for Literature was awarded him in 1956.

Augusto Mijares' great significance in modern Venezuelan society lies in his roles as author and educator, both of which he undertook with the same purpose: The ethical formation of the country's contemporary citizens. Everything he wrote pursues the goal of creating a reverent remembrance of the past among his countrymen, and when treating current subjects he wields arguments of historic root to justify his reasoning. He always speaks as a genuine patriot, an interpreter of the nation's past, at all times driven by desire to contribute to the betterment of the Venezuelan people. He invokes at every turn the most exemplary characteristics that Venezuelan history offers—generosity, pride, selflessness—as opposed to what America seems to exhibit—political disorder, despotism, and routine. In particular he uses as models eminent men (of which Venezuela has not been wanting) for their patriot qualities. He establishes as an essential principle: "If we draw no dynamic lesson from our history, we cannot hope to find it anywhere else." This is the strength, cause and purpose of all the admirable works published by Augusto Mijares.

He produced a dozen books in his lifetime over a span of forty years (1938-1977) plus innumerable essays and newspaper articles. Of these books the two most important are *The Venezuelan Affirmative* (1963, with further editions 1970 and 1979), and *The Liberator,* (1964, with five more editions to date).

In the series of provocative essays that make up *The Venezuelan Affirmative* Mijares devotes two to Bolívar: "The Caesarean Character and the Bolivarian Character," and "A Psychological Trauma in the Liberator's Chidhood." In the former, he establishes a fair interpretation of the aggregate of qualities in Bolívar's conduct, as exemplified by his relationships with Generals Salom, Sucre, etc., that completely dispel any distorted version that has been given his character. Virtues identify Bolívar, and not the devious creation of an absurd "force" of a non-existent Caesar. In the latter, Mijares analyzes ways in which Bolívar's childhood and early youth were reflected in his adult life and accomplishments.

In other passages of *The Venezuelan Affirmative* as well, Mijares refers to the Liberator's personality and thought, making sharp commentary on his love of country, but it is in the specific work devoted to Bolívar, *The Liberator,* that he develops his theme extensively.

We were witness to the vibrant emotion with which he wrote the pages that make up *The Liberator*. From the solitude of his study, in perfect caligraphy, came the hand-written legal-sized sheets upon which he set down the 35 chapters among which he divided, in laudable fashion, the chronological development and his personal interpretation of the life and work of Simón Bolívar. An examination of the sequence in which he arranges his study is instructive. Chapters are entitled with an historic event, or frequently with Bolívar's own words, which fit in magisterially with the theme he is developing.

He uses the love the Liberator felt for his native city (Chapter I: "Caracas is my Home Land," Bolívar had written, and whose passion, Mijares says, was as "a man loves a woman") as the starting point. In Chapters II and III he evokes scenes from Bolívar's childhood and the relationship with Simón Rodríguez, his tutor in Caracas. He then continues examining, with balanced judgement, the tableau that colonial Venezuela offered and the appearance in a political sense of the "homeland" concept. The events of pre-independence that arose, with the central figure of Francisco de Miranda, who had in mind a "vast ideal empire," are portrayed in Chapters IV to VI. Thereafter he analyzes Bolívar's first trip to Spain, his studies, and marriage to Teresa Rodríguez de Toro, and the return to Venezuela (Chapter VII).

Soon a widower, Bolívar returns to Europe, where he observes Napoleonic politics, meets influential people, and matures in his thinking, culminating in the oath on Monte Sacro (Chapters VIII and IX). Mijares then opens a series of three chapters devoted to Miranda (X, XI and XII), to proceed with Bolívar's presence in Venezuela (XIII), and the link with the 1810 diplomatic mission to London (XIV). The return to Caracas and incidents of the First Republic, with the loss of Puerto Cabello, Miranda's surrender and Bolívar's exile to Curaçao and Cartagena, where he formulates his theory of emancipation in 1812, are discussed in Chapters XV and XVI.

Mijares presents the "Admirable Campaign" (XVII), the ruin of the Republic at the hands of Boves, the flight to the eastern part of the country (XVIII), Bolívar's return to Cartagena and thence to Jamaica (XIX), his departure for Haiti to organize the Los Cayos expedition to Margarita, the failure at Ocumare, and the return to the continent on the last day of 1816 (XX). The eastern and Guayana campaign, the organization of State in Angostura, the relationship with Páez (Chapters XXI to XXIII), as well as the strategy that culminates in the battle of Boyacá (XXIV) and the liberation of Bogotá in 1819, give Mijares basis to explore the concept of independence, as projected in Bolívar's thought, with the decision to create the Great Colombia (XXV).

Bolívar contemplates the south. With a liberal triumvirate in Spain, the 1820 treaties are possible: Armistice and Regularization of the war. "These marvels," according to Bolívar. War is renewed, and liberty attained for Venezuela at Carabobo in 1821 (XXVI). Then the journey to the south: Quito and Guayaquil, where Bolívar meets San Martín in 1822, and on to Peru (XXVII and XXVIII). The Peruvian period, 1823-1826 (XXIX, XXX and XXXI) with the central victory at Ayacucho, is detailed.

The convocation of the Panama Congress and the creation of the Bolivian Constitution (XXXII) are seen destroyed by various factors, of which not the least is the tendency toward local disintegration in Peru, New Granada, and Venezuela (XXXIII and XXXIV), which reaches grave extremes and slowly induces Bolívar to renounce his power and wish to sail for Europe, a decision which is interrupted only by his death in 1830 (XXXV).

In the extensive Bolivarian bibliography, *The Liberator* occupies a place of honor, and already now, but a few years after publication, is considered a classic. With excellent documentation of sources at first hand, Mijares prepared this exegesis on Bolívar. It is not a simple biography, but rather a great commentary on the lessons that may be gleaned from a singular life, whose steps mark the order and development of the book. Fundamentally, what interests Mijares most, at each turn of events, is to infer the exemplary quality, stressing the value of model and counsel, for the conduct of American peoples. Expressed in another way, his aim is not strictly historical, nor a beautiful prose style, but rather the ethics and instruction that can be gained from the Liberator's existence. Always it is the teacher in Mijares who determines the character and intent of all he writes concerning the deeply felt subject of Simón Bolívar.

In narrating an exceptional life, Mijares is fascinated by the "bewilderment that the struggle of a great spirit with the whims of fate can produce." In his imagination, reality is forgotten and inspiration comes to the fore. But, "at times nature takes pleasure in building figures outside of habitual standards for ordinary human beings." He continues: "I reflect upon the Liberator's life. The violence of the situations, the improvised solutions, the changing and motley ornamentation, makes one think of a dramatic creation rather than an historical and psychological reality."

Limited, nevertheless, to historic truth, Mijares gives us a lively, attractive book, replete with reflections by a sociological historian seeking out the essentials of an existence from which to derive some standards and principles, illuminators of the feelings, convictions and conduct of the American people.

On more than one occasion Mijares commented to us upon the damage inflicted upon the general reader by Salvador de Madariaga, an excellent and well-documented author, protected by the prestige of his renown in the literary world. Mijares would say that a typographical error or an omission in an historical work must be corrected, and is excusable if incurred in good faith, but that the sin of perverse distortion has no excuse, since it causes irreparable damage in direct proportion to the reputation of the author who writes with indefensible prejudice.

In *The Liberator,* Mijares engages in a spirit to counteract the damage that the book by the famous essayist has created. But he is far from intoning a simple eulogy to Bolívar. He aspires to be lovingly just in his interpretation of Bolívar's character, with its good qualities and its defects, and to present a strict evaluation of the feats he accomplished.

For example, he brings out Bolívar's sense of friendship, as revealed in many Bolivarian texts. "Friendship is my passion," "Friendship is preferable to glory," and many more. And the consequence of affection toward his fellows: "When I give my trust, I give it completely." To accomplish the enormous task of emancipation, Bolívar required the aid and cooperation of many men of courageous vein, capable and willing to adhere to what Mijares calls the independence "project." Bolívar knew how to succeed in selecting the most suitable people for executing his plans and sharing responsibilities. Antonio José de Sucre is perhaps the most perfect and expressive example of intuition in the Bolivarian selection. Mijares also underlines the generosity with which the Liberator always treated his companions. Thus he managed to strengthen the sense of fellowship in the task of emancipation, which required proceeding in unity in campaigns of battle and organization of liberty. Mijares insists upon this fortitude of character in the strugglers for independence, forged of a collective will, without which they would not have triumphed.

The same fundamental virtues in the hero and in the people, with all social classes joined in selflessness and sacrifice, the same combativeness in the solder and in the lettered men such as Revenga and Roscio, such was the wall that was erected before the superb Spaniards.

Mijares recognizes in Bolívar an extraordinary ability to plan campaign strategy, utilizing the resources of the people. Uncommon gifts were required to conduct and mobilize a war of liberation in the vast South American continent, just as they were required to set down principles of government and international relations for the republics that were being created with each victory. Mijares explains Bolívar's success in these words:

"The whole emancipation movement had the same character. It could not fail because it represented an idea converted into a collective aim which could not be destroyed. It was the direct fruit, not so much of bravery and skill in battle, but more of the organizing ability of its greatest *caudillo*, and of his faith and enthusiasm. The Liberator displayed (in organizing the Peruvian campaign) as on no other occasion the best qualities of his character: foresight, activity, experience, the ability to make the fullest use of human resources, the quiet energy of the reflective man, and the imagination and courage with which he had fought the Admirable Campaign eleven years earlier."

Above Bolívar's stature as a military hero, Mijares stresses his characteristics of thinker, politician and statesman. "We must not see the Liberator simply as the leader of a successful military venture. He was the guide to the goals of justice and dignity without which the emancipation was meanningless," even though the author is resigned to write: "The men and sentiments used in the destruction of tyranny are not always the most suitable for the creation of freedom," a diagnosis that coincides with words by Andrés Bello, upon judging Bolívar's personality:

"None loved liberty more sincerely than General Bolívar, but the nature of things enslaved him like everyone else; for liberty, independence was necessary, and the champion of independence was and should have been a dictator."

Mijares summarizes Bolívar's personality in one happy phrase: "Bolívar was a rain-tree and not a bush; we watch him grow, persistently and slowly, in the midst of changes that life presented, as those trees in his native land grew destined to be great and lasting." An evocation of the last verse of Bello's fine poem, "Address to Poetry" upon referring to Bolívar, "the illustrious hero":

> For, like that rain-tree that is centuries old
> venerated by the neighboring people,
> that has seen around its corpulent trunk
> the forest many time renewed,
> and covers a vast space with its leafy
> branches, of a thousand victorious winters;
> thus your glory to the heavens is exalted,
> Liberator of the Colombian people,
> worthy that the sweet rhyme
> and elegant history is carried to far away time.

Mijares reiterates his confidence in the future upon reflecting that in the emancipation period "were displayed virtues fundamental to our peoples —tenacity, patience, selflessness, spiritual discipline and faith—that perhaps another great voice can convoke anew."

Mijares' thought has been labeled pessimistic, but in reality it is nothing other than the fruit of a life spent passionately serving his country with the best he felt he possessed: The hope and desire for the betterment of a deeply loved society, as reflected in his writings. We doubt that greater nobility or dignity is possible. Nor, would we say, greater optimism.

Caracas, 1983   PEDRO GRASES

FOREWORD
For the English edition

The emancipation of the New World must have been as interesting for Europe, in relation to the most tormenting cultural, moral and political problems of her civilization, as the discovery of those vast regions had been from other standpoints. It is sufficient to bear in mind that when Spanish America separated herself from her Mother Country, the republican and democratic system of government had been consolidated only in the United States of North America.

The European thinkers found themselves faced with numerous countries of mixed race but basically of European formation that were about to reconstruct political models forgotten for centuries in Europe itself, where they had been invented and where both their legitimacy and the possibilities of their survival were now being excitedly discussed.

A multitude of problems—racial, educational, social, economic and even religious—were involved in the bold initiative that this continent was trying to carry forward. This world of fundamental questions is the one in which the Liberator, Simón Bolívar, lived. Since it was he, among all the leaders of his epoch, who most vehemently and sincerely made these questions his own, his personality possesses a unique character, far superior to that which would be due him, with all justice, as a military genius.

I wrote the present biography guided by this image; and it is this that makes me think that for readers of any nation or race this work of mine will possess the universal and eternal interest that the great adventures of the human spirit never lose.

With regard to my judgement of what Bolívar was intrinsically, I must point out that the classic representation of Justice as a blindfolded statue with a balance in her hand does not attract me. I prefer the aggressive justice of the saints and heroes; that which attended by love, generosity and enthusiasm, and with open eyes, is ready to examine the world like a living goddess; not that which waits on a throne for the oppressed to bring their petitions, but that which goes out to seek them.

This was the justice in which Bolívar believed. He should be judged accordingly, rather than in the balance of the unfeeling statue.

AUGUSTO MIJARES

I

CARACAS
IS
MY HOMELAND

As A MAN REMEMBERS A woman he has loved, so Bolívar thought of Venezuela. Some of that idealizing passion and almost physical longing shines through a letter he wrote his uncle, Esteban Palacios, from Peru in 1825. The news of his uncle's return to Venezuela, he wrote, has aroused deep emotions, "everything human in me was touched yesterday." Bolívar was then at the pinnacle of his glory, warmed by the adulation born of his unrivaled success yet awed by the responsibilities of his extraordinary power. He was offered flattery, celebrations and love, but at the same time, he bore the responsibility for a geographical expanse as large as the whole of Europe. His victories had carried him to the center of the continent, where he had to deal with problems arising on all sides. Nevertheless, his thoughts returned continually to his distant native land, "my dear Venezuela, which I adore above all things," as he wrote to the Marquis of Toro.

In another letter written in the same year to General Mariano Montilla, we read: "...my right side will be at the estuary of the Orinoco and my left side will reach the banks of the River Plate, my arms grasp a thousand leagues, but my heart will always be in Caracas." In November 1826, he tells Páez: "My sole ambition now is to serve Venezuela; I have served America too much; now it is time to dedicate all my efforts, all my anxieties to Caracas; for Caracas I served Peru; for Caracas I served Venezuela; for Caracas I served Colombia; for Caracas I served Bolivia; for Caracas I served the New World and liberty..."

But if he expresses himself with such vehemence in his days of triumph, it is even more moving when, pushed to the limits of anguish and confusion by the attacks unleashed against him, he repeats despairingly the same testimony of love. "I cannot live," he claims in August 1829, "under the burden of ignominy which oppresses me, nor can Colombia be well served by a despairing man, whose spirit they have broken and whose hopes they have destroyed forever." Yet, when he refers to those Venezuelans who offend him he writes: "I declare, nevertheless, that I do not hate them, that I am very far from wishing vengeance, and that my heart has already forgiven them, since they are my compatriots and, above all, *caraqueños*..."

These quotations come not from official statements, intended for the public, but from private letters written on a variety of occasions. They show how Bolívar always thought of Venezuela as a tangible reality, as in July, 1828, when he writes with a clear sense of commitment: "I earnestly desire to improve the fate of the people of Venezuela... they are so miserable that it is essential to relieve their suffering at any price." In November 1829, he repeats to Dr. José Angel Alamo, a close friend: "Venezuela is the idol of my heart and Caracas is my homeland." Bolívar was born in Caracas on July 24, 1783. What sort of place was the capital of the province of Venezuelan then? The Count of Segur, who visited it in 1783, noted: "The city of Caracas revealed itself to us with sufficient majesty... it appeared large, clean, elegant, and well built."

Nevertheless, for a traveler used to European capitals, Caracas, a tropical town of 35,000 inhabitants, was probably far from the majesty and elegance mentioned by the French courtier. But two circumstances gave it an enchantment and miraculously transformed it for the visitor: the beauty of its setting and the exceptional flowering of creole culture and life in Caracas.

The valley of Caracas, over 900 meters above sea level, is blessed with both a richness of tropical flora and fauna and a mild, fresh climate due to its altitude. More than a valley, it is a crease or fold, a flowery basin, in the mountain mass. North of the city, separating this basin from the sea, the mass rises 2,600 meters at the "Silla del Avila." It stretches toward the south in many moderate peaks, and one has the illusion that just beyond them lie the *llanos* region and the banks of great rivers. It is only an illusion; the true Venezuelan plains are a considerable distance from the capital. The proximity of the sea does make itself felt, however, through a wide gorge, descending to the coast from the west of the city, which channels the perturbing Caribbean wind through the range. More frequent, and better appreciated by the inhabitants, is the wind from the east, dry and silky, which arrives charged with the fragance and freshness gathered during its long sweep along the mountains, across the coffee plantations, sugar estates, orange groves, and orchards of guavas and mangoes, which extended for more than two leagues along this part of the valley.

The River Guaire, then clean and powerful, bounded the city to the south, and three streams, the Caruata, the Catuche and the Anauco, flowed through it from the north, bringing fresh mountain water for both private gardens and public fountains. These streams were lined with fruit trees, such as the custard apple, and majestic shade trees called *anaucos* by the native Caribs. On the banks of the Guaire, by contrast, only a few sparse willows grew in the open meadows, giving the landscape a touch of unexpected melancholy, but they were welcome enough companions for a pensive youth who followed the river with a book of verse in his hand or the latest "prohibited book" on politics or philosophy hidden in his coattails.

The proudest possession of the *caraqueños* is their mountain, the Avila. It is austere and majestic during the dry season when its ridges rise like naked sinews out of deep ravines. This threatening appearance does not persist. The Avila is most frequently serene, a smiling and tolerant grandfather, whiskered with white and graceful clouds. Despite its rugged appearance, the Avila is a constant enticement to the *caraqueños* who know its numerous enchanting walking places. They view it from the capital and dream of cascades, fragrant groves, and enjoying brilliant vistas of the city, or, from its top, the sea. With the first rains of May, violet spiked plants blanket the mountain's gentler slopes and, in clearings among the trees, reveal their green and lilac hues. By June, new green vegetation begins to swallow up the violet color, mingling with it to produce a shade of bronze. Green soon covers most of the mountain, broken only by a few tall trees which blossom ostentatiously, despite the constricting vegetation which surrounds them. Most of them are *araguaneyes* (Yellow Pouis) and scarlet *anaucos,* so elegant that they provided the flattering nickname, *"palo floreado,"* for a man of exceptional poise and valor.

Such was the attraction of the valley of Caracas that a mere nine years after the city's foundation in 1567 the Governor of Venezuela, Pimentel, made it the capital of the province. It was enthusiastically praised by the colonial chronicler Oviedo y Baños, who was perhaps searching for a subtle moral message when he noted that the streets "neither contain dust nor tolerate mud."

This was Caracas. But the foreign visitor was as much surprised by the intellectual curiosity and political unrest of its inhabitants as by the surrounding natural beauty. Humboldt wrote: "The numerous commercial contacts with Europe and with this Antillan Sea, which I have previously described as a Mediterranean with many mouths, have had a powerful influence upon the development of society in the island of Cuba and the fair provinces of Venezuela. In no other part of America has society taken on a more European character. The many Indian peasants living in Mexico and in the interior of New Granada have given those countries a special character, perhaps more exotic. But in Havana and Caracas, despite the larger Negro population, one feels nearer to Cádiz and the United States than in any other part of the New World."

The truth is that this public character, which Humboldt thought to be "European," was the product of strongly held values which revealed themselves in all aspects of the city's life. Official education was meager and dull, but the creoles keenly sought the opportunity to instruct themselves. The historian Baralt sharply criticized the official system of education, but praised the culture that flourished outside the schools. With understandable amazement he pointed out: "In Venezuelan no class was ever given on the history or literature of Spain," and added: "The inhabitants learned their first ideas about the humanities from foreign books. The names of Racine, Corneille, Voltaire and other celebrated French writers were better known and appreciated than those of Lope de Vega, Calderón, Garcilaso, Granada, León, Mariana and other comparable princes of Castilian literature." Perhaps we should celebrate this situation today, rather than lament it, since it accelerated the country's spiritual emancipation, and perhaps even its political independence.

At the end of the eighteenth century, many aspects of the literary and philosophical work of the University of Caracas were reformed by one of the city's inhabitants, Father Baltasar Marrero, who had never traveled outside Venezuela; indeed, he had rarely left Caracas.[1] Similarly, without any assistance from the mother country, the *caraqueños* had founded a school of music, which produced talented composers, and which performed the valuable function of bringing together all social classes. Humboldt observed: "I have found among the families of Caracas a decided taste for learning, a knowledge of the important works of French and Italian literature, and a notable predilection for music which they cultivate successfully and which, like all fine art, serves as a nucleus, attracting the various classes of society." In fact the people welcomed this development with such enthusiasm that five orchestras, each with thirty players, took part in the festivities to celebrate the first anniversary of the Declaration of Independence, of April 19, 1810.

One Caracas family, the Ustáriz, held a literary salon on the French model, where the most distinguished and enlightened citizens came together to read and converse, and at times to present their own writings. Years later Andrés Bello read there his first literary works, including a translation

---

1. *Filosofía Universitaria Venezolana* by Dr. Caracciolo Parra León. Caracas, 1933.

of Voltaire's tragedy, *Zaire*. When asked by Bolívar why he had chosen that particular book, since in his opinion it had little merit, Bello replied that it was the only book of Voltaire still not available in Spanish. This incident shows how well known to the young men of the period were the works of the French iconoclast.

Comparing the creoles with the *peninsulares,* a contemporary Frenchman, Depons, suggested: "If merit were judged by the acquisition of knowledge, the is no doubt that the Creoles would have the advantage, since the people of this country are generally superior in culture to those who come out from Spain." [1]

This flourishing of artistic and cultural life was paralleled by the development of a national spirit, which was beginning to acquire cohesion and seek political expression. We will return to this later, when discussing the rapid transformation of this tendency into a clear republican consciousness. Meanwhile, a few examples will reveal a turbulence of public life, that will surprise those who see the colonial period as an era of lethargy.

By special concession the *alcaldes* of Caracas enjoyed the privilege of governing the province during a vacancy, such as would occur when a governor died in office and his replacement was delayed by the long journey from Spain. But they were able to extend this privilege in an unforeseen way, not only enthusiastically using the formal channels to oppose appointments which seemed to involve corruption, but also having unpopular governors removed from office.

In April 1623, Gobernor Juan Tribiño Guillamas died in office and the municipal magistrates of Caracas took control of the province. Five months later, Diego Gil de la Sierpe, who had been appointed temporary governor by the *Audiencia Real* of Santo Domingo, arrived in Venezuela. This was already a clear flouting of the authority of the *alcaldes,* and the situation deteriorated as Gil de la Sierpe immediately began to commit abuses. The chronicler Blas José Terrero, certainly no sympathizer with the creole spirit of rebellion, tells us how the *cabildo* behaved: "This man (Gil de la Sierpe) was concerned only with his own interests, and his excesses soon made him odious in the city of Coro. From there he went to Caracas, where the people already knew him by reputation. On December 25, he appointed Nicolás de Peñaloza to the office of *teniente general,* and two days later organized his reception by the *cabildo,* over which he presided. Until then the *cabildo's* members did nothing to arouse suspicions, at least openly, but four days later, on the 31st, the Governor was arrested and deposed, and it was proclaimed in the streets that no-

---

1. Francisco Depons: *Voyage à la partie orientale de la Terre-Ferme, dans l'Amérique Meridionale. Translated by Enrique Planchart.* Caracas, 1930, p. 400.

body, whatever his standing, should recognize him as governor or captain-general. [1]

In 1703, Governor Nicolás Eugenio de Ponte showed signs of mental disturbance, and was declared incapable of remaining in office, but the military commander, Juan Félix de Villegas, with the backing of the *audiencia* of Santo Domingo, resisted the assumption of authority by the *alcaldes*. The *audiencia* nominated Francisco de Berroterán, Marquis del Valle de Santiago, as temporary Captain-general, but when he declined to serve, the council stepped in and handed over power to the *alcaldes*. Villegas remained hostile and, when the councilors stood firm, decided to resort to armed force. He ordered his troops to ignore the orders of the *alcaldes;* instead they turned against Villegas, rallied the people with the cry, "Treason, treason, support the King," and forced him to resign and recognize the authority of the *cabildo*.

Occasionally even the king's express orders were evaded or even openly disobeyed. In 1725, for example, when the bishop of Caracas received royal orders confirming the authority of the Captain-general, Portales, who the *cabildo* had turned out of office, the council remained adamant and, according to Depons, "sent 800 troops towards Valencia, with orders to arrest Portales and bring him to the capital."[1]: Many similar examples can be found. In Terrero's opinion "the *alcaldes* became too skillful at pushing governors out of office." Whether or not one attributes great importance to these events, there can be no doubt that they reflected the vitality and vigor of a nation nearing maturity, which was testing its strength and acquiring political experience.

As far as Caracas is concerned, the brothers Luis and Javier de Ustáriz, who organized in their home the literary salon already mentioned, clearly represented the spirit of the city's young men. They cultivated poetry, the theater and music—Humboldt called them scholars. They were to become heroes, too, since they died for their country during the war of emancipation. They were artists, scholars and heroes, or to put it more mildly, thoughtful and generous enthusiasts. Like many of the guests who came to their home, they believed with blind faith that freedom could perfect both the individual and society as a whole. They prepared themselves to live this ideal or, if necessary, to die for it.

The verses dedicated to the brothers many years later by Andrés Bello reveal how they lived. It is because he knew them intimately that the poet asks if the kindly Javier will cheer himself after death with music and poetry, as he did on earth, or whether he will prefer to converse with heroes, discussing with them the coming triumph of freedom throughout the world.

---

1. *Teatro de Venezuela y Caracas,* by Blas José Terrero. Caracas, 1926, p. 114.

LE SPECTACLE
DE
LA NATURE,
OU
ENTRETIENS
SUR LES PARTICULARITÉS
DE
L'HISTOIRE NATURELLE,
Qui ont paru les plus propres à rendre
les Jeunes-Gens curieux, & à leur
former l'efprit.

TROISIÈME PARTIE,
Contenant ce qui regarde le Ciel & les liaifons des
differentes parties de l'Univers avec les
befoins de l'homme.

TOME QUATRIÈME.

A PARIS,
Chez la Veuve ESTIENNE & Fils, rue S. Jacques,
à la Vertu.

M. DCC. XLVI.
Avec Approbation & Privilége du Roy.

LA LUNETTE DE HOLLANDE
apliquée a l'Aftronomie,
en 1609.

"The Spectacle of Nature" by the Abbé Pluche, book read by Bolívar in his
adolescence.

Today, perhaps, this seems romantic. But for those young men it was a reality for which they sacrificed everything. They made their sacrifice generously and without ostentation, since they understood the need to create a strong foundation for the Republic.

Their harmonious blend of refinement and generosity was soon forced to give way to harsh action, as Venezuela suffered almost inconceivable catastrophes: The earthquake of 1812, the war to the death, the break-up of families due to political persecution, the destruction of entire families and of all visible wealth.

But the life these young brothers personified was so consubstantial with the spirit of Caracas that, in 1827, a French traveler, P. D. Martin Maillefer, detected in the half destroyed city the same atmosphere which had impressed Humboldt: "Foreigners and Americans," he wrote, "consider the city most agreeable, and the most European of the southern continent. For many years civil war has continued the ravages of nature. The Spaniards fought a war to the death, not only against men but also against the herds and even the forests. Those citizens who managed to survive the havoc of the earthquake were forced to flee from an enemy even more implacable than the volcano. The destruction caused by the war is clearly visible, and a third of the houses are still in ruins, but this mere shadow of the old Caracas is still worth more than most of the cities in the New World; the amenity of its customs, the taste for the arts, the conscious dedication to the cause of freedom, a delightful climate and the charm of its ruins stamp this city with a special character which makes a deep impression on the mind of the traveler."[1]

The house in which Bolívar was born, the property of his parents, stood 200 meters from the city's main square. Behind it was the home of his maternal grandfather, which was situated around the corner now known as "Traposos." At the northwest corner of the same block, looking onto the southwest corner of the square, was a handsome mansion belonging to the priest Juan Félix Jerez Aristeguieta y Bolívar. The house was part of a *mayorazgo* which the priest established by order of his mother, Luisa de Bolívar y Ponte de Jerez Aristeguieta, and which eventually would belong to the future Liberator. Thirty yards to the south lived the Aristeguieta sisters, commonly known as the "Nine Muses," and the whole neighborhood was made up of other friends and relatives. This close family grouping was natural in such a small, oligarchic city, and was a result and a sign of the interlocking relationships which held it together.

---

1. P. D. Martin Maillefer: *Los novios de Caracas,* p. 154. Edition of the Presidency of the Republic, Caracas, 1955.

Although graceful and pleasant, the home of the Bolívar familiy possessed little architectural beauty, apart from its sunny inner patios, most of which had been turned into gardens, and the galleries around the main patio, which formed an agreeable cloister for informal discussions and children's games. The lofty drawing rooms were cool, even in the hottest months, and appropriately solemn for the receptions and parties which the family was obliged to give from time to time.

Some idea of the house's furniture and of the life of the family is provided by an inventory of the property of the young Simón Bolívar, made in 1795, although the list refers specifically to the *mayorazgo* property inherited by Bolívar, rather than to the house in which he was born. It includes crystal, chandeliers, mirrors, cedar bureaus inlaid with ebony, silverware, 17 cornucopias in which were placed the candles that, together with the chandeliers, lit the rooms, seven china jars, two flower vases, other pieces of porcelain and a few holy images. To illuminate the hall and the corridor there were sixteen "cedar torch-holders, each one and a quarter yards tall, with tin-plate holders for the torches. There was a twenty-one square yard dais covered with embossed leather." No doubt important visitors were entertained on this low platform, where the family would gather on special days for the servants to pay their respects.

Three sedan chairs appear in the inventory. They must have been ostentatious, since we are told that they were lined and hung with damask curtains, and the most valuable was covered with embossed leather. This type of embossed leather, *guadamacil* or *guadamaci,* was introduced to Spain by the Arabs, and took its name from Gadames in Tripoli. It is painted or embossed, sometimes with intricate designs. The sedan chair which boasted such a delicate exterior had, to quote from the list, "its cedar box in which it was kept," and we think that this would have been as large as a modern garage.

A final and important point is that "two portraits of kings" are mentioned, but we are not told their identities, nor are they referred to with respect. It would seem that for a long time they had been nothing more than decorations.

"FIRST
EMOTIONS"

BOLIVAR'S PARENTS, JUAN
Vicente de Bolívar y Ponte and María de la Concepción Palacios y Blanco,
both belonged to the best families of Caracas. The very name Simón
had a history in the colony, since Simón Bolívar was the name of the
first of his ancestors to emigrate to America. He was known as Simón
de Bolívar the Elder, to distinguish him from his son, Simón de Bolívar
the Lad.
Both reached Venezuela near the end of the sixteenth century, but
the father soon returned to Spain to act as representative at court for
the cities of Caracas, Coro, Maracaibo, Trujillo, Barquisimeto, Carora
and El Tocuyo. The petitions which he took with him were intended to
promote the colony's development and secure it greater autonomy. One
of the most significant requested that the *audiencia* of Santo Domingo
should not be allowed to send judicial commissioners to Venezuela "unless their business be very pressing and serious... since the frequent
arrival of these judges wearies and molests the people, and impoverishes
them."
The importance of the Bolivars grew as they allied themselves by marriage with the families of the province's first conquerors and settlers.
One such was that of Garci-González de Silva, who so captured the public imagination that a species of bird and a fruit which bore his colors
—yellow and black— were named after him;[1] another was that of Diego

---

1. The bird is the "Gonzalito", which has yellow and black plumage, and the fruit is the
"garcigonzalo," which has yellow flesh and black seeds.

de Losada, the founder of Caracas, who was also an ancestor of the Marshal of Ayacucho, Antonio José de Sucre. Similar relationships were formed with the families of Alonso Díaz Moreno, the founder of Valencia, who was already a rich man when he went to Venezuela, Francisco Infante, another founder of Caracas, and Juan de Villegas, three times governor of Venezuela. Another ancestor of the Liberator was the fascinating Captain Andrea de Ledezma, an American Quixote, who anticipated Cervantes's hero. A few year after the foundation of Caracas buccaneers attacked the city and put its defenders to flight; only Ledezma, then an old man, remained to face them. Lance in hand, he charged on his old horse to preserve the new city's honor. He fell, pierced with wounds, but the pirates were so impressed by his extraordinary sacrifice that they formed a procession, headed by their leader with his sword held high, and carried the body back to Caracas.

Links such as these with the founders of the colony were the source of more than mere conceit. Those who were connected through their families with the hardship and struggles of the first settlers considered themselves the legitimate owners of the country, a sentiment which was one of the most important psychological elements in the formation of a national consciousness during the period of Spanish rule. In his prophetic Jamaica Letter the Liberator wrote: "The Emperor Charles V made a pact with the discoverers, conquerors and settlers of America, and this, as Guerra puts it, is our social contract. The kings of Spain made a solemn agreement with them that they should undertake the enterprise on their own account and at their own risk, expressly prohibiting them from drawing on the royal treasury. In return, they were made lords of the land, entitled to organize public administration and act as the court of final appeal, and received many other privileges and exemptions that are too numerous to mention. The King committed himself never to alienate the American provinces, inasmuch as his only jurisdiction was that of sovereign domain. Thus, for themselves and their descendants, the conquerors possessed what were tantamount to feudal holdings."[1]

Armed with this idea, the Venezuelans were far from considering themselves inferior to the Spaniards who came out from the mother country, instead they regarded them with distaste, as intruders to be kept in check. This attitude was shared by the so-called inferior classes and was extended to even the highest functionaries. In 1625, a group of mulatto rebels warned Governor Meneses: "We conquered this fair land with our bravery, our self-denial and our sacrifices. You have brought nothing

---

1. *Cartas del Libertador* (hereafter cited as *Cartas*), Volume I, p. 192.

more than your sword, and what is the sword of an adventurer worth? Think about it calmly and carefully, and make sure that your head is securely fixed to your neck."[1]

The very Laws of the Indies recorded that "to honor the persons, sons and legitimate descendants of those who fulfilled their obligation and completed their contract to found settlements, we made them *hidalgos,* and granted them all the honors and privileges which are enjoyed by the *hidalgos* and knights of these Kingdoms of Castile." The words recalled the tremendous undertaking which the conquerors had accomplished, and recognized this as the valid reason for their privileges. At the end of the colonial period, as we have seen, Depons observed the antagonism between creoles and *peninsulares.* Referring to the superiority felt by the creoles, he added: "This attitude creates in them a source of pride in having been born in the New World, and forms in them a secure affection for their native land."

The Liberator's mother, Doña Concepción, had an ancestry as illustrious as that of her husband. Her father was Feliciano Palacios y Sojo y Gil de Arratia, and her mother Francisca Blanco Heredia. Consequently she was a niece of Pedro Palacios y Sojo, the founder of the celebrated Caracas School of Music, which has already been mentioned; a man who achieved such fame in the colonial world on account of this institution that thereafter he was called simply "Father Sojo." She inherited a taste for music from her uncle, and it is known that she played the harp. In fact, both families, the Palacios and the Blanco y Heredia, were renowned for their sensibilities and intellectual leanings. Nevertheless, they also gave brave fighters to their country during the war. A particularly touching example of patriotism was provided by Josefa Palacios, a sister of Bolívar's mother. As a girl she looked after the orphan Bolívar and, although she was his senior by only nine years, it is attested to in the will of Feliciano that she and her other sister, María Ignacia, treated Simón and his brother Juan Vicente "like their own children." In 1798, she married José Félix Ribas, defender of Caracas, who earned the title of "Invincible" during the Second Republic. When he was executed by the royalists, she showed admirable fortitude. We are told: "When all of Venezuela was subjugated in 1814, a *caraqueña,* Josefa Palacios, widow of the worthy José Félix Ribas, preferred to bury herself alive rather than consent to the presence of the destroyers of her country. Although subject to attacks of dropsy, the venerable lady locked herself in a small room for six years, attended only by her servants. Her only visitor was her doctor. General Bolívar knew where she was, and at his memorable meeting with Morillo at Santa Ana, begged him to visit her when he returned to

---

1. Luis Alberto Sucre: *Gobernadores y Capitanes Generales de Venezuela,* p. 123.

Caracas, and persuade her to leave her confinement for a house to be provided at Bolívar's expense. Morillo, who seemed to repent of his crimes and want to reconcile himself with those he had abused, kept his word with Bolívar. On his return to Caracas, Morillo sent an aide to inform the widow of Bolívar's request, and to express his willingness to assist her. These overtures were repeated several times, through Morillo's aide and other people, but they were to no avail. Her reply was always the same,—"Tell your general that Josefa Palacios will not leave this place as long as her country is enslaved; she will leave only when her own people come to inform her that it is free and take her out."[1]

We should also tell a very different story about the Bolívar family. Although it deserves only a few lines, as a picturesque episode, we are obliged to present it more fully, since some writers have persisted in giving it an historical significance, basing the strangest suppositions on it. The facts are these: A hundred years before the Liberator's birth, a woman, Josefa Marín de Nárvaez, whose mother is not known, appeared on the paternal side of his family tree. She was a daughter of the rich and prominent Francisco Marín de Narváez, and, according to his will, was born of "an illustrious maiden whose name I am not mentioning for the sake of decency." A political enemy of Bolívar, the virulent Rafael Diego Mérida —the Liberator called him "el Malo", or "Evil"— claimed in a booklet that Josefa was "the daughter of Narváez and his Indian concubine, de Aroa." The information was taken from here by Riva Agüero, the man who had the shame to make a deal with the royalists after serving as President of Peru. In his *Memorias y Documentos para la Historia de la Independencia en el Perú,* a work in which he tried to justify his own conduct by slandering Sucre, Bolívar and San Martín, he gave the legend of Josefa a new twist by claiming that she was the daughter not of an Indian but of a Caracas Negress. Finally, Salvador de Madariaga, in his recent biography of Bolívar, not only accepts and adds to these distortions, but apparently in all seriousness, tries to base significant conclusions on them: "Although Bolívar was white," he writes, he had a small amount of Negro and Indian blood. Thus he was able to represent coherently a continental state of mind at a given historical moment. If his background had been different, his ideas would have been the deliria of an irresponsible demagogue or those of a madman." In other words, if Bolívar's drive as Liberator could not be explained as the resentment of a *zambo*, it would be incomprehensible to Madariaga.

This type of interpretation can be found in other of Madariaga's works. In his *Cuadro Histórico de las Indias* he tries to explain the emancipation

---

1. Story in *Biblioteca Americana,* a review published in London in 1823 by Andrés Bello and García del Río. Pedro Grases revealed it to Vicente Lecuna, who included it in his *Catálogo de Errores y Calumnias en la Historia de Bolívar,* i, p. 34.

of Spanish America in the following way: "...by a strange historical coincidence, the progressive-minded work of a few of the enlightened Spanish despots pushed the Jesuits into a strange conspiracy with the two other international brotherhoods, that of the Masons and that of the Jews, and they worked together for the destruction of the Spanish empire." Thus Madariaga sees that splendid process, which gave birth to twenty Republics in which new institutions combined with Spanish culture, solely in terms of a conspiracy and destruction. The least that one can do, by way of contrast, is to remember the words of Pitt the Elder about the rebellion of the North American colonies. He refused to be blinded by a false sense of patriotism and declared: "The Americans are legitimate children of England, not bastards, and I rejoice that America is offering resistance. Three million men whose love of liberty had decayed, who agreed voluntarily to be slaves, would be willing tools for the enslavement of everybody else."

Even if Josefa Marín de Narváez had some Indian blood, it must have been well hidden for her father to be able to claim in his will that he had begotten her by an illustrious maiden. In any case it is indeed extravagant to imagine that such "impurity" could be strong enough a hundred years later to determine the Liberator's conduct. Nevertheless, Madariaga propounds his fantastic racial argument more than once. After discussing some of Bolívar's pronouncements against Spanish despotism in America, he concludes: "If Bolívar had not had Indian blood in his veins this phrase of his would have been enough to justify his confinement in a madhouse." When one examines the long, miserable reigns of Charles IV and Ferdinand VII it is difficult to sympathize with a Spaniard who suggests that any contemporary criticism of them was exaggerated. Moreover, all liberators make the same sort of denunciations in all revolutions, and only a writer as spiteful as Madariaga is capable of basing his judgements upon them. It is also true that Spaniards themselves, even in more paeceful periods, have censured their own country even more violently. Was it not Madariaga himself who declared envy to be the key to the Spanish character? [1] And such a respected writer as Ortega y Gasset formulated the imposing synthesis that "the history of the whole of Spain, except for fleeting moments, has been the history of decadence."

Often, exaggerations like this spring from affection rather than resentment; they reflect a despair similar to that which makes a lover blaspheme at the imperfections of his loved one. They represent not cynicism but a spontaneous, unthinking moral protest against certain situations that

1. Madariaga: a comparative essay on *Ingleses, franceses y españoles.* Cited by Angel Francisco Brice in his valuable *El Bolívar de Marx ampliado por Madariaga,* Caracas, 1952, p. 7.

drive us to generalize without thinking. We Spanish Americans frequently indulge, too, in furious diatribes against each other, and those of Bolívar about Spain have no other meaning. This type of passionate despair is much more damaging when presented, as in the works of the Spaniards referred to, in terms of scientific principles. But Madariaga insists on taxing Bolívar for what he interprets as anti-Spanish sentiments, and invents for him a genealogy and a character whose only foundations are well known libels. Moreover, it is distasteful to have to prove the racial purity of the genius who dedicated his life to the cause of freedom, simply because Madariaga uses his notoriety to spread tittletattle. Even in the colonial period, when few social scandals remained hidden, the rumors were never more than unsubstantiated gossip. The Palacios themselves, Bolívar's uncles, described the matter with unembarrassed wit as "the Marín tangle." That the family lost nothing of its unblemished reputation is proved by its continuing intermarriages with the province's best families, including those with titles.

There was a wide gap between the ages of Bolívar's parents. When they married in 1773, Juan Vicente was 47 and Concepción 15. In addition to Simón they produced two older daughters, María Antonia and Juana, and another son, two years older than Simón, named Juan Vicente after his father. Another daughter died at birth. The children were orphaned while still young: their father died in January 1786, and their mother six years later. Simón lost both his parents before he was nine.

Until then he was happy. In a letter of 1825 to his Uncle Esteban Palacios he recalled his childhood: "How many recollections crowded into my mind at that instant! My mother, my gentle mother, who so resembled you, arose from the dead and stood before me. My earliest childhood, my confirmation, and my godfather at that event were focused into one as I realized that you were my second father. All my uncles, my brothers and sisters, my grandfather, my childish games, the gifts you gave me when I was innocent... all rushed back to reawaken my first emotions."

As well as these family figures who made the Liberator's early childhood so delightful, another person appears frequently in his recollections with affection and poetry: the Negress Hipólita, Bolívar's wet nurse. In a letter of July 10, 1825, Bolívar wrote from Peru to María Antonia: "I am sending you a letter from my mother Hipólita, so that you will provide her with whatever she needs. Treat her as if she were your mother, since her milk gave me life, and she was also the only father I knew." The letter is touching not only for the gentleness of its sentiments, but also because he calls Hipólita both father and mother. Usually a child's love for its father is mixed with feelings of respect and obligation, and is quite distinct from the affection it feels for its mother, who represents, above all, tenderness and encouragement —the distinction was even clearer in that epoch of strict customs. Nevertheless, Bolívar loved Hipólita in both ways, and his gratefulness to her suggests that they enjoyed a constant intimacy. In 1823, he arranged a monthly pension of thirty pesos for her, and in July, 1827, ordered that she be given a further 49 pesos. It seems that María Antonia failed to make the payments, since in September 1827, Bolívar asked José Angel Alamo to provide Hipólita with her pension, and authorized him to debit his account with the year's total. In a postscript he added, "Antonia was given the money in letters of credit for this purpose. Please be a better friend than my sister." His words show the anxiety and anger he felt at the thought that Hipólita might be in need.

The Liberator was also nursed by another woman, one from the opposite end of the social ladder, when it was found that his mother was unable to feed him. Before Hipólita's arrival, Concepcion's newborn child took his first milk from the breasts of one of her close friends, Inés Mancebo de Miyares, the wife of Fernando Miyares, who later became royal governor of the province of Maracaibo. Bolívar never forgot her, either. In 1813, he recommended her to Colonel Pulido, the Governor of Barinas, with the words: "It was she who lulled me at her breast in the first months of my life." Fourteen years later, in 1827, he wrote to Colonel Blanco, Intendent of the Department of the Orinoco: "With the greatest concern I beg of you to treat with justice my old and deserving friend, *Señora* Mancebo de Miyares, who fed me at her breast in my first days. What stronger recommendation can I make to one who understands how to love and be grateful?"[1]

We can see from the references Bolívar made to it throughout his life that his early childhood was happy and filled with affection. His father died when Simón was only two and a half, but he remembered his mother's kindness. He recalled that Hipólita served him as father and mother; he remembered the affection and the gifts of his uncle Esteban; he recommended his aunt Josefa to Morillo, despite the hostility that separated Bolívar from her husband, Ribas; and the images of his brothers and sisters, his grandfather and his godfather were all included in that rush of tenderest recollections. He felt a similar affection for his teachers, Bello, Rodríguez and Pelgrón. Even people who had entered his life for only an instant were included in these joyful memories. And, as the vast setting for the whole picture, the city of Caracas was unforgettable.

---

1. For these references see *Cartas*, iii, p. 197; v, p. 19; vi, p. 326 and vii, pp. 37-8. It was commonly said that another negress called Matea was also the Liberator's wet-nurse. But, whereas Hipólita is mentioned frequently, there is not a trace of a reference to Matea in Bolívar's correspondence. On the other hand Matea was still alive in 1883, when the centenary of his birth was celebrated, and Guzmán Blanco took her on his arm to the mausoleum. If she had been his wet-nurse, she must have been 115 in 1883 —and she was to live beyond then.

2

Perhaps this happy, secure childhood is the explanation for Bolívar's ability to give so easily his affection, respect or admiration to others. Nobody could have been further removed from the scepticism, disdain and suspicions often to be found in experienced politicians. Unlike other heroes, Bolívar was never gloomy. Even when tortured by setbacks and deceptions he was always enthusiastic and effusive.

He was ever ready to extol the virtues of others, often placing them above himself. For example, when he wanted to impress upon O'Leary Sucre's outstanding qualities, he took advantage of the occasion to praise, at the same time, four other colleagues with equal warmth. He told O'Leary: "He is one of the best officers in the army, since in him are combined the professional experience of Soublette, the generosity of Briceño, the talent of Santander and the energy of Salom. It is surprising that he is unknown and his talents remain unrecognized. I am determined to bring him into the limelight, since I am convinced that one day he will be my rival." This last reason is surprising, bearing in mind that almost all men in positions of authority, whether in government, industry, science or the arts, watch carefully to ensure that nobody is put on a level with them. But Bolívar's objective assessment of Sucre was always accompanied by enthusiasm and affection. He wrote to him in 1828: "Yes, my dear Sucre, you are one with me, except for the goodness of your heart and my good fortune." And at the end of both their lives, in May 1830, he told him: "I shall forget you only when those who love glory forget Pichincha and Ayacucho."[1]

With the same high-mindedness with which he eulogized Sucre, Santander, Salom, Briceño and Soublette, Bolívar listened to the advice of Peñalver, which, he acknowledged, had persuaded him to call the Congress of 1819, and called him Mentor and Father. Moreover, he worried like a good son about Peñalver's personal circumstances, and wrote to him frankly in May 1821: "It was with great distress that I learned of your extreme misery, since I don't have even a *maravedí* to give you. I am enclosing an order for my servant, who has my belongings, to give them to you so that you might sell them and use the money. Among them there should be some silverware which, whatever happens, will sell quickly."[2] It was with good reason that he declared: "When I give my trust, I give it completely."

Without reservation he entrusted the correction of the Angostura address to Manuel Palacio Fajardo, and accepted his suggestions. That he attributed all the virtues of his spiritual formation to Simón Rodríguez is well known, as are the affection and respect he showed towards him. He enthused over the virtue of Cristóbal Mendoza, and suffered with him in his illness and at his death as if he were his closest friend. Worried

---

1. *Cartas,* viii, p. 100 and ix, p. 267.
2. *Ibid.,* ii, p. 349.

LES INCAS,

OU

LA DESTRUCTION

DE L'EMPIRE

DU PÉROU;

PAR M. MARMONTEL.

*Historiographe de France, l'un des Quarante
de l'Académie Françoise.*

Accordez à tous la tolérance civile, non en approuvant
tout comme indifférent, mais en souffrant avec patience
tout ce que Dieu souffre, & en tâchant de ramener
les hommes par une douce persuasion.
FENELON, *Direction pour la conscience d'un Roi.*

TOME SECOND.

A PARIS,

Chez LACOMBE, Libraire, rue de
Tournon, près le Luxembourg.

M. DCC. LXXVII.

Avec Approbation, & Privilege du Roi.

"The Incas" by Marmontel, a book quoted by the Liberator in his correspondence.

about the fate of General Urdaneta, he twice offered him half his fortune. When he himself was ruined and persecuted, he showed equal trust in another friend and without hesitation told José Angel Alamo: "I will die as I was born, naked. You have money and will provide me with the means to eat when I have none." With friendly insistence he asked Salom to remain in public life, and when he agreed, thanked him as if he had done him a personal favor. "All your enemies," Bolívar told him, "I declare to be mine, since only wicked men are capable of hating virtue." [1]

He knew Doctor Vargas only by reputation, but when he met him, showed the greatest deference, invited him to his table, discussed with him the problems of popular education in Venezuela, and opened the way for him to the rectorship of the University of Caracas. Soon after he named Vargas one of his executors.

When, during Bolívar's absence in Peru, the government in Bogotá offended José Rafael Revenga, whom Santander disliked, the Liberator wrote to Santander: "The offense committed against this just man is a blow to my heart," and he ordered him to inform Revenga: "That if he wishes to join me, he will live alongside me like a brother." [2]

These effusive sentiments were extended to even the humblest people: "Do you remember," he asked Salom, "the army's joy when we shared out the bananas at Betoyes? We hadn't eaten for two days. Nevertheless, the army didn't complain. It remained steadfast in its task. . . ." He attributed the victory of Pantano de Vargas to Juan José Rondón, and on the eve of the first anniversary of the triumph wrote waggishly to Santander: "Tomorrow is the day of St. Rondón."

The Liberator was generous with praise for his enemies as well. In 1813 he fought for the first time against the Spaniard Ramón Correa. He had returned to Venezuela tormented by the atrocities being committed in his country by the royalists, and the proclamation of a war to the death was already growing in his mind yet he was still able to recognize Correa as an honorable enemy, and afterwards never failed to say so. Seven years later, in 1820, when treaties regularizing the war were signed, Bolívar wrote to his government: "I must praise the Spanish negotiators. They are all excellent men, and very human, but Brigadier Correa is outstanding, and without doubt the best man walking the earth."[3]

His outbursts of anger against those whom he considered mere political enemies soon gave way to humanity and reflection. General Mariano Montilla, a friend since childhood, became such a heated opponent that they quarreled in Jamaica for personal reasons; nevertheless, when they were reconciled the Liberator entrusted him with an important command. He

---

1. *Cartas,* v, p. 153.
2. *Ibid.,* iii, p. 272.
3. *Cartas,* ii, p. 287.

celebrated Montilla's triumphs in Magdalena. When the touchy general took offense over a detail in a letter, the Liberator charmed him with charitable explanations, and from then the bond of affection between them was never again broken. He was able to regain the support of General Santiago Mariño in a similar fashion, after they had been divided by serious disputes. As soon as the leader of the armies of the east indicated his willingness to rejoin the common Cause, Bolívar wrote to Sucre: "I strongly urge that, if General Mariño submits voluntarily, he should be treated with the greatest respect, as a man who has just performed an important service by refraining from staining Venezuela's arms with civil war." He praised and excused Santander and Córdova until the eve of the inevitable rupture with them. When he could no longer depend on the loyalty of Páez, he forgot his resentment and, pre-occupied with the need to maintain the unity of Venezuela, informed a relative: "My hope is that my relatives and friends in Venezuela have been and shall remain friendly with and support General Páez...," and he went so far as to declare, generously but suicidally: "It is better that you support him rather than me, since I have enemies whereas Páez enjoys popular support." He also recommended for service in Venezuela his adversary, later his fanatical critic, General Ayala: "General Ayala," he insisted, "has never been one of my supporters, but his integrity serves as an example to others who would judge their enemies impartially."

We will return later to a discussion of Bolívar's character. For the time being we have simply tried to sketch it in relation to the circumstances of his childhood. Although we do not share the dogmatism of those who explain the character of an adult strictly in terms of the events of his life as a child, it is possible that the Liberator's happiness as a child was the main cause of his exuberant spiritual life. This was particularly true of the spontaneity with which he bestowed affection with equal intensity on women, friends, the young men at his side, the old men who offered him advice and warnings, the humble slave whom he ennobled with the name of mother, and even inanimate objects and simple memories, such as his native city... and the people and things which helped him remember it.

Some anecdotes which circulated widely in Venezuela depicted Bolívar as a troublesome child, constantly quarreling with his guardian, Licenciate Sanz. The story went that he had been taken to live with Sanz because his ill mother was incapable of caring for him.We now have documented proof that Bolívar was never looked after by Sanz and never lived in his house. Moreover, the Liberator's precise recollections of his home life show that as a child he was not removed from the people he refers to—his mother, Hipólita, his brother and sisters, his grandfather, his aunts and |uncles—and they reveal happy emotional balance which the boy enjoyed until he lost his mother at the age of nine.

Almost all these stories about Bolívar's infancy were invented to depict him as an exceptional child. They were introduced to Venezuelan history by Arístides Rojas, an excellent narrator, who, in popularizing history enchantingly for the Venezuelans, frequently failed to restrict his imagination when he lacked documents. Both before and after him romantic historians considered it essential to give Bolívar an untamed childhood, in order to show him as a Byronic personage. In their opinion a normal child could not turn into a genius. We still have with us, even in these better informed days, writers like Madariaga, who search for fatal signs in this supposed unruliness of the Liberator. But I wish to set all of them right. According to the available documentation, Bolívar was an ordinary, normal child—normal even to the point of rebelling occasionally, as we will soon see—although it is true that even in his earliest years he was determined and tenacious.

The wealth of the Bolívar family and their spacious house must have contributed to the carefree, happy environment of his childhood which we find in the Liberator's nostalgia. All the houses in Caracas were then of one story, and their yards, or patios, had fruit trees which attracted birds. Even the wildest birds came down from the mountains, attracted by the golden and scented oranges and *guayabos* which hung there. They were a source of endless fascination for the Bolívar children, and we can imagine their cries of delight as they pointed out to each other the birds which they admired most: the *azulejos,* blue tanangers, so rapid in flight, like azure flashes of lightning among the foliage; the yellow and black *gonzalitos;* the *turpiales,* red, yellow and black, with blue-ringed eyes; the mocking-birds, who imitate bugle-calls; the *capanegra,* with its timid song like that of an apprentice canary; the daring *cristofué,* with its proud yellow breast; the *cardenales,* cardinals, dressed in rich red and black. The most admired of all were the humming-birds, or *tucusitos.* No single one resembles another in shape, size or plumage, and each with so many different colors that when the children managed to catch one they never tired of pointing out its unusual features. At times they fly so quickly that one hardly hears the hum as they cut through the air, and then sees them but an instant as they disappear like brilliant, minute darts. They can also stop instantly in full flight and hover in the air, miraculously suspended by their vibrating wings. They take their food in this way, hanging immobile in front of flowers, while their fine beaks and delicate tongues search inside them.

These tropical fruits, flowers and birds formed a mass of colors, scents and songs, a magic spectacle for the children. But they occupied themselves more with their untiring explorations among the passages and paths which joined their parents' house with that of the Palacios. A long, empty room with mysterious echoes made them tremble with thoughts of ghosts and apparitions; as they stood in front of a long-closed door, covered with cobwebs, they wondered if a garden with unseen beauties or a forgotten treasure of gold and precious stones lay behind it, or if it was the entrance to a prison where a madman or a criminal lay in perpetual incarceration. They made little huts beneath a jasmine tree, imagining themselves in the jungle, or perhaps played in an old sedan chair, pretending to be important people visiting the bishop or the marquis.

The gifts from uncle Esteban, which Bolívar later remembered, would usually be unfamiliar animals: a squirrel, a tortoise or a deer. Perhaps an ass, or even a horse, carefully selected for the first rides of Juan Vicente or Simón. It was customary for the manger at the bottom of the yard to house both fine riding horses and a cow with calf, which provided milk for the family. Another present from his uncle might have been the parrot which watched the running children from its perch, and from time to time, excited by their boisterousness, caught their attention with its sharp, deep-voiced cries: Juan, Juana, María, Simón. Unfortunately, this setting changed completely with the death of Concepción on July 6, 1792, a few days before Simón's ninth birthday. Her father, Feliciano Palacios y Sojo, took over responsibility for the children, and they began to sleep at his house, although by day they lived in their own family house. But their grandfather was ill himself by then, and when he drew up his will in August 1792, he designated separate guardians for Juan Vicente and Simón. For the eldest boy he selected Juan Félix Palacios y Blanco, and for Simón his uncle Esteban. Since Esteban was in Spain when Feliciano died, in December 1793, his brother, Carlos Palacios y Blanco, became the boy's guardian.

This was the worst thing that could have happened, since Carlos was a stern, narrow-minded man. Because of this, his own father had not chosen him as guardian for any of the children, even though he was the eldest of the Palacios Blanco, and it was only by accident that he became Simón's guardian. Moreover, he was unmarried, and was frequently away from Caracas, attending to his rural properties. It is easy, then, to picture the situation in which the eleven year-old Simón found himself. His two elder sisters had married in the year that his mother died, and the Negress Hipólita had probably gone with María Antonia. His uncle Esteban was still in Madrid, while his grandfather, the last refuge of tenderness for the children, died at the end of 1793, as we have seen. As a result, Juan Vicente and Simón were separated, as each went to live with his new guardian. So Simón was alone with the servants and the harsh Carlos. He was ill-treated and scorned when his uncle was at home, and left completely to himself during the long periods he was away in the countryside.

In view of these circumstances, there was nothing mysterious about an event which followed, although some writers have exaggerated its importance by failing to relate it to this linkage of dates and circumstances. On July 23, 1795, the eve of his twelfth birthday, Simón ran away from Carlos's house and took refuge with his sister, María Antonia. She and her husband, Pablo de Clemente y Francia, reported it to the *audiencia* the next day. The boy's neglect was such that when the tribunal began to act it could find nobody responsible for him, since Esteban, the proper guardian, was still in Spain, and Carlos, his substitute, was away from Caracas. It ordered, therefore, that Simón should stay with his sister for the time being, "instructing Juan Nepomuceno Ribas and Francisco Palacios, or whoever of them (his relatives) is responsible for his keep, to provide him with the necessary food." [1]

Carlos, however, took action to regain custody of Simón, and a clamorous lawsuit began between the two branches of the family. Carlos accused María Antonia of having encouraged the boy's flight, a possibility which would be neither surprising nor reprehensible, in view of the conditions in which he lived. The Palacios Blanco brothers believed, too, that Pablo de Clemente y Francia coveted the boy's wealth, although Pablo and María Antonia made no attempt to obtain his formal guardianship; they merely sought to be allowed to look after him. The Palacios became so violent that Esteban wrote to his brother Carlos: "Destroy the ward's income, by insisting on your rights, rather than allow these rogues to laugh at you." This excess, so repulsive at first sight, is probably less important than it seems, since Esteban, although superficial, always enjoyed the Liberator's affection. In 1830, when Bolívar was ruined and so persecuted by his political enemies that he understandably feared that he would be destitute if he went abroad, Esteban offered him 10,000 pesos, which was all he could get together. If we remember that Esteban was always short of money and feared poverty, and that by 1830 he was an old man who also felt persecuted, we see that this offer to his nephew was most generous. Probably the scandalous advice which he gave to his brother Carlos simply expressed his concern that the costs of the legal dispute would fall too heavily on his ward's income.

But Carlos's behavior was disgraceful and violent throughout the case. In one of his appearances before the tribunal, he testified: "The boy respects me and blindly submits to my authority, but I am convinced that he also feels much love and loyalty for me." This did not prevent Carlos from accusing him of being "absolutely indolent towards any kind of instruction," and attributing his flight to the wish "to escape from the

---

1. 'Expediente ante la Real Audiencia de Caracas sobre dimicilio tutelar del menor don Simón Bolívar'. *Boletín de la Academia Nacional de la Historia,* no. 149, Caracas.

decent home" in which he was kept. Similarly, despite the boy's obvious neglect, Carlos asserted hypocritically that "wards should live with their guardians, who are provided mainly for their custody, education and instruction, and also for the conservation, administration and improvement of their property." He immediately contradicted himself when he announced his intention "to put him in the house of Simón Rodríguez, master of the Public Primary School, who, as a person of well known probity and ability, professionally concerned with the education of children, can most satisfactorily provide for his instruction, keeping him always with him in his house, which is sufficiently comfortable and decent." This, too, turned out to be a lie, since, after agreeing to this arrangement, the tribunal later inspected Rodríguez's house and discovered that the following lived there with him: "his legitimate wife, María de los Santos Ronco, with three servants or domestics; his brother, Cayetano Carreño, with his wife, María de Jesús Muños, and their new-born child; Pedro Piñero and his nephew; five boy pupils deposited by their parents; Rodríguez's mother-in-law; his brother's mother-in-law, and two sisters-in-law aged eight and thirteen." This heterogeneous crowd of human beings was rather different from what Simón had known in his own house, which was still his by inheritance. Provisions were so short that "the boy declared he was regularly provided for, but his master Simón Rodríguez suggested that it would be more convenient for him to be fed from his own house, since his poverty would possibly not allow him to satisfy the boy's palate very often."

Simón's transfer from his sister's house to the boarding school was conducted in the most odious fashion. At first, an attempt was made to persuade him to go with Carlos, but he refused, "claiming that the magistrates had no right to make him live in his guardian's house... that the tribunals could dispose of his property and do what they wanted with it, but not with his person; and that if slaves had the right to choose a satisfactory owner, he at least could not be denied the right to live in the house of his choice." His sister considered this attitude a laudable example of "constancy and firmness," and she had previously declared that Simón had "extraordinary understanding and ability, and is lively and acute in understanding things," an opinion contrary to that of Carlos. According to O'Leary, who probably heard it from Bolívar himself, as a child he enjoyed joining in the conversation of adults. This, too, María Antonia might have thought a sign of his maturity, while for the stern, bachelor Carlos it would be a further proof of his disrespectful nature.

The suit was finally decided in favor of Carlos. By order of the royal *audiencia,* one of its clerks went to María Antonia's house to execute the decision at eight o'clock in the evening. Although the scene must have been awesome—the formal reading of the tribunal's order, the presence of the clerk, constables, relatives from both sides, curious on-lookers in the street and the lateness of the hour—the boy still resisted and had to be removed by force.

Pablo de Clemente and María Antonia described what happened to the *audiencia*: "For its enforcement Carlos came to my house accompanied by the said teacher at the hour arranged, that is eight in the evening. The boy still refused to leave our house, and hung on to me with cries and tears begging me not to let them take him, but Carlos took hold of him and dragged him to the street. The disturbance attracted quite a few people, including Feliciano Palacios, Carlos's brother who, seeing that the boy resisted and still held on to me, gave him a blow on the chest and made him let go." Despite this, or because of it, Simón fled from the school nine days later. Fortunately, his absence lasted only a few hours and caused no problems since he was returned peacefully by "the confessor of the illustrious bishop, who instructed me that the boy should not be punished merely for having fled," as Simón Rodríguez testified to the magistrates.

María Antonia and her husband made a strange mistake in their turn. Having given up hope of regaining custody of Simón, when the *audiencia* decided it would not be suitable "for the mentioned ward to be educated in the company of Pablo and María Antonia Bolívar, his sister, both because of her great affection (for him) and because they are too young and insufficiently experienced to overcome the problems which arise from voluntary education," they requested that the boy should be sent to the Seminary College of Caracas. This had already been proposed by the *fiscal* of the tribunal, while the *audiencia* made the atrocious suggestion that "a mature, trustworthy adult... should continually accompany Simón to the house of his teacher and outside it." Fortunately, Carlos, supported by Simón Rodríguez, resisted both this proposed virtual imprisonment and the plan to send him to the seminary. They opposed the seminary on the grounds that students there "should be and always are adults in order to withstand the hardship and toil of the community," and because they had to wear "the uniform (opa y beca) which is compulsory, but incompatible with the military uniform which Simón must always wear, since he is destined for a career in the militia." The final and most compelling reason was that the boy showed no "signs of a vocation for ecclesiastical life... which he recognizes as incompatible with the possession and enjoyment of his *mayorazgo*, which he would lose if he became a priest." The problem was unexpectedly resolved when the boy decided for himself to return to Carlos's house, and the tribunal consented to this. Although it was a very unhappy episode, it lasted for less than three months.

THE ROAD
TO PERFECTION
IS CONSTRUCTED OF
ADVANTAGEOUS
MODIFICATIONS

T HE CHILDHOOD SHOCK SUF-
fered by the young Bolívar provoked in him an emotional rather than
a rational response and had a profound influence on the rest of his life.
It has already been noted that when an attempt was made to return him
to his guardian's house the boy replied "that the tribunals could dispose
of his property and do what they wanted with it, but not with his
person; and that if slaves had the right to choose a satisfactory owner,
he at least could not be denied the right to live in the house of his
choice." The vehemence of this protest, made in 1795, is recalled by a
circular order of 1824, issued on Bolívar's express instructions to help
slaves who wished to change their owners. The order was issued at Trujillo (Peru) on March 24, 1824, and its wording is so untypical of that
normally used in official decrees that it is worth quoting in full: "All
slaves who wish to change their master, whether or not they have good
reason, and even if it is only for caprice, are to be assisted, and their
owners should allow them to do this and give them the opportunity to
request it. His Excellency orders you to give all possible protection of the
government to the poor slaves, since to deprive these miserable beings
of the sad consolation of changing their dominator is the crowning tyranny.
With this order His Excellency suspends all the laws which restrict their
freedom to choose an owner according to their will. Pass this order to
the attorney general, so that he will observe it and dispense all possible
protection to the slaves."[1]

---

1. *Decreto del Libertador*. Publicaciones de la Sociedad Bolivariana de Venezuela. Imprenta Nacional, Caracas, 1961, i, p. 289.

It is obvious that the Liberator still felt the pain of the violence he suffered when he was taken from his sister's house. To forestall the hair-splitting which might be used to evade his orders, he had no hesitation in ordering that slaves should be helped, "whether or not they have good reason." He had been taken back to his guardian's house because the law was more concerned with legal formality than with discovering what was happening in the mind and heart of the troubled boy; in 1824 he "suspended all the laws" which wronged the unfortunate Negroes, and granted them "all possible protection of the government."

This is a further proof that childhood crises are significant. Whether their effects are beneficial or harmful depends on other factors which follow in the individual's spiritual development. The human spirit, like the body, possesses the capacity to overcome or transform the adverse blows which life inevitably brings from childhood onwards. On numerous occasions the Liberator stressed the need to abolish slavery, or at least modify it, and almost invariably his declarations had a humanitarian intent which went beyond mere political considerations. In a letter to the Congress of Gran Colombia in 1821, he announced: "Those children who shall hence-forth be born of slaves in Colombia should be free, for these creatures belong only to God and to their parents, and neither God nor their parents wishes them to be unhappy."[1] He had no hesitation in risking his prestige for this cause. Commenting on his proposed Constitution for Bolivia, he said: "My treatise contains some strong ideas since I believe that the circumstances demanded them. Those without tolerance and the slave-owners will regard it with horror, but I had to speak this way, because I believe that I am right, and that on this point, politics and truth are in agreement."[2] He adopted this attitude many times because he remembered his moments of anguish as a boy, when, although apparently surrounded by every privilege, he felt as defenseless as a slave.

An important question which arises here is whether Simón in fact returned to Carlos's house of his own free will, or whether he gave in to the pressure being exerted on him from one side and the other. There is no doubt that, apart from the material pressure, the senseless lawsuit between his closest relatives could have broken the boy's spirit. That his behavior seems to have been normal thereafter suggests that at this point the beneficial influence of Simón Rodríguez on the future Liberator had begun to be felt.

The period between 1795, when Bolívar was twelve, and 1799, when, before he was fifteen, he went to Spain, is the most obscure of his life. For psychological reasons it is one of the most interesting. We know from

---

1. *Cartas,* ii, p. 321.
2. *Cartas,* v, p. 323.

his letters that he was given lessons by four teachers: Father Andújar, Guillermo Pelgrón, Andrés Bello and Simón Rodríguez. In addition, Tomás Cipriano de Mosquera, who was probably given the information by Bolívar himself, mentions Carrasco y Vides and the priest José Antonio Negrete, but it is clear that these two had no influence on Bolívar's spiritual development. The same can be said of Father Andújar who taught him mathematics. Although Andújar must have had a strong personality, since many years later Humboldt referred to him as "one of our friends," his relations with Bolívar were neither lengthy nor intimate.[1] Guillermo Pelgrón and his family were always held in esteem by the Liberator, but mainly because they, too, dedicated themselves to the service on their country. By 1814, two of Pelgrón's sons had died for this cause and another had been seriously wounded. As far as Andrés Bello is concerned, Bolívar left a piece of evidence which shows what united them as well as what separated them. He wrote to José Fernández Madriz in 1829: "Bello has just been sent 3,000 pesos so that he can go to France. I beg you not to allow this illustrious friend to be lost in the land of anarchy. Persuade Bello that Colombia is the least bad country in America, and tell him that if he wants employment there I will arrange it; he will be given a good position. His country should come first and he deserves to occupy a most important position in it. I know the superiority of this caraqueño, who is my contemporary. He was my teacher, although we were the same age, and I loved him with respect. His aloofness has kept us apart in a way, but I want us to be reconciled. I want to gain him for Colombia."[2]

Bello was only fourteen in 1795, and his ascendancy over Bolívar, which as one can see, was more of an intellectual than of an affectionate nature, must have emerged later. The true and only teacher of the Liberator was Simón Rodríguez, and we should pay full attention to the formative influence which he exercised over his pupil from their first meeting.

From his early years, under the Spanish regime, Simón Rodríguez was well known. Indeed, the respect that he enjoyed is surprising, since it must have been very difficult for a poor teacher to win recognition from that aristocratic society. For several years before the legal dispute already discussed, he had directed a public school in Caracas to which the children of Governor Guglielmi and other distinguished children of the city were sent. They included Mariano, Tomás and Juan Pablo Montilla, Leandro Palacios, Juan Paz del Castillo, Tomás Lander and Bolívar. In 1794, he had submitted to the *ayuntamiento* an ambitious study entitled *Reflexiones*

---

1. Humboldt, *Viajes*..., ii, p. 445.
2. *Cartas,* viii, p. 304.

sobre los defectos que vician la escuela de primeras letras en Ca-
racas y modo de lograr su reforma por un nuevo establecimiento.[1]
Since such initiatives were rare then, even in Spain, we should
have no hesitation in including the twenty-two year old teacher among the
thinkers who represented the country's spiritual emancipation before its
political emancipation had been achieved. Rodríguez enjoyed a reputation
as a careful and honorable man within the family of Bolívar's mother.
Although Feliciano Palacios y Sojo called him by the humble name
of clerk, he must have held him in considerable respect, since he
ordered books for him in Spain to the value of 2,088 *reales,* then a large
sum. He wrote to his son Esteban: ". . . they are for the clerk who acts for
me, Don Simón, the brother of Cayetanito Carreño. He is a very worthy
man and has sufficient ability to take care of my affairs."

In the documents dealing with Simón's flight, all witnesses praise
Rodríguez. Carlos Palacios described him as "a man of probity and
notorious ability." Referring to the school which he directed, María
Antonia Bolívar acknowledged "the well-regulated instruction and sound
wisdom of the institution and its master." The *audiencia* called him "a
subject of known probity and ability in his office." Finally, when Carlos
Palacios objected to the proposal to send Simón to the seminary, he had
no hesitation in saying: "It is difficult to see the advantage which the ward
will gain if he is installed in the seminary. Although he would be in the
care of the rector, or the vice-rector, both of whom are persons of
notable probity and sanctity dedicated to educating young men, here,
that is, in the house of Don Simón Rodríguez, the ward lives and will
continue to live under the direct supervision and control of this no less
virtuous and worthy man." This was a considerable thing to say in a period
when the priestly state did not admit comparisons.

The same documents show that when the young Bolívar announced to the
audiencia that he was willing to return to his guardian, he added the
qualification "remaining under the instruction and supervision of his
teacher Don Simón Narciso Rodríguez." In September and October 1795
respectively, Rodríguez resigned from the public school and Bolívar was
withdrawn from it. It is logical to conclude that this was so that Rodríguez
could devote all his time to the supervision and education of the boy.
This arrangement would have satisfied all parties to the dispute. Indeed
the *audiencia's* final sentence read: "In attention to what was said by
the child Don Simón de Bolívar, and the evidence of Don Pablo Clemente
y Francia, Doña María Antonia Bolívar and his guardian, Don Carlos
Palacios, the child is to live in the latter's house and remain in his charge,

---

1. *Reflections on the defects of the primary school of Caracas and method of achieving*
   its reform under a new ordinance.

as he requests. It is ordered that Don Carlos, since he is often away from this capital attending to his estates and those of his ward, should arrange for a person of standing, a priest if possible, to supervise and live with the boy, and to take charge of his education and daily attendance at his studies."

There is a further indication that Simón Rodríguez was the person chosen for this task. If his relations with the boy had ended at the time of the arranged lawsuits, it is certain that Bolívar would have retained a hateful memory of Rodríguez's house in which he had been forcibly kept in an atmosphere of poverty and promiscuity. This, however, was not the case; on the contrary, Bolívar always showed not only devotion for Simón Rodríguez but also affection and respect for his brother Cayetano and the rest of his family. In a letter to Cayetano June 27, 1825, the Liberator twice called him "my dear friend," praised Simón as a philosopher, indifferent to material things, and ended affectionately: "Next year we will go to Colombia and see each other there."[1] This was an unusual demonstration of familiarity from one so prominent.

But the clearest proof of the spiritual affinity which united them is to be seen in the unfailing veneration which Bolívar always showed towards Rodríguez. This began when Rodríguez rescued the miserable, almost embittered boy and by means of his remarkable pedagogic skill succeeded in transforming him into an enthusiastic adolescent. Ten years later, when Bolívar went to Europe as a free adult, although still young and disturbed by the crisis caused by the death of his wife and the aimlessness of his life, he sought out his former teacher on his own initiative. Together with other young Spanish Americans, he lived with him in friendly comradeship, took him to Italy, and once again submitted himself to his spiritual guidance.

In 1823, when Bolívar had already liberated a large part of America, but was terribly worried about the outcome of the Peruvian campaign and troubled by the difficulties of organizing the new states which acclaimed him as an arbiter but did not always observe his decisions, he wrote to Vice-President Santander as soon as he knew that Rodríguez had returned to America: "I have heard that a friend of mine, Simón Rodríguez, has

---

1. *Cartas*, xi, p. 281. In marked contrast is the dislike which Bolívar always showed for Carlos Palacios. Monseñor Navarro observed: "He sent only two tardy letters to Carlos, one from Bilbao, the other from Caracas itself both dry and almost acid, concerned with accounts." The second, written in 1803, when Bolívar, then free, received the accounts of his guardianship from Carlos, was more than acid. He bluntly told Carlos that he couldn't aprove the accounts without a detailed scrutiny, which would take over a month, and added: "If you had supplied the accounts when I came to the city the examination would now be over, and we would have disposed of this nuisance." One has only to remember the well known indifference of Bolívar to profit, and the constant courtesy showed in his correspondence, even to his enemies, to appreciate that this letter to his uncle was exceptional.

arrived from Paris. If this is true, provide him with whatever a wise man and a beloved friend of mine deserves. He is a perfect philosopher and without equal as a patriot. He is the Socrates of Caracas, even to the extent of suing his wife, as Socrates did with Jantipa, so as to be like him. Tell him to write to me often, and give him money on my behalf, charging it to my agent in Caracas. If he can manage it, ask him to come and see me."

He wrote to Rodríguez himself in January 1824, and began by rebuking him tenderly for not having visited him: "Oh, my teacher! Oh, my friend! Oh, my Robinson, you in Colombia! You are in Bogotá and you have neither written nor told me." He added the wonderful compliment: "You, my teacher, how closely you must have observed me, though great distances have separated us. With what elation you must have followed my steps, steps laid out long before by your very self. You molded my heart for liberty, justice, greatness and beauty." In another paragraph he provided a further proof that Rodríguez's influence was active in the years which were decisive for young Bolívar: "In short, you have seen what I have done. You have seen my thoughts in print, my soul on paper, and you must have said to yourself: 'All that is mine; I sowed this plant, I watered it, I strengthened it when it was weak...'"

When he wrote to Rodríguez in 1824, Bolívar was ill, worried and sad. Shortly before he had written to Sucre: "I am ready to fight the Spaniards to end the war in America, but no more. I am tired and old, and now I have nothing more to expect from fortune. On the contrary, I am like a rich miser, in constant fear that I will be robbed of my savings. All is fear and anxiety with me. It seems to me as if at any moment I am about to lose my reputation, which is all the reward and wealth that I have amassed at such great cost."

He was still in these uncharacteristic low spirits four months later, when he again sought Rodríguez's advice and friendship, despite the proud teacher's failure to respond to earlier approaches. In a letter of May 6, 1824, to Santander, Bolívar insisted: "Give Simón Rodríguez money on my behalf so that he can come to me. I love this man dearly. He was my teacher and my traveling companion, and he is a genius, a wonder of grace and talent for whoever knows how to recognize and appreciate such qualities. Everything I tell you about Rodríguez is nothing compared with what I leave unsaid. I would be happy if he were at my side, as every man has his weakness. Strive to get him to come and you will do me a great service, since he is very agreeable and can also be of assistance to me. I would be able to write my memoirs with his help. He is a teacher who instructs in an amusing fashion and a clerk who gives sound advice to the person who is dictating to him. For me he is everything. When I knew him he was without price. He would have had to change a very great deal for me to be mistaken. Charge the money you provide him to my account and send him to me. I need to satisfy these manly passions now that the illusions of my youth have disappeared. Instead of a mistress I want a philosopher at my side. At the moment I prefer Socrates to the beautiful Aspasia."

Bolívar was not alone in retaining such memories of Rodríguez. Another former pupil, Juan Paz del Castillo, who had reached the rank of general in 1824, passed on the news of Rodríguez's return to the Liberator in the same year, and spoke of spending the rest of his life "in his friendly company which enchanted our first years." However, although many documents reveal Rodríguez's spiritual qualities and the fact that Bolívar always sought him during his emotional crises, eminent Venezuelan historians have denied that he influenced the Liberator. This was probably attributable to the reputation for eccentricity which the incomparable teacher later acquired and to the aggresive impiety attributed to him. As a result, some writers disdained to examine his daring initiatives as a social reformer and others could not believe that Bolívar's childhood had been entrusted to the control of an unbeliever.

As far as Rodríguez's eccentricities are concerned, it has to be admitted that in his old age his natural arrogance intensified and he increasingly defied the world with a sarcasm which seemed cynical. Moreover, his mischievous nature took delight in scandalizing the most respectable people, such as Andrés Bello. But it can be proved beyond doubt that many aspects of the copious legend produced by this attitude are false, and it is reasonable to deduce from this that other parts of the fantasy have been grossly exaggerated. It was said, for example, that he gave up his paternal surname, Carreño, after a dispute over religion with his brother, Cayetano, who was a believer, and that they were never reconciled. But the papers dealing with Rodríguez's guardianship show that, although he signed himself Simón Narciso Rodríguez, he lived in the same house as his brother. Rodríguez was his maternal surname, and it was common then, even among prominent families, for some people to prefer the one to the other. It was also said that, because of his blasphemous nature, he preferred to call his children after vegetables rather than saints, but, in fact, there is no evidence that they were given odd names. The possible origin of the story is that he affectionately called a little girl, whom he introduced as his daughter, "carrot." Equally false, or at least exaggerated, is the story that Rodríguez completely deserted his wife. It is true that he did not enjoy good relations with her, as Bolívar indicated when he compared them with Socrates and Jantipa, but another of the Liberator's letters revealed that in the same period he assigned her a hundred pesos a month as soon as he began to receive a regular salary. As for his irreligion, it can be pointed out that when he discussed the possibility of Lutheran immigration to America in his work *Sociedades Americanas,* he reached a conclusion very similar to those of the most rigid Catholics: "That the plurality of religions is inadmissible in all places, at all times and in all circumstances." His burial certificate shows that he received the last sacraments. If it can be shown that the legend distorted the truth on these crucial points, is there any sense in placing much reliance on what remains of it?

It is certain that Rodríguez himself encouraged these myths to show his scorn for the prudery with which he was judged: "Explanations always seem trifles," he wrote arrogantly to Bolívar in 1826.[1] Even on the rare occasions when he deigned to justify himself, he remained defiant. Writing to friends in Ecuador who had questioned him about the supposed peculiarity of the names he gave to his children, he replied: "If I were a Jew, I would have called my sons Simón, a good Jewish name which I bear myself, or Luke, or Mark, or John, names which the Jews also use; if I were a heretic, I would have given them the names Abraham, Isaac or Jacob, which the patriarchs used many years before the coming of Christ. But the truth is that I am neither a Jew nor a heretic, and it is more than enough for me if God knows what I really am."[2]

Rodríguez's ideas on social reform seemed like eccentricities to his conservative contemporaries. In a period when Europe delighted itself with its own perfection, and other peoples sought only to import European ideas and institutions, he had the audacity to write: "Europe is ignorant, not in literature, science, arts and industry, but certainly in its politics. A brilliant curtain covers the most horrific picture of misery and vices in the old world." A century later the consequences of this misery and these vices began to make themselves apparent. And the remedy to the deep conflict which they caused has yet to be found!

Referring to the measures which the Liberator took to reform education in Bolivia, some of them under his own influence, Rodríguez wrote: "He issued a decree for the gathering together of poor children of both sexes... not in *alms houses (casas de misericordia)* to spin for the State, not in *convents* to pray for their benefactors, not in *prisons* to purge the wretchedness and vices of their parents, not in *orphanages* to spend their time learning servility, so that they will be bought by those who seek faithful servants or innocent wives... but in comfortable clean houses with rooms fitted out as workshops... Their parents were given employment if they were capable of it... Both the children and their

---

1. O'Leary, ix, p. 513.
2. *Escritos de Simón Rodríguez.* Compilación y estudio bibliográfico por Pedro Grases. Prólogo por Arturo Uslar Pietri. Caracas, 1954. See, too, J.A. Cova, *Don Simón Rodríguez. Primer Socialista Americano.* Caracas, 1947.

parents enjoyed their liberty. The children were not monks and their parents were not prisoners."

It is understandable that Rodríguez's projects, so distinct from the usual political thought of the period, and of all times, were not taken seriously, especially since their author was so aggresive in their defense. He wrote to Bolívar: "When they see me collecting poor children some think that my intention is to get myself to Heaven through the orphans... and others that I plan to deprave them so that they can accompany me to Hell. Only you, who sees the situation as I do, know that one needs new people to make republics; the most that one can expect from so-called decent people is inoffensiveness... It is possible that fate will at last come to my aid, and you will become my Queen of Spain." This comparison between himself and Columbus appears frequently in Rodríguez's writings. Although a superficial commentator might attribute it merely to simplicity or megalomania, the truth is that the repeated allusion reflected the generous, touching hope that among children, especially American children, there was a whole world to be discovered.

Perhaps this is still true! Three thousand years before the birth of Christ man was capable of conceiving and constructing marvelous edifices, and was already seeking goodwill and justice, but even today we still do not know how to educate a child. The average person knows a multitude of facts about the world in which he lives and about distant celestial bodies, but if even the wisest man lowers his gaze to his own child, he feels uncertain, as if he were faced by an unknown world. This was the enigma which obsessed the educator, Rodríguez, since he considered it the key to all human problems. Moreover, he felt it with an intensity which was full of hope. He wrote: "Today men think as they have never thought before; they hear things which they have never heard; they write as they have never written; and opinion is growing in favor of a reform which has never before been attempted, the reform of society." In this he was indomitable. Even when the Liberator had died, and he himself was an old man, miserable and oppressed by the conformity of the society in which he lived, he proclaimed: "Who can tell whether the observations of an old man, who thinks of glory rather than his funeral, might not force the Americans to open their eyes to their own fate and that of their children."

It has been suggested that Rodríguez was a follower of Rousseau. Even though fate provided him with an Emile, rich, independent and genial, who repaid him with the compliment: "You molded my heart for liberty, justice, greatness and beauty," a triumph which would have dazzled Rousseau himself, his ambition was even more grandiose. He wanted to be the teacher of poor children. "Among so many wise, talented, prosperous, patriotic men," he complained, "...there is nobody who considers poor children. Nevertheless, it is they who possess the power to provide the industry these men demand, the wealth they seek, and the army they need, in a word... the Fatherland." As if he felt he had the strength to carry all the problems of the continent on his shoulders, he demanded: "Give me the poor boys, or those whom the *hacendados* free at birth, or those they abandon as stupid idiots; give me those who are thrown out by the foundling hospital..."

If this was not going to be done, why was America emancipated? To create paper republics without "new people"? Why was the new world so ready to accept the morality and ideas of Europe, to renounce its own destiny and agree to combine its own problems with the anthill of "misery and vices" which swarmed behind Europe's glittering facade? Today we can understand the implications of these questions, but then Rodríguez could address himself only to Bolívar, with the desperate cry: "You know it because you see things as I do."

Many of these ideas were still unformed when the young teacher entered the Bolívar household with the humble title of clerk. But his project for the reorganization of primary education in Caracas indicates that he was already thinking of a wider future for his country. His demanding vision, in its turn, attracted the untapped energies of his pupil.

A consideration of the teacher's educational and political ideas gives some appreciation of what the exposure to Simón Rodríguez meant to the young Bolívar in those times of crisis. His rough guardian, Carlos, in a letter to Esteban Palacios, said that the boy should be treated firmly, but Rodríguez on the contrary insisted "a man cannot control his passion by calculation; philosophy consists of knowing rather than falsifying oneself."

He wisely and slowly dedicated himself to turning his pupil's mind away from childish pranks, so as to improve it without scarring it. His aim was not to destroy Bolívar's passions, but to give them a meaning and a purpose. He sought not to subdue the boy, as was the custom at the time, but to rearrange the vital elements of his personality in an orderly form. He proposed not to take control of his spirit, but rather to assist at its birth, carefully and skillfully to deliver it from the womb of its own confusions. It was for this reason that Bolívar later repeatedly compared him with Socrates.

Another of Rodríguez's maxims expressed the same idea of the need to accept reality in order to overcome it, to respect the shifting course of events without abandoning the effort to control one's destiny: "The road to perfection is constructed of advantageous modifications." No other single idea expresses more clearly the nature of Bolívar's character. Perfection is achieved not at a stroke, nor definitively like heavenly beatitude, but gradually, by means of acquisitions which have to be fought for and defended day by day. In fact, it is not a state, but an attitude or a way of life. By adopting it, by making "advantageous modifications," Bolívar achieved the moral greatness of the last ten years of his life. Although not all his campaigns were successful, it can be said that he was never defeated, as he was always ready to begin again with tireless faith and bravery.

This was the virtue which Bolívar preached incessantly. In his *Memoria* of December 1815, to the people of New Granada he pointed out: "The raw recruit believes everything to be lost if he loses a single battle, because he has not learned from experience that bravery, skill and steadfastness can overcome ill fortune."[1] In 1817, after three years of continuous adversity, he wrote to Briceño Méndez: "Will you not fly to break the shackles of our other brothers who are still suffering the enemy's tyranny? Yes, yes, you will fly with me even to rich Peru. Our destiny calls us to the ends of the American world... Fortune cannot fail those whom death cannot intimidate."[2] He even found a French proverb which expressed the same idea when he wrote to Santander in 1820: *"A force de forger on devient forgeron."*[3] When he was in Peru he not only had to fight an enemy who could raise 20,000 men, but also had to calm civil strife and to revive the spirit of the republicans. Nevertheless, he wrote to Santander: "The picture is horrifying, but I am not afraid, since we are accustomed to seeing the most horrible phantoms, which disappear as we draw near them."

During the first period that Rodríguez and Bolívar lived together, the greatest reward for the teacher must have been to observe the"advantageous modifications"which the boy increasingly made. The Liberator remembered him as "a prodigy of grace and talent... a teacher who instructs in an amusing fashion." Rodríguez would also have felt triumphant to see the boy taking such delight in his lessons, and particularly that he, who his pupil might have considered an inferior, was the only person who could manage him.

Many of the "foreign books," as Baralt called them, in which the creoles read about the history and literature of other countries before they knew that of Spain, and which frequently combined the enchantment of something new with the magic of the forbidden, must have revealed splendid discoveries to both master and pupil. History was still not a science, but it was more than a simple chronicle of past events. The grandiloquent "pathos" of the period gave it a particular resonance. Like one of the tragedies of Racine or Voltaire, it was an epic song, a lesson of intrepid

---

1. *Cartas,* i, p. 38.
2. *Ibid.* i, p. 250.
3. *Ibid.,* ii, p. 190.

morality, a setting for heroes and a stimulus to action. It is easy to imagine the enthusiasm with which Rodríguez—still a young man, let us not forget—used history to implant in his pupil's mind the axioms which fed his own dreams and visions. Axioms such as: "All men know that he who does nothing is above reproach, since he never errs; inactivity is an error worth many more," an argument which he was later to use in defense of the Liberator. Another, perhaps created after having read Plutarch's *Parallel Lives* together, asserted: "The man not born to undertake great deeds is never to be found in the place where they are performed." Cunning challenges like these led the pupil to think about his future, and left pointed questions engraved on his mind.

Little by little the adolescent's energy, which otherwise would have been manifested in misbehavior, was guided and controlled by his teacher's affectionate wisdom. María Antonia Bolívar complained that Carlos Palacios did nothing to prevent his ward from wandering through the city "on foot and on horse-back, and, what is worse, in the company of other boys who are not of his class." Today we should see these escapades as a lucky accident, which took him out of the artificial environment to which his social position would normally have confined him. It was during these excursions that the future Liberator acquired his skill in dealing with others, and learned to understand and love those who were to be his people, the heterogenous and dramatic people of Venezuela. We will see later how, from the first days of the Revolution, he began to reveal himself as the future leader of the masses.

It was essential, of course, to ensure that the boy's sudden emancipation did not degenerate into vulgarity, and that he would not become an irresponsible demagogue if given the opportunity to participate in the reform of society which Rodríguez believed to be imminent. His teacher understood the need to remind him continually of this danger. Beneath his premature seriousness Rodríguez often felt the surge of youth, and an irresistible sympathy drew him to the boy who, like himself, was a small boat equipped with the sails of a frigate.

Bolívar's early education is one of the themes which permits an exploration of his spiritual life and makes its events seem like fictional adventures. Despite his initiative for the reform of primary education in Caracas, Rodríguez had been hampered as a teacher by the misery and promiscuity of his house, where his pupils were exposed to the intimacies of the lives of several families, and where they were not fed adequately. But in the beautiful house of the Bolívars he found silence for reflection, gardens for thoughtful strolls, well chosen books and, above all, a pupil to whom he could dedicate himself exclusively, and such a pupil as Rousseau had asked for: An orphan, rich, healthy and of good family. The young Bolívar, for his part, found a teacher such as he had never known before: Unpedantic, enthusiastic, a pleasant companion for both strolls and lessons, so scrupulous that even the demanding Feliciano praised him for this virtue. On his lips all instruction was turned by his fiery imagination into animated evocations.

The childhood crisis which led Bolívar to flee from his guardian's house, and the subsequent contrast which he found in the company of Simón Rodríguez, was the principal cause of the minute attention which he was later to devote to the question of the education of children. It is true that this interest can be explained in political terms, as part of his long-term plans for the formation of citizens for the new republics. But his preoccupation with so many details, which he discussed like a professional educator rather than a statesman, shows that the spiritual problems of education touched him deeply. Thirty years later, when he wrote his Essay on Public Education, the enthusiasm with which he discussed his ideas revealed the importance of his childhood experiences. He wrote: "Rewards and moral punishments are the proper motivations for rational beings who are maturing; sternness and the rod should only be used on beasts." In his opinion this was the only system which "develops elevation of mind, heightening of sentiments, and decency in behavior. It contributes greatly to the formation of man's moral standard of values, creating within him this inestimable treasure and enabling him to be just, generous, humane, gentle, modest, in short, a man of principles."

The Liberator also stressed the difference between the brutal, pedantic teacher, such as most children then knew, and the generous, simple man, the "benign philosopher," whom the State should select for the formation of its future citizens: "The director of a school, that man of generous and patriotic impulses who has sacrificed his leisure and freedom to devote himself to the hard task of building citizens for the State, citizens who will defend, enlighten, sanctify and ennoble it, and who, in time, will give it sons as worthy as themselves, such a man indeed deserves the praise of his country... Of course I am not speaking of those so-called schoolmasters, those men of ordinary clay who, armed with a rod, a sinister frown and a perpetual harangue, play the part of a Pluto rather than that of a gentle philosopher.... Theirs is a school of servile minds, where among other vices, dissimulation and hypocrisy are learned, and where fear crowds every other emotion from the heart.... The government must act as it has done heretofore, selecting from the multitude not a scholar, but a man distinguished for his education and noted for the purity of his character and the naturalness of his bearing, a man who is pleasant in manner, kindly, friendly, and open-hearted; in short, one in whom there is much to emulate and little to correct.... To say to a child, we will go to school or we will see the teacher was tantamount to saying, let us go to jail or let us visit our enemy; for to place a child in school was to make of him a vile slave to fear and boredom."

The liveliness and precision of this description is surprising, particularly since it comes from an unfinished piece of work, which Bolívar left un-edited among his papers. He obviously expected too much if he thought that a wise man would take up the poorly paid profession of teacher, but he went on to insist: "A man of ability, who understands the human heart and can guide it skillfully, and a simple system, with a clear and natural method, are the effective means by which a community can make extra-ordinary and brilliant progress in a short time. If these prerequisites are lacking, precepts and labors may be multiplied in vain only to produce perplexity and confusion." He insisted on this because, anguished by the combination of tedium and fear to be found in contemporary schools, he again looked back to the memories of his childhood. His demands, in short, were nothing more than the evocation of the "pleasant-mannered, kindly, friendly and open-hearted" teacher who, in the person of Simón Rodríguez, had rescued him when he was a child.

The intimate attainments which Bolívar achieved under Rodríguez's in-fluence molded his heart for liberty, justice, greatness and beauty. One in particular of his teacher's axioms became his inseparable companion: that the road to perfection is constructed of advantageous modifications. This was the secret of his perseverance and his bravery and, in his moments of adversity, the advice which taught him how to reconcile himself with the world and with himself.

IV

THREE
CENTURIES
OF CULTURE

WHILE THE YOUNG BOLIVAR was learning to regulate the turbulent forces of his private world, a no less important, long historical process was approaching its climax in the world around him.

During the war of emancipation, the moments of intense anguish, when the Republic seemed lost and the achievements of the civilization inherited from Spain were being consumed by the horrors of the war to the death, Bolívar declared, "three centuries of culture, learning and industry have been wiped out."[1] This was a recognition of the reality of the colonial past, so different from the oft-repeated picture of an epoch of ignorance and fanaticism. The latter was a product of the aggressive rhetoric which surged up during the struggle with Spain, and of the subsequent romantic literature, both of which sought to contrast the liberty of the Republic with a black background of colonial servility. But this attitude distorted the true nature of the environment which produced the liberators.

It is misleading to continue saying that we broke the chains of bondage. The true cause of the emancipation of Spanish America was that from the middle of the eighteenth century America felt within herself a power which remained dormant in Spain. As a result, the American creoles were

---

1.   Proclamation in Caracas, 6 May 1814. See *Proclamas y discursos del Libertador.* Caracas, 1939, p. 110.

better prepared for the creation of a new world than the *peninsulares*—writers, politicians and officials—who always seemed more like their grandparents than their contemporaries.

Humboldt observed: "The youth of America has sacrificed in part its national prejudice to assume a clear predilection in favor of those nations whose culture is more advanced than that of European Spain. In these circumstances we should not be surprised that the political disturbances which have occurred in Europe since 1789 have aroused a lively interest among peoples who, for a long time, have aspired to enjoy various rights, the denial of which constitutes both an obstacle to public prosperity and a motive for resentment against the Mother Country."[1] We have already seen that the German scholar praised the European atmosphere which he found in Havana and Caracas. It impressed him so much that he referred to it again, with obvious approval, in another of his works. "To the north," he wrote, "between the *cordillera* of Venezuela and the Antillan sea are concentrated industrious cities, neat villages and carefully cultivated lands. In addition, an enthusiasm for art and scientific culture, and a refined love for civic liberty have been present in these places for a long time past."[2]

This description of the vitality of the American nations certainly does not conform with the diatribes unleashed against colonial life during and after the independence period. In fact, it is inconceivable that the intellectual and political unrest and vitality of the creoles could have been spawned overnight out of a routine, servile regime.

The Frenchman Depons, who was the agent of his government in Caracas from 1801 to 1804, analyzed the Spanish colonial system with considerable skill, and pointed out its essential difference from those created by other nations. Spain created in America true nations, with all the elements required for their own evolution, whereas "the basis of the French system, for example, has consisted of both creoles and Europeans considering the colonies as something perishable, where one goes only with the desire of obtaining riches, and from which one should depart as soon as this object has been achieved." He added: "The vocation of the French creole for the law, the church, the seclusion of the cloister, medicine or the army can be satisfied only in the Metropolis, since the colonies have no universities, faculties of law and medicine, seminaries, bishoprics, canonries, prebendaries, convents or military colleges.... Important appointments are made only in France, and a man has to return there to profit from his pride and wealth. The Spanish government on the other

---

1. Humboldt: *Ensayo político sobre el Reino de la Nueva España.* México, 1941, p. 197.
2. Humboldt: *Cuadras de la Naturaleza.* Cited by Hans Schneider in *La idea de la emancipación de América en la obra de Alexander von Humboldt,* a paper presented at the Congreso de Academias e Institutos Históricos, held in Caracas in July 1961.

TEATRO CRITICO

UNIVERSAL,

ó Discursos varios en todo género de materias,
para desengaño de errores comunes:

ESCRITO

POR EL M. I. S. D. Fr. BENITO GERONIMO FEYJOO Y MONTENEGRO

Maestro-general del Orden de San Benito,
del Consejo de S. M. &c.

TOMO PRIMERO.

Nueva impresion, en la qual van puestas las adiciones del Suplemento
en sus lugares.

CON LAS LICENCIAS NECESARIAS.

EN MADRID : En la Imprenta Real de la GACETA
Año M.DCC.LXV,

á costa de la Compañia de Impresores, y Libreros del Reyno.

"The Universal Critical Theatre" by Father Feijóo, one of the most widely read
works in the Spanish-speaking world during the XVIII century.

hand, puts no obstacles in the way of persons who have never left America, but who seek to enjoy more or less the same favors, graces and distinctions which it concedes in Europe."[1]

These observations are still of value today, 160 years later, as a rebuke and a lesson for the European colonial powers. The profound disputes which appear in the African and Asian countries which are emancipating themselves, and the consequent hatred which divides the world, are caused by those powers having always treated their overseas possessions as places to be exploited, and transplanted none of their own values to them.

But the very ease with which the American creoles lived in their own countries tended to pull them away from the Metropolis. Even before securing independence they had grown accustomed to searching in the other countries of Europe for those things which Spain was incapable of providing.

The works of eighteenth century French writers, including "prohibited" books, were better known in Venezuela than the Castilian classics. This same spirit led the creoles to found the Caracas School of Music, and the modernizer of the University of Caracas, Father Baltasar Marrero, never traveled outside Venezuela. Dr. Caracciolo Parra León demonstrated this reform of advanced humanistic studies scientifically by analyzing the university theses of the period. In addition, his work on Marrero made it clear that "modern" knowledge reached Venezuela before the introduction of free trade at the end of the eighteenth century. (Some historians have claimed that commercial reform alone caused the awakening of Venezuela.)[2]

A considerable number of books of all types reached Venezuela relatively easily. In 1794, for example, 71 cases of books from Spain and 9 from other countries arrived at Caracas.[3] We have seen earlier that on one occasion Bolívar's grandfather ordered books worth more than 2,000 *reales* for Simón Rodríguez.

It remains true, however, that education in general was very deficient. An eminent creole, the Licentiate Miguel José Sanz, complained about it to the *ayuntamiento* and identified vanity as the main factor misleading parents about the nature of the education required by their children. "Generally," he wrote, "it is considered necessary to be acquainted only with Nebrija's *Grammar,* the philosophy of Aristotle, the *Institutions* of Justinian, the *Curia Philippica,* and the theological works of Gonet and Larraga. It is considered sufficient to be able to write reports, say Mass, show off a doctorate or wear the dress of a monk or priest. Decency forbids a man to till the soil, and the mechanical arts are scorned. Out of

1. Francisco Depons *op. cit.,* p. 141.
2. Caracciolo Parra León, *op. cit.*
3. Arístides Rojas *Humboldtianas.*

mere ostentation men wear military uniform, speak bad French, and become lawyers. Some take holy orders to become respected, while others enter a monastery and take a vow of poverty precisely to free themselves from want."

Despite these defects in society, men like Sanz, who was so perceptive in his analysis and so brilliant in his denunciations, were able to emerge. Moreover, his activities indicate that society was exposed to the influence of men who were already free, and who were about to help society as a whole to emancipate itself.

Sanz added: "There are few children in Caracas who do not consider themselves more noble than the rest, boasting that they have a grandfather who is standard-bearer, an uncle who is magistrate, a brother who is monk or priest. These defects are produced by their education, and they stir up and feed family rivalries which make the citizens irrational and deceitful. Good faith, tranquillity, love and confidence cannot exist in a country where everybody tries to distinguish himself from his fellows by birth and ostentation. Instead of being taught to admire the virtues of good men and despise the vices and misdeeds of the wicked, the child hears from the lips of his parents only that Pedro is not as noble as Antonio, that Juan's family has this or that blemish, and that Diego's put on mourning dress when it was joined by marriage to the familiy of Francisco."

These words remind us of the picture of the *ancien régime* in France revealed in the Memoirs of Saint Simon. In his commentary on them, Taine wrote: "Everything was a matter of distinction, rivalries, insults... Every act was a source of honor for some and of mortification for others. Will my wife be given a place of honor? Will I ride in the royal carriages? Will I be allowed to take my carriage into the royal palace? May I wear a cloak to visit the Duke? Will I be accorded the great honor of being taken to Meudon or admitted to Marly? At my father's funeral will the preacher ask me or the officiating Cardinal to speak?"

Such extravagances were equally important when transferred to narrower, poorer surroundings. Sanz' criticism should be seen simply as a manifestation of the struggle between creole aspirations for change, essentially republican, and the courtly routine imported from Europe.

Miranda's criticisms of the best educational institutions of North America and Europe were similar to those registered by Sanz against the University of Caracas. He wrote of the University of Boston: "It seems to me that this establishment is directed more towards the production of clergymen than to the formation of useful, educated citizens, and it is certainly extraordinary that there is not a single chair of modern languages, while that of theology is the most important." In Copenhagen he observed: "Greek, Latin, natural law, history, etc., are the subjects studied, while physics and mathematics are unknown. We went to an institution founded by Borrichius.... They have his library, etc., with which they could pursue chemistry, but I was greatly surprised to see that instead they study the works of Luther in order to produce clergymen."

A further complaint frequently made against Spain is that, although the upper classes of society enjoyed a certain degree of culture, the masses remained completely ignorant. This was so throughout Europe to such a degree that at the end of the nineteenth century, despite the influence of democratic ideas, more than half of the population of England was illiterate. Similarly, in France one of the "revolutionary" ideas proposed unsuccessfully to the National Assembly in 1871 by Victor Hugo was for free, compulsory education according to Jorge Brandes. In the same period Renán ridiculed the hopes placed upon popular education. In the eighteenth century the idea that the State should educate the masses was absolutely unknown. Even Rousseau remained closely tied to a narrow aristocratic ideal as far as education was concerned. His ideal was to educate a rich, healthy, orphan youth, and to encourage a type of selection.

Initiatives to reform social conditions in Venezuela were not unknown in the eighteenth century. The chronicler Oviedo y Baños provided an indication in 1723 that popular ignorance was perhaps less absolute than is sometimes suggested when he wrote "even Negroes are ashamed if they cannot read and write." Even so, conditions were bad and efforts were made to improve them. We have seen that Simón Rodríguez presented a plan for the reform of the primary schools which did exist in 1794. In 1805, a school was created exclusively for *pardos,* and its foundation involved the discussion of important educational and social ideas, including the proposal that boys educated in the school should later become its teachers.

But the clearest indications that nationalism was acquiring surprising maturity are to be found in political unrest, which made itself evident in Venezuela from the first years of colonization.

Some of the episodes in which the creoles defended themselves against absolutism have a flavor of the best Spanish traditions about them. In 1586, for example, Governor Rojas tried to usurp the appointment of *alcaldes* from the *cabildo* of Caraballeda. Depons tells us: "Representations went unheard, but despite this when the time came for the election, the *cabildo* elected its *alcaldes* as usual. Those nominated by the governor presented themselves, but were not received. These men, so proud of their privileges, were so aroused by the abuse of authority that they showed themselves determined to defy the governor in order to preserve their prerogatives. For his part, the governor was so irritated by this attitude that he added an even greater injustice to the first, when he ordered the arrest of four councillors, who were thrown into dungeons for having fulfilled the obligations of their office. The inhabitants of Caraballeda reacted as though this injustice had been committed against each of them. All resolved to leave the town in which the law had been so criminally abused, and they left for Valencia and Caracas. The town became nothing more than a home for reptiles and birds of prey. Meanwhile, observing the system which the government had created to check violations of the law, the king censured the governor and imposed punishments which were considered sufficient to deter his successors from committing further abuses against the rights of his vassals. The councillors were freed and given all the satisfaction they could reasonably expect. The inhabitants of Caraballeda were invited to return to their homes but not one of them accepted. They replied that they would never live in a place that would always remind them of the injustice they had suffered."[1]

Some examples were given in the first chapter of the audacious methods used by the *alcaldes* of Caracas to protect their prerogative of governing the province during a vacancy. By means of this privilege creoles occupied the governorship no less than thirty times, and it would be no exaggeration to say that the leading families of Venezuela frequently controlled government long before they reclaimed it completely when they achieved independence.

These disputes reveal the rather strange combination of respect for the law and the use of force with which the Venezuelans preserved their privileges. One deposed governor was held in irons and chains, and another was reminded of this precedent as if to warn him that it was by special favor that he was not treated in the same fashion. In the case of Portales, already discussed, a determined resistance was mounted not only against the governor but also against the bishop, who was his ally: "...with great pomp the bishop presented himself to the *cabildo,* and very ceremoniously had his clerk read the royal cédula of October 15, 1723, with the aim of having Portales restored to the office of governor. The councillors replied that the *cédula* was not relevant since it referred only to Portales's first imprisonment not to his present detention, which had been ordered by the *audiencia* of Santa Fe. Portales and Escalona had foreseen that this plan would fail, and had already resolved to resort to force. When the bishop left the *ayuntamiento* he was cheered by the people gathered in the square, and at that moment the governor rode out of his palace and put himself at the head of the belligerent mob. The *alcaldes* summoned the guards and the prison garrison, and, with the support of many of their followers, marched against the governor, who was camped in the square of San Francisco. Since Portales was unpopular in Caracas, his force was small and poorly armed, while many men joined

---

1. Depons, *op. cit.,* p. 53.

the ranks of the supporters of the *alcaldes*. The latter easily won the day, and Portales took refuge in the convent of San Francisco."[1]

But the most important manifestation of nationalist sentiment in the eighteenth century was provided by the long opposition of the creoles against the Guipuzcoana Company, which was sustained for fifty years until the Company finally disappeared. This Basque business enterprise had been established by the king in order to facilitate direct communication between Venezuela and Spain and to root out contraband trade. In exchange, the Company was granted a monopoly of trade with Venezuela and a number of other economic privileges. But it soon began to interfere in political affairs, and by bribing or intimidating governors—or by having those who resisted out of honesty and rectitude dismissed—came to exercise a real tyranny. Its commissioners dictated the most important political decisions to these peninsular officials, and they also controlled the appointment of local justices who oppressed the people with abuses and impositions. The Company bought Venezuelan products for export at very low prices and charged heavily for the goods which it imported from Spain. Finally, since it was still impossible to supply all Venezuela's needs legally, the Company itself took over the contraband traffic which it was supposed to eradicate. In Caracas, according to the documents, there was "an establishment which was publicly and scandalously called the Curaçao shop."[2]

These were some of the copiously documented complaints which the aggrieved creoles sent to the king. At the same time frequent riots occurred in various towns. Some of them seem to have resembled scenes from Lope de Vega, but others were more serious, and where there was a *mulato* and negro participation, anticipated the egalitarian character of the emancipation struggle. The movements led by Juan Francisco de León in 1749 and 1751 were certainly genuine rebellions rather than simple riots. With the support of a popular army of 800 men, a large force in view of the province's sparse population, De León occupied Caracas and secured the support of the *cabildo* and the leading citizens, who declared against the Company. Although he agreed to disband his forces due to his inexperience and the wiles of the governor, and a further attempt at rebellion failed, De León succeeded in leaving all the province "disturbed

---

1. Luis Alberto Sucre: *Gobernadores y Capitanes Generales de Venezuela*. Caracas, 1928, p. 234.
2. Curaçao which belonged to the Dutch, was the source of most of the contraband which came to Venezuela. For more details of this important aspect of colonial life, see 'Boletín del Archivo Nacional', n. 85, Caracas; *Interpretación Pesimista de la Sociología Hispanoamericana*, by Augusto Mijares, Madrid, 1952; and the same author's contribution to vol. ii of the papers presented at the 'Mesa Redonda de la Comisión de Historia del Instituto Panamericano de Geografía e Historia', Caracas, 1961.

and seeking freedom", to quote one of the judges who dealt with the case. The phrase seems more like a draft for a proclamation than the expression of a judge. America was beginning to use her first subversive words.

Moreover, for the first time all social classes were joined in a common cause. De León was supported by many Canary Islanders, blue-eyed whites like himself, but also by a considerable number of half castes. When this heterogeneous mass met the members of the *ayuntamiento* and the leading citizens of Caracas at the gates of the city, the latter gave him their support, too, and declared that he was acting "in the name of the citizens of the city and province of Caracas, both nobles and commoners."[1] Subsequently, as Gil Fortoul wrote, "The Assembly met on 22 April under the presidency of the *alcaldes,* Miguel Blanco Uribe and Nicolás de Ponte, and with the richest property owners in attendance—the Marquises de Mijares, de Toro, de Torresaca, del Valle de Santiago, and members of the Bolívar, Tovar, Galindo, Solórzano, Blanco de Villegas, Ibarra, Ponte, Ascanio, Jedler, de la Madriz, and other families — agreed unanimously that the Company was prejudicial to the province and the royal treasury...."

During the period of conquest and colonization, nobles and commoners, ruined gentlemen, swineherds and simple adventurers had arrived together in Venezuela, seeking to obtain titles of nobility in return for the bravery, sacrifices and effort demanded by their task. But this promise of equality was not fulfilled: Indians, negroes and their *mestizo, mulato* and *zambo* offspring became the "lower classes," and a social structure emerged which was more unjust and more dangerous than that existing in Europe. Although the indians were not exterminated and the negroes were not condemned to indefinite slavery as in the colonies of other European powers, these social inequalities constituted an insuperable barrier to the attainment of true nationhood. The indians and the *mestizos* were officially equated with lower-class whites by Spanish legistation, but the negroid pigment was viewed as an indelible mark of inferiority. Montesquieu had written that in Europe: "The idea that God, who is such a wise being, could have put a soul, especially a good soul, in a totally black body is unacceptable...." As with many moral aberrations, the cruelty suffered by the slaves became a further motive for the contempt shown towards them; people were constantly aware of the miserable state in which they lived and their misery was used as an argument against them. Montesquieu wrote: "It is impossible for us to think of them as men, because if we did we would be forced to begin to believe that we were not Christians." As a result of this general indifference the

---

1. See the Boletín del Archivo referred to earlier, p. 40.

slaves were considered less than animals. When he was assessed for sale, a Negro was not even allowed the individuality conceded to an animal by the the phrase "a head of cattle"; he was simply a "piece" if he measured at least seven hands. Those of smaller stature were measured and the sum of their sizes was divided by seven to give the number of "pieces".[1] On one occasion an agent of the Guipuzcoana Company sought permission to unload some Negroes who were dying on board a ship that had put in at Puerto Cabello. His motive was in no way humanitarian; he was merely anxious "to protect the Royal Company against the serious nuisance which their death on board would cause it."[2]

In 1819, Bolívar pointed out to the Congress of Angostura the daring egalitarianism which would have to be practiced in order to sweep away the social dislocation caused by racial diversity. He declared: "The blood of our citizens is diverse; let us mix it to make it one." But seventy years earlier, in 1749, it must have been surprising when the "important people" of Caracas unexpectedly joined the rabble which followed De León. In previous disturbances the upper classes had been accompanied only by "their partisans"; now they joined a genuinely popular mob. Before, they had presented their complaints with subtle arguments in the tribunals or at court; now they challenged the whole apparatus which traditionally had afforded them protection. The Captain-General escaped to the coast, but the gentry remained in Caracas, participating noisily in meetings, and rubbing shoulders in the streets with the *pardos,* who arrogantly paraded past the abandoned houses of Spanish officials and Company employees, armed with lances, old muskets and *machetes.*

Some historians, having failed to study sufficient documentation, have claimed that the *cabildo* of Caracas abandoned De León after having first encouraged him. This was not the case. In fact, at the very time that the repression of the rebellion was at its height, the *cabildo* lodged a new formal complaint against the Company, and persisted with its efforts until the Company was finally abolished.

The geographical spread of the rebellion was as impressive as its all-embracing social extent. Municipal agitation appeared as far to the west as Maracaibo. In the center of the country support was forthcoming not only from Caracas and the towns where De León had a personal following, but also from the populous valleys of Aragua, whose militia marched on Caracas under the leadership of Field-Marshal Gaspar de Córdova and his brother, Sergeant-Major Lorenzo de Córdova. These same two men had led the militia in the defense of Puerto Cabello against the English in 1743, and another rebel, Mateo Gual, had driven them off

---

1. Archivo Nacional de Caracas Sección 'Capitanía General', vol. iii, ff. 269 and following.
2. *Ibid.,* f. 266.

from La Guaira. Their deeds had been hushed up so that the Spanish governor could claim the credit for these successes, and "as a result Don Gabriel José de Zuloaga was granted the undeserved title of *Excelentisimo.*" A contemporary observer, Father Terrero, enthusiastically praised the Córdova brothers as "leaders to whose valor and exertions His Majesty owes the miraculous defense recently mounted in Puerto Cabello against the English." He was indignant that their only reward for this success was to be sent to Spain as prisoners for having participated in the revolt against the Guipuzcoana Company. This evidence is particularly important, since, although a native of Caracas, Terrero did not approve of the rebellious nature of his compatriots. The revolt against the Company was the only such movement with which he sympathized.

There already existed, then, in America a genuine patriotism that was essentially creole. It operated not only against foreign invaders but also against the abuses of peninsular officials. A further feature of the incidents of these years was essentially Spanish in its nature, although the idea had disappeared in the peninsula under the weight of monarchical absolutism, while it was acquiring new strength in America. I refer to its having been provincial interests and opinion which were invoked against the Company, not the royal will, which in Spain—and in all Europe—would have been considered far more important. When De León occupied Caracas the declaration which he sought from the *cabildo* and from the "nobles and elders" was that the Company was causing "notable injury to the public and general welfare of the province." Similarly, when he summoned the townspeople to the main square he asked them "to declare who is the appellant in this suit and in whose name is he acting," and the people replied "in the name of all the inhabitants of the province." This same principle is repeated in all the documents issued against the Company.

The rebellions of 1749 and 1751 were no more than an episode in a vast commotion which disturbed Venezuela for fifty years. In these years, a continuous civic struggle developed alongside the riots and insurrections, and the political maturity and nationalist sentiment which the creoles were acquiring were clearly revealed. For example, one of the methods used by the *caraqueños* to stir up public opinion and ensure that it was heeded was to arrange in 1733 that the governor should consult "the other cities and towns of the province... so that they might declare whether or not the establishment of the Royal Company was desirable." The evidence given was hostile, but the documents "went astray" a little later when entrusted to the hands of governors sympathetic to the Company. Far from discouraging the creoles, this development gave them the opportunity to request in 1750 that "a circular order be sent to the *cabildos* and to those persons who attended the meetings held for this purpose, so that they can appoint representatives in Caracas to attend the tribunal during the hearing of the case which is in progress." This was equivalent to demanding that representatives from all over the province be allowed to attend a sort of congress of municipalities in Caracas. In fact, the *caraqueños* did not attain their objective on this occasion, but public opinion remained with them in the persistent, unanimous agitation which was to culminate in rebellion.

Details which appear here and there in the documents of the legal investigation which followed the De León rebellion are no less interesting. For example, Nicolás de León, the son of Juan Francisco and founder of the town called El Guapo, wrote to one of his followers: "So now you see that we are obliged to defend our country, since if we fail to do so we will be slaves. It is impressive that a mid-eighteenth century rural dweller in a remote colony—this is all that Nicolás de León was—could formulate the concept of "country" so clearly. In Europe nationality was still centered around the sovereign, and people were referred to as "the vassals of His Majesty" or the "subjects of the King"; the most one heard was a phrase like "the interests of the kingdom." Even in North America the idea that the country was an entity in its own right, something divorced from individual interests, and could impose obligations, was still unformed.

In the end, Juan Francisco de León was deported to Spain as a prisoner, and was declared dishonorable. The sentence ordered the destruction of his house, "and that the ground on which it stands be watered and sown with salt; where the plot adjoins the square (Plaza de la Candelaria), a stone or brick column is to be erected, visible to all, with an inscription declaring this to be the punishment ordered by His Excellency in the name of the King Our Lord." The tablet repeated that this was royal justice "enforced against Francisco de León, owner of this house, as a persistent rebel and traitor against the Royal Crown and, therefore, a criminal. It is to be destroyed and sown with salt as a perpetual reminder of his infamy."

In fact, this exaggerated punishment was of little service to the king and his representatives. Intendant Abalos reported to the court: "The natives of this land show the greatest loathing, aversion and distaste towards the names of the king, his ministers and all Spaniards. . . . The ill-will and unhappiness with which they complain intensifies daily, and if Your Majesty does not concede the freedom of trade for which they sigh he will be unable to count on their loyalty. These vassals quickly and hopefully prick up their ears at every hint or suggestion of assistance made by the enemies of the Crown, and it will be impossible or at least very difficult to remedy this situation."

The Liberator, work by the Italian sculptor Pietro Tenerani.

A further observation made by Abalos anticipated what was to happen during the war of independence. He pointed out: "This is not an empty warning, but a prediction based upon a first-hand knowledge of this land; if this part of America is lost... whoever holds this port will easily take control of the rest of the continent. Whoever dominates the provinces of Caracas and Cumaná and the island of Trinidad will be the lord of all this western part, and will easily penetrate into the rest."

Abalos was mistaken only in that he thought a foreign power would make itself master first of Venezuela and then of the rest of the continent. In fact, the power arose within Venezuela itself, which was daily moving farther away from Spain, as it sought wider intellectual horizons and as political unrest deepened. The high-born, irrepressible man who replaced the Spanish banners with new flags for five nations grew up among the creoles of Venezuela.

V

BROTHERS IN JESUS CHRIST, EQUALS BEFORE GOD

THE END OF THE EIGHTEENTH century saw the rise of that incomparable Precursor, Francisco de Miranda. He was the first Spanish American to make himself heard in Europe, where he stood alongside generals and politicians, and the first to announce the goal of a single, continental state to all America. As he traveled across Europe, sometimes in splendor and at other times in misery, he prepared himself to design this massive project by examining and studying mines, schools, ports, prisons, armies, universities, irrigation projects, libraries, fortifications, history, art and commerce. Such was his single-mindedness that his erudition frequently surprised the experts with whom he talked.

During Miranda's apprenticeship the most important development was the formation of his fascinating personality. He made himself into a classical hero and philosopher although one fortunately enlivened by a nascent romantic fervor. He was never to descend from this lofty plane, even in moments of anguish, such as occurred when he tried to impose conditions on the British government and it refused him an army. He stood firm before the Tribunal of Terror in Paris and defended himself not so much because he wanted to be pardoned, but because he sought the acclamation of the people. He defied the approach of old age to challenge Spain three times on the deserted coasts of his native Venezuela. And he always remained true to himself: when at the age of sixty-two he led raw, unruly Venezuelan troops in a sabre charge at La Victoria; during the absurd night at La Guaira, when he stood proud and indomitable before the noisy crowd; in the sinister vaults of his prison, from which he appealed for America and for his former companions, without mentioning his own sufferings; and during his final imprisonment, when, near death, he replied indifferently to the jailer who asked if his irons caused him much pain, "They trouble me less than those which I bore in La Guaira."

The fathers of both Miranda and Bolívar were among those who protested about the Guipuzcoana Company, but, although this fact is suggestive, it would be wrong to attach a symbolic significance to it.[1] Miranda himself, who was born in 1750, is obviously far more important, and we will return to him later.

The rebellious nature of the Venezuelans eventually provoked a reaction in Madrid. Soon after the *cabildo* of Caracas tried to stir up the people against Governor Portales and the bishop, the Crown created the office of *teniente de gobernador,* and, by granting to its incumbent the exercise of supreme authority during the governor's absence, effectively took away this prerogative from the *alcaldes.* But the *ayuntamiento* persisted with what Abalos called "the plausible pretext and deliberately erroneous idea that it is encharged with the welfare and interests of the public," and the government in Madrid was forced to take further steps to restrict its activities. It increased the number of *regidores* by four, and ordered that extra posts would be filled directly by the king; it insisted that one of the two *alcaldes* should always be a European Spaniard. In order to inhibit the creation of new *cabildos,* it avoided granting the title of "city" to settlements, even when they merited it. Humboldt observed that La Victoria was legally no more than a *pueblo,* although "it is difficult to imagine a village with 7,000 inhabitants, handsome buildings, a church adorned with Doric columns, and all the means of industry and commerce."[2]

Other decisions taken in Madrid, such as the refusal in 1770 to allow the creation of an *audiencia* in Venezuela, were frankly hostile.[3] In an atmosphere of reciprocal mistrust, many aspects of royal policy in this period antagonized Venezuelan opinion. One of them was the establishment of a force of *pardo* militia, which began to break down class dis-

---

1. For information on Miranda's father, see the biography of Miranda by William Spence Robertson, Ediciones Anaconda, p. 15. For Bolívar's father see 'Boletín del Archivo Nacional', n. 85, Caracas, pp. 1, 3, 5. It is interesting to note that Juan Vicente Bolívar is mentioned in some writs against the Caracas Company, since the assiduous Vicente Lecuna said that nothing was known about his activities between 1747 and 1759 (See Lecuna: *Catálogo...*, p. 19).
2. Humboldt: *Viaje...*, iii, p. 76.
3. Father Terrero considered the refusal a "punishment", although he certainly welcomed it, since he was always obsessed with "the sins of Caracas."

tinctions, by allowing the *pardos* to wear military uniforms. Traditionally, they were not allowed to carry swords or canes, nor were they permitted to use kneelers in church. *Pardo* women were prohibited from covering their heads in church (for this reason the upper-classes were given the name *"mantuanos,"* or those with mantillas). The sudden elevation of these "inferiors" to the privileges and regalia of the military state scandalized those who from habit or apprehension considered any change in society to be dangerous. The captain-general himself informed the minister of his objections against allowing white and colored militiamen to wear the same uniform. The "insolent and proud" nature of the *pardos* could lead them to forget "the most pronounced differences which exist between an ordinary white man and the most honored of them."[1]

Despite this protest, the metropolitan government took an even more radical step in 1795, when it issued a *cédula* which gave *pardos* the opportunity to obtain no less than a complete dispensation from their status, the right to be addressed as *"Don"*, and even a declaration of nobility and purity of blood, in return for the payment of specific fees. A further *cédula* ratified the scheme in 1801. These and similar innovations caused outraged reaction in Venezuela. The minutes of the *cabildo* of Caracas and its protests to the king stand out for the inhumanity of their arguments. They ascribed to the *pardos* "the infamous origin of slavery and the disgrace of illegitimacy," and argued that if they were elevated from their inferior status "they would be eligible for the public offices now reserved for whites, among other things, and would be able to occupy them without impediment, mixing on an equal basis with the whites and leading persons of greatest distinction in the republic. As a result nobody will come forward to serve in these public offices, for fear of this indignity." The *cabildo* stressed "the immense distance which separates the whites and colored, the advantage and supremacy of the former, and the meanness and subjection of the latter," and, turning back to the subject of the militia, recalled with alarm "that frequently when an officer with a little color in his face is dressed in his uniform and sword, he usurps misdirected attentions, which raise his sights to even higher things."

It is worth noting that only two or three of the creole names which were becoming prominent in Venezuela's nationalist tradition figured in the reactionary *ayuntamientos* of the late eighteenth century. In any case, although the attitude of the councillors was odious, it should not be imagined that the royal dispensations were in any way generous. They simply

---

1. Archivo Nacional, Caracas, Sección 'Capitanía General,' vi, f. 233.

involved a shameless sale of privileges and, far from moderating class distinctions, actually made them even more ridiculous and cumbersome. One order said literally: "The Bejarano Negresses are to be considered whites." This absurdity provoked such ridicule that even today one can hear in Caracas, if a ridiculous situation arises, "Yes, the Bejarano Negresses are to be considered whites."

It should also be borne in mind that the racist folly of the *cabildo* of Caracas reflected a world-wide alarm caused by the recent massacre of the whites by the Negroes of Santo Domingo. Many years later Victor Hugo told the story of how *mulatos* in the island, whose white fathers were still alive, had agreed with each other: "You kill my father, and I will kill yours." Such atrocities left Santo Domingo with a totally colored population.

In Venezuela the insurrection of the Negroes of Coro in 1795 had a marked racist character, and pillage, murders and other excesses were committed against the whites. The situation grew worse as the Spanish authorities responded with comparable ferocity. One judge wrote to the Captain-general: "I have beheaded nine of the captives, without more formality than an oral hearing." Many others suffered the same fate. The leader of the rebellion, a *zambo* by the name of José Leonardo Chirinos, was sentenced in Caracas "to death by hanging in the main square of this capital, to which he will be dragged from the Royal Prison; when he is declared dead his head and hands will be cut off; the head will be displayed in an iron cage upon a post twenty feet long on the road from this capital to the city of Coro and the valleys of Aragua; the hands will be sent to Coro itself, where one will be mounted on a post of the same height near the Caujarao, the custom-house, on the Coro-Curimagua road, and the other will be placed in similar fashion at the summit of the mountain where Don Josef de Tellería was killed."[1]

Fortunately, another movement for liberation of a totally different type demonstrated that the evolution of Venezuela towards wider forms of justice and integration had not been interrupted. I refer to the conspiracy of Manuel Gual and José María España which came to light in 1797. Both men were from distinguished families, and the former was the son of Mateo Gual, who had defended La Guaira against the English. Their movement was the first to declare independence categorically, and they proposed a democratic system for the political organization of all the continent. According to the provisional "Ordinances" which they issued, "the natural equality of all the inhabitants of the provinces and districts is declared, and it is ordered that the greatest harmony should exist between Whites, Indians, *Pardos* and Negroes, who are all brothers

---

1.   Pedro M. Arcaya: *Insurrección de los negros de la serranía de Coro.* Caracas, 1941, p. 214.

in Jesus Christ and equals before God... the payment of tribute by the Indians is abolished... slavery is abolished immediately, for it is contrary to humanity." The movement was named the "Revolution of the People," its commanders were instructed to issue their orders in the name of the "American people," and its main objective was identified as "the restoration of liberty to the American people."

The influence of the ideas associated with the French Revolution can be clearly seen in this terminology. Like other natural rights, equality was considered always to have existed. Therefore it was not "established," but "declared"; for the same reason liberty was "restored" to the people. However, the Venezuelan conspirators deviated from the French model on one fundamental point: they wanted all citizens to live together in harmony "as brothers in Jesus Christ, equals before God." Similarly, they differed from the North American revolutionaries, because of their readiness to extend natural equality not only to whites but also to Indians and Negroes.

A number of Spanish liberals who had been sent to La Guaira as prisoners for their participation in the so-called San Blas Conspiracy played an important part in the movement of Gual and España. Many historians have attributed the main role to them, and have argued that the ideology of the conspiracy was derived from Spanish liberalism. However, the short time that elapsed between the arrival of the prisoners in Venezuela and the outbreak of the creole movement seems an irrefutable proof that subversive ideas were already well advanced.[1] Moreover, it is difficult to see how political prisoners, condemned to incarceration in La Guaira, could have immediately made outside contacts to organize a subversive plot. In addition, numerous documents make it quite clear that by 1794 at the latest, José María España and others had organized an active, determined group of revolutionaries in La Guaira.[2]

A point of greatest significance is that one of the proclamations issued during this rebellion recalled the punishment which had been imposed

---

1. Dr. Pedro Grases has studied the topic carefully, with his usual acumen and reliance on sources, in his analysis of *La conspiración de Gual y España y el ideario de la Independencia,* Caracas, Edición del Comité de Orígenes de la Emancipación, 1949. His interpretation is the same as that provided above, and he provides the following dates for the arrival in Venezuela of the Spanish conspirators: Juan Bautista Picornell arrived on 3 December 1796; Sebastián Andrés, José Lax and Manuel Cortés Campomanes arrived in February, April and May 1797 respectively. Events moved so quickly thereafter that they were freed by their Venezuelan sympathizers in June, 1797.

2. Casto Fulgencio López: *Juan Picornell y la Conspiración de Gual y España,* Ediciones Nueva, Cádiz, 1955. Although this work claims that Picornell had a decisive influence on the 1797 conspiracy, it also stresses the importance of the "España group," which had been operating in La Guaira for several years. See also Héctor García Chuecos: *Estudios de Historia Colonial Venezolana,* Caracas, 1937; and Blanco Azpúrua: *Documentos...,* i, p. 370.

upon Juan Francisco de León. If we also remember that, despite his extreme conservatism, Father Terrero spoke up for the Córdova brothers, we can see how the nationalist conscience of the Venezuelans was demonstrated in a variety of ways.

In December 1797, the *audiencia* of Caracas banned the circulation of *The Rights of Man* and other seditious works which, it claimed, had reached Venezuela "from the islands of Santo Domingo and Trinidad since the English captured them." They also came from Guadeloupe, where Picornell had documents printed. In fact, the underground waters of revolution were already running so strongly in both New Granada and Venezuela that it is a lengthy task today to identify either their source or their course.

Subversive voices were heard even in the courtrooms. Juan Germán Roscio, a lawyer who later helped draw up the Act of Independence, and who in 1797 practiced in Caracas and Valencia, was accused by some rival Spanish colleagues of having made egalitarian declarations, his accusers defined them as subversive, heretical and sacrilegious, similar to those made by Gual and España. Although Roscio defended himself against the charge of complicity in their conspiracy, he had no hesitation in reiterating that "men were born free, and all are equally noble, since they are formed from the same dough, and are created in the image and likeness of God."[1] This was tantamount to repeating the fundamental principle of the "Ordinances" almost word for word.

The prosecution of the 1797 conspirators was relatively mild while Pedro Carbonell remained in charge of government, but it was intensified and atrocities began to be committed two years later with the appointment of a new Captain-general, Guevara y Vasconcelos. The sentence imposed on José María España ordered his execution and the confiscation of his property. He was to be hung and quartered, and his limbs were to be displayed on spikes in parts of La Guaira and Macuto which had been the scene of his attempted rebellion. Similar penalties were imposed on the other leaders captured by the authorities, and all those suspected of complicity were mercilessly interrogated in prison. España's wife, a woman of exceptional integrity, , was thrown into prison despite being pregnant and was later sentenced to eight years of seclusion in the *Casa de Misericordia* in Caracas. Others were given long prison sentences, and thirty were exiled. Manuel Gual managed to escape to Trinidad, but he died there from poison, which was said to have been administered on the orders of Guevara y Vasconcelos. The possibility is quite credible.

---

1. *Historia del Colegio de Abogados de Caracas,* by Dr. Héctor Parra Márquez. Caracas, 1952, pp. 574 and 446 respectively.

The execution of José María España horrified Venezuela. The writer Juan Vicente González, who obtained reports from many eyewitnesses, described the dreadful scene: "On May 8, 1799 the city of Caracas went into mourning. The doors to houses were closed and windows were hung with black. The sorrowful voices of the women who moaned within, the mournful ringing of bells, and the grave and fearful countenances of the people announced a unique and terrible occurrence.

"A few townspeople, some soldiers, and children in the carge of their teachers, watched from the main square as a confused group of praying friars and armed soldiers anxiously emerged from the public prison which stood on the site of the present palace of government. As they slowly drew near they were accompanied by brothers of the Orders of Charity and Sorrows, who carried wine and water, or alms bowls, and cried funereally: 'Do good deeds for the soul of a man they are about to execute.' An unrecognizable bundle lay on a blanket being held by some friars and pulled by horse. Two priests spoke to the object alternately. It seemed to listen intelligently and allowed itself to be taken where they led it. It was José María España being hauled to his execution. He was a man of about forty, and, without his white shroud, would have been admired for his resolute look and his elegant, pleasing figure. The harsh voice of the town crier, who walked ahead reading the sentence, rose above the rattle of the weapons, the chants of the clergy, the tolling of the church bells and the doleful tones of those who prayed for his soul.

"When España reached the foot of the gallows, one of the accompanying priests, his old friend Dr. F. José Antonio Tinedo, brought him to a halt with his eyes lowered and his hands bound among a ring of officials. The priest bid him to cast out pride as he prepared for death. Then the curate of the cathedral church mounted the steps with him, embraced him, and tenderly covered him with his vestments. Before the curate descended, the man convicted of *lese-majesté* had died at the hands of the hangman.

"The ordinary, simple people were still unaccustomed to witnessing death, and they remained still and quiet for some time. The frightened children huddled together around their teachers. Many of the main participants began to move away, silently and sadly. . . ."[1]

The story goes that as he stood in front of the scaffold José María España exclaimed: "My ashes will be honored in this very spot by my country." This prophecy was honored by his contemporaries, and it was doubtless out of respect for it that the martyr's sons were given the privilege of bearing the Venezuelan flag when, in 1811, it was raised

---

1. Juan Vicente González: *Biografía del General José Félix Ribas.* Caracas, 1946.

for the first time in the main square of Caracas. Perhaps España's exclamation was the "surge of pride" which the priest made him expiate.[1]

In this way Venezuela was forming her political features in the late eighteenth century, and there is no doubt that many creoles were already genuine patriots. Possibly they did not yet think in terms of separation from Spain, but they had acquired an awareness of the public good and were concerning themselves with trying to secure the transformation which America clearly required. As a result of their efforts, plans for social reform, which to an extent came before those for political emancipation, emerged in increasing numbers. As we have seen, the Licentiate Miguel José Sanz accurately criticized the prevailing system of education and identified the flaws in the national character which it caused. Moreover, he was already thinking in terms of an agrarian law which would transform conditions in the Venezuelan countryside. This was one of the first projects which he announced after Venezuela secured independence.[2] Simón Rodríguez tried to reorganize elementary education and make it available for all children, while the Count of Tovar sought to transfer the cultivation of the land from slaves to white laborers and proprietors. Humboldt commented on his efforts: "Nobly occupied with the necessary measures for the gradual abolition of Negro slavery in these regions, the Count of Tovar took pleasure in the prospect that slavery would become less essential for landowners, and that the freed Negroes would be given the opportunity to remain on the land as farmers. . . . It pleases me to discuss the details of colonial agriculture, because they prove to the inhabitants of Europe something which has long been known to the enlightened inhabitants in the colonies, namely that the Spanish American continent can produce sugar, cotton and indigo with free labor, while the unfortunate slaves are capable of becoming farmers, planters and landowners."[3] Inspired with these ideas the Marquis of Mijares had founded the village of San Antonio de los Altos near Caracas by giving free land there to forty families from the Canary Islands.

Humboldt's observations rightly stressed the social significance of initiatives such as these. Before slavery could be abolished, it was essential to prove that is was dispensable. The contrary view was still held in Europe, and even Montesquieu wrote calmly: "Sugar would be too expensive if the plant from which it is produced were not grown by slaves." The admired author of *L'esprit des lois* considered this a sufficient justification for the abominable institution. In contrast, some Americans dedicated themselves to destroying these prejudices by effective, practical

---

1. This is the interpretation put forward by Casto Fulgencio López in his biography of Picornell.
2. See the biography of the Precursor by Dr. Juan Saturno Canelón. Caracas, 1956.
3. Humboldt, *Viaje...*, iii, p. 94.

examples, since, although they were held throughout the world, they were incompatible with the future of the American states.

The increasing maturity of Spanish America inspired some Spanish statesmen with the idea of forestalling a violent rupture in the colonies by conceding a certain autonomy to them. The plans of the Count of Aranda are well known. Later, even the mediocre Manuel de Godoy claimed in his memoirs to have foreseen the problem, and stated: "When in charge of government, I observed and understood the abundant evidence that the inhabitants of America had reached the age of adolescence, and I lost no time in deciding that it was essential to govern them as young men." He proposed, therefore, "that the viceroys should be replaced by the royal children, who, with the title of prince-regents, would make themselves loved, and by their presence would satisfy the ambition and pride of those people. I further proposed that they should be accompanied by a sound council of responsible ministers, and that a senate, half of whose members would be Americans and half Spaniards, should govern there."[1]

These proposals went too far for the Spanish Bourbons, but not far enough for the Americans, whose ideas were already republican and democratic. Thus Venezuela herself, then the most vital and alert part of the Spanish empire, had to decide which way she was to go. The change which was about to occur in Spanish America was to be so decisive that what followed would in no way resemble what went before. People were well aware of the importance of this transcendental dividing line. Behind them they were leaving three centuries of culture and the narrow colonial existence given to them by Spain, in the future unlimited possibilities for the individual and for society as a whole were again to give America the exciting enchantment of a New World.

---

1. Manuel Godoy: *Memorias del Príncipe de la Paz*. Madrid, 1836.

VI

ALL
EVENTS
AT ONCE

FROM 1794, WHEN HE WAS only eleven years old, Bolívar showed a persistent desire to travel to Spain. There is no doubt that his main motive was to rejoin his uncle Esteban, whom he loved because he was so like his mother, for he felt abandoned after her death in 1792 and that of his grandfather in 1793. The prospect was particularly attractive when compared with the harsh reality of life with his uncle Carlos.

But travel to Spain was long and dangerous, especially during the long warfare on land and at sea in which Spain was involved against France, and later against England. Moreover, it would have been difficult for the bachelor Esteban to care for a young boy in a country whose climate and way of life were so different from those of Venezuela. Cold winters were unknown in Venezuela, but the icy wind that blows from the Guadarrama mountains onto Madrid, "so keen that it snuffs out a life but leaves a candle burning", was liable to cause pneumonia, which was nearly always fatal.

For reasons such as these, Esteban resisted Simón's plans, but he understood why the boy wanted to join him. He wrote to Carlos and advised him: "in order not to disappoint him, you can pretend that I will soon return to Venezuela, although travel is very dangerous because of the war."[1]

---

1. *Correspondencia entre los hermanos Palacios Blanco.* Boletín de la Academia Nacional de la Historia, no. 52, Caracas.

By 1798, however, Esteban had changed his mind, and he suggested that both Simón and his brother Juan Vicente travel to Madrid. He told Carlos: "I have also informed you that, since I am in Madrid and well connected with the Court, it would be very suitable for Juan Vicente and Simón to join me. They could be well instructed here, and we can see what fate will provide for them, since their fine qualities give them a great advantage." The change of heart was caused partly by both boys being then four years older, but another factor was the improvement in Esteban's personal prospects. Until 1798 he was always short of money, and if he had allowed Simón to join him in Madrid he would have had to live off his ward's income. In 1798, however, he took office as a minister of the Tribunal of Accounts in Madrid. Although the position was of only average importance, Esteban looked forward to rapid promotion, thanks to the patronage of his friend, Manuel Mallo. As a result he decided to remain in Madrid and to present his nephews at court. Like his father and his sister, Concepción, Esteban was both generous and correct, and he was anxious to protect his nephews' interests. An indication of these characteristics had been provided in 1797, when he opposed his brother Carlos's plan to move into the family home of the Bolívars. He explained frankly to Carlos that it was better "not to suggest to the public that you are taking advantage of your guardianship to live in his (Simón's) house."

Esteban again suggested that the boys join him in February, 1799, but by then Simón was already on his way, accompanied by a Venezuelan friend, Esteban Escobar, who was traveling to Spain to take up military studies. Juan Vicente Bolívar chose not to go with them.

A lot of attention was paid to selecting a ship and a route which offered the greatest security, since the ship in which uncle Pedro Palacios had sailed a short time before was twice intercepted by privateers. In contrast, Bolívar's voyage was uneventful. He left La Guaira on the *San Ildefonso* on January 19, 1799. The ship reached Veracruz on February 2, and since Havana, the next port of call, was being blockaded by the English, remained in New Spain for six weeks. Far from being a disappointment, the long delay gave Bolívar the opportunity to go up to Mexico City, where he stayed in the house of an *oidor,* to whom he had been recommended by the Bishop of Caracas. His ship finally sailed on March 20, calling only at Havana, which was then open, before reaching Spain. The passengers disembarked on May 31 at Santoña, near San Sebastián.

From Veracruz Bolívar wrote the first of his extant letters to his uncle Pedro. The ignorance revealed by its crude style and deplorable spelling has surprised many historians, while others have tried to balance these defects by stressing "the regularity of the script." Lecuna, for example wrote that the letter was "admirable for its harmony." In fact, it reads like the work of a schoolboy, and has the labored regularity which a child can produce with a great deal of effort. But it would be pedantic to be disappointed by this, since in the eighteenth century the letters of relatively cultured adults, and even official documents, showed the same carelessness over spelling. Moreover, there was a marked distinction between the education provided for a "young noble," destined for a military career, and that of a future lawyer. In fact, as Maurois shows in his biographies of Byron and Shelley, the English aristocracy of the period deliberately neglected the scholarly aspect of their children's education, lest an excess of culture, scruples and doubts impaired the strength of character and powers of decision required in a future lord. It is true that Simón Rodríguez did not believe that the cultivation of intelligence was so radically opposed to firmness of will, but he disapproved of traditional, routine instruction for other reasons, due to the influence of Rousseau. For Rodríguez, all instruction had to consist of action or stimulus for action, and even advanced disciplines, history, criticism, ethics, had to have as their goal the perfection of the individual or of society.

Bolívar's letter, then, was neither more nor less than could be expected from a boy of his class without special training for a profession. At least he realized himself that it was not well written: "You will not be surprised by the bad penmanship," he wrote, "it is only moderately good, for I am tired by the movement of the carriage in which I have just arrived, and since I am in a hurry I have written it very badly, and all the events are happening at once." He had no idea when he wrote that he was "the future Liberator" or that historians would dissect his laborious essay and judge him on the basis of it.

It is particularly interesting in this context to recall that Bolívar always resisted the idea of publishing his correspondence. He wrote to Santander in October 1825: "Do not have my letters published, either during my lifetime or after my death, as they have been written in a style far too free and disorganized." Similarly, he ordered in his will: "The papers in the possession of Mr. Pavageau are to be burned." Nevertheless, it was in his private correspondence that the best of Bolívar was revealed: the spontaneous and lively expression of ideas, the evidence of what he suffered in his efforts to organize his country as a republic, the sentimental exuberance with which he bestowed affection or appreciation on friends and subordinates, the constant awareness of moral values which gives such a heart-rending pathos to his political vacillations. O' Leary wrote: "I would submit the Liberator to a test which few men would choose for themselves, namely an examination of his private correspondence, and I doubt if anybody, even if he were less frank and passionate than General Bolívar, would emerge as pure as he from such an ordeal if one many call it such." Indeed, the very fact Bolívar thought his correspondence would never be published makes it an impeccable historical source.

O'Leary related one anecdote about Bolívar's stay in Mexico: "General Alava, who was in Mexico at the same time and who met Bolívar in the viceroy's palace, informed me that one day, when the conversation touched on the French Revolution, the young Venezuelan expressed himself with such audacity that he surprised his listeners, and, if similar opinions had been voiced by somebody older or with more influence in the country, they would have greatly offended the viceroy."

The story is attractive, but absolutely no significance should be attached to it. One would have to be ignorant of the caution with which any political question could be discussed in the period to accept that the French Revolution would be openly debated in the viceregal palace, especially in the presence of casual visitors. Even less convincing is the suggestion that a boy who had such difficulty writing a proper letter to his uncle would dare to venture an opinion on events which were barely mentioned in America, except in clandestine publications. Most absurd of all is the idea that the rigid etiquette of the period would have permitted him to do so in front of adults of such standing. Even if he had attempted to do so, the conversation would have been switched immediately to a less controversial topic.

Other writers have presented what is at first sight a more likely explanation of the episode, with the suggestion that it was provoked by questions put to Bolívar about the revolution of Gual and España. If this were the case, the imprudence of the questioners could be explained by their curiosity to know more about something hardly reported in Mexico. None of them would imagine that the boy's answers might be embarrassing, and even less that he might have approved of the conspiracy, but, out of either sympathy for the victims or a certain regional pride, Bolívar might have defended his unfortunate compatriots. But this interpretation, too, has its fatal flaws, notably that when Bolívar was in Mexico the prosecution of the conspirators, who had been virtually forgotten for two years, was just in the process of being reactivated, and none had yet been executed. Consequently, neither the suggested interest in the viceregal court to know what had happened in Caracas nor Bolívar's supposed vehemence in defending his fellow-countrymen can be satisfactorily explained.

These points have been stressed in order to repudiate this anecdote, which was intended to adorn Bolívar's childhood with poetic rebellion. The same search for the truth will make it necessary to refute similar stories, some of which are frankly ridiculous. A sound study of Bolívar's gradual development to the fullness of his powers, so interesting both psychologically and historically, depends upon discarding the confusion and embellishments accepted by many writers out of laziness or a misdirected enthusiasm for their subject. The formation of Bolívar's character in the last years of the eighteenth century coincided chronologically with the clear progress of Venezuela towards independence. But this chance coincidence should not tempt the historian to join the two processes into a near synthesis, depicting the boy as a miniature of the future Liberator.

In fact, it is highly unlikely that any ideas of emancipation penetrated the house where Bolívar lived, since all the male Palacios Blancos were royalists, except for one Francisco, who died for his country in 1814 with the rank of lieutenant-colonel. The two uncles with whom Simón came into most contact were the most rigid of all in their aversion to the republican cause. In 1819 Feliciano (who should not be confused with his father, Feliciano Palacios y Sojo, Bolívar's grandfather) even signed the so-called Manifesto drawn up by the Spanish authorities against the Liberator; and Carlos, Bolívar's guardian, combined personal crudity with the most narrow political conservatism to such an extent that he ended a letter to Esteban about the revolution of Gual and España with the frenzied gibberish: "In America, since we lived surrounded by this rabble, it became necessary to have them humbled, and every one of them put in his place."[1]

Any suggestion that Bolívar was a revolutionary as a boy, despite the spiritual confinement and the close supervision to which he was sub-jected, is pure fiction. As far as Simón Rodríguez is concerned, his in-fluence ended in 1797 when he went to Europe, but in any case he was more of a social reformer than a political agitator, most vehement when discussing general ideas, but disinterested or disdainful when faced with concrete situations. It has been suggested that Rodríguez fled from Ven-ezuela because he was involved in the conspiracy of Gual and España, but there is no evidence to support the theory. On the contrary, he is not mentioned in the bulky file of documents dealing with the affair, and he was not a man who could be easily overlooked.

The only clear intention shown by Bolívar until his adolescence was to travel to Spain, and this in itself hardly suggests an aversion to the mother country. Several years later, he still retained his religious beliefs. So, despite the suppositions of various writers, it seems that neither in religion nor politics did Rodríguez attempt to turn his pupil into a pre-mature Jacobin. Indeed, such an idea could not have been further re-moved from the teacher's educational ideas. His aim was to instill in Bo-lívar the fundamental virtues of a manly character which, later in life, would allow him to judge for himself problems which were still beyond his comprehension. Rodríguez entrusted everything to the unfettered,

1. Boletín de la Academia Nacional de la Historia, no. 52, p. 541, Caracas.

spiritual development of his pupil, and there is no doubt that, when the boy first put his foot on Spanish soil at the age of sixteen, he was neither a premature genius nor a young hero. He was about to enter a world known to him only through vague reports, and it it easy to imagine the pictures which filled his mind: The pomp and pleasures of court life, the important personages who resided there, women, studies, magnificent spectacles, and the dangers which made life in Madrid an adventure. He must have felt a fear of being lonely or out-of-place in his new surroundings, as well as a natural ambition and determination to overcome his shortcomings and emerge triumphant.

Those who write about great men frequently fall into the error of trying to show that they progress in a straight line from childhood to the fame which awaits them. It is only valid to anticipate events in terms of their characters, since basic qualities are usually revealed at an early age, but, as far as everyday life is concerned, heroes, like everybody else, fluctuate from one moment to the next in early life. Constancy consists not in always doing the same thing, but rather in always directing oneself towards the same goal. Many forks are to be found in the path of genius! And how many times MacBeth's witches try to deceive him with their cunning auguries!

Except for those youths whose forces are prematurely polarized upon a single goal by violent crises, or for geniuses like Johann Sebastian Bach, raised in an artificial environment, adolescents in general experience only confusion when they make their first contact with life. They see themselves in the future as splendid gentlemen, surrounded by magnificence, or as idealists suffering extreme privations. Their dreams move from the enjoyment of many women to an undying dedication to one. They are equally entranced by the glorious ostentation of the soldier and by the patient, honest dedication of the intellectual. In short, they still do not know whether they will be stern leaders of men or mystical brothers of all their fellows, because they still retain an innocent egoism, to which they themselves are blind. If they yearn to sacrifice themselves to save the world, it is because they hope thereby to achieve universal acclaim.

It is only later, sometimes much later, that they learn that the price of glory is almost invariably terrible suffering, and that true heroism is proved not in the delightful hour of glory, but in the bitter hours, or years, in which all seems lost. The future was to bring the young Bolívar frenzied adulation, but this was followed by a flood of calumnies and intrigues, which so tormented him with the prospect of the imminent destruction of his life's work that he even feared for his reputation before posterity. As we have seen, he was to describe himself in 1829 as "a despairing man, whose spirit they have broken and whose hopes they have destroyed forever." Nevertheless, he continued his struggle, and was able to lighten his sadness by forgiving the compatriots who had deserted him. Although the adolescent will have read of such reverses, he conceives of them not as a reality which tears body and soul asunder, but only as a joyful contrast, which makes heroism even more beautiful.

Bolívar himself experienced this adolescent confusion on the two solemn occasions when he saw Napoleon. He admired the emperor's simple uniform, but realized that it would not have interested him so much if not for its contrast with the brilliance of the dress of the general staff. He thought that the emperor's crown was irrelevant and anachronistic, but was fascinated by "the universal acclaim and the interest which his presence inspired."[1]

The only picture, then, which can honestly be painted of Bolívar on his arrival in Madrid in June 1799, is that of a youth very proud of his uniform of a second lieutenant in the Aragua Militia, frequently amazed by the magnificence of the capital, but at times affecting indifference towards the things shown to him, lest he give the impression of being an oaf from the Indies.

The journey from Santoña to Madrid through the monotonous wheatlands and the desolate, eroded plains of the Spanish countryside perhaps made him homesick for the brilliant Venezuelan forests and the birds and flowers which had delighted him all year round. But it is more likely that his mind was filled with stories of Roland at Roncesvalles and of the Cid at Burgos, and his curiosity captured by the vineyards and olive groves. He must have passed near Puebla de Bolívar, the birthplace of his ancestors. In fact, Esteban Palacios had originally traveled to Spain with the intention of completing research on the family's genealogy, so that the marquisate granted to Juan de Bolívar y Villegas at the beginning of the century could be made effective. In 1799 the pretender to the title was Juan Vicente Bolívar. On June 16, shortly after his arrival in the capital, Bolívar was taken by Esteban to visit the court at Aranjuez. There is no record of what the boy thought, or whether he was more impressed by the luxury of court life or stupified by the shameful lives of Charles IV, María Luisa and Godoy: the abject monarch, the queen imprisoned by her love of luxury, and the inept, arrogant favorite. The trio so disgusted the colonials that, years later, such a thoughtful man of letters as Roscio simply called Ferdinand VII "the son of María Luisa." Almost without dissimulation, this was the most damning insult he could make in the Spanish language.

Bolívar and his uncle had close links with the court, since it seems that Manuel Godoy had then been replaced at the queen's side by Manuel

---

1. *Diario de Bucaramanga por el General L. Perú de Lacroix,* edited by Monseñor Nicolás E. Navarro, Caracas, 1935. *Passim.*

Mallo, the young New Granadian, who had spent his childhood in Caracas. He was a close friend of Esteban, who lived in his house in Madrid, and Simón was also taken there. Mallo did not replace Godoy in the political sphere, but he did become María Luisa's lover. It seems that Godoy encouraged this affair, since it relieved him of the most distasteful of his duties. This simply made the scandal spicier, and the French ambassador in Madrid recorded an anecdote which has been published several times. The king, the queen and Godoy were on a balcony in the palace, when the king asked, "Manuel, who is this Mallo? I see him every day with a new carriage and new horses. Where does he get all his money?" "Your Majesty," Godoy answered, "Mallo hasn't an *ochavo;* but it is well known that he is maintained by an ugly old woman, who steals from her husband in order to enrich her lover." The king, shaking with laughter, said to the queen, who was present: "What do you have to say about that, Luisa?" "Carlos," the queen replied, "you know quite well that Manuel is always making jokes."

The management of public affairs in Madrid was no less shameful. Large sums were spent on court life at a time when the treasury was exhausted and the government had been obliged to issue paper money. Administration was so chaotic that even the navy was not properly maintained, although imperial communications and the very existence of the empire depended upon it. After failing to make any progress in war against revolutionary France, the Spanish gevernment made peace, but this brought in its train new disasters and humiliations. In order to appease the French, Spain declared war on England. Among the first results was the defeat of the Spanish squadron at Cape San Vicente and the loss of Trinidad. The colonials were particularly hard hit by the war, since English ships impeded their commerce and threatened their ports. By prohibiting trade with neutrals, the government in Madrid ruined colonial agriculture and left the colonies dependent for supplies upon contraband merchants. It was rumored in Madrid that the Marquis de Ustáriz was to be taken into the Ministry, a development which would have benefited his fellow Venezuelans; but it was also said that his chances of high office were considerably reduced by his being an American. It was becoming quite clear to the creoles that in bad times they suffered most, and that they would never be given the opportunity to help remedy the situation.

The correspondence of the Palacios Blanco brothers, some were in Madrid and the others were in Caracas, contained frequent references to these events, although they soon realized that their letters were intercepted and read.

Godoy became so hated that he was attacked by the clergy and the Council of Castile and the court was so lax that it agreed to the demand of the Directory that French royalist refugees be expelled from Spain, a decision hardly contrived to encourage support for monarchy within Spain itself.

The general moral degradation of life in the Spanish capital must have made a deep impression on Bolívar, although its impact would have been softened by the lack of public discussion of affairs of state. It was also inevitable that the most notable scandals would be obscured by the daily trifles emanating from the court to feed the idle curiosity of the nation. Public opinion was frankly monarchical, just as it was for most of the nineteenth century. Some indications of the innate conservatism of the Spaniard can be found in the works of the great historian, Menéndez y Pelayo. Writing about the conspiracy of San Blas, he expressed surprise at the "complicity" in the movement of a Spaniard whom he considered otherwise respectable. When he discussed later developments he was so violent in his attitude towards the constitutionalists in early nineteenth century Spain that he accused them of having been in league with the Spanish American revolutionaries. He wrote that the American deputies in the Cádiz Congress "hired out" their services to the "faction" which seemed most likely to be triumphant, and he called Miranda "an old terrorist." If an intellectual of such powers, writing so many years after the events, could show such bitterness towards one of the few liberal movements which flourished in nineteenth-century Spain, and felt the need to attack the American republicans so blindly, we can easily imagine how reactionary was general public opinion in the late eighteenth and early nineteenth centuries towards any initiative for reform. Even in the twentieth century, Salvador Madariaga, a politician as well as a writer, considered the independence of the New World a product of a "conspiracy" among Jesuits, Jews and Masons, and saw the Liberator's emergence in terms of an obscure racial prejudice.

In fact, the emancipation of Spanish America represented a healthy reaction against the corruption and stagnation of metropolitan Spain from that part of the empire which was the most developed politically. This was explained clearly by Bolívar and other revolutionary thinkers. They also created the concept of "American Spain," which they wanted to join with Spain after in a common effort to achieve political perfection. But, with rare exceptions, Spanish commentators ignore or reject this aspect of the independence movements, have called the American republicans "insurgents" and "rebels" and, as part of this same attitude, have labeled the liberals in Spain as "traitors" and "sympathizers with the French" (afrancesados).

Esteban Palacios was too superficial to concern himself with the moral defects of court life, but he had sufficient dignity not to copy Mallo's bedroom intrigues, remunerative though they were. According to a letter from Pedro Palacios to Carlos: "Esteban still retains the first, temperate qualities instilled in him by our good father and, as the present circumstances demand, controls himself in all things without getting involved in much intrigue and mischief." Given the casual language of this personal correspondence, the comment was a striking reminder of the strict family influence which still weighed upon Esteban.

Pedro's evidence, showing as it does that Esteban was rather different from his friend Mallo, also undermines a myth created by O'Leary and spread by other historians, possibly because it gives credence to the story that, as a child, Bolívar played with the future Ferdinand VII and knocked off his hat in symbolic anticipation of snatching the American crown from his head. According to O'Leary, Bolívar "agreed, although always with repugnance, to accompany Mallo at court and at the royal residences around Madrid. On some of these occasions he was an involuntary witness to the depravity of María Luisa. She liberally paid the expenses of her favorite and had his table served from the royal kitchens. If a dish pleased the queen she sent it from her own table to Mallo's, and she frequently came to his apartments when Bolívar was there."

This supposed intimacy between Bolívar and Mallo does not ring true, partly because of the difference in their ages, and partly because of Esteban's reported caution in imitating Mallo's activities at court. The correspondence of the Palacios shows that although they continued to visit Mallo's house and occasionally dined there after moving into their own house, they rarely saw him, since he lived at court. A further indication that O'Leary's story was incorrect was the French ambassador's comment that Mallo was "always surrounded by spies and without liberty to meet anybody."

Esteban and Simón left Mallo's house when Pedro Palacios arrived in Madrid. Together with three servants, the three of them took a house in Jardines Street in July, 1799. In August, Pedro wrote to Carlos about Simón's life in Madrid: "Esteban keeps the boy very busy; he applies himself with relish and success to Castilian, writing, in which he is very proficient, dancing, history in sound books, and he is about to take up the French language and mathematics. He is obedient, his conduct is reasonable, or, to be more precise, good, and he leads a quiet life."[1]

This picture is confirmed by Esteban's recollection of this period in Bolívar's life, written many years later: "Since we were connected with the court in Madrid, it was very easy to find teachers who provided him with skills and training appropriate for a youth. By turns, and in his own house, he was taught by the fencing master, the French language

---

1. *Correspondencia entre los hermanos Palacios Blanco.* Boletín de la Academia Nacional de la Historia, no. 52, p. 656, Caracas.

teacher and the dancing instructor. He spent part of the afternoon in the mathematics class and always applied himself obediently and happily."

This way of life was suddenly interrupted by a most unforeseeable development. Uncle Esteban was put in prison. It has proved impossible so far to discover the reason for such a strange event; some think it was caused by palace intrigues related to Mallo's affair with the queen, but even as assiduous a researcher as Vicente Lecuna was forced to admit that he had failed to discover any credible explanation. The episode is particularly mystifying, since it seems that Mallo failed to intercede on behalf of his close friend. On the other hand, although Esteban was treated so harshly that he was kept in solitary confinement for a year and a half, he continued to receive his salary from the state. Bolívar wrote on 13 January 13, 1802: "My uncle Esteban... is well, but deprived of all communication. This is all I can tell you about the affair. He has no attorney, so there is a great deal of work involved just in collecting his salary."[1]

The whole episode is a good indication of the type of government then existing in Spain. An individual with influential friends could be imprisoned, kept in solitary confinement, continue to collect his salary as a public employee and after a long period regain his liberty, without any explanation ever being disclosed.

---

1. *Cartas,* xi, p. 1.

VII

MY LADY
DOÑA TERESA

Ａ FTER ESTEBAN'S IMPRIS-
onment, his brother Pedro moved to Cádiz, and the young Simón
went to live in the house of the Marquis de Ustáriz, with whom he already enjoyed close contact. This brought into his life another person of
exceptional character and impressive culture, whose influence was as decisive as that of Simón Rodríguez in the spiritual formation of the
Liberator.

Ustáriz was a *caraqueño,* but he went to Spain as a young man and
occupied a prominent position there for fifty years. A notice published in
Seville on the occasion of his death reveals that he served as intendant in
several provinces, and, on the basis of this experience, "he presented to
the Ministry a long, learned report, suggesting the most opportune methods of increasing population, improving agriculture, bringing much hilly,
arid land into cultivation, establishing honest administration of justice,
and ensuring the due separation of judicial and political authority, thus
avoiding the problems which their confusion would bring. This report
earned superior approval, and led to the creation of the *Audiencia* of
Cáceres; in many of its aspects it was adopted as a general guideline for
all the peninsula."[1]

When Spain was invaded by Napoleon, "the Marquis de Ustáriz, far from
imitating the timidity and selfishness of so many other magistrates in the

---

1. Quoted by Vicente Lecuna in *Catálogo de errores y calumnias en la historia de Bolívar.* Caracas, 1956, i, p. 117.

kingdom, immediately added his voice to those of the people of Aragon. . and became one of the first members of the governing committee." He worked with "the fire and enthusiasm of youth" for this movement, which briefly redeemed Spain from her earlier humiliations and brought to the surface political ideas which could have transformed public life.

The same notice reveals that "at the same time he secretly produced plans for a political constitution for the kingdom. He possessed for this task an invaluable knowledge of historical events, criticism and philosophy. The last of these was his final field of study, for he repeated frequently: We will have achieved nothing, unless, before this war is over, we have a constitution which frees us forever from tyrants and favorites, and restores dignity to the people."

In 1778, when Ustáriz was intendant of Badajoz, he was visited by Miranda, who noted in his diary: "I discovered there a friendly, knowledgeable subject, anxious for the good of his country."[1] Such a comment was tantamount to exceptional praise from Miranda, who rarely found anything praiseworthy in the Spanish functionaries of the period.

Ustáriz was not a republican. Like many contemporaries he reacted against the excesses of revolutionary France, but we can accept without qualification the conclusion in his obituary: "He was outstanding for his honesty and his love for the King and the public good; his simple manners, and his frank, friendly nature; his profound understanding of moral and political sciences; his tireless attention to all his duties; his wide, discriminating knowledge of literature; his clear and unaffected mind, and his rare public and private virtues."

This fortunate combination of kindness and uprightness, of lordship and democratic sensibility, made it possible for Ustáriz to control Bolívar. His critical mind and his experience were like a window, opened for the first time in the youth's life, to reveal the paths for which he was beginning to search. Like Rodríguez, Ustáriz was a gracious and talented prodigy, but he also possessed the experience acquired in an extensive political and administrative career. According to O'Leary, "Bolívar regarded him like one of the wise men of antiquity. He was delighted by his company and abandoned his books in favor of it, for, he said, he learned more in conversation with the Marquis than in his scholarly tomes. There is no doubt that Ustáriz exercised a great influence on Bolívar. Even in his last days he remembered him with pleasure and spoke of him with veneration. The two friends frequently discussed the possibility of separating South America from the Metropolis. On these occasions the elderly Ustáriz, although not disapproving of the idea, pointed out the difficulties of the undertaking with such strong arguments that they would have

---

1. Miranda, Archivo, i, p. 133.

weakened the resolve of his young companion if he had not held his convictions so firmly."

This judgement was undoubtedly based upon recollection heard frequently by O'Leary from Bolívar's own lips, with the exception of the final point, which seems to attribute to Bolívar ideas which were still unformed; and we will see that the qualities possessed by Ustáriz were precisely those which Bolívar sought and praised in his future friends and advisers, such as Peñalver, Palacio Fajardo, Roscio, Mendoza, Sucre, Revenga, Camilo Torres, Mosquera, Vargas and Salom.

At about the same time that Bolívar moved into the house of Ustáriz, another development of a personal nature contributed to the continuing vagueness of his nascent political unease. He fell in love. It seems to have been a fiercely passionate affair, for having arrived in Madrid only in June 1799, he wrote to his uncle, Pedro Palacios, in September 1800, shortly after his seventeenth birthday, and informed him of his intention to marry. Simón's letter was very formal, and began by pointing out that he was obliged to marry in order to retain his *mayorazgo,* but he added, "and because I have formed a passion for a *señorita* of the finest background and most recommendable talents, my lady Doña Teresa Toro, daughter of a compatriot and a kinsman." Her father was Bernardo Rodríguez del Toro, uncle of two of Bolívar's lifelong friends, the Marquis del Toro and Fernando del Toro. Despite these favorable circumstances, Bernardo decided that, in view of the suitor's tender age, the wedding should be put off for some time.

As a result of this decision, Bolívar again turned his attention to his studies, which were increasingly influenced by the Marquis de Ustáriz. Years later a bitter enemy, Ducoudray Holstein, was forced to admit: "In the course of his voyages he had acquired that worldly manner, that courtesy and suavity which distinguished him from other men, and so impressed all who dealt with him."

Only six of the letters written by Bolívar during this first visit to Europe still survive, but they are sufficient to reveal two points of considerable psychological interest. The first is the spontaneity with which he bestowed affection and respect upon those who merited it. He called the Marquis de Ustáriz, for example, "the only guardian I possess here," meaning—for Ustáriz was not his legal guardian—that he had the right to guide him in the absence of his two uncles. When he informed Pedro Palacios of his intention to marry, he acknowledged, "nobody can equal your concern for and mastery of my affairs," and he always ended his letters to him with the tender phrase "from your most affectionate nephew who loves you with all his heart." He was particularly effusive in his relationship with Esteban. He was deeply hurt by his uncle's imprisonment, and, in reply to Pedro, who had informed him of measures taken on Esteban's behalf, he wrote: "I know that nobody is more concerned than yourself about the fate of this unfortunate man; I can only offer my most devoted thanks for the step you have taken for the relief of my worthy godfather. I am unable to express my happiness. A feeling that we will succeed fills me with the most delightful hopes." These affectionate declarations, like those dealing with his childhood, are noted because they anticipate one of the psychological characteristics which Bolívar always retained, despite the setbacks of later life. He lavished the same sentimental exuberance, as much out of respect as affection, on all who surrounded him, both when he was at the height of his glory and in the hours of his abysmal despair.

It is a common error to suppose that a revolutionary is always obsessed with destructive rages, that a genius is incapable of normal human sentiments, that friendship and affection are incompatible with an energetic character. It seems, in fact, to be accepted as a general rule that the respect of the servile masses can be won only by ill treatment and scorn. By exploiting this flaw in man's collective nature and by means of propaganda, individuals who are really no more than vain madmen are frequently converted into heroes. Unfortunately, before their true weakness becomes apparent, they succeed in bewitching the masses, and causing much misery and bloodshed. Applying this criterion to history, some writers attribute to great men imagined outrages and indiscretions, simply because they believe these to be indispensable for their heroes to be recognized as truly great. Bolívar has suffered more from such stupidity and bad taste than from the deliberate calumnies of his enemies. In order to depict him as an "irresistible" man, neither respecting nor taking advice from anybody, many writers have distorted the truth to make him an unmanageable child and a reckless youth.

It would be equally wrong to depict Bolívar as a child without problems and even less as an adolescent without fire. What we have attempted to do is to show, with documental proof, how the confused agitation of his formative personality was consciously seeking higher goals. He was helped in his days of crisis by the unselfish and loving encouragement of his grandfather, Simón Rodríguez, Esteban and the Marquis de Ustáriz. Their generosity, family solidarity and commitment to the public good served as an example to him. When he was still an adolescent his character was already sufficiently strong and mature for him to pursue concrete and serious objectives: his studies, his travels, his first romance. Above all, he had acquired a firm respect for certain moral values. He admired and respected Rodríguez and Ustáriz, and loved Pedro and Esteban Palacios, because be was already sufficiently adult to recognize and appreciate their talents, wisdom and goodness.

The second interesting point about Bolívar's spiritual life emerging from the letters written in this period is that his religious faith remained intact and was expressed with an impeccable devotion and humility. In the letter to his uncle Pedro, in which he expressed his exhilaration on learning of the measures taken on Esteban's behalf, he wrote: "My prayers are insignificant and ineffective, nevertheless, I will continue to dedicate them all to the success of the zealous interest which you have taken in this affair."[1]

This again brings to mind Simón Rodríguez. Bolívar's religious beliefs came from his mother and his maternal grandfather who had opposed Simón's projected voyage to Europe, for fear that he would be contaminated by the agnosticism which, he believed, had been made fashionable by the French Revolution. But they both died while he was still young, and the boy soon passed into the hands of Rodríguez. If the teacher had been the aggressive atheist that some horrified historians have claimed, it would have been easy for him to destroy or weaken Simón's religious faith. We must conclude, therefore, either that Rodríguez was not as violently atheistic as is sometimes supposed, at least not in his youth, or that on this delicate point he had the integrity not to impose his ideas on his pupil.

The happiness which Bolívar enjoyed in Madrid as a result of his romance and his delightful conversations with the Marquis de Ustáriz, was disturbed by a mysterious attack made on him by some of the city's constables. O'Leary described the incident as follows: "In the autumn of 1801 Don Bernardo and his family went to Bilbao, and their absence caused Bolívar deep distress. Soon after the departure of the Toro family, an incident occurred which, apart from the great annoyance it caused, obliged him, too, to leave the capital. One day, as he was riding by the Toledo gate, he was detained and examined by order of the Ministry of Finance, which claimed, as a pretext for the outrage, an infraction of the ordinance prohibiting the use of a large number of diamonds without permission; but the real motive was that the Queen, burning with jealousy and aware of the young American's intimacy with Mallo, believed it would be possible to find evidence of some amorous intrigue of her favorite among Bolívar's papers. Bolívar was filled with indignation by the outrage committed against him, refused to submit to the search, and, drawing his sword, threatened to strike the first constable to approach him. Some of his friends, who happened to be passing, intervened, and the incident was sorted out; but after this nobody could induce him to stay in Madrid any longer. After obtaining a passport, he set out for Bilbao, and by the end of the year was reunited with the object of his love. But he could enjoy such pleasurable company for only a few days, since Don Bernardo was obliged to return to the capital."

---

1. *Cartas,* i ,p. 7.

A similar account of the event is provided in the Memoirs of General Tomás Cipriano de Mosquera, who, like O'Leary, possibly heard it from Bolívar. Vicente Lecuna pointed out that the incident must have occurred not in the autumn but before March 20, since in a letter of that date Bolívar announced that he would be leaving in the evening for Bilbao. Lecuna also considers the reasons for Bolívar's detention suggested by O'Leary and Mosquera to be mere "ridiculous, illogical suppositions." He prefers to believe that Bolívar "was wearing a uniform when not on active service," and that the incident arose from exaggerated military precautions caused by preparations for war with Portugal. But this argument is even less convincing, since such precautions, including the right to search a uniformed officer, would not be entrusted to irresponsible constables. Moreover, it fails to explain why, once his identity had been established, instead of receiving an apology, Bolívar was prohibited from remaining in Madrid. Details of the ban are obscure, but Lecuna writes that, "The prohibition lasted from March 20, 1801 until April 29, 1802." And it is the only possible explanation for Bolívar's plan, in August 1801, to marry by proxy. In a letter written then he announced: "My marriage will take place by proxy in Madrid, and after it Don Bernardo and his daughter will join me here, and we will leave in a neutral vessel which is sailing to North America."

It is obviously difficult to prove that Esteban's imprisonment and the abuse committed against Bolívar were both caused by a simple bedroom intrigue. But if the country was governed in such a way that events like these could occur without even the victims being aware of the reasons for them, we have to accept that any explanation, no matter how flimsy, cannot be more absurd than the facts. Moreover, there was a certain synchronism between the two affairs. Esteban's imprisonment seems to have begun in September 1800, and the incident at the Toledo gate occurred the following March. Bolívar obtained a passport to return to Madrid in April 1802, while a letter of January 1803 shows that Esteban was then free. If we wanted to attribute greater significance to the events, it might be possible to relate them to the persecution in Venezuela provoked by the conspiracy of Gual and España. Such a connection would help explain a remark made by Bolívar in the letter of March 20, 1801 to his uncle Pedro: "I do not know what happens to your letters, which are always delayed. I haven't had a letter from you in this post, but perhaps they will come with the next. This annoys me greatly, since it is a clear sign that they collect them, read them, and then return them to the post." But, without stooping to sarcasm, we venture to suggest that, although the peninsular authorities in Venezuela were capable of such vigilance, the Madrid police were doubtless more concerned with palace intrigues than with the fate that might befall the empire.

It is worth noting, too, that just as Esteban remained in the employ of the government while held in solitary confinement, Bolívar, although prohibited from going to Madrid, was allowed to go to Paris and then return to Spain. He was away from January to March 1802, and was in Paris for the celebration of the Peace of Amiens. This made an extraordinary impression on Bolívar for, as is well known, all France was stirred with enthusiasm for the treaty, and Napoleon, proclaimed "restorer of the State and genius of the peace", took advantage of it to establish the lifetime Consulate, thus breaking, at one and the same time, with both revolutionary and "legitimist" France.

Unfortunately there are no extant letters for this period of Bolívar's life, but the references he made in later years to Napoleon recorded by Perú de Lacroix and others, suggest that the proclamation of the empire made more of an impression on him than the festivities of 1802, possibly because his political ideas were more defined at the time of Napoleon's coronation, whereas on his first visit to France his mind was absorbed with his plans to marry and return to Venezuela. The visit to Paris was accidental, in that it was brought about by the incident in Madrid and by his fiancée's return to the capital from Bilbao. When he wrote to his uncle Pedro in August 1801, he spoke only of marrying and returning immediately to Venezuela. In any case, he remained in Paris for only two months. He left for Spain at the end of March 1802, traveled from Bilbao to Madrid in April, and was finally able to marry on May 26. He was still only nineteen; María Teresa was twenty.

At the ceremony the bride produced as her witness a haughty uncle, "Sr. Don Luis Quijada Quiñones y Moreno, Marqués de Inicio, Conde de Revolledo, Contador Mayor de los Reinos y Secretario de la Diputación." None of Bolívar's immediate relatives were present. His uncle Esteban was still in prison, and Pedro was unable to leave Cádiz. While Bolívar was doubly happy with the marriage and the prospect of returning to Venezuela, his young bride must have been apprehensive about the perilous voyage and her future life in an unknown land which Europeans imagined to be full of mysteries and dangers.

Bolívar's determination to return immediately to Venezuela is very revealing in a psychological sense and of historical significance when we remember that he represented the creole oligarchy, proud of being American and about to seek independence. It is true that the terms under which he had inherited his *mayorazgo* required him to live in Venezuela, but the Palacios Blanco brothers had managed to overcome similar obstacles, either by pleading service to the crown or by purchasing dispensations. Their letters show that from the time that he first went to Spain, they planned a career in Madrid for Simón, for in their opinion, he would find at court opportunities for glory and advancement which Venezuela could not offer.[1] Moreover, after his marriage to Teresa her aristocratic relatives had the power to open the most aristocratic houses to him. If he preferred it, the Marquis de Ustáriz, who treated him like a son, could introduce him to a career in government or public administration. If he had submitted to pressures such as these, Bolívar would have taken his bride to Paris, which was once more a city of security and happiness, but his mind was upon other things. He wanted to settle in Venezuela, and, now that he was educated and able to understand the importance of America, felt impatient to discuss the future with his compatriots. To marry and to establish himself in Venezuela were two inseparable goals. His love for Teresa and the wish to take her to the country which would be her homeland were fused into a single deep desire. Venezuela was calling him; the ancestors who had endured dangers and hardships to make this new world theirs were calling him.

This, basically, was what his determination to return to Venezuela signified. And from this solid American creole, which he now was, would emerge the Liberator. It must again be stressed that, during his stay in Spain, he was not the unbridled youth or the premature Jacobin depicted by careless authors.

In accordance with his wishes, the newlyweds sailed from Spain soon after the wedding, and reached Caracas by the end of August. Bolívar had been away for three and a half years. He had left as a boy to return, at the age of twenty, as a married man, ready to assume full ownership of his property. He took María Teresa to live in the house belonging to his *mayorazgo,* situated on the corner called Las Gradillas on the southeast of the main square of Caracas. Parties and celebrations awaited them, for in addition to their youth and attractiveness, Teresa no doubt aroused the curiosity and the envy of all the young women in the province. Everybody hoped for stories about Napoleon or endless tales of life at court.

It is also easy to picture Bolívar's enthusiasm as he showed his wife Venezuela's tropical beauties: the strange trees and fruits; sugar-cane, coffee, the ancient rain-trees, some of which, like the one at Güere in the Aragua valley, could provide shade for a whole battalion; the *cacao* shrub, with its fat pods, full of sweet nibs, growing directly from the stem, and the multi-colored, noisy birds, which he had not seen since his childhood. María Teresa also found a cousin, the Marquis del Toro, in Caracas, and she discovered in the city's salons that she had entered an elegant, cultured society that loved music and read verse. It is true however, that the men were taciturn and overly serious, and at the other extreme, scandalously incautious with their comments on prohibited books and their vehement criticisms of local affairs.

---

1. Boletín de la Academia de la Historia, N° 52, Caracas.

Medallion of Bolívar by David D. Angers, 1832.

Count de Segur drew attention to the seriousness of the men of Caracas compared with the grace and vitality of the women, while Humboldt commented upon the daring with which they discussed politics, and the interest of all classes of society in public affairs. He reported that when he first visited Caracas he met some people on Mt. Avila: "They were *caraqueños,* and were arguing among themselves about the independence movement. . . I was surprised by the unrest which reigned in their minds. . . When we entered the inn an elderly man who had spoken more calmly than the others, reminded them how imprudent they were, both on the mountain and in the city, to embark on political discussions in these dangerous times."

The Bolívar family had a holiday residence on the banks of the Guaire at the southern edge of the city. At its gate was a Latin inscription chosen by Andrés Bello, who had become Bolívar's tutor when Simón Rodríguez went to Europe. It read: "Here you will find the comforts of the city joined with the delights of the countryside." The house, gardens and stables covered more than three hectares; two giant cedars which stood there were named after Tamanaco, an Indian chief who had fought, it was said, one of his battles in their shade during the Conquest. Another family property, always mentioned by historians, was the *hacienda* of San Mateo in the Aragua valley, although its fame is derived mainly from the battles fought there during the Independence period. The young Bolívar preferred the *hacienda* of Yare, nearer to Caracas, where he established extensive indigo plantations. To the north and east of the city lay Bolívar's favorite walks, along the banks of the Catuche and the Anauco. A leafy rain-tree, originally a cutting from the tree at Güere, under which Bolívar again began to meet Andrés Bello, still stands alongside the Catuche.

As these delights were revealed to Teresa, the young couple dreamed and planned for the future and made their home in the Venezuela so loved by Bolívar. Teresa's father, also a *caraqueño,* must have been delighted by her letters describing her discoveries and her happy life in her new country. But their correspondence was brief. Yellow fever was then endemic in Venezuela. It killed in a few days, sometimes in hours, and Europeans were particularly at risk. The unfortunate Teresa contracted the terrible disease and died on January 22, 1803, after only five months in Caracas.

Nothing of what has been written about Bolívar's grief seems exaggerated. He had loved Teresa with dedication, and for her sake had resisted the temptations and frivolities of life in Madrid. His plans to establish himself in Venezuela had been built around her. All this had been destroyed in the five days that she had been able to hold out against the sickness. Fearful Europeans described the fever as "tropical", but in a sense it was Venezuelan, a part of "his Venezuela" that he had shown to her with such affection. He never again sought a love like that which he held for Teresa, so fierce in its constancy and purity. He had written to his uncle Pedro as he planned for the future with Teresa: "May God grant me a son." After her death he never again considered such a durable union. He loved other women briefly without considering them important, while his young wife always lived in the intimacy of his conscience. He was unjust in this sense with even the fascinating Manuelita Sáenz, whom he called "the lovable madwoman." He rediscovered Teresa only towards the end of his life in the young girl whom he called "la gloriosa," and who called him "mi glorioso." Her real name was Joaquina Garaicoa, but she lovingly signed herself "Gloriosa Simona Joaquina Trinidad... y Bolívar." The Liberator showed such exaggerated concern for her innocence that he must have been motivated in part by the memory of his first-love.

Bolívar was not inconsolable in the romantic sense. He did not make a spectacle and cry out his grief, but an analysis of his subsequent love life can persuade us that he was always Teresa's widower, without realizing it himself. But this was later. So many things were to occur later! At the time, the only feeling as he saw his young wife lying in her coffin was one of disbelief. She had been dressed in a rich gown of white brocade and her head rested on the robe in which Simón had been christened. She was barely twenty-one, and, before her illness, her features had possessed all the freshness of a young girl. Now Bolívar did not venture to lift the cloth which covered her face, so as not to see her adorable countenance scarred by the bilious yellow color spread throughout her body by the fever. For two years he had courted her in Madrid with unflagging enthusiasm. With what solemnity he had first addressed her, "my lady Doña Teresa!"

VIII

ON THE ROAD
TO POLITICS

T ERESA'S DEATH SHATTERED all Bolívar's plans. Even the question of his accomodations became an irriting problem. He could remain alone in the vast mansion intended for a large family, or move temporarily into the house of Juan Vicente, or of one of his married sisters. But the very prospect of remaining in Venezuela, previously anticipated so eagerly, had been made odious by the tragedy. He decided to return to Europe. He was aided in his crisis by an ability to recover quickly from misfortunes, a quality which he was to demonstrate frequently later in life, and he immediately began to prepare for the voyage. On August 9, 1803 he asked the treasury to provide him with 20,000 pesos, to be repaid in Cádiz after the sale there of products from his *haciendas*. The money was required not for the expenses of his journey, but for the maintenance of his estates in his absence. Even in peacetime it was inadvisable to transport money across the Atlantic if it could be avoided, and such arrangements were commonly made for the convenience of both landowners and treasury officials. Landowners thus avoided the dangers involved in shipping their receipts back from Spain, and the dispatch of revenue from Venezuela was facilitated for the treasury. But the system was sometimes difficult to operate, especially when war at sea disrupted shipping and caused a shortage of coinage in America. Thus, on this occasion, the treasury ordered on August 11 that Bolívar's request could not be met, "because, when the Superintendency received the first news about the present circumstances, it decided to make no further payments from the capital collected for remittal to Spain."[1] But it ordered on August 31 that he should be allowed 12,000 pesos.

---

1. Quoted by Lecuna in *Catálogo...*, i, p. 140.

It seems that Bolívar invested all the money in the coffee and indigo plantations that he had established on his Ceuce and Yare estates. He was so concerned about them that as soon as he arrived in Cádiz he asked his agent in Caracas to send a detailed report on them, including "even the least significant thing that happens on these estates." He added, with his customary enthusiasm: "Every day I am more anxious to see a beautiful coffee estate at Ceuce."[1]

It is clear that Bolívar made a brave effort to overcome his personal misfortune. The interest showed in his estates, by a man who was never corcerned about money, was simply one of the avenues which he was exploring in the struggle to find his destiny. It also reflected an instinct, inherited from his ancestors, to build and create.

Arrangements for the journey to Spain were completed by October. Bolívar must have sailed almost immediately after formally vesting his brother Juan Vicente with responsibility for his affairs on October 23, for he was in Cádiz by the end of December 1803. This second visit to Europe was made in very different circumstances from the first, when his tender age, his inexperience and his early romance led him to think only of himself and his future with his wife. By 1803 the emptiness in his life had, in a sense, liberated him from selfish preoccupations. The spectacle which the Napoleonic world presented was such as to awaken even the most idle imagination; for the dynamic Bolívar it must have been like a sunny, open field suddenly appearing before a prisoner.

Even Napoleon's enemies were fascinated by his genius and his almost incredible career. After the gradual spread of monarchy and the chaos produced by the French Revolution, Europe was shaken for the first time by the will of one man, who showed what could be achieved by a personal, improvised power, dedicated simultaneously to the restoration of order and the continuation of revolution. At the beginning of the Revolution Mirabeau had declared: "Opportunity is being reborn. Ambition is now permitted." Under Napoleon this prophecy was fulfilled, since the opportunities for promotion and glory were opened to all men, and all were stimulated by his own incomparable drive. Most of the marshals and administrators of the empire had risen to office from the lower and lower-middle classes. The only qualification demanded of them was ability; and their emergence was, in effect, part of a world-wide democratic revolution, certainly more thorough than anything that egalitarian legislation could have achieved. There was no toleration of inefficiency, ineptitude, or intrigues caused by fear and faction. War was declared on the favoritism and stagnation that had sheltered the nobility

---

1. *Cartas,* xi, p. 3.

in all the courts of Europe. Even in England, the model of political organization for the rest of the world, commissions in the army were sold
openly until the middle of the nineteenth century, despite the repeated
observation that the superiority of the navy was due to the fact that
naval promotions were achieved only by ability and merit.

In Bourbon Spain and Italy the whole of secular life was marred by the
corruption and negligence emanating from the courts, while in the absolute monarchies of Russia, Prussia and Austria the palace cliques were
isolated from the people. But everywhere routine and parasitism were
the rule, except on the rare occasions when the whims of a monarch
accidentally coincided with national needs.

The French Revolution made the first crack in this outdated system.
By demonstrating the superiority of the "people in arms" over courtly
armies, it promised to force aggresive reform in the political sphere,
but it failed to create an efficient administrative machine to provide
the stable base for this gigantic reformation. The same problem still
confronts all radical political movements. Indeed, the strongest opponents
of social justice are not its deliberate enemies, but those who forget, in
their enthusiasm for reform that, without an administrative foundation
to give concrete reality to political principles, errors soon have to be
covered up with lies, and lies with abuses and cruelty. This happened
with the French Revolution, and it happens with many twentieth century revolutions.

It seemed that Napoleon had found a new way through these dangers,
and it was certainly true in 1803 that if he could make his administrators
work as ably and efficiently as his untrained generals had on the battlefields, there would be no limit to the fulfillment of the aspirations of
the people. There was nothing in any field of human activity, including
business, politics, arts and science, that could not be achieved in an open,
equal struggle. This, in fact, was the real revolution that men wanted,
something tangible and immediate, with direct benefits for all men. By
holding out such a prospect, Napoleon aroused tremendous enthusiasm
in France. As we will see, his system was not entirely without corruption and intrigue. An even greater problem, growing in the background,
was that his own excesses and his angry reaction to individuals and institutions who refused to submit to him were to turn his movement away
from peace and organization.

When Napoleon first appeared, many nations welcomed him as a liberator, and for all people he represented the hope for a fuller, worthier
life in place of the ignorance and immorality in which the former governments had kept their subjects. But these promising horizons grew
more distant as Napoleon became increasingly preoccupied with strictly
French interests. Victor Hugo later recalled the days "in which the name

of France made the world tremble." Many men continued to search for freedom, and, particularly in those countries which rejected both the despotism of their own monarchies and the "foreign" Napoleon, were forced to seek a new political system. The creation of the Republic in France had terrifying consequences; but these were only circumstantial, for in America the new institutions created by revolution operated within a framework of social stability and dignity for all men.

The movement which produced the French Revolution was inspired by an idealized vision of the Roman republic and the aim of combining private morality with public happiness. When Franklin was ambassador to the court of Louis XVI, the French aristocracy was delighted by his cotton stockings and shoes without buckles, and some were even prepared to renounce their splendor to live the honest, simple life of the other side of the Atlantic, which they imagined to be free of worries and problems. Later, many leaders of the Revolution, beginning with Mirabeau and Robespierre, turned in into a bloody farce. Later still, the unashamed irregularities of the Directory, which saw the emergence of a new, privileged class, offended many former supporters of the Revolution.

Those who refused to compromise reiterated in family conversations, or in discussions with workers and peasants, that the perversion of the French Revolution was an unforeseen disaster. In these semi-clandestine discussions men also talked at times about Miranda, the extraordinary South American, who had traveled throughout Europe in his efforts to pave the way for the emancipation of the Spanish colonies, promising to devote his expert knowledge of military affairs, politics, history, philosophy, public administration, and even music and antiquities, to the organization of the states he would liberate. He achieved high office during the French Revolution, captured the fortress of Amberes, and confronted Dumouriez when he tried to betray the Republic. He also opposed the excesses of Robespierre and, despite the latter's power, succeeded in clearing himself before the implacable Revolutionary Tribunal. The people of Paris carried him back to his residence in triumph. With the same inflexibility of character he refused to serve Napoleon, who recognized his ability, and he disappeared from public life. Stimulated by his ideas and by his example, the South Americans were able to share the hopes which the North Americans preserved intact.

The most serious contemporary thinkers were united in the search for a better life for the individual and for society. Condorcet had devoted all his skill as an economist, mathematician and philosopher to forming a thesis that affirmed without qualification the perfectibility of human nature. His insistence that accidental retrogressions in human development were caused solely by superstition and tyranny became an unquestioned creed. Jeremy Bentham devised ideal legislation for America, which would allow justice and reason to reign in the new world, uncorrupted by the greed and hypocrisy which destroyed all institutions in Europe. This was the confused and unstable world full of promises and excitement that Bolívar was about to enter. Many roads lay open to the enthusiasm of a young man. Nevertheless, when he disembarked in Cádiz, he could see his future only in terms of Venezuela and probably imagined himself there looking after his "beatiful estates," about which he wanted to know "even the least significant things." The confidences which he entrusted to Perú de Lacroix twenty four years later about his state of mind when he began his journey can probably be accepted literally. He said: "See how things happen. If I had not been bereaved, my life would perhaps hare been different. I would have become neither General Bolívar nor the Liberator, although I agree that my nature would not have been satisfied with the magistracy of San Mateo."

Even more interesting are the following observations which show without a doubt that Bolívar's concrete political ideas, although imprecise at first, were formed during these travels: "Orphaned, at the age of sixteen and rich, I went to Europe after visiting Mexico and the city of Havana. It was then, when in Madrid and in love, that I married Teresa Toro y Alaiza, the niece of the old Marquis del Toro. I returned from Europe to Caracas with my wife in 1802, and I assure you that my head was then filled only with vapors of the most fierce love and not with political ideas, for these had still not caught my imagination. After the death of my wife I was desolated by my sudden, unexpected loss and I returned to Spain. From Madrid I went to France and later to Italy. I was then beginning to take an interest in public affairs; political life interested me, occupied my mind, and I followed its shifting developments. In the final month of 1804, I saw the coronation of Napoleon in Paris. The magnificent ceremony filled me with enthusiasm, less for its pomp than because of the sentiments of love which an immense crowd showed for the French hero. That general effusion of all their hearts, that free and spontaneous popular movement aroused by his glories, the praise of Napoleon, acclaimed at that moment hero by more than a million people, seemed to me the highest aspiration, the final desire, the ultimate ambition of man. I thought the crown which Napoleon put on his head a miserable object of Gothic style. What seemed great to me was the universal acclamation and the interest which his presence inspired. This, I confess, made me think of my country's enslavement and of the glory which would be bestowed upon the man who liberated it. But I was far from imagining that such fortune awaited me! Later, I began to flatter myself that one day I would be able to assist in its liberation, but not that I would play the leading role in that great process. If my wife had not died, I would not have undertaken my second journey to Europe, and I believe that the ideas which came to me during my travels would not have been formed in Caracas or San Mateo; in America I would not have acquired the same experience nor undertaken the studies of the world, of men and of things, which have served me throughout my political career. The death of my wife put me on the road to politics at an early age; it made me follow the chariot of Mars rather than the plough of Ceres: so you can see how it influenced my fate."[1]

In spite of this autobiographical account which indicates so precisely the difference between Bolívar's first and second voyages to Europe and shows how his political aspirations developed gradually, almost all his biographers have insisted on confusing the process. The actual pattern is clear: Bolívar's spiritual formation began when he was a child; he acquired knowledge and experience on his own account and with the assistance of Ustáriz, then went on to develop ideals with much human and patriotic content. Bolívar himself explained the natural, balanced development of his personality without reference to egocentric dreams or anticipation of glory. It is difficult to understand, then, why some writers feel the need to distort the truth by substituting for this calm evolution a confused mixture of vision and prophecies. The author has no intention of refuting in detail the fantasies which have accumulated about Bolívar's life in this period, since to do so would tire the reader and cause confusion rather than enlightenment. In almost all cases they will be simply ignored.

Bolívar read widely during the long voyage from Venezuela to Spain. According to Mancini: Plutarch, Montesquieu, Voltaire and Rousseau were among the authors whose works he selected. He disembarked in Cádiz at the end of December, and remained there until the beginning of February, arranging business matters with his commercial agents in the port. According to Mitre, he was also admitted to the "Gran Logia Americana," and swore an oath of loyalty to the republican system as "the most suitable for the government of the Americas." But it seems unlikely that the Cádiz liberals would have risked confiding in a young American aristocrat who was only in the city for a month. It is more realistic to accept Bolívar's own statement that his political ideas were still undefined. What is certain is that he went to Madrid in February 1804. There he met his lifelong friend, Fernando Rodríguez del Toro, the cousin of Teresa. They traveled to Paris together in April.

Bolívar lived for a year in France, until he set out for Italy in April 1805. He returned in December 1805 or early in 1806, and lived there again, almost certainly in Paris, until September 1806. He then went to Ham-

---

1. Perú de Lacroix, *op. cit.*, p. 226.

burg, and in October sailed for the United States on a neutral vessel. After spending four months in the main cities of North America, he returned to Caracas in June 1807. He had spent almost two of his three and a half years in Europe living in France, although his time there was broken by the eight months spent in Italy.

In the French capital Bolívar and Fernando Toro made contact with a number of other young Spanish Americans, including Carlos Montúfar and Vicente Rocafuerte from Ecuador. Montúfar, who was to die in the struggle for independence, was the son of the Marquis de Selva Alegre, who in 1809 became president of the Revolutionary Junta of Quito, the first to be formed in South America. Rocafuerte did not play an active role in the emancipation, and for this reason later felt himself to be in a "false position" in front of his former companions. He became an enemy of Bolívar during the last years of Gran Colombia.[1] An unexpected member of the intimate circle which these young expatriates soon formed in Paris was Simón Rodríguez. He was little more than thirty years old; so, in age at least, there was little to distinguish him from other members of the group. He wrote to Bolívar in 1826: "I do not know if you remember that when we were in Paris I always took the blame for what happened to Toro, Montúfar, you and all your friends,"[2] words which suggest that friendly disputes frequently arose between the young men and the turbulent but respected educator.

It is believed that Rodríguez had left Caracas for Europe in 1797. There is little concrete evidence about his life there, although there are numerous legends about his activities. The only thing certain is that he continued to teach under the assumed name Samuel Robinson and was inspired by the idea of promoting a general reform in education. He wrote many years later in *Luces y virtudes sociales* (1834 and 1840 editions): "my rough drafts for *Instrucción Pública* were prepared at the end of the last century in Europe, where I lived and taught for many years." His failure to mention the memorandum submitted to the municipal council of Caracas suggests that his later works, which unfortunately have not survived, must have been much more important. He taught Spanish in Bayonne and Paris and prepared the first translation into Spanish of Chateaubriand's *Atala* under his assumed name. The translation appeared in 1801, and although Fray Servando Teresa de Mier claimed the credit

---

1. In 1830 Fanny de Villars wrote of Rocafuerte to Bolívar: "Only self-love keeps him allied to you... the false direction he would have taken as a result of the divisions in the different Republics isolates him from everybody, and in these circumstances you could attract him to you for his own sake and for the general good; he cannot offer himself, because he finds himself in a false position with respect to his former compatriots and to you" (Boletín de la Academia Nacional de la Historia, no. 52, p. 668, Caracas).
2. O'Leary, ix, p. 513.

for it in his memoirs, there is now no doubt that it was the work of Rodríguez.[1]

Soon after Bolívar arrived in Paris, another woman came into his life, the married Fanny Dervieu du Villars. Her family name was Trobriand, and she also occasionally added the name Aristeguieta, claiming to be Bolívar's cousin. Nobody has ever found evidence of any family relationship. This amorous adventure has given rise to the most extravagant fantasies, and a digression is necessary to present the truth about it. Fanny's husband was made both a count and a colonel after the Restoration, but apart from an appointment to the Lyons garrison, his main activity was as a contractor to the army, an occupation which certainly did not carry much honor. As Queen Hortensia wrote in her memoirs, in Paris "the Terror was followed by balls, parties and happiness. The fortunes of France had passed into the hands of the army contractors. They took honors in the capital, and spent their easily acquired money often at a singly party."

Reliable information about Fanny is provided by her letters, although those available were written in the most miserable period of her life when she no longer enjoyed the attentions of Bolívar, who was occupied with political life. She pestered him with ridiculous requests and irritating little lies. In 1821, for example, she asked him for "between one hundred and fifty and two hundred thousand francs," a sum she considered "not beyond your actual and future greatness, especially now that peace has allowed you to recover your fortune in Caracas." She made similar requests in other letters, and in 1825 offered Bolívar "the services" of her son Augusto in the following terms: "If you wish to extend our family ties, by choosing for him a woman of your family, he would go to collect her, and you could return him to me in France with the title and duties of Consul General of Colombia...."[2]

These extravagances are easily explained; Fanny was a product of the confused salons of the Directory and the Consulate, where vain new-rich rubbed shoulders with ruined nobles and confused newcomers with political or military authority. All were degraded by the changes introduced to public life with unprecedented rapidity and none knew—nor wished to know—whether they belonged to the *ancien régime,* the revolution, or the empire. Struggling madly for favors, they recreated

---

1. See the oustanding study of Dr. Pedro Grases in *Escritos de don Simón Rodríguez,* Caracas, 1954.
2. Boletín de la Academia Nacional de la Historia, n° 52, Caracas. This same source reveals that Fanny's brother-in-law, also a colonel, was in Colombia at the end of 1827 and early in 1828. After witnessing riots against Bolívar in Cartagena, he sailed for New York, from where he asked Bolívar for 4,000 piastres, pleading the damage to his honor threatened by outstanding debts and the ruin of his bankers in Paris.

the way of life which Saint Simon observed in the reign of Louis XIV, about which Taine commented: "We, who are educated in equality, will never understand the frightful distance, the pounding of the heart, the veneration, the profound humility, which a man felt before his superior; the vehement passion with which a man resorted to intrigue, favoritism, lies, adulation and even infamy to clamber up a step above his station."[1] During the Directory, before the egalitarian revolution was completed, money began to re-establish that frightful distance. Napoleon introduced new forms of control, many of them legitimate, but court customs tended to survive.

Only a setting like this can explain Fanny's willingness to offer her son to Bolívar, so that he could be forwarded to her, as if by return post, married to a woman he did not know, but with the office of Consul. The young man was no more than twenty-nine years old, and, according to the letter, "he has been a cavalry captain for two years, and is well regarded by his superiors and his comrades," etc., etc.

Bolívar must have been even more angered by his former mistress's attempts to compromise him with childish inventions. On a number of occasions she lamented that she had suffered political persecution for her loyalty to him, while at other times she offered him her influence at the court of the restored Bourbons. She wrote to him in 1825: "My position in society and even in the French Court is good. It is no longer considered a crime that I belong to you, and there seems in this to have been a change for the better." She wrote the following year, referring to 1820, "...but what will surprise you most, my dear cousin, will be to learn that on April 20, 1820 the person who questioned me with the most lively interest about your character, your ability and your birth was King Louis XVIII, who granted an audience I had requested with the aim of dispelling charges made against my son. His colonel, the Marquis of Rochedragon, had threatned him with expulsion from the regiment because a friendly, enthusiastic letter which he sent to you had been intercepted. The King, full of kindness and with his solicitous nature, told me to calm myself; he asked for your portrait, which I delivered to the Duke of Chartres, his first gentleman, and they kept it in the Tuileries palace for eight days."[2]

Bolívar must, indeed, have experienced surprise, and more, to read that Louis XVIII, the protégé of the Holy Alliance, the champion of "legitimacy," the monarch who sent Ferdinand VII the "hundred thousand sons of St. Louis" to re-establish absolutism in Spain, had asked Fanny for his portrait in 1820 and had kept it in the palace for eight days.

---

1. H. Taine: *Essais de critique at d'histoire.* Paris, 1920, p. 201.
2. O'Leary, Narración, i, p. 62, Caracas, 1952.

No doubt he wanted to show it to his courtiers "with the most lively interest," "full of kindness," etc. Some North American and European adventurers still tell such cock-and-bull stories to deceive certain South American presidents. But it is clear that Bolívar was not fooled. This explains why he only replied to his former mistress "now and then," to quote her. In 1820, she reproached him for not replying to her letters; she repeated the complaint in February 1821 and again in April 1823; in August 1825, she observed that the first and last letter received from him was dated July 20, 1822. In her 1823 letter she told Bolívar that she still had his portrait, probably one that he gave her before he returned to Venezuela, and Bolívar's letter of August 14, 1830, to Leandro Palacios reveals that he sent her another. [1]

This distressing spectacle of Fanny when she had lost both her youth and her fortune should not be allowed to obscure the fact that when she was rich and surrounded by a brilliant, if not very select, society, her home offered a pleasant refuge to the unknown *caraqueño*. Fanny did not need to be a Cornelia to be an enchanting lover in Paris; and Bolívar was content to enjoy his conquest without questioning the nobility or the military prowess of Fanny's husband. This analysis is intended to refute the attempts of certain authors to depict this amorous adventure and others which are more or less authentic, as decisive events in Bolívar's life. Bolívar himself wrote: "To be the Liberator means more than everything else; and for this reason I will not degrade myself before a throne." It was obviously futile to attempt to flatter him by inventing stories about kings and aristocrats. Bolívar was a rain-tree, not a vine. He grew stubbornly and slowly, amidst the change which life brought, just as those trees in his native land grow to be great and lasting. It is both false and ridiculous to show him creeping up like a vine, with stories that he knocked off Ferdinand VII's hat and argued with this or that prince in Fanny's salons, or that Louis XVIII was anxious to know him.

O'Leary included many of these stories in his valuable work, thus giving them great authority, since it could be assumed that he had heard them from the Liberator. In fact, the source was Fanny. She told them to General Leandro Palacios, who later passed them on to O'Leary. From his infancy and his youth, Bolívar's life was a battle, and his greatness was achieved only with much effort, constancy and valor. Only an incompetent biographer or a vulgar reader finds it necessary to substitute paper adornments for the natural poetry in the lives of great men. The adventure with Fanny did, however, acquire importance and provoked various legends because of two letters which Bolívar was supposed to have writ-

1. Boletín de la Academia Nacional de la Historia, no. 52, pp. 655, 657, 659 and 660 respectively, Caracas. For the letter to Palacios, see *Cartas*, ix, p. 286.

ten to her. It is now known that they were not intended for Fanny; and they contain so many anachronisms and errors of fact that it is very difficult to accept that Bolívar wrote them. In any case, there is not a single paragraph in them that can serve as historical material. For these reasons they are not discussed here but, because of their notoriety, are analyzed in the *Appendix*.

These letters and the extravagant commentaries which accompanied them each time they were published, provided the main source for the legend that Bolívar abandoned himself to a life of endless, aimless dissipation in Europe. The story that he imprudently disseminated ultra-radical political ideas in the Paris salons, stirring up arguments with the most prominent people in the empire, is equally groundless. As Vicente Lecuna wisely pointed out, nearly all Bolívar's fortune was tied up in the *mayorazgo,* and he did not enjoy free access to it. His expenditure was restricted to the income from his rents, although this was no doubt sufficient to permit a comfortable life, at least equal to those led by the other rich South Americans in Paris.

The stories of his prodigal life in the French capital should be seen in this context. As far as romances and dissipation are concerned, General Serviez, who later accompanied him in some of the campaigns for independence, related: "His recollection of Paris was like that one retains of a first passion. In the midst of the Liberator's serious worries, it was like a scholar's recreation for him to take a mental stroll past the Royal Palace. He was then filled with intense ardor for pleasure, and in particular for small pleasures, and it was a really extraordinary thing to hear the Liberator of one's country cite, one by one, the female beauties he had known in France with a precision and exactitude that did credit to his memory. He quoted the puns of Brunet, sang the fashionable verses, and laughed about his youthful pranks with a truly ingenuous expression."[1] All this was very natural, but of no great importance. Serviez added: "But he showed the greatest enthusiasm when he recalled memories of another sort. He told me of his sense of glory and liberation when he watched the First Consul's military parades in the Place du Carrousel and, impressed by the glory which shone through all the ceremonies, repeated the patriotic airs of the music of the French regiments."[2] A further point which contradicts those who try to give great importance to Bolívar's youthful frolics is that when he returned to Europe, he took with him his young nephew, Anacleto Clemente, who was about to begin his education there. The voluntary assumption of this responsibility

---

1. Quoted by Jules Mancini in his biography of Bolívar, Paris, 1923, p. 136. It is taken from the work published in Paris in 1832, under the title *L'Aide de Camp ou l'Auteur Inconnu. Souvenirs de Deux Mondes,* generally considered to be the memoirs of Serviez.
2. Quoted by Lecuna, *Catálogo . . . ,* ii, p. 46.

indicated a strong feeling of family solidarity. It also belies the state of spiritual nihilism in which some authors insist Bolívar found himself after his wife's death. Years later, in 1826, Bolívar referred in one of his letters to his plans for his nephew's education and showed how conservative were his ideas on what a young man could do and what was forbidden. He wrote: "Lima, May 29, 1826. Señor Anacleto Clemente. Anacleto: I am tired of hearing complaints from your mother and your family, and I am going to talk to you for the last time through my aide-de-camp, O'Leary, who will bear this letter to you. He will tell you to your face how disgusted I am by your bad conduct, and will acquaint you with my order that you return immediately to your family in Venezuela, if not to care for it, at least to protect it from the discredit you have been causing it in Bogotá. I tell you for the last time, Anacleto, if you fail to leave Bogotá immediately, if you do not give up this accursed vice of gambling, I will disinherit you for ever; I will abandon you to yourself. It is a disgrace for you and your family to see your scandalous behavior in Bogotá, making your poor mother responsible for sums which even a potentate does not spend, deserting your wife and, to complete the picture, discrediting the Vice President. You are failing your country, your honor, your family and your blood."[1]

Another paragraph of this letter, in which Bolívar held up as an example to Anacleto the *llaneros* who out of self-respect "have made themselves gentlemen," will be discussed in more detail in a later chapter. But enough of it has been transcribed to suggest that Bolívar's conduct in Paris probably lay somewhere between what Serviez described and what he himself insisted to his nephew were the obligations imposed by honor and blood. Despite his youthful carelessness and the vigor of his temperament, his self-respect held him back from vulgarity and looseness. It should be remembered that the visit made to Paris during his first stay in Europe was accidental. He stayed there only two months, so preoccupied with his plans to return to Venezuela and raise a family that even political events in France made little impression on him. It was natural, then, when he returned, that he should be fascinated by the enchanting city and attracted by the women and other diversions. He enjoyed the easy women with ingenuous surprise, but they did not capture his spirit, which was already committed to other matters.

It was from the end of 1804, in fact, that Bolívar's intellectual development began to accelerate. Many long hours of doubts and argument separated the conventional, rather fashionable creole so far encountered from the brilliant writer and political thinker of 1812 who committed himself, with a clear aim, to the revolution. There were also long dis-

---

1. *Cartas,* v, p. 319.

Simón Bolívar (1811-1813?) by an anonymous artist.

cussions with Rodríguez, with other Spanish Americans living in Paris, and with eminent scientists such as Humboldt and Bonpland. The intimacy enjoyed by Bolívar with these scholars was an indication of his own intellectual abilities. In 1822, Humboldt recalled: "The friendship with which General Bolívar deigned to honor me after my return from Mexico, in a period when we were praying for the Independence and the liberty of the New Continent. . . ." A year later Bolívar asked the dictator of Paraguay to release Bonpland, saying that he awaited this "with the anxiety of a friend and the respect of a follower."

This was the path to politics then opening before Bolívar, he confided to Perú de Lacroix. It was still to take the form of historical studies and reflections on men and events for a number of years; but it was sound preparation for the direct political action he was later to follow in Spanish America.

IX

I SWEAR...

THROUGHOUT HIS LIFE BO-
lívar was an avid reader. Mancini tells us that when he left Venezuela
for Europe, he took the works of Plutarch, Montesquieu, Voltaire and
Rousseau to read on the voyage. According to Perú de Lacroix, more
than twenty years later, in 1828, Voltaire was his favorite author.
"After lunch," he recorded in his *Diario de Bucaramanga,* H.E. went
to his hammock, and he summoned me to hear him translating French
verse into Castilian. He read from the *War of the Gods* as if it were
written in Spanish. He read easily, quickly and eloquently. I listened for
more than an hour, and I confess that I did so with pleasure. H.E. had
to ask me to translate only a very few words. At dinner H.E. praised
the works of Voltaire, his favorite writer. He went on to discuss a
number of English writers, particularly Walter Scott. He ended by commenting that he did not like Jean Jacques Rousseau's *Nouvelle Héloise,*
because, although the style was admirable, the work itself was dull,
whereas Voltaire had everything: style, great and profound thoughts,
philosophy, fine criticism and wit."[1]
Bolívar himself occasionally mentioned the works that he read. When
he wrote to Santander on May 20, 1825 he was untypically violent, because a "servile, lying *godo*"[2] had suggested that he was poorly educated.
Referring mainly to the time that he spent in Paris, Bolívar told Santan-

---

1. Lacroix, *op. cit.,* p. 305.
2. *"Godo"* means conservative.

der: "My mother and family made every possible effort in order that I might have proper instruction. They secured for me the foremost teachers in my country. Robinson, whom you know, taught me reading and writing. Our celebrated Bello taught me the art of composition and geography. Father Andújar, of whom Baron von Humboldt had a high opinion, created an academy of mathematics especially for me. I was sent to Europe to continue my study of mathematics at the Academy of San Fernando. I studied foreign languages with selected teachers in Madrid —all under the direction of the learned Marquis de Ustáriz, in whose home I lived. While I was still very young, perhaps too young for such arts, I took lessons in dancing, fencing and horsemanship. It is true that I learned neither the philosophy of Aristotle nor the codes of crime and error. But it may be that M. de Mollien has not gone as deeply as I into Locke, Condillac, Buffon, D'Alembert, Helvetius, Montesquieu, Mably, Filangieri, Lalande, Rousseau, Voltaire, Rollin, Berthot, and the classicists of antiquity, whether they be philosophers, historians orators or poets, as well as the modern classics of Spain, France and Italy, and not a few of the English."[1]

The remark about Aristotle reflects the world-wide reaction against his authority which free inquiry had been eroding since the Middle Ages. In America this reaction was combined with a frantic search for new methods in all activities, a state of mind very clearly reflected by Juan García del Río's observation that: "In Europe philosophy began to break the chains of terminology, but for us it created a subtle, euphistic, abstract method of reasoning. Aristotle, banished from Europe by Bacon, took refuge in America. Scepticism reigned in the land of Galileo, Descartes, Newton and Leibnitz, but the most blind credulity remained supreme on the other side of the Atlantic."[2] As in every movement of liberation, those who took pride in "the new philosophy" distorted what had gone before. But Bolívar was too sensible to submit blindly to new trends as part of the process of rejecting the formalism personified by Aristotle. On the other hand, nearly all the authors that he mentions were, in their time, the source of the most dynamic ideas, and his letters and writings show quite clearly that he read them. These writers helped stimulate the period's intellectual curiosity, and this was the first stage in the diffusion of an understanding of science and politics.

Bolívar's other favorite writers have been skillfully identified by Manuel Pérez Vila, who points out: "The names of José de Acosta, Antonio de Solís, Herrera (author of the famous *Decades),* and Las Casas appear in Bolívar's writings, together with those of Robertson, Humboldt and

---

1. *Cartas,* iv, p. 337.
2. *Revista del estado anterior y actual de la instrucción pública en la América antes española.* Repertorio americano, i, p. 235, London, October 1826.

Fray Servando Teresa de Mier, all of whom wrote about America. The ghosts of Pizarro, Almagro, Garci-González de Silva, Cortés, Carlos V and the Welsars come face to face with those of Atahualpa, Huaina-Cápac, Manco-Cápac, Manaure, Montezuma and Tupac Amaru. Colocolo springs from the pages of *La Araucana;* the dazzling figure of Quetzal-coatl, about whom the Jesuit historian Acosta wrote, is taken from native legends." He goes on: "Dr. Pedro Grases reports that he has found analogies with one of the *Sueños* of Quevedo —*El Mundo por de dentro y por de fuera*— in *Mi delirio sobre el Chimborazo,* which Bolívar wrote about 1822. He explains that, although the two pieces are basically different, 'the construction with abstract characters is in the style of Quevedo, whose works Bolívar read'. There is also evidence that Bolívar was familiar with the works of Padre Isla *(Fray Gerundio),* Ercilla *(La Araucana)* and possibly Góngora, as well as with those of moralists and pamphleteers like Gracián and Saavedra Fajardo. During his stay in Madrid he went to see Ramón de la Cruz's famous parody, *Manolo,* and years later, in June 1825, he referred to it in his letter to Olmedo: 'Manolo and El Cid, although sons of different fathers, are blood brothers.' The works of modern French writers and philosophers were the most important influence on Bolívar's cultural development or, to be more precise, they were the most referred to in his writings. The names of Montesquieu, Rousseau and Voltaire, the first two especially, appear frequently, and their ideas are discussed, sometimes approvingly, sometimes not. One has the impression —so far no more than an impression— that Montesquieu appealed to Bolívar's intelligence, while Rousseau found a response in his sensibility. Another influence was Count Volney, whose dedication in the Spanish edition of his works was quoted by Bolívar in the Angostura Address. Bolívar remembered him again in Cuzco in 1825. The list also includes Raynal, Marmontel, Baronness de Staël, Carnot, Benjamin Constant, the poet Casimir Delavigne, Abbot De Pradt, Bishop Gregoire, Count Guibert, La Condamine, Abbot Carlos de Saint Pierre, Sieyés, Racine, Corneille, Boileau, La Fontaine, Descartes, and others mentioned by Bolívar in his oft-cited letter from Arequipa."[1]

O'Leary too referred to the philosophers studied by Bolívar at the time of his second visit to Europe: "Helvetius, Holbach and Hume were among the writers recommended by Rodríguez... Bolívar admired the austere independence of Hobbes, despite the clear monarchical bias in what he wrote; but he was more attracted by the speculative opinions of Spinoza, and it is there, perhaps, that we should look for the source of some of his political ideas." O' Leary's conviction on this point suggests

---

1. Manuel Pérez Vila, *La formación intelectual de Bolívar: estudios y lecturas* in *Escritos del Libertador,* Caracas, 1964, p. 442-3.

that Bolívar discussed these authorities with him at some length. We know that Bolívar sent some works of Voltaire, Locke, Robertson and other writers to Chile for him in 1823. It is now fashionable to think that a man of culture must possess much "information"; then, however, a man with few books could have many ideas, because he absorbed what he read and savored it like a spiritual meal.

Another piece of evidence about the Liberator's literary tastes refers to the last few days of his life. When, according to Cornelio Hispano, he arrived half-dead at Joaquin Mier's house in Santa Marta, he looked for books to read in the library and remarked to his host: ". . . here you have the history of mankind. Here is Gil Blas, that is, man as he is, and *Don Quixote,* man as he should be." A few days later he exclaimed in deep melancholy: "Jesus Christ, Don Quixote de la Mancha and I have been the world's three greatest fools."

Bolívar had Simón Rodríguez to guide his studies and to animate what he read, although the teacher's Socratic method consisted in disguising his concern. In the well-known letter of 1824, in which Bolívar acknowledged that Rodríguez molded his heart "for liberty, justice, greatness and beauty," he also wrote: "I have followed the path you traced for me. You were my pilot, though you remained upon the shores of Europe. You cannot imagine how deeply engraved upon my heart are the lessons you taught me. Never could I delete so much as a comma from the great precepts that you set before me. They have been ever present in my mind's eye; I have followed them as infallible guides. In short, you have seen what I have done. You have seen my thoughts in print, my soul on paper, and you must have said to yourself: All that is mine; I sowed this plant, I watered it, I strengthened it when it was weak. . . ."

There is no doubt that Rodríguez's influence upon his pupil was as much intellectual as moral, and that it was important both when Bolívar was a child and when he was adult. On both occasions Rodríguez became the future Liberator's liberator: When he prevented the persecuted boy's rebelliousness from becoming a serious defect in his character, and later, in Paris, when he guided Bolívar away from mere pleasure seeking. In both cases he strove to direct Bolívar's disparate spiritual impulses towards new horizons. Rodríguez's intellectual mastery did not come from his factual knowledge or from formal lessons; it sprang from the enchantment with which he animated history and from the vivacity and insight with which he judged men and events.

The pseudo-classicism, characterized by the glorification of Greek and Roman republicans which became fashionable after the reign of Louis XIV, and the Romantic reaction of the early nineteenth century which rejected Aristides, Brutus and Cato, were divided by a transitional movement in which the best features of both were present. This movement was predominant during the North American and French Revolutions, and it survived even longer in South America. In this period the great Classical heroes, soon to be rejected, were given greater authority than ever before by the nascent Romantic impetus. The ideal of living "like an ancient" was no longer a great tragedy, and it became genuinely attractive to young people. When Miranda went to North America, for example, he and a young country woman were able to seriously compare Franklin with Aristides; the assimilation of the past into the present was in everybody's heart. The young men at the Ustáriz salon in Caracas or at concerts in the School of Music, the Carreños, Ribas, Montillas, Buroz, Salias, Pelgróns, Bolívars, Tovars, thought in the same fashion. They later went out to die for the revolution, as both ancient Stoics and modern Romantics.

These stupendous combinations frequently appear in periods of great vitality, but the transitional period between the demise of theatrical Classicism and the full flowering of literary Romanticism had other no less important characteristics. Reason, for example, was exalted in a very unreasonable way during the French Revolution. Moreover, the zeal of thinkers and politicians, from Locke to Bentham, to destroy and rebuild the State *rationally* was much more *passionate* than they realized. It was romantic, although it predated Romanticism. Their proposed reformation of society took no account of passions or of historical accidents. It was based only upon essential, fundamental factors; Reason, Justice and Liberty were the only objectives worthy of a superior mind. There is no doubt, however, that these ideals, although completely classical and anti-romantic in origin, were pursued with a totally romantic commitment.

One can even say that Romanticism was already dead by the time that it triumphed in the theatre and in France in 1830; thereafter it was merely theatrical and artificial. The real Romanticism was what had existed earlier, when men had gone insane in the name of Reason, and the Roman Republic had been considered perfect. The real Romanticism glorified the heroes of classical antiquity: they were sometimes completely false heroes, but they were admirably falsified to provide models for men to emulate.

Plutarch and his heroes were still in fashion when Bolívar reached Paris in 1804, and they saved many young men from vulgarity and routine. Humanity has always defined as heroism not merely ordinary struggles, but rather an intimate, ethical quality, which raises a man above his fellows. The hero is the man who continues to resist when others surrender, the man who believes when others doubt, the man who remains true to himself when others prostitute themselves, the man who rises up against the routine and conformity in which cowards live in comfort.

This was how Simón Rodríguez saw heroism; he often presented as examples of valor the constancy, the mental anguish and the generosity of the great men whom he skillfully plucked out of the past for his amazed pupil.

Some of these heroes were Americans. It is true that most of them did not figure in the few chronicles available to the creoles, and Rodríguez had to reconstruct their lives from oral traditions, but this gave his stories an exciting, legendary flavor. It was in this way that Bolívar first heard the sonorous Indian names of Cuauhtémoc, Caupolicán, Guaicaipuro and Sorocaima; he learned, too about the Canary Islander, Juan Francisco de León, and his Venezuelan son, Nicolás, and about the *comuneros* of New Granada and Venezuela, so Spanish in demanding "good government," but nevertheless sacrificed as rebels. He heard the story of Tupac Amaru, who unexpectedly came forward as an Inca leader at the end of the eighteenth century, and about Manuel Gual and José María España, the first men to give the revolution a democratic character. Many of these patriots —patriots before the birth of their *patria,* patriots who began by creating their own *patria*— had been slandered, scorned and generally depicted in the darkest colors by the royalists, and it was perhaps an almost unbelievable revelation for Bolívar to learn the truth about the history and people of his homeland from the mouth of Rodríguez.

It was not always necessary to look to the past for oustanding men. Some living men, like Kosciusko, were already Plutarchian heroes; Washington had died only recently; the fighters for freedom in Greece and Italy were all considered equal to the paladins of classical antiquity. Fascinating individuals could be seen in the streets of Paris. When Napoleon invaded Italy he told his troops: "Soldiers, you are naked and hungry; the Government owes you much, but it can give you nothing. I will lead you to the most fertile plains in the world, where you will find honor, glory and wealth . . . ." This bold promise is reminiscent today of the odious depredations that marred the dubious honor of the *conquistadores*. But few stopped to think of this at the time.

Their youthful minds preferred to concentrate on Napoleon's fabulous expedition to Egypt, the victories that overthrew twenty centuries of antiquity, and the hazardous return to destroy the weak corruption of the Directory. War was still a dangerous, brilliant sport, and military glory had lost none of its prestige. When one nation attacks another today, it is usually condemned for its greed or the megalomania of its leaders (who nearly always escape the disasters that follow). It is amazing to read how many times Europe went to war merely so that France could take the left bank of the Rhine and to keep it until her defeat in the next war. But even the suffering masses reacted with enthusiasm to the sound of drums and trumpets. The cautious burger who put his children or his property first was condemned as a coward.

These attitudes can be understood when it is remembered that the masses were still denied access to the scientific, literary and artistic fame that today, thanks to free public education, is within the reach of even the poorest child. Nor was it possible to achieve success through sport, journalism, the cinema, television,—avenues to fame and triumph now open to all. The opportunity to acquire wealth and position through industry or commerce was also restricted to a very small circle.

For the lower and lower-middle classes, war was the only means of escape from poverty and subordination. When the masses went into raptures at martial parades, headed by princes and generals who had previously been anonymous peasants, every man shared the dream of the most obscure soldier that he carried a marshal's baton in his knapsack.

Bolívar, as we have seen, witnessed Napoleon's coronation. His memories of it, recorded by Perú de Lacroix, reveal a confusion of feelings, with admiration and enthusiasm predominating. He also experienced, with a young man's inevitable egotism, clear doubts about what the event signified for his own future. A determined young man assimilates everything that he sees and, although he would not admit it, on even the most grandiose occasion thinks only of how he might profit from the example. If Bolívar were already beginning to form political attitudes, he must have been sad or angry when he thought of the dullness of life in America. In addition, he must have felt a choking anxiety when he compared his own insignificance with the omnipotence of Napoleon,—he was barely twenty-one years old, a face lost in the crowd,—but he was confronted with the gigantic task of emancipating America.

An apparently much less significant incident that occurred at the same time must also have stimulated Bolívar's ambition. When he discussed the possible emancipation of Spanish America with Humboldt, the *savant* told him, "I believe your land is now sufficiently mature, but I have yet to meet the man who can secure it."[1]

This wounding challenge came from the man who had lovingly revealed the beauties and the prospects of the New World to Europe, and the reproach was timely, for Bolívar was still enmeshed in his escapades at the Palais Royal. Rodríguez later repeated the same disdainful message in an effort to stimulate him: "The man who was not born for great things never appears in the place where they occur."

Bolívar went to Italy in April 1805, accompanied by Simón Rodríguez and Fernando Toro, two friends whom he preferred above all

---

1. Account of Cristóbal Mendoza in the preface to his *Colección de Documentos relativos a la vida pública del Libertador de Colombia y del Perú, Simón Bolívar, para servir a la historia de la Independencia de Sur América,* i, p. vii. Edición de Devisme Hermanos, Caracas, 1826.

others. The letters of the Dervieu du Villars show that they met him in Milan, and Fanny's husband reminded him in 1830: "I often recall our walks in Milan and your comments on the state of this nation, which already revealed the genius that has illuminated your life." A reference of Fanny's to the same period was much less poetic, although it was perhaps intended to suggest something to Bolívar about the paternity of her son, Eugenio: "My Eugenio, with whom I was pregnant in Italy."

This evidence suggests that Bolívar spent some time in Milan, and he was there, according to Lecuna, on May 26, 1805, when Napoleon was crowned King of Italy. Du Villars and his wife were probably there for this very event, perhaps in Napoleon's entourage. Bolívar must have attended many of the festivities, and we know from the *Diario de Bucaramanga* that he attended "a great parade of the Italian army, watched by Napoleon on the plain of Montesquiaro (Monte Chiaro,) near Castiglione." It was on this occasion that Bolívar was struck by the contrast between the simplicity of Napoleon's uniform and the gold and brocades of his subordinates. Perú de Lacroix recorded his impressions: "I devoted all my attention to Napoleon and I saw nobody but him among the multitude of men gathered there. My curiosity was insatiable, although I assure you that I was far from foreseeing that one day I would command the attention or, if you prefer it, the curiosity of almost a whole continent."

Some historians, anxious to stress Bolívar's republicanism, question the veracity of such statements. They overlook how attractive Napoleon was, surrounded with glory, particularly because of the discredit brought down upon the Republic by the excesses of the Revolution. Bolívar was simply excited by and interested in a man admired by the whole world, although he was far from a monarchist or a Caesarist himself.

O'Leary states that Bolívar refused to attend Napoleon's coronation in Paris: "The Spanish ambassador invited Bolívar to join his party at the ceremony, but he refused the invitation and stayed inside his house all day." His evidence about the coronation in Milan is similar: "Napoleon's triumphal entry into Milan was no less splendid than the festivities in Piedmont, and his coronation as King of Italy was no less brilliant than his crowning as Emperor of the French. But, despite its magnificence and luxury, Bolívar, who watched the ceremony, reacted as he had in Paris. He found it more rewarding to contemplate the noble city and its delightful suburbs." This version of Bolívar's actions and reactions seems to be inspired by sentimentality. Perú de Lacroix's account rings truer.

Another of O'Leary's invented anecdotes, relating this time to Bolívar's visit to Rome, bears a close resemblance to his account of Bolívar's attitude toward Napoleon. He states: "Bolívar went with the Spanish ambassador to the Vatican to be presented to Pius VII. As they drew near His Holiness, the ambassador whispered in Spanish that Bolívar should kneel and kiss the cross on the Pontiff's sandal. Bolívar refused to perform this part of the ceremony. It was in vain that the distressed ambassador insisted that it was essential to conform to etiquette. Bolívar indicated that he would not give in by firmly shaking his head. The Pope noticed the ambassador's surprise and embarrassment and, guessing its cause, said with friendly condescension, 'Let the young American do as he pleases.' He held out his hand, and Bolívar kissed his ring most respectfully. When the Pope learned that he was a South American, he put various questions to Bolívar and was well satisfied with the replies. When they had left the palace, the ambassador rebuked Bolívar for refusing to observe the ceremony of the papal court. Bolívar replied: 'The Pope must have a low opinion of the sign of the Christian religion, which he displays on his sandals, while the proudest Christian sovereigns wear it on their crowns.' "

For O'Leary's tales to be true the Spanish ambassadors in both Paris and Rome would have taken Bolívar in their retinue, the first of them, moreover, on an occasion when invitations must have been fought for by all the Spaniards and Spanish Americans in Paris. It is also almost unbelievable that, if Bolívar had been taken to the Vatican, he would not have been informed beforehand of the procedure that he should follow. Even the suggestion that a Caracas youth of no particular importance should walk alongside the ambassador on such an occasion is unconvincing.

The travelers proceeded from Milan to Venice, Ferrara, Bologna, Florence, Perugia and Rome. The insatiably curious, imaginative Rodríguez had arranged that part of their journey should be on foot, and Bolívar must have enjoyed strolling along, book in hand, savoring the country's history. One of Italy's enchantments, in fact, is the way in which varied emotions aroused by the mysticism of Asisi, the magnificence of Rome, the ambigous fascination of Venice, the exquisite turbulence of Florence and the incomparable sensuality of Naples all seem to harmonize. Whether this is because of the beauty of the surroundings or their appropriateness to the events that have occurred there, it is possible to experience the most varied impressions without confusion or discord, as if they have been diluted by their long immersion in history or sifted by the gentle beauty of nature.

It was perhaps in Florence that Bolívar read Machiavelli for the last time. According to O'Leary, he was unable to admire Machiavelli, because his name was synonymous with political trickery and crime. He reports: "Shortly before his death, Bolívar visited me in Cartagena one day, and, seeing a volume of the new edition of Machiavelli's works on my desk, told me that I could employ my time better than in reading it. We discussed Machiavelli's works and, when I realized that Bolívar was familiar with the contents of the new edition, I asked had he read it recently. He replied that he had not read a single line of Machiavelli's writings since leaving Europe, twenty-five years earlier."

Machiavelli's life was ennobled by his sufferings and his patriotism, but it has to be remembered that as a political theorist he stressed that deceit and crime are the paths to and the price of greatness. Caesar Borgia, whom he so glorified, proved beyond a doubt that Machiavelli's maxims were much more than vague theories by applying them as a reality of tricks, depredations and assassinations. Nobody could want to be a subject of a Ceasar Borgia, far less his friend, neighbor or ally, nor could anybody wish to live in a world ruled by princes like him. But in any case, Caesar Borgia's temporary success was due more to the protection of his father than to his own ability or bravery. Alexander VI seems to have been a more vigorous man, although he, too, resorted to uncontrolled infamy. Despite this, the temporary effect of his achievements was the abuse of human values.

There is abundant evidence in the modern world that popular admiration for unscrupulous governments is based upon the cowardice and servility of the common man. Individuals with real energy are rarely seduced. Many men enthusiastically support upstart despots in the foolish belief that they can share their success and escape the dullness and restraints of normal existence. Such men are not only incapable of individual greatness, but they are also unaware that their mediocrity is produced by their own limitations. They frantically endorse the tyrant's persecution out of desire to wreak vengeance on the rest of society for their own insignificance.

This brittle support collapses on the day of defeat, when the "irresistible" leader of the previous day is suddenly forced to flee the mob. Eulogies give way to taunts and insults, as the same mob that acclaimed him hastens to sneer. We know, in fact, that there was a reaction of this type against Alexander VI almost immediately after his death, and Caesar Borgia, without his father's protection, was relegated to an obscure position.

Bolívar's reluctance to endorse popular praise for Machiavelli is quite understandable, although his own aversion to trickery and opportunism in politics was, in practical terms, more of a defect than a virtue. In 1822, for example, when he controlled half a continent, he wrote to Colonel Briceño Méndez: "My attitude toward the elections in the South will be the same at it has been everywhere. What I mean is that, as always, I will not try to exercise the slightest influence." This was an honest, confident attitude, but it was also suicidal, because his enemies had no such reservations about using their influence to control Congress. The result was that Bolívar and his supporters were crushed by an irresponsible coalition of self-interested groups. Even then, an agreement with Santander could have undermined this coalition, but Bolívar did not want to deny his adversary the friendship he had formerly bestowed on him. He later acknowledged: "Our failure to make terms with Santander has lost us everybody." On numerous other occasions he suffered similar reverses and disappointments, because of the dishonesty of his rivals and his own reluctance to engage in political intrigue. Even at the end of his life, when he wanted nothing from America except a haven for his last days, he refused to live in Ecuador because he knew that to do so would make him a focus for intrigue and faction.

Nevertheless, Machiavelli's desires to expel foreigners from Italy and to unify the country must have appealed to the Venezuelan travelers, while the sharp contrast between Italy's glorious past and her present subjection reminded Bolívar of his hopes for the future of America. But his vision embodied the principles of liberty and human dignity, not the tortuous intrigues and despotism of a Caesar Borgia.

As the party reached Rome, Bolívar was clarifying his ideas in daily discussions with Rodríguez and Toro. In the middle of August, the three of them visited Monte Sacro. It was there that he swore his famous oath. Excited by his awareness of Rome's glories and miseries, he suddenly appeared transformed, and swore to his astonished companions that he would consecrate himself to the independence of America. It was then that the Liberator was born; for, as Simón Rodríguez later wrote to him, anticipating a similar observation of Nietzsche: "The benefactors of mankind are born not when they first see light but when they begin to shed it."[1]

Bolívar reminded Rodríguez of the occasion when he wrote to him from Peru nineteen years later: "Do you recall how we went together to the Monte Sacro at Rome, to pledge upon that holy ground the freedom of our country? Surely you have not forgotten that day of eternal glory for the two of us, a day when prematurely, I might say, we swore a prophetic oath to a hope we could not expect to see fulfilled." This moving recollection, written alongside the multitude of happy phrases with which Bolívar greeted Rodríguez's return to Venezuela, is sufficient proof that the oath was much more than a romantic gesture. It was a genuine commitment which Bolívar always remembered.

In all published accounts the wording of the oath is flowery and rhetorical, but these are unreliable since they are based upon the version published in 1883 by the Colombian writer Manuel Uribe on the basis of

---

1. Manuel Pérez Vila, *op. cit.*

information from Simón Rodríguez. The obvious objections are that it was second hand and written a very long time after the event.[1]

It is not difficult to imagine the scene, as the three Americans, uncertain about their own future and that of America, looked down on Rome. They were seeking a sign, an augury, and they expressed their anxiety in an oath.

At that time liberty was not a cold political concept to be analyzed by critics, nor did men invoke it with qualifications and sophisms. Instead, all men regarded it as a new way of life which would change public and private morality. It was impossible to conceive of dignity, justice or happiness without liberty, and men would achieve fame merely by fighting for it. There are numerous examples of the devotion with which men everywhere sustained these ideals, and of the way in which the hope of bringing liberty to the whole world united the most dissimilar individuals. Beethoven thought that "liberty is the goal of art, just as it is of all life." The North American Colonel William S. Smith, son-in-law of John Adams, supported Miranda's cause with such enthusiasm that he risked all he possessed for it: his fortune, his political position, his family name and even his son, whom he offered to Miranda as aide-de-camp with the endorsement that he had been "raised in the cult of liberty." Smith wrote that it pleased him to help "contribute to the liberation of countries from the yoke of oppression, to provide a refuge against persecution and to found nations freed from the lash of tyrants and the vices of corrupt courts." Humboldt put science at the service of the same ideal, and he wrote: "In affirming the oneness of the human race, we are also declaring our opposition to the repugnant concept of superior and inferior races. All are equally destined for freedom."[2]

There is little to add about Bolívar's stay in Europe. He may well have accompanied Humboldt and Gay Lussac in their ascent of Vesuvius. The French scientist Boussingault declared this to be the case in his *Memoirs,* and Bolívar's subsequent relations with Humboldt indicate that they were on relatively close terms at the time.

Bolívar returned to Paris at the end of 1805. There, in January 1806, he was made a Brother of the Lodge of St. Alexander of Scotland. The minutes of the ceremony note that he had been "recently initiated" and that his promotion was "on account of the journey that he is about to undertake."[3]

Once again Bolívar was feeling the call of Venezuela, and he decided to return, despite the dangers of a sea voyage because of the Napoleonic

---

1. Mancini, p. 150. *Catálogo of Lecuna,* i, p. 154.
2. *Kosmos,* i, p. 385. 1845-62.
3. A copy of the minutes, taken from the facsimile of the 'Fundación John Boulton', was provided by Dr. Pérez Vila. See, too, his study of Bolívar's intellectual development.

Wars. He was doubtless more concerned for his nephew, Anacleto, who was traveling with him, than for himself. The journey was uneventful, although the weather was bad and for the first time he complained about fevers, possibly malarial, from which he was to suffer increasingly. In October 1806 he traveled from Holland to Hamburg, where he embarked on a North American vessel. Although some historians give detailed accounts of the voyage, the only details that can be documented are that by January 1, 1807, he was in Charleston, that he went on to Philadelphia where he left his nephew in a school, and that he was in Caracas by June 1807.

The United States made a deep impression on Bolívar. Years later he declared: "During my brief visit to the United States I saw rational liberty for the first time in my life."[1] The liberty admired in Europe was the English variety, which was praiseworthy only when compared with continental absolutism. The common people did not participate in public life, neither through elections nor any other means. Social pre-eminence, wealth and fame were still the hereditary privileges of a few, and even elementary education was beyond the reach of most people. In the United States, however, all such rewards were obtained by individual effort. The President of the Republic, no less a man than Thomas Jefferson, one of the founding fathers, set the tone by riding unescorted to his office on a mount no better than that ridden by his father on his farm. This was a demonstration of the natural, honest way of life that all Americans accepted.

The Republic created its own traditions without aping the aristocratic structures of Europe, and it created a new morality rather than merely a new political system. Many of the scenes witnessed by Bolívar, like that of the soberly dressed President riding a common horse as if he were a country lawyer, could well have been illustrations from an enlightened European treatise on good government and republican happiness. Who knows!—he thought—perhaps one day Simón Rodríguez's unlikely vision of an America setting an example for Europe will be reality.

He made two further observations: That in the United States equal education for all had not proved inferior to the aristocratic education of Europe, and that the opening of access to fame, prosperity and control of government to the lower classes had caused neither violence nor disorder. At the time this was the only democracy in which the ideal and the practical combined to produce harmonious progress. Today we would call it functional democracy; Bolívar used the rather more French description, "rational liberty."

---

1. According to letter from United States representative, Beaufort F. Watts, to Henry Clay. Quoted in William R. Manning, *The Independence of the Latin American Nations* (1925), ii, p. 1322.

Although only twenty-three, Bolívar had grown wise from his experiences, and was approaching maturity. One can begin to see the future Liberator in him. O'Leary's description, although written years later, gives a good idea of how he must have looked on his return to Caracas: "Bolívar had a high but rather narrow forehead. The wrinkles that he had from an early age marked him out as a thinker. His eyebrows were thick and well-shaped. His black eyes were lively and penetrating. His nose was large and perfectly-shaped, but he had a little wen on it, and it bothered him a lot until it disappeared almost without trace in 1820. When I first met him in 1818, his face was already hollow and his cheek-bones were prominent. He had an ugly mouth, and his lips were rather thick. The distance between nose and mouth was noticeable. His teeth were white, even, and beautiful, and he looked after them carefully. His ears were large but well-positioned. He wore his black, fine, curly hair long until 1821. It then began to gray and thereafter he wore it short. He first shaved his fair side whiskers and moustaches in 1825 in Potosí. He was five feet six inches tall, narrow-chested anl slim. His legs were particularly thin. His skin was dark and rather rough. Any woman would have envied his small, well-formed hands and feet. When he was in a good humor he looked placid, but his appearance was terrifying when he was angry. The change was unbelievable.

"He talked well and often. He had the rare gift of conversation, and enjoyed telling stories about himself. He wrote in a flowery, correct style; his writings and discourses are full of bold, original images. His proclamations are models of military eloquence, and his dispatches are marked not only by clarity and precision but also by an elegant style. When he issued orders to his lieutenants he calculated and foresaw everything, not overlooking even the slightest detail.

"He also knew how to persuade others and inspire confidence. These are the qualities which largely explain the surprising triumphs he achieved in such difficult circumstances. A lesser man, without Bolívar's gifts and state of mind, would have lost heart. He was an outstanding creative genius who could make something out of nothing.

"He understood human nature, and could immediately assess the capacity of every man; he rarely erred in this. He spoke and wrote French perfectly, and Italian reasonably well. He knew little English although he understood what he read. He was familiar with the Greek and Roman classics, which he had studied, and he always enjoyed reading them in good French translations."

This was how Bolívar appeared when he returned to Caracas. He had changed since leaving the city; so much in fact that, to use a Venezuelan phrase, "nobody would recognize him."

X

GREAT
WORK

WHEN BOLIVAR RETURNED to Caracas in the middle of 1807, the abortive invasion attempt of Francisco de Miranda in the western part of the country was still a keen topic of conversation. Miranda is rightly recognized as the Precursor of independence throughout the continent, and in view of his importance, it is now appropriate to devote some space to his activities. When he sailed from La Guaira on January 25, 1771, before his twenty-first birthday, to begin a military career in Spain, Miranda began to preserve documents about himself as if he could foresee the important role that he was to fulfill in both Europe and America. The total collection, which he always carried with him, reached sixty-three bound volumes.[1] As a result there is no shortage of detail about his career, and his diary, for example, shows that he disembarked in Cádiz on March 1, 1771.

Miranda, like Bolívar, was a native of Caracas. His house stood about two hundred yards southwest of the Plaza Mayor, while that of the Bolívars was about the same distance to the southeast. But there was a difference not only in their ages—Miranda was born on January 28, 1750,

---

1. Miranda's papers, which cover the period up to 1810, were published in 23 vols. by the Venezuelan Government between 1929 and 1950. A 24th vol. is devoted to the documents published in Paris in 1884 by the Marquis de Rojas in *El General Miranda;* the latter are grouped into 'Documentos referentes a la campaña de Francia', 'Documentos referentes a la campaña de 1806' and 'Cartas inéditas referentes a la campaña de Venezuela.'

thirty-three years before Bolívar—but also in their family backgrounds. Bolívar's creole forebears had been established in Venezuela since the early sixteenth century. Although Miranda's mother had a similar ancestry, his father was born into a Spanish family in the Canary Islands.

Miranda began to preserve his papers from the age of twenty not simply because he foresaw the great events in which he was to play a leading role, but more precisely, because he was determined to achieve world-wide fame. His career seemed to lack the risk and improvisation found in most men's lives. With Miranda everything seemed to be deliberate, the product of his ambition and tenacity, the expression of a grandeur that he learned to control at an early age and subsequently imposed upon events. External circumstances were liable to change, but Miranda remained constant in misfortune and triumph, like an elevated bronze statue around which other men moved. Like his contemporaries, Miranda venerated classical antiquity, and he believed almost religiously that public and private morality came together in the ideal of living like an ancient, like a Roman. But he was untainted by the sentimental affectation which was also fashionable at the time, the budding romanticism that not only aimed at the exaltation of emotion in all aspects of life, but also demanded veneration for the very words which expressed this exaltation. Napoleon himself enthused over the affected sentimentality of Ossian. But Miranda did not succumb to the fashion. On the contrary, he seems to have been austere and self-possessed in all he did. A careful examination of his career, his ideas and his papers shows that only two things, science and liberty, aroused his passion. He was surprisingly knowledgeable about art in general but, with the exception of music, which he actively pursued because he liked to play the flute, he studied simply to acquire information.

Miranda identified himself so closely with an ideal in which reason and will were like the hammer and chisel of an indefatigable sculptor, that even the women who fell under his fascination were able to look beyond his physical qualities and his immoderate sensuality to see him as a philosopher and a hero. One of his French admirers compared him to Scipio. The English poetess, Miss Williams, who told the story of Miranda in the dungeons of revolutionary France, where he studied history and science "under the constant threat of death," was seduced above all by "this philosophical quality of mind which he possesses in the highest degree."

But it is even more revealing to find that for the exciting and turbulent Delphine de Custine, Miranda was Socrates.[1] This beautiful French aristocrat inherited her spirituality and her sensuality from her mother, Ma-

---

1. See the delightful monograph *Miranda et Madame de Custine,* by the Venezuelan historian, C. Parra Pérez, París, 1950.

dame de Sabrán, who is still famous for these qualities in French literature. For example, when Anatole France discussed a book on Madame Custine by M.A. Bardoux, he wrote: "Since M. Bardoux pleasantly devotes himself to his heroine's early years, we will talk about her mother, worthy of immortal praise. We will recall her enchanting spirit from the depths of the past." And referring to her daughter, he exclaimed: "What marvellous culture was that which created a Delphine de Custine."[1]

Before Delphine gave herself to Miranda she had shown admirable tenderness and affection for her husband and her father-in-law, both of whom were killed during the French Revolution. After her affair with Miranda she became the mistress of Fouché and Chateaubriand. "Nevertheless," notes Picón Salas, Delphine could detect differences in her men; while the Venezuelan remained her 'Socrates' she gave her new lover (Fouché) the more domestic, less classical nick-name of *Cheché*." With the lovers who came after Miranda the enchanting marchioness lost none of her fine human qualities. It was not only by comparison with her "Cheché," moreover, that she appreciated her "Socrates." Even when she was in the arms of the author of *René*—in those days an achievement comparable to an Olympic triumph—she did not forget her South American. Although he was being pursued by Napoleon, she wrote: so Miranda: "Time, which never stands still, will perhaps bring us together... I hope that we will see each other again and that we will still enjoy together those delightful moments which, thanks to your eloquence, I will never forget and which remain both in my mind and in my heart. Mama says that she could listen to you all day."

If Miranda could so impress these women, of whom some, like Madame de Sabrán, represented the *ancien regime* in its most stylized form, while others, like Delphine, and Madame Staël and Madame Tallien, gloried in gathering the exciting celebrities of the new age into their salons, it was with even more reason that the men of Europe, when not offended by his imperiousness, were taken by his rare combination of ardent fantasy and vast knowledge.

The verses that Lavater dedicated to him admirably express the effect that he had on everybody. Lavater was at the peak of his fame when Miranda visited him. The most important people in Europe were discussing his theory of *Physiognomy,* which was accepted by such eminent men as Goethe, Jacobi, Herder and Stolberg. Catherine of Russia wrote to him so often that their correspondence, when published, filled two volumes. Miranda by contrast was a mere "ordinary Spanish Colonel, traveling for pleasure and out of curiosity," to quote Parra-Pérez. Nevertheless, the austere, passionate Swiss thinker recognized him as more

---

1. Anatole France, *La vie litteraire,* i, pp. 471 and 479. Calman Levy edition, Paris, 1950.

distinguished than his multitude of European visitors, asked to be allowed to have his portrait drawn, and endorsed it with a dedication describing Miranda's character as he saw it: "Almighty man, you live in the feeling of your vitality. You see the secrets of the heart better than you hear them! Who can penetrate reality like you, when so few things escape you? Who can understand the frailties of the weak like you? Who can understand the fortitude of the strong like you? What resolution, what energy, what talent, what disdainful pride, what valor nature has given you!"[1]

There is no doubt that Lavater found the Venezuelan's "disdainful pride" particularly attractive. Like Miranda, he was not prepared to leave his world of thoughts and ambitious whims to the mercy of the pesterers who came from all over Europe to visit him, despite their flattery. But he asked Miranda to visit him, and he described his company as a compensation for "so many tedious foreigners incapable of giving or receiving ideas." He later wrote of Miranda: "He is a man who carries a world of men within him . . . a world of inspiration and energy."

In his *The Life of Miranda*, Robertson says of the portrait drawn for Lavater: "This drawing depicts Miranda as a young dandy attired in a frilled shirt, a white waistcoat, and a coat of dark cloth. A forehead ample but slightly receding, luminous eyes, a prominent nose, a bold mouth, and a chin round and determined—these were the most striking traits of a clean-shaven, handsome and vivacious face. His physiognomy was admirably set off by artistically arranged and powdered hair which was worn long and fastened in a pigtail. With this crayon portrait before us we can more readily understand why Miranda occasionally depicted himself in his diary as one who was very popular with the ladies."

In 1771, Miranda began to acquire books with the aim of "perfecting my incomplete education." A year later he purchased a commission as captain and entered the Infantry Regiment of the Princess.

The titles of the books he obtained are listed in his papers, and their range reveals his wide ambitions. They included French, English and Italian dictionaries and grammars, treatises on mathematics and military science, and geographical and historical studies. It is significant that among the latter were four volumes on the English revolutions and two on Russian revolutions. There were also literary works, one favorite was his copy of Virgil. He always carried it with his flute among his conspiratorial papers to calm his spirit at anxious moments. More than thirty years later, on the eve of his invasion of Venezuela, Miranda included in his letter of farewell to Jefferson, the North American

---

1. The portrait was discovered among Lavater's papers in the National Library of Vienna by the eminent Venezuelan historian, C. Parra Pérez. The dedication and other quotations are taken from his *Miranda and Madame de Custine*.

President, the lines in which the Roman poet declared, perhaps in anticipation of Republican America, that felicity and harmony would return to inhabit the world of men: *"Ultima Cumai venit...."*

Miranda knew how to enjoy literature conscientiously. Once, according to Parra-Pérez, "in Vevey, after arranging comfortable lodgings in the inn *Las Tres Coronas,* the Colonel (Miranda) went out to buy a copy of *La Nouvelle Héloise.* In the bookshop he read passages in which Rousseau talks about these "delightful places," and the hospitable bookseller took the trouble to show him the beautiful countryside from the terrace of his shop overlooking the lake. Later in his room, Miranda spent the night reading what he described as "the perfect and exact description that the skillful, poetic writer gives of these places."

Miranda's papers show that the works of Hume, Locke, Bolingbroke, Raynal and Las Casas were among those purchased in 1771, and that he later listed them himself. Robertson points out: "As his purchases included cedar cases for his books and globes, it is evident that Miranda had begun to treat his belongings with loving care." Throughout his life he carefully and skillfully added to his impressive collection. Pijoán tells us in his *Historia del Mundo:* "When the agents of the Convention made an inventory at Miranda's house in Paris they found *une bibliothèque immense, composée des libres les mieux choisis et les plus rares, les cartes de tous les pays et des meilleurs géographes...* Miranda was able, in 1806, to borrow £2,000 in London on the security of his library."

The acquisition of knowledge was not Miranda's sole objective. It was believed in his time that a man perfected his character by enriching his mind, just as it was hoped that if people were rescued from ignorance they would abandon their prejudices and bad habits. Public and private life were considered inseparable. The cultivation of the mind was thought to be just as important as the control of behavior in the formation of the individual. This lofty concept of perfectability had never been lost, but it was only at the end of the eighteenth century that it reacquired its original dynamism. The important difference then was that it was no longer the secret of a few philosophers, but accesible to all men.

Miranda purchased, as we have noted, the rank of captain for the sum of 8,000 *pesos.* The sale of office and honors surprises many modern readers; respectable writers have condemned it as a sign of Spanish venality. But it was then a universal practice, and it persisted in England until the middle of the nineteenth century. In any case, Miranda purchased his commission not because he wanted a flashy uniform, but so that he might be given opportunities to distinguish himself. In June 1774 he asked to be sent on active service, for which he was well fitted by his advanced knowledge of military science, geometry, geography, English, French, Italian and Latin, so that he could "display his zeal and energy."

As a result of his request he was sent at the end of the year to help defend Melilla against the Moslems.

This was his baptism by fire, and Miranda used the opportunity to prove his bravery and daring to his superiors and perhaps to himself. But he also revealed his impatience and pride. He began to make enemies. On the voyage from Málaga to Melilla bad weather aroused fears for the safety of the ship, and the pilots and officers were of the opinion that it should return to the Spanish port. Miranda protested that this would delay the relief expected in Melilla, and he obtained a copy of the proceedings of the Council of War, which he presented to the Captain General of Málaga to justify his attitude. No sooner had he reached the front line than he urged his commander to give him a party of thirty men, with which he promised to render useless the enemy artillery. In his own words: "I formed my men into a small, well-ordered platoon, led by a corporal and four brave men who had the task of surprising and killing the first sentinels they met. At the same time, I attacked the battery, sabre in hand (because pistols were to be used only in an emergency to avoid alarming the nearby posts), followed by the rest of my men who put the guards to the knife."

In 1812, when he was aged sixty-two and at the end of his career, Miranda repeated his youthful feat at the battle of La Victoria. According to Colonel Austria, who was at his side in the campaign, the commander-in-chief "at the head of some lancers threw himself into the center of the skirmish."

Immediately after the siege of Melilla, Miranda suggested the formation of a special force of officers who had fought there to attack Algiers. Although his ambitious project was not accepted, he took part in the expedition that landed on Algiers in July 1775. The Spanish forces were defeated, and Miranda had a miraculous escape. Three bullets hit him in the leg and another shattered the musket he was carrying. He did not earn promotion, although the official report on his unit recognized that "he possessed proven valor, great application and clear capacity." It also noted "but he should show more prudence." This final comment was either another proof of his daring or a subtle sign that his ambition and his ideas were making him a nuisance.

It would seem that the contrast between his hopes and the routine to which he was condemned made the impetuous creole impatient and perhaps resentful. The result was that new commendations alternated with serious accusations of insubordination and other irregularities in the reports of his superiors. Miranda's life was becoming an incessant struggle, in which, when he felt trapped in and held back by the tangle of mediocrity, favoritism and animosities, his pride turned into contempt and scorn.

He acquired new books on politics, history, law, literature, languages and music, by Montesquieu, Helvetius, Grotius, Puffendorf, Corneille, Moliere, Pope and, once again, Virgil. He continued to study Latin, and also obtained a Greek grammar and dictionary. But his intellectual activities caused him difficulties. It was known that he had acquired some French philosophical works, and he was accused of possessing "prohibited books and indecent pictures." It seems that privately the inspector-general of the Spanish army made a much more serious charge against him: no less than trying to "subvert the Laws of the Kingdom."

Miranda finally found another opportunity for active service in 1780 when Spain joined France to assist the struggle for independence of the English colonies in North America. Miranda's request to be allowed to join the expeditionary force being assembled in Cádiz was granted. Although he did so initially only as a "supernumerary of the Aragon regiment," in June of the same year he was made a captain in the regiment.[1]

Miranda served in the force under the orders of Bernardo de Gálvez, governor of Louisiana. After capturing the English frontier posts of Baton Rouge, Natchez and Mobile, they besieged and stormed Pensacola. Robertson points out: "Whether or not he commanded the American volunteers in this operation as has been alleged, Miranda entered the city with the victors." He adds a detail of great psychological interest. "On May 12, he bought some volumes of English literature from a Pensacola bookseller."

But the most important development for Miranda, both for his career and his spiritual life, was that he was made aide-de-camp to General Juan Manuel de Cagigal who, some years earlier, as Colonel of the Princess Regiment, had been his commanding officer and a fatherly friend. As Governor of Cuba, Cagigal led the expedition that took part in the attack on Pensacola, and in 1781 he made Miranda lieutenant colonel as a reward for his conduct during the campaign.

For Miranda, the most rewarding aspect of his promotion was that his commander trusted him completely and defended him tenaciously against the intrigues sparked by his success. The first calumny alleged that Miranda, as "a passionate enthusiast of the English," had allowed the British General Campbell to inspect the defenses of Havana. He had to present a detailed dossier to prove that he was not in the city when Campbell visited it. Later Cagigal himself and Miranda were accused of illicit trade, and Miranda's arrest was ordered, while the investigation of Cagigal's

---

1. The basic sources for this chapter are: *The Life of Miranda,* by William Spence Robertson, University of North Carolina Press, 1929. *Francisco de Miranda y el antiguo español,* by Santiago García, S.J., Caracas, 1961; *Francisco de Miranda* by Mariano Picón Salas, and the works on Miranda and his family of the Venezuelan historian Angel Grisanti. The most abundant and useful source is Dr. C. Parra-Pérez, whose studies cannot be surpassed.

conduct was reserved for the Crown. It seems that Miranda had visited Jamaica on Cagigal's instructions to arrange an exchange of prisoners, and had conspired with a merchant there for the supply of contraband to Cuba. His aim was to obtain, in return, information about the situation in Jamaica, because Cagigal intended to attack the island. In any case, accusations of contraband activities were very common in this period. The truth is that the so-called "illicit trade" was inevitable, because Spain did not possess the necessary industrial development to sustain the monopoly of trade with her colonies that she insisted upon trying to preserve. Moreover, difficulties and delay in maritime communications, which were sometimes interrupted for long periods by warfare, made the monopoly even more unrealistic. In Venezuela, as we have seen, even the Guipuzcoana Company, which had been established by the Crown to eradicate contraband, began to indulge in it quite openly. The situation was no different in the English colonies, where public opinion was so much in favor of illegal trade that it was considered "detestable" to try to suppress it.[1] Cagigal had no hesitation in supporting Miranda. He promised to vouch for his good conduct to the court in Madrid, and assured him that he would be rehabilitated. And so he was, but not until final sentence was pronounced sixteen years later, in 1799. The irony is that when he was innocent and a favorite of Cagigal, Miranda was unable to obtain justice; but when he was finally cleared of the charge of illegal trading, he already deserved capital punishment for conspiracy!

It was always Miranda's destiny that jealous mediocrities tangled themselves around his legs or tried to climb onto his shoulders; taunting punishment for this arrogant man who remained impassive through dangers and misfortunes but was exasperated by everything weak or coarse.

For the time being these intrigues did not do much damage to Miranda's career, for he served alongside Cagigal in the capture of the Bahamas and was promoted to the rank of Colonel.[2] But the haughty *caraqueño* was not prepared to waste his time in intrigues and haggling, and he decided to leave the service. He told Cagigal, in a letter which reveals the ambitious plan to which he had dedicated his life, that the reason for his decision was: "...not only to escape from the outrage that is

---

1. This is the word used by Maurois in his *Histoire des Etats-Unis,* which contains interesting information on attitudes to contraband, which is sometimes seen as a vice exclusive to the customs and the commercial organization of the Spanish Americans.
2. There is some contradiction in the documents on this point, because, although Miranda is sometimes referred to as a colonel, Cagigal informed him in a letter that he had nominated him for this rank, "with the corresponding colonel (coronel graduado), and that Cagigal had proposed that he be made "coronel vivo y efectivo", with the salary appropriate to the rank.

designed against me, but also to begin at the same time those travels in foreign countries which you know it was my intention to undertake on the completion of the war. Because of this design I have cultivated the principal languages of Europe.... All these principles (so far this is all they were), all these seeds that with no little labor and expense have been sown in my mind during the thirty years of my life, remain as yet without fruit because of the failure to cultivate the plants at the proper season." Reflecting upon the universality to which the great spirits of the age aspired, he added: "The experience and knowledge that men acquire by visiting and examining with active intelligence the most wise and various societies that compose the universe, their laws, government, agriculture, public administration, commerce, military art, navigation, science and art, etc.... is the only thing that can mature the fruit and complete the great work of forming a firm, useful man."

Cagigal feared that Miranda's decision might imply a clear break with the Spanish government, and he replied: "Follow in a happy hour your own plan but, as a special favor, I beseech you in the name of my friendship and affection that, until I inform you from Madrid of the outcome of this affair, you will neither make any decision nor alter your promises in any particular."

It is evident that Cagigal must have respected Miranda to press him as he did. He did not hesitate to remind him of "the advantages that the State might derive from your knowledge and constant application." He pointed out, "your experience is not unusual, for all persons who excel in the world journey by that road," and he again stated categorically: "I hope that upon my arrival at the Court this recommendation (for promotion) will be followed; that when His Majesty is better informed of your character and services... you will gain greater recognition; that your friends will have the pleasure of seeing you the object of general applause in our country; and that I shall be able to gratify the paternal tenderness with which I have always regarded you."

This was in 1783. In 1782, according to a document among Miranda's papers—a copy without authentic signatures—three citizens of Caracas, Juan Vicente Bolívar, Martín Tovar and the Marquis of Mijares, had sent him a communication in which they announced their decision to shake off the "insupportable and infamous oppression" under which Venezuela lived, and acclaimed Miranda as the "first-born" to lead the struggle. They mentioned other reports that they had sent to him in July 1781 and, in conclusion, authorized him, "in our name and that of all the province," to seek the aid of foreign powers if necessary "for our rescue from such a wicked captivity." Although it is very tempting to accept this letter as authentic, it should be considered apocryphal. It is impossible that in 1782 the young Miranda's far-off countrymen could see him as the leader of the emancipation. It is equally implausible to imagine that his hopes for independence could be known in Caracas while the Spanish authorities remained ignorant of them. Apart from his, the sentiments expressed in the letter do not fit in with the conservative reaction that, as we saw earlier, was strong in Venezuela in this period.[1]

It is doubtful, moreover, whether Miranda had yet made up his mind to lead the struggle for independence in South America, although it is clear that he was aware of Spain's backwardness from an early age. Severely critical phrases, like "wretched Kingdom" and "unhappy province" appear frequently in his diary of his travels in the mother country. He was aware, too, that this attitude aroused suspicions against him. "It is not the offender whom they seek, but my person," he wrote to Cagigal in 1783. Soon after, a general plan for emancipation did begin to take shape in his mind: "In the year 1784," Miranda recorded in the memoir quoted by Robertson, "in the city of New York, I formed a project for the liberty and independence of the entire Spanish-American continent with the co-operation of England."[2]

It was appropriate that the recently emancipated colonies of the North should be the first country to be visited by Miranda after he cut himself off from Spain. He went to pursue the "great work" of perfecting himself that he announced in his letter to Cagigal. The new spiritual impetus that Miranda drew from an environment of fervent renewal is evident. He observed everything with ardent curiosity: battle-fields and fortifications, the operation of tribunals and the system of government in each state, the development of agriculture and public education. He was even able to make some rather primitive customs, which must have shocked him, fit in with his idealized visions. He noticed at a public banquet that all classes of people, magistrates, common men and aristocracy, were fraternizing, eating pork and drinking rum together. "It is impossible, he noted, without seeing it to imagine a more purely democratic gathering. It illustrates all that Grecian poets and historians have told us about similar celebrations among the free peoples of Greece." This was an uncharacteristic response for a man who never subsequently showed demagogic tendencies; but how could he judge otherwise if he had his Homer and Virgil with him, probably having read them again that very evening?

---

1. See the study of the Venezuelan historian, Alfredo Boulton, in *Boletín de la Academia Nacional de la Historia,* no. 173, Caracas, January-March, 1961. The so-called "carta de los mantuanos" is in vol. i, f. 120 of Miranda's papers, and in vol. xv, p. 69 of the published collection (Caracas, 1938). Robertson quotes it with some discrepancies.
2. Robertson, *op. cit.,* i, p. 43 gives "I formed the project"; in the Spanish translation of his work (editorial Anaconda, Buenos Aires, 1947, p. 46) this becomes "se formó el proyecto" (the project was formed).

What interested him most, however, was to study men and discover the secret of those who had achieved prominence in any sphere. Judges, soldiers, theologians, politicians, diplomats and men of science were added to the museum of celebrities that he carefully assessed and collected in his portentous papers. Most of them, moreover, made it clear that they respected and even admired Miranda. Dr. Andrew Turnbull considered him an intelligent traveler and exacting observer of everything that can instruct the spirit or add dignity to human nature. Major Eustace wrote him of "the anxious ardor with which I have sought your society on all occasions." The historian David Ramsey wrote to a friend as follows: "I have had so much pleasure and have acquired so much information from the bearer, Colonel Miranda, that I am desirous of the honor of introducing him to you. He is a native of South America and of high rank in the army of his most Catholic Majesty. He loves liberty with an ardor that would do honor to the freest State in the world. He arrived here lately and has been respectfully noticed by the best people of this metropolis. . . . I am certain that men of sentiment and of inquisitive dispositions will be much delighted with his company."

Philadelphia made a favorable impression on Miranda. He called it a beautiful, free and commercial city. It was there, moreover, that he met Washington and dined with him. But perhaps as a reaction against the emotion that he must have felt in anticipation of the exceptional meeting, he was cold in his judgement of the liberator of the North. He considered it "a usurpation as capricious as it is injust" that, "although there are many illustrious persons in the United States who by their virtue and talents promoted the great and complicated work of independence," all the glory was bestowed on Washington. He ended with the icy observation: "His demeanor is circumspect, taciturn, and inexpressive but a suave manner and great moderation make it endurable."

The truth is that their meeting occurred in December 1783, when Washington was faced with serious worries. He had gone to Philadelphia to resign command of the army. During the ceremony the deputies wore their hats to underline the supremacy of the civil power, but the weakness of the institutions that were emerging did not justify such arrogance. Conflicting opinions and many problems were then disturbing what was soon to be a great, exemplary democracy. Six months before the ceremony, "in June 1783, according to one historian, a group of drunken soldiers so scared Congress that it took refuge in Princeton where the College provided hospitality for the disbanded legislators." There was nothing strange, then, in Washington's being "taciturn and inexpressive." If only the young Venezuelan colonel, then impatient and filled with so many ideas, could have foreseen what fate had in store for him!

Miranda was disconcerted by Washington's excessive taciturnity. But he judged Lafayette severely for a completely different reason. He called him "a mediocre character" and described his great zeal to obtain honors as "a ridiculous political farce." General Henry Knox, who had organized the new republic's artillery during the war and who later became the confederation's Minister of War, created a different impression when Miranda met him in New York. The judgement that Miranda recorded in his diary is very characteristic of the importance that he always attributed to intelligence and learning. He wrote: "Among all the military chieftains whom I have met in this country, even including the *Idol,* General Knox is one of the best informed on the theory and practice of war. His bearing is agreeable and his conversation is interesting." Knox, for his part, wrote to a friend that Miranda "possesses an extensive knowledge of men and things, and his opportunities have been exceeded only by his eagerness to improve them." A genuine intimacy was established between them, and it is clear that Knox treated Miranda with consideration. He wrote to him on one occasion: "I beg a thousand pardons for not having seen you during the week past. It was my fixed determination to have called upon you almost each day but a number of perverse accidents frustrated my intentions. If you are unengaged, and could do me the pleasure of spending the day at Dorchester, the servant with the carriage has orders to wair for you. We have no company." Miranda also became acquainted with Thomas Paine, the popular political agitator, who had exercised a considerable influence upon public opinion during the North American Revolution with his pamphlet *Common Sense,* and who was also to extend his influence to Spanish America.

Miranda later reminded Alexander Hamilton of the "frequent discussions" they had on South American emancipation. Hamilton was a cultivated, refined man of great intellectual daring, very similar, in fact, to Miranda. A further similarity was their rigid aristocratic outlook, the almost choleric disdain with which they regarded everything that was weak. Despite their love of liberty, this deep-rooted characteristic always impeded their fraternization with other men.

The political situation in the United States was then so confused that an association of French and North American officers, the Society of the Cincinnati, sought to make itself an hereditary organization. This caused so much alarm and suspicion that John and Samuel Adams condemned it as a "new and insidious form of nobility." Miranda, however, accepted an invitation to dine with some of its members.

We do not know what Miranda said to Samuel Adams, to whom he would be able to address pressing questions about American life, but he does tell us: "We conversed at length about the Constitution of this Republic and, after chewing them over well, he agreed with two objections to it which I proposed to him." The two points were characteristic of Miranda: that the institutions attached greater importance to property than to virtue and, that although freedom of religion was recognized as a right of man, the non-Christian was barred from all legislative or representative offices. Miranda described Adams as "the famous republican," and he noted with gratitude: "He gave me much interesting information about the origin, principles and occurrences of the recent Revolution, and treated me in a familiar manner."

It is not surprising that Miranda's opinions were sometimes inconsistent. It must be remembered he had just left a narrow, hierarchial world to enter another in which the results of democracy were still uncertain. On the one hand he enthused over the open-air banquet, which seemed to be recreating the democracy of heroic Greece. Similarly he noted in New England that despite the poverty of the soil " . . . such is the industry and the spirit with which liberty inspires the people that from a small plot of ground they raise enough produce to support their large families, to pay heavy taxes, and to live in comfort and enjoyment—a thousand times happier than the proprietors of fertile lands and rich mines in Mexico, Peru, La Plata, Venezuela, or indeed in any part of the Spanish-American continent." The same reforming spirit can be seen in his observation that the books in the public library at Hartford were read more than those guarded so zealously in the Escorial. But he became intolerant if the application of these principles interfered with his ideal vision of the Republic. He wrote in Massachussetts: "On various occasions I attended meetings of the State's Legislative Assembly where I beheld in patent fashion the defects and inconveniences which this Democracy suffers because it places the Legislative Power entirely in the hands of *ignorance*. In the midst of a debate that he did not understand, one legislator was reciting verses that he knew by heart. After the assembly had been discussing a subject for two hours, another legislator asked what was the motion on which they were to vote. Most of them are like this. In these democratic assemblies the most absurd and unjust measures have been proposed, debated and approved throughout the continent."

On another occasion he pointed out that a Negress, originally from Guinea, who had received some education in America and who had been admired in England for her ability to compose prose and verse, eventually "suffered the same neglect experienced by talented people everywhere. . . and she is now dying in poverty. . . Rational beings are alike, whatever their shape or appearance." But he promptly returned to his aristocratic customs when egalitarianism affected him personally. He wrote about a New England inn: "I shall not refrain from mentioning here that the spirit of republicanism is so strong in this country that the coachman who drives the stage and all the other guests sat together at the same table. It was with no small difficulty that I arranged that my servant should eat by himself." He forgot that Nausicaa, although the daughter of a king, drove the chariot in which she went with her maids to wash her own clothes at the edge of the sea.

Miranda was also severe in his intellectual judgements. He was scornful of Commodore Hopkins, whom he considered ignorant and lacking in geographical knowledge. At Rhode Island College he recorded that the library and the scientific apparatus were very deficient. He wrote of Harvard: "It appears to me that this establishment is better adapted to train clergymen than to mold capable and well-informed citizens, and it is certainly extraordinary that there is not a single chair of modern languages, while the chair of theology is the most important in the college."

As he wrote this, Miranda must have reflected that, all in all, the University of Caracas was not so bad, although he made similar criticisms of it. He showed evidence of his affection for the institution in his wills of both 1805 and 1810, in which he instructed: "The classical Greek books in my library are to be sent to the University of Caracas as a token of my gratitude and respect for the wise principles of literature and Christian morality with which they nourished my youth."

When he noted in Salem that witches had been executed there "in times of crass fanaticism," Miranda would have realized that by contrast, despite the legends that he himself was spreading about Spanish fanaticism, such aberrations had not appeared in Spanish America. The Inquisition did not issue a single death penalty in the whole of Spanish America. And as far as Caracas was concerned—the smiling tropical town that Miranda still saw in his dreams—it was impossible to imagine witches in such a sunny valley. Nymphs there were, certainly; Miranda had seen them along the banks of the Guaire and the Anauco, when he read *Telemacus* as a boy. Nymphs yes; but wicked witches existed only in stories, and even children smiled when they spoke of them, more out of curiosity than fear.

Many women figured in the friendships formed by Miranda in the course of his travels. Some of them seem to have been reasonably intellectual, and exchanged books with him. Others give the impression of less serious relationships. Eliza Livingston teased him: "Surely when in this city you greatly approved of female society." A year later she wrote: "Sayre stays this winter with your friends the Duers. I never meet these men but they speak of you and drink the health of the Queen of the *Incas*." This last remark suggests that Miranda had already talked to his close friends about the Inca state that he was to propose to Pitt some years later. If so, this was one of the few occasions in which a woman appeared in his political plans. Perhaps Eliza herself was the Queen of the Inca state that was to remain in the realms of Utopia.

Miranda's ability to conduct himself with such aplomb in the wide world of the new republic despite having only just escaped from the narrow soldier's life, must be attributed to his incessant reading and to his zeal to prepare himself for high office. It is also possible that the confidence with which he seemed to assess men and events subjecting them to his demanding standards, may have been exaggerated. But what he was doing was to prepare, for his own guidance, a Plutarchian world, and it was natural for him to put the heroes assembled in it to repeated tests. He had just passed the age of thirty and he was trying to categorize the world he was entering, in order to establish the moral and intellectual values that he could place alongside the classical models in his books. He had modestly confided to Cagigal that the object of his travels was to perfect his "incomplete education," and one could say that there was often more enthusiasm than petulance, and respect and hesitation rather than ease in the insistence with which he set out to judge all the people he met.

What is surprising is that many of them responded with fervent praise for Miranda. John Adams, whose position as Washington's successor in the office of President as well as his prominent role in society, should have made him a skillful judge of men, wrote: "Miranda acquired amongst us the reputation of having studied the classics, of possessing universal knowledge and of being a master in the art of war. He was said to be very wise, with a lively imagination and insatiable curiosity. Miranda knew more of every campaign, siege, battle, and skirmish that had ever occurred in the whole war, than any officer of our army, or any statesman in our councils."

Robertson considers such rare eulogies "extravagant." But he tells us himself that Miranda examined the fortifications of Charleston, Philadelphia, New York, Newport and Boston, that he inspected the battlefields of Bunker Hill, Brandywine and Saratoga, and that he sought explanations and detailed descriptions of the whole war from outstanding soldiers. In addition his diary entries show that he stubbornly questioned many men about laws, customs, tribunals, education, history, geography and other matters. That the retention of such a mass of facts by his lively and acute intelligence impressed his biographer is not surprising. Robertson also gives us another assessment of Miranda—by William Duer in a letter to the Secretary of the Treasury in London—which bears a striking resemblance to that from Adams. Duer's letter of introduction ended with the words: " . . . You will thank me when we have the pleasure of meeting for giving you so valuable an acquaintance, who will be able to give you not only a very accurate detail of that unexplored country of which he is a native, but a much more just account of the resources, genius, and state of politics of the United States than you would be able to obtain from most of its natives."

The letter from General Knox to Miranda quoted previously concerned a proposal to emancipate the Spanish colonies which, in the course of discussion, had developed into a detailed project. A document in Miranda's collection shows that they thought in terms of 5,000 recruits from New England to serve for five years, and that they also discussed arms, munitions, expense and other details. It is clear that the project was a long-term one, because in the very month that it was formulated, November 1784, Miranda completed his preparations to sail to England. He left Knox a secret code for their future correspondence. Hamilton was also involved in the scheme, and it is probable that it was his idea to obtain the support of England. This was the immediate objective of Miranda's voyage, although he also hoped to be able to establish contact with possible malcontents within the Spanish colonies.

Was there really an appreciable number of dissident colonists? Would there be men with the capacity to translate passive discontent into effective action? How would the clergy and the upper classes react? These questions, and many others which must have kept Miranda awake, were complicated by the dispersion of the inhabitants in the enormous expanse of the South American continent. Communications between cities like Caracas and Bogotá, apparently so near to each other, took months. Unless careful preparations could be made for several of the most important cities to rise up simultaneously, those which did so in isolation would soon fall to the Spanish regulars. Perhaps there would be need of a Precursor, who would sacrifice his life to arouse the whole continent, a Decalion to make men spring from the ground, a Moses willing to see the Promised Land only from afar. Just as the devil tempted Jesus, so God himself tempted Moses. To inform him that he would not enter the Promised Land, while asking him to continue leading his people towards it, was a way of testing his qualities, a challenge and a temptation. But perhaps the secret of greatness must always remain inconclusive.

It would not be enough for the Revolution to be a military success. Society would have to be organized afterwards. It is one thing to destroy tyranny, quite another to create freedom. Miranda had searched in his history books anxiously for a solution to what might happen in America, but he was unable to find one that was without risks. Perhaps he would find it in Europe where a group of superior intellects was directing all the resources of philosophy, historical criticism and the nascent pedagogy towards the task of solving social and political problems.

Miranda pointed out in his letter to Cagigal that the purpose of his travels was to study "the most wise and virtuous societies," while completing the great work of forming his own personality. Towards the end of his life he declared in his will that his papers "contain my travels and researches in America, Europe, Asia and Africa, undertaken with the object of seeking the best form and plan of government for the establishment of a wise and prudent civil liberty in the Spanish American Colonies." It was typical of the eighteenth century that this was essentially three ways of looking at the same thing.

Miranda tells us that during a roadside halt in New England he met a pretty young woman who was reading Rollins's *Histoire Ancienne*. They discussed the work, and she told him that Franklin was superior to Aristides. The woman, the traveler, the place, the theme of the conversation and the final comparison paint the spirit of the period better than several tomes could. People spoke like this sometimes even in roadside inns, during the dawning of romanticism. They sanctified history and they over-idealized men. But it would be unkind to smile. Many admirable qualities were born both then and even in the century of extreme credulity that was to follow.

XI

THAT
I CAN NEVER
ABANDON . . .

ALTHOUGH MIRANDA HAD made contact with men of first rank in North America and had been able, in a sense, to build the foundations for his ambitious projects while he was there, he did not imagine when he sailed for Europe in December 1784 that within a decade his fortunes would improve to such an extent that he would become one of the figures in the proscenium. It is even less likely that he could foresee that he would achieve his fame, not in the America to which his gaze constantly returned, but in Europe, and in the country—France—which at the time did not figure in his plans and desires.

Miranda filled his time on the voyage with his customary reading of historical and philosophical works, and as soon as he reached London he sent a grammar and a dictionary to General Knox. A short time afterwards he wrote to his brother-in-law, Arrieta: "At present, philosophy, government, academies of science, sessions of Parliament, and the society of statesmen and of learned men occupy all of my time with much profit and to some extent mitigate the pain of stern adversity."

The adversity of which he complained arose largely from his persecution by the agents of the Spanish government. Although he visited the Spanish legation in London, and the minister, Bernardo del Campo, returned the courtesy, Miranda soon realized that he was being spied upon. Del Campo described him to the government in Madrid as a man of "much talent, great discernment, and more than ordinary intelligence," a fanatical champion of liberty capable of collaborating in "any audacious project" against the Spanish empire. He suggested that it would be a good idea to steal or burn Miranda's papers. Respect for English laws and for the influential contacts that Miranda was beginning to make—a number of lords and various officers had become friends of the Venezuelan—held Del Campo back from anything more extreme. At the end of the year the *Political Herald and Review* described Miranda as follows: "In London, we are well assured, there is at this moment a Spanish American of great consequence and possessed of the confidence of his fellow citizens, who aspires to the glory of being the deliverer of his country. He is a man of sublime views and penetrating understanding, skilled in the ancient and modern languages, conversant in books, and acquainted with the world. He has devoted many years to the study of general politics: the origin, progress, and termination of different types of governments, the circumstances that combine and retain multitudes of mankind in political societies, and the causes by which these societies are dissolved and swallowed up by others. This gentleman, having visited every province in North America, came to England, which he regards as the mother country of liberty and the school for political knowledge. As friends to freedom we forbear to be more particular concerning this distinguished personality."[1]

Moreover, Miranda came into contact with two men who were to be the most faithful of all his friends. They were to help him for many years with the greatest abnegation and efficacy. One was John Turnbull, an English merchant who had met the then captain Miranda in 1777 when he visited Cádiz with some friends. He had sent Miranda some books and music in return for his kindness. The other was Colonel William S. Smith, son-in-law of John Adams. Adams, whose passionate portrait of Miranda was quoted above, was then his country's minister in London, and in 1797 he was to succeed Washington as President. Miranda had met Smith in New York, and he had obviously made a strong impression upon him since, despite his prominent position, Smith hurried to the traveler's lodgings to leave a card which declared his wish "to pay his respects to Col. de Miranda as a friend to the rights of mankind and the Happiness of Society."

Miranda found Smith's company congenial and invited him to accompany him on a journey to the continent. After obtaining Adams's permission —Smith was his secretary—the two left England for Holland in August 1785.

Miranda's plans for emancipation had made little progress. He explained in a memorandum written seven years later: "With this object I proceeded to England early in 1785, but the embarrassment and disgust that

---

1. Robertson, *op. cit.* (Chapel Hill edition), i, 62-3.

prevailed there because of the loss of the their colonies and the heavy expenses of the past war did not promise an opportunity for the presentation of a design of such magnitude. Accordingly I resolved to occupy myself temporarily with an attentive examination of various government and political systems of Europe."

The Spanish government, however, intensified its persecution. Although Del Campo pretended to maintain good relations with Miranda, and even gave him a letter of introduction to his colleague in Prussia, he offset it by a secret message, sent directly. At the same time, an attempt was made to persuade the French Bourbons to detain him if he entered France. In the future, Miranda was to be constantly surrounded by trickery of this sort, and in danger of disappearing into one of the state prisons into which the paternalistic governments of the time cast their wayward sons for the rest of their lives.

The journey which began in August 1785 lasted almost four years, until June 1789. The itinerary was recorded in Miranda's diary: Holland, Prussia, Saxony, Austria, Hungary, Venice, Bologna, Florence, Pisa, Rome, Southern Italy, Greece, Egypt, Turkey, Russia, Sweden, Norway, Denmark, Holland again, various German cities, Switzerland and France. The robust creole traveled the badly maintained roads of Europe in all sorts of ways: on horseback, in coaches with his friends and even in his own carriage which a Russian prince had given him. He read imperturbably as storms tossed his boat on the Black Sea, and he joyfully climbed a peak near Corinth from which, with the aid of his telescope, he could see Mount Helikon and the Parnassus, the sea of Lepanto, the island of Salamis and the hills of Athens.[1] Few travelers had achieved anything comparable. Several years later Chateaubriand traveled from Paris to Jerusalem and dedicated a book to him.

Miranda took with him a gentleman's wardrobe: formal suits, overcoats, silk stockings, wigs, slippers, riding boots, rapier, pistols, etc. He forgot neither his flute, which had soothed him in his hours of torment since he had been a captain in Spain, nor his Virgil, which was his companion in the countryside and during his hours of rest. Music scores, souvenirs of women and sketches of fortifications and monuments were crammed into his baggage along with papers that had to be carefully guarded: his diary, documents connected with his plans for emancipation —a list of Jesuits expelled from America, useful military notes, reliable reports of the rebellions of Tupac Amaru and of the *Comuneros* in New Granada— and the correspondence that he received or had to send to keep the log of life up to date.

As far as books were concerned, he fell into the habit of buying them in each city that he passed through, literally devouring them, according to

---

1. *Diario,* ii, p. 119.

his notes, and, unless they were essential, like his Virgil, sending them immediately to London. His library grew to 6,000 volumes. How many of them did he read on this tour?

It is revealing to glance through Miranda's commentaries to see what interested him during this period of his life. At first sight it is hardly possible to detect preferences. When he was in Switzerland he read Calvin on theology and Mengs on art. When bad weather delayed him at his inn in Geneva he read Winkelmann, Becarria's discourse on commerce, a history of the city, a "most imaginative and humorous" satire on friars, a study of hospitals and the work of Howard. He noted on the last of these that it had been "translated into French and disfigured," indicating that he had read it previously and could compare the two texts from memory. He also read some *Letters on Denmark,* Filangieri's *Science of Legislation* and a book on Greece by Choiseul, but he was naturally most interested in Rousseau and Voltaire. The works of these two writers are so well-defined that it is almost possible to infer the character of an educated man of the period by his preference for one or the other of them. It has been said that Rousseau was Bolívar's favorite, while one might well think that Miranda's nature, more analytical than sentimental, would make him a Voltairian. But the few reliable scraps of evidence we have suggest that Miranda preferred Rousseau, and Bolívar, Voltaire.

Perhaps there was more passion than calculation in Miranda, the statue of bronze, even when he adopted the statuesque pose that was derived from his passionate commitment to antiquity, while the reflective and critical aspects of his nature came to predominate in Bolívar, the man of irresistible rages, as a reaction against the temperamental impulses that he began to curb as a child.

Indeed, it was perhaps too simple to state, as we did above, that for Miranda art was above all a matter of information and instruction rather than pleasure. His papers reveal a profound artistic sentiment. His interest in the theater and in concerts was such that sometimes when he had no time to change after traveling, he hurried to the auditorium in riding boots. He recorded this fact without any sign of repentance for what must have been an unpardonable breach of etiquette. He had numerous books on music in his library and, apart from his skill with the flute, his appreciation of music must have been sound, because when he was in Hungary he talked at length with Haydn on the merit of Boccherini and on other musical topics. Among painters, Raphael so fascinated him that he wrote in Milan that a copy of the painting 'Saint John, Virgin and Child' was superior to Leonardo's original. He went on: "Afterwards to the Ambrosiana to gorge on Raphael's design, which I consider to be the best pictorical composition in existence."

He savored the beauty of statues and monuments with the same passion. When Lord Elgin took the marbles of the Parthenon to London, Miranda hurried to admire them again, even though he had already seen them in Athens. Picón Salas tells us: "When he did not have an appointment with Vansittart or some other person, he spent whole afternoons in the British Museum admiring the friezes, the heavenly proportion of the figures and the rhythm of the large sculptures. With the zeal of a collector, he kept among his papers penciled sketches and printed descriptions of all he saw and inquired about."

Miranda enjoyed literature with the refinement of an intellectual Sybarite. We have already seen how he took the trouble to compare the Swiss scenery with Rousseau's "perfect and exact description," which he had just re-read. Similarly, when he was in Rhein-felden he was delighted "by the rural idea of picking cherries from the tree next to the windows and eating them while reading Virgil."

Raphael, Virgil and the flute were strange companions for the creole Titan who was striving to destroy the pillars of the Spanish empire. He never forgot that this was the prime objective of his life. His notes include numerous references to work on military instruction. Whenever he could he studied the organization of troops, marches and maneuvers, he sought detailed explanations, and he inspected battlefields, arsenals and fortifications. He continued to show the independence of mind that he used when he judged men. Just as he lamented the excess of accessories and adornments in some Roman churches, including St. Peter's, so, too, he criticized Vauban when inspecting fortresses.

The books that he read most frequently dealt with history, jurisprudence, the origin and development of revolutions, the organization of societies and public administration. "The immortal Montesquieu," as Miranda called him when he visited La Brède, had an altar for himself in his mind. His diary entry continues: "I looked through the windows to observe the objects that his imagination saw, in case I could find in them something of that *energy* and *vigor* that animate his writings... I did not tire of looking at the place in which the *most brilliant* work of the human spirit had been produced."

But not even in the case of Montesquieu was Miranda prepared to renounce the right to judge for himself. Parra-Pérez comments, in connection with an incident in French politics: "It is clear that Miranda, enamoured by Montesquieu and his separation of powers, did not hesitate to share the opinion of the many men who, after applauding the rebellion of the parliamentarians, began to consider them impertinent. Here the colonel followed his favorite authors, especially Voltaire, Helvetius and

Marmontel, who were not particularly friendly towards those bodies composed of crafty and scheming men inclined towards usurpation."[1]

From an early age, Miranda regarded Montesquieu and Beccaria as models of "solidity," but he was happier with the second than with the first, who he was able to meet him in Milan. Miranda noted that Beccaria received him with "the greatest pleasure," and asked about Franklin; they discussed the Inquisition, which Beccaria had feared when it functioned in Milan, and his attitude towards the existing government. Miranda noted that "he has written other things, but he does not dare to publish them," and that he had refused an invitation from the Empress of Russia "out of fear of despotism and of Siberia, of which he had heard so much." But the learned Italian "was so happy to talk about America."

A little later Miranda visited Gibbon: "Homer was on his table!" he noted, and he called Gibbon "the Tacitus of our time." Despite this deference their discussions were quite relaxed. They had a "long debate" on Gibbon's assertion that England had lost nothing with the independence of America, and they went on to discuss various historical works, although Miranda knew one of them only indirectly. They surveyed at length people and political events in America and Europe, and they naturally dwelt upon the lack of freedom in Europe. Gibbon told Miranda "that an English noble whose books had been confiscated in Vienna in the reign of María Theresa had asked Minister Kaunitz to return them as a favor. Kaunitz had replied that although he was powerful in the government he did not even dare to speak to the sovereign on the subject of *prohibited books*."

Miranda's diary contains the following entry revealing from the psychological standpoint: "I am reading Vattel's *Droit des Gens* to determine whether or not I have deluded myself in regard to my conduct. I have always wished to regulate it by *natural law,* which is *justice* and *reason.* In truth, I do not know what motive impels Spain in her attempts to injure me. Neither do I know in which essentials I have fallen short. To look for them is to seek for that which is impossible to find. Nevertheless I have seen with pleasure and consolation my rights defended with the rights of other men by such an able author." He undoubtedly meant that independence was a right of the Americans, and that as such it could be neither an offense nor a crime against Spain.

But Miranda, unlike many of his contemporaries, was not solely interested in political problems and in the formal modification of the state. He showed in his first complaints against the Spanish regime made when he was still a serving captain in the Metropolis that he was more interested in public administration. Those first comments in his diary—"wretched

---

1. From *Miranda et Madame de Custine.*

kingdom," "unhappy province"—invariably refer to deficiencies in this sphere: in industry and agriculture; in road maintenance and municipal administration because of negligent or corrupt officials. He later began to reflect on social organization when he had the opportunity to compare the new regime in North America with the regimentation to which he was accustomed. "Wise and virtuous societies," "prudent and honest magistrates," "enlightened and worthy citizens"—combinations of words that were then inseparable—formed the images that were his reflections on reality. This mixture of good sense and idealism shaped his mind and guided him as he sought instruction for his America. It contained not only much of both Franklin and Rousseau but also, although Miranda did not realize it, much of the traditional Spanish longing for "good government."

This practical concern for the collective good produced Miranda's abundant notes on such topics as the cleaning of cities, popular education, exploitation of mineral resources, agricultural techniques, organization of prisons and asylums, and the care of destitute or delinquent children. He studied architecture along the banks of the Rhône and then went on to question peasants about viticulture and wine-making. When he found children and adults together in the same prisons he protested with words that could have been spoken by Simón Rodríguez. "God knows how many of these innocents will lose their health forever," he noted on visiting a workhouse where the children inhaled the dust from the wool that they were made to beat. He was offended by antiquated legal codes and by the deficiencies of prisons. He rejoiced when he came across libraries that were open to the public. When he observed the ignorance of the people in the south of France he considered it a proof of their degradation.

When Miranda toured Europe he became intimate with the Empress Catherine, he dined with the king of Poland, he was regaled by men such as Potemkin and Esterhazy the Magnificent, and he formed a friendship with the Prince of Hesse who forecast a happy future for him and later addressed him by letter as "my dear Count." Despite these attentions he seems to have been less preoccupied with the importance of his gentlemanly status. He casually noted in his diary in Pistoya: "I said that I was a merchant (which is the same as saying a plebeian), and so the guards made fun of me for nearly an hour." Soon after he wrote in Lucca: "having said that I was a noble, they opened the gate without bothering me."

The most celebrated episode of the tour was Miranda's reception in Russia. The Empress Catherine treated him with such affection that legend insists they were lovers. It seems to us, however, to have been pure invention, rather similar to the story that Bolívar played ball with the future

Ferdinand VII, which arose from the belief that friendship with a royal bumpkin was an honor.

It is true, of course, that both Miranda and Catherine had voracious sexual appetites. But whether or not she shared his bed is of no importance. Although the empress told him that she "loved him like a mother"—an expression made suspicious by Rousseau and Madame Warren—and although she once made the suggestive gesture of offering him an orange, an appropriate tropical symbol, with her own hands, we are inclined to think that their relationship was purely intellectual. They both collected celebrities. Catherine had formed an intellectual court with all the notable men of Europe, and Miranda always was on the lookout for a rare creature that he could add to his collection of classical archetypes.

When Miranda announced his intention to leave Russia the empress demonstrated her affection for him in a most unqualified, categorical way.

He was authorized to use the uniform of a colonel in the imperial armies, and he was given a large sum of money and letters of recommendation to imperial representatives in other countries, who were instructed to assist him and, if necessary, even to shelter him in their own houses, *"lui offrir le cas échéant sa maison même pour asile."* If Catherine and Miranda had been lovers, it would have been very difficult for that northern Dido to agree to her Aeneas abandoning her after only seven months. Neither as a woman nor as an empress would she have allowed him to break off an affair in full view of everybody.

It should also be borne in mind that before being presented to the empress, Miranda enjoyed the exceptional hospitality of Prince Potemkin for more than a month. The prince took him in his own carriage to visit his estates and the recently conquered Crimean peninsula, and he presented him at court. If Miranda's personality, talent and knowledge could win the prince's favor in this way, why should it be assumed that these qualities alone were not responsible for the warm reception he received from Catherine? It is well known that she took pride in corresponding with all her talented, distinguished contemporaries. Her correspondence with Lavater alone filled two published volumes. It was natural, then, that she should wish to associate herself with the destiny of that extraordinary man who represented and proposed to emancipate a continent about which Europe was becoming more aware. Miranda could talk to her about the land of the Incas and he could describe Washington and Adams. He could tell her about the tropical lands of America, and he could recount the details of his campaign against the Moors in North Africa. He could recite Homer, and compare him with what he had just seen in Greece. He could discuss the Roman senate, or give his opinion on the English parliament. Was this not sufficient to make him fascinating for the sovereign whose intellectual curiosity was acknowledged by all? Dr. Guthrie, an eminent English surgeon in Catherine's service, attested to the impression created by Miranda, and he also confirmed that the Venezuelan left Russia of his own free will. He wrote to a colleague in Edinburgh," It is difficult to discover in what branch of ancient or modern learning he is deficient," and added, "He answers the historian, the philosopher or naturalist all such questions as can throw light on their respective researches... Our Great Lady has been joking with him about the flames of the Inquisition and even invited him to stay in Russia, an honor she seldom confers on any officer however distinguished.... The King of Poland wished also to make his acquaintance on his last journey and made him similar offers. In short it appears that all lovers and protectors of letters take an interest in the first thoroughly instructed South American who has appeared in Europe."

The Spanish Bourbons, who neglected everything but their persecutions, were still endeavoring to catch Miranda. It is miraculous that their relations and alliances with the other European courts did not bring them success. They now had an even stronger reason to pursue him because, according to the reports of the Count of Cobentzel to Vienna, Miranda was in close contact with foreign diplomats and with the Russian court. He added: "He is a man with a haughty disposition and vast knowledge who speaks very freely about everything, but particularly denounces the Inquisition, the government of Spain, the King, and the Prince of Asturias. He makes many offensive allusions to Spanish ignorance."

Catherine cut short the impertinent overtures of the Spanish ambassador, informing him that her respect for Miranda arose from his personal qualities, which she had been able to judge for herself, and not from the rank he had held in Spain. She added, according to Miranda, that if he represented a danger to the Spanish empire, "there was no region where I might better sojourn than in Russia, for this country was at a great distance from Spain."

When Miranda bade farewell to Catherine he told her that "nothing but the great and interesting purpose that currently occupies me" could deprive him of the pleasure of repaying the empress's kindness with his services. It seems that he was sincere when he expressed these sentiments, because he always remained a passionate defender of Russia and of Catherine herself. It is true, of course, that Catherine's protection did not cease when the interesting traveler left Russia, and Miranda even took up the offer of lodging in the house of the Russian ambassador. This continuing imperial favor shows, in its turn, that their relationship was based upon neither frivolous curiosity nor upon love. In the first case it would not have survived Miranda's departure while in the second it would have turned into spite or scorn.

Miranda's continental tour ended with a visit to France. He was daring to go near Madrid in this way, because he had been warned on several occasions that Spanish agents were trying to catch him, and he knew that French diplomats almost invariably collaborated with the Spaniards in their persecution. He was so wary of them all that he treated Lafayette himself, whom he met in Prussia, and Count Segur, in Russia, with offensive reserve. He wrote in his *Diario:* "I was visited by Count Segur this morning and we were alone together. He seems to be a man of judgement. He showed me much affection and I do not believe any of it...."[1] Segur, for his part, described Miranda as "an educated man, ingenious, intriguing and audacious," but he repaid the hostility that the Venezuelan had shown him with little gossipy tales.

Miranda, however, threw caution to the winds because of his desire to visit France, and he entered the country under the name of Meiroff with a Russian passport. After traveling in quite leisurely fashion through the south of France, he sailed up the west coast from Bordeaux to Le Havre and finally reached Paris.

Although the year was 1789, Miranda seemed not to notice the revolution that was beginning. The truth is that the same applied to most Frenchmen, including those who must have considered themselves better informed or better equipped to judge events. Thus, when Miranda visited Abbé Raynal in Marseilles, a man who had gained world-wide fame for his revolutionary ideas, the vehement renegade considered that France was not ripe for revolution, and saw the existing unrest as just another "fashion," which would soon be forgotten. He told Miranda: "When the fashion of *Agriculture* was in vogue, I saw in Paris that the boudoirs of the ladies were filled with books on it, and on ploughing, to such an extent that one would have thought that the whole nation would take up farming... and within six months fashion changed and everything disappeared as if it had never existed. Another season was devoted to *education,* and Rousseau's *Emile,* and everything that touched upon it was found everywhere. Fashion changed and they disappeared like those that had gone before."[2] When he made these comments, Raynal did not know that his own renown, a product of this rotation of fashion, was to disappear very soon, while those events that he belittled were to bring about others of such importance that he himself would be terrified by them.

When he reached Paris, Miranda would have followed the installation of the States General and the decisive events that followed it with great

---

1. *Diario* in p. 264, official edition.
2. Miranda, Archivo, edición oficial, iv, p. 187.

interest, but the police vigilance to which he was subjected no doubt persuaded him to refrain from expressing his thoughts in writing. This is the opinion of Parra-Pérez, who points out in support of it that, once he was safe in London, Miranda broke his silence, and wrote to Potemkin that France had a "detestable" government, and that whatever resulted from the existing anarchy would be better than what had gone before.

Miranda returned to the English capital in June 1789. He soon renewed his correspondence with his friends in North America, and he tried to establish contact with Spanish Americans who might be interested in his schemes. As always, he rapidly formed sound friendships with the important men whom he met. General Melville, a retired soldier who filled his leisure by writing, frequently invited him to dine and consulted him on history and geography. Sir Frederich Haldimand, a former British governor in North America, declared that he daily found Miranda more interesting, and entertained him in his home. Dr. Marshall, a surgeon, wrote to him: "I met you in town with pleasure, and I left you with regret. I consider you now as the modern Puffendorf: the history of Europe has in you a perfect master." Turnbull again showed his readiness to serve Miranda with his influence and money, and he introduced him to another former British governor, Thomas Pownall, who after long and detailed discussions with the Spanish American conspirator, showed great interest in his plans and put him in touch with the prime minister, William Pitt.

It was thus that Miranda came to meet Pitt on February 14, 1790, a few months after returning to England. As always, he was at his ease, and while he waited to come face to face with the formidable minister who at the time was perhaps the most powerful man in the world, he examined his library so as to form an opinion on his intellectual standing. He would have been satisfied by Titus, Livy and Euripides, which he found among Pitt's favorite books.

Miranda submitted to Pitt a vast plan for the emancipation of South America, based on the premise that the continent, although entitled to independence by its wealth and population and capable of winning it for itself, needed the aid of England to check Spain's naval power and because the geographical isolation of the South American countries made it difficult for them to aid each other. The new state, which Miranda had always referred to in his notes as COLOMBIA, would stretch from the Mississippi to Cape Horn, excluding only Brazil. He intended it to have a form of government "mixed and similar to that of Great Britain," with an emperor at the head of the executive branch, and with a two-chamber legislature, one chamber of which would be elected by popular suffrage. An original institution, a product of Mirandas's reading, would consist of two censors to watch over education of the young and morality of customs, while a corps of magistrates would be entrusted with the most important aspects of public administration. Naturally, many other details were given, dealing both with the future of this new world and with its population, exports, contraband, mining, etc. Miranda considered that 12,000 to 15,000 infantrymen and fifteen ships of the line would be sufficient for the British contribution to the enterprise, and he promised that the new nation would pay for these services punctually. It would agree to a "reciprocally advantageous" plan of commerce with England and a canal across the Isthmus of Panama would facilitate European maritime communication with the Pacific and the Far East. He added: "Considering the analogy that exists in the character of these two nations, and the effects that naturally must flow from *Liberty* and a good government, giving instruction to the general mass of men... we must expect to soon see growing up a respectable and illustrious nation worthy of being the close ally of the most wise and celebrated power upon earth."

Yes; very attractive. Except that England did not aspire to see the emergence of respectable and illustrious nations on any continent, nor was Pitt interested in liberty and instruction for the general mass of men. There was too much "equality" in the plan, and the English were accustomed in their adventures to securing better rewards at less risk. If we add that thereafter England embarked on a policy of stimulating or restraining Miranda, according to the state of its relations with Spain, it is easy to understand that the negotiations were bound to fail. "I have been sold for a treaty of commerce with Spain," Miranda exclaimed when he was finally informed that Pitt would not adopt his scheme.

Fortunately, if Miranda placed too much trust in Pitt—which disturbed Pownall, who at times seemed to be shamed by his compatriot—the duplicity and opportunism with which he was treated made him react violently. This preserved his dignity and the rectitude of his intentions. He declared categorically in relation to Spain: "And I expect, since my intentions are purely *patriotic,* with a view only of offering services to my country and promoting the interests and advantages of Great Britain, in so far as they are compatible, that services should not be requested from me against Spain for any other cause. This is a point of delicacy for me, even though such services might be authorized by the law of war and the example of great and virtuous men in modern and ancient times." He never gave way on this point in his negotiations with the English politicians, and in his correspondence with Castlereagh he stressed that he would not serve against Spain "for any other purpose but the emancipation of South America."

We will look at other manifestations of Miranda's nationalist suscepti-bility a little later. We now return to 1792, when our hero was in the unfortunate position of having to discuss his financial position with the English government. In this case, as in many others, a document in his prodigious collection sums up the situation perfectly. The noble Pownall wrote to him: "I have been in situations similar to those in which you find yourself at present. I can, therefore, and do, understand your feelings, and perfectly agree with your reasoning. You are correct when you say that you do not wish to accept monetary offerings in any form unless based on a plan to contract your services. Yet, remember you have a great project in view and I hope you will never lose sight of it. Thus, as much as you scorn money, and are even offended by the person who offers it, accept it before placing yourself in a position that may prevent you from pursuing your objective."

Miranda was also annoyed that the papers entrusted to Pitt were not returned to him. At first the Venezuelan was given evasive answers and then came the shameless excuse that some of them had gone astray. He informed the English minister: "I hope that all will be returned to me without a copy, translation, or anything being retained," and as if the insulting insinuation of this remark was not sufficiently clear, he wrote personally to Pitt: " . . . perhaps you think that when I leave this country you can use my projects as you like. No, Sir, you ought never to forget that all the ideas embodied in these plans were expressly communicated to you in order to promote the liberty and happiness of the Spanish American people and the welfare and honor of England as objectives that were entirely compatible with each other . . . Sir! papers transferred personally to the Prime Minister of Great Britain and judged by him to be of great national importance, —lost! Allow me to refrain from making the reflections provoked by these peculiar circumstances. . . ."

Meanwhile, the indefatigable Miranda had decided to go to France, in the hope that the revolutionary principles declared there would induce the government to support his project for South America. With these ideas in mind he reached Paris in March 1792. He spent some weeks establishing contact with the country's new leaders: Roland, Minister of the Interior; Dumouriez, Minister of Foreign Affairs; Petion, Mayor of Paris; Brissot, one of the most influential politicians of the time. At the same time, he did not neglect the visits that formed his daily intellectual sustenance: visits to the royal library, to the studio of the sculptor Houdon, etc. He made so much progress with his new friends that he wrote in his diary on August 11: "My friend the Mayor of Paris (M. Petion), seeing that I had decided to leave for England where I had engagements of the greatest importance, asked me why I did not enter the service of France in the cause of that liberty that I loved so well. . . . He said that she would give me a lucrative post and that I would be able to render her essential aid."

To appreciate the significance of these proposals it is necessary to recall that the last shadow of Louis XVI's remaining authority had disappeared two days earlier. After the invasion of the Tuileries by the mob on the night of August 9, the royal family sought asylum in the National Assembly which removed the king from his duties. At the end of September, the first decree of the Convention declared the abolition of the monarchy.

Nevertheless, Miranda was not dazzled by the magnificent opportunity that was offered him. He pointed out to the new leaders of French politics that he was a foreigner, and after more meetings with Petion and the Minister of War, Servan, he presented the latter with a memorandum that listed the conditions upon which he would accept: that he should be given the rank and salary of major-general, that at the end of the war he should be given a civilian or military appointment which would allow him to live comfortably in France, and that he should be allowed to devote most of his time to his objective of emancipating the Spanish American colonies. He argued: "It is necessary that their cause should be effectively protected by France, being the cause of Liberty, and that France should give me permission, as soon as occasion arises, to promote their welfare by establishing Liberty and Independence. . . ."

The final touches were put to the agreement at a dinner with Servan and the Minister of the Navy, Monge. Miranda was given his orders on September 5, 1792, to join the army of the north, then commanded by General Dumouriez.

But, as if even in those moments of triumph he needed to renew explicitly the promises made in his youth, Miranda repeated in a letter to Count Voronzow: "It should not astonish you to see me united with the defenders of liberty, for you know that she is my favorite divinity and that I was devoted to her service before France became interested in her. What has most strongly influenced me to accept this post is the hope of some day being useful to my poor country, that I am unable to abandon."

XII

A QUIXOTE...
WITHOUT EXCLUDING
THE MADNESS!

Miranda's new career followed a meteoric path just as that of Dumouriez and other politicians and soldiers of this period when the slightest error could bring dishonor and death. Miranda was one of the more fortunate. He remained alive, and the people of Paris loudly endorsed the honors he won with his triumphs on the battlefield.

Almost as soon as he arrived at the front, the Venezuelan had his first encounter with the enemy at Morthomme where, with 2,000 men under his command, he defeated a Prussian force three times larger. He noted in his personal records: "The different groups under my command returned to the camp at night, satisfied with having fought the Prussians for the first time and, although inferior in number, having defeated them." This victory was the first won by the raw volunteers of the Republic over the regular troops of the enemy; for this reason its moral effect was far superior to its strategic importance. A year later, when he was tried before the Convention, Miranda cited this triumph in his defense with words very similar to those noted above, "I had the honor to obtain the first victory of our arms against the Prussians on the outskirts of Grand-Pré on September 12."[1]

---

1. I am closely following the interpretation of Dr. C. Parra-Pérez, who is an incomparable authority in the field. Some French writers, especially Paul Adam, who glorified Miranda in an extraordinary way, consider the encounter at Valmy to have been more important. But, according to Parra-Pérez, this encounter, which occurred two days later, was a simple artillery exchange, in which the soldiers were mere spectators. See his *Miranda et la Revolution Francaise* (Paris, 1925) and *Miranda et Madame Custine* (Paris, 1950).

But those enthusiastic, raw recruits, so brave and generous, could also be easily disorganized. A few days later in Wargemoulin, they were on the point of deserting because of a rumor that their generals were betraying them. Miranda, sword in hand, mingled with his men, harangued them, and stopped the panic. The flowery words he used the following day to praise the battalions that had formed around him to save the army still retained the heat of the moment. He told them: "General Miranda feels obliged to declare publicly the warm approbation deserved by the forty-third battalion of the line and the first battalion of the National Guard of Mayenne et Loire for their conduct on September 15. They merit the thanks of the whole army, which have already been expressed by the commanding general-in-chief, and those of all men who, like him, are true friends of liberty and equality." In this fashion the army was formed that was to fight for many years against a coalition of the rest of Europe.

Petion was delighted by his friend's early successes, and he commented: "Miranda has conducted himself like an experienced officer and excellent citizen. He knows how to win the confidence of the soldiers under his command." He added, as a final encouragement to the South American's deepest hopes, "We are concerned not only with the liberty of France, but also with the liberty of the whole world. We will never fight for a greater or a nobler cause." As for Dumouriez, the fervor with which he commended Miranda and praised him personally is surprising. Parra-Pérez tells us: "His correspondence with Paris in this period was full of dithyrambic praises for his subordinate, to whom he attributed, quite simply, true genius." And we read in a letter from Dumouriez to Miranda, "Your friendship, my dear Miranda, is my most precious reward... Your sublime philosophy is what unites us."

The attitudes of Servan, Monge and Brissot were similar. Paradoxically, however, this unanimity in support of Miranda almost cut short his career and brought him to disaster because his friends sought to have him appointed Governor of Santo Domingo so that he could revolutionize Spanish America from the island. Monge and Brissot asked Dumouriez to release Miranda for this purpose, and Brissot wrote to him (Dumouriez): "It is necessary to promote revolution in Spain and in America at the same time. The fate of the movement in Spanish America depends upon one man. You know him, you esteem him, you love him—Miranda! The ministers have been searching for someone to replace Desparbes at Santo Domingo. A ray of light struck me. I said: 'Appoint Miranda.' Miranda will soon put an end to the miserable quarrels of the colonist, he will soon bring the turbulent whites to reason, and he will become the idol of the colored people. Then with ease he will be able to revolutionize the colonies that the Spaniards possess in the West Indies or on the American Continent. At the head of twelve thousand troops of the line now at Santo Domingo and of ten or fifteen thousand brave mulattoes from our colonies, will he not be able easily to invade the Spanish dominions, having also a squadron under his orders, while the Spaniards have no forces with which to oppose him?"

This, apparently, was the plan cherished by Miranda for many years but, although he seemed to react to it with a certain enthusiasm and even consulted Knox, Hamilton and Smith about it, he soon rejected it. He explained to Brissot that although he was very familiar with the Spanish possessions, he was completely ignorant about conditions in the French colonies which would have to serve as base for operations and, secondly, that his appointment to Santo Domingo would provoke the most violent reaction from the governments in Madrid and London.

All this was reasonable, of course, but hardly enough to dissuade that hard-hearted dreamer, who was always ready to undertake great enterprises with few resources, and who in 1806 was to challenge with only three small ships and a few recruits all the might that Spain could muster in South America. The real reason for his refusal is to be found in his repugnance towards fighting against Spain as the tool of another power. We have noted how violently he made this attitude clear to the English. Although on this occasion new principles could be invoked—the world-wide revolution of which men talked—Miranda must have been alarmed at the prospect of serving a foreign government against Spain. He was so sensitive on this issue of foreign intervention that he always insisted that any foreign troops that might aid him to emancipate Spanish America would have to be prepared to take orders from the government formed by the creoles. During later negotiations with the English, he wrote in his diary, "I have replied that I would not agree even for a minute to a foreign force exercising any authority or acting like a conqueror in the country, and that only under the American flag would I serve or call upon my countrymen to band together." It is clear that he would have felt obliged to give the same warning to France, and that he would have been prevented from so doing if he had agreed to command such an enterprise with a French commission and in a French uniform.

For these reasons Miranda turned down proposals which at first sight were attractive. Fortunately, the skill with which he rejected them, coupled with his conduct at the front, outweighed any bad impression that his refusal might have caused. As always, he was surrounded by enthusiastic admirers, including the veteran Duval who had fought with him at Wargemoulin, and who wrote: "I hope, my dear General and friend, that you will remain with us as General-in-Chief of our army, and that you will not go to America.... Remain in France...." Far from falling into disgrace, Miranda was promoted to the rank of Lieutenant-General, and was given command of eight brigades of the Army of the North. He went on to replace

General La Bourdonnaye at the head of the forces operating against Antwerp and, after intensifying the siege, he obtained the city's surrender on November 29, 1792.

During the occupation of the city, Miranda once more displayed his almost magnetic ability to attract friends in the most extraordinary circumstances. On this occasion it was the Bishop of Antwerp who befriended the amazing revolutionary general. When Miranda visited the episcopal palace, he probably went straight to the library, or perhaps his first questions to the prelate were about the latter's favorite books. At any rate, the bishop presented the stormer of his city with various Spanish and Latin classics as a token of "the homage due to the man of letters, the philosopher full of charm and extensive knowledge, the great military personage of whom Homer and Horace would have said: *Quid mores hominum multorum vidit et urbes.*"

This triumph was for Miranda an appropriate revenge for the distress caused him by Pitt. Antwerp, one of the most coveted fortress in Europe, had always been a nightmare for England. Over the centuries many of her wars with Spain, France, Holland and Austria had been fought to prevent any of these powers from establishing itself in this part of the coastline of western Europe. The seizure of Antwerp by France once again turned the antagonism between the two nations into open war, and Holland, Prussia, Russia, Austria and Spain joined England in what came to be known as the First Coalition. France stood alone, but she took the offensive and invaded Holland. Something new now became clear: that "the people in arms" were capable of defeating the best professional armies of the rest of Europe, and that the improvised generals of the Republic were superior to the dukes and princes who commanded elsewhere by right of birth. If the Republic could succeed in making the old monarchies revise their secular class structures and recognize merit and learning as the basis for political and military preeminence, the triumph of democracy would be assured, even though the Republic itself might disappear. And this, in fact, was what was to happen. The Republic killed itself with its excesses, but its early triumphs, although apparently ephemeral, introduced a new social valuation which was to be the basis for European democracy in the century which followed.[1]

Miranda's task in the next campaign was to capture Maestricht, but even though he announced on February 25, 1793, that he was besieging the city and that it was on fire in five places, the Dutch would not surrender. Dumouriez, too, was held up at Dordrecht, despite some early successes.

---

1. We distinguish the scale of social values established in North America from that created by the French Revolution, because we believe that the former would have been considered inappropriate for Europe, even if the French Revolution had not occurred. The democracy that gradually emerged in nineteenth century Europe was very different from the North American variety and even today there are still essential differences between them.

These delays gave the Duke of Coburg time to bring Austrian reinforcements to the Roer, where they crushed the forces of General Valence. After this defeat, new contingents of enemy troops advanced towards Maestricht, and Miranda was forced to abandon the siege.

The invasion of Holland, then, was a failure, but the French still held Belgium. Their reverses, however, sparked off rivalries between Miranda and Valence, while Dumouriez, who according to a contemporary had turned against the Republic after the execution of Louis XVI in January 1793, "hastened to hazard a battle in the hope, if he were victorious, of making himself redoubtable to the Convention or if he were defeated, of allying himself with the enemy in order to march against the Mountain."[1]

For this reason Dumouriez abandoned positions that Miranda considered impregnable, to attack the enemy at Neerwinden with inferior forces. Miranda wrote to Petion: "I am astounded that Dumouriez should have been capable of such an error." Dumouriez, in turn, criticized Miranda, whose troops were the first to give way to the imperial attack. He obtained an order for "the foreigner," as both he and Valence had begun to call Miranda, to be judged before the Revolutionary Tribunal.

Two points relating to the defeat at Neerwinden were later proved in Miranda's favor: that the troops under his orders who broke ranks and created disorder in the army were raw recruits who could not be controlled by their immediate superiors, and that his forces were much smaller than those of the enemy. The veterans Roualt and Champmorin, who mingled with the troops swords in hand in a vain effort to arrest their flight, declared, "The majority (of the recruits) deserted in cowardly fashion, despite our efforts to regroup them." And Baron Jomini comments in his *Histoire Critique et Militaire des Guerres de la Révolution:* "The assertion of Dumouriez is unjust; he was doubtless unaware that Miranda had been fighting against very superior forces which outflanked him and that as all of Miacznisky's soldiers had not yet arrived upon the battlefield, Miranda's retreat was made even more inevitable." For his part Miranda claimed that he had made the following observations to Dumouriez: "A reconnaissance of the left side had not been ordered; we had a river without a fordable spot in front us; the enemy was favorably situated on the heights of Halle and Vildere. I asked him if he knew the approximate number of the enemy forces. He replied that he calculated them to be 52,000. (Ours were 35,000). And do you think it was likely that we could dislodge the enemy from such a position? But I saw that he did not want to think about it and that he had decided to fight the battle at all cost."

Parra-Pérez tells us that Dumouriez entrusted Miranda with the task of covering the retreat after the defeat, and that the official report of the

---

1.   Louvet de Couvrai: *Memoires.* Quoted by Robertson.

imperial command stated that this operation was conducted "coolly and with much order."

It is well known that both Dumouriez and Valence deserted the Republic. Although Valence had the delicacy to make clear that he would never fight against his countrymen, whatever their excess, Dumouriez attempted a coup with the forces entrusted to him, and afterwards simply went over to the enemy. According to Miranda's story, Dumouriez had told him "that it would be necessary to march on Paris with the army to re-establish liberty."

And Miranda replied, "I believe the remedy to be worse than the illness and I would certainly prevent it if I could."

"Would you fight against me?"

"Perhaps, if you try to destroy liberty."

"You would be a Labienus, then?"

"Labienus or Cato, you will always find me on the side of the Republic."

It was to avenge himself for this reply and to anticipate any denunciation that Miranda might make against him that Dumouriez hastened to accuse him at the very time that he entrusted him with the delicate task of covering the retreat of the whole army.

Despite so much evidence in his favor, Miranda's future looked bleak. It was with good reason that the Conciergerie prison in which he was confined was known as the "ante-chamber" of the tomb. Few of its inmates escaped the guillotine. Moreover, Miranda had to answer not only for Neerwinden but for his conduct throughout the campaign. This gave his enemies and the bloodthirsty fanatics who swarmed in the press and around the Tribunal and the Convention the opportunity to select any details which could prejudice his case. He was accused, in turn, of being an accomplice of Dumouriez, a negligent general, a "Brissotist," and an agent of England. But the worst feature was that Miranda's enemies were trying to destroy him not because they thought him guilty, but because he was, as Michelet later said, "the sword of the Gironde." Thus, for Marat, Danton, Robespierre and all the hotheads around them, Miranda's disgrace and elimination would in a stroke mean the destruction of the Girondins and freedom to embark upon the terror which they invoked as a savior. In this context, then, the vindication of Miranda was the last victory of the Girondins. This point has not been stressed sufficiently in the past.

The trial was one of "sublime" drama, to use the adjective then in vogue. Miranda's counsel was Chaveau Lagarde, who later achieved fame when he defended Marie Antoinette. The prosecuting counsel was Fouquier Tinville, who did everything he could to preserve his reputation as unrelenting. The fiercest attacks upon the accused came from Marat and Anarchasis Clootz in the press, from Robespierre in the Convention, and from Danton of the Jacobins. Miranda remained haughty, laconic, precise and icy. He defended himself with curt statements, such as, "Attack on Maestricht, by order; my retreat, approved; battle of Neerwinden, against my judgement."

In another incident he unintentionally achieved a theatrical effect when he spoke in favor of General La Bourdonnaye, a personal enemy. His statement caused murmurs of disapproval because La Bourdonnaye was then in disgrace, but at the same time, all had to admire Miranda's detached sincerity. The judges and the spectators must also have been moved when the old General La Noue testified that the mistakes of the French at Liège were the fault not of Miranda, but of Valence.

In its final verdict, the court unanimously absolved Miranda of the charges against him. The *Moniteur* praised the verdict on May 21, 1793, and it added: "The people applauded the judgement concerning Miranda and also his speech; they took him in their arms, carried him in triumph, and crowned him." Even Fouquier Tinville himself and the jury joined in the applause, and the President of the Revolutionary Tribunal, J. B. Montane, congratulated Miranda by letter and invited him to "a republican dinner."

Thus again we see Miranda's ability always to impress those with whom he had dealings. During the trial Joel Barlow, the North American poet and patriot, had declared: "My friends in London were also Miranda's. They were the most pronounced friends of liberty, the most zealous defenders of the French Revolution. They always lauded this philosophic warrior and they made known their profound satisfaction when they learned that he had entered the service of freedom in France." At the end of the trial General Pille, although formerly Dumouriez's lieutenant in Belgium, congratulated Miranda and told him, "One can say to you with Seneca, *Virtus cum violata est, refulsit.* Your enemies have not been able to ruin you by their persecutions; they have merely demonstrated to France your true worth." Chauveau Lagarde, who proclaimed that the day on which he had defended Miranda was the happiest in his life, described him as follows: "One cannot imagine more grandeur in character, more elevation in ideas, or more of true love for all the virtues.... I maintain that there is not a single man who followed the trial who has not become convinced that Miranda is not only guiltless but that he is a man who is most moral and virtuous. I avow on my honor that several witnesses who accused him with great bitterness have since proclaimed his innocence and have deposited in my hands their most formal retractions."

A further testimony to Miranda's character, included in Cochelet's report to the Convention on the French generals, contained the criticism that was to be made of him with increasing frequency throughout his career:

"Miranda has a genius which is vast and profound. He loves liberty and equality as a young man loves his dear mistress... He was ceaselessly occupied with his duties. I did not behold him distracted for a single instant. To me he seemed to possess all the moral qualities of a good general: activity, intelligence, watchfulness, discernment, probity, patriotism, love for the soldiers, regard for discipline, and a comprehensive vision. One might only reproach him because of his vivacity, because of an air of hauteur in his bearing, and because he does not display enough sympathy for those men who are less discerning, less intelligent, and less active than himself."

Europeans of the highest rank had shown their resentment of Miranda's haughtiness. It seems that the inflexibility of which Cochelet complained was the main reason that few of his compatriots were to sympathize with him in Venezuela in 1812. It is true that in 1812 Miranda performed wonders of self control to temporize with men like Roscio, who although sincere, attacked him unjustly, and with others like Mérida, who deserved only contempt. But his efforts, born of patriotism and self-discipline, were probably insufficient to obliterate in his behavior and daily conduct, the severity with which he judged those who were less intelligent and less capable than himself. And there must have been many of them, in Venezuela as in Europe!

We return to France and to 1793, the year of the Terror. Miranda had little time to enjoy either the apotheosis of his trial or the delightful retreat he had obtained outside Paris where he began to bring together his books, papers, music, portraits, porcelain and sculptures. A few days after his release, the Girondins were swept from power, and Miranda once again found himself one of the "particular objects of Robespierre's rage," to quote the English poetess Helen Marie Williams, then his fervent admirer.

The antagonism between Miranda and Robespierre was understandable given their contrasting characters. The infatuated demagogue, the lying, powder-smeared, badly spoken terrorist, who was about to bathe France in blood and who provided posterity with not one worthy action or memorable saying—or even an original saying—must have hated the imposing, vigorous General, who evidently held him in contempt. Moreover, Miranda was a danger for the new government which looked for enemies on all sides, both because of his own personality and because of his numerous friends and admirers. The Committee of Public Safety, therefore, ordered his arrest at the beginning of July 1793 and he was taken to the prison of La Force.

This prison, from which cartloads of victims flowed incessantly to the guillotine, but which was kept packed with new prisoners, lodged one of the most extraordinary spectacles in history. The political anarchy of the time was reflected in the prison's ever changing, heterogeneous population: aristocrats, Girondins, intellectuals, and not infrequently extremists labeled "suspect" by Robespierre, but who themselves had been demanding the guillotine for the weak the previous day. All were preparing for death, but each man wanted his death brave and eloquent, to give testimony to his beliefs. Some told frivolous stores and laughed, even as the grim jailers laboriously spelled out their names and prodded them into the cart. Some looked down from the cart upon the mob with insulting affection, smiling disdainfully at its insults. Others meditated furiously upon man and liberty and arranged the final details or their memoirs. Others trembled with impatience to discover the secret of how those beautiful dreams of universal brotherhood had led to what they saw before them. Almost all the Girondins heatedly reiterated their faith in the Republic so that nobody would think they had turned against it or considered it lost because of their own miserable sufferings.

It is easy to imagine what Miranda did. He gathered together what books he could find, and he surrounded himself with a select group of fellow-thinkers with whom he talked politics, art and philosophy. We know that he thought of death, because his companions noticed that he had a flask of poison. He was not interested in defying the raving Jacobin crowd from the cart or the guillotine; he preferred death by his own hand because such an end would be, in a sense, voluntary and appear freely chosen. If circumstances denied him the sword of Cato, the man who had sought to live by classical models would choose the poison of Socrates as a final dignity.

Miranda was anticipated in this course of action by the young Achille Du Châtelet, of whom Picón Salas gives this delightful sketch: "He was barely thirty-four, one of those intellectuals whom the Revolution turned into a military leader. He compiled the report that his fellow provincialists sent to the National Assembly in 1789. He stirred up artisans and peasants and he jumped from his province's political clubs to command troops in the Army of the Rhine. His knee almost became gangrenous from a cannon wound suffered at Courtray, and he was taken to the prison of La Force, the victim of political intrigues. He was a follower of Condorcet, skilled in ancient and modern languages, and managed to take a whole encyclopedic library to his cell." And Madame Rolland tells us that the two prisoners, Miranda and Du Châtelet, discussed an Elzevir edition of Seneca. Du Châtelet knew too much about books, not enough about life, and sought greater understanding of human nature in his friendship with Miranda. Before killing himself, Du Châtelet compiled a document in which he declared that he had sold to Miranda all that he possessed in La Force. Miranda wrote: "This is the manner in which this virtuous and unfortunate friend, who had determined to swallow poison, undertook to leave to me his books and other valuable property as a token of remembrance."

Du Chatelet had often acted as a judge in the debates on politics and strategy between Miranda and another of the erudite prisoners, L.A. Champagneux, who fortunately survived to record his recollections. Whereas Du Châtelet left Miranda his books, Champagneux wanted to entrust to him his son, who was destined for a military career. "If he has the opportunity of seeing you," he wrote to Miranda after his release, "I beg that you will inspire him with a love for labor and for the cause which he has embraced...."

Other members of Miranda's circle in prison were the Girondists, Vergniaud and Valazé, Adam Lux, the impetuous deputy who admired Charlotte Corday, and the young Armande de Custine, around whom appear various figures of a similar romantic stamp. His father was General Adan Philippe de Custine, who on his way to execution replied mockingly to the mob's "To the guillotine! To the guillotine!" with "Now we will see, rabble, now we will see!" Armande, too, although he had remained true to his republican ideas, was to be taken from La Force to the gallows. While he waited he was sometimes visited in prison by his young wife Delphine. Her beauty was so radiant that when her mother, the spiritual Madame de Sabran, saw her after an absence of four years, she exclaimed: "My God, my daughter, how beautiful you are!" This delicate flower of the aristocracy was also surprisingly cultured. Parra-Pérez tells us that she had read Corneille, Racine and Voltaire by the time she was eight. She later immersed herself in the classics and we know from a letter she wrote to her brother that she enthused over Pliny. She was just as capable of meditating with Diderot and Holbach as of dreaming with Goethe and even with Ossian. As for her courage and enchantment, Anatole France describes her attitude during the trial of her father-in-law: "... the old General de Custine had been brought before the Revolutionary Tribunal. Although his daughter-in-law had cause for complaint against him, she aided him before the judges and, as we have said, she was his most eloquent defender. She was in the Palace of Justice every day at six in the morning; she waited there for her father-in-law to emerge from the prison, threw her arms around his neck, and gave him news of his friends and family. When he was summoned before the judges, she watched with her eyes bathed in tears. She sat facing him on a small seat at the foot of the bench. As soon as the interrogation was over, she hurried to offer the attentions that his state demanded. After each session she secretly spent hours with the judges and the members of the committees. Her grace could move the hardest hearts."[1] We can imagine the impression that her visit created in the gloomy con-

---

1. Anatole France: *Oeuvres completes*. Paris, Calman Levy, 1950, ii, p. 480.

finement of the prison. Miranda met her there, but never dreamed that within two years he would have her in his arms as a lover.

Miranda was saved from execution because the recent and clamorous acquittal he had received made it difficult to send him immediately to the gallows. Fouquier Tinville himself, according to the poetess Williams, put off "the second trial required by Robespierre, until the tyrant would hear of delay and excuses no more and personally inscribed Miranda's name on the fatal list for the twelth of Thermidor." Fortunately, time was running out for Robespierre. His fall and death brought an end to the Terror. Miranda was freed in January 1795, and he wrote almost immediately to General Knox: "I take up the pen only to tell you that I live, and that my sentiments for our dear Colombia as well as for all my friends in that part of the world have not changed in the least in spite of the events which are bound to ruin France."

There began at this point in Miranda's career an interlude unrelated in many ways to the global significance of his life. In reality neither the American patriot nor the dreaming Girondist within him was at home in the environment of corruption and intrigue that followed the Terror. Miranda was admired by the public, and there were times when he seemed to be the only man capable of forming and leading healthy reaction against the collective laxity. Intelletuals and soldiers, some of them restless with ambition, others out of patriotism, visited him. Monarchists and discontented republicans in Switzerland and Germany sent him proposals which coincided with what rural, uncorrupted France hoped for.

Miranda was again briefly imprisoned in 1795 because the authorities were afraid of him. A little later a law restricting the political activities of foreigners was invoked against him, threatening him with expulsion from France. What really held him in check, however, was something less concrete and at the same time more powerful than all these police measures: Political activity had shifted to the salons of women, who formerly had been better known for their loose morals than for their spirituality. The contacts between those who controlled public life were made through men like Fouché, intriguers elevated to the rank of politicians, or through the work of the "army-suppliers," who sacked the country and enriched corrupt officials and soldiers. Miranda capitulated in part to this trend, and set himself up in luxury, but fortunately he still preferred Madame Staël and Petion's widow. And he did not forget even for a moment—a saving memory— that faraway country that he had promised never to abandon.

Miranda met Napoleon at one of these salon gatherings. According to the Duchess of Abrantes, the future emperor said in her presence: "I dined there with men of the greatest importance. There is one whom I should like to meet again. He is a Don Quixote except that he is not mad." When the owner of the house insisted upon knowing the man's name, Napoleon added, "It is General Miranda; that man has a sacred fire in his soul."

This incident was interesting, but, unfortunately, it has been distorted. Parra-Pérez relates that after Napoleon had left, one of those who had heard his opinion of Miranda, Salicetti, commented that the two had met in the house of a "rascal," apparently a Mexican hostile to Spain. Parra-Pérez discovered that Salicetti's comment was later attributed to Napoleon himself and, to cap it all, as if he had indicated that the rascal was Miranda.[1] This clarification from the erudite Venezuelan investigator, supported by the correct quotation from the Duchess of Abrantes, is important, because no less a person than Robertson uncritically accepted the distorted version in his *Life of Miranda*.

Napoleon's good impression of Miranda was not reciprocated; our Girondist never showed enthusiasm or admiration for Napoleon. It is possible that he shared the opinion of his friend, Madame de Staël, that Bonaparte's happy successes were due as much to the virtues he lacked as to the gifts that he possessed. This harsh assessment would have been reinforced by, among other things, a comment that Miranda must have heard increasingly at the time: that the ambitious General took as his wife the loved one of the inept Barras in order to obtain the command of the Army of Italy as his dowry. This was only half true. Napoleon loved Josephine madly and it would be more correct to say that the command of the army was Napoleon's dowry, offered to persuade the turbulent Josephine to accept him. Whatever the truth, Napoleon's importance was bound to increase thereafter, and it was difficult for a man like Miranda, who was then approaching fifty, to condone such a humiliating beginning for a young man.

Miranda left France in 1798. He was not to return, except for a few months, November 1800 until March 1801, with the "tacit permission" of the First Consul, only to be subsequently expelled on suspicion of conspiring against the government. Napoleon wanted no Quixotes around him; he wanted conquerers with a clear understanding of their self-interest. One imagines that he wanted nothing of "sacred fire," although his own rapacity, seemingly so practical, was divorced from reality. His own mother, with Sanza-like philosophy, commented after each victory: "Provided that he lasts!" In the end, Miranda's dreams proved to be more durable than Napoleon's empire.

With the exception of the four months spent in France, Miranda was to remain in England pursuing his design of emancipating the Spanish colonies. In 1797, while he was still arranging his departure from France, he had prepared the so-called "Pact of Paris", whereby "the deputies of the towns and provinces of South America" commissioned him to arrange with England for the dispatch of an expedition which would aid the Spanish

---

1.   C. Parra-Pérez: *Miranda et Madame Custine*. París, 1950, p. 240.

Americans to obtain their independence. In fact, these fiery deputies numbered only three: Pedro José Caro, José del Pozo y Sucre and Manuel José Salas. They were completely unknown and, like good revolutionaries, without credentials of any kind. The Peruvian Pablo Olavide had also agreed in Paris to help Miranda. He had acquired a certain fame in Europe because of his liberal ideas and because he had been pursued by the Inquisition. He was a sort of Spanish American Abbé Raynal, who ended up horrified with his own "ideas" when he saw the excesses of the Jacobins. Olavide could have given the project a certain sparkle, but he was already an old man on the verge of making public his repentance, and therefore refused absolutely to go to London.

These circumstances, which we have sketched very roughly, have led some historians to conclude that the Pact of Paris was a trick to wrest from Pitt the collaboration that Miranda desired. But the text of the agreement and Miranda's firmness with regard to England lead us to a contrary interpretation. In reality the Precursor sought to use the fragile agreement to ensure that Spanish America, his Colombia, could deal with England as nation to nation on a basis of absolute equality. If he could manage to negotiate on this footing, all the cheating that had tormented him—the lost papers kept by Pitt, the ambiguous proposals, the rumors in Spain and France that he was "an agent of England"—would be put aside, and the bilateral discussions with England would acquire increased status. In this sense, the Act of Paris was very significant. The final objective was not simply an English expedition, but a genuine tripartite alliance between England, the United States and South America, which at the outset would imply the rejection of any transfer of territory or sovereignty. The exclusive direction of military operations and of the agreements with England and the United States about the aid that other "allied" nations would provide was left to General Miranda. Was Miranda naive in his belief that England would help him selflessly? As if to answer this reproach, he referred in his will of 1805 to his "correspondence and negotiations with the ministers of His Brittanic Majesty from the year 1790 until the present about the absolute independence and establishment of civil liberty in all the American continent *on the same terms that France made with the United States of America.*" This final phrase, which underscored the principle established by the Pact of Paris, was also intended to justify the confidence that he placed in England. Why should Miranda not hope to see repeated something that he had already witnessed, with the sole difference that the tutelary power of the new Republics on this occasion would be England rather than France. It is odd that this interpretation of the Act of Paris should not have been noticed previously.

If the authority conferred upon Miranda in Paris was somewhat dubious, in 1798 he received a new commission of extraordinary moral significance in a letter from Manuel Gual, who had taken refuge in Trinidad after the discovery of the conspiracy which he had planned with José María España. Gual demanded passionately: "Miranda! If, contrary to what a newspaper has reported, it is not true that, because of the wickedness with which men have treated you and because of your love for reading and a private life, you have renounced these beautiful climes and the glory of being your country's savior, answer the call fo the American people! Come as their savior . . . Miranda! My only passion is to see this beautiful work completed, and I desire no other honor than to serve under you."

Miranda replied in 1800 that the goal of his efforts would always be the same: to secure "the happiness and independence of our beloved country, by honest means, so that *all* might enjoy a pure and honest liberty . . . We will tackle this noble enterprise, with perseverance and righteous intentions, leaving the rest to Divine Providence, the supreme arbiter of human activities. When we receive no more personal glory than that of having drawn up the plan and established the first foundations of such a magnificent enterprise, we will be sufficiently rewarded . . . ."

Miranda had reached the age of fifty, and one can detect an unexpected trace of melancholy in his reply. Was it because of the re-emergence within him of the Christian Spaniard, who incorporated the new devotion to country to the feeling of eternity and absolute consecration of his old beliefs? Or was he trying to remain the Stoic, scornful of external contingencies, and placing rectitude and constancy above all else? Or were his words simply an expression of a constant aloofness that refused to subordinate his austere ideals to the hazards of triumph or defeat then being juggled by the hands of other men? There must have been something of all of this shaping Miranda's words which at once were tender and harsh, humble and proud. In them an apparent resignation was transformed into a claim for eternal glory.

In London, Miranda dedicated himself to ideological preparation for the noble enterprise with perseverance and abnegation. Like Gual, many other Spanish Americans descended upon him, anxious to discuss their projects or obtain his guidance. The most pathetic case was that of Bernardo Riquelme who later liberated Chile under his paternal surname of O'Higgins. This son of faraway Arauco was very unhappy in London, and he later wrote to his father from Cádiz: "I am filled with envy when I see all my countrymen receiving letters from their relatives, while I, poor unfortunate that I am, receive them from nobody!" Miranda treated him like a son, taught him mathematics, and sublimated his loneliness in the magnificent dream of a free, united America. For his part, O'Higgins called Miranda "father of the oppressed," declared that he wanted to kiss the hands "destined to break the fetters that burden our compatriots." He later described his unforgettable initiation as follows: "Without loss of time Miranda initiated his discipline into the secrets of the cabinets of America and Europe respecting Spanish-American affairs. A fine library was the place in which the master studied the policies of nations. He devoted most of his time to the art of war. During long winter nights he told his disciples anecdotes of the French Revolution and reminded them of the errors which stained with blood and smothered in its cradle the liberty that should have been extended to the whole world." The future Liberator of Chile also always kept with him the final instructions given to him by Miranda when they parted. They were entitled: Advice given by an old South American to a young compatriot upon his return from England to his native land." According to Vicuña Mackenna, O'Higgins kept them hidden in the lining of his hat.[1]

Numerous secret societies were charged with the diffusion throughout America and Spain itself of liberal ideas, which at the time were more suppressed than ever, even in England, because of the reaction to the French Revolution. It is difficult to determine the influence of these societies, or to decide whether they were truly Masonic, or in "the Masonic style," as some historians describe them. Virtually all commentators exaggerate or minimize their importance, according to their own prejudices. Miranda founded one in London called "Gran Reunión Americana." Its members called themselves "Rational Gentlemen," and branches were set up in America under the name of Lautaro, the Araucanian chieftain. Moreover, almost all the precursors of independence and many of the liberators were Masons. The historian Alfonso Rumazo González, compiler of a copious bibliography on the subject, attributes great importance to Miranda's relations with Adams, Hamilton and other North American Masons, and to the activity in London of the "Lautaro Society."[2] Bolívar, too, apart from his supposed but unlikely initiation in Cádiz, seems to have been promoted from the rank of "brother" to that of "Gentleman Officer Mason of the Respectable Scottish Lodge of Saint Alexander of Scotland, according to a document of January 1806 which also states that he had been "recently initiated."[3]

A most lamentable loss for the Spanish Americans in London was the death there in 1798 of Juan Pablo Vizcardo, the Peruvian ex-Jesuit who left, among other important papers entrusted to Miranda, his "Letter to the Spanish Americans." For many years this was to be the revolutionary document that received the warmest reception in South America. It was printed the following year in Philadelphia and, when Miranda sent it to Trinidad for distribution in all the Spanish American countries, he told

---

1. Archivo de don Bernardo O'Higgins, Santiago de Chile, 1946, pp. 7, 13, 22.
2. Rumazo González, *Biografía de Manuela Sáenz*. Buenos Aires, 1945, p. 52.
3. We thank Dr. Manuel Pérez Vila for information about this document and permission to quote from it.

– 163 –

Gual, "You will see with what solid, august, and evident reasons our compatriot Vizcardo victoriously supports the justice and beauty of our cause." Gual replied that he had read it with "holy enthusiasm."

In this way, Miranda's activity in London in these years served to link, directly or indirectly, all the Spanish American liberators to his work of indoctrination and example. The scene in his library, described by O'Higgins, when the General became a teacher, was to be repeated many times with other "compatriots" from his vast Colombia, until 1810 when Bolívar, López Méndez and Bello arrived in London to inform the Precursor that Venezuela had proclaimed her autonomy and was awaiting him.

Throughout the continent the most difficult aspect of the emancipation process, that of synchronizing the initial impulses so as to impress the power of the revolution upon Spain and the rest of the world, was pursued in this fashion. Miranda's ideological preparation led to the strengthening of what were to be the basic principles of the continental reorganization: the solidarity of the Spanish American countries, the creation of civil institutions untainted either by Jacobinism or Bonapartism, and the categorical insistence that "the influence of no foreign power whatever should be allowed to interfere in the management of the country. Otherwise Spanish America would be coveted and despoiled by maritime powers that desired to engage in a partition." Miranda stated this in a letter to Gual, and he repeated it tirelessly to all who approached him.

But if the "sacred fire" which burned in Miranda alarmed Napoleon, England's politicians were not even interested in confirming that it existed. The tension in which England lived, thanks to Napoleon's advance to world-wide domination, obliged her to concentrate all her efforts upon this one vital concern. Some outstanding Britishers—the detached Turnbull and Vansittart—continued to support Miranda's projects. But his various proposals whereby Britain would help him to land in Venezuela and revolutionize it fell on deaf ears. Miranda resigned himself to 3,000 rifles, 3,000 sabres, and the right to recruit six hundred slaves in the English Antilles. He offered to pay for everything by sending cattle and mules to the same islands from Venezuela. On another occasion the mere offer of a passport to go to Trinidad filled him with enthusiasm, and he wrote: "This concession seemed to be a great point gained. Count Voronzow encouraged me to take this step, for if a post should be captured in South America, we should soon gain supporters. This good friend added that if it were not for the eccentricity of Paul I, or if the Empress Catherine still lived, he would procure for me two Russian frigates and two thousand soldiers which were all that would be necessary."

In effect, Miranda was a captive in England, although the attentions which he received gilded his captivity. The fluctuations of European politics frequently made it seem that a rupture between Spain and England was inevitable, and that he would be given the command of the coveted expedition of emancipation. He finally abandoned this hope in 1805 and decided to go to the United States. When it was suggested to him that he should wait a little longer, Miranda replied with his habitual arrogance that he could not be accused of haste, for in the short space of a year he had "four times witnessed the breaking of promises" given him "by His Majesty's Ministers."

Before leaving for the United States, Miranda made a will, because he had decided that he would subsequently proceed to Venezuela one way or another. Nothing is more moving than this inventory of what he left behind when he embarked on his uncertain adventure. He owned in Paris "a precious collection of paintings, bronzes, mosaics, *gouaches* and miniatures," and he calculated that France owed him about 10,000 louis for unpaid salaries. His property in London included his furniture, his silver, the ornaments in his house, and a library of 6,000 books, of which the Greek classics were to go to the University of Caracas. Above all, he left behind an eighteen-month old son, Leandro, and the as yet unborn Francisco. He fathered them, after so many amorous adventures, as he was approaching old age. Their mother was his housekeeper, the humble Sarah Andrews. These children had brought forth in Miranda feelings of tenderness not before experienced. His deep affection for Leandro led him into another unexpected return to Spanish roots, when he asked the Protestant mother to have the baby baptized a Catholic, despite the opposition that the ceremony might provoke among his friends. Picón Salas observes that he took his decision "as if Spanish race and tradition were to prevail above everything else in his descendants."

Miranda arrived in New York in November 1805. The marvelous William S. Smith and other friends arranged festivities in his honor. General Knox wrote of his "great pleasure" on learning of his arrival. Washington's family and numerous politicians and businessmen entertained him. But neither President Jefferson nor Secretary of State Madison would offer more than "to wink at" the arrangements he might make for his future enterprise. Miranda then decided to buy what he could for his own expedition. He had £2,000 which he had obtained in London on the security of his valuable library, together with a smaller sum given to him by the English government. Smith offered to collect $50,000 for him, and a number of merchants agreed to provide credit for the rest of his needs. Even with this, he was able to purchase very little: A ship, armed with twenty-one cannon, which he named *Leander* after his son; two small craft, *Bacchus* and *Bee,* which he obtained later; less than six hundred muskets; fifteen carbines and a few sabres and machetes. His human resources consisted of two hundred

North American recruits without any military experience. Some were unselfish volunteers, but the majority were recruited by the methods normally used in such cases, trickery and payment.

It is touching that Miranda could raise no more than this for the enterprise which he had told Pitt would require 12,000 to 15,000 infantry men and fifteen ships of the line. He did not even have the 2,000 men and the two frigates of which he had spoken with Voronzow, or the minimum of 600 recruits and 3,000 guns agreed a short time before. He was about to challenge on sea and land all the might that Spain could muster, with a second-hand ship, two schooners and 200 men. When Don Quixote noticed, as he was about to put on his armor, that he had no helmet to protect his head, he had to fashion one with his own hands. If Miranda had known that Napoleon had called him a Quixote "apart from the madness" perhaps on this occasion he would have corrected him arrogantly, in a very Spanish way: A Quixote, without excluding the madness!

The picture, one of those in which fact surpasses fiction, is completed by the presence at Miranda's side of another splendid knight, the North American Colonel William S. Smith, who offered his son to Miranda as aide-de-camp with the recommendation, which only the two of them understood, that he had been "raised in the cult of liberty."

The adventure was quixotic, but only to a point. Miranda was still a man of harsh, inflexible reasoning. His decision was not dictated by desperation, anger or thoughtless enthusiasm. Rather he knew that it was only by voluntarily risking his life that he could "make good his words," show that he was ready to die for them, and prove the sincerity of what he offered and what he asked. The uncertain international situation suggested that he should wait, his position in England tempted him to wait, and the apostleships he was fulfilling gave him the right to wait, but he was already on the threshold of old age. Unless he acted now to offer his life his ideal, an ambiguous shadow could descend upon him. At the end of the century, another Spanish American knight-errant, José Martí, was to be impelled by the same "sentiments" to prove the meaning of his whole life with a gesture, to offer himself to death, despite the entreaties of his fellows, in an equally bold enterprise. Martí explained that he did so "to make good his words," and because "for me the *Patria* will never mean triumph, only agony and duty." Miranda's thoughts were the same when he wrote to Gual that he sought no other glory than that of having laid the foundations of the magnificent enterprise.

On the other hand, Miranda also possessed the quixotic faculty of transforming external circumstances and adapting them to his own personal reality, which was bound to prevail, and he behaved on board ship, surrounded by his motley band, as if he were in his library in London, instructing those select disciples who were to become the continent's liberators. And the surprising thing is that, spiritually, he triumphed once again; an eye-witness tells us: "He assumed the manner of a father and instructor to the young men. He spoke of the prospect of success, and of the preparations made, with great confidence. The glory and advantages of the enterprise were described in glowing colors. At another time he detailed his travels, his sufferings and escapes in a manner that aroused both their admiration and sympathy. He appeared the master of languages, of science and literature."[1]

The Spanish minister to the North American government, who had kept watch of Miranda and was hostile to him, intensified his efforts as soon as he learned of the departure of the expedition; he alerted the Viceroy of Mexico, the Governor of Cuba and the Captain-General of Venezuela, and, together with the French Minister, he protested to the government in Washington. The Spanish Minister in Paris also complained of what he considered the benevolent attitude of the United States government; Colonel Smith was removed from his official position, and both Jefferson and Madison had to deny having aided Miranda. In short, the unprotected convoy left behind an indifferent or hostile world and, when Miranda hoisted on bord the *Leander* the first flag of the world that he was going to lift up in his arms, he did not have at his side a single Spanish American worthy of passing with him into history.

Failure, then, was inevitable. The schooners *Bacchus* and *Bee* were captured in an encounter with the Spanish coastguards near Puerto Cabello. Miranda returned to the English islands in search of aid, and obtained some reinforcements in Trinidad, but when he landed on the Venezuelan coast near Coro, he found the shore deserted, with nobody to read his proclamations and nobody to hear his voice. The only human being to come near, apart from two fugitive slaves and a Negress whom he found imprisoned for murder, was a horseman who brought the reply of the Bishop of the Diocese to his requests. Miranda learned that the prelate not only remained faithful to the king but also that he had excommunicated the "heretic" invader—he called him "new Belial," "monster," "atheist"— and all who read his seditious documents.

This solitude that Miranda found could have been voluntary on the part of Venezuelans, deceived by Spanish propaganda, which presented Miranda as a heretic, a Jacobin and an agent of the English government; but the authorities were accustomed to using this scorched-earth strategy against invaders. In 1779, according to documents in the National Archives, Caracas, it was feared that the English would invade the same coastal area around Coro, and the regional authorities were ordered by the

---

1.   Quoted by Robertson, p. 262.

Captain-General to prepare the landowners to take their slaves and animals inland—and, of course, to flee themselves—if the attack materialized.[1]

It was impossible for Miranda to venture into the interior with his small, untrained band of foreigners. After spending a few days vainly scrutinizing the emptiness that lay before him, he decided on August 13, 1806 to re-embark from the port of La Vela. He was to leave the printing press that he had brought for Venezuela in Trinidad, where he took refuge before returning to England. Two years later, it was to become Venezuela's first press when it began to serve the cause of liberty after April 19, 1810.

---

1. Augusto Mijares, *Hombres e Ideas en América*. Ensayos, Caracas, 1940, p. 114.

XIII

COLOMBIA
WAS BORN

THE POSITION OF FIRST RANK
that Miranda came to occupy in Europe, and the impression that he left
on all who met him has led us to suppose that Bolívar and Rodríguez must
have heard his name in the salons of high French society and in the circles
of old republicans.

But, although it is impossible to think that Bolívar was ignorant of Miranda's activities, we have no grounds for supposing that he was familiar
with his precise ideas for the emancipation of the continent. These projects
must have been kept secret because of Miranda's very nature. Some European politicians were aware of them, as were a number of American liberals
and the followers and initiates recruited here and there by Miranda in the
course of his unlucky planning. It may be even that the information which
filtered through to the public was not that provided by the Spanish
Americans living in Paris, but a distorted version, disseminated by Spanish
officials, Napoleonic courtiers and conservative creoles. His relations with
the English, although conducted by Miranda with Hispanic correctness,
were the basis for propaganda used against him for years by the Spanish
authorities. The French revolutionaries' project to send Miranda to Santo
Domingo, and the subsequent racial rebellion in the island which terrorized
all the Caribbean, could also have alarmed the creoles. Their mistrust
became so intense that in 1803 the Governor of Curaçao reported to the
English government: "I can do no less than insist upon respectfully calling
Your Lordship's attention to the true sentiments of the inhabitants of
Caracas respecting General Miranda. I assure you that his appearance as

an agent of the British government would tend more than any other event to weaken the bonds that today unite Terra Firma with Great Britain."[1]

Such circumstances could explain why Bolívar showed excessive caution when he learned in France of Miranda's 1806 invasion. His only comment was contained in a letter to his friend Alexandre Dehollain, sent from Paris on June 23, 1806: "All the news that we receive about Miranda's expedition is a little sad because it is claimed that he plans to revolutionize the country, and this can cause much misery for the colony's inhabitants."[2] Of course, this reserve could also be explained by the hostility to Miranda of the French and Spanish police who were working closely together. Bolívar knew that the privacy of his correspondence was not respected. In any case, it is significant that his letter contained no earnest protestations of loyalty to the king or abuse of "the traitor," which the caraqueños so readily supplied the Captain-General of Venezuela. Under the implacable pressure of this official—the same Guevara y Vasconcelos who had sent Gual and España to their deaths—the leading citizens of Caracas contributed 30,000 *pesos* as a price on Miranda's head. His portrait and his proclamations were burned by the hangman in the city's main square, and the clergy, following the example of the Bishop of Mérida, clothed the terrifying image that was being created for the Americans with the words "heretic" and "atheist."

It was wise then, for Bolívar to avoid recording his judgement of Miranda's enterprise in his letter, and to limit himself to lamenting the material damage it might produce. We will see below that Miranda owed his return to Venezuela in 1810 almost entirely to Bolívar, who ignored the instructions of the Supreme *Junta* which had sent him to London. He accomodated Miranda in his own house, despite the opposition of his intimate friends and relatives, the Toros.

The absence of documentation of these events gives rise to queries, making it necessary to disgress. It is good for the author to do this, if only to refute writers who strive to prevent readers from reasoning for themselves. For example, would Bolívar's prejudices against Miranda weaken as a result of what he must have heard in the United States in 1807, during his journey back to Venezuela? It is not rash to suggest this. Although the North American authorities had regarded Miranda's expedition of the previous year coldly, other republicans welcomed him enthusiastically. Moreover, Bolívar could have been told things about his extraordinary compatriot in the lodges and other secret societies of the United States, which completely contradicted the calumnies he had heard previously.

---

1. Archives of *Colonial Office,* Curazao, 1808. Quoted by Gil Fortoul, *Historia Constitucional de Venezuela,* i, p. 149.
2. *Cartas,* i, p. 17.

In any case there are gaps in the life of Bolívar between 1807 and 1810 which should not be passed over as if he were already the Liberator, completely mature and ready to join battle.

Moreover, the lack of reliable information about another very interesting aspect of his psychology—his romances, his feminine relationships—during these same years arouses our imagination. We saw him in his adolescence, passionate but with a surprising emotional balance, dedicated to one love, and striving to conserve his *mayorazgo* and ensure the continuity of his family by means of marriage. This period was followed, as a natural reaction to his wife's death, by the parenthesis of his second voyage to Europe, when fleeting, unimportant romances took second place to his intellectual development and to the political unrest which was beginning to crystallize within him. Later in his career, even during the most hazardous moments of his campaigns, he was always to be involved in affairs, some of which seemed deep and permanent. What then was his emotional state in 1807, when he returned as a young man to Caracas, and met so many women of his own culture and social position? Count Segur tells us that these *caraqueñas* were "renowned for the beauty of their faces, the richness of their clothes, the elegance of their fashions, their love of dancing and music, and for the vivacity of their coquetry in which they skillfully combined pleasure with decency." Did they make no impression on Bolívar?

Why did he not fall in love again? Did he no longer feel the family duty to perpetuate his name and his fortune, which had accompanied his passion for "my lady Doña Teresa?" The young women of Caracas would eagerly ask themselves similar questions as, seated on their balconies, they saw Bolívar riding through the paved streets during the sweet, restless tropical evenings. The historian, anxious to penetrate his personality, can only do the same.

Perhaps what does emerge is that the political situation in Venezuela was becoming Bolívar's sole, absorbing passion. He was already a convinced revolutionary, but many of the compatriots who formed his most intimate circle, such as his uncles, the Palacios, were crudely reactionary. Others hid their discontent after the humiliations imposed by Guevara y Vasconcelos, and pretended a sincere devotion to the monarchy. Many, inevitably, were confused and uneasy, trying in good faith to orientate themselves in the midst of that revolution which was spilling out of books to be expressed in action. Not a few of these restless spirits drew near to Bolívar, whom they believed capable, because of his position and his recent travels in Europe, of giving them the decisive password.

On his return Bolívar felt more at home in the Ustáriz circle because the learning acquired in Europe equipped him to join in the discussion of politics and philosophy with appropriate references at his fingertips, to express his opinions on art and the theater, and to recite verses in French. But, although the Ustáriz circle had emerged unscathed from the brutal recruiting conducted by Guevara y Vasconcelos against Miranda, it could feel the howling wind of the Revolution rattling its doors. Its members were no longer able to regard as merely a beautiful dream the reforming zeal with which Rousseau seduced them, nor could they echo the pointed criticisms of Voltaire as though they were merely attractive mental acrobatics. Hobbes had warned them against revolution, pointing out that man was evil and anarchic by nature and that everything tending to weaken the omnipotent authority of the State implied a return to the disorder and depredations of primitive societies. This attitude was refuted not only by Rousseau but also by Bentham, who put his faith in the perfectibility of society and even proposed that criminals could be redeemed in rationally based establishments.

Venezuela had her own problems: racial heterogeneousness, a small, scattered population, political vices inherited from Spain, and ignorant masses. But on this last point optimists argued that all that was required was to penetrate into that oceanic realm of popular education, which nobody had explored previously. It had just begun to be realized in Europe that even the education of the privileged classes was extremely defective. What could not be achieved, then, when with new methods and a wise use of spiritual resources, education were rationally orientated towards the perfection of the individual and the triumph of the public good?

Confusion and enthusiasm alternated in men's minds, and contradictions were no less evident in concrete events. When the French Revolution turned into an orgy of blood and the impact of its excesses unleashed devastating racial strife in Santo Domingo, nationalist opinion in Venezuela, which in the middle of the century had been clearly revolutionary, changed its direction. The conservative reaction of Venezuelans was undeniable. It was evident in the affair of the *pardo* militia in opposition to the royal *cédulas* for the purchase of privileges, and in the passive response of public opinion towards the appeal of the 1797 conspirators. All this had as its base the alarm which had been caused by the excesses of the "atheists and regicides" who had suddenly emerged striving for Liberty, Equality and Fraternity. But when the Spanish Bourbons allied themselves overnight with the executioners of Louis XVI, the Spanish Americans found themselves obliged to smile upon the regicides in order to remain faithful to their king. The same was to happen with Napoleon; the fear of these "good vassals" that Spain might fall into his clutches promptly turned into amazement when they learned that the very kings of Spain had handed over the crown to the parvenu. A new twist was given to the tourniquet that constricted their temples when they were told that in order to remain faithful to their king they had to accept another. Charles IV in his ignominy accused his own son before the French emperor, adding: "I will lose no time in dutifully reporting to Your Imperial Majesty, whom I respectfully ask to assist with his wisdom and counsel." Ferdinand VII, for his part, asked Napoleon to marry him to a "princess" of the Bourbon family and promised: "I venture to say that this union and the publication of my intentions, which I will reveal to all Europe if Your Majesty permits me, can exercise a healthy influence on the destinies of Spain and can take away from a blind and furious people their pretext for flooding the soil of their country with blood in the name of a prince, heir to their ancient dynasty, who has converted himself through a solemn treaty, by his own election and by the most glorious of all adoptions, into a French prince and a son of Your Imperial Majesty."

Many of these documents were published at the time by the Spanish Court itself, and Miranda included them for the benefit of the Americans in *El Colombiano,* a journal he had begun to edit in London.

Another change of heart which disturbed the creoles was to be demanded of them with respect to England. England was not only the self proclaimed "heretic" nation, the traditional adversary of Spain, it was also an enemy which the Americans always had at their gates and which, with good reason, they had learned to hate and fear. The pirates who used to sack the young cities of the Indies were nearly always English. England armed the fleets which unexpectedly seized Spanish ports and islands, and refused to hand them back. Curaçao and Trinidad, both near Venezuela, had fallen into her hands in this way. During the frequent wars between England and Spain, American produce rotted on the trees or in warehouses as English ships cut off trade. Even in peacetime it was never certain that a ship loaded with these goods would not be attacked at sea by a lawless English pirate or trapped by a sudden declaration of war. In these struggles "against the English," a special type of patriotism developed in Spanish America, based as much upon local interests and attitudes as upon those of Spain. We have seen how ardently the Venezuelans protested in the middle of the century that it was they and not the Spaniards who had defended La Guaira and Puerto Cabello against the attempted invasion of the English. The activities of Miranda and his invasion in 1806 permitted the Spanish authorities to arouse this nationalistic pride and to put a Luciferian halo of wickedness around everybody who sympathized with the blasphemous, plundering English. Yet when the Spanish people rose up against the shameful abdication of their kings, English troops landed in the peninsula to help them. And the Spaniards and Spanish Americans were to forget that some years earlier during a similar conflict, England had seized Gibraltar and had still not returned it. Since the creoles believed that Charles and Ferdinand were "captives" of the Emperor, it its not surprising that the British ships which had always aroused hate and fear were welcomed as friends in the ports of America.

Agents of Napoleon and English emissaries reached Caracas simultaneously, the former to demand submission to the French, in accordance with the example of the legitimate monarch, the latter to remind the creoles that the Spanish people had risen up on their own account, led by their mayors and generals, and were winning victories over the invincible French.

The first reaction of the *caraqueños* in 1808 when they learned of the abdications of Charles IV and Ferdinand VII was, as could be expected, one of ingenuous loyalty. The people ran to the doors of the *ayuntamiento,* cheering Ferdinand and abusing Napoleon, and the collectivity immediately organized a solemn reaffirmation of loyalty to the "legitimate king." Led by the *Alférez Real,* Feliciano Palacios, Bolívar's uncle, who held aloft the royal banner, *cabildo* and people paraded together through the main streets and squares of Caracas, crying: "Castile, Castile, Castile, and Caracas, for the lord Don Ferdinand VII and all the descendants of the House of Bourbon."

It required considerable determination to swear allegiance to monarchs who had abandoned their subjects in so cowardly a fashion. Although they were not yet aware of it, the people of America were emulating the example of the Mayor of Móstoles who, at th head of his small hamlet, declared war on his own account against Napoleon. This attitude, however, presented Captain-General Juan de Casas with a problem, because the instructions which he received from the Metropolis legitimized the Bayonne abdication. This is a point which some historians overlook, and because they do they repeat the accusations of duplicity and sympathy with the French made at the time by the creoles, first against Casas and then even more strongly against his successor, Emparan. The perfidy, in fact, was that of the "legitimate king" himself, who had ceded his title to the usurper. Charles IV wrote categorically to Ferdinand: "My son, the perfidious counsels of those who surround you have put Spain in a critical position, and now she can be saved only by Napoleon." Ferdinand, in turn, congratulated Joseph from his "captivity" on his accession to the Spanish throne, and had Napoleon's victories over the Spanish people celebrated with festive lights. The Captain-General of Venezuela, therefore, could not be expected to share the attitude of his credulous subjects.

When news reached Caracas of the formation of *Juntas* in Spain for the defense of Ferdinand and the struggle against the invader, Casas seized the opportunity to go along with the wishes of the city. He suggested to the *cabildo* the formation of a *Junta* for the province. The *ayuntamiento* accepted this invitation, but proceeding with more enthusiasm than Casas would have liked, proposed that the *Junta* should have eighteen members, including a representative of the farmers, one of the merchants, and one of the ordinary people. For the first time the right of the people to participate in government was recognized. Moreover, it was anticipated that new elections would be held every two years. This was too much for the embarrassed Casas; those more reactionary than he described these proposals as "terribly dangerous and an open door to the most serious agitation."

In this way even those who followed the path of loyalty ended up on that of revolution. Moreover, as always happens in such situations, ultra-radicals emerged, led on this occasion by the strange figure of Manuel Matos who, although a retired militia captain and rich landowner, proclaimed: "The time has arrived for us Americans to enjoy our liberty. On this occasion we must get rid of all the Spaniards and allow only the creoles and the Islanders, who are good people, to remain."

The English Captain Beaver, commander of the warship *Acasta,* had been sent at the time to examine the state of public opinion in Caracas. He reported: "I can venture to say that they (the creoles) are loyal in the extreme and passionately addicted to the Spanish branch of the House of Bourbon, and that so long as there is some probability of the return of Ferdinand VII to Madrid, they will remain united to the Mother Country. But if this does not occur soon, I believe that I can affirm with equal certitude, that they will declare independence for themselves... These inhabitants are in no way the indolent and degenerate race that we find in the same latitude in the Orient. On the contrary, they seem to possess all the intellectual vigor and strength of character normally considered characteristics of inhabitants of more northerly regions."[1]

Colonel Robertson, sent to Maracaibo for the same purpose, wrote: "All the inhabitants are desirous of a close and intimate union with Great Britain, but they are in no way resolved to submit to her. If a prince of the House of Bourbon does not ascend the throne of Spain, their desire is to make themselves independent. Even today it seems to me that the idea predominates of preferring to constitute themselves a sovereign state under a prince of their ancient dynasty."[2]

The minds of the Venezuelans doubtless oscillated between their old loyalty, now untenable, and the need to assume responsibility towards events which were calling them. The temperature rose with each day that passed, and although Governor Casas now considered the plan to establish a *Junta* subversive, the *cabildo* insisted upon it. A new attempt to form it at the end of 1808 involved all the prominent families of the city which, because of their social contacts and their extensive properties in

1. Quoted by Gil Fortoul, *Historia Constitucional de Venezuela,* i, p. 148, and with slight differences by O'Leary, *Preliminares* i, p. LXIV.
2. Gil Fortoul, *op. cit.,* i, p. 149.

Aragua, the valleys of the Tuy and Barlovento, really formed the effective leadership of the province.

The *audiencia,* however, invoking its traditional authority, took action against them, arrested the principal conspirators, confining some to their homes, some to their estates and others to the city's barracks, and reported to Spain that the true object of their ill-advised action was "to establish the independence of these provinces, separating them from the Metropolis."

Details of the case bring to mind the traditional turbulence of the Caracas oligarchy. Count Tovar had gone to the secret meetings, "carried in a chair because of his advanced age," and when a statement was taken from him—his two sons had already been arrested with the other conspirators—he arrogantly explained: "Four infamous men, for whose vices the establishment of the *Junta* would be untoward, have divided the people into parties. They have told the Europeans that we were trying to kill them, and the *pardos* that we wished to make them our slaves. The Europeans became alarmed because the vile sectarians of the government told them that we are their enemies. The *pardos* aspired to destroy us because they had been told that we were attacking their liberty. The only blame to be attached to either group is that of being extremely credulous. . . . I see no other remedy to save us from the precipice into which the wicked wish to hurl us but a speedy decision to create a governing *Junta.* Whereas previously we requested it as a means of avoiding our ruin, today we consider it absolutely essential. . . . I have reached the age of eighty-three without ever involving myself in public affairs because I never witnessed any as important as the present matter. . . ."[1]

The "vile sectarians of the government" to whom the old man referred with such archaic language were without doubt the Spanish inhabitants of Venezuela and the conservative creoles, who were later to be the most unrelenting in the struggle between the two sides. But his words also show that events were already moving with a revolutionary rhythm.

The *Junta Central* of Seville declared in vain the following January that the American dominions would no longer be "strictly colonies or factories like those of other nations, but an essential and integral part of the Spanish monarchy." Apart from this implicit recognition and even exaggeration of the condition in which the Americans had lived, the creoles could well imagine that when Ferdinand returned to the throne these fine words would bring only persecution and death to those who believed in them. This was the experience of the liberals in Spain itself. Nor were the *caraqueños* reassured by the decision that, in accordance with this new policy, the measures taken against those who had tried to establish the *Junta* should be suspended. The unease all of them felt was so intense

1. *Ibid.,* i, p. 156.

that, according to eye-witness accounts, not one, but several plots were hatched at the same time by different groups which otherwise competed with each other.

Events moved on in this way until April 18, 1810, when in accordance with ancient custom the *cabildo* was chosen by the people and the plotters managed to depose Captain-General Vicente Emparan, Casas's successor. Emparan himself was the protagonist for an episode which raised enthusiasm even higher, as in one of those collective risings recorded by Lope de Vega in classical Spain. Confined within the *ayuntamiento* by the conspirators, Emparan appeared on the balcony overlooking the public square and asked the people if they were happy with his government. "No, no," replied the mob. "I do not want the command either," answered Emparan indignantly, and with this thoughtless resignation recognized the people as the arbiters of the revolution.

Other scenes of the new times had this same flavor. Early in the morning Emparan had attended a meeting of the *ayuntamiento,* which explained to him the necessity of establishing the projected *Junta*. He retorted that the Council of Regency established in the Metropolis was the legitimate authority and sufficient to represent the monarchy, and he precipitately ended the session on the pretext of having to attend the religious ceremonies for Holy Thursday in the cathedral. Emparan believed that he had succeeded in foiling a new conspiracy but, as he reached the front of the church, he was accosted by one of the most determined plotters. Francisco Salias, who demanded that he return to the *ayuntamiento*. Seeing that his personal guard, commanded by Captain Luis Ponte, a creole, showed no signs of a willingness to defend him, Emparan agreed. Once again, however, he was on the point of saving the situation, because during the first deliberations he managed to arrange that he would be made Presidente of the *Junta* which was to be formed, and that the *Audiencia* and other royal authorities would remain untouched. "But," Ramón Azpúrua narrates, "Roscio, considered the thinker of the Republican Party and who was beginning to record these details in the minutes of the session, had a happy inspiration. It was to propose, through the priest, José Félix Blanco, a young and fiery revolutionary, that another of the most notable revolutionaries be called in to assist the patriots."[1] This was the canon José Cortés de Madariaga, a Chilean living in Venezuela, who was recognized along with the priest, Francisco José de Ribas, as a representative of the clergy. Doctors Juan Germán Roscio and José Félix Sosa were added as deputies of the people, and they were joined a little later by José Félix Ribas who, although white and from one of the

---

1. Juan Germán Roscio, *Obras*. Caracas, 1953, i, p. XXI. Azpúrua could have obtained his information directly from the priest José Félix Blanco. It agrees substantially with the *cabildo* minutes and it corrects the versions of Gil Fortoul and other historians, according to whom Emparan found these representatives already seated in the *ayuntamiento* when he arrived.

capital's leading families—he was a brother of the priest Francisco José and Bolívar's uncle-in-law—was summoned as a representative of the *pardos*. Reinforced with these persons clearly identified with the revolution, the *cabildo* began to deliberate a course very different from that desired by Emparan. It was at this point that he went to the balcony to make his surprising appeal to the people.

The government of the province remained "deposited" in the *ayuntamiento* which, strengthened by the above representatives and by others who were added later, took the name of "Supreme *Junta,* Conserver of the rights of Ferdinand VII."

Despite this mention of the king who had abdicated, there could be no doubt that April 19 marked the beginning of the Revolution. The official minutes of what occurred record that, because of the situation in Spain and in accordance with natural law, it had been decided "to erect in the very heart of these countries a system of government which supplants the announced faults, and exercises the rights of sovereignty *which by the same act have devolved upon the people.*" A manifesto issued a day later promised the inhabitants of Venezuela that they would be summoned "to take part in the exercise of supreme authority." A secretaryship of state for foreign affairs was created to be filled by Doctor Juan Germán Roscio. Less than two months later, on June 10, the *Junta* summoned all the people of Venezuela to elections. It is difficult to state precisely Bolívar's participation in the conspiracies that led up to April 19. According to legal documents drawn at the time by the Spanish authorities, the two Bolívar brothers, Juan Vicente and Simón, had frequent meetings with the conspirators in the "Bolívar Block," and also in the house of José Félix Ribas. Bolívar had also been a close friend since childhood of Matos, the only person to whom he sent his regards when he wrote from Mexico at the age of fifteen. It was not proved, however, that he was involved in Matos's conspiracies. José Ignacio Casas, son of the Captain-General, declared that on the night of July 27, 1808, he learned that something was being plotted by the Bolívar, Ribas and Palacios Sojo families, and he decided to discuss it with Simón Bolívar, "to whom I spoke these words: You know that I am your friend and that I respect you, although I do not often visit you. It would be very painful for me if you were to find yourself in any grief, for which reason I believe you will refrain from receiving guests or friends in your house, because they do you much harm." Bolívar replied to this: "I am desperate to escape from parasites who trouble me; I summon nobody and I am innocent of any slanderous charge."[1] We do not know if this was the truth or the natural reaction of a conspirator who had been discovered.

---

1. Boletín de la Academia Nacional de la Historia, no. 52, p. 616, Caracas, Oct.-Dec. 1930.

The investigation of another conspiracy at the end of the year established that the Bolívar brothers were decided supporters of "overthrowing the established authorities and establishing independence." Yet they continued to vacillate, and did not sign the representation which was prepared.[1]

This interpretation fits in well with the attitude of both brothers, especially Simón, to subsequent events. The Regent of the *Audiencia,* José Francisco Heredia, affirmed in his *Memorias* that Bolívar "was one of the leaders who secretly hatched the revolution of April 19. The Marquis of Casa León reported to me that in an effort to persuade Bolívar and others of his companions of the dangers in which their imprudent activity was placing the province he invited them to a meeting, in which José Domingo Duarte, assessor to the Intendant, explained their error with all the force of reason. Bolívar, after hearing him in silence, replied that *all that was very well explained, but that he and his associates had declared war on Spain, and they would see what happened.*"[2] The uncertainty we observe in the documents reflects that which existed in events themselves. We find, significantly, in the confused 1808-10 period that the Bolívar brothers at times disagreed with their relatives and close friends, the Toros. At the same time the ultra-conservative Feliciano Palacios associated with the most radical, revolutionary young men, like the Bolívars, Ribas, Tovar, Salias and Montilla. The Marquis of Toro, who a short time before had handed to the Spanish authorities a letter from Miranda, whom he described as a "traitor," became a revolutionary. This does not take into account the divisions deliberately fomented by "the vile sectarians of the government," as the Count de Tovar indignantly described them.

The Bolívar brothers played no part in the events of April 19, because, like the Montillas, Toros, and other members of their group, they had been restricted at the beginning of the year, after the failure of another plot, to various places outside the capital. It seems, moreover, that the movement was accelerated by the arrival on the previous day of two commissioners of the Regency Council whose purpose was to have this new authority recognized in Venezuela. Fernando Toro explained in a manifesto published in May 1811, "We had taken all the measures necessary for the success of the enterprise, when the *caraqueños,* acting on April 19, left our initiative stranded." Despite this, Bolívar retained such memories of April 19, that in 1820 on commemorating its tenth anniversary, he said in a solemn proclamation to the liberating army: "Ten years of liberty are solemnized this day... On April 19, Colombia was born."[3]

---

1. See the documental study of Dr. Angel Francisco Brice, *Bolívar en la Revolución de Abril* in his *El Bolívar de Marx ampliado por Madariaga.* Caracas, 1952.
2. *Memorias del Regente Heredia.* París, 1895, p. 123.
3. We should explain, for the benefit of those unfamiliar with our history, that the word *Colombia* has several meanings: Miranda invented the idea of using it to mean all the American continent; it was the name given to the state formed in 1819 by

We shall examine the differences which separated the revolutionary groups in 1810 and which existed even between individuals. It is known, for example, that the Licentiates Miguel José Sanz and Antonio Nicolás Briceño were enemies of Bolívar for various reasons. Shortly after April 19, José Félix Ribas was expelled from the government and the country because he was considered excessively radical. Lawyers like Roscio later became bitter opponents of Miranda, because they feared that he might remove them from the leadership role they had asumed. All this was very natural in men who had suddenly found themselves exercising political power. The fall of the first Republic was due in large measure to this hostile surge of ideals, passions and interests. Long years of failures and suffering were to follow before the victories of the Liberator, his constancy and his ability to touch the human heart, to paraphrase his own words, were to organize those forces released by the revolution and carry them to triumph.

There were also very profound differences among the different groups and their attitudes towards the question of social equality. We will see how Roscio, although a *mestizo,* was alarmed or appeared to be alarmed by the "indiscreet murmurings of equality" which he attributed to Miranda and the Ribases. In another paragraph of the same letter written to Bello, he included Bolívar in this group. It is known that Ribas, in addition to having presented himself as the representative of the *pardos* on April 19, was accustomed to roaming Caracas, his head covered with a Phrygian cap, trying to attract "the common people"—as Roscio would have called them— to the cause of the revolution. We can assume that Bolívar agreed with this attitude, because in these early years the Bolívars and the Ribases were united on everything, including Bolívar's democratic ideas on major questions such as slavery.

For the moment at least, the young Simón Bolívar aroused the same suspicions as his uncle, José Félix Ribas. This mistrust was so marked that, according to O'Leary—who probably heard it from the Liberator himself—when Bolívar suggested shortly after April 19, that the Supreme *Junta* send him to London to secure the aid or the neutrality of the British government, "the *Junta* acceded to his request, but it did so reluctantly. Many of its members, as well as several other individuals who had taken an active part in the movement, had no kindly feelings towards him. But, since he had offered to pay the expenses of the mission and there was no money in the treasury, they had to accept his generous offer, giving him as a companion Don Luis López Méndez, in whose experience and capabilities

---

the union of Venezuela, New Granada and the presidency of Quito, and it is in this sense that it is used here; it also designates the actual republic of Colombia, the former New Granada, which adopted the name in the middle of the last century. *Gran Colombia* is also used today for the 1819-30 state.

they had more confidence."[1] In fact Bolívar persisted, in contravention of the express instructions of the *Junta,* in arranging the return of Miranda to Venezuela, a development which constituted a decisive step towards the break with Spain.

The *Junta* granted Bolívar the rank of Lieutenant Colonel in the infantry militia, a high office considering his lack of military experience and the fact that in the Spanish system such promotions required many years of service.[2] It was a gratuitous, decorative title, but it was to be the last of its kind for the spoiled youth, who was voluntarily abandoning the privileged regime which protected him to take the rough road of revolution. With each of his subsequent steps towards glory he was to leave behind him the prints of his bloodied feet. As General-In-Chief he had to fight at times with a lance, like an anonymous soldier, in the whirlwind of a war to the death. The conquest of moral greatness was even more arduous; he was to overcome countless doubts and sufferings, but when he reached the harsh peak he found only loneliness and anguish.

1. O'Leary Narration, i, p. 25.
2. *Ibid.* Lecuna says in his *Catálogo de errores y calumnias en la vida de Bolívar,* Caracas, 1956, p. 209, that the rank was that of lieutenant colonel in the infantry; in the same work, vol. iii, p. 324, he says that he was "appointed colonel in the royal army". As we have already seen, an officer in the Spanish army could be both a "teniente coronel vivo y efectivo" and an "acting colonel"; his next promotion would be to "coronel vivo y efectivo". This could partly explain the contradictions on this point.

XIV

JOINED BY KNOTS
WHICH HEAVEN
FASHIONED

A T BOLIVAR'S REQUEST,
Andrés Bello, whose exceptional genius was already recognized in Caracas,
was appointed secretary to the mission which he and López Méndez were
to lead to London. But the representatives of Venezuela could obtain
nothing from Great Britain, because at the time the English needed to
use Spanish forces in their struggle against Napoleon. The British Foreign
Secretary, Richard Wellesley, explained to them frankly and openly that
his government was opposed to any innovation in the American provinces.
A little later England prohibited the trade in arms in the Caribbean in
order to leave the "insurgents" defenseless.

The only improvement this time was that the English Cabinet did not
need to lie. Two years earlier Miranda had suffered the most atrocious
of his disappointments because of the fickleness of English policy. At
the beginning of 1808, everything was ready for England to support a new
liberating expedition by the Venezuelan when the unexpected rising of the
Spanish people against Napoleon once again caused a change in plan
of the government in London. The shameful submission of Charles IV and
Ferdinand VII had seemed to destine Spain to be simply one more of the
conqueror's fiefs, but the formidable reaction of the Spanish people
completely changed the situation. It converted the peninsula into the best
battlefield against the Emperor. England hurried to declare that the
Spanish nation was her "natural friend and ally" and prepared to help her.
Naturally, everything promised Miranda was forgotten. No less than General Wellington, Wellesley's brother and the future victor of Waterloo, was

selected to ask the Precursor to postpone his plans. His rank was flattering, but it made Wellington's mission more difficult, because he was well aware of the concrete promises which had been made to Miranda, and he had encouraged him personally. Wellington took Miranda for a walk through the streets of London, as if they were two friends enjoying a carefree stroll. While the Englishman was mentally seeking a way to get to the point, Miranda, who without doubt was already well-informed, was hardly able to control himself. As Wellington began to skirt the subject, Miranda violently threw at him all the recriminations he was no longer able to keep within his breast. Wellington felt so ashamed that he hurried his pace, almost running away from his enraged companion. "When I joined him again he was cooler," he later related, and we can almost feel his sigh of relief. "I think I never had a more difficult business," he confessed.[1]

Wellington, however, had a new proposition for the Venezuelan shortly before he left for Spain at the head of the English auxiliaries, "Why do you not come to Spain with me?" he asked. "I will not interfere in the affairs of Spain," Miranda replied sullenly. Wellington could have argued, in accordance with Miranda's earlier declarations, that in this case he was going to fight not againsts Spain but for independence. For this reason the Venezuelan's reply has always been considered a demonstration of delicacy towards France. His stating that he did not want to interfere in the affairs of Spain calls to mind his refusal to serve against Spain in Europe; and he could hardly forget that on a similar occasion England had seized Gibraltar and afterwards had refused to return it.

Even if the Venezuelan commissioners had obtained new promises from the English government in 1810, they would have been able to place very little faith in them. Nonetheless their journey provided the opportunity for a historic scene which captivates our imagination: the meeting in London of three Spanish American geniuses, Miranda, Bolívar and Bello.

The lives of these three exceptional men from the New World were to be curiously interwoven chronologically. Miranda began his apostleship of liberty around 1783, and until he surrendered in 1812, he was the central figure of the continent he unified and revolutionized. In the year he disappeared from public life, Bolívar was brought to the fore as a thinker and leader by the Cartagena Manifesto and by his first victorious campaign. Bello began his civilizing work precisely in 1830 when Bolívar died, and its breadth and continuity marked him as an unequalled figure in the Spanish-speaking countries until his death in 1865.

The respected Spanish critic, Marcelino Menéndez y Pelayo, wrote many years later: "The former Captaincy General of Caracas, now the Republic of Venezuela, has the glory of having given Spanish America its best man of arms and its best man of letters: Simón Bolívar and Andrés Bello."

---

1. Robertson, *op. cit.*, ii, p. 23.

These three who met together in Miranda's London library in the summer of 1810—the library in which O'Higgins had been given lessons and so many other young enthusiasts had received their political indoctrination— were to dominate the history of Spanish America for almost a century. The encounter with their imposing compatriot must have been an extraordinary spiritual experience for Bolívar and Bello. Miranda must have been no less moved to see that America, represented by those two young men of the top social and intellectual class, was seeking him out at last.

Bolívar was to say of Bello years later: "I recognize the superiority of this *caraqueño,* my contemporary. He was my teacher when we were the same age and I loved him with respect." Although lamentable divisions were later to separate Bolívar and Miranda, at the time the new revolutionary went with enthusiasm in search of the fabled man who had been preparing the emancipation of America for almost twenty-seven years, and whose mere presence in Caracas would be enough, Bolívar believed, to ensure triumph for the great enterprise.

Bello, until then confined to the limited colonial environment made particularly narrow by his poverty, was dazzled by the 6,000 volumes in Miranda's library where Greek and Latin classics, which Miranda himself had filled with marginal notes, appeared alongside authors whose works on politics and philosophy were shaping world thought at the time. When Miranda and Bolívar returned to Venezuela, Bello stayed behind to study in the library, thus, in another sense perpetuating Miranda's influence upon the continent for many years after his death.

López Méndez was the most skilled of the three emissaries in forming valuable contacts with important officials and financiers in London, and he was to continue to serve the Republic unselfishly in this role. Restrepo wrote in his history: "On various occasions we heard General Bolívar say that the true Liberator of Colombia was López Méndez. He assured us that he would have been able to do nothing in the celebrated campaign of 1819 without the opportune and effective assistance that López Méndez provided from London by pledging his own responsibility and that of the still insecure government of Venezuela." In fact, López Méndez was imprisoned in London for debt as a result of personally guaranteeing credits granted to Colombia. Although he returned to Venezuela in poverty and died in that state, he never claimed anything for his services. We can assume, then, that he was charged with extending and cultivating the first contacts arranged by Miranda, while the other three *caraqueños* dedicated long hours to imagining and discussing what America might become. So many things to decide, so many things to do! Their eyes—Miranda's were gray, Bello's blue and Bolívar's black—lit with enthusiasm as their words brought to life the past, present and future of their continent.

Miranda and Bolívar talked in particular about politics and administration. Miranda had begun to study public services at the age of twenty-one, when he saw its backwardness as he traveled through Spain. He continued to pay attention to this subject in all the countries he visited. Now ideas and projects—for mines, agriculture, irrigation canals, museums and libraries, military and technical schools, penitentiaries, municipal hygiene and improvement—were effortlessly plucked from his memory, and Bolívar avidly fell upon them. They also discussed the continent's special problems, such as the plan for a canal across Central America linking the two oceans. Miranda had first proposed this idea to the English government in 1790. He also thought the capital of the "Colombian continent" should be established on the Isthmus of Panama.

Such vast schemes were needed to jolt the continent's collective spirit, which had been contaminated by the negligence and favoritism of Spanish rule and tended to drift towards a policy of empty words and sophisms of inaction.

They talked about the political organization to be provided for the new states, and the public morality which was to be its foundation. They understood that these two problems were inextricably linked. For this reason the riddle put to them by the sphinx at the gates of the ideal society they saw before them was this: was it possible to alter public morality by means of new political institutions or should they wait for the collective morality to evolve gradually before attempting to create the perfect republic? Should they wait until a more developed and enlightened society provided a stable foundation for the new state or could they rashly reverse the equation and found a state which would become the basis of a new society? Perhaps there was a middle way. In the plans submitted to the English government Miranda had provided among the key officials of the proposed political organization for two censors, charged with watching over public morality, directing education and maintaining the purity of institutions. This idea strongly appealed to Bolívar. It might seem nonsense to a Europe bound by so many traditional shackles—class rivalries, international hatreds, moral and religious prejudices—but this did not matter! The truth was that Europe represented an old culture, too concerned with preserving its antiquity. To dare was justifiable in America, where everything was still to be done.

Bello listened to these discussions in silence, but his dreams were no less ambitious. He thought that a moral and intellectual purpose should be established for the new countries as a justification for and goal of their political sovereignty: "Will the American republics have no role in the general progress of the sciences, will we play no greater part than the tribes

of Africa and the islands of the ocean in promoting human understanding?"[1]
This was the question posed by the emancipation of America. To proclaim
independence without knowing what to do with it would be a grotesque
calamity. To call ourselves free nations without securing true sovereignty
—that of the spirit—would reduce independence to the chattering mirth
of a San Juan night, when ingenious freed men forget that the ground upon
which they walk is not theirs, because they do not know how to work it,
that their very thoughts are not their own, since they lack originality, and
that their education, their economy, their public administration, and even
their devotion to heroes are but a parody of what they should be in a
truly free nation.

We must begin of course, Bello's thoughts continued, by nurturing the
first tool given to us by Spain, her language. If Castilian were abandoned
to the differing customs and ways of life created by nations so isolated from
each other, it would perhaps develop into "embryos of future languages,
which over a long period would reproduce in America the situation which
existed in Europe during the dark period of the corruption of Latin." In the
heat of revolutionary turmoil this linguistic disintegration might be regarded
as a happy development. There would also be those who would demand a
separate language for each of the new nations as a sign of strength and as a
confirmation of absolute sovereignty. Would they understand in the end
that to save the language was to save the soul? Would they accept that the
standards of a rich, developed language, far from signifying servility, provide wider scope for thought; that it was the only means of remaining
united to the universal culture which Spain had given us?

Bello's meditations coincided with those of his two companions on a subject which the three of them considered basic: popular education. Miranda
had introduced them to Joseph Lancaster, a pedagogue obtaining surprising
results by means of a method called "mutual instruction," which allowed
economies in teachers and money, two elements America lacked. Bolívar
immediately proposed taking him to Caracas and paying the expenses of his
journey and his establishment there from his own fortune. This would have
overcome initial difficulties, but would have been a humble beginning,
since in Bello's opinion Lancaster's system was only appropriate for ele-

---

1. It should be pointed out to readers who are not specialists in American history that
   this attempt to reconstruct the discussions of Miranda, Bolívar and Bello in London
   is strictly based upon what they wrote or were to try to achieve. This quotation,
   for example, is from the discourse or *Memoria* of Bello, when he was rector of the
   University of Chile in 1848; and his meditations on the language are based upon
   the polemic which he sustained with Sarmiento on the topic. Similarly, Bello's thoughts
   on American law and literature, human law, the university, journalism, etc., follow
   the contours of his work from 1830. In this way I am partly anticipating and synthe-
   sizing the essential aspects of the political ideas of the three great Americans whom
   fate brought together in London. What doubt can there be that this was the favorite
   theme in their conversations?

mentary education. Bello's goal was a system of education absolutely new in its methods and in its social and political aims that would be able not only to engender a richer, juster, more agreeable way of life in America but also, in its turn, to influence Europe and secure universal democracy.

Bolívar also spoke about the education of women, and he heatedly insisted that this could be the most efficacious force for a complete reformation of our customs. He related to Miranda how, before he had left Caracas, he had seen women attending the early revolutionary meetings and popular celebrations. They went not to demand blood but, with the sober abnegation of heroines of antiquity, to offer their belongings, their husbands and their sons to the common cause. One of his cousins, a member of the Aristeguieta family, wrote to her husband, Antonio Nicolás Briceño, the most fitting words for the beginning of a revolutionary epoch: "I ask God to guide your judgements." Selflessness and justice. Why could not our women also display these fundamental virtues in peacetime, and become enthusiastic and austere republicans?

Miranda had told them that public education was not much more neglected in America than in Europe itself. He pointed out that when he visited the south of France in 1789 he had hardly been able to find anybody among the common people who could read or write. As far as universities were concerned, he showed them his notes on those of Boston and Copenhagen, both of which were better adapted, according to his observations, "to train clergymen, than to mold capable and well-informed citizens."

Bolívar, for his part, remembered a daring observation on the same general theme by Simón Rodríguez, which, like many others of his teacher, he could repeat almost word for word: "Europe is ignorant, not in literature, science, arts and industry, but in its politics. A brilliant veil covers the most horrific picture of misery and vices in the old world. Europe's great work has been achieved without design. It has been constructed from fragments. Improvements have been *heaped together without order,* not *neatly arranged*; art glitters more in intrigues than in combination. The most sublime things mixed with the most contemptible provide a contrast... beautiful for the perfection of the parts, but disagreeable because of the impropriety of the whole."

Many years will pass and Europe, conceited as she is in her brilliant setting, will have to suffer much before she learns how to judge her own errors.

All this brought them back to the problem of the form of government most suitable for the new states. They proclaimed that politics would not be a daily patchwork of incoherencies but a plan of harmonious development. The dream of virgin America was of a new age of happiness and order. Miranda, wo always had his beloved Virgil at hand, recited to them:

Ultima Cumai venit iam carmini oetas;
magnus ab integro soeculorum nascitur ordo;
iam redit et virgo, redevit Saturni regno.

Bello was moved by the juvenile fervor of the old republican. But, although he too loved Virgil, he returned to his restless meditation. He believed that in literature it was not good enough meekly to accept models from Europe. We would become wise not by passive acceptance but by incorporating into our own experience that of the rest of the world. We would have to begin in literature with the landscape, revealing the true America to Europe, correcting the distorted picture of America which Chateaubriand had made fashionable. It was necessary to give literary expression to the everyday American countryside—cocoa, sugar-cane, coffee, cotton, cochineal, indigo, shade trees and rain-trees—but by means of direct images, giving things their proper names. Similarly, the liberty of which men dreamed in America was not that of the Rousseau jungle or that of Chateaubriand's savages, but civil liberty, based upon reciprocal tolerance and communal effort. Oh, to put all this in a poem... a song to America to its nature, to its heroes and to the noble equality of all men, a concept accepted for the first time only in the New World.

One must not create illusions. The cultural richness of Europe, of which its literature was only an example, had developed over a long period due to innumerable secular contributions. In America, however, a small group of enterprising men had to improvise everything. They themselves were self-taught, and they felt isolated and misunderstood. Our universities had to be academies too, both centers of teaching and research and places of dialogue for the formative generations. The man who undertook to reorganize and direct them would have to struggle to spread culture to the common people, so that the works produced by the universities would be appreciated, and would give their unknown authors fame and influence.

As he gazed at the full shelves of Miranda's library and the centuries of culture accumulated there, Bello trembled with controlled excitement. He could not remotely suspect that the man in his speculations would turn out to be himself. He could imagine even less that, although he was already twenty-nine, he would have to wait another twenty years to begin his magnificent work. It was not until he was forty-nine, an age at which most men look forward to a time of problem-free repose, that fate was to give him the first opportunity to test his strength. Many times in Caracas he had thought bitterly that the knowledge he had accumulated so avidly had fitted him only for a minor post in the offices of the Captaincy-General, with no opportunity to transmit it to his compatriots or to speak to America in their name. And now he had before him a world so vast that it made him swoon.

The American nations also needed new laws. If they continued to observe Spanish law they would be in the absurd position of daily invoking rules of conduct derived from authorities they no longer recognized. Moreover, one of the creole grievances had been the slowness and the great expense of legal process, which always favored the richest or most cunning litigants. This arose from the obscurity and contradictions in the innumerable legal texts which had to be consulted in every case. What was required, then, was both to provide new laws for the republic and to codify them, following the brilliant example which Napoleon had just provided in France. In America, moreover, this work should have a social purpose; it should complement emancipation: "Without this preliminary step, the laws will not be recognized as widely as they need to be if they are to control men's behavior effectively, nor will it be possible to prevent their being turned into tools of oppression employed by the powerful against the weak. Without this first step, the labyrinth of legislation like ours will always make constitutional guarantees illusory and meaningless. . . ." But, Bello asked himself, where can erudite, prudent men be found to carry out this unprecedented task? He was to assume the formidable undertaking himself.

America could make important contributions to international law, because her people were free of the traditional hatreds that divided the Europeans. Miranda and Bolívar hoped to unite the continent into a single political entity, and Bolívar said that for the Americans the Isthmus of Panama should be what that of Corinth was for the Greeks. Bello would be content with a continental unity built upon standards of justice recognized by all the sister countries: inviolability of established boundaries, compulsory arbitration of disputes, American congresses meeting periodically to re-adjust and confirm the results obtained, and the common defense of demo-cratic principles.

Themes like this drew the three colloquists together. They were also united by their concern for the immediate future. If protracted, the war would intensify bad political habits. It would be impossible to expect the people to guarantee the republic if, over a long period, violence was praised, mis-behavior was tolerated, and military obedience was demanded. We did not possess an experienced and industrious bourgeoisie as did Europe. The small group we did have was to be sacrificed during the war. Our evils were linked in a vicious circle: the poverty of the people, an impracticable system of education, the parasitic attitudes of the privileged classes, the *caudillismo* produced by the war, the new wars which *caudillismo* was to produce, the iniquity of slavery, and the difficulty of abolishing it without provoking other problems.

The awesome weight of these problems made the three friends lower their voices. At times they halted their passionate dialogue, but they did not lose confidence. Bolívar observed: "Americans have risen suddenly, without prior understanding and, what is more serious, without experience in public life, to play on the world stage the roles of eminent dignitaries, such as legislators, magistrates, treasury administrators, diplomats, generals and all the other supreme and secondary officials who form the hierarchy of a well-organized state." An era of hurried creation, whose demands seemed to exceed human abilities, awaited them. The republican reorganization would require new laws, effective administration of justice, a definition of what democratic equality should be, popular education, newspapers, science and arts, agriculture, industry and commerce. Even the most elementary instruments of public administration—a national currency, banks and a capable bureaucracy—had to be developed. And while this was being done, Europe would watch and encourage our errors with the cunning hope that if we failed, our emancipation would lack justification, and we would become once more targets for booty and conquest. The century which was beginning was bound to be hard and painful for South America, but the people would deserve to feel proud if they could achieve nothing more than the most urgent aspects of their enormous task in the years ahead.

During these discussions, which were not always coherent, Miranda's tone was no less rapturous than that of Bolívar, and only Bello, whose rosy, almost red face and blue eyes made him look younger than he was, remained calm. When the dialogue between the other two was interrupted by anxious questions or digressions, it was Bello who put it back on course. Many of the ideas they discussed are now familiar to any educated man, but then only a few "ideologists" considered them attainable. Some of them, for example those relating to international law, which were recognized in mid-century by the so-called *Declarations of Paris,* were still considered novel years later.

Their hopes for political and social improvement—mass education, collective morality, the almost direct participation of the people in everyday political life, and the moral stimulus provided by mothers and wives—cannot stand up to the reigning scepticism of our day. The means intellectuals and politicians now possess to influence the people are used more to confuse rather than to promote morality. The people are treated to propaganda rather than education. It is easier to devise a slogan than explain an idea. The constant repetition of a lie is more effective than submitting issues to popular deliberation. Deceit, like force, can condition nations to almost complete passivity. The greatest tragedy of our contemporary world is that, although it continues to believe in spirituality, justice and liberty, it no longer has faith in the measures necessary to secure them. For this reason it rejects them in despair and impotence. This was not the case at the beginning of the nineteenth century when men ardently believed in both a new social and political order and in the spiritual dedication required to guarantee it.

But we return to the immediate reality confronting the four Venezuelan patriots. Apart from England's commitments to Spain, the dominant tendency in her government at the time was towards harsh reaction. Bertrand Russell tells us: "During the long years from 1793 to 1815, when any sympathy for French ideas was considered criminal, and men branded as Jacobins were sentenced to long periods of detention, some of the most prominent Whigs continued freely to express opinions, such as a belief in liberty and in the need for drastic parliamentary reform, which had carried humbler men to prison."[1]

In these circumstances, Bolívar and his companions were given a lukewarm reception by the press and some aristocrats, and they soon realized that it was useless to press their demands. It was perhaps then that Bolívar learned that the American people would have to make their own revolution, alone against everybody, hungry, naked and without arms. Then, too, he realized that he was ready to lead them. He was soon to discover, moreover, that the Venezuelan mission to the United States had also failed. It was unable even to buy arms, and Juan Vicente Bolívar, the leader of the abortive mission, died in a shipwreck on the return journey. López Méndez and Andrés Bello remained in London, but Miranda and Bolívar returned to Venezuela by different routes in December 1810.

The leaders of the new situation in Venezuela after April 19 showed no enthusiasm whatsoever for Miranda. They were obliged to adopt this attitude because if they declared open rebellion by summoning the old revolutionary, on whose head the Spanish government had put a price, the English government would begin by refusing to let him leave the country and then might even join in the blockade of Venezuela. In the instructions to its representatives before the English government, the *Junta* informed them that Miranda was "a rebel against Ferdinand VII and, therefore, if he was in London or in any other place where the commissioners halted or landed, and they approached him, they would know how to treat him in the light of these principles, and according to the immunity of the territory in which they found themselves."[2]

---

1. Bertrand Russell: *Libertad y organización*. Madrid, 1936, p. 60.
2. The documents dealing with the mission of Bolívar and his companions were published with a critical study by Dr. Cristóbal L. Mendoza with the title *La Junta de Gobierno de Caracas y sus misiones diplomáticas en 1810*, Caracas, 1936. Luis Correa later added the War Office documents copied by Dr. Carlos Urdaneta Carrillo (Boletín de la Academia Nacional de la Historia, no. 81, Caracas, 1938). In 1957 Dr. Pedro Grases published, with pertinent observations, the report to the Supreme *Junta*, mentioned below, which he had discovered in Bogotá. He points out that the report was written after Bolívar left for Caracas; Luis López Méndez signed it but it was written by Andrés Bello and, as its text indicates, it represented the unanimous opinion of the three commissioners.

However, Bolívar, López Méndez and Bello rebelled against the timorous conduct imposed upon them. In their report to the *Junta* they did not attempt to hide the enthusiasm and veneration which Miranda aroused in them. It said: "From the beginning... we realized the errors and dangers to which our adventurous acts had exposed us. We decided that we could obtain the information we needed only through Miranda, who was the only person we could consult openly." They stressed "the virtue and merit of our fellow-citizen, wronged so unworthily," recalling that "not even his enemies have dared to deny his extraordinary superiority in learning, experience and talent." They went on: "Envious persons have attacked his personal qualities with particular force, but what we have seen in London has been more than enough to reveal to us the injustice of the way in which he has been censured. We have seen him in the company of persons of the first rank, and with almost all the respectable society to be found in London. We have observed his domestic conduct, his sobriety, his frank and honest behavior, his application to study, and all the virtues which characterize a worthy man and citizen. We have often seen him moved to the point of shedding tears when we told him of our experiences! So great has been his interest in becoming informed of even the smallest details! He has been eager to serve us with his knowledge, his books, his faculties and his contacts!"

Three lines, however, almost at the end of the report are terribly painful for us because they indicate that the commisioners were afraid not that Miranda's merits were unknown in Caracas, but that his presence there could provoke envy and jealousy. They pointed out: "He does not ask for any part in public affairs; he wants nothing more than to die with the satisfaction of having seen the dawn of liberation in his country." We will see below the decisive influence which this attitude of Bolívar, López Méndez and Bello had in Caracas.

When Miranda arrived at La Guaira, the people acclaimed him. In Caracas, he stayed at Bolívar's house. Thus, in spite of all the disillusion he had suffered, the Precursor was persuaded that the revolution was finally triumphing in his country.

All social classes seemed to be united in their enthusiasm. The first anniversary of April 19 was celebrated as "the birthday of the revolution," to quote Antonio Muñoz Tébar, the young tribune of extraordinary intellectual capacity, who four years later gave his life on the battlefield for his country. Another contemporary wrote: "The people of Caracas demonstrated the importance they attached to the benefits they believed they had obtained for themselves and their posterity. Jubilation was general. After the religious services the inhabitants in festive garb and displaying cockades of red, white and yellow ribbons in their hats, dispersed into the streets. Bands followed by dancers paraded through the city playing lively airs. Members of a patriotic club marched in procession through the main streets, carrying flags suitable for the occasion. The most respectable citizens of Caracas joined in the universal rejoicing. Groups of Indians were seen singing and dancing with more ingenuity than grace. The faces of the people showed their delight as they vigorously exchanged good wishes. Nightfall brought a change of scene; Caracas was completely illuminated. The public buildings competed with each other in ingenuity and good taste. Bands continued to fill the air with melodies and, as the heat of the day disappeared, happiness seemed to increase. Small theaters in different parts of the city served as places of relaxation, where the people were entertained with songs and plays. The merriment continued long into the night, and when the festivities came to an end the hearts of all were filled with the most lively and pleasing enthusiasm."[1]

The Patriotic Society had become a revolutionary center from which public opinion was aroused. It was open to all classes of society, and no less daring for the period was its policy of allowing women of all levels to be present at its debates, even in the evenings. The women were just as committed as the others when the sessions ended, and orators and audience dispersed in groups throughout the city, carrying their joy, their discussions and their ideas to even the quiet streets of the suburbs.

Miranda presided over the meeting on the anniversary of April 19, and his arrogant bearing, his exotic manners and his ardent, domineering gaze attracted the interest and admiration of the people who, until then, had known him only through vague reports. All were aware that for many years and even in his moments of triumph, he had been constantly threatened by the intrigues of the Bourbon courts of Spain, France and Italy and had run the risk of being cast into one of the dungeons of the *ancien régime,* which "reasons of state" sealed forever condemning its victims to neglect and death. The listeners were captivated at hearing from his own lips the splendors and miseries of the French Revolution, the details of his escape from the Tribunal of Terror, and what Napoleon, who then held the world in bondage, was like when Miranda knew him. But when the discussion moved beyond topics which, after all, were mere trivialities for Miranda, to the more urgent matter of what should be done to deal with the country's problems, not a few felt hesitant in the presence of the imperious, experienced conspirator. Some still had not rid themselves of the idea that he was an "agent of the English", and others —fastidious provincial lawyers—resented the self-possession of the man who had traveled so much in history and in the world.

It was in the Patriotic Society that Bolívar, too, first made himself known as a public orator. The speech he delivered there on July 3, 1811, is the first

---

1. Manuel Palacio Fajardo, *Bosquejo de la Revolución en la América Española* (Caracas, 1953), p. 70.

"The Signing of the Declaration of Independence" by Juan Lovera.

of his recorded addresses. The subject of debate was the need to persuade the congressmen to proclaim independence. Bolívar replied to a suggestion that the Patriotic Society might turn itself into another congress: "The question is not whether or not there are two congresses. How can those who are most keenly aware of the need for union promote division? What we desire is that the union be effective, so that it may give life to the glorious struggle for freedom. To unite and do nothing, to sleep in the arms of apathy, was yesterday but a disgrace, while today it is treason. The National Congress is arguing issues that should long since have been settled. And what is being said? That we must begin with a confederation, as though we were not already confederated against foreign tyranny, and that we should await the outcome of Spanish policy. What does it matter to us whether Spain sells her slaves to Napoleon or retains them, if we are determined to be free? These doubts are themselves the sad consequence of our ancient fetters. It is also said that great enterprises should be planned over a period of time. Three hundred years—is that not time enough? The Patriotic *Junta* respects, as it must, the Congress of the nation, but the Congress must hear the Patriotic *Junta,* for it is the center of inspiration and the headquarters of revolutionary interests. Let us fearlessly lay the cornerstone of South American liberty. If we hesitate we are lost. I propose that a committee representing this body convey these sentiments to the sovereign Congress."

While these discussions went on, other work was underway. Miranda, who had brought the first press to Venezuela, and who later founded in London *El Colombiano,* a journal intended to stimulate American independence, must have been moved to see that, in addition to *La Gaceta de Caracas,* which began to be produced on that press in 1808, four other periodicals appeared in Caracas after the revolution: the *Semanario de Caracas,* the *Mercurio Venezolano, El Patriota de Venezuela,* and *El Publicista de Venezuela.* Pamphlets and books, both scholarly and propagandistic, arrived from abroad in relative abundance. In addition, William Burke's *Rights of South America and Mexico,* Condillac's *Logic,* and the *Rights of Man and the Citizen* were published in Caracas itself. The *Diario Político* of Santa Fe de Bogotá was reprinted there, and an advertisement in the *Gaceta de Caracas* announced a translation of the *Social Contract.*[1]

Two works translated and published in Philadelphia by the Venezuelan Manuel García de Sena; *The Independence of Costa Firme Justified by Thomas Paine Thirty Years Ago* and the *Concise History of the United States from the Discovery of America Until the Year 1807,* had a great

---

1. Some writers state that this was the work completed at the end of the colonial period by the learned Dr. José Vargas. *The Rights of Man and the Citizen* was accompanied by "various republican maxims," but, according to Dr. Pedro Grases, the Rights of Man adopted by Constituent Congress of 1811, and published separately in the same year, were those of the Gual and España conspiracy."

impact. Some assertions of Burke on religious tolerance unleashed a passionate polemic. The creole intellectuals showed themselves wisely concerned by the social problems that were bound to accompany the political upheaval. Muñoz Tébar warned the people in the same speech which excited them on April 19, 1811: "As we have escaped from tyranny, only its restoration concerns us; but anarchy is also tyranny, complicated by disorder. . . ." The Licenciate Miguel José Sanz demanded an agrarian law which would make the distribution of rural property more just and more fruitful: "Why," he asked, "do some cattle-owners have to occupy lands whose extent would seem unbelievable to those who have not seen them? Why should they not be made to sell or let on long leases those parts of their estates which are useless for raising and keeping cattle, but which divided would bring great productivity? The Government should consider this matter with much greater attention, given that a very important part of the Province's happiness rests upon it. How scandalous it is to see fertile valleys and highlands lying useless in the hands of a single owner who, out of incompetence, disinterest or extravagant caprice, neither cultivates them nor sells them to other men who would contribute to the common abun· dance, to their own welfare and to the income of the State. Ah for a just, equitable and wisely-meditated agrarian Law to destroy a custom so prejudicial to other men and to the proprietors themselves."[1]

But the most important point is that Venezuela had decided to give constitutional form to the revolution. The Congress summoned by the Supreme *Junta* was installed on March 2, 1811. On July 5, it declared the Independence of Venezuela; on the 14th it solemnly published the Act and the national flag was hoisted for the first time in Caracas. The design was that drawn by Miranda, and it was raised in the main square by the sons of José María España, thus fulfilling the prophecy that his memory would be honored on the very spot of his execution. The fundamental law of the new State was approved in December of the same year.

It is not without significance that this constitution was the first in Spanish America. In subsequent years the Venezuelans, aided only by their neighbors in New Granada, had to defend themselves against powerful expeditions sent by Spain for the reconquest of America. This terrible effort and the subsequent emancipation of Peru by Venezuelan generals, so elevated Venezuela's military prestige that her thinkers and politicians were forgotten. Writers have glorified Venezuela as the land of *caudillos,* some artfully, but others, including not a few Venezuelans, out of ingenuous admiration. It is important, then, to point out that ours was the first Spanish American constitution. Venezuela took action to give a lawful base to her revolution with the same vehemence that she later displayed in defense of it.

---

1. Juan Saturno Canelón, *Licenciado Miguel José Sanz* (Caracas, 1956), p. 126.

It is also appropriate to point out that the constitution had a continental significance, because it determined categorically that the revolution should be republican and democratic. Even while the Declaration of Independence was still being debated, Martín Tovar maintained that the question had already been decided by Congress. He said, "the proof is that it has commissioned some of its members to draft a democratic Constitution." In Venezuela the republic was not the work of the *caudillos,* nor was democracy imposed by the accidents of war. Both were born of a doctrinaire determination which the founders of the country considered the moral justification for their struggle for independence.

The principles of this Constitution reveal the noble aspirations with which the emancipation of America began. Not only Americans but also Spaniards and Canary Islanders could become members of the Supreme Executive Authority, a triumvirate, on the sole condition that they had recognized and sworn fealty to independence. The Supreme *Junta* had written to all the *ayuntamientos* of America shortly after April 19, asking them "to contribute to the great work of Spanish-American Confederation." It sent commissioners to the neighboring country of New Granada to arrange a treaty of "friendship, alliance and federative union." The Constitution of 1811 defined these proposals even more closely, for while declaring its precepts inviolable, it promised "to alter and change these resolutions at any time, in due proportion to the desire of the majority of the people of Colombia to unite in a National Body for the defense and preservation of their liberty and independence." Colombia meant for them, as it did for Miranda, the whole of Spanish America or, to be more precise, "American Spain," a phrase coined by the Jesuit Vizcardo that became fashionable. It was appropriate, because it underlined the spiritual unity of the Spanish World, including the Metropolis, and, at the same time corrected the error that Spanish America was so called because it "belonged" to Spain.

Patriotic airs carried the same sentiments of continental unity to the people. The most popular, written at the time by Vicente Salias, which was to become the National Anthem of Venezuela, proclaimed with the ingenuousness of a Christmas carol:

Joined by knots
which heaven fashioned,
the whole of America
exists as a nation.

Heaven. They did not suspect that hell, too, was preparing to intervene.

XV

WOUNDED
IN THE HEART

LIKE MEN HURRYING ALONG
the shores of a lake, unaware that they had returned to their starting point,
the revolutionaries at times reestablished features of the regime they had
just overthrown.

Mainly for this reason the Republic proclaimed in Venezuela in July 1811
was to disappear just a year later, in July 1812. Preoccupied with fears that
a strong government might make itself despotic, and anxious to prevent the
central authority from oppressing the provinces, the legislators created a
weak national executive in the form of a triumvirate and enshrined federalism as the basis of the new State. Each province in the confederation was
given its own deliberative body with the right to create its own constitution.
These precautions prevented the leaders from making themselves tyrants,
but they hampered the stabilization and defense of the republic.

Some wise patriots vainly opposed these measures. They included Miranda,
who had bitter personal experience of them, and Bolívar, whose political
vision had begun to manifest its courage and its precision.

Also, serious difficulties were approaching. The Spanish Regency had
declared war upon the new republic, and had decreed the blockade of its
coasts. Moreover, it was likely that if Napoleon secured the complete submission of Spain, he would also attempt to conquer these overseas dependencies. The cities of Coro and Maracaibo, which to a great extent
dominated the west of the country and controlled its access to the sea, had
remained in the power of Spanish officials who commanded veteran troops.
In the southeast, Guayana returned to royalist control after a brief flirtation

with the patriot cause, and a counter-revolutionary movement had to be suppressed in Caracas itself before the end of 1810.

The Supreme *Junta* sent a force under the Marquis del Toro against Coro where the active Spanish Governor, José de Ceballos, had entrenched himself. Del Toro was defeated and his untrained militiamen were scattered. In the east and in Guayana, royalists and republicans fought to a stand-off.

In July 1811, another revolt was attempted in Caracas, and the city of Valencia returned to the royalists after a surprise uprising. The movement in Caracas was a grotesque mutiny by a few "Islanders,"[1] but the rebels in Valencia succeeded in defeating the Marquis del Toro, to whom the government had again entrusted its army. An expedition under Miranda was then organized, and Bolívar went with it as Colonel commanding the Aragua Battalion. General Miranda, who according to Scot Semple, "exposed himself considerably," mentioned Bolívar three times in his dispatches to the government. He reported that on July 23, he and Fernando del Toro atacked the two strong-points of the enemy. Del Toro was wounded and made a permanent invalid, and Miranda included him among the officers who had distinguished themselves in action. On August 13, Miranda reported that Bolívar had "distinguished himself in the various tasks entrusted to him," and announced that he was traveling to Caracas with Captain Francisco Salias to deliver verbal reports to the Executive.[2]

Valencia was captured only after bloody assaults. Although the Canary Islanders in Caracas had been severely punished, the Valencia rebels were pardoned by Congress. Bolívar commented in the Cartagena Manifesto: "The pacification cost us about a thousand men, and not a single rebel was brought to justice. All retained their lives and most their property."

But the approach of the legislators to the organization of the military forces was even more lamentable. Bolívar related in the same document: ". . . innumerable, undisciplined militia units were formed. The salaries paid the staff officers of these units exhausted the funds of the national treasury. Farmers were torn from their homes and their crops lost. This made them despise the Government that had forced them to abandon their families and take up arms. 'Republics,' said our statesmen, 'have no need for hirelings to maintain their liberty. Every citizen will turn soldier when the enemy attacks us. . . .' What followed in Venezuela was bitter evidence of the error of their calculations. The militia that went to meet the enemy did not know how to handle arms and, unaccustomed to

---

1. The Venezuelans have always called the natives of the Canaries "Islanders"; sometimes the name is also used for the natives of Margarita, an island in eastern Venezuela.
2. For Semple's comment see Parra-Pérez, *Historia de la primera República de Venezuela*, Caracas, 1939,. ii, p. 66. Miranda's dispatches were published in the *Gaceta de Caracas*, Thursday July 30 and Friday August 16, 1811. The Academy of History published a facsimile edition, Caracas, 1960.

discipline and obedience, was routed at the very beginning of the last campaign, notwithstanding the heroic and extraordinary efforts of its leaders."

These calamities undermined public morale, while the government's weakness deprived it of the respect it should have enjoyed from the masses. The privations inherent in a wartime situation surprised a people who had always lived in peace. Maritime traffic was interrupted as much because of the Spanish blockade as the warfare in Europe. Communication by land became more difficult because of increasing guerrilla activity and banditry. With trade paralyzed, agriculture ruined, and the future uncertain, it was natural for the people to decide that the deprivations and miseries they were suffering formed too high a price for political innovations few of them could understand.

The crowning evil was a step commonly taken in such cases, and which is always calamitous. The government decided, with the public treasury ruined, to resort to issuing paper money. Severe penalties were introduced to support the system, but this merely increased the general panic without improving the situation. We quote once again from Bolívar's manifesto: "In the eyes of most people this new money was a direct violation of property rights. They felt that they were being deprived of objects of intrinsic value in exchange for others of problematical worth. The paper money aroused discontent among the otherwise indifferent people of the interior and they called upon the commandant of the Spanish troops to come and free them from a currency which they regarded with a horror greater than slavery."

The Republic was already suffering from internal decay when a Naval Captain, Domingo de Monteverde, who had come from Puerto Rico with regular troops sent to reinforce the royalists in Coro, obtained authorization to march on the interior of the country. On the outskirts of Barquisimeto an Indian called Juan de los Reyes Vargas went over to his side along with the advance guard of patriots. Two Spaniards in the service of the Republic, José Martí in Guanare and Bernardo Goroyza in San Juan de los Morros, soon followed his example. These betrayals, and the inexperience of the republican leaders, whose troops frequently scattered without a shot being fired, contributed to an atmosphere of uneasy fear which the few officers who were becoming veterans struggled in vain to arrest.

It was then that the greatest catastrophe of all occurred and almost literally seemed to open a grave for the dying Republic. On March 26, 1812, at seven minutes past four in the afternoon, an earthquake leveled almost half the country, the most populous half, which was in the hands of the patriots. The cities of Caracas, La Guaira, Maiquetía, Mérida and San Felipe were completely destroyed, and Valencia, La Victoria, Barquisimeto and other cities were severely damaged. In Caracas, the churches of

La Pastora, Altagracia, La Merced, Santo Domingo or San Jacinto, and La Trinidad collapsed. Others, like that of San Francisco, were so severely damaged that divine worship was suspended for a long time, and the cathedral itself lost a third of its tower. Since the day was Holy Thursday and the churches were filled with worshippers, the mortality was frightful. In addition, thousands of soldiers and civilians were buried beneath the ruins of barracks and private houses. About 10,000 people died in Caracas alone, and for several days bonfires were lit to burn the corpses. Since it was impossible to attend to the sick and wounded, many more died on the days that followed. Fifty years later many ruins still remained in the razed cities to remind the fearful people of the cataclysm.

The opponents of independence hurried forward to argue that the disaster was a heavenly punishment upon the rebellious provinces. They stressed two coincidences which strongly affected popular opinion: that the earthquake, like April 19, 1810, had occurred on Holy Thursday, and that the cities held by the Spaniards had been spared. Fervent Spanish priests paraded through the ruins demanding repentance and submission to the king. Many creoles and laymen, some genuinely terrified, joined them. Some confessed their sins aloud or resorted to grotesque forms of self abasement, increasing the confusion and the feeling that God himself was scouring the rebel country.

There then occurred an incident which has become a symbol in Venezuelan history. In the midst of this general depression, Bolívar climbed onto the ruins of the church of San Jacinto and proclaimed: *"If Nature is against us, we will fight her, too, and make her do what we want."*[1]

The royalist, José Domingo Díaz, who was intent on increasing the panic, described these words as profane and claimed that they were directed as an insult to him. But, for history the incident foreshadows the constancy with which Bolívar was to surmount all obstacles and even dominate the forces of nature to secure the emancipation of America: as, in 1814, when he trekked in defeat through the jungles of Barlovento, personally helping the despairing masses flee from Caracas and even descending from his horse to take an abandoned child in his arms; when he saw, shortly afterwards, that the republicans in New Granada, although threatened on all sides by the formidable expedition of Morillo, were weakening themselves in a blind civil war; during the campaign of 1818 and 1819 in the plains, when water sometimes reached the girths of the horses, and his enemy uttered the magnificent eulogy, "more redoubtable vanquished than victorious;" in the icy heights of the Andes, where naked, hungry, and poorly armed soldiers followed him to the dazzling triumph of Boyacá, awed by his

---

1. José Domingo Díaz, *Recuerdos sobre la rebelión de Caracas,* Madrid, 1829. The quotation is taken from the edition published in Caracas in 1961 by the Academia Nacional de la Historia, p. 98.

unquenchable energy; in Peru in 1824, when he improvised an army in four months, crossed the Cordillera Blanca, scaled 5,000 meter peaks, and marched two hundred leagues to defeat the enemy at Junín. When the time arrived for the civil reorganization of his great work and opportunist *caudillos* split the country, his genius took a formidable leap and, in the Congress of Panama, anticipated the unity of the whole continent. During these shifts of fortune Bolívar's response was always the one which had sprung to his lips in the ruins of Caracas.

At the end of his life, Bolívar even conquered nature within himself. It did not seen human for him to give up the struggle as he saw his work being destroyed, but he did abandon it, and the explanation he gave to Sucre was a lucid, arrogant synthesis of the serenity he had achieved: "The Republic is about to break up, and in whichever part I find myself, they will try to make me their *caudillo,* to lead them in rebellion. Neither my dignity nor my position allows me to make myself a leader of factions." He preferred exile and death.

The earthquake, coming on top of earlier disasters, decided Monteverde's triumph. Palacio Fajardo relates: "The troops quartered in Barquisimeto, under the command of Jalón, were preparing to march against the royalists at the time the earthquake occurred. Most of them were buried beneath the ruins of the barracks which collapsed as they were trying to get out. Their leader was seriously injured."[1] The city then fell to Monteverde without resistance. The patriot detachment garrisoning the neighboring town of Araure refused to fight, and handed over its commander, Colonel Palacios Sojo. The fort of San Carlos in the plains was bravely defended by Colonel Carabaño, "but the cavalry of the *independientes* went over to the royalists, and they secured victory." All the west of the country and the plains, where various guerrilla bands had appeared, was thus in royalist hands. Since communication between Caracas and the east was difficult by sea and possible by land only across the plains, the Republic was reduced to a narrow coastal strip reaching barely beyond Valencia to the west, ending to the south at San Juan de los Morros, and to the east in the jungles of Barlovento very near Caracas.

It was then that the politicians decided to entrust command to Miranda. But even so, they failed to abandon the contradictions and suspicions which had paralyzed the defense of the Republic. It was already too late. Congress granted extraordinary powers to the Executive on April 4, 1812, but it was not until the 23rd that they were delegated to Miranda, who was given the rank of Commander-in-Chief. By the end of June two developments had made the republicans' position untenable. On June 24, the Barlovento

---

1. Manuel Palacio Fajardo, *Bosquejo de la Revolución en la América española.* The author, who witnessed all the events which occurred in Venezuela in this period, was a consistent patriot, and so respected for his talent and learning that in 1819 the Liberator entrusted to him the correction and translation into English of his Angostura address.

Negroes revolted, threatening Caracas from the east, and on the 30th, the fortress of Puerto Cabello, which held most of the republicans' munitions, was delivered to the royalists by a traitor. Miranda's so-called dictatorship lasted barely two months, and it was restricted to a small part of the national territory.

But here, we should examine more closely the situation of general dissatisfaction that ruined the Republic of 1811.

Acting through the politicians he had helped and the agents he dispatched, Miranda had had great influence over the pronouncements which aroused the main cities of South America in 1810. In Caracas, paradoxically, he did not enjoy this authority, at least not directly, mainly because the Spanish propaganda, depicting him as an "agent" of the English, had been most intense, naturally, in his own country. On the occasion of the 1806 invasion, the calumny was renewed. The overall result was that the Venezuelans, some out of excessive credulity, others because they had been persuaded by Guevara y Vasconcelos to denounce Miranda, viewed the possibility of his predominance with distrust or fear. Many historians add, as a principal cause of the hostility towards Miranda, at least among the leading citizens, that fifty years earlier the upper class of Caracas had sued the Precursor's father, Sebastián de Miranda, to prevent him from wearing military uniform and carrying a baton, on the grounds that he was a merchant. Such suits were so commonplace in the colonial period that this one doubtless would have been forgotten if the extraordinary position which Miranda achieved on both continents had not stirred up intrigues and the envy that such men unfortunately attract. We add, as a curiosity, that the prejudices displayed by the oligarchy of Caracas in the late eighteenth century had so changed by 1802 that Bolívar saw no stigma in being described as a merchant in an administrative document, nor did anyone else.[1]

Despite this, the errors, prejudices and wicked attitudes that alienated Miranda in his own country became so violent that in 1808, when the Precursor wrote to Marquis del Toro about the events at Bayonne, the Marquis delivered the letter to the Captain-General, describing Miranda as a "traitor."

It was even more regrettable that after April 19, in the first communication sent to Miranda by the Supreme *Junta* after he arrived in Venezuela, the phrases with which he was greeted were courteous but restrained. Instead of welcoming the unselfish revolutionary with the enthusiasm he deserved, it simply told him that "the recommendation made in your

---

1. I refer to a communication to the Treasury ministers about a cargo sent from La Coruña to "Don Simón Bolívar of this body of merchants." Boletín de la Academia Nacional de la Historia, no. 143, p. 279, Caracas, July-Sept. 1953. Of course, in this period Bolívar habitually described himself as *"hacendado,"* when he had no need to use his military title.

favor by the commisioners in London, Don Luis López Méndez and Don Simón Bolívar" had persuaded the *Junta* to grant him "the corresponding permit to proceed to this city as soon as you wish."[1]

Miranda was received triumphantly by the people of La Guaira, and Bolívar put him up in his own house. But his first brush with hostility awaited him on the road from the port to Caracas: "An Islander who received him in La Guaira, and who accompanied him to Caracas, noted that he spoke ill of the government of the United States of America, and that on the *Venta* road, and elsewhere where repairs and improvements were need, he boasted that he would arrange everything, as though he already had the rudder of the New Republic of Venezuela in his hand."

The statement is from a letter from Roscio to Bello, dated June 9, 1811. It provides us, far better than a whole volume of narrative could, with the key to what ensued in Venezuela.[2] Roscio was one of the most eminent —and without doubt the most influential—of the lawyers who controlled the new political situation. His letter shows that from the moment Miranda entered the country there existed a tacit but unrelenting conspiracy against him, directed towards spying on him, isolating him, and misrepresenting all his words and deeds.

After recounting the surprising testimony of "an Islander," Roscio traced the old revolutionary's steps, and he noted that the Canon Madariaga "was the only member of the government who went out of the city to greet him as he descended the mountain." He gloated: "After the installation of the Congress of Venezuela, the agents of the other branches were appointed, and in none of them was our compatriot given office." He added with equal malevolence: "On the day of the appointment of those who were to compose the executive branch, Miranda awaited the results in his house. In the election he received eight votes from thirty-one members of Congress." Roscio must have had another Islander reporting to him from Miranda's house, for he added that Miranda veiled his regret at the news by saying: "I rejoice to learn that there are in my country persons more suitable than I for the exercise of supreme power."

Roscio was also annoyed that Canon Madariaga, sent by the government of New Granada on the mission mentioned earlier, "was recommending and applauding the person and conduct of Miranda . . . he applauded and recommended him much more in the capital, where he had his applause and recommendations published in the official newspaper . . . these eulogies, written and printed with craft and cunning, made, by low means, a favorable impression upon the common people." The eulogies described with such rancor were those Madariaga published in Bogotá to support the

---

1. Juan Germán Roscio, *Obras,* Caracas, 1953, ii, p. 204. Roscio signed the document as Secretary of State.
2. *Ibid,* iii, p. 23.

reprinting of a manifesto by Miranda on the emancipation of America. It is clear that the indirect glorification of "our compatriot" could not be tolerated, even if it was in the service of the common cause.

When he mentioned the Patriotic Society, Roscio insisted upon celebrating the opposition to Miranda: "Miranda was a member of this body from its foundation, but when he was nominated as its President in May, he did not even receive votes for the Vice-Presidency." Roscio revealed that he also knew that when Miranda visited the Archbishop "he went dressed in a very religious manner." He was alarmed by "the gossip, tales and indiscretions of our compatriot with regard to the colored people, who are over-flattered by his visits, conversations and his very liberal ideas." Roscio considered it equally dangerous for Miranda to identify himself with the aristocratic families, and he told Bello: "I return to Miranda to inform you that his present conduct is arousing the distrust of the most numerous and wisest section of the population. His most conspicuous friends are the Toros, the Ribas Herreras and the Bolívars."

The differences among the revolutionaries were already evident on April 19, 1810, and they perhaps explain why Bolívar played no part in the movement. Like Ribas, he was feared for his radical ideas on the question of social equality. Roscio also attacked Miranda on this point: "On the very day of the installation of the executive, a group of *pardos,* led by Fernando Galindo, were surprised and arrested at a private meeting arranged for the discussion of government affairs and unlimited equality and liberty. The leader had an inflammatory proclamation on the subject which contained a reference to Miranda, so complimentary that it seemed Miranda's own work. All who read it reached this conclusion, even if they were ignorant of the contact and frequent communication between the two."

Roscio was no common man. He occupied an important position. He had helped write the Act of Independence, and until he died he completely dedicated himself to the Republic with valor, probity and abnegation. It is, therefore, astonishing and distasteful to see the imprudent, cruel and unsparing attack that he unleashed against the man who had been fighting for the emancipation of America for thirty years. Miranda's enemies succeeded in portraying every one of his actions as suspicious. He was excluded from office, and even his inevitable political activities were twisted into new grounds for suspicion and pretext to immobilize him.

But it is not surprising to discover a swarm of evil passions beneath the surface, because political upheavals always provide the opportunity for the emergence of worthless men, who naturally conspire to constrain and destroy anyone who tries to raise them from their petty desires and grudges to the service of a greater cause. Such occasions also produce men who scramble around the feet of great men, seeking opportunities to elevate themselves. The third group, consisting of individuals who, whatever their character, talents and energy, are perverse, jealous intriguers, is always the most dangerous. The latter are terribly destructive at times of unrest and, unlike the others, they survive for many years, always well-placed to do the greatest harm. Individuals of all these categories combined in the attack on Miranda: a certain "Trader," and the no less notorious Escorihuela; the "little Biscayan Gragirena," to quote Sanz; "the perverse Intriguer" of Tejera; Rafael Diego Mérida's "el Malo"; and Miguel Peña, "the eternal Iago of the Republic."

Roscio's letter to Bello reveals the atmosphere in Caracas in June 1811. In July Miranda was entrusted with the command of the army against Valencia after the defeat of the Marquis del Toro. But his victory became a further obstacle. According to Palacio Fajardo, the Executive accepted Miranda's plans to attack the royalists in Coro, "but his enemies, irritated by his latest triumph, opposed the project in every way possible, and they were supported by the Congress."

The politicians constantly opposed the creation of a regular, permanent army. When a force was required in the field, it had to be determined before it marched whether it would consist of militiamen, federal troops or provincial troops, because it depended upon this whether or not it would be allowed to leave, and whether it would be used in the defense of the city, or the province, or the whole country. According to Espejo, frequent discharges were ordered from the ranks so that Miranda would be prevented from acquiring effective power.[1]

It would take too long to describe all the details of this inflexible obstruction. It increased dramatically until the very eve of surrender, and can be seen most clearly in the final stages.

Miranda was given power and the title Commander-in-Chief on April 23, 1812, after the earthquake and the loss of Barquisimeto, although it was first offered to the inevitable Marquis del Toro. But Miranda embarked upon his so-called dictatorship without an army to help him, and he could do nothing against the interminable intrigues which obstructed him. On May 16 he invited the federal government and that of the province of Caracas to a conference designed to end anarchy in government. Even then, his enemies tried to prevent him from being heard, provoking the Licentiate Sanz to comment bitterly, "To be denied at a stroke that which is not denied to one's greatest enemies!"[2] Miranda finally obtained the suspension of the Constitution and the introduction of martial law, which authorized him to

---

1. The reader will have noticed that I am relying on the testimony of eye-witnesses, such as Bolívar, Palacio Fajardo, Roscio, Espejo, etc. I am also relying heavily on the information provided by the eminent Venezuelan historian, C. Parra-Pérez, in his *Historia de la Primera República de Venezuela* (Caracas, 1939).
2. Juan Saturno Canelón, *Biografía del Licenciado Miguel José Sanz* (Caracas, 1956).

appoint military commanders. In the middle of June, however, the government of Caracas was still refusing to accept martial law, and was proposing new discussions with the Commander-in-Chief and representatives of the federal government.

Even Roscio, who had been so injust to Miranda, and who had been sent by him to Caracas, together with Madariaga, to deal with the "Provincial Government and its Honorable Council," became exasperated. He confessed to the Commander-in-Chief: "We have still not obtained a reply from the Council, despite pressing for one with the urgency demanded by the dangerous circumstances in which the *Patria* finds it self. It looks to your patriotism, your valor and your military skill to secure its salvation and the enjoyment of its independence and liberty." Colonel Juan Nepomuceno Quero, appointed military governor of Caracas, was unable to use his authority, and an eye-witness commented "never have I seen a man so excited or in such a state because of his inablity to have his orders enforced, for he was not far from crying with rage."

Even Miranda's correspondence was maliciously delayed, and in a meeting of the executive, legislative and judicial authorities of the province of Caracas at the end of May, he was insulted and told "that they had finished with him."

Those who wanted to help Miranda despaired. Miguel José Sanz, for example, denounced the politicians for their "indecent and gross jealousy and rivalry." Espejo referred to "the accursed Council of Caracas." Although he was a brother-in-law of the Montillas, who were enemies of Miranda, Luis Delpech ardently tried to help him, but on June 12, he was obliged to report: "All of them, my General, except for a small number, seem sworn to destroy the *Patria* which you seek to save."

This did not discourage Miranda. He energetically tried to remedy the economic difficulties which, together with the earthquake, had brought about the country's spiritual collapse. He began to train the army, making good use of his few regular officers (unfortunately, they were nearly all foreigners, a fact that was used as a further pretext for criticism), and skillfully encouraging the outstanding creole recruits, such as Ribas, Bolívar, Ayala, Soublette, Carabaño and Paz del Castillo. As Roscio's letter indicates, he had tried since his arrival to draw near to the people and neutralize the influence of the higher clergy. He also had discussions with his opponents, winning over some by calling them to his side as advisers and buying off the less sensitive with appointments and commissions. He won the support of numerous civilians and soldiers, men of the highest moral calibre, by making them see the miseries, mistakes and dangers which were destroying the Republic. Subsequently, nearly all of them expressed their admiration for him.

After taking Barquisimeto, Monteverde advanced on Valencia, and the city fell to him in a manner characteristic of the whole campaign. The republicans, led by Miguel Ustáriz and Miguel Carabaño, lay in wait for the royalists near the city at Los Colorados with a force of 1,300 men which, although untrained and poorly-armed, was larger than that of the enemy. The leader of the patriot cavalry, however, a Spaniard called Juan Montalvo who pretended to serve the Republic, had already arranged with Monteverde to cross over to his side. He did so at the height of battle, and the republicans were defeated and dispersed. Every episode of this type increased the demoralization of the patriot forces, and what followed was not surprising. The ill Ustáriz remained in charge of the defense of the city of Valencia at the head of a new, hastily assembled force. Miranda, who until then had been kept in Caracas by political affairs and the need to reorganize the army, anxiously planned to go to his aid. But there was not enough time, for, as Parra-Pérez tells us: "As the *Corianos* advanced, the people declared against the Republic, and the patriot soldiers who ventured alone onto the streets were attacked and killed. The frightened Ustáriz decided to abandon the city, and did so precipitately, thoughtlessly destroying large quantities of supplies of all types, including the powder and cartridges, rather than sending them to Maracay."

Ustáriz was intelligent, brave, and an impeccable patriot, but he lacked military experience. Many years of reverses and suffering were needed for real leaders to emerge from the inexperienced officers who went out to command the republican troops without any other qualification than their courage. At the time, Miranda was obliged to write to José Félix Ribas, later "the Invincible": "Listen to veteran officers who are used to war, pay attention to their orders, their personal honor and their sound judgement. Do not allow yourself to be taken in by the reports of faint-hearted men. Return to your post. What has happened is a disgrace." Miranda was referring to a case very similar to that of Valencia. After retreating to Portachuelo de Guaica, a patriot force beat off Monteverde's attacks, but a meeting of officers unaccountably decided to abandon their strong position and retreat to Yuma. Ribas, who served Miranda loyally, was not at all to blame for the decision, but his qualities of oustanding bravery and military capacity were only beginning to show themselves. Upset by what had happened, Miranda preferred to send two experienced officers, the foreigners MacGregor and Du Cayla, to retake the position. Fortunately, Ribas himself had already done this. He was not offended by Miranda's decision, although he insisted on clarifying what had happened.

Meanwhile, where was Bolívar? We know only that after his first taste of battle at Valencia, he remained idle on his San Mateo estate. Why? This is a question which still cannot be answered with documentary evidence. Dr. Cristóbal Mendoza, the venerable *prócer* who was the first man named to the Republic's triumvirate executive, wrote that Miranda considered Bolívar "a dangerous young man" and had asked, when he was organizing the first expedition against Valencia, that he should be removed from the army on any pretext.[1] This explanation has been accepted by almost all Venezuelan historians, but it would need to be much more detailed to be convincing. Bolívar had brought Miranda from London, ignoring the deliberate disinterest of the Supreme *Junta* and the hostility of the politicians then in charge of goverment. He lodged Miranda in his own house and, disregarding the old antagonism which his relatives, the Toros, felt for Miranda, dedicated himself to obtaining a warm reception for him from the people of Caracas. He also introduced Miranda to his other relatives the Ribases and the Herreras. Moreover, and this is the crucial point, all contemporary documents show that Bolívar and Miranda agreed on the key issues which decided the fate of the Republic. They opposed the weak constitution of 1811 which established the federal government and a tripartite executive. They opposed administrative inefficiency and paper money. They called for an expedition against the Coro royalists before they became entrenched, and they stressed the urgency of replacing the fragile citizen militia with a regular, integrated army. They agreed, too, on the need to apply severe sanctions against conspirators, the robbers of public funds, and those who brought anarchy to the army and public life. One argument is that despite their agreement on these important matters, Bolívar and Miranda were divided by irrational differences of temperament and by secondary disagreements over the conduct of military operations. Dr. Lecuna, the most eminent of the Bolivarian critics, states that it was the "difference in military opinions" which caused Miranda's ill-will towards Bolívar. But what possible value could Bolívar's opinions on military affairs have had at the time specified by Mendoza, that is, before the expedition against Valencia, when he had still to experience his first taste of battle?

It is more logical to see Miranda, Bolívar and Ribas as the victims of the same political intrigue, bearing in mind that the leaders of the revolution completely opposed taking Bolívar into the government, and that they removed Ribas from authority shortly after April 19 and that, even after giving Miranda dictatorial powers, the government stubbornly resisted his right to grant military titles and promotions. In his letter to Bello, Roscio maliciously claimed that all three were united and formed a powerful combination. We know, too, that they were competent, decisive soldiers, at times excessively strict, whom the civilians watched with suspicion and fear.

Moreover, despite the supposed differences between them, Miranda sent an officer to San Mateo and later went in person to offer Bolívar the

---

1. Quoted and discussed by Lecuna in *Catálogo de errores y calumnias en la historia de Bolívar,* ii, p. 215.

command of the fortress of Puerto Cabello. Dr. Cristóbal Mendoza, and those who support his interpretation, see this as a trick to remove Bolívar from the scene by "condemning him to inaction." We will see below just how important Puerto Cabello was at the time. In any case the basic flaw in this approach is the anachronism of seeing Bolívar as the future Liberator. The truth is that at the time he had experience of only one battle, and there was little to distinguish him from the many other officers, elevated precipitately by the creation of the Republic, who although at times capable of acting boldly, could not be regarded as sound, experienced leaders.

Fortunately, Bolívar was not conceited and he did not experience the resentment against Miranda attributed to him by Mendoza's argument. When he learned of the danger to Valencia, he hurried to Maracay, and he wrote to Miranda while on the road: "I am going immediately to arouse the troops who are in La Cabrera. I have lifted these people from their depression. I hope to be able to do the same with the troops. Reply to me with your orders at La Cabrera. Your subject and friend, Bolívar. It seems to me that you would do unimaginable good if you came to these parts. *Ut supra*."[1]

Meanwhile, the Spaniard Antoñanzas had taken San Juan de los Morros, and was threatening the long patriot front between Caracas and Guaica. Moreover, his presence made Guaica useless, since it was no longer feasible to think of undertaking the recapture of Valencia from there. Miranda decided, therefore, to concentrate his forces in the town of La Victoria, and it was there that he awaited the royalists.

Monteverde attacked from June 20-29, strengthened on the latter date by Antoñanza's troops and by regular soldiers recently arrived from Puerto Rico. But he was repulsed, and the patriots caused such heavy casualties that they regarded their success as a clear victory. They were beginning to realize that their bravery and enthusiasm could in large measure compensate for their inexperience. Colonel Austria reported: "Without any co-ordination or order, the infantrymen entered the battle, loading their muskets. The artillery moved its guns and carriages with urgent speed. The officers and leaders, full of bravery and with a noble disregard for danger, left their positions to urge on their men. The Commander-in-Chief himself, at the head of some lancers, threw himself into the thick of the fighting. All advanced together with heroic courage, until the royalists were forced to seek their salvation in a disorderly and shameful flight." Another eye-witness, Fr. Martel, noted that the soldiers admired Miranda's "serenity and his smiling countenance."

But the Commander-in-Chief did not let himself be carried away by the enthusiasm of his men, and when they clamored for the pursuit of the enemy and a general offensive, he made the army return to the town, which he began to fortify for a defensive action. He feared that, if his

---

1. *Cartas del Libertador,* xii, p. 22.

troops were sent back to the open country where they would have to split up for separate operations, they would again make mistakes and the desertions and breakdowns in discipline he had seen so often would reappear. He proposed, therefore, to organize and train officers and men behind the shelter of the fortifications, creating the "professional army" that both he and Bolívar had demanded in vain from the politicians. Parra-Pérez draws an apt comparison between Miranda and San Martín, although he is not referring specifically to events at La Victoria. "Miranda undertook the organization of his army with the same spirit that San Martín, the professional soldier, displayed when he trained the troops entrusted to him at Tucumán in 1814 by the government of Buenos Aires. After the defeat of Belgrano, San Martín prepared a fortified place and dedicated himself to instructing officers and soldiers. As we know, the Argentine general did the same thing successfully in Cuyo. The differences are that San Martín's troops did not desert, and that the royalists were far away."

The patriots, however, stimulated by their recent triumph, would have preferred one of the dazzling campaigns later to be undertaken by Bolívar. Those who had already criticized Miranda for the retreat to La Victoria were furious when they realized that he was refusing to take advantage of the general enthusiasm. They were unaware that it was already too late for an offensive. On June 30, the day after Monteverde's last attack on La Victoria, a traitor led a revolt by part of the garrison of Puerto Cabello, freed the royalist prisoners, and was able to control the city from the castle which he had captured. Palacio Fajardo, a worried spectator of the drama, wrote: "Miranda's wise policies were just beginning to restore order in Caracas and discipline in the army, when the Spanish prisoners in the fortress of Puerto Cabello seized control of it. . . ."

Bolívar, who was in command of the fortress, tried desperately and valiantly to defend it, but what took place there was a local reflection of what was happening to Miranda at the national level. The city's *Cabildo* obstructed his measures, and, if Bolívar had acted violently against it, the accusations of despotism which were already being made against him would have caused a scandal. Various officers were incompetent or plotting openly against Bolívar. There was no time to select those who were able and loyal —the war itself was soon to do this—and Bolívar knew that if he placed his trust in others they might turn out to be even worse.

According to the evidence of the traitor Fernández Vinoni, who led the revolt, the Commander of the republican artillery, Domingo de Taborda, "led a popular party, hostile to the public authorities," and the *Cabildo* was implicated in "the move to capture Bolívar."[1] Bolívar has been criticized on

---

1. Vicente Dávila, *Investigaciones Históricas,* i. This is the best of the many documented studies devoted to the loss of Puerto Cabello. See, too, Lecuna, *Catálogo* . . . , i, p. 215, and Bolívar's official report in *Cartas del Libertador,* xii, p. 24.

JUZGADOS MILITARES

DE ESPAÑA Y SUS INDIAS.

POR DON FELIX COLÓN DE LARRIÁTEGUI.

TOMO I.

Contiene las personas que gozan fuero militar: los delitos de
desafuero, el modo de seguir las competencias con las ju-
risdicciones extrañas: la de formarlas con la eclesiástica
cuando los reos se refugian á sagrado: su extraccion de él:
el juzgado eclesiástico castrense, y los testamentos militares
y civiles, con todas las Reales resoluciones hasta fin
del año de 1816 y parte del 17.

TERCERA EDICION CORREGIDA Y AUMENTADA.

MADRID.
IMPRENTA DE REPULLÉS.
1817.
CON SUPERIOR PERMISO.

The work "Military Tribunals" by Félix Colón, one of the books which the
Liberator kept in his library.

points of detail: for keeping the prisoners in the castle rather than in the town, for failing to live in the castle himself, and allegedly for both leaving the cell doors open and for mistreating the prisoners. But, given the above situation, these reproaches are clearly of no importance.

Although the royalists were reinforced from Valencia and dominated the town with the guns of the invincible castle, Bolívar and his men fought for seven days to save Puerto Cabello. He explained in his official report: "The soldiers, despairing to see themselves surrounded by dangers and alone in the midst of ruins, thought only of escaping wherever they could. Thus, those sent out on missions failed to return, and those at their posts marched off in groups."

The *Cabildo* tried to get Bolívar to surrender, but his report continued: "I replied that the city would be reduced to ashes before I took such a shameful step, and I added that my hopes of saving it had never been higher because I was beginning to receive favorable news about the army and about the defeat of the enemy at Maracay and San Joaquín. To make this fiction more plausible, I had a bulletin published. To announce the news, gun salutes were fired, and drums and fifes were played in order to raise public morale, which was extremely low. I achieved my aim to an extent, and the troops began to hope for improvements."

But on the fourth day they began to suffer the torments of thirst: they dug in the grounds of the fortress but found only salty water. By July 6, Bolívar had only forty men left, and he was forced to abandon the city and sail for La Guaira.

His despair was extreme. On July 12, he ventured to write to Miranda: "General, my spirits are so depressed that I do not feel that I have the courage to command a single soldier. My vanity forced me to believe that my desire to succeed and my burning zeal for my country would serve to replace the talents which I lacked as a commander. I therefore beg you, either place me under the orders of an officer of the lowest rank, or grant me several days to compose myself and to recover the confidence that I lost at Puerto Cabello. To this should be added the state of my physical health, for, after thirteen sleepless nights and extreme distress, I find myself in a state of collapse. I shall commence at once the detailed report of the operations of the troops which I commanded and the misfortunes which destroyed the city of Puerto Cabello in order to justify your selection of me, and to clear my honor in the opinion of the public. I did my duty, General, and had but a single soldier stayed, I would have fought on, but they abandoned me through no fault of mine. I did everything in my power to hold them and oblige them to save their country, but, alas, the country has been lost at my hands." Two days later he was already hopeful of recovering his "normal temperament." He repeated to Miranda: Although filled with shame, my General, I venture to send you the enclosed report, which is hardly a shadow of what actually happened. My head and heart are useless. I beg you, therefore, to allow me a period of a few days, to see if I can restore my mind to its normal temperament. After having lost the country's last and best fortress, my General, how can I fail to be half-witted? You are generous in not making me face you! I am not to blame, but I am unfortunate, and that is enough. I remain, with the greatest consideration and respect, your passionate subject and friend, Simón Bolívar."

Those who wish to depict Bolívar as invincible, or try in this particular case to clear him of responsibility, do him a disservice by ignoring or glossing over documents like the letter quoted above. We repeat that his greatness lay in his ability to rise from extreme misfortune to the heights of power and glory, carried up by his invincible force of character, which grew firmer and stronger after each defeat. In 1812, he considered himself worthy only of serving under "an officer of the lowest rank." A year later he was the Liberator, with his own officers and men, who were transformed by the glow of his genius and were considered invincible. The whole of Venezuela was delirious with enthusiasm for the victories that he created out of nothing. The whole of his career was to reveal these contrasts, like a romantic poem filled with violent antitheses and unforeseen conclusions. Bolívar's first letter to Miranda contained a paragraph which at another level was also characteristic. Despite the humiliation which dazed him, his first concern was to support the officers who had served with him and to exonerate them from blame. He told Miranda: "I trust that you will be kind enough to tell me what is to become of the officers who have come with me. They are extremely fine men, and in my opinion there are none better in Venezuela. The loss of Colonel Jalón is irreparable; he is worth an entire army."

When Miranda learned in La Victoria of the loss of Puerto Cabello he exclaimed, "Venezuela is wounded in the heart." Without doubt he was already aware that the revolt of the slaves of Barlovento was threatening Caracas and had reached Guarenas and Guatire. He decided then to make use of his remaining forces to enter into negotiations with Monteverde. His representatives agreed with those of the royalist commander on a treaty under which the persons and property of all would be respected; nobody would be arrested or tried or lose his belongings; those who wished to leave the country would have three months to ask for a passport; and both sides would release their prisoners. These were the main points of the capitulation signed in the general headquarters of San Mateo on July 25.

The royal *audiencia,* restored in 1813 despite Monteverde's opposition, regarded the treaty as acceptable, but the royalist commander cynically violated it. He imprisoned the patriots, subjecting them to torture and humiliations, and he handed over the defenseless towns to the rapacity of his men. Not even women and children and the aged were immune from sense-less persecutions. Human dignity suffered outrages which even the Span-iards denounced with surprise and shame.

For this reason the war, which had apparently ended, was actually renewed in a new form, fed by hatred. Civilians were to suffer perhaps more than soldiers,for there could be neither traitors nor waverers. Respect for law, faith in promises, and all the legal and moral order maintained by Spain for three centuries were to disappear in the tragic whirlpool. The brotherhood between creoles and Spaniards, enshrined in the Constitution of 1811, disappeared, as did the compassion which is always aroused by defeated and defenseless creatures. The war to the death was beginning.

XVI

INDULGENCE
WAS
A CRIME

"THE INHABITANTS OF
Siquisique received us with great rejoicing, much cheering and ringing of
bells. We entered Carora. Here the troops were allowed to plunder, with
considerable profit. The date was the 23rd. Afterwards we carried the
portrait of Ferdinand VII, our King, in procession."

This description of one of the first episodes in Monteverde's campaign,
written by Lieutenant Luis Ginetti, who left Coro with him, is in many
ways symbolic, because it sums up the three basic characteristics of his
authority: cruelty, rapine and insensitivity. The towns were in a desperate
situation. They were still royalist, but, nevertheless, they were sacked and
Ferdinand VII's portrait then carried through the streets. There was no
better way of ensuring that his image would be forever associated in the
popular imagination with these atrocities.

In the *llanos* the evil Eusebio Antoñanzas behaved in a similar fashion,
meting out horrifying punishments. His natural cruelty was made worse
by his drunkenness, and he possessed a further defect, rarely found among
the Spanish commanders. He was a thief. What he did not do out of
wickedness, therefore, he did out of greed or insanity. He tortured and
killed not only all the the combatants who fell into his hands, but also
defenseless civilians, and he sacked and burned whole towns.

The truth is that all the members of the horde that Monteverde hurled
against the Republic rivaled each other in wickedness. When they were

in Valencia their chaplain "loudly exhorted the soldiers in a company leaving for San Carlos *to spare nobody above the age of seven.*"[1]

Heredia also wrote about a certain Pascual Martínez, who, although "not worthy even of captaining a galley," soon won Monteverde's confidence because he was a fellow Canary Islander. Heredia reported: "They say that he took pleasure in mistreating the natives of the country in the villages along the route, insulting them with the name of *"creole dogs."* This and similar acts, such as the murder of an old man and his grandchild near La Victoria, was merely a start. "Because of these qualities, Monteverde made him Governor of Caracas in 1812, and Martínez took pleasure there in abusing his former friends and punishing the poor and obscure. The punctilious Luzón, officer of the *pardos,* was exposed to public humiliation in Capuchinos Square, with both his legs dangling from the ignoble stocks, for some gesture he made when Monteverde passed his house. Martínez ordered a colored man, who was crossing the street, to seize hold of Dr. Juan Germán Roscio, who was in the same stocks alongside Luzón and others, and turn him to face the fierce midday sun.... " Martínez was later appointed Governor of the island of Margarita where, according to his report to Spain, "his desire was none other than to annihilate all who conspired against the Crown." His treatment of Arismendi and other peaceful *margariteños* gives some idea of how he set about his task. The royalist Urquinaona tells us: "Thoughout the revolution of 1810, they were no more than passive spectators of events in Caracas. The violence and barbarism of the despicable Martínez turned Arismendi into a monster, thirsty for human blood.... He was gaunt with hunger (in the forest) when he was surprised by the news that the Governor had imprisoned his sons, aged barely eight and nine, and was threatening to shoot them if they did not quickly reveal their father's whereabouts. He emerged from the undergrowth to surrender to his pursuers, who took his goods and put him in a prison from whence he was transferred, together with forty-nine other inhabitants, to the dungeons of La Guaira. His wife lay buried, his sons were orphans, his property was lost and his household was filled with sorrow and worry."[2]

All the Venezuelan provinces were handed over to malefactors of this type, elevated by the caprice of Monteverde. An obscure lieutenant, called Cervériz or Zerbériz, was appointed commander in Cumaná, and his excesses were so scandalous that when he contributed to a public collection after his return to Spain, his own compatriots refused to accept money they believed

1. José Francisco Heredia, *Memorias sobre las revoluciones de Venezuela.* Heredia, born in Santo Domingo, was Regent of the *audiencia* of Caracas and a royalist. He risked his career by attempting, out of respect for the law, to check the barbarism unleashed by Monteverde.
2. Pedro de Urquinaona y Pardo, *Relación documentada del origen y progreso de las Provincias de Venezuela.* Urquinaona, a royalist, was an agent for his government in Venezuela and New Granada.

to have been acquired in an ignominious fashion. Colonel Emeterio Ureña, one of the victors at Bailén and Royal Governor of the province, later claimed that when Cumaná was under his own control, "The loyal vassals were always heard when they sought justice, but not when they suggested nonsense, for there were some hot-heads who thought that their support for the King entitled them to seize the properties of those who belonged to the other party without going through legal channels." But, when Monteverde's nominee took over, "He was given an authority which could not and should not have been given, particularly since Zerbériz had been indicted for his notorious excesses. He was shown favor when he should have received an exemplary punishment, and from a simple lieutenant became a great lord with innumerable jewels, slaves and properties. It is clear that the province rebelled because of these activities, his unpublicized cruelties, and those of similar men."[1]

Throughout the province the judicial system of which Spain was justifiably proud was replaced by arbitrary excesses. Urquinaona tells us: "When the list of suspects was ready, the names of the victims were given, without signature, instruction or any formality, to unruly gangs of the viles Islanders, and they were free to add any names that occurred to them." On another occasion, according to the same source, 1,500 people were imprisoned. The *audiencia,* for its part, wrote to the Regency: "The inhabitants were imprisoned on the basis of verbal reports, their goods were taken and deposited with irresponsible people, and they were exiled without legal process. They thus found themselves criminals without being tried. The justification of some was unknown, it was not known who had ordered the arrest of others, and in other cases the person who had arrested them could not explain the reason for their imprisonment." José Costa y Galli, *fiscal* of the *audiencia,* wrote: "In the land of the Kafirs men could not be treated with greater contempt and disdain."

Some historians have suggested that Monteverde was more weak than cruel, and that what he allowed to happen was much greater than what he did personally. But, in fact, the situation was even more sinister in Caracas. Regent Heredia reported that Monteverde's ante-chamber was filled with "delicate children, the most beautiful women and respectable matrons, all begging for protection even from the *zambo* Palomo, a bully with disgusting habits from Valencia, whom Monteverde had chosen as a constant companion." A corrupt doctor, Antonio Gómez, who ventured to attend the meetings between the regent of the *audiencia* and Monteverde, was the person encharged with converting cruelty into profit. In return for a little money paid to him, those who failed to secure legal protection could persuade the zealous royalists to forget that they were

---

1. Archivo Nacional, Caracas. Sección 'Causas de Infidencia', tomo xxxiii. The rebellion to which Ureña refer is that of 1813, which will be discussed below.

"traitors to the King," "insurgents" and "monsters." José Domingo Díaz filled the comic but repugnant role of mischief maker. An unsuccessful doctor and writer, who turned against the patriots after first supporting them, he had pretensions as a poet, and was commissioned to write sonnets to Monteverde's generosity. According to Heredia he was possessed by the *insanabile vulnus scribendi cacoethis*.[1] He employed his madness in libeling patriots, and as a result of his crafty falsification of events and documents, the history of Venezuela is still filled with cock-and-bull stories. The circumspect General Miyares, Royal Governor of the province of Maracaibo, also complained in a *Manifesto* that "under the authority of Monteverde there was neither security nor repose. The threat of being charged with insurgency quieted unrest, and the slightest complaint was a proof of infidelity."

Nearly all the observers whose opinions have been quoted were royalists, partly because if they were not, what they wrote would lack credibility, but also to stress that many Spaniards genuinely disapproved of Monteverde's wicked policies. It should also be noted that they all pointed out that his violence was the cause of the subsequent creole declaration of war to the death.

Even Antoñanzas, whose cruelties were appalling, but who felt the need to justify himself when the tragic consequences of the situation became apparent, reported to the Regency: "Within twenty-four days of the surrender of Caracas, despite the proclamation of security, the principal families were stricken with grief, as fathers, sons and husbands were carried off to the dungeons in chains. Their laments and fear were attributed to occult machinations."

Monteverde, on the other hand, did not shrink from making his attitude clear. He informed his government: "When I entered this capital and became aware of the character of its inhabitants, I realized that indulgence was a crime, and that tolerance and reserve made criminal men insolent and bold." He decided therefore, that the Constitution of Cádiz should not be applied in Venezuela, which "should be treated according to the law of conquest."[2]

Many patriots suffocated in the dungeons where they were crowded together in chains, and other died from hunger and thirst. In Puerto Cabello the customs superintendent threw chemicals into the castle dungeons to asphyxiate the prisoners. When the prison commandant reported this to Monteverde, he replied simply: "That is the fate of those whose turn it is to die."[3]

---

1. Quoted in Mario Briceño Iragorry, *El Regente Heredia* (Caracas, 1947), p. 120.
2. Quoted by Gil Fortoul, i, p. 275, and by Blanco Fombona in his prologue to J. V. González's *Biografía de Ribas,* p. xxix.
3. Quoted by Dr. Angel Francisco Brice in his *El Bolívar de Marx ampliado por Madariaga* (Caracas, 1952), p. 55.

Other prisoners were shipped to Spain in the most inhuman conditions, with a report from Monteverde describing them as "monsters, the origin and cause of all the problems and innovations in America."

This sordid setting was momentarily touched by noble pride when Juana Padrón de Montilla, a woman of attractive personality, "endowed with great talents, a lively imagination, and a strength of character capable of overcoming the most grave difficulties in any circumstances" went to demand of Monteverde that he should observe the terms of surrender agreed with Miranda, in the case of her sons, the young republicans Mariano and Thomas Montilla. After waiting a long time without being given an audience, she departed, indignant. In a note she left for Monteverde, she reproved him for his discourtesy and asked: "Why do you want to govern, if you do not listen?"[1] Like one of the heroines of Lope de Vega or Calderón, she was defending not so much her sons as the Spanish tradition of "good government."

Given episodes like this, which were less rare than is usually believed, it can be seen that Monteverde destroyed not only the Republic's political structure but also its basic principles, which in part were inherited from the Spaniards. It was under Monteverde that the laws and moral principles which had always been respected in Venezuela were violated for the first time. It was his fault that the nascent resentment between the two sides degenerated into war to the death. It was in his ante-chambers that government was first stained with acts of complicity and favoritism, because men like Antonio Gómez and Palomo had never before had the opportunity of turning terror into a lucrative traffic in influence. Monteverde usurped the authority of his own superiors, Miyares and Ceballos, and he mocked the military hierarchy with appointments such as that of the abject Cervériz over Colonel Emeterio Ureña, victor at Bailén, and royal governor of the province of Cumaná.

The treatment of Miranda was the worst feature of this destruction of human ideals and justice. He had not been responsible alone for the surrender. On June 14, 1812, when the patriots still held Puerto Cabello and the east of Caracas, the licenciate Miguel José Sanz, who was without doubt the most acute political thinker in Venezuela, considered that the situation was already untenable. On this date, he wrote to Miranda: "After I became acquainted in the Secretariat of State with the political condition of Venezuela, I formed the idea that her liberty and independence could not be achieved without effective aid from European powers. The situation in which our soldiers, our agriculture, our commerce and our revenues are placed, the partisan spirit that animates our compatriots, and the

---

1. Archivo Nacional de Caracas. Sección 'Capitanía General,' uncatalogued documents.

scarcity of men to carry out the enterprise have convinced me of that truth. It is impossible to furnish and equip the necessary military forces, with so small a population and with only the revenues that the province of Caracas actually affords. . . We cannot sustain ourselves without agriculture, commerce, arms and money. The greater part of our territory is occupied by our royalist enemies while our internal enemies make crude and perilous war upon us. These internal enemies are ignorance, envy, and pride. Such evils not only render your measures ineffective, but disturb and confound everything. If you wish to have the glory of making your native land independent and of securing for her the enjoyment of liberty, do not depend upon the means available here. Seek help abroad. . . It is a mistake to try for extraordinary results with ordinary methods. It is essential to consider extraordinary means. . . ."[1]

If we consider that Sanz was right in his lucid analysis, in judging that Venezuela was incapable of securing independence by her own efforts, why should Miranda be reproached for reaching the same conclusion? It is true that Bolívar was later to achieve the impossible, but if, like Miranda, he had been eliminated after his early failures, en 1814, or 1816, or 1818, the independence of South America might well have been set back for a long time. In Miranda's time, moreover, the people had not steeled themselves to withstand the sacrifices they were later to accept, and Miranda, unlike Bolívar, could not count upon a proper army with trained officers to overcome the political anarchy and sustain the desperate twelve-year long effort which culminated in Ayacucho. Miranda's situation was so difficult that even though he would have preferred to resign as Commander-in-Chief rather than surrender, it was impossible to find a replacement. The federal government had nobody to put in his place.

Miranda intended, therefore, to use his remaining forces to obtain from Monteverde a treaty that would save Caracas and the patriots. He consulted with representatives of the federal executive, the judicial authorities and other high officials, according to a formal Act signed in La Victoria. Several files in the Archivo Nacional de Caracas (sections 'Causas de Infidencia" and 'Ilustres Próceres') show that many politicians and soldiers shared his attitude.

As far as his own future was concerned, Miranda intended to go to New Granada, as Bolívar did in 1812 and 1814, and recommence the struggle there. He could count on his friend Nariño in the neighboring country, which had signed a treaty of reciprocal aid with Venezuela. He hoped also to be able to obtain aid from England or the United States.[2] But when the surrender was signed, with many patriots ignorant of what had pre-

---

1. Marquis de Rojas, *El General Miranda* (París, 1884), p. 275.
2. Miranda personally confided this plan to Pedro Gual. Gual, who remained passionately faithful to him, published the information in 1843. See Blanco y Azpurúa, iii, p. 758.

cipitated it, the rumors which had always circulated about Miranda were intensified. The anger and fear of the great majority was expressed in a flood of hostility toward him, and many of those responsible for the defeat joined in the incriminations to absolve themselves.

Miranda finally decided to sail abroad from La Guaira. On the night of July 30 he arrived at the port, where he was awaited by the English corvette *Sapphire.* He did not embark immediately, however, and at dawn a group of his junior officers, including Bolívar, succeeded in their wretched plan to arrest him. While it was still dark, they went to the house where he was sleeping. "The conspirators first approached Soublette, the Commander-in-Chief's secretary and aid. The General was sleeping soundly when Soublette knocked at the door of his chamber, and, mistaking the reason for the call, asked, *'Isn't it too early?'* When he realized his mistake he said calmly, "Tell them to wait; I will be with them soon.' When this reply was passed to them the leaders were willing to wait because they had taken full precautions, and both the house and the street were surrounded. A few minutes later, the Commander-in-Chief appeared before them. He was dressed from head to toe, and both his appearance and his gestures revealed the firm tranquillity of his spirit. Without preamble, Bolívar told him that he was a prisoner. With his left hand Miranda took hold of Soublette's right arm, which held a lantern, raised it high, as if to help his vision, and after surveying the participants one by one, said simply, *'A tumult, a tumult, these people are only capable of stirring up tumults.'* Without more ado, he handed himself over to the guard waiting at the door, which escorted him, as arranged, to the castle of San Carlos."[1]

Those responsible for what took place were Dr. Miguel Peña, political governor of the city, Colonel Manuel María de las Casas, its military commander, and Bolívar, leader of the officers who decided to arrest Miranda and who actually committed the deed. But their subsequent behavior showed that the motives of each of them were quite different. On July 31, Colonel de las Casas informed the Commander of the *Sapphire,* "by order of the Commander-in-Chief of the troops of His Catholic Majesty, Domingo Monteverde," that, in order to prevent the flight of people involved in the revolution, no ships would be allowed to leave the harbor.[2] Shortly afterwards he handed over the fortress and he remained on the Spanish side for the rest of the war. It is difficult to justify his weakness or his offense. Historians who try to reduce his responsibility can point out only that, instead of trying to distinguish himself with the royalists, Casas lived

1. Ricardo Becerra, *Vida de don Francisco de Miranda* (Editorial América, Madrid), p. 386. Becerra married one of Soublette's daughters, and was given this dramatic account by him.
2. Quoted by Mariano Picón Salas in his *Biografía de Miranda.* Of course both Peña and Casas had been appointed by Miranda to the posts which they occupied when they arrested him.

"quietly on his *hacienda* in Tuy," to quote Lecuna. Dr. Miguel Peña remained faithful to the republican cause, despite some hesitation, and dedicated his whole life to it. Nonetheless, many observers have regarded his conduct as particularly odious, because he had a reason for personal resentment against Miranda, namely a fine imposed by the latter upon his father during the Valencia campaign. He showed himself subsequently to be a vindictive intriguer, which leads one to the conclusion that he committed his crime out of petty spite.[1] If this was his motive, it makes him more repulsive in a way, but at the same time it acquits him of treason against his country.

The case of Bolívar was very different. He was incapable of either treason or personal resentments. We have already seen that the differences of opinion about the conduct of military operations that supposedly alienated him from Miranda were invented, or at least exaggerated subsequently with the aim of justifying involvement in the arrest. His letters to Miranda about the loss of Puerto Cabello, written only a few days earlier, showed his continuing affection and obedience. So the reason for Bolívar's turn about must be sought in the state of mind which the letters revealed. If he considered himself deserving of being put under the lowest officer because he had lost Puerto Cabello, then it is not surprising that, amazed and enraged at Miranda's capitulation, he should have directed this same attitude against Miranda, attempting, with his fellow-officers, to obtain an explanation for his conduct.

Although it was clearly unjust to blame and condemn Miranda for what had happened, this explanation is the one suggested by all the reliable documents. Biographers are asked too frequently to humanize their heroes, that is, to reveal their weaknesses and mistakes, but the process should also involve showing them the tolerance that is considered valid for other men. We all insist that our acts are legitimate or excusable, if they can be "explained." Should not great men be judged by this same standard in the realization that they too experience the confusion, anger, fear and anxiety which make other men irresponsible? All these elements were present in the whirlwind of events that occurred in the last ten days of July 1812, between the capitulation of San Mateo and the murky dawn of La Guaira. Most historians who have examined the confrontation between the two men seem to have thought either that Bolívar's conduct could be explained only by presenting Miranda's behavior in an equivocal light, or that any lament about Miranda's fate or any stress upon America's debt to him could be only to Bolívar's detriment. We do not accept this

---

1. Mario Briceño Iragorry is particularly severe with him. He says in *La tragedia de Peñalver* (Caracas, 1949), p. 26: "He did not forgive Miranda for the punishment imposed upon his father during the Valencia campaign, and, despite having received favors from him subsequently, he imprisoned the Precursor in La Guaira and handed him over to the royalist authorities."

dilemma. A straightforward narrative of what occurred is sufficient to exonerate both heroes.

Bolívar was depressed by the loss of Puerto Cabello, but his natural combativeness soon stimulated him. He was far from thinking that the struggle was over. This is made clear by a personal letter to his sister-in-law, Josefa María Tinoco, who had written to him on July 27, expressing her anxiety at his absence and seeking his protection for her three sons. He replied: "My dear Josefa María: My first concern has been to arrange that Juan Vicente's property goes to his sons, and that you receive a pension of fifty *pesos* a month until it yields revenue, when you shall have all of it. Antonia has orders to assist you as she would me, and I know that she will do it better than I could. I am in a hurry and perhaps I will not be able to see you, for honor and my country call me to their assistance."[1]

It seems that Bolívar and his La Guaira companions planned to arrest Miranda, stir up a reaction against Monteverde, and make a surprise attack upon Caracas. This was the explanation given by Restrepo and O'Leary, the two historians closest to the events. It seems reasonable to accept that this was Bolívar's intention, and that he was foiled because Casas handed over the fortress to Monteverde's men on the morning of July 31. What is quite clear is that there are no grounds for supposing that Bolívar intended to deliver Miranda to Monteverde. It would have been physically impossible for him to do so, given that he intended either to renew the struggle or flee the country.

This foolish calumny arose from Bolívar's unfortunate association with Casas, whom he joined in the belief that he was a sincere patriot. Monteverde contributed to the confusion when, after granting Bolívar a passport to leave the country, he tried to justify himself to the Spanish government by expressly identifying Casas, Peña and Bolívar as members of the group who should be "pardoned of their misconduct" for having arrested Miranda. He reported: "Included in this category, Your Excellency, are Manuel María de las Casas, Miguel Peña and Simón Bolívar. Casas and Peña were charged with the governing of La Guaira, the former with military government and the latter with political control, when, in the days before my army entered Caracas, the rebels of this province and their dictator Miranda tried to escape from this port, taking with them the contents of H. M.'s treasury."

"As soon as I reached this city, I gave peremptory orders for the detention of the rebel leaders who were at La Guaira, but fortunately by the time that I reached that port, although I had marched with the greatest rapidity, Casas had, with the advice of Peña and by the aid of Bolívar, thrust

---

1. *Cartas del Libertador*, i, p. 26.

Miranda into a prison and also detained all his companions who were in that port. In this transaction Casas risked his life, which he would have lost if his orders had not been carried out. Peña and Bolívar ran a similar risk. Casas finished his task in a most satisfactory manner. He had previously disobeyed the orders of the despot that he should place the Europeans and Canary Islanders of the vicinity on a pontoon which should be scuttled upon the slightest occasion, that he should not demand receipts for the sums of money embarked, and other related instructions. .... I cannot forget the interesting services of Casas nor those of Bolívar and Peña. Because of these services I have not touched their persons, simply conceding to Bolívar passports for foreign countries; for his influence and connections here might be dangerous in the present circumstances. I hope that Your Excellency will bring this decision to the attention of the Supreme Council of Regency for its sovereign approval, and so that, if it sees fit, it might show its gratitude for the important services of Casas."[1]

Despite some inaccuracies, such as the claim that Miranda had ordered that the Europeans and Canary Islanders be put upon a pontoon to be drowned, this document is important because it underlines the differing attitudes and subsequent conduct of Casas, Peña and Bolívar, and that Monteverde considered Bolívar dangerous.

Several months later the cruel Canary Islander informed the Minister of War: "...When I entered this capital I was short of good troops, and at the same time I had to send some of my men to deal with the rebellion of the Negroes of Curiepe, which fortunately soon ended. So I did not court-martial and shoot Miranda and those who tried to flee with him, taking the State's money with them. This was the powerful motive which led me to be lenient and to give passports to three or four of them despite my regret and my fears."[2]

There can be no doubt, then, about Monteverde's reason for giving Bolívar a passport. But the Liberator's enemies subsequently insisted upon stressing his complicity with Casas, glossing over the fundamental differences which separated them. It should also be remembered that Monteverde granted a passport to José Félix Ribas, and even recommended him to the governor of Curaçao, because they were related. The same motive would have induced him to be lenient with Bolívar, who was Ribas's nephew-in-law.

But the decisive factor in Bolívar's favor was the influence of a generous Spaniard, Francisco Iturbe. Nine years later Bolívar described what had happened, when he wrote to Congress asking it not to confiscate Iturbe's property: "In the year 1812, the treasonable act of Colonel Manuel María Casas, then Commander of La Guaira, placed that

1. Gil Fortoul, *Historia* (1930 edition), i, p. 267.
2. *Boletín de la Academia Nacional de la Historia* (Caracas), no. 16, p. 460.

town and all our leaders and officers who had been attempting its evacuation in the hands of General Monteverde. I was not able to avoid the unhappy fate of being introduced to a tyrant, as my companions-in-arms would not venture to join me either in castigating that traitor or in selling our lives dearly. I was presented to Monteverde by a man as generous as I was miserable. Don Francisco Iturbe presented me to the victor in the following manner: *'This is the Commander of Puerto Cabello, Simón Bolívar, for whom I have given my bond. If he is to be punished, punish me instead. My life is pledged for his.'* So, if the properties of Francisco Iturbe must be confiscated, I pledge mine for his, even as he pledged his life for mine. And should the Sovereign Congress be willing to pardon him, I am the person who would be favored and my possessions would benefit."[1]

Iturbe told Bolívar's first biographer, Felipe Larrazábal, that, when he presented his petition on behalf of Bolívar, Monteverde replied, "All right" and, turning to his secretary, Bernardo Muros, said: "The gentleman is granted a passport in recompense for the service he did the King in arresting Miranda." Bolívar had remained silent until then, but when he heard what Monteverde said, he promptly responded that he had seized Miranda in order to punish a traitor to his country, not to serve the King. This retort annoyed Monteverde, but Iturbe insisted that he deliver the passport since his word was pledged. After paying his respects he said jocularly to Muros, a close friend: "Come on, take no notice of this hot-head; give him his passport and let him go."[2]

Although at this tragic time Bolívar must have been more exasperated than ever with Miranda, it is difficult to believe that he would have called him a traitor. It is very possible that Iturbe applied to Miranda the word that Bolívar used for Casas.[3] But if Bolívar really did refer to Miranda in these terms it might have been because of the influence of the Marquis de Casa León. We know from a letter Bolívar sent from Cuzco in 1825 to his sister, María Antonia, that in 1812 he hid from Monteverde in the house of Casa León, who had been Miranda's Director General of Finances. Although this seems to have been after the La Guaira affair, there is no doubt that Bolívar, like all the other revolutionaries of 1810, was on intimate terms with Casa León, who was soon to show, to borrow Gil

---

1. *Cartas del Libertador,* ii, p. 385.
2. Felipe Larrazábal, *Vida de Bolívar* (1883 edition), i, p. 137.
3. It seems, however, that with respect to Casas himself, Bolívar finally acknowledged the extenuating circumstances which he alleged, and that they re-established friendly relations in 1826. This is confirmed by various affidavits, including one from Juana Bolívar, which Casas's sons published in Caracas in 1843 in a pamphlet entitled *Defensa documentada de la conducta del Comandante de La Guaira, señor Manuel María de las Casas.* It argues convincingly that at least Casas cannot be regarded as a traitor to his country. A facsimile edition was published in Caracas in 1965.

Fortoul's caustic phrase, "that since 1808 he had been betraying both the Republic and the Monarchy." He hurriedly joined the winning side, and did not shrink from drawing up for Monteverde a list of the leading patriots, his former colleagues, who were to be rounded up and imprisoned. He said of Miranda: "Since Miranda is a person whom the wicked would choose to lead them in any tumultuous enterprise, I consider it very dangerous to allow him to remain in this province, even as a prisoner. Like all the rest, he should be sent to Spain without a moment's delay." Considering this behavior and every thing which Casa León did subsequently—he became known as the Venezuelan Fouché—there is some foundation for believing that he might have turned Bolívar against Miranda in those chaotic days as part of his design of dividing the patriots.

Bolívar was certainly unaware of Miranda's intention of continuing the war from New Granada. Indeed, it is probable that since he had no official post, he was ignorant of many of the major developments which had precipitated the surrender, such as the scandalous desertion of the patriot troops at La Victoria or the depredations of the revolting slaves to the east of Caracas. With that vile intriguer whispering into his ear night and day, it did not take much to make him believe that Miranda was a traitor.

Monteverde admitted, as we have seen, that he intended from the first to violate the terms of the surrender. With great regret, as he put it, he gave passports to three or four patriots, but the rest were imprisoned or sent to Spain in very cruel circumstances. Miranda was put in the subterranean dungeons of La Guaira and later in those of Puerto Cabello. Although there was absolutely no possibility that the prisoners might escape, they were "secured" with irons and chains. Miranda, a contemporary tells us, was "for some time reduced to a diet of bread and water, because this seemed the least harmful to him and he feared being poisoned. But he was not left without company for long. His cell and all the others were crammed with miserable victims of all ages and classes without any segregation. The Spaniards made a show of doing this to mock the liberty and equality proclaimed by the patriots. Their fears of poison then disappeared."[1]

Conditions were made worse by the tormenting heat, which at that time of year is unbearable on the Venezuelan coast. It was impossible to keep clean and Miranda, who was accustomed to taking a daily bath, suffered terribly. The unbreathable air of the damp cells was made even fouler by the overcrowding, and by the fact that the prisoners had to perform their natural functions in a communal pit within the enclosure. Rats, flies, bugs

1. Rojas, *El General Miranda* (París, 1884)., p. 773, William White to John Stevens of London, Puerto España, Trinidad, July 6, 1813.

and other pests troubled the prisoners day and night, and the majority of them were in a terrible state because of dysentery, rheumatism, infected wounds and bruises, and the weakness caused by their deficient diet.

Perhaps Miranda remembered the prisons he had known in France. There, at least, it had been possible to remain decent and feel free to think. Monteverde's vile favorites would have been furious to hear him reciting Virgil or commenting on Tacitus. In France a delightful woman, the beautiful, fragrant, luminous Delphine de Custine, had appeared before the prisoners like a heavenly vision. In Venezuela they heard only the obscenities of the soldiers. When they picked out the dark shadow of a Negro slave emerging from the gloom which seemed to hang from the walls, they never knew whether he was coming to exercise the terrible prerogatives with which the jailers were invested. In this prison, as in those of the cities, the republican "monsters" were abandoned to the caprice of the "faithful vassals," and their fears of new sufferings and humiliations increased with every moment. As we have seen, some patriots even died from nauseating and asphyxiating substances thrown into their cells.

For eight months Miranda was allowed no contact with the outside world until the *audiencia,* which was striving to re-establish the traditional judicial system and to have the terms of surrender observed, was finally able to secure permission for him to submit a petition to it.

Miranda had to write it on his knees with his feet in fetters, and he could work only at midday when the gloom of the prison lifted slightly. But his pride was unshaken and he remained true to his stern intellectual discipline, treating the surrender as an important matter of state, rather than as a personal matter which involved his own fate. He argued convincingly that it should be observed for both moral and political reasons, pointing out that a reconciliation between Spaniards and creoles "would open to peninsular Spaniards a secure and permanent asylum, no matter how the struggle that they were waging against France might terminate." He observed, too, that the newly-promulgated constitution would be laughable if Spain began by denying its benefits to America. The sweat running beneath his shirt with the persistence of the filthy insects which tormented him at night brought his attention back to the immediate situation and he turned to the abuses he had seen: "... These victims were conducted to the port of La Guaira. Some, mounted on beasts of burden, were tied hand and foot on pack saddles. Others were driven on foot. All were threatened, outraged, and exposed to the indignities of the persons who escorted them. While in transit they were even prevented from responding to the demands of nature... Then, with horror I beheld scenes repeated in Venezuela which my eyes had witnessed in France. I saw at La Guaira droves of men belonging to the most illustrious classes treated like bandits. I saw them buried near me in those terrible prisons.

I saw both rich and poor, venerable old men, tender maidens, artisans and even priests bound with chains and condemned to breathe the mephitic air that extinguished artificial light, contaminated the blood, and inevitably prepared the way for death. Lastly, I saw sacrificed to this cruelty citizens distinguished for probity and talent who perished almost immediately in those dungeons, not only deprived of the aid that humanity dictates for the alleviation of physical suffering, but also deprived of the spiritual succor prescribed by our holy religion. They died in the arms of their comrades, citizens who would a thousand times rather have died with arms in their hands when they surrendered than have submitted to such outrages and treatment." Perhaps Miranda thought for a moment of describing the infected prison in which he was kept in shackles, but he said nothing at all about it. He shrank from the idea, because an account of what the Spaniards had done to him would also involve a discussion of his sufferings at the hands of the Venezuelans, and he would not allow his experiences to be used to shame them. Had he not seen comparable injustice in the United States, where Washington was surrounded by rivalries and petty intrigues? In France, had he not felt sad when he contrasted the heroism perceived by the outside world with the cowardly fear of Robespierre, the fickleness of the mobs and the power of wicked men like Fouché and fools like Barras? He remembered, too, that in his afflicted Venezuela, despite everything, he had been given respect and affection by generous men who were comparable to the purest among the Romans, men like Bello, Sanz, Gual, Espejo, the enthusiastic Delpech and the brilliant Vicente Salias. At Valencia and La Victoria anonymous mulattoes had stood at his side, zealously learning to fight and to be republicans. He was determined, therefore, that his name should not be used in the future as a symbol of sensational complaints against his country. When he turned to his own experiences in the petition, he said simply that he believed he had fulfilled his duties "with the honor and zeal of which I was capable."

Throughout his life Miranda had remained faithful to the demanding standards of honor, patriotism and bravery, found in his books and on his travels. The great men of history were now calling him to join them, for he felt that he was already condemned, as good as dead, about to become an exemplary hero. He raised his gaze, again shook his white, leonine head in a firm negative, and signed: "Dungeons of the Castle of Puerto Cabello, March 8, 1813. M.P.S. Francisco de Miranda."[1]

Miranda thus showed once again that despite a life of adventure, there was nothing of the adventurer in him. Wherever he went he seemed to prove the rule which Emerson was later to express: "If a man remains firm in his

---

1. Rojas, *op. cit.*, p. 764.

convictions, the world will revolve around him." For this reason his life was filled with proud refusals. He declined to remain in Russia, although Catherine herself offered him flatteries which would have dazzled any man. He risked his career and his life in saying "No" to Dumouriez. He rejected both Pitt and Wellington, in order to avoid serving against Spain or France. When he realized that he would not get the aid he sought to liberate "Colombia", he refused to continue enjoying the gilded refuge of his London house, and he left with three miserable ships to risk his life for his goal. In the same way, two pathetic negatives marked the end of his career. When he reached La Guaira, his friends and the captain of the *Sapphire* pleaded with him to go on board the ship immediately, but he did not want to show indecorous haste, and this doomed him. The document he was writing for the *audiencia* offered him his last chance to justify his conduct for posterity by denouncing the cruel villainy which had paralyzed his efforts to defend the Republic. And once again he refused.

Despite his unfortunate circumstance, destiny, which had been so generous with him in the past, gave him a further opportunity to demonstrate his irresistible personality. He was taken to Castillo del Morro in Puerto Rico, where the Spanish Governor, Salvador Meléndez, and a Venezuelan royalist, Andrés Level de Goda, like so many men before them, fell under the spell of the stupendous philosopher-General. They tried to make his confinement less rigorous. Meléndez sent him books and food from his own table, while Level de Goda visited him often, sharing with him numerous cups of lemon tea, a favorite drink of Miranda's since his youth, and discussing with him news from Europe, politics, history and philosophy. "He enslaved everybody with his voice, his logic and his fame," this admirer wrote later. Miranda had had the same effect throughout Europe and the United States on politicians, soldiers, men of the world, women, artists, Catherine of Russia and Madame de Sabran, Adams and Napoleon, Lavater and the bishop of Antwerp, when they saw him in the full force of his manhood, apparently predestined for great things.

At the end of 1814 Miranda was transported to Spain, where he was confined in the castle of La Carraca, near Cádiz. He arrived at the height of conservative reaction. Ferdinand VII believed, as he later announced, that liberalism and democracy were the "fertile source" of all misfortunes. The palace advisers demanded an "absolutely absolute" king, and the mobs in the streets cried "death to the Constitution; long live chains."

Nevertheless, Miranda still managed to make secret contact with his English friends, John Turnbull and Nicholas Vansittart, who had always believed in him and were now trying to save him. After the failure of efforts they and other faithful friends made to persuade the British government to intercede on Miranda's behalf, an escape plan was worked out. A woman, referred to in the secret papers as Antonia de Salis, risked her life at the Spanish end. Everything seemed ready, and in the middle of March 1816, Miranda wrote to Duncan and Co. that he had arranged to leave "next Wednesday or Thursday on that little journey about which you know." But suddenly, on March 25, three days before his 66th birthday, he suffered an apoplectic fit.

At his side was another of those men who enoble the human species, his faithful attendant Pedro José Morán. It is not clear whether he was a Spaniard or, as some suppose, a Venezuelan from La Guaira. Morán reported the misfortune to the Englishmen connected with Miranda, adding: "He recovered his senses, but he was left with a severe, putrid fever. Forty-eight hours later he was seized by an inflammation in the head and a hemorrhage from the mouth which reduced him to the last extremity. I helped him with the greatest care, because my happiness depends upon his health."

It was all in vain. On July 14, Morán wrote again: "This day, at five minutes past one in the morning, my beloved master Don Francisco de Miranda, delivered his soul to his Creator. The priests and friars have not allowed me to perform any funeral rites. In the same condition in which he expired, with mattress, sheets and other bedclothes they seized hold of him and carried him away for interment. They immediately afterwards came back and took away his clothes and other belongings to burn them."

XVII

TO BE
THE LIBERATOR
MEANS MORE THAN
EVERYTHING ELSE

ITH VENEZUELA DOMINATED
by Monteverde, Bolívar left for Curaçao, and in October of the same
year, 1812, he left this island for Cartagena, in New Granada.
The New Granadans had been no more successful than the Venezuelans
in their first steps towards independence. Although the Spanish
leaders had failed to exploit the situation to restore their authority, the
dissension which divided the patriots had brought civil war. The principal cause of, or pretext for, the split was the preference which many
politicians and almost all the provinces felt for the federal system, while
the central government had to ensure that the means of defense were
not dispersed. It also happened in some cases, of course, that one province tried to dominate another, invoking first one principle and then
the other, or that several of them tried to seize control of the federation.
These misfortunes were crowned by the fact that even the men who had
the capacity and experience to create national unity —the venerable Nariño, for example— had had to compromise their prestige in the bitter
contests.
It is easy to imagine the impression that this situation made upon Bolívar. He had realized from the beginning of the revolution that the military defeat of the Spaniards was the first priority, but that this victory
could not be won without unity of command and bold, speedy action. He
had been filled with despair to see the Republic collapse in Venezuela
because of the failure of the politicians to recognize these principles. He
now found in New Granada the same shallow discussions and the same

suicidal obstruction that had doomed his own country. The memory was to remain with him forever, almost as an obsession, and it is vital to be aware of it in order to understand his attitudes, especially up to the year 1819.

It was this spiritual shock which led to the flourishing within him of what in the future was to be his most important characteristic, namely his duality as a *caudillo* and a political thinker. When he reached Cartagena, like most of the Venezuelan officers, he asked the government for military duties, but he also planned to analyze the causes of the disaster suffered by Venezuela, present them as a lesson to the republicans and, reaffirming the idea of continental unity, convince them that the emancipation of America and the future of these nations demanded that they abandon forever regional egotism and jealousies. These were the aims of an declaration that he sent to Congress and of the *Memoria* which he began with the pathetic words: "I am, Granadans, a son of unhappy Caracas...."

Today the unprepared reader cannot easily understand the intellectual importance of these first expositions of Bolívar's political ideas. Their basic principles subsequently penetrated the collective awareness so thoroughly and have been repeated so often that it is difficult to appreciate their novelty when they were first propounded. But we can understand their impact if we compare them with other documents of the period which incorporate the imprecise stammering of a continent which had not produced political thinkers. Other proclamations and expositions, whether produced by important American functionaries or by jurists trying to justify and stimulate the nascent cause of independence, had invariably followed the model of meticulous Spanish casuistry applied to the defense of the rights of Americans, or almost slavishly reproduced North American or French ideas. Bolívar resolutely ignored both paths and with an extraordinarily precise, direct and arresting style—something previously unknown to the Spanish Americans—embarked upon an exposition of our problems which was as wise in its appreciations of detail as it was daring in its general conclusions. His analysis, although directed in the first place to an examination of the immediate past which tormented him, anticipated implicitly the future character of the war, posed questions about collective psychology, and extended to the most serious political problems which the republican reorganization of these countries was to cause.

The causes to which Bolívar attributed the loss of Venezuela have been adopted by all subsequent historians: The federal system, "which enabled enemies to penetrate deep into the heart of the State and to occupy a large part of the province before the question of whether federal or provincial troops should go out to meet them was settled;" the costly and inefficient system of popular militias, established because of "the firm opposition to raising seasoned, disciplined troops, prepared to take their place on the field of battle and indoctrinated with the desire to defend liberty with success and honor;" the excessive tolerance, thanks to which "every conspiracy was followed by acquittal, and every acquittal by another conspiracy;" and finally, paper money and the earthquake.

He emphasized that the first indication of weakness shown by the Supreme *Junta* was its failure to subdue Coro, the city from which the royalist expedition which destroyed the Republic was to depart. He concluded from this that New Granada and the rest of America were in danger of suffering the same fate, because "Coro is to Caracas as Caracas is to all America.... With Spain in possession of the territory of Venezuela, she can easily draw upon it for men, provisions, and munitions of war, and her armies, under the direction of leaders who have had experience against those great masters of warfare, the French, can move inland from the provinces of Barinas and Maracaibo to the farthest confines of South America."

At first sight this conclusion seems chauvinistic but it endorses almost literally what intendant Abalos had secretly reported to his government sixty years earlier. The same route of penetration was also indicated in Miranda's plans for the liberation of the continent. The Spanish government attempted to follow it, when it sent the Morillo expedition and, finally, Bolívar himself was to use it.

These early writings of Bolívar are also significant because they contain important clues to his psychology. His two fundamental ideas —that all the people of America were linked to a common destiny, and that they needed, provisionally, to subject themselves to efficient, energetic government which would guide their republican reorganization—later seemed suspicious because they were seen in the context of his personal control. In 1812, however, there were no grounds for doubting his sincerity. He was simply one of many patriot officers dispersed by defeat, an anonymous "son of unhappy Caracas." He felt the unity of America so intimately that he addressed the Granadans as "follow-citizens," and although he showed that he was still bitter towards Miranda because of the surrender, he adopted the latter's phraseology by twice referring to Caracas as "the cradle of *Colombian* independence."

As far as the constitutional organization of the new States was concerned, he said what he was to repeat at Angostura in 1819 and in Bolivia in 1826: "I believe that, unless we centralize our American governments, our enemies will gain every advantage. We will inevitably be involved in the horrors of civil strife... The popular elections held by the simple people of the country and by the scheming inhabitants of the city add a further obstacle to our practice of federation, because the former are so ignorant that they cast their votes mechanically, and the latter so ambitious that they convert everything into factions."

He pointed out: "We were given philosophers for leaders, philanthropy for legislation, dialectic for tactics, and sophists for soldiers," and he expressed the hope that "the terrible and exemplary lessons which that defunct Republic has supplied may induce America to mend her ways and correct her shortcomings in unity, strength and energy."

The passion with which Bolívar wrote made his observations more pointed but he rarely exaggerated. He stressed: "What weakened the Venezuelan government most was the federal form it adopted in keeping with the exaggerated precepts of the rights of man. By authorizing self-government, this form disrupts social contracts and reduces nations to anarchy. Such was the true state of the Confederation. Each province governed itself independently. Following this example, each city demanded like powers. . . ." He then formulated the question which Americans were to repeat ceaselessly in the years to come: "What country in the world, however well trained and republican it may be, can, amidst internal factions and foreign war, be governed by so complicated and weak a system as the federal? No, this system cannot possibly be maintained during the turbulence of battle and political strife. It is essential that a government mold itself, so to speak, to the nature of the circumstances, the times, and the men that comprise it. If these factors are prosperity and peace, the government should be mild and protecting; but if they are turbulence and disaster, it should be stern and arm itself with a firmness that matches the dangers, without regard for laws or constitutions until happiness and peace have been re-established."

A few months earlier Bolívar had been nothing more than the humiliated leader at Puerto Cabello and, at La Guaira, the truculent leader of mutineers. Now, he was discoursing on the problems of the continent with the aplomb of an experienced statesman. The transformation began during his years of study and meditation in Paris. It was completed during the three years in Caracas between 1807 and 1810 that preceded his political initiation, years in which the influence of the strict rationality of Andrés Bello was important. It was this intense intellectual preparation that gave Bolívar the capacity for systematic thought, searching for ideas, or rather realities instead of simple words. He was turned into a man capable of creating his own concepts.

Even more impressive was his emergence as a military leader, which occurred at almost the same time. His first posting was to the small town of Barrancas, with seventy men under his command and subordinant to a French adventurer called Pedro Labatut. He took to the field immediately and began to increase and improve his forces while fighting the enemy bands that controlled the banks of the Magdalena River.

He took the town of Tenerife, defeated several groups of enemy guerrillas, and flushed them out of Guamal, Banco, Tamalameque and Puerto Real de Ocaña. Sometimes the enemy was tricked or intimidated by Bolívar's aggression. In the encounter at Chiriguaná he captured four well-equipped vessels that they had on the river, and then went on to occupy the city of Ocaña. On some days he marched hundreds of kilometers in triumph, and the result was that his forces, now five hundred strong, controlled the whole of the Magdalena River.

It was at this point that Colonel Manuel del Castillo, Commander-in-Chief in Pamplona, asked for his assistance against the royalists led by Colonel Ramón Correa, whose 1,400 men were threatening the Granadan frontier from Venezuela. Bolívar prepared to go to his aid, but he though that he should first consult the government in Cartagena, to which he was responsible. On this occasion, fortunately, the common cause was not compromised by delay and regional selfishness. The President-Governor of Cartagena, Manuel Rodríguez Torices, immediately issued the required authorization and ordered, moreover, that Bolívar's forces be strengthened. The government of the Union also formally requested Bolívar's aid, and he set out for Pamplona.

Bolívar was now confronted by the forces of nature which he had sworn on the day of the earthquake to overcome. Even the best roads in America were poor, but the route facing him across the *cordillera* was to be a definitive test of his temperament and his organizing ability. Lecuna describes it as follows: "The only route from Ocaña to Salazar crossed a rugged plateau for some leagues before ascending to the ridge through the channels or clefts cut by water, which were wet and slippery underfoot. It continued along the steep mountain face through a cold, empty region in which rains fell frequently. It was the first march of this type for the *caudillo* who was to cross the *cordillera* of the Andes in all directions."[1] Bolívar managed to preserve his little army despite desertions and enemy attacks. He took it across the powerful River Zulia, with the aid of only one canoe, and immediately attacked Correa at San José de Cúcuta. Once again he won a complete victory, and he captured the enemy's artillery. The Granadan government granted him the title of citizen of the Union, promoted him to the rank of Brigadier-General, and gave him command of the Cúcuta division.

Bolívar had argued in his Cartagena *Memoria* "that every defensive action is harmful and ruinous for those who wage it, as it weakens them without hope of recovery." The best proof of this principle was provided by these triumphs, which had saved the Granadan frontier by means of a bold offensive against superior forces. Although his memorial was addressed to the people, this lesson was meant for the politicians who were

---

1. Lecuna, *Crónica razonada de las guerras de Bolívar,* i, p. 11.

still the arbiters of the war. Although he was now on the threshold of Venezuela, and anxious to cotinue his triumphal gallop, towards "unhappy Caracas" —he again used this phrase in a proclamation issued after the victory— he had to wait once more for permission to advance. Because of his impatience he had already broken with Labatut, and he was on the point of breaking with del Castillo. He managed, however, to restrain himself, and he acknowledged in his proclamation that he had been "generously protected by the governments of Cartagena and the Union." His report to the confederation noted obediently: "I understand that I must not advance any further than La Grita."

Bolívar had to remain in Cúcuta from February to April 1813, held up by these legal difficulties and by the mistrust of General del Castillo with whom he shared command of the frontier zone. He insisted: "To work with the greatest speed will be of most benefit to both States. The most terrible calamity that could befall us would be for the tyrant in Caracas to become alarmed at the defeat suffered by Correa, for we are giving him time to organize a strong force to come out to meet us and defeat us on our own frontiers." But neither Nariño, President of the province of Cundinamarca, nor the Congress was prepared to help him, despite sympathy for his plan. Apart from the divisions which debilitated the Granadan patriots—Bolívar was already involved in these because of his differences with Castillo, which daily grew worse—the country faced the threat of a royalist invasion from the south. Also, the province of Santa Marta, mistreated by Labatut, had rebelled against Cartagena. Moreover, the type of war proposed by Bolívar, based upon a strategy of constant offensive, was so new in America that it inevitably made soldiers and politicians hesitate. Castillo, for example, complained of "men with delirious heads, authors of the ruin of Venezuela."

Castillo finally took a step that could have been decisive. Together with other officers, he accused Bolívar of infidelity towards the federal system and demanded his resignation from the army. Bolívar warned the government that such behavior threatened the entire army with total ruin, "and with it perhaps New Granada, for there can be no belligerent state without troops, and there are no troops without discipline." It was at this point that the Venezuelan Colonel, Rafael Urdaneta, wrote to him: "General, if two men are enough to emancipate the *patria,* I am ready to accompany you." This demonstrated the abnegation and moral bravery that this austere official was to sustain always. If Bolívar described himself as "the man of difficulties," he might well have called Urdaneta "the man of responsibilities," because he was always ready unhesitatingly to assume the most arduous and dangerous tasks.

Bolívar already possessed an effective force which inspired him with confidence. All the Venezuelans in New Granada, including the vehement

José Félix Ribas, his uncle-in-law eight years his senior, recognized him as their leader. A brilliant group of Granadan officers was also ready to follow him in the reconquest of Venezuela. They all worked together as comrades on the task or organizing the incipient army. Bolívar cannot have failed to realize that he was witnessing the true basis for American brotherhood in an impetuous selfless collaboration that made frontiers meaningless.

Bolívar had acquired confidence as a leader, an ability to see opportunities quickly, a precision in improvising the plans demanded by each new situation, and the boldness to execute them. He was already the *caudillo,* and he felt entitled to the role.

The governors of New Granada, moreover, came forward with endless generosity to sustain him morally and to help him materially. He received aid from Rodríguez Torices in Cartagena and Nariño in Bogotá, while the venerable Camilo Torres supported him with his influence in Congress. Bolívar acknowledged their contributions with language which was clearly intended to record his gratitude for posterity: "Oh! What a beautiful spectacle is being enacted, *Señor Presidente,* on the theater of the New World. It will be a struggle perhaps unequaled in history. To see, I declare, all the people of New Granada spontaneously and simultaneously join in the task of re-establishing the liberty and independence of the former Republic of Venezuela, with no other stimulus than humanity, without greater ambition than the glory of breaking the chains that degrade their compatriots, without hope of any reward other than that which virtue gives to heroes who fight for reason and justice."

This declaration was dictated by neither rhetoric nor opportunism. Bolívar was always to retain a fond memory of New Granada's generosity. His correspondence shows increasing annoyance and impatience with Caracas, but never with the Granadans. He gave fiery eulogies to them when he was triumphant, and even in the days of adversity when his enemies tried to take control of New Granada from him, he did not utter a single criticism against the nation that gave birth to his glory.

But May had already arrived, and Bolívar was still waiting in Cúcuta for permission to advance. It is easy to imagine his impatience, aggravated by the beginning of the wet season in Venezuela. The rains would seriously impede his army's march along routes which were impassable even in the dry season, and he could expect little aid from a country which the royalists had already sacked several times. Authorization finally arrived on May 7, but it was limited to permission to liberate the Venezuelan frontier provinces of Mérida and Trujillo. The army began its march on May 14, the vanguard commanded by the Granadan Colonel Atanasio Gi-

---

1. Bolívar to Nariño, Cúcuta, May 10, 1813. O'Leary, xiii, p. 219.

rardot. The advance troops occupied the city of Mérida four days later, and they entered Trujillo on June 10. Once again hundreds of kilometers had been occupied in less than a month.

In Mérida Bolívar was acclaimed for the first time with the title of Liberator. Of all the honors he was to receive in his career, that was the one in which he took real pride. Only the responsibility and the glory of being the Liberator could make him more aggressive and constant than he was by nature. Similarly, when he was faced by long years of anguish and hesitated over the question of accepting an imperial throne offered to him as the only remedy for the civil dissensions America was suffering, the invocation of this title was his salvation. He wrote to Páez in March 1826, refusing the crown he had been offered: "The title of Liberator is superior to any that human pride has ever sought." In September of the same year he told Santander: "To be the Liberator means more than anything else; for this reason I will not degrade myself before a throne."

Bolívar should have waited in Trujillo for new orders from the Granadan government, but the long distance between them, and the large forces available to the royalists obliged him to seek a bold, prompt solution to his difficulties. Baralt observed: "The position of the patriots was insecure. On the left flank they had Maracaibo, from which an invasion could be launched at any time against the territory from Cúcuta to Trujillo. On the right was Barinas, where Monteverde had stationed 2,600 men under Tíscar for the purpose of invading New Granada. In front was Monteverde himself with all the troops he had used to subjugate Venezuela, and with the ability to obtain supplies of all sorts from the richest provinces. Coro, finally, remained a constant threat on the other side. It was in royalist hands and commanded by Ceballos.

At the same time the arrival of other news from Venezuela encouraged Bolívar to speed up his campaign. In February 1813, while he was preparing to invade Venezuela from the west, a group of patriot refugees under Colonel Santiago Mariño invaded the eastern provinces from the island of Trinidad. They defeated the forces sent against them, including some led by Monteverde, and made themselves masters of the region and subsequently of the island of Margarita, which revolted on its own account. Despite these victories, the eastern patriots were in no hurry to march on the center of the country. There the royalists revenged themselves for their setbacks with increased exactions and cruelties, without realizing that these outrages in turn increased the exasperated patriotism of the creoles.

Although these objective factors encouraged Bolívar to continue towards Caracas without awaiting the permission of New Granada, the most powerful influences pushing him forward were his own convictions and character. If he believed that the presence of Spanish troops in any part of America was a threat to the independence of the rest of the continent, how could he agree with the decision of the regional leaders to leave Caracas and the richest, most populous provinces in the hands of the royalists? He had already told the government of the Union in April: "If Correa was a fool for not taking New Granada with only 700 men, then I must be an idiot if I do not liberate Venezuela with such a sizeable and victorious army."[1]

The decision of Mérida to acclaim him Liberator not only gave him a title superior to all others, but also provided his enterprise with a national character. He decided, therefore, to go on. By the end of June he was in Trujillo, and on August 7, he entered Caracas in triumph. Girardot had beaten the Spaniards at Aguaobispos; Ribas and Urdaneta defeated them at Niquitao and Los Horcones; and Bolívar himself won the battle of Taguanes in the province in Caracas. Monteverde fled to take refuge in Puerto Cabello.

The campaign was rightly entitled the "Admirable Campaign". For the first time Bolívar and the eastern leaders had proved that untrained recruits, inferior in number, could defeat the best royalist officers. His concepts of defensive war and a direct appeal to the people to join the struggle had given America a triumphant strategy. He had left Barranca with seventy men and he now had a genuine army. Experienced officers, none of them vacillators or traitors, followed him with absolute confidence, and he knew clearly what he could expect of them in terms of skill and bravery. The civilian population was becoming aware of what it would have to give for the common cause, while the fugitive masses of the first Republic had been turned into soldiers, capable—as had just been proved at Ocaña and Mérida—of fighting in both arid lowlands and at a height of 4,000 meters, with machetes, lances and muskets that they learned to fire on the very field of battle.

Bolívar's triumphal entry into Caracas opened the patriots' eyes to a horrible reality. The 1,000 members of the volunteer battalion of Ferdinand VII, all Spaniards and Canary Islanders, had believed, according to Colonel Ureña, that calling themselves "loyal vassals" gave them the uncontrolled right to dispose of creole lives and property as they wished. As Bolívar advanced, the battalion dissolved itself without facing battle and almost abandoned the city in disorder, fearing patriot reprisal. The road to La Guaira and the port itself were again filled with thousands

---

1. *Cartas,* i, p. 49. The description of Correa as a fool was a reflection of the Granadan attitude rather than Bolívar's opinion of him. In fact, the same report put him a long way above Monteverde, and Bolívar stated: "I am compelled to accord Correa the respect he has earned by bearing himself with the valor of a soldier and the dignity of a noble leader. Monteverde has never surpassed Correa in these virtues."

of frightened refugees, sad victims of the cruelties brought by civil wars. They were more fortunate than the republicans of 1812, in that some of them were able to escape to Curaçao in the fourteen ships that were in the harbor. The patriots, for their part, were transported with delight and planned victory celebrations. In Caracas, of course, there were neither triumphal arches nor magnificent *fiestas,* because two migrations of despairing people had left the city deserted, and the devastation caused by the earthquake was still visible everywhere. This atmosphere of sadness was made even more poignant by the groups of girls who went out to greet the Liberator with baskets of flowers and simple patriotic emblems fastened to their white dresses.

The day after his entry into the city Bolívar's first task was to inform the government of New Granada of the liberation of Venezuela, "which the heroic feats of the New Granadan army have created from nothing."

He then had to organize the government. He had been thinking about this since leaving Mérida, and he had already written to Dr. Cristóbal Mendoza: "Come without delay. The *Patria* needs you. I will lead, conquering, and you will follow me, organizing, for you are the man of organization just as I am the man of conquest."[1] Bolívar's fundamental aim was always to separate political and military authority, giving the former responsibility for legal organization, and leaving the latter with the freedom of action that war made necessary. But co-operation with Mendoza was also invaluable because of this steadfast patriot's ability and honor, and because he had been the first person to exercise executive authority in Venezuela during the triumvirate with which the Republic began. Miguel José Sanz, who was so learned that Humboldt esteemed him with rare praises, and Francisco Javier de Ustáriz, who had also been a member of the triumvirate, committed themselves to Bolívar. Mendoza was appointed Governor of Caracas, and Ustáriz and Sanz both worked out plans for a provisional government which delegated supreme authority to the chief of the army.

Sanz and Bolívar had been enemies before the revolution for family reasons. Sanz's friendship and admiration of Miranda could have deepened this animosity. Since Sanz's rectitude and moral courage were above suspicion, his decision to support Bolívar can only be explained by his considering indispensable for the salvation of the country the "extraordinary measures" he had urged upon Miranda and which Bolívar now embodied. Many other eminent politicians thought the same, including the firm, austere Fernando Peñalver, who, as we will see below, acquired such ascendancy over Bolívar that he was called "Mentor" and "Father" by him.

---

1. Vicente Dávila, *Próceres Trujillanos,* p. 231.

Finally, in accordance with the colonial tradition whereby the *ayuntamiento* of Caracas assumed responsibility for the representation of the whole country, an extraordinary *cabildo* met on October 14 to solemnly ratify Bolívar's title of Liberator and to appoint him Captain-General of the republican army.

Bolívar was thus able to add the moral authority of the principal governors of the first republic to his personal prestige. Political institutions were altered, insofar as they could be. The federal constitution of 1811, the plural executive, etc., were ignored, not only because of Bolívar's opposition to them, and his prior experiences in Venezuela and New Granada, but also because it would have been farcial to attempt to re-establish them in the state of war which existed throughout the country. The situation was so bad that Bolívar stayed in Caracas for only two weeks before again going on campaign. Apart from the regular armies which both sides put in the field, innumerable guerrilla bands had sprung up throughout the country, fighting for both the King and the Republic.

A new epoch was beginning. The whole of the legal political structure had been destroyed, first by the revolution and then by the collapse of the Republic. The Republic was about to be reconstituted by victorious military leaders whose authority rested simply upon their personal power. They rooted out the enemy with fire and sword from what was to become republican territory so long as it remained under their control, but nobody had time to think of promulgating stable laws or of establishing rules of conduct other than those demanded for each day's precarious survival. The *caudillo* thus emerged, supported by his numerous possessions—his troops, his officers, his victories, his prestige and frequently "his people"—which made him both feared and fascinating. They could make him either a savior or a despot, and sometimes both at once. As a sociological phenomenom this was *caudillismo,* a by-product of the war of emancipation, the worst aspects of which were to survive for almost a century as the greatest obstacle to the reorganization of Spanish America.

The war had also become total in an even more lamentable sense. In response to the cruelties of Monteverde and his favorites, Bolívar had declared it "to the death."

Bolívar had received hair-raising information of abuses before invading Venezuela. In addition to the assassinations and extortions discussed in the previous chapter, some Spanish leaders had developed almost unbelievable refinements of cruelty. One of them, Antonio Zuazola, was described as follows by Baralt, on the basis of reports sent to Spain which horrified royalists themselves: "A worthy subordinate of Antoñanzas, he committed the greatests abuses as he advanced, persecuting as enemies all the Americans he encountered without distinction, burning their houses and destroying their crops. After shooting the prisoners, he called upon the town's inhabitants, who had fled in fear by land and sea, to return peacefully. Many had learned from previous treachery, and did not trust him, but the incautious and the naive returned with their families, reassured in the thought that they were peaceful people who had not involved themselves in anything. Men and women, young and old, had their ears cropped or were skinned alive. Their feet were skinned and they were made to walk on fragments of glass or stone. Their faces or one or more of their limbs were mutilated, and they were then mocked for their ugliness. They were stitched together, shoulder to shoulder. The punishments were not always the same. Zuazola varied them and worked out a thousand different combinations to give himself the pleasure of novelty... Because of his cruelties the ferocious Biscayan was given the title of good and gallant subject. The many boxes of ears that he sent to Cumaná were received by the Catalans with cheers and applause. And those wretched men, who had been renowned for their modesty and probity, used the ears to decorate the doors of their houses, or wore them in their hats like cockades."[1]

Reports of these horrors were handed down orally from generation to generation in Venezuela. Because of this, many Venezuelans believed them to be exaggerated. The story of the ears, for example, seemed to be based upon the "rosaries of ears" seen in France during the Revolution. It is authentic, however, beyond any shadow of doubt, because it was denounced by the royalist contemporary, Urquinaona. Moreover, all the documents published after Independence, far from minimizing or disproving the abuses, have confirmed them. The memoirs of the creole royalist Andrés Level de Goda, for example, which he composed shortly before his death to explain himself to his sons, confirmed the ears incident and described other punishments employed by Zuazola and Cervériz.[2]

Baralt pitied the Catalans as much as he condemned them. In this sense the behavior of the Canary Islanders was even more lamentable. They had been welcomed throughout Venezuela as settlers because they assimilated themselves to the creole way of life quicker than any other group, even in their manner of speech. Numerous Venezuelan families were descended from Canary ancestors. But Monteverde, whose role was decisive, succeeded in corrupting the Canary Islanders, turning them into the scourge of Venezuela. In the reprisals that followed they were persecuted just as much as the Spaniards.

The royalist zeal to exterminate reached such extremes that Cervériz wrote quite calmly to Monteverde: "Sir, there is nothing better than a military government to shoot all these knaves (creoles); and I assure you that

---

1. Baralt (1939 edition), i, p. 137.
2. *Boletín de la Academia de la Historia*, Caracas, 1932. No. 59.

none of those who fall into my hands will escape." General Manuel del Fierro wrote to another Spaniard: "More than 12,000 men have perished in the recent actions in one place and another. Fortunately, most of them were creoles, and very few Spaniards. If it were possible, it would be best to exterminate every American."

It is easy to imagine the mentality of these royalist leaders when we see that it is still shared, more than 150 years later, by writers like Salvador de Madariaga. Madariaga is hostile towards Bolívar because his feelings are really the same as those of Ferdinand VII, although he occasionally manages to hide them. For this reason his unembarrassed comment on the cruelties, including the ear-cropping, is as follows: "In this war Monteverde's royalist leaders were inspiring the people of Venezuela with the spirit of resistance and independence, which the separatist *caudillo* had been unable to eradicate."[1]

The metropolitan government unfortunately legalized these excesses and paralyzed the *audiencia*'s admirable proposal for a return to legality. An official communication of the Secretary of War, published by Monteverde on March 13, approved his conduct in Venezuela, authorized the putting to the sword of stubborn insurgents, ordered that all who had accepted employment under the Republic or co-operated in any way with the revolution should be tried for crimes against the State and condemned to death, and established penalties, including confiscation of property, for anybody else judged guilty of involvement in sedition.

Such measures, which reinstituted the beheading of all rebels, "without more process than an oral hearing," which had been used years earlier during the rising of Chirinos in Coro, showed that Spain was not prepared to alter her policies. They also revived memories of atrocities committed by other royalists, in Peru, Quito, Popayán and Mexico.[2]

The first enraged Venezuelan to respond with a policy of war to the death against Spaniards was Dr. Antonio Nicolás Briceño, an eminent jurist who had turned himself into a soldier to organize a corps of volunteers, which he led into Venezuela from New Granada. In April 1812 before he acted, the plural executive of the republic had issued a "Penal Decree against traitors, rebels and opponents of our government," which established the death penalty for those who by act, and even word, showed themselves hostile to the republican system. But this decree did not make a distinction

---

1. Discussed by Dr. Angel Francisco Brice in his *El Bolívar de Marx ampliado por Madariaga* (Caracas, 1952).
2. Bolívar referred to them in a proclamation in Mérida. Admiral Cochrane reported in his *Travels in Colombia* that President Montes, the Spanish leader who took Quito in 1812, "not content with the execution committed by the royalist forces when they reached the city, ordered that one in every five of the inhabitants should be shot, a monstrous act, of which he boasted in a letter of November 11 to the Governor of Guayaquil."

between Spaniards and creoles, and it was not even enforced against those captured at Valencia with arms in their hands. Briceño, then, was the first to make this distinction, and he was determined to ratify it mercilessly.

Briceño, like Arismendi, another patriot who fought a war to the death, was a mild-natured man. (In Caracas he was humorously called "The Devil" simply because as a young man he had acted this role in a religious play.) As deputy in the Republic's first Congress, he had been one of the most determined to ensure that Spaniards and Canary Islanders should be made welcome in the new State, even enjoying access to the highest offices. Nonetheless, the plan that he worked out in New Granada was the wildest imaginable. It held that the aim of the war was "to destroy in Venezuela the accursed race of European Spaniards, including the Islanders." It denied them the chance of joining his expedition. Finally it established a macabre scale for promotions whereby "the soldier who presents the heads of twenty such Spaniards will be promoted to the rank of second lieutenant, he who presents thirty to that of lieutenant, and he who presents fifty to that of captain."[1]

Briceño wanted to serve under Bolívar and Castillo, who at the time were still in Cúcuta, preparing for the invasion of Venezuela. When Briceño sent them the heads of two Spaniards, Bolívar severely warned him "that in the future you may in no circumstances execute or enforce any serious sentence against any individual without first sending me the papers which, in conformity with the laws, must be prepared before sentence." Castillo replied: "I return the head that you sent me. Content yourself with seeing it, and send it to whomever has pleasure in seeing victims sacrificed in desperation."

Only desperation could have led the gentle lawyer to such extravagances, a point clearly indicated by his reply to Castillo, whom he told: "My friend, take a look at the large number of patriots now groaning in the dungeons of Puerto Cabello, La Guaira, Cumaná, Puerto Rico and the Maracaibo prison-ship, as in the other places that the *godos* occupy in our America, and tell me that we should describe the shooting of two Spaniards as cruelty.... Remember for a moment |the fate of virtuous Roscio, of patient Ustáriz, of eloquent Espejo, of brave Francisco Carabaño.... Recall the death of wise and illustrious (document torn,) of active and ingenious (document torn.) Imagine that you can see how they have been kept, and how some of them still are kept, deprived of light, roasted with heat, sleeping in the filth of their own bodies, and perishing with only God's aid, without confession, without doctors, and for no other crime than having been born in America...."

---

1. Vicente Dávila, *La Guerra a muerte,* in *Investigaciones Históricas* (Caracas, 1923). This book is without doubt the most detailed of those written on the war to the death, and it is the source for other data used above.

These were the images that ceaselessly tormented the minds of the Venezuelan patriots. Every day the invaders received maddening news of what was being suffered by their families, their friends and the most respected men in the country. It was not surprising that Bolívar was to threaten the Spaniards with a war of extermination, hardly two months after rebuking Briceño. On June 15, 1813, in Trujillo, he declared in a proclamation: "Justice demands vengeance, and necessity compels us to exact it... Any Spaniard who does not, by every active and effective means, work against tyranny on behalf of this just cause, will be considered an enemy and punished. As a traitor to the nation, he will be shot by a firing squad. On the other hand, a general and absolute amnesty is granted to those who come over to our army with or without their arms... Those Spaniards who render outstanding service to the State shall be regarded and treated as Americans... Spaniards and Canary Islanders, you will die, though you be neutral, unless you actively espouse the cause of America's liberation. Americans, you will live, even though you have trespassed."

It is a common mistake to describe this proclamation as a "Decree of War to the Death." Of interest is the similarity that exists between some of Bolívar's terminology and the *Law of Suspects* promulgated in France in 1793, whereby "those who, although having done nothing against liberty, have done nothing for it" could be condemned to death.

On the other hand, Bolívar's proclamation was nothing more than a threat, for he immediately tried to suspend its execution. As soon as he entered Caracas in triumph, he proposed to Monteverde according to the regent Heredia, "a general reconciliation, ignoring the past entirely, with permission to emigrate for those who desire it." But, even when he removed the condition that Puerto Cabello be handed over, he was unable to reach any agreement with the inflexible Islander who continued to insist on treating the patriots as traitors, subject only to the "law of conquest." Monteverde refused to exchange the republican Colonel Diego Jalón, a Spaniard, for the ferocious Zuazola, who had been captured by the patriots. He refused to accept the offer of two Spaniards for every American, and he also turned down Bolívar's offer to exchange the 2,000 Spaniards imprisoned in Caracas for the 400 patriots held in Puerto Cabello. Bolívar also tried to rescue those who had been exiled to the Bahamas and Barbados, hiring four schooners to bring them to La Guaira, and ordering that the operation be paid out of the money taken from the Spaniards and Canary Islanders.[1] Unfortunately, the project could not be realized; it is not known if this was because of a lack of money, the refusal of the islands'

---

1. *Boletín de la Academia Nacional de la Historia,* Caracas, no. 69, pp. 82 and 87. See too Lecuna, *Catálogo,* i, p. 276.

governors to co-operate, or the press of military affairs that forced Bolívar to leave Caracas after only a few days.

The reason advanced to justify a war to the death are as follows: that it was just for both sides to be exposed to the same risks; that otherwise the patriots would be intimidated while the royalists grew bold; and that it contributed to the growth of a feeling of nationalism in the Venezuelans, dramatizing the revolutionary path that the country had to follow. We consider the last of these arguments, which is the easiest to adorn with futile rhetoric, false and dangerous. False, because the feeling of nationalism and the spirit of sacrifice that had to go with it were already so strong in Venezuela that after the fall of the Republic in 1812 the country immediately rose again in both the east and the west at the same time. Furthermore if the majority of the masses remained royalist, they later turned to the republican cause not because of the war to the death, but because of the influence of patriot proselytism—formerly prohibited by the Spaniards—and because of the emergence of creole *caudillos*, such as Páez, Monagas, Zaraza and Sedeño, who acquired prestige among the rural masses. The argument is dangerous because it ignores the moral considerations which underly the debate about the war to the death, and also because it is the nearest to the present day argument used to justify political violence.

In our opinion the war to the death was the only way to make the royalists give up, either by means of partial agreements, such as Bolívar sought immediately, or through a general treaty, like that which was subsequently secured, also on his initiative. It is easy to see, moreover, in all the royalist documents, that it was they who began the war to the death, not only out of cruelty but also because of their contempt for the Americans, whom they wished to regard as traitors rather than belligerents. As a result, the Venezuelans felt humiliated as well as afflicted, and they saw more clearly every day that unless they replied with equal vigor, the Spaniards would never parley with them.

There are many examples of impunity making men and nations lose all sense of culpability and moral sensitivity. It is as true of common delinquents and corrupt politicians as of *caudillos* and kings. Arrogance leads even honest men as well as imperialist nations to condone the merciless squeezing of weak countries and their inhabitants. The slavery of the past and today's exploitation of raw material producers by industrialized nations are clear examples. The Spaniards had this sense of impunity in America (as a race, that is, because their respect for the law in private relationships was admirable) and it was necessary to remind them with severe punishment that justice, tolerance and compassion could be demanded as rules for public life on this side of the Atlantic, too.

It was thus under dark, threatening clouds that the year 1813 came to an end. There was fighting throughout the Republic. During the siege of Puerto Cabello, the patriots repelled several attempts by the defenders to break out, but they were unable to attempt an assault on the impregnable fortress. They were in considerable danger and frequently had to fall back, because the defenders, reinforced with 1,200 regulars sent from Spain, were more numerous than the troops the patriots could spare for the siege. Girardot, the brilliant Granadan colonel who had fought with the vanguard during the Admirable Campaign, died in one of these actions. Among other honors granted by Bolívar was the decision to take his heart in triumph to Caracas where it was to be put in a mausoleum in the cathedral. Ribas and Urdaneta again showed the skill and daring that was to take them to the highest military post, while in the east, Mariño, the Bermúdez brothers, Piar and Arismendi enhanced the fame they had acquired in their first battles. Other leaders emerged, including Monagas, Zaraza, Sedeño and the eighteen-year old Antonio José de Sucre, the future victor at Ayacucho.

Bolívar tried to see to everything, moving from the siege of Puerto Cabello to Caracas to deal with the city's defense or with general policy, and thence joining the campaign in the interior. In addition to numerous minor engagements, he personally directed two battles at the end of the year, at Barquisimeto and Araure. At the former, the victorious patriots had already entered the city and bells were ringing when a bugle sounded the retreat. It is not known whether this was done treasonably or in error, but the infantry panicked and certain victory became a rout. To punish their cowardice Bolívar formed a new corps, which he called the *Nameless Battalion,* out of those who fled. Soon after, his reorganized army was victorious at Araure, where he personally led a charge or several squadrons against the enemy. He then pursued the enemy with such zeal that he overtook them, intercepting them at night thirty kilometers from the battlefield. The *Nameless Battalion* fought courageously and captured from the enemy the standard called *"Invincible of Numancia."* It was thereafter known as *"Victor at Araure."*

It was in 1813 that the true Venezuelan army was born, boasting a trained infantry. Heredia pointed out in his *Memorias* that a Spanish officer was surprised at the battle of Araure to find that the republican soldiers possessed the qualities of regular troops. "This man and other intelligent officers," he wrote, "assured me that the insurgents had performed wonders of bravery, and maneuvered with as much speed and fortitude as the more battle-hardened European troops." The patriot infantry, of course, was always short of arms, at least until 1819 when the Republic was able to purchase some. For this reason the cavalry continued to dominate throughout these early years. It fought with improvised lances, pikes, and sometimes with simple staffs of wood, sharpened and hardened with fire.

It was in this period, unfortunately, that the dark figure of José Tomás Boves appeared upon the horizon of the *llanos*. He was to become the most dreadful of all the Spanish guerrillas. Boves was a rare individual, a native of Asturias in Spain, accustomed to the life of the Venezuelan *llanos* where he engaged in smuggling and similar activities. He originally supported the republican government, which pardoned him for his "crimes of piracy," but he was attracted to the royalist cause by Monteverde's triumphs, and in 1812 a republican judge sentenced him to death. The sentence was not carried out—an increasingly common occurrence in those difficult days—and after obtaining his freedom, Boves joined the army of Monteverde, who made him Commander-in-Chief of the town of Calabozo. He advanced himself from this position with surprising energy. Brave, skillful with horse and lance, and possessing a detailed knowledge of the plains, he had no hesitation from the start in encouraging the excesses of the semi-savage hordes that he led. He dedicated himself with unequaled ferocity to sacking, murder and torture in the defenseless villages that lay in the path of his first campaign.

By the end of 1813, Boves led a real army which he replenished after each battle, whether or not he won, from the apparently inexhaustible *llanos*. He fought against two of his compatriots in the service of the Republic: Colonel Vicente Campo Elías managed to defeat him at Mosquitero, but Lieutenant-Colonel Pedro Aldao lost his life in a heroic but vain attempt to hold up Boves's army of 4,000 with barely 700 men. Commandant Pedro María Freites of the eastern army, also defeated Boves, but shortly afterwards Boves defeated Colonel Carlos Padrón who died with his sword in his hand.

These were just a few of the hundred or so fights and battles that occurred at the end of 1813. It would be pointless to try to describe this incessant combat or to define the precise importance of individual actions. Regardless of the size and strength of their forces, patriots and royalists fought wherever they met. The losers were almost always exterminated. Victories were worth very little, for as soon as the victors thought that they had secured an extensive area, they were forced to abandon it almost immediately by either the arrival of larger forces or the appearance all around them of numerous guerrillas.

The guerrillas were a problem for the patriots in particular, because their shortage of arms and the hostility of the rural population meant that no victory brought them relief. At the beginning of the Araure campaign Bolívar wrote to Mariño: "I have reason to fear subversion in La Guaira or Caracas, where there is not a musket to be had, and I consider it almost inevitable in the *llanos*." No sooner had he left, in fact, than the slaves and some peasants declared for the royalists and sacked the towns of Santa Lucía, Santa Teresa and Yare, close to the capital.

On every side those avid, cruel bandits were throwing themselves against the civilized part of the country like infernal hordes emerging from the craters and rubble left by the cataclysm of the previous year. Bolívar realized in despair that the cities were being ruined and depopulated by the endless sacrifices demanded of them. Would he have to admit that it was impossible to succeed without English or North American aid? England would not even allow the republicans to buy arms in her West Indian colonies, and the United States no longer had a Smith to act as a Lafayette for his brothers in the South.

At the turn of the century Caracas had about 40,000 inhabitants. The other Venezuelan cities were much smaller. In some of them the earthquake had killed up to a quarter of the population. But the cities had to give and give, day after day, in the hope of containing the raging torrent for a short time. How long could they go on giving?

XVIII

THE KILLING
CONTINUED FOR
SEVERAL NIGHTS

A MAP OF THE ROUTES OF the rival armies in 1814 and of the actions that they fought would resemble a child's aimless scribbling on a sheet of paper. What happened to Urdaneta at the beginning of the year can serve as an example. Although he was busy in the center of the country, fighting the numerous guerrillas who surrounded him, he managed to organize his army for a march against Coro, the royalist stronghold in the extreme northwest of the country. He defeated the Indian Reyes Vargas, who was blocking his path, and was nearing the city when he learned that Barinas, hundreds of kilometers to the south, was in danger. Afraid of arriving too late, he hurriedly changed direction and marched ahead into the *llanos* with a small force. As they were crossing the Portuguesa River, a fugitive officer told them that Barinas had been taken, and most of its defenders and inhabitants put to the sword. After sending most of his men to the assistance of the city of Ospino, Urdaneta went with only nine troopers to Barquisimeto where he set about organizing a sizeable force for the recapture of Barinas. When it was ready, however, he received orders from Bolívar to send his best men to Caracas because Boves was marching on the city, with 7,000 men. If this unfortunate itinerary were transferred to a European map, the army might have left Paris for Amsterdam, decided in Holland to return to Switzerland, only to return from there to Paris. And all this without having been able to fulfill any of its objectives.

On February 3, in La Puerta, Boves crushed Colonel Vicente Campo Elías, who had only 3,000 men, and descended on the valleys of Aragua. Caracas was also being threatened from the south by the army of a no less ferocious guerrilla called Francisco Rosete. When he captured and sacked Ocumare del Tuy close to the capital's southern boundary, Rosete indiscriminately killed men, women and children, and those who had taken refuge in the church were killed there.

Caracas was saved on this occasion by José Félix Ribas, who defeated Boves at La Victoria on February 12, and soon afterwards twice defeated Rosete in the Tuy valleys. The republicans were so outnumbered at La Victoria that they were pushed back to the city's main square. After they had beaten off one attack the most that Ribas could say to Major-General Mariano Montilla was, "There is no need to despair, my friend, we can resist two more attacks like this one before we are completely destroyed." The remaining youths in the university and seminary in Caracas had been sent to fight, and the victorious leader himself regarded his triumph as nothing less than miraculous. He told the City Council of Caracas, which had expressed its gratitude: "The *Patria* was saved that day by the blood that the *caraqueños* shed at La Victoria and by the protection of María Santísima de la Concepción."

This statement was typical of Ribas's revolutionary personality. He was so fiery that, when he joined the *cabildo* of Caracas on April 19, 1810, he described himself as the representative of the *pardos* despite belonging to one of the capital's leading families. Afterwards he showed himself in the streets wearing a Phrygian cap, exhorting the people to join the revolution. He was expelled from the Supreme *Junta* and from the province because of his radical ideas. His inflexibility later led him to oppose Bolívar, who was both his nephew and his commander, to threaten him with death, and even slander him. But he was submissive and unselfish after his triumph at La Victoria. He asked Bolívar to decide upon the honors to be accorded him while he closed his reply to the *ayuntamiento* of Caracas with the following words: "I earnestly beg you to assign the whole of the reward due to me to the relief of the many widows and orphans, who justly deserve their country's assistance. I expect the municipality to set aside this day for devotion to the Mother of God, Our Lady of the Conception, promising to hold a solemn *fiesta* every year in the Holy Metropolitan Church." Ribas fell ill soon afterwards but he insisted, nevertheless, on lending his prestige to the aid of his country. He had himself carried in a hammock-carriage to do battle with Rosete. In Caracas he was called the Invincible.

Among the heroes who fell at La Victoria were two of the Republic's best veterans, Colonel Luis María Rivas Dávila, who at the head of the Magnificent Dragoons of Caracas had secured the victory at Araure, and Captain Rudecindo Canelón of the infantry, who was the first to engage and disperse the enemy with an advance force of eighty men in the same battle. The Minister of War recorded, in his comments on the battle of La Victoria, that when the bullet that caused his death was removed, Rivas Dávila said, "Take it to my wife, and tell her to keep it and remember that I owe to it the most glorious moment of my life, when I died defending the cause of my land."[1]

The danger to Caracas was the cause of an incident in Bolívar's career that has been just as much debated as, for example, Napoleon's killing of the 3000 Turks who surrendered at Jaffa or his sacrifice of his soldiers who were stricken with plague. Afraid that the Spaniards and Canary Islanders who had been imprisoned the previous year in Caracas and La Guaira might organize an uprising, Bolívar ordered that they be shot. This bloody deed claimed 800 victims, most of them civilians, and it forces even those writers who are inclined to justify the war to the death in theory, to hesitate.

In fact, this was the only case of the patriots' enforcing the terrible Trujillo threat on a massive scale and in cold blood. Two grave considerations pushed them to it: the memory of what had happened in 1812 in Puerto Cabello to Bolívar himself, when the royalist prisoners won over a number of junior creole officers, and the fact that Caracas and La Guaira were completely undefended except for a few badly-armed old men. Even the seminarians and the university students, who were little more than children, had been conscripted into the forces going out to meet Boves and Rosete.

Nor could the patriots forget that these Spaniards and Canary Islanders, although civilians, had formed the corps of volunteers who, as "loyal subjects," had attacked the creole population when Monteverde was triumphant. The Americans asked themselves whether they should continue to threaten a war to the death vainly when their failure to carry it out was making their enemies crueler and more arrogant. It is very easy to rationalize passion, and on this occasion either reason or passion was sufficient to convince the desperate defenders of Venezuela. Bolívar asked the Archbishop of Caracas: "What benefit have we gained from holding these men prisoners and even from freeing a large number of them? The answer is that yesterday they entered Tinaquillo and murdered twenty-five of its garrison, not sparing one. Boves has not yet given quarter to a single one of out men taken prisoner. Your Reverence will be horrified to learn that Boves sacrifices men and women without distinction."

---

1. Blanco y Azpurúa, v, p. 57.

This last accusation was no exaggeration. Boves, Yáñez, Puy, Zuazola, Rosete, Antoñanzas, Cervériz, Pascual Martínez and almost all the other royalist guerrillas sacrificed men, women and children without distinction. Even worse, the Spanish insistence upon treating the Americans as rebels, outside international law, made them cruel even when they observed legal processes. Their victims included those who should have been respected, such as the wife of José María España who, although pregnant, was imprisoned and mistreated as a punishment for her fidelity to that martyr of the country. María Josefa Torres was also imprisoned and had her property confiscated for having granted asylum to Vicente Salias, even though he was protected by the terms of the San Mateo surrender.[1] This was the rule that was applied in all cases because the Spaniards insisted dogmatically that neither treaties nor considerations of simple humanity could be invoked in favor of the insurgents.

In accordance with this criterion, Monteverde refused to make any agreement for the exchange of prisoners and he replied to the victorious republicans with the greatest ignorance: "Neither the decorum, nor the honor, nor the justice (!) of the great Spanish nation permits me to make any reply or to listen to any proposal that is not directed towards returning these provinces to my control, under the domination in which they legitimately exist."[2] He even imprisoned some of the patriots sent to discuss terms with him.

Bolívar and his men insisted, nevertheless, in avoiding the atrocious sacrifice as long as they could. When Colonel Tomás Montilla captured Calabozo, one of the first cities to suffer the war to the death at the hands of Antoñanzas, he freed all the royalists who could not be guarded. The number of Spanish and Canary Islander prisoners in Caracas was reduced from 2,000 to 800 by giving some of them passports to leave the country and by freeing large numbers. Ribas, too, treated the wounded and prisoners with the greatest humanity after his victory over Rosete at Ocumare. The *Gaceta de Caracas,* in reporting this, also praised the conduct of the royalist leaders Correa and Ceballos, and the republican government declared, in what was a new invitation to regularize the war, that if all the enemy leaders had been like them "the war to the death would never have been declared, and not a drop of Spanish blood would have been spilled."[3] On January 28, 1814 Bolívar himself made a further

---

1. Vicente Dávila, *Investigaciones Históricas,* i, p. 95. Salias, composer of the patriotic song which became the Venezuelan national anthem, was tried as "a revolutionary and editor of tracts." After a trial which lasted only seventeen days, he was condemned to death, without the right to appeal.
2. Blanco y Azpurúa, iv, p. 699.
3. See Lecuna, *Crónica razonada...,* i, p. 110, and *Catálogo de errores y calumnias...,* i, pp. 315, 317; and *Gaceta de Caracas* no. 411 (vol. iv), March 1814. (Edited by Academia Nacional de la Historia, Caracas).

"The House where the Decree of War to the Death was signed" in 1813, in Trujillo.

effort, when he announced in a proclamation: "On December 7, 1813, I issued an amnesty. . . . I now extend the aforementioned pardon and general amnesty to include fugitives and others persons, Americans, Spaniards and Canary Islanders. . . and I further declare the said amnesty to be unlimited. . . . I therefore order all military, civil and political leaders under no circumstances to execute, to threaten death, or to treat arbitrarily any individual who should voluntarily surrender, regardless of nationality, status or condition."[1]

But the royalist guerrillas replied to these republican overtures with new and more horrifying cruelties. And the most powerful of the Spanish leaders, José Tomás Boves, not only managed to exceed all previous ferocity, but also conceived the wicked plan of dividing the Venezuelans by means of a war of classes and races, so that they would destroy each other.

Evidence for this is the report which was presented to the crown in 1815 by Dr. José Ambrosio Llamozas, the chaplain to Bove's army. His aim was to indicate to the king the urgent measures required for the spiritual pacification and the reconstruction of miserable Venezuela, but his testimony of what he saw from Boves's side gives us an unequaled general panorama of the war. Even the lack of organization in his narrative seems to reflect the nightmarish confusion of events. He related: "From the start of the campaign Commander-in-Chief Boves revealed the plan that he had made, and from which he never deviated. It was based upon the destruction of all whites, and the protection, flattering and praising of the other castes, and it was demonstrated by the following deeds. In Guayabal, soon after the battle of Mosquitero, he sentenced death to all the whites, an order which he enforced as far as the town of San Mateo. The 87 whites captured in Calabozo were killed, and he left a list of 32 others who were to receive the same treatment. As he left the town, he ordered its military commander to kill any white man who turned up there and to send the white women of the town and the surrounding villages to the island of Arichuna. This was done, and the houses and property of the dead and the exiles were distributed among the *pardos,* who were given property deeds. In the town of Santa Rosa the white members of the companies that had been formed in the area were taken at night to the countryside and killed in secret, without confession. Those who came to sell supplies to the army in the town of San Mateo suffered the same fate. When Boves left Cumaná for Urica, he found that there were a number of whites in the companies that had been formed, on his orders, from the men who had recently arrived from the towns. He had them all killed by night in the countryside. They included Don N. Armas, a resident of Barcelona,

1. *Proclamas y discursos del Libertador* (Caracas, 1939), p. 89.

son of the Military Commander of San Mateo, and the Military Commander of Margarita, called Morales. Salaberria, the Military Commander of Cumaná, who had more than 200 white people secretly killed by night and without confession, observed this same conduct. Bove's thirst of blood was not solely for that of the whites, although it was against them that he was most determined. Almost unprecedented horrors were committed on his orders on the fields of battle and in the pacified towns. After a siege, the city of Valencia surrendered to Boves, who solemnly promised, in the name of Your Majesty, to pardon lives and to respect and preserve property. But as soon as he entered the city, between eight hundred and a thousand men were taken at night to Pato Hill where they were executed without confession, and the city was then sacked. The city of Caracas, which surrendered without resistance, suffered the same fate, and every night while Boves was there and afterwards on his instructions, a party of men was taken out for execution."

The chaplain gave details of similar atrocities committed in the east of the country, and he added: "Boves's conduct was in accordance with his words. He constantly reminded his troops in public of his declaration in Guayabal of war to the death against the whites. He always repeated that their property belonged to the *pardos*. This practice formed an important part of his military calculations and of his style of government. He said in the *llanos* that not a single white should remain for two reasons; first, because the territory was destined for the *pardos,* and, second, to cover his retreat in case of a defeat, for he did not trust the whites, whose company always displeased him. He ate with the *pardos,* and it was with them that he sought his entertainment. As a complement to this conduct, he gave verbal and written orders to all the military commanders that any white patriots who surrendered or could be captured should be secretly killed without legal process or any other formality. He always added that the one who killed the most would be his best friend. As a consequence the whites have disappeared. Only 5 or 8 of those born in the country have survived in Cumaná. Even a large proportion of the ladies were arrested and sent to Caracas for transportation to the deserted isle of Arichuna. At the beginning od December 1814, when Boves's army was 7,500 strong, only 60 to 80 of the soldiers were white, and there were 40 to 45 Spanish and creole officers of the same color. After the capture of Maturín, in the middle of December 1814, there followed the same pattern of butchery and killing that was observed invariably while Boves lived. Commander Gorrín killed 130 people captured in the four days that followed the occupation of the town, and the same fate was suffered without distinction by all who were captured or who returned to town after the publication of an amnesty that promised them security. The insubordination of the army was general and scandalous and, without orders from any officer, the few peaceful whites in the towns were killed. The determination of the *pardos,* negroes, mulattoes and *zambos* who made up the army to exterminate the white race was proved by several examples. Their lack of discipline and subordination was also clear. When they wished to disobey the orders of any commanders and officers, they resisted them and demanded their removal. Commander-in-Chief Boves cooperated and appointed others who soon suffered the same fate when they tried to check the excesses of their men."[1]

From the end of February until March 25, 1814, Bolívar fought Boves in the hilly territory of San Mateo where his family had an *hacienda.* Although the royalist forces were three times larger than his own, Bolívar was victorious in several encounters. In the last of these actions, the royalists had taken the heights and were about to capture the patriots' ammunition when the Granadan Antonio Ricaurte blew it up, with the loss of his own life. After discovering that the eastern army, led by General Santiago Mariño, was approaching, the chastised Boves retreated. Soon afterwards Mariño, too, defeated him at Bocachica. Bolívar pursued Boves, scattered his army, and managed to send help to Valencia, where, with less than 1,000 men, Urdaneta had withstood a siege by 4,000 men under Ceballos and Calzada. Bolívar had instructed him: "You will defend Valencia, Citizen General, until you die."

Bolívar and Mariño together won another fine victory, at the so-called first battle of Carabobo. In this action both sides were equal in number. The royalist army was led by the Captain-General himself, Juan Manuel de Cagigal, a professional soldier, and it included regular troops sent from Spain. Bolívar had his best subordinates with him, including José Félix Ribas, Rafael Urdaneta, Florencio and Leandro Palacios, and the unselfish Spanish republican, Colonel Diego Jalón. Mariño's leading officers were the fearful Colonel Francisco Bermúdez, Francisco Carvajal, the *Resting Tiger,* who was famed for his habit of fighting with a lance in each hand, Manuel Sedeño, later described by Bolívar as "the bravest of the brave," and José Tadeo Monagas, who personally seized the royal standard from the enemy during the battle. More than 2,000 royalists were killed, wounded or captured, and they also lost several pieces of artillery, 500 muskets, all their ammunition and eight standards, including that of the Granadan regiment.

During the battle an extraordinary example of heroism was set by Captain José María Carreño. Larrazábal tells us: "He was very weak, recovering from fourteen wounds received at Cerritos Blancos, where he lost an arm. But when he learned that an important action was being

---

1. *Boletín de la Academia Nacional de la Historia,* Caracas, no. 17. After the death of Boves, Fr. Llamozas was sent to report to the king by General Morillo. Significantly, one of his requests was that Venezuela should be repopulated with white settlers.

prepared which the Liberator would command in person, he asked to be let up, and took part in the glorious action of Carabobo. He looked like a ghost, bloodless, mutilated, with a weak voice and slow gait. . . ." This gallant captain was son of Commander Julián Carreño who, with his four sons and his slaves, joined the republican ranks at the beginning of the revolution. Two of those sons died on the field of battle, as did the father in 1817 during the defense of the Castle of Barcelona. As far as Captain José María is concerned, the information on his certificate of military service is even more astounding than his having fought at Carabobo with fourteen wounds.[1] It shows that of the many wounds he received, no less than nine had to be regarded as mortal. One of them opened his skull, while another damaged his lung and destroyed his shoulder blade. Nonetheless he outlived Bolívar, and in 1842, when he was a General, he was a member of the mission that brought Bolívar's body to Caracas. The admiring and affectionate *caraqueños* said that the remains of Carreño went to collect the remains of Bolívar.

The republicans won victories when they were able to combine their forces, but their triumphs brought them little respite. They were obliged almost immediately to separate their forces again to deal with the covetous rural masses who were hurling themselves against the center of the Republic from all sides. They also had to attend to Puerto Cabello, through which the royalists could receive aid from Spain or other colonies, and attack them from behind. The patriots had to fight simultaneously on several fronts and were thus restricted to the semi-mountainous territory near the cities, where they had some protection. Despite their efforts, the endless wave of invaders sapped their strength, and every day brought a further decline in manpower and money, in stocks of arms and in food.

Boves, in particular, seemed to be everywhere with inexhaustible forces. He was defeated on a number of occasions, and his army was even destroyed, but he managed to vanish like the contrabandist that he had been. He would re-appear a few days later, more powerful than all the other royalist leaders, ready to spill in new battles the American blood that he despised just as much in his own soldiers as in the republicans.

These circumstances explain the fact—at first sight inexplicable—that, less than one month after the triumph of Carabobo, a single defeat suffered by Bolívar and Mariño at the hands of Boves, at the second battle of La Puerta on June 15, decided the fate of the country. The Republic was exhausted.

Boves, as usual, killed all the prisoners taken in the battle, including the gallant Colonel Diego Jalón, a Spaniard like himself. This identity of blood simply inspired the ferocious victor to a new form of brutality. He

---

1. Archivo Nacional de Caracas, Sección *Ilustres Próceres*, vol. xvi. The information about his father and brothers is also taken from these documents.

invited Jalón to lunch with him at Villa de Cura the day after the battle and, when the meal was finished, had him beheaded in his presence.

Boves then moved against Valencia, where Colonel Juan de Escalona held out for twenty days until his supplies of food and water were exhausted. The terms of surrender, which promised protection to the city's inhabitants, were guaranteed by Boves's "most solemn and sacred oath to the holy Evangelists before the Divine Majesty,"[1] and Captain-General Cagigal was anxious to observe them. But the royalist Heredia tells us: "The night after his entry into Valencia, Boves summoned all the women to a dance, while the men, who had been guarded to prevent their escape, were rounded up and taken outside the town where, without spiritual assistance, they were lanced like bulls. Only Dr. Espejo (the political governor) was allowed time to confess and the distinction of being shot. The ladies at the dance, afraid of what was happening, sobbed and trembled when they heard the hoofbeats of the cavalry parties, while Boves with a whip in his hand made them dance the *piquirico* and other local dances of which he was fond. The tenderness they displayed was incapable of softening his heart of iron, and the killing continued for several nights."[2]

After the defeat at La Puerta, "General Bolívar, accompanied by a large number of officers and soldiers, on horse and on foot, was able to break through and escape along the royal road. Briceño Méndez, Leandro Palacios, Captain Ambrosio Plaza, and his aides Plaza and Herrera also saved themselves. Bermúdez threw a rich cloak to the *llaneros* who were about to surround him and fled from the field while they fought over it. Mariño, Valdés, Monagas and other easterners escaped along the Pao de Zárate road."[3]

The fall of Valencia cut off from the center of the country General Urdaneta, who was operating in the west. He managed to save his forces only by means of a most skillful and brave retreat to New Granada during which he marched 166 leagues through the enemy armies. What about Bolívar and his officers, who had been practically forced back to Caracas and its environs?

For a few days they considered resistance. The Liberator decreed martial law and ordered all citizens to present themselves within three hours with the arms and beasts they possessed. Another proclamation ordered them to hand over whatever they had in money, jewelry and provisions. In a daring raid against the royalist bands who were pillaging to the south of the city, the republican Captain Artero Rachadel succeeded in seizing the jewels that they had taken from the churches, and he took the

---

1. Bolívar, *Cartas,* i, p. 176.
2. Memorias del Regente José Francisco Heredia.
3. Lecuna, *Crónica razonada...* His account is based upon the report of aide-de-camp Marcelino de la Plaza, and other contemporary documents.

treasure to the capital. The city's churches gave all their valuables, the gifts of faithful Venezuelans over three centuries, for the country's defense. Three infantry battalions and three cavalry squadrons were formed from the troops who had escaped from the battlefield and the remaining citizens capable of bearing arms. An entrenched space in the middle of the city, upon which work had started in January, gave the most daring the hope that they might still be able to hold back the enemy. But it was impossible. The six so-called battalions and squadrons together numbered hardly 1,000 men. A pathetic appeal to the English Governor of Barbados for 2,000 muskets and 1,000 men to save Caracas from devastation proved fruitless. Only one of the many efforts to obtain arms was successful. A Swedish schooner sold the republicans 290 muskets, 20 pairs of pistols and 79 sabres. What mockery!

The policy followed by Boves and other royalist guerrillas of encouraging the hatred and greed of their men resulted in pillage, rape and murder as they entered the places abandoned by the patriots. We regard as foolish the attempts of some writers to treat this phenomenon as peculiar to America and to draw over-simplified conclusions from it. In even the best organized countries there exist entire social strata which are held in check only by the moral and physical pressure brought to bear on them in peacetime. Their latent criminality triumphs as soon as this compulsion is removed, or when there is a change of emphasis, whereby what was previously condemned becomes laudable and is expressed either in anarchy or in repressive government machinery of despotic regimes. In Venezuela the crisis was aggravated in this period by social heterogeneity and the uncivilized state of the rural masses. The terrified families of the smaller cities fled, therefore, to Caracas in search of protection, increasing the despair and disorder that surrounded the patriots. The churches remained open day and night to receive the multitude and the pitiful procession of refugees even sought shelter in the ruins left by the earthquake.

The state of mind of the men in the city is revealed by a letter written by Martín Tovar Ponte, a patrician, who had inherited his integrity, patriotism and sincere democratic convictions from his father, the Count de Tovar. He had been one of the first and keenest creole revolutionaries and, after heading the government established on April 19, had led a squadron in the war to the death. He now wrote to his wife, Rosa Galindo: "Save yourself and our children, and do not be afraid of the perils of the sea. If you are unable to find a ship, flee to the depths of the forest before the enemy sees you, with whatever you need to hide yourself for three or four days, in order to escape the first moments of fury. We will soon go on campaign; you will always find me on the field of honor."[1]

---

1. Quoted by Lecuna, *Crónica razonada...*, i, p. 290.

Since he had nothing left from his large fortune to give to the family that he was forced to abandon, he advised his beautiful young wife to take up needlework and washing to earn her bread abroad.

But this pugnacity also weakened the republicans, because the complaints about the leaders which always arise on such occasions and the fantastic projects of the demagogues threatened them with destruction. José Trinidad Morán, later to become one of the outstanding Venezuelan leaders in the Peruvian and Ecuadorean campaigns, described what he saw then in his *Memorias:* "The Liberator called together the most notable men of Caracas. They met in *cabildo abierto,* in the presence of the common people and the heads of families and, after making a truly patriotic speech, Bolívar deposited his authority in their hands. He offered to serve with the best good faith and with identical constancy under the orders of whomever they elected to command in his place. I was still a child when I witnessed this calamitous scene, leaning against a column of the St. Francis church, supported by my crutches, and it was almost impossible for me to form an opinion on what *the sovereign people was debating.* A thousand candidates proposed themselves for the supreme command... the rabble wanted to start looting, claiming that all whites were *godos,* but the Liberator checked them by ordering that two of those who began this *patriotic* act should be shot.... When the sensible people, and particularly the organized factions, grew tired of annoying each other with candidates and proposals, there was a general move to re-acclaim the Liberator as supreme leader of Venezuela. He was entrusted with saving the *Patria,* but now there was no time left. Boves was marching on Caracas with a victorious army, sowing death and destruction on all sides. Six thousand men were threatening Caracas, while the city's defenders numbered only two thousand, including the weak and the convalescents from the hospital. It was decided, therefore, to abandon the capital. The silverware was removed from the churches and sent to La Guaira to be taken aboard our squadron of six small ships, brigs and schooners."

On the wet miserable morning of July 7, 1814, just eleven months after his triumphal entry into Caracas, the Liberator began the retreat to the eastern part of the country where he hoped to be able to reorganize his forces. Almost all the population of the capital, and many of the people from the surrounding villages who had sought refuge there, fled with him rather than expose themselves to the atrocities of the victor. Morán goes on: "Twenty thousand souls of both sexes and all ages followed our steps. Almost all of them were on foot and, as the road from the highlands of Capaya to Barcelona is most difficult, it dismayed us to see the women and distinguished young ladies accustomed to the comforts of civilized life, up to their kness in mud, finding strength in their weakness, in order to save their honor and their lives from the villainous horde led by Boves. Our soldiers gave them what we had for their assistance, but it was not possible to help all of them. Many women died from hunger and exhaustion, were drowned in the rivers or were devoured by the beasts that abound in those forests."

This region was so dangerous and inhospitable that a hundred years later it still lacked roads that were regularly open, and communication between Caracas and Barcelona was by means of a long detour to the south. But it was precisely these almost virgin jungles, the swampy paths, and the fear of wild animals and poisonous snakes that provided the fugitives with their sole protection against the royalist commander's swift cavalry. Bolívar personally helped those who were most in need. The young Luisa Cáceres, a model of heroism and fidelity, was carried on his own horse through the floodwaters of Tacarigua lagoon, and he carried in his arms the small baby who was to become the famous mathematician, Miguel María Urbaneja.

This tragic flight from Caracas to Barcelona lasted for twenty-three days. The survivors had just begun to rest, and Bolívar, with the aid of Mariño and other eastern leaders, was starting to reorganize his forces, when Bove's army led by his second-in-command, José Tomás Morales, appeared from the plains to the south. The Liberator and General José Francisco Bermúdez made a stand against the royalists at Aragua de Barcelona, but even here the republicans were weakened by their internecine animosities. Since 1813, Bolívar, as western leader, and Mariño, as commander in the east, had enjoyed separate authority and military jurisdiction although they had always been broadly in agreement. Bermúdez, along with the eastern army, had reached Aragua de Barcelona before Bolívar, and he refused to accept Bolívar's advice on how the defense should be organized. Thus, although the royalist army was twice the size of the combined republican forces, Bolívar and Bermúdez fought separately, with independent strategies. Naturally, they were defeated, and Morales proceeded to act in the now customary fashion. An eye-witness recorded: "On all sides there was killing, rape, burning and pillage. The executioners used their swords mercilessly in the town, the woods and the church, where the wounded and the sick, women, old men and children took refuge. The slaughter was general, and the church was soaked with blood."[1]

This disaster, far from teaching the patriots a lesson, exacerbated their mutual recriminations. Ribas and General Piar, respectively, tried to displace Bolívar and Mariño as western and eastern commanders. If Ribas had been successful, the title would have been *in partibus,* since all the

---

1. *Las víctimas de Barcelona,* by *Un Caraqueño* (Caracas, 1853). Quoted by Lecuna in *Crónica razonada...,* i, p. 306.

west was already in royalist hands. For his part, Piar was hated by the most prestigious easterner, Bermúdez.

To crown their problems, a privateer in the service of the republicans, José Bianchi, tried to seize the ammunition and the small amount of patriot treasure that had been sent to his squadron by Mariño. Bolívar and Mariño risked their lives in boarding his ship, but as soon as they made him return part of what he had taken, he made fresh accusations against them. Passions were so aroused that Ribas wrote the most senseless libels about the Liberator and Mariño to Martín Tovar; while at Margarita, Piar fired upon the ship in which they arrived. Ribas finally imprisoned the two leaders, and in his letter to Tovar he described their plight as follows: "Bolívar and Mariño and their followers arrived at Carúpano suffering from hunger and thirst because they had no provisions. There I surprised and arrested them, and I took the money, equipment and muskets that luck had befallen them." Ribas was still the patriotic, selfless, fearless, admirable leader who was defeated only when the enemy's numerical superiority was irresistible, but grief and anger were blinding him.

Bolívar persuaded Captain Pedro Villapol, charged with guarding him, to set him free. He then released Mariño and, followed by forty-two officers, sailed for Cartagena in New Granada. They left their country with their pistols in their hand, ready to defend themselves against their own companions and subordinates.

The daring leaders who remained could do little with their weak forces. Bermúdez and Sedeño defeated Morales at Maturín after five days of fighting, but when Boves returned to lead his army he defeated first Piar and then Bermúdez. On December 5, he vanquished Ribas and Bermúdez at Urica, in the province of Barcelona, but, happily for the patriots, Boves was killed in this action. His death came too late. On December 11, Morales again defeated the few troops led by Ribas and Bermúdez, who tried to resist in Maturín. By the end of 1814 all Venezuela was in the hands of the royalists. Ony a few guerrillas, including the future General Piar in the *llanos* of Apure, and Monagas, Sedeño and Zaraza in the east, kept the yellow, blue and red flag of the country flying here and there like a spluttering torch.

Ribas, who fled after the defeat at Maturín, was handed over by a slave to royalist guerrillas who killed him, fried his head in oil, and sent it to Caracas. The Spanish authorities there ordered that this pitiful trophy be hung in an iron cage at the northern entrance to the city, and it was kept there for several years. However, those dark days were lightened slightly by the humanity of two Spaniards, Salvador Meléndez, the Governor of Puerto Rico, and Mariano Ramírez, the island's *intendente*. They provided the Venezuelan refugees in St. Thomas with money and food and took many of them to Puerto Rico. Meléndez had already shown his fine moral qualities with the attentions he paid Miranda during his imprisonment on the island.

As in 1812, Bolívar went to New Granada where he was received with exceptional generosity by the President of the Congress, Camilo Torres. The Liberator wanted to appear before Congress to report on his activities in Venezuela, so that it might pass judgment on him, but Torres told him: "General, your country has not perished as long as your sword survives. You will return with it to rescue her from the rule of her oppressors. The Granadan Congress will give you its protection, because it is satisfied with your conduct. You have been a luckless soldier, but you are still a great man."

The fact that General Urdaneta, and the force that he had saved, recognized Bolívar's authority was also of considerable assistance to him, for it meant that he could put those magnificent veterans under the orders of the Granadan government which, as in 1812, found itself almost impotent in the face of the endless antagonism that divided the provinces. Although the Spaniards occupied part of New Granada and were capable of extending their control from Venezuela and in the south, the republican leaders were unable to find a peaceful solution for their conflict. The confusion was intensified by an increasing number of more-or-less personal disputes within each province.

Bolívar found himself involved in these internal differences as soon as he reached Cartagena from Venezuela. This was the most irritating thing that could happen to a person of his character. He would perhaps have been willing to accept a subordinate role in an army that was to be used for the liberation of the continent. He could control his impetuosity and submit to a national government with broad aims, as he did with respect to the Colombian government on the eve of Ayacucho. But he considered it insulting to himself and fatal for the Republic to be put in the position of a regional *caudillo* or the leader of a faction. We can well imagine, therefore, the eagerness with which he accepted from the general government of New Granada the task of forcing the province of Cundinamarca and its capital Bogotá to rejoin the federation.

Fortunately, the task was accomplished after brief military operations and two days of fighting in the capital. Bolívar then devoted himself to erasing the resentment that the *bogotanos* felt at their defeat. He had written to the President of Cundinamarca: "Providence has destined me to become the Liberator of the oppressed peoples, and thus it is that I will never be the conqueror of a single village. The heroes of Venezuela, who have triumphed in hundreds of battles, have not crossed the wastelands, the plateaus and the mountain ranges only to impose chains upon their compatriots, the sons of America." He repeated that his sole aim was to unite the New World to secure freedom and independence. Bolívar proceeded with such tact after his victory that even the political leaders in Bogotá wanted him to stay. The federal government, which also acted nobly and generously, sent commissioners to discuss the situation with him, and he was given the rank of Captain-General, one not previously recognized by the republicans.

But what must have given him most satisfaction was that the bestowal of this extensive authority meant approval of his larger military plan. He proposed to send an expedition to the northern province of Santa Marta, which was still in the hands of the Spaniards, go from there into Venezuela to liberate it again, return through Cúcuta and march south to Lima.

This vision of the American undertaking frightened the shortsighted politicians, as well as many of Bolívar's fellow soldiers, but it was a stroke of genius that prevented the destruction of the spirit of revolution by the provincialism of local interests. Moreover, it was such a consuming idea for the Liberator that he committed himself to it more eagerly precisely in times of greatest adversity. On December 24, 1814 he told General Custodio García Rovira, who had been elected to the triumvirate that was to govern Santa Fe: "This is the most critical moment for Santa Fe, and all, therefore, want to have some patronage from the government for their protection. . . . I must march within fifteen days at the latest. . . . I need instructions designed to make them obey my orders. . . . Believe me, my friend, I need wide authority in relation to the war, because I am determined to take Santa Marta, Maracaibo and Coro, return through Cúcuta, and free the South as far as Lima.[1] But it was to be a long time before that dazzling accomplishment, which fate let him enjoy for a few moments, became reality. Five testing years awaited him. The year about to begin, 1815, was to be one of the hardest.

---

1. *Cartas,* i, p. 113.

XIX

BRAVERY,
SKILL AND
PERSEVERANCE

"THE NOVICE SOLDIER BE-lieves all is lost when he has once been routed. Experience has not proved to him that bravery, skill, and perseverance can mend misfortune," Bolívar had told the Granadans in his Cartagena manifesto. He was a novice soldier himself, for his first command had ended in disaster, an he still had no victory to authenticate his bold assertion. But he recommenced the struggle with the only thing he still possesed, his tenacity, and eight months later he entered Caracas in triumph. Now, 1815, he would need to repeat his heroic maxim to himself frequently, because despite the favorable auguries with which the year began, all was soon to seem lost. His plan to combine the New Granadan forces for a comprehensive campaign against the royalists was enthusiastically received, not only by the General Government, which was prepared to make the required sacrifices, but also by private individuals, whose generosity was endless. Some examples were most moving, such as that of the Girardot family, about wihch Bolívar wrote to the government: "The services of Colonel Girardot have not been well repaid. All New Granada and Venezuela mourn his death and honor his memory. The grants made in favor of his family have been generously renounced for the good of the country. The loss of two sons on the field of battle might have made his father anxious to preserve the rest of the family, but he offered me, as soon as I arrived, his only remaining son."

Once again, however, internal grudges were about to frustrate the great enterprise. Cartagena, whose government had passed into the hands of Bolívar's personal enemies, including Colonel Castillo, his rival from 1812, refused to provide the assistance required for the start of the campaign against Santa Marta. It was decidedly hostile, even to the point of prohibiting the Union troops from crossing its territory just when the royalists in Venezuela were threatening their right flank, while in the south another enemy expedition was expected at any moment.

Bolívar exhausted all possible means to find a solution. He wrote to Dr. Pedro Gual, who had offered himself as a mediator: "I pursue the glorious career of arms only to garner the honor it affords, to free my country, and to merit the blessings of its peoples. Why, then, would I care to tarnish the laurels with which fortune favors me on the field of battle and allow myself to be carried away like a woman by emotions truly feminine? Not only with Brigadier Castillo, who supports our cause, but with Ferdinand VII who opposes it, am I ready to become reconciled for the sake of the Republic's freedom."[1]

He made this pathetic appeal to the President of the state of Cartagena: "The funds that I brought are being spent uselessly; the uniforms are wearing out; the *reinosos* and *momposinos* are deserting because of the ease with which they can do so; the enemy is preparing to repel us; the troops from Cartagena are decreasing in number considerably because they are unpaid and there is no action; distrust and fear are on the increase; public opinion is losing the confidence that we must inspire; the General Government is very worried to see that it is not obeyed; our internal enemies are fomenting discord; and with our own hands we are pulling down the edifice of liberty, and we will bury ourselves beneath its ruins. . . . Let us save the Republic, *Señor* President. I invite you to join in this generous, just and glorious task. Let us reach agreement. You will have all possible deference from me. I am even ready to sacrifice the honor of being the liberator of my country. I will renounce the command of the army, if you do not have confidence in my good faith. I will do everything; but I am determined not to delay operations any longer. Such a fine army does not deserve to perish in inaction because of the caprice of suspicious men, who fear that which they should not fear, while they are not afraid of their responsibility before God and man of being the destroyers of their country."

As always with civil strife, nothing could calm the suspicions and fears of the factions, which had already abandoned themselves to scandalous

---

1. *Cartas*, i, p. 130. Castillo had had an infamous libel published, in which he not only attacked Bolívar's public conduct but also grossly smeared his private life. Bolívar said: "He denies me even my manhood."

scenes of violence within the city itself. Even the veteran and selfless D'Elhuyar was one of their victims, because, after being expelled from the city by Castillo's party, he died in a shipwreck at the end of the year as he returned to the defense of his country. Bolívar boldly decided to lay siege to the city, not, as was later claimed, with the intention of taking it by force since he did not have enough troops for the task, but in the hope that his arrival would lead to the triumph of his followers within the city. He had the excuse that Castillo had successfully used the same strategy, but this was not a sound argument. He should have understood that this action would further compromise him in a pernicious, inglorious civil war.

It is clear that he attached more importance to his despair and anxiety than to reason, and he said in self-justification: "They want my army to perish. My army desires this too, but with glory on the field of honor fighting the enemy, if they help me, or against traitors, if they refuse."[1] He repeated, in another communication to the general government: "I have come to liberate New Granada, not to receive insults. My army is resolved to die on the field of honor, at the foot of the trenches of Santa Marta or at the walls of Cartagena. It is determined not to perish like vile slaves from fevers, poxes and miseries."[2]

Finally, after failing to provoke the reaction that he sought within the city, Bolívar resigned his command of the army on March 25. The Venezuelan and Granadan officers in the *junta de guerra* unanimously refused to accept his resignation, so he reiterated his decision on May 8, and sailed for Jamaica. As he took his leave, he wrote to the President of the United Provinces: "I shall always remember the gratitude I owe the government of the Union, and I shall never forget that the men of New Granada started me on the path to glory."[3]

Distressing news reached him from Venezuela before he left. The general ruin of the country, controlled by the royalists since the end of 1814, was almost indescribable. Whole families had perished. Of the five Buroz brothers who enlisted in the patriot ranks, three died in the first years of the war. Those slaughtered at Maturín included Miguel José Sanz, the illustrious Francisco Xavier Ustáriz and two of his younger sons, Dionisio Palacios Blanco, the Liberator's cousin and brother-in-law, and the officers Francisco Palacios Blanco and Dionisio Blanco, all from the same family. Mariano Ustáriz, still a boy, was saved by an Indian woman, who hid him in her hut. José Félix Ribas caught sight of him as he fled and called to him: "Mariano, if you see my wife tell her that I am still alive." We know

---

1. O'Leary, xiv, p. 139.
2. *Ibid.,* p. 150.
3. *Ibid.,* p. 236.

that he did not survive for long. Ribas's wife and Mariano Ustáriz's mother were sisters, Bolívar's aunts, and both found themselves among the multitude of wandering families and desperate combatants who fled before the implacable lancers of Boves.[1] Twenty-four men of the Ribas family had perished in less than two years. Four sons of Catalina de Tovar, Vicente Salias, two brothers of Colonel José María Carreño, Luis María Ribas Dávila, Dr. Francisco Espejo, Bernardo Bermúdez, García de Sena, Aldao, Freites, Campo Elías and Villapol also gave their lives on the battlefields or were shot as "insurgents," Antonio Muñoz Tébar was only twenty-two when he died in the battle of La Puerta, and he had already been Secretary of War and Navy. Common people like Francisco Carvajal, the *Resting Tiger,* and Juana Ramírez, *The Attacker,* had risen from anonymity to fame by their heroic deaths as had thousands of humble artisans in Caracas, such as those who had dreamed of a school for the *pardos,* and the musicians who played in the five orchestras on April 19. There were also many others who had been simple slaves!

Many of the slaves, in fact, were freed by their owners so that they could join the republican army. As soldiers, rubbing shoulders with the family sons in the ranks, they contributed to the conquest of equality that their masters wished to convert into a political idea. They did so, however, at the cost of their lives. It seemed that all, rich and poor, famous and obscure, had to die.

Royalists and patriots, locked by their bitterness in a furious, blind embrace, had gone through the whole country, exterminating each other. Each time the fields became more desolate and the cities hungrier. Dr. José Manuel Oropeza, a creole royalist and assessor to the *intendente,* reported: "There are now no Provinces! Towns with thousands of souls have been reduced to hundreds, others to tens, and in others there remain only traces that rational beings once lived there.... The roads and fields are filled with unburied corpses, the towns are leveled.... Agriculture is entirely abandoned, with the result that neither grain nor essential crops can be found in the cities.... I have seen the churches defiled and full of blood, with even the tabernacles looted."

The Spanish General, Manuel del Fierro, also described the situation: "If there were many men like Boves in the other parts of America, I assure you that we would soon achieve our aims. His conduct in Venezuela has seen them virtually accomplished, for we have finished off all those who presented themselves to us."

Such was the state of Venezuela when, in April 1815, the largest of the expeditions organized by Spain for the reconquest of America reached its shores. Its total strength was about 15,000 men, of whom 10,642

---

1. *Francisco Javier de Ustáriz,* by Emilio Antonio Yanes, *Crónicas de Caracas,* no. 31, Oct.-Dec. 1956, p. 377.

were combat troops. The remainder were administrative employees, servants and specialists in the artillery and engineering corps. When added to those already arrived from Spain and other colonies, and to the large body of creole royalists, they formed an imposing army.

The expedition was intended for the pacification of all the American colonies, not just Venezuela and New Granada. Its officers and men, like the commander, Field-Marshall Pablo Morillo, were veterans of the struggle against Napoleon when, without arms or leaders, their guerrilla bands had decimated and demoralized the French armies. They were capable of fighting as guerrillas or in long-range campaigns, and their experience and resources made them the equals of the best regular troops in Europe.

Morillo had risen from the rank of private to the highest position in the militia. He had fought the French at Toulon, Trafalgar and Bailén. He led the heterogeneous multitude—"soldiery and peasantry" was his description—that captured Vigo and, after accepting the French surrender, was promoted from Second Lieutenant to Colonel. After driving back Ney at Sampayo, he formed the Union regiment, which he brought to Venezuela. Its standard portrayed the bridge where the action was decided. He followed the ups and downs of the campaign for the liberation of Spain, at times with barefoot, naked troops, at others with a Portuguese or English battalion in his army, and he was among the victors at Vitoria. Morillo was as skilled and tenacious an organizer as he was a daring fighter. On one occasion during the war in Spain he wrote to Castaños: "Here we are trying to make all possible use of time, continually training troops in the school of battle and guerrilla activity, so that in the future they can begin to fight in the line."[1] The Venezuelan royalists were dazzled by his arrival. Heredia wrote: "The great expedition led by Morillo was formed of the victors over Napoleon at Arapiles and Vitoria. The corps consisted of Spanish veterans who had fought in the campaign from the Portuguese frontier to the other side of the Garonne. They came fully equipped and with a magnificence never before seen in our armies. Such a brilliant and numerous expedition had never before left Spain for America."

They felt so splendid that, when the creole *llaneros* of Morales joined them, a colonel of the Union regiment commented: "If these are the victors, who are the vanquished?" The sarcasm was later repeated with hilarity by the other commanders, including Morillo himself. Despite their misery, however, Venezuela and New Granada were going to absorb and even destroy this expedition which, when it arrived, intended simply to march across them to the ends of the continent.

---

1. Antonio Rodríguez Villa, *El Teniente General don Pablo Morillo, primer Conde de Cartagena, Marqués de la Puerta.*

In revolutionary France the "people in arms" had destroyed the king's professional armies. Later, during Napoleon's invasion of Spain, it was the French who possessed experienced, well-armed forces led by first-class commanders with the prestige of innumerable victories. They were defeated and humiliated several times, nevertheless, by hastily assembled popular troops without experience and almost without arms, led by general "no matter who." In America in 1815 the professional, disciplined army, led by one of the most experienced generals in Europe, was composed of the destroyers of the French. It had equipment, arms and supplies that the despised creole "insurgents" could not hope to obtain. The creoles, however, were going to defeat them. The proud regiments, the historic standards, the trains of artillery and the gallant body of officers were to be destroyed on the battlefields of Venezuela and New Granada.

But this was all in the future. At the end of 1814 Bolívar had declared in a proclamation: "Thus it appears that providence, to our humiliation and glory, has determined that our brothers shall be our conquerors and that only our brothers shall triumph over us." How would he feel now, alone in Jamaica, when he learned that those Venezuelans inexplicably "faithful to the King," were receiving such reinforcements?

For a short time Bolívar thought that he might obtain assistance from England, and he even had a plan to go to London. He spoke of his plans and of the commercial benefits that an independent America could offer Great Britain in letters to the Duke of Manchester; Governor of Jamaica; Richard Wellesley, with whom he had dealt in London; and Maxwell Hyslop, a Kingston merchant who was particularly friendly to him. He told Hyslop: "These extensive benefits can be obtained with the most insignificant means: twenty or thirty thousand rifles, a million pounds sterling, fifteen or twenty men-of-war, munitions, several envoys, and any volunteers who wish to fight under the flags of America. This is all that is needed to bring liberty to half the earth and set the world in balance."

But that prospect and the argument that these countries "seek freedom only in order to receive the continental Europeans at their breast, and turn America into another Europe within a few years," failed completely to move the English leaders of the period. The blackest reaction dominated in Europe after the fall of Napoleon. Even in England liberty was synonymous with Jacobinism, racial strife, world-wide subversion and other difficulties that could seem terrifying to the merchants and politicians who for more than twenty years had kept up the struggle against revolutionary France. The new cult of *Legitimacy* reigned throughout the continent, and the international congresses that met thought only of using this collar to choke any manifestation, however mild, of the dreaded "popular will." The persecutions and punishments imposed on liberals in Russia, Prussia, Austria and Italy delighted Ferdinand VII, who, naturally, strove to improve upon them; but they also made England smile, for, although she had no need of them to restrain her own people, she felt no repugnance in approving their use elsewhere. At precisely this time the English governor of the island of Trinidad announced that the supply of arms to the insurgents on the mainland was a crime, and that "any fugitives from the Spanish provinces admitted to this island only on a temporary basis for their own security and protection, who are found to be involved in such crimes, will be immediately imprisoned, their properties will be seized and confiscated, and such persons will be banished and expelled from this colony..."[1]

Bolívar witnessed this attitude at close hand. "Not only the Europeans but even our Northern brothers have remained immobile spectators of this contest...," he wrote, and he leveled against England the accusation: "Every recourse, military and political, denied to us has been made abundantly available to our enemies. To cite only one example *The Courant* of Jamaica and *La Gaceta de Santiago de la Vega,* copying from the former, have published the list of arms, munitions and clothing that the Spanish have received."[2]

It was this atmosphere, without doubt, that persuaded Bolívar to abandon his plan to go to London. Once again, as in 1810, he realized that his America stood alone, and that she would have to win the war through her desperation, in the creole style. With his mind filled with new plans for the recommencement of the struggle, he spent the last months of 1815 analyzing the situation in America and explaining it to the world. In addition to the letters mentioned above and various communications sent to the government of New Granada, he had published in the *Royal Gazette* a number of letters which explained his ideas on the social structure of Spanish America and on its political future.

In one of these studies, apparently not published, Bolívar referred to South America's racial heterogeneousness. In view of the unfortunate events in Santo Domingo in the previous century, this was the subject discussed with most alarm whenever any revolutionary plan was proposed for these colonies. Then, as now, there was a tendency to see this social characteristic as an insoluble problem, denying the Spanish American nations the possibility of a way of life like that of Europe and, in the political sphere, condemning them to permanent anarchy and despotism.

Bolívar condemned this dogmatism with two observations that still contain critical value today. He said, first, that, although the white race was

---

1. Blanco y Azpúrua, v, p. 328.
2. *Cartas del Libertador,* i, pp. 187, 208.

less numerous than the others, it possessed "intellectual qualities which give it a relative equality," with the result that the population of America was "balanced... now by number, now by circumstance, and above all by the irresistible dominion of the spirit." The racial imbalance of America could not be an obstacle to the stabilization of new governments, because "its composition produces in the inhabitants the most favorable support for harmony and union among all." His second point was: "We are told that our civil war proves the opposite. No, sir. The domestic conflicts of America have never originated from the difference of castes. They have been born, like those that have afflicted all other nations, of differences in political opinions and of the personal ambition of some men."

This point was of particular interest to Bolívar, as though he could foresee that Spanish America's misfortunes would give rise to a depressing and unjustly pessimistic interpretation of its history. He strove to demonstrate that our conflicts are neither greater than nor essentially different from those of the world's more fortunate nations, protesting: "What free nation has never suffered from disunity? Could any history be more turbulent than that of Athens? Factions more blood-thirsty than those of Rome? Civil wars more violent than those of England? Dissensions more dangerous than those of the United States of North America? Yet these are the four nations that the human race most honors for their virtues, their freedom and their glory."

He concluded with the following observations, which seem to have been written for the present-day crisis of America and the world: "That which, in my opinion, is really terrible is the indifference with which Europe has watched so far the struggle of justice against oppression, because of her fear of increasing anarchy. This attitude is an obstacle to the attainment of the order, prosperity and brilliant future that awaits America. The forlornness in which she has left us is the factor that, one day, might disillusion the independence party to the point of driving it to proclaim demagogic maxims in order to espouse the popular cause. This indifference, I repeat, is an immediate cause capable of producing subversion, and which, without doubt, will force the weak party in some parts of America to adopt the most pernicious, but most essential, measures to defend its *patria* against a persecution unknown in every country other than Spanish America. Despair cannot choose the means to save her from danger."[1]

Bolívar spoke of despair and forlornness. Today we could add the merciless exploitation that economic imperialism has brought to these countries. When an industrial dispute occurs in Europe or the United States, it can be resolved by increasing the cost of the products, which are paid for

1. From the rough copy published by Lecuna in *Papeles de Bolívar* (Caracas, 1917,) p. 271.

mainly by the other countries in the world. But these countries cannot do the same with their rubber, their sugar, their cocoa beans, their coffee, or even their gold, diamonds or petroleum.

It is untrue to assert that these conditions can be overcome by inventiveness, work and common-sense, for they are derived from an internationally organized oppression. The misery that they cause, and the attendant depopulation, ignorance and epidemics, help to perpetuate them. Even the wars that produced romantic exaltation or boasts of racial superiority in Europe became for Spanish America one more affront, a means of obtaining scandalous indemnifications, or a pretext to send warships to blockade our ports and expeditions to conquer our shores. Crowning all this is the attempt to create for "the little countries" a fatalist sociology which is eagerly adopted by writers like Ortega y Gasset. The mistake is fatal. Today it is important, with the struggle between communism and the old civilization of Europe and North America, for the whole world as well as ourselves to understand that our disputes represent the same "struggle of justice against oppression" of which Bolívar spoke, and that our excesses can be explained purely and simply by the phrase "despair cannot choose the means."

The most valuable of the Liberator's reflections on the reality of America are, nevertheless, those contained in the prophetic, so-called Jamaica Letter dated September 6, 1815, in Kingston.[1] The precision with which he foresaw the immediate future of almost all the nations of the continent is truly surprising. Among his predictions to be clearly confirmed by the history of America in the nineteenth century were the following: that in Mexico an attempt would be made to re-establish the monarchical regime in some form; the union of the Central American republics in a single state; the establishment of a common government for New Granada and Venezuela; that Peru would have difficulties with her republican reorganization because of her wealth and the great inequality between social classes; the danger of military rule or oligarchy in Argentina; that Chile, because of the morality of her inhabitants and her geographical isolation, would establish stable, liberal institutions, of a markedly conservative character.

Some of his other observations are still of interest. Although he was trying at the time to secure the goodwill of England, he did not hide his desire to avoid in America the spirit of conquest which the other great monarchical states seemed to possess. He wrote: "Mr. de Pradt has wisely divided America into fifteen or seventeen mutually independent states, governed by as many monarchs. I am in agreement on the first suggestion, as America can well tolerate seventeen nations; as to the second, though it could easily be achieved, it would serve no purpose. Consequently, I do

---

1. *Cartas del Libertador,* i, p. 181.

not favor American monarchies. My reasons are these: The well-understood interests of a republic are limited to its preservations, prosperity, and glory. Republicans, because they do not desire powers which represent a directly contrary viewpoint, have no reason for expanding the boundaries of their nation to the detriment of their own resources, solely for the purpose of having their neighbors share a liberal constitution. They would not acquire rights or secure any advantage by conquering their neighbors, unless they were to make them colonies, conquered territories, or allies, after the example of Rome. But such thought and action are directly contrary to the principles of justice which characterize republican systems. What is more, they are in direct opposition to the interests of their citizens, because a state, too large of itself or together with its dependencies, ultimately falls into decay. Its free government becomes a tyranny. The principles that should preserve the government are disregarded, and finally it degenerates into despotism. The distinctive feature of small republics is permanence; that of large republics varies, but always with a tendency toward empire. Almost all small republics have had long lives. Among the larger republics, only Rome lasted for several centuries, for its capital was a republic. The rest of her dominions were governed by diverse laws and institutions. The policy of a king is very different. His constant desire is to increase his possessions, wealth, and authority; and with justification, for his power grows with every acquisition, both with respect to his neighbors and his own vassals who fear him because his power is as formidable as his empire, which he maintains by war and conquest. For these reasons, I think that the Americans, being anxious for peace, science, art, commerce and agriculture, would prefer republics to kingdoms. And, further, it seems to me that these desires conform with the aims of Europe."

Bolívar also recognized that, although it would be grandiose to unite all the American nations under a single government, the geographical, economic and psychological differences that divided them made such a union impossible. He preferred to think of the contribution they could make to the creation of a happier humanity, when they could support reciprocal tolerance and free deliberation in international relations. He explained: "It is a grandiose idea to think of consolidating the New World into a single nation, united by pacts into a single bond. It is reasoned that, as these parts have a common origin, language, customs, and religion, they ought to have a single government to permit the newly formed states to unite in a confederation. But this is not possible. Actually, America is separated by climatic differences, geographic diversity, conflicting interests, and dissimilar characteristics. How beautiful it would be if the Isthmus of Panama could be for us what the Isthmus of Corinth was for the Greeks! Would to God that some day we may have the good fortune to convene there an august assembly of representatives of republics, kingdoms and empires to deliberate upon the high interests of peace and war with the nations of the other three-quarters of the globe. This type of organization may come to pass in some happier period of our regeneration. But any other plan, such as that of Abbe St. Pierre, who in laudable delirium conceived the idea of assembling a European congress to decide the fate and interests of those nations, would be meaningless."

But he did believe that Venezuela and New Granada, which he described indiscriminately as his *patria,* could unite themselves more intimately: "New Granada"—he pointed out—"will unite with Venezuela, if they can agree to the establishment of a central republic. Their capital may be Maracaibo or a new city to be named Las Casas, in honor of that humane hero, to be built on the borders of the two countries in the excellent port area of Bahia-Honda. This location, although little known, is the most advantageous in all respects. It is readily accessible, and its situation is so strategic that it can be made impregnable. It has a fine, healthful climate, a soil as suitable for agriculture as for cattle raising, and a superabundance of good timber. The Indians living there can be civilized, and our territorial possessions could be increased with the acquisition of the Goajira peninsula. This nation should be called Colombia as a just and grateful tribute to the discoverer of our hemisphere. Its government might follow the English pattern, except that in place of a king there will be an executive who will be elected, at most, for life, but his office will never be hereditary if a republic is desired. There will be a hereditary legislative chamber or senate. This body can interpose itself between the violent demands of the people and the great powers of the government during periods of political unrest. The second representative body will be a legislature with restrictions no greater than those of the lower house in England. The constitution will draw on all systems of government, but I do not want it to partake of all their vices. As Colombia is my country, I have an indisputable right to desire for her that form of government which, in my opinion, is best."

It can be seen that on many topics the Liberator expressed himself—above all in this letter—as if he were musing by himself on the future of America. His reflections, therefore, are particularly important, despite the doubts that occurred to him, and we believe that it would be mutilation to try to explain them without reproducing them fully.

In this document, as in other writings of the same period, Bolívar passionately stressed the censurable aspect of Spanish colonization, not, as some Spanish writers allege, because he hated Spain, but because he was being tormented by the devastation that he had just seen in his country, and which was still continuing. Nor is it sensible to use his comments as valid historical criticism of Spain, as some Spanish Americans have tried to do.

It is more interesting to note that, despite his unfavorable state of mind, Bolívar's analysis of the significance of Spain's spiritual contribution to our culture, and of how the war of independence should be understood, was profound and perspicacious. He explained: "We are a young people. We inhabit a world apart, separated by broad seas. We are young in the ways of almost all the arts and sciences, although, in a certain manner, we are old in the ways or civilized society." He rejected, therefore, the simplistic formulation, already becoming popular, that we were "primitive" people without the antecedents to give us a stable and worthy organization. Our experience of civilized society was based upon the laws received from Spain, and the institutions that she brought to America such as universities, *cabildos,* tribunals, and the press. Spain also brought what we might call habits of legality in public life. These certainly existed under her rule, although, as in all periods and all countries, the laws were occasionally violated.

Bolívar never denied this life-giving nucleus of our nationality, which linked us to Spain and to the millenary civilization received from her. In one paragraph he recalled it with obvious nostalgia: "The habit of obedience, a community of interest, of understanding, of religion, mutual goodwill, a tender regard for the birthplace and good name of our forefathers, in short, all that gave rise to our hopes, came to us from Spain." He hurriedly added: "At present the contrary attitude persists: we are threatened with the fear of death, dishonor, and every harm; there is nothing we have not suffered at the hands of that unnatural step-mother, Spain." Despite his reference to the images of animosity that torture him, that mutual goodwill of which he speaks remains as a testimony of the sentiments that had been building up in him and his creole ancestors for three centuries. And is it not clear that he calls Spain step-mother because of his sadness at being unable to continue calling her mother?

We have stressed the basis of affection in these judgements of the Liberator because in some cases sentiments are more revealing than ideas. His concept of the experience of civilized society, which we held in common with Spain, also led him towards other conclusions with which he formed a comprehensive, connected picture. Such was his assertion that the struggle of the Americans against Spain was really a civil war. He wrote: "Surely unity is what we need to complete our work of regeneration. The division among us, nevertheless, is nothing extraordinary, for it is characteristic of civil wars to form two parties, *conservatives* and *reformers.* The former are commonly the more numerous, because the weight of habit induces obedience to established powers; the latter are always fewer in number, although more vocal and learned."

Bolívar did not lightly call the struggle for independence a civil war, nor did he describe it thus because of the transitory circumstance that some Spaniards fought on the republican side and many creoles for the royalists. When this peculiarity no longer prevailed, in November 1820, and even though he was negotiating with Morillo on a government to government basis, he repeated the same idea. In his instructions to the republican commissioners who were going to discuss an armistice with the Spaniards, he said: "Propose that all prisoners should be exchanged, including spies, conspirators and opponents, for it is in civil wars that international law should be most strict and vigorous." It is clear, then, that Bolívar saw the war as an episode in the struggle then taking place throughout the world between *conservatives* and *reformers* (the underlining is his). His interpretation was so perspicacious that it is applicable today, for in our time, too, anti-colonial wars are mixed up with civil disputes and international conflicts, when all of them, in fact, are aspects of the same crisis of reform.

This universality with which Bolívar embraced the war of independence was important to another of his basic concepts: that if Spaniards and Americans were divided only by a civil war, the superior unity that had joined them should not be considered broken. This idea appears in many of his writings; and all the enlightened creoles shared the conviction with such an intensity that in 1842, twelve years after Bolívar's death, Simón Rodríguez expressed it with surprising spontaneity. Referring to the importance of education in America, he wrote: "We are discussing nothing less than the fate of a large part of the Spanish Nation, separated from the other part by the ignorance of the last King of Spain and the avarice of the peninsular merchants."[1] Even though the republics had become sovereign states, recognized by all the world, for Rodríguez they continued in another sense which was superior to that of the political reality, to be part of the Spanish nation.

The tendency of the American jurists involved in the early revolutionary movements to call America "American Spain" has the same significance. As far as they were concerned, there was only one Spanish nation, divided by the Atlantic into peninsular Spain and American Spain.

We thus arrive at the final synthesis to which these concepts led. Bolívar and the other advanced creoles understood with perfect clarity that the Spanish nation was dividing, not because of animosity or past disputes, but simply because the part endowed with greater political vitality and the most disposed to join the worldwide movement of reform, American Spain, felt that metropolitan Spain was unjustly holding her back.

---

1. Simón Rodríguez, *Sociedades americanas* (Lima, 1842), p. 37 of J. A. Cova's facsimile edition (Caracas, 1950). The idea is repeated quite frequently in other of Rodríguez's writings.

9

The sons of those creoles who had demanded in 1749 that the wishes and interests of the province should determine whether or not the Guipuzcoana Company should remain, were no longer content to be governed by officials selected for them by the court of Madrid. And what they knew of Spain did not increase their confidence. When Fr. Llamozas, the chaplain to Boves's army, was sent to Spain by Morillo with the important task of reporting to the government on the American situation, he was not received by Ferdinand VII. Instead he had to deliver his celebrated *Memoria* to the king's favorite: the servile, disloyal, lazy, dismal canon Escoiquiz. One has to imagine what could be discussed with Escoiquiz! Above him Ferdinand VII was simply more obstinate and abject than his favorite.

Rodríguez agreed with this interpretation of the independence of America, writing: "Bolívar, unlike the common people, saw neither opprobrium nor shame in the dependence from Spain, only an obstacle to the progress of the society of his country."[1] This judgement should not be considered in isolation. It represented the conclusion and final expression of a consciousness, mainly collective but expressed most clearly by Bolívar, whereby the Americans accepted with pride that their culture was a continuation of that of Spain, but, at the same time, fought the civil war to proclaim the need for the American *reformers* to urge Spain away from her obstinate absolutism.

This interpretation, moreover, changes the position in history of Bolívar, because we see him no longer contemplating the past but looking towards the future, motivated not by bitterness but by legitimate hopes for a better world. His mission was not to destroy a dark colonialism, but to set America on the path towards her own future. Our independence from Spain was secured not out of vengeance, but in accordance with those "ways of civilized society" brought to us by Spain, and to give them opportunity and freedom of development. The final result was not, as some blinkered critics saw it, the destruction of the Spanish empire, but the reorganization of American Spain into twenty republics.

This awareness of the American situation showed the Liberator's extraordinary spiritual elevation, particularly since the immediate reality that surrounded him was such as to confuse the serenest of men. There was now added to the horrors he had seen in Venezuela the lamentable spectacle of creole families wandering through the Antilles, literally without anything to eat. Women could not work outside the house, nor was there anywhere for them to work. They could not even earn their living as servants, because in America these positions were filled

---

1. Simón Rodríguez, *El Libertador del Mediodía de América y sus compañeros de armas defendidos por un amigo de la causa social* (Arequipa, 1830), p. 3. Facsimile edition by Sociedad Bolivariana, Caracas, 1954.

by slaves. It seemed then, that prostitution or beggary would be forced upon those Venezuelan ladies who fled from their country, sometimes accompanied by children or even more defenseless old people. They embroidered, spun, and sold the trifles that they made themselves, but without hope of surviving very long by these means. We have already seen how Martín de Tovar advised his wife on this point. Horrifying letters have survived of the brilliant daughters of the Aristeguieta family, the young women relatives of Bolívar, Sucre and the Marquis del Toro, who had been called the Nine Muses. One of them, Belén, who was so beautiful that she had sat as a model for a painting of Nuestra Señora de las Mercedes, spent seven years "wandering about with her family from town to town." In Caracas in 1827 she was still so poor that she wrote to Bolívar, "I do not even have an outer skirt in which to show myself... there are days when I do not even have a light to see by."[1]

On several occasions Bolívar himself had to ask for money lent by Hyslop, for himself and for the operations that he planned. On one of these occasions he told him frankly, "Your generosity will have to be gratuitous, because it is impossible for me, after losing everything, to offer you any recompense...."[2]

He was also almost assassinated. A Negro called Pío, whom he employed and protected, stabbed to death the patriot José Félix Amestoy, who had gone to receive his orders from Bolívar, and was sleeping in his hammock while waiting for him. Bolívar's life was saved by the coincidence that he did not sleep in his lodgings that night because of a quarrel with the landlady. According to the royalist Level de Goda, *fiscal* of the *audiencia* of Caracas, Morillo had arranged the murder with a Catalán to whom he paid 5,000 pesos.[3]

At this point Bolívar was involved in the most daring exploit of his military career, an attempt to go to the aid of Cartagena, which was being besieged by Morillo. He would first have to get past the blockading Spanish squadron; and, once inside the fortress, what would he do? He had only the desperate hope that his presence would encourage the defenders, and that a mass sally or some similar solution might be found. When commissioners of Cartagena, including Hyslop, decided on their own initiative, without the authorization of the province's government,

1. Boletín de la Academia Nacional de la Historia, Caracas, no. 94, April-June 1941.
2. *Cartas del Libertador,* i, p. 216. In 1830 Bolívar repeated his thanks to Hyslop for his services, and, as the generous Englishman was then in economic difficulties, offered him his assistance.
3. Boletín de la Academia Nacional de la Historia, Caracas, nos. 63 and 64. For the complete account of what happened, see Navarro (ed.), *Diario de Bucaramanga* (Caracas, 1935, p. 174).

to ask for his aid, Bolívar began by warning them: "No danger deters me, save the fear that my presence might revive the differences that drove me from Cartagena." But he immediately added, "If Cartagena should call me, I would fly to defend her or to seek my tomb among her ruins!" He decided to depart even though this summons did not come. We see here Bolívar's surprising duality: a few days earlier he had been involved, like a sedentary scholar, in analyzing the history and the possibilities of the New World; suddenly, he returned to his role of the impetuous guerrilla—in this case a guerrilla on the sea—going to fight without hopes. He took little with him apart from his own presence. It is not even known who helped him and with what, except that Hyslop provided some money and that Captain Luis Brión as always gave him all he had.

Captain Brión was a rare individual comparable in admiration only to that aroused by the North American William Stephens Smith, who compromised his fortune and his political future for Miranda and offered him his son for his enterprise. Although Brión was born of Dutch parents in Curaçao, and enjoyed an easy life, he consecrated himself to the independence of South America with such enthusiasm that Cartagena gave him the title "beloved son" of the city and Bolívar called him "the magnanimous Brión." Bolívar wrote to him: "I know not what I should most admire in you: your generosity, your patriotism, or your kindness. Yours must be a character quite extraordinary for you to sacrifice yourself without stint in the interests of a cause which is being torn asunder by its own offspring. To you, friend Brión, must be accorded the honor of being the foremost patron of America and the most liberal of men." Brión was educated in Holland, where he also acquired some military experience, and he later studied navigation in the United States. In 1805 he distinguished himself in the defense of Curaçao against the English, and in 1811 he offered his services to the Venezuelan Republic. He was a strong supporter of Bolívar, and in 1814 bought and armed at his own expense a ship which he called the 'Intrepid Bolívar': In 1815 his privateer 'La Popa' was considered the fastest and best armed in the Caribbean, and it was in this ship that Bolívar set out for Cartagena.

He left Jamaica at midday on December 18, with this one ship, a handful of Granadans and Venezuelans, and the arms and provisions he could gather together. They had been sailing for more than twenty-four hours towards their destination, when they had the good fortune to encounter 'El Republicano,' a privateer in the service of the patriots, which informed them that Cartagena had already fallen to the Spaniards. Chance, therefore, once again saved Bolívar's life, just as it had preserved him a little earlier from the attack of Pío.

Cartagena had resisted for a hundred and six days, tormented by hunger. The Spanish Captain Rafael Sevilla, who was among the besiegers, wrote: "The state in which we find the rich Cartagena de Indias is indescribable. . . . Men and women, living portraits of death, grasped the walls to walk without falling, such was the horrible hunger they had suffered. . . Women who had been rich and beautiful, men who belonged to the most illustrious of that rich mercantile center of both worlds, all of them, without distinction of sex or class although hardly able to move, threw themselves pushing and fighting onto our soldiers, not to attack them, but to search their knapsacks in search of a crust of bread or a few biscuits. . . . The foul smell was unbearable, as though there were many houses full of rotting corpses. . . . The first thing that General Morillo did was to order the digging of a large trench, and that the heaps of corpses that were infesting the city should be buried in it. Many cartloads of them were taken from the houses. . . ."[1]

Despite this extreme misery, General José Francisco Bermúdez had managed to organize an evacuation by sea, and he passed through the blockading squadron with thirteen ships carrying 2,000 people. This inconceivable adventure of the Venezuelan Ajax was assisted by the fortuitous withdrawal of some of the enemy ships, but the fugitives were bombarded by the royalist batteries controlling the bay. Their situation was so extreme that they welcomed a storm which scattered their ships that night, because it also saved them from being pursued.

It was thus that the year 1815 came to an end, with no more encouragement for the republicans than the spectacle of their own heroism. More than ever before, everything seemed lost. The Liberator, however, had new plans, and to realize them he changed course for Haiti after meeting *El Republicano* on the high seas. He arrived at the capital, Port-au-Prince, on December 31, 1815.

---

1. Quoted by Andrés Revesz in his biography of Morillo (Madrid, 1947), p. 97.

XX

THE MAN
OF DIFFICULTIES

A POET WORKS WITHIN the dramatic personage he has conceived. He is interested not in reality but in the creation of a vassal spirit through which he can sing of the greatest miseries and the most beautiful exaltation. With subtle artistry he prepares the tests that his hero has to face, all the contrasts that test the human soul, cajolery and licentiousness, sadness and shameful impotence, easy and brilliant success, and undeserved, total misfortune. This poet is not concerned with what is probable or opportune. He wants to sing of an exceptional life; he is fascinated by the dazzle that can be produced by the struggle between a great spirit and the whims of fate. The poet wants "to create," concentrating in his hero everything that human imagination has dreamed of, and vainly pursues—somewhat cowardly—in everyday ordinary life.

The poet, we repeat, works outside of reality. Nevertheless, at times nature, too, takes pleasure in constructing exaggerated figures as if under the influence of a lyric rapture, abandoning the rules she normally applies. I am thinking of the life of the Liberator. The violence of the situations, the unforeseen outcome, the changing, variegate scenary, make one think of a dramatic creation rather than a historical and psychological reality.

When the first test was put to his young, ambitious spirit in the violent initiation of 1812, failure kept him in Puerto Cabello with mocking sleight of hand. Despair threw him into an equivocal "tumult" consummated in the ruin of the Precursor Miranda. . . . Suddenly, the Admirable Campaign from the Magdalena to Caracas, a triumphal gallop of hundreds of leagues in less than eight months, and, for the defeated and uncertain subaltern of the previous year, the prestige of the invincible General with discretionary authority. EL LIBERTADOR!, the most personalist improvisation which for the first time separated the fascinating figure of the *caudillo* from the measured progress of the collective revolution.

Afterwards, five years of consecutive failures, from the despair of San Mateo where he wished to die, to the impotent anger of the third defeat of La Puerta, where he killed the fleeing standard-bearer with his own hands. In 1818, when he returned defeated from the valleys of Aragua to the heart of the plains of Apure, it doubtless must have seemed to him that the fleeting successes of the early years had been simply the joke of a malicious genius, which with cruel delight was using him for defeat. Perhaps his officers would regard him with suspicious fear, and it would be his turn to lose the respect and obedience of his men because the persistent dark shadow of defeat could be dispelled by neither prudence nor valor.

His most daring exploit then restored his mastery of fortune. It would have seemed cowardice if prudence had foreseen limits to the giddy ascent from Boyacá to Ayacucho. He became the arbiter of Spanish America, worthy of the magnificent boast: "I know the roads of victory and the people live under my justice."

He visited the liberated country: "He began at Arequipa. The Municipality came out to receive him with demonstrations of delirious gaiety. It offered him a richly harnessed horse for his entry into the city. The stirrups, the bit, the breastplate, and the trappings on the saddle and the bridle were of solid gold. The Incas never made more magnificent parades than those for the Colombian hero. At the end of July he was in Cuzco...."[1]

Why do we think of Napoleon, a depressing example? Miranda had already foretold the fabulous Inca state that would unify independent America. In Peru it had a double base in the tradition of the indigenous monarchy and in that of the Spanish empire. This was in 1825. Three years later Bolívar himself was to say: "When one's duty is almost done, to waste insults on me..."; and on another occasion: "All America resounds with complaints about me...."

There were contrasts even at the hour of death. He left behind the enduring reality of five independent nations, and projects that would begin to be realized a century later. But in his last declaration he ventured only to invoke the negative hope that his departure would reconcile the parties.

His character was that of the hero. He was meticulous to the point of taking pleasure in the detailed, reiterated orders of the best administrator and,

---

1. Gil Fortoul, *Historia Constitucional de Venezuela*, i, p. 345.

when fortune did not force him into desperate action, he was capable of submitting himself to all the dictates of prudence. In the Peruvian campaign he found gratification in the discipline of heroic abstention and in foreseeing and calculating all possible vicissitudes. But he did not love these virtues and, moreover, he did not believe in their efficacy. He loved constancy and valor. The force that inspired his actions and directed his life was expressed in a simple observation made in 1823 to Sucre, referring to the possibility that the Spaniards would defeat Santa Cruz: "If the enemy did not pursue him before, it will do so now, for to do things properly it is necessary to do them twice; that is to say, the first attempt teaches experience to the second." This was the true idea that dominated in that obstinate and aggressive spirit: "To do things properly it is necessary to do them twice . . . the first teaches the second." The spontaneity of this reflection gives it the value of revelation. Triumph depends not upon logical precision or foresight. It is obtained only by dauntless effort and by constancy. Adversity has a relative importance. It ensures the first failure, and it is scorned; when the hero returns to battle he already possesses, in his consciousness, the irresistible weapon.

If it can be said that each of us possesses within himself a dominant force, which is revealed in all our psychological reactions, there is no doubt that in the Liberator this nucleus of character was an indestructible confidence in the power of action. All men possess the potential for lucid thought and vigorous impulse. This force is the true creator of character, not only because it orientates all its qualities, but also because it recreates itself after every crisis. This virtue of renovation was evident in Bolívar. At his critical moments we can see a sort of spiritual retreat after each adverse confrontation with reality which restored the hero's contact with his life-giving principle.

Bolívar called himself "the man of difficulties." Morillo described him as "less dangerous victorious than vanquished." Both judgements express-ed an awareness of Bolívar's most constant psychological characteristic, his admirable capacity of overcoming failure. The taunt of 1812 against nature was a spontaneous reaction, not a literary device. The "to tri-umph!" at Pativilca was for him a straightforward proposition. His pro-mise at Casacoima seemed delirious but, in a similar situation in 1814, a fugitive in New Granada from his ruined country and the leader of simply one force in a civil war, he maintained his goal of "liberating the South as far as Lima." Soon after, in exile, he had to petition depressingly for even the means of subsistence, but he had not lost the gift for abstract thought. In the Jamaica Letter the hero analyzed the possibilities of his America, debating and judging with the same serenity that he would show in 1825 when his hegemony over the Bolivarian nations permitted him to summon the Congress of Panama.

The intellectual has a sad confidence in the infallibility of calculation. Men with little combativeness take shelter in this confidence. They prepare their actions scrupulously, and they embark upon them only when this intellectual preparation gives them the confidence that their foresight has eliminated any possibility of failure. Their scruples are nothing more than an unconscious manifestation of the fear they feel at the prospect of commencing a new venture. The road ahead always seems difficult and they will follow it only when they have convinced themselves that it is the *right road*. Their dismay is overwhelming when chance demolishes their carefully constructed plans. The combative man, however, always counts upon the intervention of the unforeseen. His calculations always represent a provisional assessment, based upon immediate circumstances, and he is always ready to modify or completely alter them. This gives him a confidence and a flexibility denied to those who depend upon definitive, rigid calculation. And it is clear that the man who recognizes that the ground beneath his feet is crumbly, but is prepared to jump nimbly and bravely from one firm spot to another, has put his faith in his own action. If he fails, he is always prepared to begin again. "To do things properly it is necessary to do them twice...." Nothing surprises such a man, and he is not dismayed to find that the road he is following ends in an abyss.

Unamuno considered Bolívar *theatrical*. We might say that his life was theatrical, like the creation of a poet who takes pleasure in antithesis. The Liberator—a member of the cast—simply emphasized the drama in the situations, and expressed the lyricism of his adventures with appropriate high-sounding language.

When we hear him preparing himself for the heroic task, his ideas seem like hallucinations little related to visible reality. His aggressiveness gives the impression that he deliberately sought to deny the limits of the possible. His efforts to alter reality seem grandiose and sometimes senseless. The indominability of his attitude grew in inverse progression as he moved from success to defeat. He gives the impression that even in his moments of greatest misfortune he could calmly foresee his triumphal entry into Cuzco. In his exile, his unquenchable optimism let him forget the apotheosis of 1813, just as it permitted him in 1818 to overcome the sudden, total, confusing reverse of fortune which seemed rather like an arbitrary change of scenery. It might even be said that he became fond of the instability of fate. When he seemed to have conquered it, he found pleasure in provoking it. In 1823 he worked throughout the night on plans for the American confederation, and in the morning he led his escort in a charge against the guerrillas of Agualongo. It gave him an intoxicating thrill to risk both his life and the great plans he was carrying with him. The force within him not only erased external reality but also altered or eliminated feelings in his own consciousness. Sadness did not exist for him. He ventured to say: "My fortune has improved so much that now I cannot be unhappy." He suffered severely from adversity, but he watched it from afar, his mind occupied with work accomplished and new possibilities.

Between 1815 and 1819, however, the Liberator did not need this steely elasticity of character. Despite the miserable situation that we have examined, the republicans were able by the end of 1818 to take control of a vast stretch of Venezuelan territory from the island of Margarita and the eastern coast, Guayana and the mouth of the Orinoco on one side, to the plains of Apure and part of New Granada in the extreme southwest on the other. Although the royalists still held the center of Venezuela, the mountainous region of the west, New Granada, which Morillo had conquered, and the most important cities and ports in both countries, the patriots had created an extensive base for operations from which they could attack various points. In 1818 the geographical situation of the two sides represented an almost complete reversal of the 1814 position.

There was also a reversal in another important sphere. In 1818 the *llaneros* of Apure followed a *caudillo,* José Antonio Páez, who had brought them under republican standards. Other factors also gave hope to the defenders of freedom. The patriotism of the cities occupied by the royalists remained hidden but alert. The arms given to Bolívar by President Petión, and those that could now be bought with increasing facility in Europe, following the defeat of Napoleon, alleviated the tremendous inferiority formerly suffered in this sphere. The supplies of tobacco and cattle in the territory occupied by their forces provided the means of obtaining arms and other essential supplies for shipment up the Orinoco River. Most important, the relatively secure control of the city of Angostura on the banks of the river permitted the Liberator to summon a Congress which, together with his personal prestige, restrained the anarchy of local *caudillismo* and gave new force and legitimacy to the republican government.

At the end, all were to attribute this transformation which paved the way for the great victories that followed, to Bolívar, but in fact, he was responsible for none of the republican successes between 1815 and 1818. On the contrary, three dismal failures at Ocumare de la Costa, Clarines, and the third battle of La Puerta, in 1816, 1817 and 1818, destroyed his army and on several occasions almost cost his life. Arismendi was responsible for the liberation of the island of Margarita in 1815 and 1816, and his success was consolidated by General Francisco Esteban Gómez who, in 1817, defeated Morillo himself. The republican flags were kept flying in the eastern *llanos* by the constant fighting of Monagas, Zaraza, Sedeño and other local leaders. In 1816 Piar and MacGregor defeated Morales at the battle of El Juncal, which gave the patriots control of the province of Barcelona. Piar went on to win Guayana in 1817 with his victory at San Félix. José Antonio Páez emerged as the unchallenged *caudillo* of the *llanos* of Apure and won them for the Republic by his own efforts. He was so isolated there that Bolívar and the other leaders, fighting in the east and in Guayana, did not become aware of him until the end of 1817, when he had already been in control of his area for three years and had defeated General La Torre, Morillo's second-in-command, at Mucuritas.

Bolívar reached Port-au-Prince, the capital of Haiti, on December 31, 1815. He was soon joined by some of the few defenders who had managed to escape from Cartagena. Only four of the thirteen ships that left the heroic city were saved, and conditions on board were so bad that, according to notes made by General Salom, "In the 13 or 14 days we remained on board the *Constitución,* the Cartagena warship commanded by the French privateer Ori (Aury), more than thirty people were thrown into the sea, dead or apparently dead."[1] The Haitian senator Marion, who watched the arrival of the refugees, recorded later: "With most of them ill and suffering from hunger and thirst, they could hardly stand. It was sad to hear the cries of the children and the laments of the women and the aged. . . ."[2]

The worst aspect was that families were scattered among the different islands by the confusion of the tragedy instead of having the consolation of being together with their relatives. People despaired even more as they received news of their families' sad fate. To take one example from many: the ladies of the Sojo y Herrera family, relatives of the Liberator, earned a living by playing the harp and the guitar at the Negro dances on the island of St. Thomas.[3]

Bolívar applied himself immediately to the tasks of reviving the spirit of the republicans, calming personal resentments caused by the recriminations that always appear among the vanquished, forming new plans for a return to Venezuela, and obtaining aid from Alexander Petión, the President of Haiti.

Three causes of discord had to be overcome before the patriots could reorganize: the rivalry, and even hatred, which divided many of the military leaders, and which at times led them to join forces against one of their number, not excluding Bolívar; the attitude of the politicians and jurists, the fathers of the revolution, who attributed its collapse to the anarchy of the *caudillos,* but who had also contributed to it with their doubts and their illusory plans for constitutional reorganization; finally, although on a smaller scale, the intriguers and the wicked, who are always to be found in such circumstances.

1. Quoted by Lecuna, *Crónica razonada,* i, p. 417.
2. Account reproduced in Blanco y Azpurúa, v, p. 398.
3. *Crónica razonada...,* i, p. 432.

Simón Bolívar in Haiti, 1816, by an anonymous artist.

Bolívar strove to find and use all the means available to him to remedy this spiritual dispersion. He wrote to canon José Cortés de Madariaga, who had great influence with the civilians because of his decisive intervention on April 19, 1810: "I close with the hope of seeing you soon in the refuge of our country, co-operating effectively in the construction of the great edifice of our republic. Our arms will destroy the tyrants in vain if we do not establish a political order capable of repairing the ravages of the revolution. The military system is that of force, and force is not government."[1] He cajoled Roscio in the same fashion and invited him, too, to co-operate.

But he was unbending when he considered it necessary. He went so far as to expel General Bermúdez from the expedition that he was organizing and he reiterated to him in July 1816: "After the difficulties and strife which you caused in *Los Cayos,* and which obliged me to discharge you; after your persistence in forming factions to oppose the expedition, and your attempt to obtain command of it against the general will of all its members and against the decision of the *Junta general* of commanders and notables who had entrusted its direction to me, and, what is no less important, against your express promise; after the formal and express decisions that you and your companions made publicly to make an attempt on my life in order to give you supreme command; finally, after the many examples you have provided of insubordination and sedition, I do not wish to allow you to enter the Army or the territory of the Republic."[2]

General Petión, fortunately, responded splendidly. Although he was involved in a civil war with Christophe, that France was threatening him and it was dangerous to provoke Spain, he generously sheltered the unfortunate republicans and decided to help Bolívar prepare his expedition. The total amount of aid is not known, because, to quote General Marion, "It is not pleasing to tell foreigners the country's business"—the fear of provoking Spain was also significant—but there is no doubt that it was Petión's support and new donations from the magnanimous Brión that made possible the organization of Bolívar's proposed expedition. An assembly of the republicans who were to participate proclaimed Bolívar Commander-in-Chief, as Captain-General of Venezuela and New Granada. On March 31, the expedition sailed from the haven of La Beata in Haiti for the island of Margarita on the eastern coast of Venezuela.

Despite its importance for the liberation of Venezuela, the expedition from Los Cayos, the name of the Haitian town where the assembly met, was not

---

1. *Cartas,* I, p. 256. Although this letter was written in November 1816, Bolívar mentions in it another that he sent, in the same terms, at the beginning of the year.
2. Boletín de la Academia Nacional de la Historia, no. 62, Caracas April-July 1933, p. 184.

large. It consisted of only a few schooners, armed with what could be improvised, and the total number of combatants was less than 250, all of them officers. The veteran General Salom who never retreated from anything and who in 1826 was to have the glory of storming Callao, the last fortress that Spaniards held on the continent, later confessed: "We found the Liberator in Los Cayos organizing the expedition with which we invaded Venezuela in 1816. I confess that at first I refused to join it because in my opinion it was a Quixotic expedition. When I later enrolled, I was deceived by the hope of going to Jacomelo to receive a considerable number of troops, but it was not to be, and we went ahead with more or less 240 leaders and officers." He added, referring to the ships: "One of them, called the *Decatur,* in which I served, had only 14 to 20 crew, and some 40 leaders and officers. In the guards that were mounted daily the second lieutenants and captains served as privates, the sergeant majors and lieutenant colonels as corporals, and the colonels as sergeants of the guard."[1]

Another detail, although amusing, is touching because it reveals the privations they suffered. Lecuna tells us that, as they were sailing along the coast of Santo Domingo, they captured a small sloop, "and the sailors did not want to set free two friars captured on board without exchanging them for two cows, the only livestock obtainable on that coast."

When the expedition reached the eastern shores of Venezuela, a Spanish brigantine and a schooner tried to intercept it. The patriots fought furiously and boarded the brigantine, *El Intrépido,* whose captain, Rafael La Iglesia, died fighting. The schooner soon surrendered with its captain, Mateo de Ocampo, seriously wounded. Lecuna comments: "The surprise of the Spaniards, when the patriots arrived from an unexpected direction, meant that Bolívar had to fight only two ships. If all the ships employed in the blockade of Margarita had been involved in the encounter, the outcome would have been different."[2]

Arismendi had led the revolt of the island of Margarita a year earlier. The Spanish brigadier Pardo discussed his resources in an official report: "They defend themselves with slings and stones, of which they have made little piles at every step. The delirium extends to the accumulation of stores of slings and other devices which were used only in the time of the Moors."[3] According to another royalist leader who fought them, Colonel Joaquín Urreistieta, the island's patriots waited for Morillo's veteran infantry without arms, "and there was an insurgent who snatched the bayonet from the rifle of our soldiers, which is the sort of boldness of

---

1. *Crónica razonada...*, i, pp. 434-5.
2. *Crónica razonada...*, i, p. 441.
3. Mariano de Briceño, *Historia de Margarita* p. 104 Pardo to Moxo.

which a fearless man is capable."[1] By means such as these, the patriots were triumphant on several occasions, and after their victory at Guacuco, near the island's capital, they sang arrogantly:

Where are the ten thousand Spaniards
who defeated the great Napoleon?
On the beach of Guacuco lying in
the 'Barbastro,' 'Corona' and 'Union.'

An assembly of the island's soldiers and leading citizens, over which Arismendi presided, endorsed Bolívar's election as commander-in-chief by the members of the expedition. The Liberator soon crossed to the mainland, but not before giving those modern Spartans 1,000 muskets and a field gun, for which "their enthusiasm knew no bounds." The *margariteños* did not want him to leave, but Bolívar explained: "If I stay here after an expedition has left for the mainland, they will ruin this island simply to pursue me."

However, he accepted for Venezuela the sacrifice that he was unwilling to impose on Margarita. One of the happy consequences of his 1816 expedition for America was that it obliged Morillo to return to Venezuela from New Granada, instead of continuing his advance on the rest of the continent. The alarmed royalists in Caracas demanded his return as soon as they learned of Bolívar's preparations. But, in any case, the bravery and triumphs of the *margariteños* had made such an impression on Morillo that one of the few military reproaches made by his biographers is that, in his haste to subdue Margarita, he neglected Apure and Guayana. When he reached the island a second-rate general, Francisco Esteban Gómez —the equivalent of the Spanish "no matter who"— defeated him.

In the east of Venezuela, the insurrection had been sustained by leaders like José Tadeo Monagas, Manuel Sedeño, Pedro Zaraza and Francisco Vicente Parejo. Even after Morillo's arrival, they refused to lay down their arms, and survived by making desperate forays from remote Guayana to the sea. But they were so short of everything that they were armed only with lances, the points of which were hardened with fire, because they were unable to obtain iron.[2]

Bolívar landed at the port of Carúpano, where he captured the brigantine *Bello Indio* and a schooner called *La Fortuna,* a name that could have seemed an augury. The town and its fortifications were taken by force. Bolívar kept his promise to Petión, and also followed his own convictions by

---

1. Briceño, *op. cit.,* p. 95.
2. Archivo Nacional, Caracas. Sección *Ilustres Próceres.* Passim.

immediately decreeing the liberation of the slaves. He invited them to take up arms in defense of what might now be called their country. He also sent some squads into the interior, while trying to strengthen and train the forces that remained. However, he had only 800 men, almost all of them recruits, when he learned that the Spaniards were preparing to attack by land and sea with a squadron of fourteen ships and troops far superior to his own.

It was then that Bolívar formed the idea of re-embarking, landing at Ocumare de la Costa, to the west of Caracas, taking the war to the center of the Republic, and perhaps capturing the capital. Although the plan was dangerous, it could give him access to the rich, populated valleys of Aragua, and there was no doubt that it would worry the Spaniards. Above all, if he could take Caracas, he would hold a political center of decisive importance. We will return to this final objective, which has never been pointed out before and which explains many other of Bolívar's decisions, usually attributed to a thoughtless preference for the city of his birth.

Once on board a schooner which Brión had named *Bolívar,* he informed Arismendi that his plan was "to march rapidly to the heart of Venezuela and end the war." He added: "This project has evolved from the change in circumstances. Success will justify the enterprise. If I fail, I will lose nothing more than my life, because it is always a great thing to attempt the heroic."[1]

He almost succeeded. He landed, as proposed, at Ocumare de la Costa, and his advance forces, led by General Soublette, reached Maracay in the valley of Aragua. But an accumulation of chance circumstances suddenly snatched away the victory. Soublette unexpectedly retreated because of a false alarm, although his prudence was not unjustified, for the royalist general threatening him was Morales, Bove's active and cruel second-in-command, who could reasonably have been expected to have a sizeable force. Because of his rank, Bolívar rebuked Soublette, telling him: "Whatever you deem too daring will be your best course of action, for today, rashness is prudence." Soon afterwards, Morales defeated Bolívar and Soublette in a position they had chosen to defend. The principal cause of this defeat was to torment the patriots for a long time, namely the necessity of using newly-formed forces against the experienced royalist infantry. This lack of experience meant that the disorder caused in the patriot camp by the defeat and other reverses was frightful. What could be called the main body of the army marched inland under MacGregor, while Bolívar, who planned to follow later, remained behind to salvage the ammunition. But he was abandoned by the privateers when he tried to embark it, and

---

1. *Cartas,* i, p. 244.

he found himself alone, at the mercy of the royalists, who were already entering the town.

Bolívar wrote in 1830: "What happened at Ocumare is the most extraordinary thing in the world. I was tricked by both an aide of General Mariño, who was a traitor, and by the foreign sailors who committed the most infamous act in the world, leaving me among my enemies on a deserted beach. I was about to shoot myself, when one of them (Mr. Vidau) returned from the sea in a rowboat and picked me up to rescue me."[1]

This occurred on July 14, 1816, the same day on which the Precursor Francisco de Miranda died in Cádiz and his jailers, with all speed, wrapped him in his blankets as if they were dealing with an untouchable animal, and threw him into an unmarked grave.

Many years later Soublette told O'Leary that "love intervened" in the Ocumare disaster, adding "and you know that, despite the danger in which he found himself, Anthony wasted precious moments at the side of Cleopatra." He was referring to the presence of Josefina Machado, then Bolívar's fiancée or mistress, in the expedition. Lecuna, however, thinks that Soublette made the insinuation to cover up his own blunders during the campaign. It is said that Wellington, too, was late in arriving at Waterloo, because of Lady Frances Webster. But Wellington won, while Bolívar lost most of his equipment, a printing press and the prestige that he was again beginning to impose over his unruly subordinates. This final loss was the most serious, and after his return to the east, Mariño and Bermúdez rose against him at the Güiria camp. Uttering indecorous cries, the rioters advanced on him and, as in 1814, Bolívar had to use his sword to gain access to one of the ships in the port. "Burning with rage, Bermúdez drew his sword when he saw that Bolívar was about to save himself, but he was held back by Colonel Manuel Isaba and Licenciate Gaspar Marcano."[2]

What must Bolívar have felt when, once safe, he looked from his ship upon the land from which he had been ignominiously expelled? Was he dazed with anger? Did sadness predominate, as he reflected on the rush of mistakes that had snatched away his country's last hopes? Some of his contemporaries found his eyes sparkling and others, extremely sad. What we know is that he immediately began to revive the struggle. Without thinking about the royalist patrols which were patrolling the Venezuelan coast and the Caribbean in all directions, he returned to Haiti.

---

1. *Cartas del Libertador,* ix, p. 243. According to Lecuna, *Crónica razonada...,* i, p. 468, he was saved by Comandante Videau, who was well known for his exploits and bravery.
2. Larrazábal, in Lecuna, *Crónica razonada...,* i, p. 482.

Showing as much generosity as perspicacity, Petión welcomed him with these words: "With enterprises great and small, an inexplicable fate affects even the wisest steps, causing unforeseen reverses which destroy every precaution and ruin the best-laid plans. Your Excellency has just experienced this harsh, sad truth, but if fickle fate has destroyed your hopes for the second time, it may favor you the third time. I, for one, foresee this, and if I can in any way minimize the pain and distress of Your Excellency, you may immediately count upon whatever consolation is within my power."[1]

The splendid Negro kept his promise. With the means made available, and others that his own prodigious activity was always able to produce, Bolívar arranged to return to Venezuela.

He then received two summons: one from Arismendi, who was still in control of Margarita, and the other from MacGregor and various leaders who had joined him. MacGregor had conducted a most successful campaign, describing a large semi-circle of 150 leagues to the south of Caracas, from Ocumare de la Costa in the west to Barcelona in the east. On several occasions he defeated the royalists who came out to intercept him. In the east he joined Monagas, Zaraza and other leaders, and further successes in combat made them masters of the province of Barcelona. They went on, under the command of General Manuel Piar, to decisively defeat Morales at El Juncal. Immediately afterwards, they decided to summon the Liberator.

Bolívar arrived at Juan Griego in Margarita on December 28, and three days later he disembarked at Barcelona. Once again General Mariño refused to submit to his authority. Despite this, at the end of 1816 the best republican *caudillos* recognized him as their leader, and he found himself at the head of a victorious army.

---

1. Boletín de la Academia Nacional de la Historia, Caracas, no. 77, p. 110.

XXI

A
YOUNG
PEOPLE

IN A PROCLAMATION OF
January 1, 1817, Bolívar once again promised his companions in arms:
"You will fly with me even to rich Peru. Our destiny calls us to the ends
of the American world."
But he then suffered the second and most inexplicable of his reverses.
He had ordered Monagas and Zaraza, who were operating in the interior, to concentrate in Aragua de Barcelona. Piar, who was planning
an expedition against Guayana, was offered naval resources for the control of the Orinoco, but Bolívar asked that, if it proved impossible to
take the province, Piar should join him or at least send him the officers
of the Ocumare expedition who were with his forces. Only Arismendi,
of the leaders he had summoned, remained, and Bolívar had managed to collect a force of only 700 men, but he decided to advance on
Caracas. He was motivated by the need to give his incipient forces the
experience of battle that would turn them into a proper army, by the
fear that the royalists would attack him if he remained inactive and
allowed them to concentrate and, according to Lecuna, by the aim of
drawing the attention of the Spaniards towards the coast, thus facili-
tating the concentration of the patriots in Aragua de Barcelona. Lecuna
also considers that Bolívar planned only a small-scale maneuver, and
that his proclamation promising prompt liberation to the *caraqueños* was
simply a trick to alarm the enemy. In any case, even if the idea of the
campaign was foolhardy, as some critics claim, Bolívar's decision to
attack a smaller royalist force, led by an unknown commander, certainly

was not. But it was in this action, fought at Clarines on January 9, that he was completely defeated. Bolívar and Arismendi, on foot at the head of their troops, led three unsuccessful assaults against the enemy defenses. At the height of the fighting, an Indian *cacique* called Chaurán came to the aid of the royalists and the patriots panicked and fled. Other causes of the disaster were the inferior quality of their forces, the fact that a column sent to outflank the enemy got lost in a wood, and the excessive boldness of the patriot Colonel Tomás Hernández, who died in a frontal attack on the enemy.

The republican leaders, who had grown accustomed to seeing Bolívar triumph in the most difficult circumstances, were not surprised by the unexpected defeat. An insurmountable fate seemed to be venting its fury on Bolívar. Even his most loyal subordinates began to think that a mysterious, malicious influence was involved in what had happened. Previously they had been astounded to see him create resources and victories out of nothing; now, with no less amazement, they thought that fate seemed to have come to engage in a personal battle with Bolívar and to cruelly inflict repeated failures upon him. Bolívar himself learned of this depressing fairy-tale, and he confided to Perú de Lacroix many years later: "The rumor spread that I was out of favor, and that everything went badly for me."[1]

In these circumstances, and because operations were still dominated by guerrillas, Bolívar found himself leader of an army one day, and a solitary fugitive the next. After the defeat at Clarines he was so impatient to secure unity among the patriots by any means that he even offered command of the army to Mariño. But when he saw that not even this could secure concerted action against the enemy, he decided to leave Barcelona and join Piar in Guayana.

Bolívar was accompanied by only fifteen officers and their assistants as he set out to cross a very large area full of royalists. To lessen somewhat the danger of an ambush, he ordered the officers to carry the carbines of their aides. A royalist party did prepare an ambush, but Colonel Parejo, who was riding ahead, opened fire and jumped to the ground as did Bolívar and the others. Using an old guerrilla trick, the Liberator then shouted: "Forward, infantry, to the right and the left!" The enemy, who doubtless thought that he had soldiers with him, fled after a few shots. Nevertheless, Colonel José María Carreño and Parejo's aide fell wounded at Bolívar's side. Unable to continue the march, the aide took refuge in a nearby town and shortly afterwards was killed by the royalists.

In July of the same year, Bolívar suffered another reverse at Casacoima. He and his staff officers had to swim across a channel of the Orinoco

1. Nicolás E. Navarro (ed.), *Diario de Bucaramanga* (Caracas, 1935) p. 390.

to escape from the royalists, who had cut off their retreat. The last to take to the water were Bolívar and General Lara. According to Lara's account, this led to fears that the Liberator had been killed or captured, and the army was about to disband. It seems that on this occasion, as at Ocumare, Bolívar thought of killing himself to avoid capture. Afterwards, although still numb from his long immersion in the water, he harangued his companions, promising them new, victorious campaigns, and some of them thought that he was delirious.

But the gravity of these reverses and suffering meant that the situation confronting the Liberator had become much more difficult. After the destruction of the legal structure formed in 1811, the *patria* had been reborn in 1813 by the activities of the *caudillos,* but their authority which was personal, unstable and localist, could not provide a foundation for the Republic. Profound vices, derived from this glorification of the *caudillo,* were beginning to disturb this collective mentality. Blind obedience to the leader, or ostentatious individualism in some cases, was beginning to displace the freedom of choice characteristic of times of peace. Virtues considered essential for social life—reflection, tolerance, learning, respectability—were becoming less important than the qualities demanded by war—aggression, obedience, destruction and force. Healthy judicial and moral scruples upon which the normal life of a nation depends were giving way to the military need for rapid decision. Harmony of opinions under law was not yet able to overcome the spiritual disintegration engendered by the ideological disputes of politicians or the blind decisions imposed by *caudillos.*

Thus the antagonism which was to become the fundamental tragedy of the reorganization of Spanish America began to appear. The men and sentiments used in the destruction of tyranny are not always the most suitable for the creation of freedom.

Bolívar, then, had to struggle from the beginning against two currents which, although opposed to each other, combined against any attempt to secure stability: that of the thinkers and politicians, who demanded the urgent legal reconstruction of the state, and that of the military leaders, who were unwilling to obey anybody.

Even before the 1813 campaigns were over, he had to face the first attempt to re-establish the federal system in Venezuela, which had contributed so much to the fall of the Republic in 1812 and which had been no less disastrous in New Granada. The movement was led by Manuel Antonio Pulido, a rich landowner from Barinas and an eminent patriot who had provided the Liberator with material support for his campaign. Bolívar pointed out to him in vain: "How can small, impotent and poor cities aspire to sovereignty at this time and hope to maintain it? In New Granada the struggle involving claims similar to yours degenerated into a horrible civil war which caused American blood to run, and which might have destroyed the independence of that vast region but for my efforts in effecting a reconciliation and the recognition of a supreme authority." Soon afterwards he had to dismiss Pulido from his post as governor of the province, and to order, while the war continued, that political and military authority should be invested in one individual, "as in time of conquest."

Also in 1813, Bolívar was confronted by General Santiago Mariño who, after liberating the east of Venezuela while Bolívar was fighting the Admirable Campaign as far as Caracas, believed that he was entitled to govern that part of the national territory. In fact, Mariño could produce sound arguments: as a *caudillo,* and according to the federal principles, his authority was as legitimate as that of Bolívar, although he was not prepared to recognize that the authority of both of them was equally illegitimate as long as the constitution was not restored. The restoration of the constitution was impossible; Bolívar stayed only a few days in Caracas, for the war was raging on all sides. Under these conditions it would have been an unworthy farce to re-establish the plural executive and the federation of 1812. The negotiations with Mariño were long and troubled. They delayed his assistance to the republicans fighting in the center of the country, and the agreement that came out of them was both imprecise and impermanent. In December 1813, Bolívar addressed him as "Commander of the Eastern Provinces," but he pointed out in the same letter: "If we establish two independent authorities, one in the east and the other in the west, we will create two different nations which, because of their inability to maintain an independent existence, and to take their place among other nations, will look ridiculous. Only a Venezuela united with New Granada could form a nation that would elicit from others the decorous consideration due her. How could we think of dividing her?"[1] A few months later, Bolívar and Mariño, united by misfortune, were being angrily pursued by Ribas and Piar.

The political attitude of each of these personalities was also influenced considerably by his character. One of the most surprising cases was that of Manuel Montilla. He was patriotic, selfless, gentlemanly and, moreover, a friend of Bolívar since childood, but he acquired such hatred for Bolívar that he did all he could to oppose him in the difficult days of 1815 and 1816. While Bolívar was preparing the Los Cayos expedition, Montilla went to his house for the express purpose of challenging him. According to Larrazábal, Montilla acted out of vanity and ambition, but his subsequent career makes this explanation unlikely. We suppose that he must have been extremely touchy, and this weakness, which had made

---

1. *Cartas,* i, p. 88.

him an irreconcilable enemy of Miranda during the first Republic, manifested itself again in his relations with Bolívar.

Another personal friend of the Liberator who always opposed him in the poltical sphere was Martín Tovar Ponte. A man of the highest moral qualities, he offered himself and his family to his country unreservedly. We have already discussed their heroism during the disasters of 1814. One of his sons, Florencio, who in 1818 returned to Venezuela from the United States where he was educated, was captured in the campaigns of that year and Morillo shot him. But Martín Tovar's political ideals were so radical that for him anything short of the federal system was equivalent to monarchy and slavery. He was to write in 1829: "What we are discussing is not how many States there should be in Colombia, but whether we should have a federal Republic. This is a great crisis in which the definitive decision must be made between our life or our death, between our slavery under a centralist or monarchical system, for both are the same, or our freedom under the federal system, and it is impossible to compromise between these two extremes... etc."[1] It is not surprising that, guided by this criterion, he attributed the fall of the Republic in 1814 to the tyranny of Bolívar and the Ribas family. But it is most odd that he also accused Miranda of despotism, even though in 1811 the republicans simply showed him hostility and obstruction. Roscio attempted in 1816 to attract Tovar to other ideas, telling him: "I have been very sorry to find that you accept this mistake and, for this reason, I have explained to you that the source of our problems is religious-political fanaticism, not the arbitrary power with which Miranda governed in 1812, and Bolívar and the Ribas family in 1813 and 1814."[2] But Tovar was unshakeable. It is said that when Bolívar embraced him on his return to Caracas in 1827, he told him: "Martín, only the Avila and you do not change!" If he was referring to the selfless patrician's temperament, there could have been as much admiration as friendly reproach in the remark.

Some *caudillos* rebelled, or were always ready to do so, simply because this was their character. An example was Bermúdez, the disconcerting and congenial Ajax of the contest, who was daring and generous but incapable of controlling his passions. And, of course, much further down, in the region of the reptiles, swarmed men like Rafael Diego Mérida, *el Malo;* among the patriots he always played the role of Thersites, sometimes so skillfully that, according to Bolívar, he almost destroyed the Los Cayos expedition.

Although it was difficult for the Liberator to maintain harmony among the different republican leaders, unity of command was totally impossible

---

1. Essay entitled *A los colombianos.* Quoted by Gil Fortoul (1930 edition), i, p. 651.
2. Roscio, *op. cit.,* p. lxxxv.

when he went away or when they ignored him. From 1814, Arismendi was an enemy of the other eastern *caudillos*. Bermúdez was prepared to recognize an authority other than his own only on a provisional basis, until he finally reconciled himself with Bolívar in 1814 and remained loyal to him thereafter. Piar had the unfortunate distinction of falling out with all his companions in arms and his suspicious nature led him to insult, unjustly, commanders like MacGregor, Monagas and Parejo. Mariño, although with well-deserved prestige in the east, would not have been able to depend upon Arismendi or Piar. Even Bermúdez, who was accompanying him from 1813, finally turned against him and Páez was even less disposed to recognize him. The military leaders who stood out as men of principle—Urdaneta, Soublette, Anzoátegui, the young Antonio José de Sucre, the Granadan Francisco de Paula Santander— did not hide their repugnance for this anarchy, and consistently followed the Liberator. The men of the pen who accompanied the armies had even more reason to support Bolívar, for, although they were not always in agreement with him, he was the only *caudillo* who was also a political thinker.

Monagas, Sedeño and Zaraza were *caudillos* of a different type, always ready to fight for their country whatever the circumstances. From 1813, Monagas shone as a bold lancer who formed his own troops and continued the struggle in the desperate period of 1815. He contributed decisively to the victory at El Juncal, and afterwards put up with the injustices of Piar who dismissed him from the army and ordered his arrest. On not a few occasions, he also gave troops to the other commanders, and on others he accepted a subordinate role when he might have demanded control. The same attitude was adopted by Sedeño, who was master of the western part of Guayana, alongside the *llanos* of Apure. In 1817 he even gave some of his troops to Zaraza, and remained with the others under the orders of Piar. After the battle of Carabobo, where he gave his life, Bolívar held him up as an example of loyalty and "the bravest of the brave." On many previous occasions he had described him in similar terms. Zaraza had become a legend because of his charge against the dreaded Boves at the defeat of Urica, when he or one of his men killed the Asturian. The royalists were never able to dislodge him from his territory, the *Alto Llano,* between the eastern plains and Caracas. His soldiers adored him for his paternalism, and because his head was crowned with a lock of white hair like the snowy crest of a mountain, they called him *Taita Cordillera.*[1] Despite his skill and bravery, the indiscipline that he tolerated in his men was so extreme that Bolívar had to reprimand him on several occasions. According to the

---

1. *Taita:* Venezuelan family name for the head of the household.

English legionary Vowell, who saw him at close quarters and left a sympathetic record of his customs, even Páez and his *llaneros* laughed affectionately at the chaos in Zaraza's army. Nevertheless, it could be said without the slightest exageration that Zaraza and his men were the first to attack and the last to retreat.

In the midst of ebullient, young people, and forced to fight a war to the death against a more numerous, better armed enemy, the Liberator had to display as much patience and tact as energy and valor. The more he was assailed by suffering and dangers, the more alert and tenacious he became, and to use his own phrase, the more he "remained steadfast in his work."

Some historians have reproached Bolívar for the excessive importance that he attributed in these years to the possession of Caracas and for the rashness with which he tried to recapture the city on three occasions: at Ocumare de la Costa, at Clarines, and again in 1818. It is possible that these attempts had in them something of the exalted *caraqueñismo* which Bolívar always expressed with vehemence. But it is undeniable that he was also motivated by a calculated political purpose. He was trying to establish a center to give unity to the disorderly activity of the *caudillos,* which represented the gravest threat to the stability and strength of the Republic. Geographically, this center had to be Caracas, just as in the moral sphere, as the experience of these years indicated, it could be only Bolívar. His plan, like his insistence on the need "to liberate the South as far as Lima," which he repeated at even the most critical moments, clearly reflected an almost obsessive, deeply felt impulse, but it also did much to distract his subordinates from trifling regionalist plans and to recruit them for a greater enterprise.

It was with the same object of gathering together whatever spiritual and political resources could be of aid to the Republic that Bolívar tried to summon a congress in Margarita in December 1816. But the project was evidently premature. The cities occupied by the patriots were falling to the royalists all the time, and Margarita itself was to be invaded by Morillo the following year.

The Liberator, therefore, abandoned the idea. But a few months later, while he was occupied in Guayana, a number of politicians and *caudillos* took it up again in the form that he feared most. Their intention was to re-establish the "government in recess," namely that of 1811, under the federal system and with an executive of three members who would rotate every month. The spokesman for the plan was Canon José Cortés de Madariaga, recently returned from abroad, who promised that the restoration of constitutional government in this form would ensure recognition and aid from England. He was supported by a number of civilian patriots of certain importance, and the military men in favor of the plan included Admiral Brión, who was such a strong supporter of Bolívar. But the most important backing came from General Mariño. When those who considered themselves most entitled to form the assembly which was to organize the government met in the town of Cariaco —there were only eleven of them—Mariño resigned in his own name and in that of Bolívar the authority conferred upon them at Los Cayos. The little Congress, accepting this, named three men to exercise executive authority: first, Fernando del Toro, brother of the Marquis, who had been a refugee in Trinidad since being crippled in 1811; second, the civilian Francisco Javier Mayz, and third, Bolívar, who had had nothing at all to do with it. Mariño was acknowledged, naturally, as commander-in-chief of the army. Since those elected to the triumvirate were to remain in the capital of the Republic, which was to be the city of Asunción in Margarita, Bolívar would have had to stay there, waiting to govern every third month. The assembly is known in Venezuelan history as the *Congresillo de Cariaco*. Despite the diminutive, the name seems rather misleading.

It was impossible, of course, for such a foolish plan to make any progress. It was soon undone by the indifference of the other patriots and, unfortunately, by some royalist triumphs. But it did have the effect of provoking and widening the differences between the commanders, which represented the greatest danger to the patriot cause. The anarchy that Mariño's attitude caused in the army led, among other serious consequences, to the loss of the city of Barcelona, where the heroic republican General Pedro María Freites was forced to fight without the reinforcements that might have saved him, in a desperate attempt to save his ammunition and to protect the many civilians from the cruelty of the royalists. Lecuna tells us: "As soon as the troops reached Aragua, they began to receive reports from Freites of the approach of the enemy, and since he could not evacuate the town until he had removed the guns and munitions, a request for help in defending himself. Urdaneta repeatedly urged the others to countermarch to help Barcelona, but it seems that Mariño was no longer in command and, in the general anarchy, no decision was taken. Freites's messages became more urgent, until one said that it would be the last. The order to return to Barcelona was expected at any moment when at midnight the alarm was raised, announcing the approach of the enemy. General Urdaneta says that this was untrue, but that Bermúdez, Valdés and Armario had decided to go south to Chaparro, leaving Mariño alone with the Güiria battalion, which was the only force then in the charge of Jugo. They went, and the following day Mariño, without bothering about Barcelona, left with Jugo for Cumaná, along the Santa Ana route. The army that had been formed with such difficulty was thus dispersed and, as we will see, two thirds of it were to be lost without fighting a battle."[1] Lecuna adds, referring to the capture of the city: "Because of their few numbers the defenders concentrated in the castle, abandoning the other fortifications used on February 8. Altogether there were probably no more than 500 men, although the report of the Spanish commander puts the number at 700. A large number of the people, mostly women and children, were locked in with them. Freites, expecting help from the army, decided to resist in order to save the ammunition. Help did not arrive, the enemy surrounded the castle, and on the 7th they established two batteries a thousand paces from the walls and began to bombard them. When the walls were partly demolished, the enemy attacked. The defenders fought fiercely but they could not hold them back, and only those who managed to escape in the confusion saved themselves from execution. Freites, who was seriously wounded, and Ribas were taken to Caracas, where they were hung. More than 1,000 patriots died in the struggle, including Colonel Meza, the former aide Chamberlain and his wife, the heroine Eulalia Ramos, and the Granadan Gutiérrez de Piñeres. The Spaniards captured 1,000 muskets, 20 cannons of various sizes and a large amount of ammunition."[2]

Bolívar's concern at these symptoms of decay must have been profound, when the most serious of all occurred: General Manuel Piar left him. Like Brión, this bold fighter had been born in the neighboring island of Curaçao, a Dutch colony, although it was sometimes occupied by the English. Despite this origin, Piar considered himself a Venezuelan, and he had consecrated himself to the cause of independence since 1810. He won important victories in the eastern part of the country in 1813 and 1814, and he defeated Morales at El Juncal in 1816. In April 1817, he inflicted a decisive defeat upon General Miguel de la Torre, Morillo's second-in-command, at San Félix, thus giving the patriots control of Guayana. He remained faithful to Bolívar after this triumph, and it was thanks to him that the Liberator was able on July 17, to occupy the city of Angostura, the capital of the province, using mainly the troops that had fought at San Félix. Piar was a brave patriot, unselfish, and a skillful military tactician. But he was haughty and timid at one and the same time, pulled in different directions by doubt about his origins—it was said that he was descended from a Braganza prince, but it was also known that his mother was a humble *mulatta*. He was uneducated, and his personal behavior was so improper that he made enemies of even his closest subordinates. On several occasions he had quarreled with Bolívar, Mariño, Bermúdez, Arismendi, MacGregor, Monagas and the other republican leaders.

1. Lecuna, *Crónica razonada...*, i, p. 538.
2. *Ibid.*, i, p. 543.

After San Félix and the capture of Angostura, Piar became involved in bitter disagreements with the colonel and priest, José Félix Blanco, whom the Liberator had appointed administrator of the rich Caroní missions. The letter that Bolívar then sent him merits complete transcription, because it paints both their characters admirably.

"San Félix, 19 June 1817.
"To General Manuel Piar.

"My dear General:

"I have just received your esteemed letter of the 16th, as a result of which I have written immediately to the Commissioner for the Missions, recalling him, for I have decided to relieve him of the post that he was given on your orders and mine. This will resolve any embarrassment with Fr. Blanco, a useful servant in any other position. I have done this to please you, although you are in error when you tell me *that now Blanco could not be your friend.* You are even more mistaken to think that he is prejudiced against you. Unlike you, I know Fr. Blanco. The point is that he can be inflexible *even with me* over regulations.
"You are also mistaken about General Arismendi, although I am not surprised, for until now distance has made it difficult to examine his conduct. Those mules to which you refer, which like other animals went to Pueblito with those sent by General Sedeño, and because of which you accuse him, were not stolen. My God, General! What will our enemies and detractors say? Are you not aware that they have stolen mules, cattle and other items in the colonies, and that they have obtained war materials right here that we did not have, and provisions and coats for their bodies?
"General, I prefer a fight with the Spaniards to these disputes among the patriots. It is you who is suspicious of your companions, when you should know that they are your friends, from whom you should not separate yourself for the sake of the cause. To do otherwise is to serve the cause of oppression.
"Yes, if we divide, if we become anarchic, if we destroy each other, we will thin the republican ranks. We will strengthen those of the *godos,* Spain will triumph, and with reason we will be called *vagabonds.*
"Do not insist upon resigning your post. If you were in charge, I would not abandon you, just as I will not abandon whoever leads us tomorrow, no matter who it is, as long as his authority is legitimate and the country needs him. The country needs you today, as you are, and tomorrow it will need you for what your services will have made you.

"Do not doubt my sincerity. Let me know of any other measure we should take in connection with the government of the Missions.

"I am your affectionate friend. *Bolívar*

"P. S. Father Blanco is your friend. I assure you because I know."[1]

It was in vain. Piar insisted on resigning and, finally, motivated mainly by what happened in the Cariaco Congress, he tried to come to an agreement with Arismendi to disregard Bolívar's authority. Moreover he was to be accused of much more serious sedition, and condemned to death as a "rebel deserter, mutineer and conspirator."

This lamentable event has provoked passionate debates, and the historian, depending upon his criteria for judging it, still finds it perplexing. The Council of War that pronounced the sentence was composed of honorable soldiers, including friends of Piar. None of them were his enemies. Independent-minded historians, who do not hesitate to censure Bolívar in other cases, abstain from criticizing him for his decision to ratify the sentence. However, we cannot avoid some doubts. The most serious charge made against the accused—and, morally, the only one that could justify the punishment—was that he had sought to lead the *pardos* in a movement to exterminate the whites, particularly the upper class of Caracas. Although there is no doubt that the impetuous general, believing himself a victim of intrigues and persecution, attributed this to his being a *pardo* and said so with anger and bitterness, this was no real proof that he was guilty of the charge. Three of those who gave evidence professed genuine hatred for him for serious reasons. Piar himself did not challenge them—out of ingenuousness or gallantry, or because he had no opportunity to do so—but his counsel did. And he added: "Everybody exaggerates false rumors, and it often happens that the unjust world strives to make a criminal out of an innocent. There is much of this in the case of the defendant. If we examine the grounds for the charge calmly and coolly, we will find nothing more than personal resentments, unimportant expressions uttered with passion and indiscretion, private complaints against his friends to ease his mind, in short, trances of the type from which, as everybody knows, General Piar suffers. This leader, today so miserable, was slandered atrociously by his enemies, who even claimed that he had stolen eighty thousand pesos. These accusations wounded him deeply. His heart ached. He grew tired of being told that it was planned to kill him. Confused by it all, he spoke like a fanatic or madman, without knowing what he was saying. He cursed his enemies. He spewed forth terrible complaints, and he shouted furiously against those whom he suspected of wanting to do away with him, but without the depraved motives and the criminal intent that are alleged. Where are his

---

1. *Cartas*, i, p. 278.

conspiratorial plans? Where is the list of conspirators? Where are the proclamations to urge the masses to rise? Where are his accomplices in this enormous enterprise? Where are the soldiers with whom he discussed his plans? Where, finally, are the preparations for such a colossal, foolish scheme?"[1]

This counsel who spoke with such fire, Fernando Galindo—he went so far as to describe Piar as "the Venezuelan general who has never been defeated"— belonged to that Caracas upper-class which, according to the charge, had been condemned to extermination. A brother-in-law of Martín Tovar Ponte and holder of the rank of lieutenant-colonel, Galindo was to lose his life at Rincón de los Toros, just six months after Piar's execution. He was endowed not only with generosity but also with clear talent. This can be seen in the way he skillfully defended Piar against the charge of desertion: "Surrounded on all sides by personal enemies, aware that he was being pursued by the very men who had most admired him, under fire from rivals or secret enemies, falsely informed by his friends at head-quarters that it was planned to kill him, and endowed with a suspicious nature which was violent and timid at one and the same time, he believed himself lost.... Is it surprising, then, that at such a critical moment a person without great peace of mind should seek asylum among his own brothers?"

He was referring to the fact that Piar, instead of presenting himself at headquarters, as requested, sought refuge with Mariño, who was then in open rebellion. Although this clearly made his defense more difficult, it did show that he had not insisted on fighting a racial war, since Mariño was white, a member of the privileged class in the east.

Twelve days before Piar was executed, Bolívar considered commuting the sentence. Why did he not do so? He told Bermúdez, in a letter dated October 4, "My personal, private wish is that the council should rec-oncile the rigor of the law and the credit of the government with the merits of the defendant. I will select for the Council of War from among the general officers with the qualifications required by law, those whom I know to be without cause for resentment towards Piar. Brión, his compatriot and his closest friend, will preside, and the other members will include some of Piar's men. Would to God that if the Council imposes the ultimate penalty, it will leave me the opportunity, the clear opportunity, to commute it; and that the army or the units nearest the capital should ask for it, through normal channels, without losing discipline. The responsibility for the pardon, should this be indiscreet, will then be shared by those of us who are building and supporting the edifice of the republic."[2]

---

1. *Memorias del General O'Leary* (Caracas 1881), xv, pp. 351-424, *Proceso de Piar*.
2. *Cartas,* i, p. 310.

Why did he abandon this generous intention? It seems certain that Piar's downfall was planned by many intriguers, who strove after his triumph at San Félix to convince him that Bolívar was suspicious of him and was pursuing him; while others exaggerated to Bolívar the danger that Piar would incite the *pardos*. The saddest detail is that a part was played in both processes by Dr. José Domingo Díaz, the wretch who, according to Heredia, suffered from *insanabile vulnus scribendi cacoethis*. He was then employed by the royalists to mix up and adulterate documents captured from the patriots, which were then published in the Gaceta de Caracas with the aim of fomenting discord among them. In his "Memoirs of the Rebellion of Caracas," he cynically reported that "a chance combination of fortunate circumstances permitted me to make him (Piar) disappear several months later. He turned Bolívar against him "by means of intermediaries and by a chain of papers and real or imaginary events." And he added, "A Gaceta de Caracas, put in his hands, encouraged him. . . . A little later he knew the truth of things; but then there was no remedy."[1]

Of course, Díaz inserted falsehoods in even this criminal boast in the belief that it would give him importance. But it is true that he twisted events and adulterated documents. Modern historians have worked hard to expurgate the forgeries, many of which appear as genuine in the compilations of the last century. Doubts remain over those which cannot be compared with the originals.[2]

It would be a stupid frivolity to present Piar as a possible rival to Bolívar. None of the military leaders had switched allegiance to him. A brilliant general but uneducated and impulsive—he would have found it impossible as commander-in-chief to lead the thinkers and politicians who accompanied the Liberator on his continental mission. The struggle, then, was not between Bolívar and Piar in the limited sphere of military capacity, but between the Liberator and the anarchy of the *caudillos,* which had already caused so many problems for the Republic. And perhaps Bolívar believed, in accordance with the ideas then accepted unanimously in ordinary criminal law, that it was essential to make an example to arrest that social disintegration.

We hasten to add, in Bolívar's defense, that at the same time his policy towards the rebels in the east was quite different. He told Sucre: "Politics rather than force must work in this province. I instruct you to move all the resources of the human heart to persuade the dissidents led astray by General Mariño to submit to the government. Your only enemies should be public ones, as has always been the case with me. Who

---

1. José Domingo Díaz, *Recuerdos sobre la rebelión de Caracas* (Caracas, 1961, Academia Nacional de la Historia), p. 336.
2. See Lecuna, *Catálogo* . . . , ii, p. 68; *Cartas del Libertador,* i, p. 265.

can regard his brothers as enemies?"[1] Shortly afterwards he reiterated: "I have received with great pleasure in Maturín your letter of the 5th, in which you inform me of your dealings with General Mariño. You have conducted yourself with the delicacy and skill I expected. . . I strongly recommend that, if General Mariño submits voluntarily, you should treat him with the greatest dignity and as a man who has just performed an important service by refraining from staining the arms of Venezuela with civil war. The lessening of evil is a virtue, and this should be rewarded insofar as it is compatible with the honor of the government. It is this that causes the greatest difficulty in the exercise of clemency."[2] Not only the honor of the government but also the safety of all made it necessary to sacrifice Piar. And although it might seem brutal, we should say that Bolívar was able to be tolerant towards Mariño precisely because he had been strict with Piar. Tolerance towards them both would have been seen as weakness, and the army would have been destroyed by indiscipline and anarchy.

It also seems that Bolívar never doubted that Piar sought to unleash a "race war." Today this accusation seems exaggerated, or a fabrication, because such a threat never emerged in Venezuela after independence. Then, however, it was in the mind of all men, as numerous documents show. In 1826, when Sucre learned of the events called *La Cosiata,* he commented that he had always feared "African trouble" in Venezuela, although only military trouble had appeared. Among the benefits to be secured by the Inter-American Congress of Panama, Bolívar included the prospect that "differences of origin and color would lose their influence and power. . . . America would have nothing more to fear from. . . . that tremendous monster who has devoured the island of Santo Domingo." In the *Diario de Bucaramanga,* written in 1828, Perú de Lacroix attributes to him the following observation: "The death of General Piar was then a political necessity, and it saved the country, because without it a war was going to begin between the men of color and the whites. The extermination of all would have brought the Spaniards to triumph. General Mariño deserved to die like Piar, on account of his dissidence, but his survival did not present the same dangers and, for this reason, political necessity could give way to sentiments of humanity and even of friendship for a former companion."[3]

In any case, Venezuela owes a debt of recognition and admiration to Piar. Three years after his execution, Bolívar let slip, in a letter to Santander, the following remark, which could be the best epitaph for the

---

1. *Cartas,* i, p. 316.
2. *Ibid.,* i, p. 319.
3. *Op. cit.* Edited by Navarro (Caracas, 1935), p. 315.

victor at San Félix: "We must be just; without the valor of Piar the Republic would not be able to count so many victories."

Another adverse development for the republican cause at the beginning of this same year, 1817, was the arrival of 2,800 Spanish regulars under General José de Canterac. This expedition, like those that preceded it, was composed of men selected from that legendary Spanish infantry which had recently triumphed over the French. In America, moreover, they were to demonstrate a prodigious capacity to adapt to conditions of life and climate, and forms of combat, which would have dismayed the most experienced armies. Páez wrote of General La Torre's campaign from Bogotá to the Apure *llanos:* "The march of La Torre from Bogotá in the space of forty-four days was considered an extraordinary achievement by Morillo, for he never slept in towns, he had only meat to eat, he suffered continuous rains, and he crossed swamps and the most powerful rivers, like the Negro, the Upía, and many others, the smallest of which is, as he said himself, wider than the Ebro at is mouth." If Morillo admired the fourteen republican cavalry charges at the battle of Mucuritas, in which Páez defeated La Torre, we should regard as no less admirable the ability of the royalist infantry to stand up to them after that exhausting march. At the end of the battle they were almost ringed by fire, for Páez had set fire to the plain, but they retreated in good order.

Fortunately, the patriots, too, were strengthened soon after the arrival of Canterac by contingents of foreign legionaries, mainly British, recruited in London by the unselfish López Méndez. Most of them were adventurers and officers who had been made idle by the end of the long revolutionary and Napoleonic wars in Europe. Some of them were unable to adapt to the harsh conditions of war in Venezuela, and a few tried to compensate for their failure or to unburden their resentment by writing bitter *Memoirs* about these lands or against the Liberator. This was the case with Ducoudray Holstein and George Hippisley, whose comments are quoted with passionate voracity in the recent work of Salvador de Madariaga. But the majority, it is pleasant to note, showed a remarkable sense of honor in fulfilling the obligations that they had accepted. Many gave their lives for their new country with as much self-denial as the creoles. Others survived and founded illustrious families in Venezuela.

One of them, the Irishman Daniel Florencio O'Leary, deserves to be remembered with special gratitude. He arrived in Venezuela in 1818, aged sixteen or eighteen —the precise date of his birth is not known— as an ensign in the British unit called the *Red Hussars,* and he fought thereafter in the Venezuelan and New Granadan campaigns. He was the Liberator's personal representative in Chile during the Peruvian campaign and, despite O'Leary's youth, Bolívar demonstrated confidence in his wisdom by subsequently giving him other difficult commissions. He was already a General when the Liberator died in 1830, and on several occasions he had served as his first aide-de-camp. O'Leary was familiar with all aspects of the great process of the emancipation of America. He had fought on the battlefields, he had lived for twelve years alongside the creole soldiers and *caudillos,* he had seen the intrigues of political life, and he had observed the Liberator himself directly and intimately. Nobody, then, was better qualified than O'Leary to write the history of those years. Not satisfied, however, with his personal records, he dedicated himself to the task of supplementing his material with whatever documents he could obtain from the other leaders —especially from his brother-in-law, Carlos Soublette, who served the Republic from 1810. He finally produced thirty-two volumes of narrative, letters and other documents which still form a source of the first quality for all historians.[1]

For the patriots, 1817 was a year of mixed fortunes. As we will see in the next chapter, the happiest event of all was the recognition of Bolívar's authority by the *caudillo* who had made himself master of the *llanos* of Apure, José Antonio Páez, who thus brought to the patriot cause the terrible lancers who had destroyed it in 1814.

By the end of the year, the patriots had consolidated their possession of eastern Venezuela. In the south they controlled Guayana, its capital Angostura, and the river Orinoco, giving them access to the sea. The support of Páez completed the extension of their authority into a vast arc of territory, stretching as far as the plains of New Granada in the south-west, around the center of the country.

At this time, Tomás Montilla wrote to his sisters: "Despite his reverses, Bolívar has a great reputation and is much loved."[2] Tomás Montilla himself was an example of Bolívar's ability to inspire respect and affection, because he remained an intimate friend of the Liberator despite what had happened to this brother, Mariano.

Bolívar, in fact, remained the inspiration of everything that happened, as the decision of Páez to submit to him clearly proved.

---

1. 1879 to 1888. It is divided as follows: vols. i-xii, *Corespondencia de hombres notables con el Libertador;* xiii-xxvi, *Documentos;* xxii, xxviii and Apéndice, *Narración;* xxix-xxxi, *Cartas del Libertador.*
2. Boletín de la Academia Nacional de la Historia. Caracas, no. 80, p. 500.

XXII

STEADFAST
IN
ITS WORK

JOSE ANTONIO PAEZ WAS
born not in the Apure *llanos* of which he was to make himself master,
but in Curpa, near Acarigua, at the entrance to Venezuela's mountainous
region. He spent his childhood near Caracas, in the town of Guama,
but when he was still very young, he fled to the *llanos,* after killing a
highwayman who had tried to rob him. There he entered the service of
Manuel Pulido as a *peón* on his ranch on the banks of the Apure.

This life was hard for a boy who was not accustomed to it, and his misfortune was compounded because the foreman, a Negro slave called
Manuelote, believed that Páez had been sent to spy on him and
took pleasure in making work even more difficult. Páez himself
narrated in his *Autobiografía:* "I remember that one day, when we came
to a river, he shouted to me: 'Jump into the water and lead the cattle.'
When I hesitated, declaring that he knew nothing, he answered in an
angry voice: 'I am not asking you what I know; I am ordering you to
jump into the water and lead the cattle.' Much, much I suffered from that
treatment. My hands were cracked as a result of my efforts to control
horses with the horse-hair halter that is used to break them when their
necks are secured and their muzzles are fastened in a sort of bridle. I had
to struggle with those indomitable animals, riding bareback or seated on
a wooden saddle with straps of untanned leather. My thighs suffered so
much that they were often covered with bleeding abrasions. As often
happens in those deserts and with that savage life, even worms came out
of my wounds. The multitude of flies that abound there in the wet season

produce similar horrors. When the day's work was done, Manuelote, lying in his hammock, used to say to me: 'Catire Páez, fetch water, and wash my feet.' Afterwards he used to order me to rock him until he fell asleep. He called me by the name of *catire* (light-haired person), and he chose me rather than any of the other *peones* for anything particularly difficult or dangerous that had to be done with the herd."[1]

Páez was to rise from this infamous state to the rank of Commander-in-Chief and to the office of President of the Republic, which he exercised several times. But what was truly remarkable was that, in the process, he was able to uplift his moral and intellectual personality to the point where he was able to enjoy easy, unembarrassed relations with leading scholars and politicians when he held high office.

He was aged twenty when the revolution began in Venezuela in 1810, and it seems that he immediately decided for the republican cause, for it is known with certainty that in 1813 the royalists held him prisoner in Barinas. He was freed by a detachment sent to the city by Bolívar after his triumph at Araure. Páez then held the rank of captain, although it is clear that, in these early years of his career, he detested the discipline of the regular armies and would not submit for long to the authority of a commander. He preferred to lead his own guerrillas, although being still very young and unknown, he was able to attract only a few desperate men, at times no more than five, who either recognized the incipient *caudillo's* astuteness or were driven to him by necessity. Within a short time he found himself alone, and he had to begin again. After fighting in Urdaneta's division, which was retreating towards New Granada, and despite winning an encounter of some importance near Mérida, he decided to leave the force in 1814, "without Urdaneta's permission" to quote from his *Autobiografía*. Shortly afterwards he refused the command of a corps offered him by the Granadan García Rovira.

His narrative also tells us that he quarreled with Francisco Olmedilla and Fernando Figueredo, his two subsequent commanders. Although he gives good reasons for the disputes, he was also able to find them to justify his next quarrel, with General Joaquín Ricaurte and, later, that which occurred with Commander Miguel Guerrero.

In 1816 Páez was involved in a serious usurpation of authority. A group of eminent patriots, Venezuelans and Granadans, who had fled to the *llanos,* wanted to establish a civil structure of government with a more or less legal appearance. They elected as president of their precipitate republic the Granadan Colonel, Fernando Serrano, the former Governor of Pamplona. Generals Urdaneta and Serviez and Dr. Francisco Javier Yanes were elected as councillors of state, and the command of the army was entrusted

---

1. *Autobiografía*, i, p. 10.

to Colonel Francisco de Paula Santander. After a few days, Páez, who was the real leader of that "government's" only forces, either prepared or accepted a mutiny which deposed all the elected officials. Without more ado he thus found himself in authority over them. This typical "pronouncement," like so many others that were to bring disaster in Spain and America, not only destroyed the attempt to create civil government, dubious though its legality was, but also overthrew the military hierarchy. No less than two generals and several colonels were ignored, as Lieutenant Colonel Páez—his rank had been conferred by the Granadan government—took control.

One of the deposed leaders was Rafael Urdaneta, who in 1814 had led a retreat of 166 leagues from the center of Venezuela to New Granada, and who had held the rank of divisional general since 1815. He gave a further demonstration, however, of the abnegation with which he always served his country, and accepted command of a small cavalry squadron, which he led into battle in the next combat, at El Yagual.

By 1816 Páez was a strapping young man of twenty-six, just beginning to raise himself from the semi-savage state in which he had grown up. He could hardly read or write. As for manners, he was still ignorant of how to eat with a fork, as he admitted in his *Autobiografía*. On the other hand, he must have felt dizzy when he looked down from the heights to which he had raised himself despite almost unbelievable dangers and obstacles. His prestige had almost completely overshadowed that of the other guerrilla leaders, both royalist and republican, who had been fighting for several years in the Apure region. He led an army of hardened fighters whose valor and skill, as well as the anarchic independence of their characters, would allow them to accept as their commander only a man whom they could consider their better in all circumstances. This was a consequence of his success in numerous combats, which were beginning to qualify as battles. On January 28, 1817, at Mucuritas, he inflicted on Morillo's invincible infantry the first serious defeat of their American campaign. A year earlier, at El Yagual, two fugitive generals and nine colonels had fought under his orders. At Mucuritas he had with him only the officers he had trained himself.

Páez's career contained many episodes, more or less hidden by his cunning, in which law and circumspection were pushed to one side by his personalistic predominance. But it would be ridiculous to expect anything else for this period. Instead, we should marvel that he and his *llaneros,* many of them former soldiers of Boves, renounced the disorder and pillage that had been allowed them when they were "loyal vassals," and accepted the laborious service to the country. When that deprived rural mass entered a city, where the comforts of civilization and the delicacy of the women must have fascinated them, under the royalist banner nothing was denied them. They enjoyed vengeance, rape, looting. But they could not permit themselves to do this once they accepted those defenseless citizens as their compatriots and brothers.

Bolívar reiterated at the time: "I desire the most exact discipline from the troops of the Republic, for without it we will lose both the love of the people and the morality of the soldier."[1] Would these poor men have accepted this imposition if they had not realized that this love of the people and this morality of the soldier was something more than an appeal for constraint in their behavior?

But for Bolívar, Páez would never have emerged from the *llanos*. If he had been simply a common fighter, he would never have thought of leaving, or having thought of it, would have done nothing about it, for the Apure *llanos* were a rich fief. What is certain is that there is no example in the history of America comparable to Páez's greatness of character in overcoming his origins and the flatteries that tempted him later. Historians who have censured him occasionally feel obliged to justify him for this reason, not out of sentiment, but because he controlled that peculiar, turbulent world—in war as in civil disputes it was always a question of all or nothing—without the blemishes of vulgarity, ostentation, rancor or arrogance displayed by men with similar careers.

The ceremony that he organized at the end of 1817 to recognize Bolívar's authority seems like a scene from the Crusades. He tells us: "Considering only the good of the country, bearing in mind the military gifts of Bolívar, the prestige of his name, already known even abroad, and understanding above all the advantage of having a superior authority and a center to direct the different *caudillos,* who were operating in diverse places, I decided to submit my authority to that of General Bolívar. I arranged the troops that I had in El Yagual, and I asked Fr. Ramón Ignacio Méndez, later Archbishop of Caracas, to come, so that in their presence he could receive my oath to recognize General Bolívar as supreme commander. I then ordered the troops to follow my example, and that the units in other places should do the same."[2]

A little later, on January 30, 1818, Bolívar and Páez met and embraced for the first time at the ranch of Cañafístola. As if they were watched by an occult poetic genius who had decided to accumulate episodes that would adorn future narratives, one of the most astonishing incidents in the war occurred a few days later, on February 6, when Páez, amidst a cavalry charge, swam the river Apure and, watched by Bolívar, captured a number of enemy craft which were preventing the patriots from crossing the river. A British legionary described the unbelievable exploit as follows:

---

1. *Cartas,* xii, p. 132.
2. *Autobiografía del general Páez,* i, p. 136.

"Bolívar was in the Apure *llanos* with his men. They were weak from hunger and, unless he could cross the river Apure, were without the means to obtain supplies without making a torturous march of many leagues, an impossibility in their state. The hungry troops could see a multitude of cattle grazing on the opposite bank, but they were unable to cross because Bolívar had neither craft of any type nor wood to build them, and also because the enemy had seven well-armed and well-manned boats in the middle of the river. Bolívar observed everything from his side of the river and, full of despair, was walking along it. Páez, who had been watching him, rode up and asked the reason for his anxiety. His Excellency said to him: 'I would give the whole world to capture the Spanish squadron, for without it I cannot cross the river and the troops cannot march.' 'It will be yours within an hour,' replied Páez. 'Imposible!' said Bolívar, 'and the men will die.' 'That's my business,' said Páez, and he galloped away. Within a few minutes he returned with his Guard of Honor, composed of three hundred lancers chosen for their proven honor and strength. Leading them to the bank of the river he spoke these words to them: 'We must take these boats or die. Follow *your uncle* those of you who wish to.' Applying his spurs to his horse, he plunged into the river and swam toward the squadron. The Guard followed him, their lances in their mouths, swimming with one arm, and hugging the necks of their horses with the other, urging them to swim against the current and shouting to frighten away the many caymans in the river. They thus reached the boats and, mounting their horses, jumped aboard from their backs. Led by their commander, they seized control of all the boats, to the great admiration of those who were watching from the bank of the river. It will seem impossible to English officers that a body of cavalry, armed only with lances and without other means of transport than horses in the rapid current of a river, could attack and capture a squadron of gun-boats in the midst of a multitude of caymans. Although the deed seems strange, it happened, and there are many officers in England who can testify to it."[1]

O'Leary, who was little inclined to praise Páez, also commented as follows upon the cavalry charge into the water: "Naked, lances in hand, and riding bareback, Aramendi and fifty Hussars de Apure plunged into the water, seized the boats amidst the applause and admiration of the patriot army and heavy fire, and took them to their general. Opposite San Francisco the river Apure is 206 *toesas*[2] wide. At the spot where Aramendi crossed, three quarters of a mile away, it is wider. The speed of the current and the nature of the river, which is filled with dangerous fish and caymans, heighten the merit of this daring stroke. But it was not

---

1. Quoted in the *Autobiografía de Páez*, i, p. 144.
2. A *toesa* was an old measure equivalent to 1 meter 946 millimeters.

the first time that Aramendi had performed such a deed. A year earlier he had done the same thing with equal success and in the same river when he captured the Governor of Barinas, Francisco López."[1]

The only thing that can explain the success of such feats of bravery is that those lancers were already considered almost invincible, even by the most experienced officers in the enemy forces. One of them, Captain Rafael Sevilla, who wrote *Memorias* about his campaigns in Venezuela and New Granada, did not hide the unease felt throughout the *pacifying* army when it entered the *llanos* for the first time to face Páez. It was this feeling of almost superstitious fear that these lancers inspired which led him to describe them with a phrase which Revesz rightly considers Shakespearean. He called them "a forest of lances spread out at the gallop." The obstinate Morillo also declared them invincible, although unwillingly, when he confessed in a report to Spain: "I have never managed to attack them with success in their territory. In addition to what I suffered from the distances and the climate, the infantry has never obtained decisive advantages over them on any of the occasions that they have come to hand."[2]

This was even though, as noted by Páez: "The Spanish soldiers fought with such desperation that our *llaneros,* discussing the day's events at night, told me (I will permit myself to repeat it in their own words) that 'when four of them remained, they defended themselves arse to arse'. That is to say, they formed a square. It is certain; they did not surrender and it was necessary to kill them."

O'Leary has given us a portrait of Páez at the time, which does him justice, although a few lines, inspired by the reservations with which he always judged the Apure *caudillo,* should be removed. He tells us: "He was of medium height, strong and well built, although the lower half of his body was out of proportion to his torso. His chest and shoulders were very wide, and his short, fat neck supported a large head, covered with short, curly, dark brown hair. His dark eyes did not lack sparkle. He had a straight nose with wide nostrils, thick lips, and a round beard. His skin had a healthy appearance, and it would have been very white but for the effects of the sun.... As a guerrilla leader he had no equal. Fearless, active, brave, cunning, quick to form ideas, resolute in execution and rapid in his movements, he was most frightening when his forces were smallest."

With more sympathy and flexibility, Vowell narrates an episode in his campaigns, describing Páez and his men for what they were at the

---

1. O'Leary, *Narración,* i, p. 443. Lecuna who says he follows Vowell, also gives the number of attackers as 50, and states that Páez divided them into two groups, led by Colonels Francisco Aramendi and José de la Cruz Paredes.
2. Revesz, *op. cit.,* p. 72.

time. He tells us: "From experience acquired at great cost in the plains of Calabozo and El Sombrero, Morillo was well aware of the incapacity of his cavalry to take on the *llaneros,* so he ordered the Spanish hussars and lancers to take up positions in a number of small clearings along the edge of the forest on the banks of the Arauca. Two field guns were placed in front of each detachment, and the gunners stayed at their posts with fuses lit, ready to open fire. The infantry was deployed, forming a dark line along the edge of the forest where the plain begins... Páez halted his men about half a mile from the edge of the forest, and advanced on horseback, followed by three or four of his black warriors, riding the spirited, elegant horses that are caught wild on the plain. Each of these officers also carried a lance with a black pennant, similar to that of the soldiers, upon which a skull and cross-bones was roughly embroidered in white cotton. The leader himself rode a prancing, silver-grey charger, its mane and tail flying, for the *llaneros* do not disfigure their horses by cropping their tails. His dress was the same as that of his companions in arms, consisting of an open-necked shirt made of English cloth with red horizontal stripes and very wide frills and sleeves, and separate trousers of white cotton, which reached just below his knees. His calves were uncovered and his feet were bare, but he wore silver spurs with sharp rowels about four inches in diameter. His head was covered with a low-crowned hat, woven from palm leaves, with a wide blue ribbon fastened beneath his chin in the manner of a chin-strap. His lance was light and manageable, its shaft made from a hard, elastic, black cane that grows in several places in the plains. It was carried for him by a boy of about twelve, who was riding a very fat and strong horse. The boy served the commander as an orderly, and was much loved in the army, thanks to his great indifference to danger and to his skill in riding and swimming.

"Páez, the terrible *llanero* leader, showed no trace in his generous expression of the ferocity that has been attributed to him! His short, curly hair fell onto his forehead, and he had little black moustaches, but no beard. Only his black eyes showed signs of those rages that could drive him to deeds of excessive rigor —to describe them in the best way possible— although in his case they could well be extenuated by invoking the right of reprisal. His cheeks, usually rather pale, were now burning, because of his exertions and the exaltation caused by the prospect of an imminent battle with the enemies of his country. He rode slowly, calmly examining the royalist positions, seated side-saddle (his usual posture in such circumstances) with one leg crossed over the bow of his saddle. Although Páez and his staff were a hundred yards from the forest, the Spanish infantry did not aim even a musket at him, for an intense curiosity and perhaps a feeling of respect for his resolute, tranquil attitude fixed the attention of the enemy on the movement of this exceptional man. Having passed finally along the whole enemy line, much like an officer reviewing his own troops, he took his lance from the hands of the boy who was carrying it and, sitting erect in his saddle, returned at a half gallop, waving aloft the well known and terrible symbol of *War to the Death* as a challenge to the Spanish cavalry to emerge from the forest in which it had taken refuge and face him on the plain. Meanwhile his guard, which was watching him attentively, burst into enthusiastic shouts of *'Long live Páez!,' 'Death to Morillo!'* When he rejoined his lancers, they all dismounted and, as additional insult to the Spanish cavalry, removed the bridles from their horses, controlling them by means of the *cabestro,* or rope of twisted horse-hair, that they used among themselves. The *llaneros* then took out their small wooden cups and their tobacco, lit a fire and began to smoke with as much calm as if they were in their encampment."[1]

With these troops incorporated into his army, and with the co-operation of the best patriot commanders —Urdaneta, Monagas, Anzoátegui, Sedeño, Zaraza—Bolívar attacked Caracas for the third time at the beginning of 1818, this time from the south, across the Guarico *llanos.* Although Zaraza had just been defeated at La Hogaza, an action in which Guillermo Palacios Bolívar, the Liberator's nephew, lost his life, the campaign began auspiciously. Morillo was surprised and defeated near the city of Calabozo, and had to make a hurried retreat towards the center.

Everything gave rise to the hope that Bolívar was about to repeat the brilliant campaign of 1813. Morillo managed, with great difficulty, to hold up the patriots with two rearguard actions, fought at La Uriosa and El Sombrero, and thus gained refuge in the center of the country. The alarm among the royalists was so great that many of them rushed to La Guaira to embark for overseas, and the authorities in Caracas destroyed a large part of the public archives. But Morillo was no less determined than Bolívar, who found three armies larger than his own threatening him when he reached the valleys of Aragua.

Páez had refused to accompany the campaign beyond the *llanos,* on the pretext that he first had to capture San Fernando de Apure, and that his cavalry was unable to fight in semi-mountainous terrain. This last argument is accepted by many historians, and a present-day *llanero,* our esteemed friend José Rafael Viso, who is well-versed in history, has reminded me that Páez's lancers came from the Apure, a region of sedimented terrain, where until recently it was a curiosity for children to find a stone. The horses, therefore, had very soft hooves. Since they were unshod, they would have been unable to stand up to the broken, stony ground of the Aragua valleys. As we will see, the Liberator was to find himself in a similar situation in Peru when he had to use horses

---

1. *Las sabanas de Barinas* (Caracas), p. 29.

from the coast in the mountains of the interior. Other historians, however, regard Páez's reasons as cunning pretexts to abandon Bolívar. The truth is that Bolívar came to despair so much at his inflexibility that he wrote to Páez at the end of the year: "I assure you under my word of honor that I have neved distrusted you; but I also assure you, with the greatest frankness, that in my opinion you have never obeyed my orders. Perhaps this is the reason for your fancy that I distrust you. The proof to the contrary is that I have put my only available troops at your disposal; I have given you powers enjoyed by no other commander; and finally, I have done whatever you have wanted since you recognized me."[1]

The same arduous task always confronted Bolívar. He could not win a supporter, buy a musket, or take a step forward, except at the cost of infinite sacrifices, moving all the resources of the human heart, and suffering wounds in the flesh and in the spirit from the stones of that harsh reality.

Whether or not Páez was justified in his decision, what is certain is that he deprived Bolívar of his best forces at the most critical moment. The Liberator was obliged, therefore, to retreat, and on the field of La Puerta, which had already been fatal for the patriots on two occasions, he was defeated by Morillo and Morales on March 16, 1818. The struggle was so furious that both the Liberator and Morillo threw themselves into the fight. The British legionary Richard L. Vowell, who fought on the republican side, recorded: "At a certain moment, when the enemies were crossing the stream, Bolívar picked up a banner and, advancing at a gallop, called to his soldiers to hurry to retrieve it. They did so after an impetuous charge in which one of the foreign officers lost his life. Colonel Rooke, who was wounded twice at Bolívar's side, told us that the Libertador behaved as though he wished to die in the battle."[2] It was also said that Bolívar personally killed a fleeing standard-bearer.

Morillo was wounded by a tremendous thrust with a lance, "which pinned him to the saddle." According to Páez it came from "the then Captain Juan Pablo Farfán," while Larrazábal attributed it to "the bold Colonel Jerano Vásquez, afterwards killed in the Ortiz combat." Morillo himself reported the incident to Spain, and the words he used to excuse his temerity indicate that the republicans were rightly convinced that they had already won the day, when the arrival of Morillo with fresh troops and his personal charge, changed the outcome of the battle. He wrote: "I was pierced by a lance-thrust, that I received at the critical

1. *Cartas,* xii, p. 103.
2. *Campagnes et Croisières dans les Etats de Venezuela et de la Nouvelle Grenade,* par un officier du 1er. Régiment de Lanciers Vénézuéliens (Paris, 1837), p. 92.

moment of charging the intrepid enemy.... This has been one of the occasions on which it is necessary to risk the person of the Commander-in-Chief, so as to prevent a disgrace and restore order... My wound is extremely large, because of the frightful damage that the lance caused where it entered and came out, and also because of the place in which I received it, in the left side between my hip and my navel; the lance came out through my shoulder."[1]

After this defeat the patriots regarded the campaign as lost. Bolívar led them in an attack against General La Torre at Ortiz, but both sides did badly there and abandoned the battlefield. It made patriot hopes for a decisive victory even more remote.

This was the situation when Bolívar, encamped at a place called Rincón de los Toros, was surprised on the night of April 17, by a bold royalist officer who got into the camp without difficulty after obtaining the password from a patriot deserter. At almost point-blank range, he shot into the hammocks containing the Liberator and his companions. Miraculously, Bolívar escaped unhurt. Several bullets went through his hammock, two of his companions were killed and another wounded.[2] There was such confusion that Bolívar was separated from his troops, and found himself alone and lost on the plain at night. Páez commented in his *Autobiografía:* "It should not surprise us that the Liberator could not find the camp, for even the best *llanero,* when he becomes lost there in the dark, is in the same situation as the navigator in the middle of the ocean who loses his compass on a dark night. I have been in the position of believing myself wandering in the *llanos* at night, only to find with the dawn that I had passed many times by the foot of the same tree."

At dawn, the patriots were again attacked by the royalists, and concerned as they were at the absence of the Liberator, whom they believed to be dead or a prisoner, they were unable to resist effectively. Fighting desperately, Colonel Silvestre Palacios and Lieutenant Colonel Mariano Plaza lost their lives. Other young republicans, including Florencio Tovar, Martín's son, were captured and executed later. However, Leonardo Infante, the noted *apureño* lancer, performed wonders of bravery in several oustanding incidents despite the disorder, and his orderly shot the Spanish commander and captured his horse, which had a harness of silver. Shortly afterwards, Infante met Bolívar, who was still on foot, and he offered him the mount. Consequently Bolívar rode into Calabozo on the horse of the enemy who had been about to finish him off, but who had lost his own life in the attempt.

---

1. Rodríguez Villa, *op. cit.* See too Revesz, p. 133.
2. Lecuna, *Crónica razonada...*, ii, p. 192. Perú de Lacroix gives a slightly different version in his *Diario de Bucaramanga.*

Such was the final episode of that campaign, in which adverse fate tested to the limit the Liberator's spirit. Who could have foreseen that the following year he would triumphantly enter far-off Bogotá, and that uninterrupted victories would then carry him on to that Lima of his dreams, which he had set for himself as the goal of his liberating activity.

In 1824, during the Peruvian campaign, he told Sucre: "The picture is horrifying, but I am not afraid, since we are accustomed to seeing the most horrible phantoms disappear as we draw near them." The phantoms were those of these five years, 1814 to 1818.

But we would distort history if, to exalt the hero, we were to remain silent about the selflessness and the absolute dedication with which the Venezuelan people, without distinction of military or civilian rank, rallied to his side.

The sacrifices they made seem unbelievable today. The Italian Captain Carlos Castelli, who was with the republicans and who later became a General, noted in his diary that in 1817 he and his troops in Barcelona were living off rain drops and ass's meat. He noted in 1819, as a special event, that after three years' service he had received his first pay: 16 pesos.[1] When the republicans gained control of Guayana in 1817, the relative wealth of the area and the possibility of trading down the Orinoco filled them with hopes. We find, however, that they had to haggle with and cheat even the privateers to get a few miserable supplies. They had captured an enemy brigantine, and Bolívar had to excuse himself to Admiral Brion because ". . . at the request of all the officers, who were unclothed and hatless, I ordered the commissioners to deliver to the General of the garrison some suits of old clothes that were found in the trunks and some hats, so that they could be shared among the officers and the troops. . . ."[2] In 1819, Vicente de Sucre, Governor of the province, wrote to one of his companions demanding the return of a sack of young corn and bananas, lent to him for his troops, which he claimed was all he had to feed himself.[3] They all accepted this way of life quite naturally. O'Leary, who saw it at close hand, commented: "Generals, commanders and officers were, with respect to their way of life, on a footing of complete equality with even the private soldier. They shared the same tasks and ate the same rations, water and meat, prepared in the same fashion. They were all equals even in their dress, and the Liberator wore nothing to distinguish himself in the *llano*. There were even occasions when he was short of clothing."

In some places, they ate only meat. Elsewhere, they had none at all. In 1818, the republicans were exporting beef and tobacco from Barinas down

1. Archivo Nacional, Caracas, *Ilustres Próceres*, xviii, f. 23.
2. *Cartas*, xi, p. 106.
3. Archivo Nacional, Caracas, Gobernación de Guayana, vol. iv.

the Orinoco, but all they obtained in return was dedicated to the purchase of arms. They despaired at the thought that the traders who ventured to bring the arms might take them back if there were insufficient funds to pay for them. On one occasion Roscio wrote to Bolívar: "We are in danger of seeing muskets going back for lack of money.... There are no cattle, mules or anything else for freighting and it is necessary to live by and defend the river. We feed the garrison, the hospital and the navy by taking the beasts of people in La Soledad; and for the supply of the Apure people we have had the fortune to obtain by false pretenses four hundred barrels of flour that an American ship brought from North America. I sent it to thirteen forts...." And he added: "I am suffering, but I would not want the Republic to suffer this degree of misery to which we have sunk here. Since I received your orders on salaries, I have limited myself to a meat ration of three pounds...." According to a report to Bolívar from Dr. José Rafael Revenga, he and Roscio were called "the miserable persons," because of their meanness in the management of public funds but, he added, "the service has continued to progress, unhindered by a shortage of resources, and this misery, as they choose to call it, has allowed me to fulfill this contract for muskets, which I firmly believe will lead to many others."[1]

Several years later, this Revenga, an eminent statistician and an enthusiastic patriot, was to give proof of altruism which seems like a novelist's invention in these days of scepticism. He was sent to London on a government mission, and one of the Republic's creditors had him imprisoned for its debts. When Revenga was released, he demanded and obtained damages. The money was obtained at the cost of his freedom, and it would have served to free him forever from the privations that he had suffered, but Revenga decided to use it to purchase materials for free normal schools, which he had always wanted the government to establish. A thousand blackboards, forty thousand pencils, hand-bells and inkwells made up the strange cargo with which he returned. He also took a trained teacher, although he confessed "I am not authorized to make him offers on behalf of the government, and he does not demand them."[2] They had no arms, no clothes, no food, but it was important to them to obtain teaching materials and a trained teacher.

Really, those glorious austerities that the republicans suffered were never to end, and they gave rise to an anecdote told as follows by Simón Rodríguez in his Defensa de Bolívar: "...that when the Colombian soldiers reached Peru, they mutinied because an attempt was made to pay

1. Juan Germán Roscio, Obras (Caracas, 1953), passim. For the quote from Revenga, see O'Leary, vi, p. 453.
2. Armando Rojas, Ideas educativas de Simón Bolívar (Madrid, 1952), and Manuel Pérez Vila, José Rafael Revenga (Caracas, 1953).

Oil on canvas, painted in Bogotá by the Colombian artist Pedro José Figueroa, in 1819, shortly after the Liberator's entrance in the capital of New Granada. This portrait belongs to the Colombian Academy of History and measures 0.96 x 0.72 metres.

their wages in *money;* that the Commander-in-Chief immediately sent schooners to bring *funds* from Colombia; that they returned loaded with *yuccas* and that the mutiny turned into *hurrahs!*" Although it was not meant to be very charitable, this amusing invention has a basis of truth, which, far from humiliating the Venezuelans, should fill them with enthusiasm and pride. Yes; the use of money, and the pleasures and vanity that it procures, were almost unknown to those yucca and banana eaters who went from the coast of the Caribbean as far as Ayacucho, and for fourteen years withstood hunger and nakedness in order to secure the independence of America.

What does seem unbelievable is that, despite such privations, they retained a vigor and a skill that dazzled the imagination of the most experienced Spaniards. Morillo wrote to Spain about the inhabitants of Margarita: "These wicked men, full of rage and pride, seemed like tigers after their first success in defense, and they exposed themselves to fire and bayonets with a boldness unequaled among the best troops in the world... Not content with the infernal fire that they started, they hurled stones of great size, and since they were strong, gigantic men, they were seen to throw an enormous stone with as much ease as if it had been very small. Thus we had some men killed and many wounded from the stone-throwing."[1] Giants! No. Merely long-suffering, valiant *mestizos,* hardened by their work at sea, who went to war with the same quiet intensity with which they embarked on their work. Nor were they "wicked men." When the Spanish commander came to know the country better, he no longer regarded the heroism of his enemies as savage, and his expressions became almost respectful. He confessed, referring to the defeat of his second-in-command, La Torre, at Mucuritas: "Fourteen consecutive charges against my tired battalions made me see that those men were not, as I had been told, a small gang of cowards."

Above all, the spiritual forces revealed in such unselfishness and constancy turned those wars into a stage for indefatigable heroes. Morillo described Bolívar as "an indomitable being, for whom the smallest triumph is enough to make him master of five hundred leagues of territory." He added in another report that "attention should be paid to the land of Venezuela, which provides all the other revolutionary provinces with commanders and officers who are more audacious and better trained than those of other countries."[2] And he told his government about the people who supported them: "In Spain it is commonly believed that the leaders who have aroused this country are only four in number. It is essential, Excellency, not to think in these terms, at least as far as the provinces of

---

1. Revesz, *op. cit.,* p. 127.
2. Rodríguez Villa, *op. cit.,* i, 252.

Venezuela are concerned. . . . The said people are vigorous and valiant. They will eat anything. They are without hospitals, and they do not wear clothes. . . . In this territory of men who need nothing, who are favored by the climate, who are determined, who have arms and capable leaders, it is necessary to smother them with forces to subject them. When forces are not available in this proportion, the goal will not be fulfilled."[1]

Such was the wall that appeared before the arrogant Spanish commanders: the hero and the masses displaying the same fundamental virtues, all social classes united in their altruism and sacrifice, and learned men like Revenga and Roscio displaying the same combativeness as the soldiers. And it was this that convinced them a little more each day that an admirable ofshoot of their own race was growing among the despised "insurgents."

Bolívar felt this solidarity profoundly, and in his letters and confidences he increasingly depersonalized the work he was undertaking and, proud and grateful, exalted the contribution of everybody else. On one occasion he said to Salom: "Do you remember, Salom, the army's joy when we shared the bananas at Betoyes? It is true to say that we hadn't eaten for two days. Nevertheless, this army didn't complain. It remained steadfast in its work because it had been told that it was going to destroy the tyrants. When the history of these combats is written, and an account is given of the marvels of valor of our soldiers, of their courage in all adversities, ancient history, full of heroes and exaggerated scenes, will lose much of its importance, for it will be seen to be outstripped by reality."[2] Similarly, when his uncle Esteban Palacios returned to Venezuela, Bolívar wrote to him: "You left behind a large and happy family. It has since been cut down by a bloody scythe. You left a country that, newborn, was still nurturing the first fruits of its creation, the first elements of a nascent society, and now you find it all in ruins... all a memory. The living have disappeared. The work of man, the houses of God, the very fields of the earth have suffered the terrible havoc wrought by the quaking force of nature. You will ask, 'Where are my parents, my brothers and sisters, my nieces and nephews?' The most fortunate have been buried within the sanctuary of their own homes. As for the less fortunate, the fields of Venezuela have been watered with their blood and littered with their bones. Their only crime was their love of justice." He ended: "I have reaped the fruit of all the efforts of my countrymen, relatives and friends. I have been their representative before mankind, and I shall continue to represent them before posterity."[3]

---

1. Revesz, *op. cit.,* 113 and 120.
2. *Manuscrito del General Salom, adjunto a sus itinerarios y campañas,* quoted by Antonio Arráiz, *Culto bolivariano* (Caracas, 1940), p. 63.
3. *Cartas,* v, p. 21.

This awareness that he represented the efforts of all his compatriots was at times expressed in an open-hearted solicitude which extended to even the most humble of them. He concerned himself with the needs of the army, and he provided for the welfare of the soldiers with detailed instructions, pointing out on one occasion: "The columns should not march a lot, only three, four or five leagues a day, resting in a wood or by a river from ten o'clock until four in the afternoon. At this place they should make their camp. When day breaks they should march for tow or three hours, and for a similar time in the afternoon. They are to carry lemons, so that when they halt they can drink lemon juice with sugar or honey, in order to avoid suffering from the bad climate and the excessive heat of the day and of the country."[1]

He wrote to Páez in 1828: "I anxiously desire to improve the lot of the people of Venezuela. . . the people are so miserable that it is essential to relieve them at all costs."[2] The same attitude led him to hold up the most forsaken *llaneros* as an example to his nephew, Anacleto Clemente, whom he asked, in the well-known letter from which we have already quoted: "Are you not ashamed to see that poor *llaneros,* without education or the means to obtain it, who have been to no other school than that of the guerrilla, have made themselves gentlemen? They have become worthy men. They have learned to respect themselves simply because of respecting me. Are you not ashamed, I repeat, when you consider that, being my nephew and with a woman of the strictest morality for your mother, you are inferior to such a poor guerrilla fighter who has no other family than his country?"[3]

This final phrase was so apt and delicate that only affection was capable of producing it. In the cold registers of the Republic those men appear as born "of unknown parents." It is still customary to use the phrase "sons of nobody." But Bolívar did not see them in this way. For him the soldier with whom he had lived was, in a tight synthesis of praise and warning, the man "who has no other family than his country."

He also said that they had made themselves gentlemen. Gentlemen, with such coarse manners? Gentlemen, "with feet in the soil," to use the popular Venezuelan phrase? Yes, because they were brave, long-suffering, imperturbable and generous. In remarks to Salom that we have already examined, Bolívar characterized them with another admirable phrase. He said that they did not complain, because the army was "steadfast in its work." Their determination increased with their suffering. And, if he had observed this, why not describe them as gentlemen?

---

1. *Ibid,* xi, p. 371.
2. *Ibid,* vii, p. 373.
3. *Ibid,* v, p. 318.

Despite the failure of the campaign against the center, by the end of 1818 Bolívar could see himself approaching the culmination of a long period of reorganization for the Republic, in which he achieved two fundamental successes: the submission of the anarchic *caudillismo* and the legal reconstruction of the State. The second, which was to be achieved at the beginning of 1819, was really a result of the first. If it had been attempted earlier, the effect would have been simply to compound the separatist activities of the *caudillos* who, because of the source of their power, were regionalists and autocrats, and who carried on ideological disputes like lawyers and jurists. It also became possible because the patriots captured Angostura, a city relatively isolated from the theater of war and with easy communications not only with the outside world but also with all parts of the territory that they controlled.

Each change reinforced the other. As the growing prestige of the Republic attracted the allegiance of the numerous creole guerrillas fighting the royalists, the war became more closely defined as an international conflict. It became possible, moreover, to plan military operations, previously haphazard local adventures, on the basis of large campaigns, which offered more scope to the genius of the Liberator and to the strategy of Sucre.

We end this chapter with something that we have not forgotten, but which we have deliberately held back until we reached this decisive stage in Bolívar's career: the description of his physical appearance and of some of his personal habits.

Páez can supply this better than anybody. He tells us in his *Autobiogra-jia:* "Bolívar was then in the best of his years, and in full possession of the limited strength that city life can give. He was not tall, but his stature was sufficient for it not to be disdained by the sculptor who sought to depict a hero. His two principal characteristic features, which more than compensated for what he lacked in stature in distinguishing him from his companions, were the excessive mobility of his body and the brilliance of his eyes, which were black, lively, penetrating and restless, giving him the gaze of an eagle. His hair was black and somewhat curly. His hands and feet were as small as those of a woman, his voice was sharp and penetrating. His skin was toasted by the sun of the tropics but it retained the limpidity and lustre that the rigors of the climate and the continuous, violent changes of latitude experienced in his marches had been unable to destroy. Those who believe that the man of arms can be recognized by his athletic strength would not have imagined that Bolívar could have achieved what he did. But it is no less true that an artist, or any observer who studied him, could see with a glance the signs of a tenacious man, suited to accomplish any task that requires great intelligence and the greatest perseverance. Despite the agitated life capable of weakening the strongest constitution that he had lived until then, he remained healthy and full of vigor. His disposition was friendly and jovial. His character was normally pleasant, but he was impetuous and dominating when he was trying to accomplish an important enterprise. He combined in this way the affability of the courtier with the fire of the warrior. He liked to dance; he was gallant and strongly addicted to women. He was a skillful rider, and he used to like to go at full speed across the Apure plains, chasing the snakes that abound there. In camp he retained his good humor, making appropriate jokes; but on the march he was always rather restless and he managed to divert his impatience by singing patriotic songs. He loved combat, perhaps too much, and while it continued he displayed the greatest serenity. He did not spare example, voice, or sword, to check the defeated."[1]

Various historians state that Bolívar was ambidexterous and that when he fought he used to change his sword from one hand to the other. According to eye-witnesses he did this at Araure in 1813 and at La Puerta in 1818.

It is much more interesting to note that in one fundamental respect the portrait provided by Páez differs completely from a description written at the same time by the legionary Vowell. Páez found Bolívar friendly and jovial, disposed to remain good-humored in camp and to make jokes. He made a very different impression on Vowell, who wrote: "When he passed in front of us, he replied to our greeting with the melancholy smile which was habitual with him... he was aged 35, but he looked seven or eight years older. His thin face displayed patience and resignation, virtues of which he has given many proofs during his long political career and which do him so much more honor, insofar as his character is by nature impetuous."[2]

Which of the two descriptions penetrated more deeply the intimacy of Bolívar? Our heart grieves to think that perhaps those jokes in the camp were intended only to soften or hide the melancholy that had already become habitual. Perhaps that joviality was simply one more example of the patience and valor with which he made himself steadfast in his work.

1. *Autobiografía de Páez,* i, pp. 139-40.
2. *Campagnes et Croisières* (Paris, 1837). Quoted by Lecuna in *Crónica razonada...*, ii, p. 164.

XXIII

SIMILAR TO
A ROBUST
BLIND MAN

ON AUGUST 6, 1817, BOLIVAR
wrote to Martín Tovar: "At last Guayana is free and independent...
This province is an excellent point of vantage. It is well situated for
defense and even more so for offense. We threaten the enemy's rear from
here to Santa Fé, and we control an immense territory on either bank
of the Orinoco, Apure, Meta and Arauca rivers. We also have horses
and cattle. Since the struggle is now a matter of holding territory and
prolonging the campaign, whoever gains the greater advantage will be
the victor."
Increasingly, events were proving him right. At the beginning of
1819 he dedicated himself to the moral and political reorganization of
the Republic. Already, at the end of 1817, he had decreed the formation
of a Council of State "considering that it is impossible for now to establish a sound representative government and an eminently liberal constitution." Although the body's powers were very limited, it gave a certain
deliberative character to the unipersonal authority that Bolívar was exercising. Of greater importance, because it renewed the doctrinaire discussion of public affairs while still serving as propaganda for the republican system, was the foundation of a periodical called *Correo del
Orinoco*. Bolívar was particularly keen in having it published, but the
printing press that he obtained was lost at Ocumare. In 1817 another
press arrived from Trinidad, and the first number of the *Correo* finally
appeared on June 27, 1818. It was to last until 1822 and, in addition to

Bolívar himself, the most eminent republican thinkers worked on it, including Palacio Fajardo, José Luis Ramos, Roscio, Zea and Peñalver. Although it was regarded as an official newspaper, it did not bear this title, and in the first number the editors scrupulously pointed out: "We are free. We write in a free country, and we do not propose to deceive the public. For this reason we do not make ourselves responsible for official announcements; but, publishing them as they are, we leave it to the judgement of the reader to decide whether they deserve greater or lesser credence."[1] This freedom was respected on an important point. When the Liberator's political ideas were discussed, adverse opinions were welcomed by the *Correo* just as much as those that were favorable. It is also surprising that, despite the violent passion of the period and the fact that the *Gaceta de Caracas,* under José Domingo Díaz, was unleashing libels and provoking intrigues against the republicans, the *Correo del Orinoco* maintained an unshakeable composure. As Luis Correa noted in his prologue to the facsimile edition, "There appears nowhere a peevish conclusion, an uncultured note, a resort to disgraceful procedure. Everything there is peaceful, clean, transparent. Everything bears the stamp of the unequaled provenance which gave it life and movement."

It was doubtless to avoid disturbing this tone that Bolívar refrained from publishing in it a fantasy that he wrote at the time, which cast him in the most unexpected role of a satirical writer. The document was found, unpublished, among his papers, and it consists of a supposed dialogue between a "brother" Juan Trimiño and José Domingo Díaz. Among other things, Trimiño says to Díaz, referring to a decoration granted to him by the king of Spain: "Ha, ha, ha!, you make me laugh with your decoration and your proclamations. I now remember a very apposite case. They say that in Spain in the filthiest places, particularly on street corners, they place decorations to restrain the people from urinating and excreting on them.... I think that it was with this intention that your King Ferdinand tossed you this decoration."[2] The smile of Rabelais seems rather strange on the lean, passionate face of the Liberator.

At this time, the independence of Spanish America seemed to be threatened by a serious danger that the great European powers, led by the Holy Alliance, would intervene on Spain's behalf. The reaction in Venezuela was most violent, and an asssembly of all the authorities, con-

---

1. *Correo del Orinoco.* Facsimile edition ordered by the Venezuelan government in 1939.
2. Vicente Lecuna (ed.), *Papeles de Bolívar* (Caracas ,1917), p. 276. Some critics believe that the document was not written by Bolívar, partly because Juan Trimiño actually existed, and lived then in Angostura.

Bolívar during the time of the Congress of Angostura. Engraving by M. N. Bate, over an original drawing which belonged to Mr. W. M. Walton. Published in London in 1819 (courtesy of Alfredo Boulton).

voked by Bolívar in Angostura, solemnly declared that the Republic would never negotiate with Spain, "except as equal to equal," and that "the people of Venezuela are resolved to bury themselves completely beneath their ruins, if Spain, Europe and the world try to bow her under the Spanish yoke." This was an exasperated boast, but very similar to the spirit that Venezuela had already displayed.

Fortunately, those monarchs who had embarked again on a spree of re-establishing their *legitimacy* after the overthrow of the French Revolution and the empire, remained as inept as ever. In 1818 a Russian fleet arrived at Cádiz to help with the reconquest of America, but the ships were unseaworthy, and even Ferdinand VII was disillusioned. On the other hand, England and the United States were showing, for the first time, a slightly favorable attitude towards the South American nations. In England, although the Tories were still hostile to "all French ideas... the education of the people, the liberty of the press and seditious oratory," to quote Bertrand Russell, commercial interest was now advising them to favor the emancipation of America. They at least no longer opposed the purchase of arms and the enlistment of volunteers, activities in which Luis López Méndez and Andrés Bello were engaged in London itself.

As for the United States, although complaints were published in the *Correo del Orinoco* about her intervention on the island of Amelia, she had finally decided not to ignore the war being fought in the rest of the continent, and she recognized the "insurgents" as belligerents. In addition, according to Gil Fortoul and other historians, she sent a friendly agent, John Baptiste Irvine, to Bolívar. This commissioner, however, proved unfriendly, for "although the official documents state that he was frank, spoke with friendliness and sincerity, and stressed the friendly disposition of the government of his country towards the Venezuelan patriots, his mission had no political character and no practical result. He left behind only the bitter memory of a sour dispute by correspondence with the Commander-in-Chief, concerning dubious mercantile demands of some Americans."[1]

The North American's demands were so unjust and his language so unsuitable, that the Liberator replied to him: "It seems that your intention is to force me to exchange insults with you. I will not do so; but I insist that I will not permit you to abuse or scorn the government and the rights of Venezuela. A large part of our population has disappeared defending them against Spain, and those who remain yearn to be worthy of the same fate. It is the same for Venezuela to fight against Spain as against the whole world, if all the world offends her."

---

1. Lecuna, *Crónica razonada...*, ii, p. 224.

From all sides threats fell upon the desperate group of patriots, forced back to the banks of the Orinoco. In the middle of 1818 there was another attempt at sedition in the Apure, led by a British colonel called Wilson, apparently with the complicity of Páez. But support for the different units on campaign was provided by the Liberator—with Angostura as his base, he was in Maturín in November, and in the Arauca area two months later—and neither these difficulties nor the extreme misery experienced by everybody could distract him from the two projects which he considered of capital importance: The assembly in Angostura of a Congress, which would reorganize the political life of the Republic on a stable basis, and the invasion of New Granada which would provide, as always, men and new resources for the patriot cause.

Elections to the Congress were held at the end of 1818 and the first session took place on February 15, 1819. It was to mark this event, and to expound his ideas on the constitution that would be suitable for the Republic, that Bolívar delivered the address which represents the fullest and most precise expression of his political thought.

The fundamental principle that he stressed energetically was that Venezuela could not continue to imitate the legislators of North America, and that she could afford even less to preserve the Constitution of 1811, which combined the weakness of a collective executive with the dispersion of the federal system. But before establishing these principles, which were rather unpleasing for his audience, he provided sharp observations on Venezuela's political antecedents and, in general, on the fickleness of all nations and the difficulties that had been encountered in some of them with the stabilization of freedom. He had said in the Jamaica Letter that the American world was "in a certain manner old in the ways of civilized society." Contradicting this, he now asserted that, "subject to the threefold yoke of ignorance, tyranny and vice, the American people have been unable to acquire knowledge, power, or (civic) virtue." Terrifying possibilities appeared before his eyes as he lamented: "An ignorant people is a blind instrument of its own destruction. Ambition and intrigue abuse the credulity and experience of men lacking all political, economic, and civic knowledge. They adopt pure illusion as reality; they take license for liberty, treachery for patriotism, and vengeance for justice. This situation is similar to that of the robust blind man who, beguiled by his strength, strides forward with all the assurance of one who can see, but, upon hitting every variety of obstacle, finds himself unable to retrace his steps."

Such deviations, in his opinion, were consequences of the colonial regime, which he condemned as the worst in the world for leaving the people not only ignorant and inexperienced but also corrupted. He went on: "If a people, perverted by their training, succeed in achieving their liberty, they will soon lose it. It would be of no avail to explain to them that happiness consists in the practice of virtue; that the rule of law is more powerful than the rule of tyrants, because, as the laws are more inflexible, everyone should submit to their beneficent austerity; |that proper morals, and not force, are the bases of law; and that to practice justice is to practice liberty."

But his gloomy images were not limited to Spanish America, and he reminded his audience: "The history of bygone ages affords you examples of thousands of governments. Visualize the nations that have shone in brightest splendor and you will be grieved to see that virtually all the world has been, and still is, the victim of their governments. You will note numerous systems of governing men, but always their purpose has been to oppress them. If our habit of looking upon the human species as being led by its own shepherds did not diminish the horror of so distressing a spectacle, we should be stunned to see our docile species grazing upon the surface of the earth, like meek flocks destined to feed their cruel keepers."

Too strong? We can see that it was no more than imprudent frankness if we reflect upon the devastating impressions left on Bolívar's mind by the accumulated experiences of his life: What he saw as a boy at the corrupt court of Charles IV; shortly afterwards the spectacle of the Directory in France, which changed the revolutionaries' dream of living "like the ancients" into peculation and libertinage; later, the gigantic farce of the empire with armies followed by carts full of booty, Europe sacked in the name of glory, and in Paris, regicides becoming dukes and princes; when he returned to Venezuela, the first Republic ruined by four pedants and malicious men, destroyed by the inept Monteverde, and bathed in blood by a horde of Islanders, the Negro Palomo and Cervériz; since then, a war to the death which all regarded as absurd and horrible, but which none could avoid. At that very time, the most powerful states in Europe were trying to help Ferdinand VII establish in America the gallows that he had set up in Spain. And the United States had sent its first commissioner to Venezuela to threaten the unprotected patriots, simply because a privateer had captured a miserable schooner and it considered this prejudicial to "its interests." What then were justice, humanity, compassion, decency, and where were they? At the same time, while these things were crowding in on his mind, what was happening in his own country? He saw that the legionary Wilson, recently arrived and knowing nothing of Venezuela, was trying madly to seduce Páez in order to elevate him to the office of commander-in-chief; that the *Gaceta de Caracas* was still falsifying documents, this time with the object of arousing in Arismendi the distrust that had doomed Piar; that Morillo was sending commissioners to Zaraza, proposing that he should transfer to the service of the king; and that, at the same time, Martin Tovar and many other revolutionaries —all very respectable, which made things worse— believed that the country was doomed to perdition if it abandoned the principles proclaimed in 1811. Was humanity, transported at times by generosity and at others by greed and deceit, bound always to advance likes a heedless blind man? Where was it safe to step in the midst of that shifting ground? Tacitus, who had been Bolívar's juvenile companion, and Machiavelli, whom he detested, fought for his spirit, as he added, heartrendingly: "It would appear that we have every right to persuade ourselves that most men hold this humiliating maxim to be the truth: It is harder to maintain the balance of liberty than to endure the weight of tyranny."

But, although these "bitter reflections", as he called them, could have been inspired by the political factors discussed above, there is no doubt that radicalism had degraded the assembly of 1811. The federation, the plural executive and the other nonsense of the first republic were so deeply rooted that Bolívar had to refer to them and to the constitution as though they were still in force. For this reason he used the present tense, when he said: "Our executive triumvirate lacks, so to speak, unity, continuity and individual responsibility."

The possibility that the anarchic institutions of 1811 would have been maintained in 1819 seems so absurd that it is necessary to pay attention to the considerable effort that the Liberator dedicated to refuting them, to appreciate the danger that they still represented. Neither Bolívar's political attitude until 1819 nor the Angostura address itself can be understood without an appreciation of this anguish, which was manifested in many of his letters from 1813 onwards.

Having made this reservation, however, we must mentally separate his ideas from the pressure that deformed them, so that we can analyze them more clearly.

Faithful still to revolutionary rationalism, Bolívar thought that the mission of the legislators should be "to lay the political foundation for a newly born nation." What was involved was not simply the writing of a constitution, but the creation of an entire society. He did not hesitate, therefore, in asking for an original work, a body of "Venezuelan laws." Already this confidence in what could be attempted indicated that his initial pessimism was only transitory.

Bolívar analyzed Venezuela's ethnic structure: "It is impossible to determine with any degree of accuracy where we belong in the human family. The greater portion of the native Indians has been annihilated. Spaniards have mixed with Americans and Africans, and Africans with Indians and Spaniards. While we have all been born of the same mother, our fathers, different in origin and in blood, are foreigners, and all differ visibly as to the color of their skin, a dissimilarity which places upon us an obligation of the greatest importance." But he did not see this peculiarity as an insuperable difficulty, for, like Humboldt, he believed that no races were fundamentally inferior, and that all could perfect themselves in freedom. We have already discussed his thoughts in the Jamaica Letter on this subject. He now suggested an even more audacious remedy: "The blood of our citizens is varied; let it be mixed for the sake of unity."

He also defended civil liberty, which he wanted to see established in the constitution. He pointed out, giving an ingenious twist to an old controversy: "Nature makes men unequal in intelligence, temperament, strength and character. Laws correct this disparity by so placing the individual within society that education, industry, arts, services, and virtues give him a fictitious equality that is properly termed political and social." Then it was often said that men could not declare themselves equal, because nature had made them unequal. Bolívar accepted the second half of the argument, that nature had made men unequal, but he argued that the laws should try to make them equal in order to minimize that injustice and convert it into harmony within society. His approach was not only more generous but also more correct, for the law, when it organizes society and establish standards of justice for peaceful co-existence and even morality, rectifies and corrects nature. Equality among men should be established, therefore, not out of obedience to the natural order, but to reduce it to a legal order more suited to the proper development of society as a whole. Bolívar was thus able to convert an argument regarded by most people as reactionary because of its premises, into a most skillful affirmation of democracy. He felt it so sincerely that many years later he repeated, in a letter to O'Leary: "Legal equality is indispensible where there exists physical inequality, so that it can correct to a certain extent the injustice of nature."[1]

From the beginning of the revolution, Bolívar had emancipated all his slaves, and he had issued various decrees directed towards the definitive suppresion of that atrocious institution.[2] He now told the legislators: "You know that one cannot be both free and enslaved at the same time without simultaneously violating every natural, political, and civil law. I leave to your sovereign decision the reform or the repeal of all my statutes and decrees; but I appeal for the confirmation of the absolute freedom of the slaves, as I would plead for my very life and the life of the Republic."

He was worried more by the ignorance and political inexperience of the majority of the population, which could lead to the triumph of corruption

---

1. Quoted by Antonio Arráiz, *Culto bolivariano* (Caracas, 1940), p. 141.
2. See especially: *Decretos del Libertador* (Caracas, 1961), p. 55; *Cartas,* x, p. 110; Boletín de la Academia Nacional de la Historia, Caracas, no. 143.

and disorder, than by the question of racial heterogeneousness. In his opinion, "The Venezuelans love their country, but they cannot love her laws, because these, being sources of evil, have been harmful. Neither can they respect their magistrates, as they have been unjust, while the new administrators are scarcely known in the calling which they have just entered. Unless there is a sacred reverence for country, laws, and authority, society becomes confused, an abyss, an endless conflict of man versus man, group versus group."

He thought that only bold, new institutions could prevent this social chaos. He insisted: "Morality and enlightenment are the foundations of a republic. Morality and enlightenment constitute our primary needs." The constitution should establish a moral authority, or "fourth power" to preserve good public customs and to watch over education. They should also be protected by "moral penalties, just as criminals are punished by corporal penalties. Such action should be taken not only against that which conflicts with customs, but also against that which mocks them; not only against that which attacks them, but against that which weakens them; not only against that which violates the Constitution, but also against that which outrages public decency." He added, however: "The jurisdiction of this truly sacred tribunal should be effective with respect to education and enlightenment, but advisory only with regard to penalties and punishments."

Bolívar stressed in the most concrete form the importance of child education. As we have seen, this subject was always close to his heart. In his plans for a moral authority, he defined "the co-operation of mothers for the education of their children" as "absolutely indispenable," and he requested the production and publication of simple instructions to help them in their task. This appeal to mothers was unexpected in an educator-politician considered by many to be a follower of Rousseau, for Rousseau not only frowned upon the idea of learned women but also believed that the ideal pupil should be, among other things, an orphan. Bolívar's suggestion, then, showed an independence of mind. It also suggested fond memories of his mother, and perhaps of the intuitive and friendly Hipolita, who had been both mother and father to him.

The Liberator also departed from ideas then popular, with his proposals for political institutions which he considered suitable for Venezuela's social state. He proposed a popularly-elected chamber of representatives and a hereditary senate; a lifetime president, elected by the people or by their representatives; and a judicial authority which, bcause of its strength and respectability, would be, with the senate, the best guarantee of freedom and institutional equilibrium. Flanked by these two authorities, the executive, which would be given powers no wider than those enjoyed by the British sovereign, would not be able to exceed them. "Moreover," he added, "as the judges are responsible for the enforcement of the laws, they do not depart from them; and the administrators of the exchequer, being subject to prosecution not only for personal infractions but also for those of the government, take care to prevent any misuse of public funds."

His fundamental conclusion was as follows: "Venezuela had, has, and should have a republican government. Its principles should be the sovereignty of the people, division of powers, civil liberty, prohibition of slavery, and the abolition of monarchy and privileges. We need equality to recast, so to speak, into a unified nation, all classes of men, political opinions, and public customs."

In the midst of his anguished search for remedies for the evils that he could foresee, Bolívar's thoughts returned to the subject of education, and he suggested that future senators should be educated "in a college designed especially to train these guardians and future legislators of the nation." Anxious to leave no doubts about the scope of his plans, he stressed: "The creation of a hereditary senate would in no way be a violation of political equality... What I propose is an office for which the candidates must prepare themselves, an office that demands great knowledge and the ability to acquire such knowledge." Similarly, he emphasized that this select body would exercise a stabilizing authority: "A hereditary senate, I repeat, will be the fundamental basis of the legislative power, and therefore the foundation of the entire government. It will also serve as a counterweight to both government and people. As a neutral power it will weaken the mutual attacks of these two eternally rival powers.... The Venezuelan senate will give strength to this delicate political structure... and it will maintain harmony between the head and the other parts of this body politic."

These ideas are still of great interest for Spanish America, because some writers, by making a superficial comparison, have created the sad myth that Bolívar's "lifetime presidency" anticipated and justified the "indefinite presidency" of the nineteenth century *caudillos*. The unipersonal regime of the *caudillos* was, by its very nature, unstable, discretional and irresponsible and, as we have just seen, it was precisely this that the Liberator was trying to prevent. The most striking thing about the rule of the *caudillos* was its simplicity, similar to that of a primitive government. However, the complaint that could be made about the Liberator's ideas is that they were extremely complex. Because he believed that the society of his time was incapable of providing a stable basis for the reorganization of the state, he boldly and desperately inverted the terms, and tried to forge a state that would be the basis for a new society.

Despite the fact that in the United States, whose model was the only one that had survived for the republicans of the world, there had also been supporters for lifetime institutions—notably Hamilton—Bolívar's ideas were not accepted by the Angostura Congress. The constitution signed on August 15 rejected the lifetime presidency, despite, or perhaps because of, the Liberator's victory at Boyacá, and established it for only four years. The hereditary senate was also turned down, and, although it was then accepted that the senators should serve for life, their tenure was reduced to eight years in 1821. Opinions were divided over the question of the moral authority, and the final judgement of the Congress said: "The moral authority, established in the project for the Constitution presented by General Bolívar, as Commander-in-Chief of the Republic when the Congress was installed, was regarded by some deputies as the most promising idea and as best suited to influence the perfection of social institutions. It was seen by others as a moral inquisition, no less dismal and no less horrible than the religious. All agreed that it would be very difficult to establish, and absolutely impractical at the present time. After lengthy debates the majority opinion was that in the infancy of our political life, when we are dealing with matters of such importance for the State and even for humanity, we should publish our theories and reasonings without either approving or rejecting the project, and that, through the press, we should consult the opinions of the experts in all other countries. It was agreed to make some partial tests, and to collect facts that prove the advantages or drawbacks of this new institution and, on this basis, to proceed to put it into practice or to reject it. It was decreed, therefore, that the title of the Moral Authority should be published as an appendix to the Constitution, and that all experts should be invited to consider it, not only in this capacity but also as citizens of the world, and to communicate their opinions to this beautiful part of their immense domain."

This appeal to world opinion should not make us smile. It was typical of the revolutionary exaltation of the period, when even these small nations saw themselves as a beautiful part of the common domain. What was confusing and dismaying was that some deputies saw the Moral Authority as a new inquisition. Bolívar himself had stated that it was taken from Greek and Roman antiquity —he even called it Areopagus— but even more curious was that, as far as the vigilance over customs was concerned, he had followed the ideas of Miranda, who had been the Inquisition's most passionate opponent. Moreover, in treating his project so lightly, the Angostura legislators did not even mention the most important aspect of it, that relating to education.

At any rate, the jolt that Bolívar gave to the routine with which the politicians were tackling our constitutional problem did prevent them from bringing back the triumvirate, about which they had enthused at Cariaco. Momentarily, at least, it drew them away from the mystical federalism which, far from strengthening freedom, as they believed, had divided the Republic into fiefs for the benefit of the *caudillos*.

This failure of Bolívar at the Angostura Congress also preserved something of great importance for the public morality of Spanish America, for it proved that the Congress was neither a personalistic farce nor a political device to present a facade of constitutionalism to international opinion. It represented, instead, the installation of a genuine, deliberative government, which proceeded with complete independence and which later, rather than hesitating in the face of the Liberator's military victories, was to show an excessive determination not to give way to his prestige.

But these reflections would have been of little consolation to Bolívar when he received the statement from the Congress, which did not fall far short of saying that, like Ferdinand VII, he wanted to re-establish the Inquisition.

We can picture him, lying in his hammock, unable to sleep, thinking throughout the night. Angostura, today Ciudad Bolívar, was then a small town, unhealthy because of the fevers endemic in the region. But the surroundings were attractive, and it enjoyed a good position on the banks of the Orinoco. Moreover this great river, which drained all parts of Venezuela, made the city rather like the heart of the country. The river starts in the south, among the virgin forests of our farthest frontiers. The Uribante and the Apure bring it water from the west, and the Portuguesa, the Guárico and the Apure again flow into it from the center. The Pao and numerous other tributaries come from the east. The Orinoco itself flows towards the eastern shores, after being joined, just beyond Angostura, by the Caroní, the turbulent envoy from the mountains of the southeast. The voices of the whole of Venezuela could thus be heard on the banks of the Orinoco.

Bolívar, perhaps the only person awake, was trying to listen to these voices, in the midst of the solemn silence of the night, hoping that they would provide him with an augury for the future. The military triumph of the independence movement was secure. He had never doubted this; he could already see it coming. But what would these people do with this precious gift? The questions that he, Miranda and Bello had posed in London, eight years earlier, now demanded an immediate reply. Others, with puerile enthusiasm, could celebrate victory over Spain as if it would magically begin a new life for America; but he knew that this was not the case. Those long campaigns, those endless sacrifices, were leading to this rendez-vous with fate, and the total meaning of the emancipation enterprise depended upon what the Americans could obtain there.

The humid heat of the riparian city increased his anxiety. As he lay there he heard the words of a distant ballad:

There were no Negroes in the Passion;
Indians then were unknown;
Mulattoes, there were none:
It was an affair for white men!

When he had heard the song on previous occasions, he had simply smiled at its innocent malice. Now, suddenly, it became a sarcastic allegory. "It was an affair for white men!" In reality, it was not a question of whites and coloreds, as the song mockingly suggested, but of those who are led and those who lead; of those who come to public life only with their miseries and hopes, and those who, because of their culture and position, possess power, understanding and responsibilities. Were the latter prepared to fulfill the obligation that their superiority imposed upon them? The same questions and same doubts repeated themselves with the insistence of feverish visions. He recalled that he had stated in Jamaica that the whites would remain in control of America because of their culture and other factors. But could they guide the revolution that they had unleashed so that the human contribution that they had to give to the other social classes could be incorporated into the active life of the nation? The masses had given all that they had: faith, valor, enthusiasm. What would the leaders give in the future?

It was to answer this that he had thought so much about the development of popular education as the only legitimate means of placing the problems of all in the hands of all. But he had been told that his whole project was impracticable. Was it because to most men everything that is not easy is impossible?

They preferred to continue repeating words that, simply because of the act of routine repetition, they were accustomed to regarding as principles. In fact, they had no plan at all. There returned to his mind the obsessive image of the robust blind man, who strides forward with all the assurance of one who can see, but upon hitting every variety of obstacle, finds himself unable to retrace his steps.

It was not without reason that Vowell spoke of the "melancholy smile which was habitual with him."

XXIV

ST. RONDON

WHILE HE WAS WORKING
on the political and administrative reorganization of the country—he had
issued other important decrees, including one on land distribution—
Bolívar was also preparing the great military enterprise, the invasion of
New Granada, that, in his opinion, would change the course of the war.

He had already thought of collaborating with a talented Granadan
officer, a good organizer, upright, patriotic, constant and disciplined, who
since the beginning of the revolution had fought campaigns both in his
own country and in Venezuela. He was Francisco de Paula Santander,
and he was to become, in succession, one of the Liberator's best
collaborators and his most dreadful enemy. On August 12, 1818, Bolívar
promoted him to the rank of brigadier-general, appointed him governor
and military commander of the Granadan province of Casanare, which
bordered the Venezuelan Apure, and provided him with 1,000 muskets,
munitions and uniforms for the advance troops that he was to organize.
Three days later he announced, in a proclamation to the people of New
Granada: "The sun will not have completed the course of its present
round without beholding in all your territory the proud altars of liberty."
The promise was kept, before a year had passed, with the victory at
Boyacá on August 7, 1819.

The diligent Colonel José Félix Blanco had also gone to New Granada,
disguised as a merchant, to collect information on conditions in the viceroyalty and to distribute propaganda for the republican cause. For the
latter purpose he took with him a book published in Philadelphia in 1817

by Juan Germán Roscio, entitled *Triunfo de la libertad sobre el despotismo*.[1] According to Roscio, the people in America continued to support absolutism because they regarded it as inseparable from their religious beliefs. His book was intended to prove that, rather than condemning popular sovereignty, religion and the sacred scriptures actually supported it. Although tedious, the book was written with passion, no doubt because it reflected the inner conflicts that the author had had to overcome in his youth. We have no information on what influence it might have had in this period, but we do know that it later secured an unexpected triumph. In the middle of the century it contributed to the liberal formation of Benito Juárez. According to the Mexican writer H. Pérez Martínez, Roscio and Benjamin Constant were the two most important influences on Juárez, and he tells us, referring to Roscio's book: "Juárez made this last book his faithful companion. He liked to discuss the Venezuelan author's themes ardently with small groups at the Institute; on his lips the word liberty took on a serious intonation, a mysterious meaning. It seemed like an invocation...."[2]

On April 2, 1819, before the invasion got under way, the patriots secured a triumph which has become legendary and which considerably increased the prestige already enjoyed by the *llaneros of Páez*. The opposing armies met at a place called Queseras del Medio, with the Arauca River between them. Bolívar was unwilling to risk an open battle because Morillo's force was much larger than his own, and he had limited himself during the previous days to harassing the royalists from a distance and cutting off their supplies. But Páez decided upon a daring adventure. He had learned from a Spanish deserter that if he began again to expose himself in skirmishes, Morillo was determined to use all his forces in an attempt to kill him or capture him. Far from frightening him off, this information gave Páez an idea of how to destroy all the enemy cavalry. After swimming across the river with 150 of his best lancers, he rode fearlessly towards the Spanish lines until he was within range of their guns. Morillo, as he hoped, then moved his forces against him. The patriot lancers, divided into groups of 20 men, then began to retreat in good order. With remarkable precision they alternated attacks against the royalists with hurried retreats, each time drawing their pursues farther away from the body of the army.

---

1. Ramón Azpúrua, *Biografías de hombres notables de Hispanoamérica* (Caracas, 1877). According to Azpúrua, Blanco went to New Granada on his own account, having realized before Bolívar the need to make the viceroyalty the theater of war. Both Páez and Santander also claimed credit for being the first to propose the 1819 campaign. But this role in the expedition can be kept in proportion by recalling Bolívar's constant insistence that he regarded all of northern South America, as far as Lima, as his natural sphere of operations. For Roscio's *Triunfo de la Libertad*..., see *Obras de Roscio* (Caracas, 1953).

2. H. Pérez Martínez, *Juárez, el impasible* (Editorial Espasa Calpe. Colección Austral), p. 31.

They attacked the enemy on the flanks, or fled as if they were about to disband, only to reform rapidly to threaten the infantry or confront the cavalry. Finally, when Páez saw that he had succeeded in drawing all the enemy cavalry into one group, away from the musketeers, he cried to his irresistible *llaneros:* "About turn!" They hurled themselves against the unprepared royalist squadrons, easily slaughtering and routing them, and then turned on the accompanying infantry. Only the darkness of the night and the presence of a wood, which helped Morillo's retreat, prevented the total defeat of the Spaniards. The field of battle was left to the *llaneros,* who continued to provoke the fugitives among the shadows with their cries. They then recrossed the Arauca, peacefully, as though on an exercise, and rejoined Bolívar's army.

It is easy to imagine how this triumph must have aroused the imagination of the victors. Bolívar consecrated it for history with a ringing proclamation: "Soldiers! You have just performed the most extraordinary feat that the military history of the nation can celebrate. One hundred and fifty men, or, I should say, one hundred and fifty heroes led by the intrepid General Páez have deliberately mounted a frontal attack against the whole of Morillo's army. Artillery, infantry, cavalry, none of them were enough for the enemy to defend himself against the one hundred and fifty companions of the most fearless Páez. The cavalry columns have succumbed to the blows of our lances; the infantry has sought refuge in the forest; the firing of their guns has halted before the breasts of our horses." Páez, three colonels, twelve lieutenant colonels, eighteen captains, and forty-four junior officers fought at the head of the patriot squadron. The sergeants, corporals and privates numbered seventy-two. Bolívar granted all of them the Star of the Liberator.

In the description of the encounter contained in his *Autobiografía,* Páez identified only one of the patriot commanders, Juan José Rondón, an irresistible Achilles, who was capable by himself of turning defeat into victory. He came not from the Apure area but from the *Alto Llano* to the southeast of Caracas. Páez narrates how he selected him for one of the most daring maneuvers: "Our situation was then very dangerous, for the enemy was surrounding us on both sides with its cavalry, and we were under fire from their muskets and cannons. Then the valiant royalist commander, Narciso López, fortunately offered me the opportunity of crossing with some advantage to the offensive. López was approaching the infantry with the squadron of carabineers that he commanded. I immediately instructed Commander Rondón, a brave leader, to lead twenty men in a charge against him, with lances out, and then to retire rapidly in order that he not be surrounded by the two divisions of enemy cavalry, which I wanted to combine into a single mass so that I could turn around and attack them violently." Rondón succeeded in doing what Páez wanted, and the Apure *caudillo* commented: "When I saw Rondón win so many laurels on the field of battle I could do no less then exclaim: 'Bravo, bravísimo, commander!' 'General,' he replied, alluding to a reprimand I had given him a few days earlier, after a charge he had made against López, 'that is how the sons of the *Alto Llano* fight.'"

That "valiant royalist commander, Narciso López" to whom Páez referred was also destined for immortality. Born in Caracas, he was only thirteen when the revolution began in 1810. One of his uncles was the commander of the royalist guerrillas in the *llano* and Narciso followed him. Wearing then the Spanish uniform, which he was afterwards to call "brilliant but ignominious livery," he fought in the Venezuelan campaigns and reached the rank of colonel. When the emancipation of his country was secured, he went to Spain, where he fought with Isabella's reformers during the civil wars in the peninsula. He served successively as governor in Cuenca, Valencia and Madrid. He was renowned as "the first lance in the army," and counted among his achievements victory in a duel with Colonel Carlos O'Donell, fought in front of the Carlist and Isabelline armies.

As a youth López liked to demonstrate his extraordinary strength by bending a coin or tearing in two a packet of playing-cards with his teeth. He was as much at home among the formal politicians at court as with the easy comradeship of the army camp. His valor and skill followed him everywhere in the shape of flattering legends. Later in life, when he held the rank of field-marshall, he suffered spiritual crisis. He had served a country which was becoming increasingly strange to him, and he was still the instrument of a miserable personalist policy which, particularly in Cuba and Puerto Rico, Spain's remaining colonies in America, was odious. He left the army, therefore, and, after devoting some time to business affairs in Cuba, began to plot for the island's independence. He had perhaps been thinking of this for years, ever since Bolívar had planned to send an expedition to emancipate Cuba, and the "Suns of Bolívar" and other secret groups had started the Cuban patriots on their long calvary towards freedom. It was in one such meeting, led by Narciso López, that Cuba's present flag was created, and it fell to him to unfurl it for the first time on Cuban soil when he led the invasion of the island in 1850. This attempt failed, because of the indifferent response of the local population, but López did not lose heart. It is said that when one of the Cuban patriots cried pessimistically: "They are giving up, López, they are giving up...," he replied, with the appealing malice of the veteran: "The Cubans know how to swim, Don Pepe; what we have to do is to push them into the water." He was defeated, however, heading a new expedition that encountered a Spanish force five times its own size. He was taken prisoner and the Spanish again demonstrated their disregard for "insurgents." Despite his status as a general and his former services, López was condemned to death by garroting, like a common criminal. His last, defiant words were: "My death will not change the fate of Cuba."

We return to our story. The Apure had become so patriotic that, according to one Spanish commander, when the royalists entered town they were received by only "a few dogs which, because they were crippled, had been unable to join the emigration." Although he had been forced to give up the refinements to which he had been accustomed, Bolívar was happy, or appeared to be, in this region. O'Leary tells us: "It is very difficult to give a complete idea of the sufferings of the army on its marches over those sun-scorched plains, where not a cloud is to be seen throughout the day. Tortured by the heat, deceived hour after hour by the mirages so common in these places, and with neither a single shrub to give them shade nor a drop of water to refresh their lips, the troops arrived late at the bivouac, where a meager ration of poor, unsalted meat was waiting them. There they slept in the open air, exposed to the unhealthy climate; but not one complaint was heard from that brave, unselfish army, which was inspired by the example and steadfastness of its general-in-chief.... During these marches Bolívar arose at daybreak, mounted his horse to visit the different units, and encouraged them as he passed with a few friendly words or pleasant recollections. Accompanied by his staff, he followed the army, dismounting at midday to bathe wherever it was possible. Like the others, he lunched on meat alone, and then rested in his hammock. Afterwards he dictated his orders and dispatched his correspondence while swinging in it. When the troops had eaten their short ration, they continued their march until they found, if possible, a tree or a small wood where they could camp. Otherwise they camped in the open. Bolívar was then thirty-seven years old, at the height of his physical and mental powers. We who accompanied him during that period—at the time I was aide-de-camp to General Anzoátegui—can testify to his incomparable activity and his vigilance, not only for the fate of the Republic, but also for that of the very least of his soldiers."[1]

But it was still whispered in the army that he was pursued by a fatal spirit, and, because of this superstition, even the gunner's cap that he wore was disliked. O'Leary also wrote: "One day it fell in the river Arauca, and was swept away by the current, to the loud cheering of the English, who saw it as a bad omen and the cause of the recent setbacks."

This alternation of splendor with almost humiliating situations that we see in the life of the Liberator suggests the superficiality of any parallel that might be drawn between Bolívar and Napoleon. Both the rise and fall of Napoleon were vertical and, when he reached his peak, the stability of his destiny was sustained by uninterrupted triumphs, which seemed

---

1. O'Leary, *Narración*, i, p. 539.

gratuitous gifts from a supernatural force. On the other hand Bolívar had to struggle for many years with himself and against innumerable adverse factors. He rose to greatness slowly, painfully, and we can almost see the effort with which he climbed, step by step, the punishing road to reach it. His motto could not be the "I came, I saw, I conquered," which was as apt for Napoleon as for Caesar. The phrases with which he fortified himself, and which also sum up his career, are: "Bravery, skill and perseverance can mend misfortune," "to do things properly it is necessary to do them twice," "because without energy merit never shines, without strength there is no virtue, and without bravery there is no glory."

Simón Rodríguez had taught him that "the road to perfection is constructed of advantageous modifications." His enemy Morillo almost unconsciously synthesized the secret of his triumphs with the eulogy that Bolívar would have preferred to all others: "Bolívar triumphant follows a familiar path; but, when he loses, it is impossible to know where he will appear, more active and formidable than ever. For this reason he is less dangerous victorious than vanquished."

If we were to seek another man of genius with qualities similar to those of Bolívar, we should have to select Frederick the Great, who, because of the overwhelming difficulties that he had to face, and the tenacity and valor with which he challenged adverse fortune, provoked his biographers to make remarks that could be applied almost literally to Bolívar. Napoleon said of Frederick something very similar to Morillo's phrase about Bolívar: "He was great particularly at the most critical moments." It is well known that the Corsican's admiration for the great Prussian organizer was one of the keenest and most constant of the ideas that inspired him.

The Liberator's campaign of 1819 has the appearance of a prodigious leap, similar to those that brought Caesar or Napoleon to triumph, and the victory at Boyacá also seems like one of the sudden victories of those military geniuses; but its true meaning is to be found in those long years of trial, suffering and courage that preceded it. Those years also clearly identified Bolívar with the soldiers whose sufferings he shared. On innumerable occasions he repeated the conviction that he was nothing more than one of them, and that they were all being carried forward by the same destiny to achieve the independence of America. Profoundly submerged in the collective, this Frederick was above all an American creole, which was also all that he wished to be.

In this period the mobility of the army was extraordinary. General Anzoátegui referred to it in a letter to his wife, whom he had left in Cumaná: "We left Angostura in March and went to the Apure, where we did not spend a single day in the same camp. We stopped for a few days only at Rincón Hondo, after the display of valor by Páez at Las Queseras. We left there on May 14, and reached Mantecal on the 21st. We turned back from there on the 25th towards Guasdualito, so as to make Morillo think that we were heading for Barinas. We departed from Guasdualito on June 2 and reached the Arauca River on 5th. It will be impossible for you to imagine what it was like during these three days when we were marching through the water, swimming at times. The plains were flooded; they literally looked like a sea, like that which you see from your balcony. We had to ford and swim across rivers, channels and inlets, particularly the Cachicamo, which extends for about two leagues."[1]

This picture of the plains given to us by Anzoátegui is quite different from those provided by descriptions quoted earlier. The rainy season, known as winter in the tropics, had begun. Bolívar deliberately chose this season for his invasion, both because the Spaniards in New Granada would not expect him to attempt the crossing of the *llanos,* and then of the Andes, in such difficult weather and also because he could be certain that Morillo would remain immobile on his flanks.

Although he had announced that he would enter the viceroyship through Cúcuta, Bolívar's real intention was to go through Casanare, which lay much farther south, cross the Andes and descend almost directly on Bogotá. The operation against Cúcuta which was entrusted to Páez, was intended, according to Bolívar's instructions, "to divert the attention of the enemy to that region, cut his communications with Venezuela, open communications with me and send parties towards Mérida, both to strengthen our forces there and to observe the movements of the enemy." Páez was also "to reserve for the troops under my command the blankets, wraps and clothing that they might need, for it will not be easy to cover their nudity except with booty from Cúcuta." He was to provide from the same source, "all the cattle that can be obtained for the subsistence of the army, for it is impossible to move cattle from here because of the shortage of men and horses." His final duty was to send to Bolívar from Casanare all the arms and ammunition that he could obtain either there or from Angostura, because "I have no more than 1,400 (muskets) and I need many more." Bolívar, therefore, entrusted his fate and that of his army to Páez. Despite the detailed explanation given by Bolívar of the difficulties that the army would face if help were not forthcoming, Páez failed completely to obey his orders.

He later wrote that the mission entrusted to him was "as impossible to fulfill with cavalry as taking hold of the sky in one's hand."[2] But Vicente Lecuna rightly comments, "the Liberator met Páez at Guasdualito, and

---

1. Boletín de la Academia Nacional de la Historia, Caracas, no. 90, p. 236.
2. *Campañas de Apure. Narración del General Páez.* Boletín de la Academia Nacional de la Historia, Caracas, no. 21, p. 1201. Here, as in his autobiography, Páez shows a great anxiety to justify himself.

there gave him verbal instructions identical to those repeated by letter from Arauca.... Why did the *llanero* leader not tell him then that to march to Cúcuta was like taking the sky in one's hands? The simile was reserved to excuse himself to posterity. Moreover, he tries to make us believe that Bolívar offered him the command of the main expedition to Casanare and Sogamoso, which was much more difficult than the march to Cúcuta with his column of lancers and musketeers."[1]

Such was Bolívar's confidence that Páez would enter New Granaɑa through Cúcuta that he warned him, characteristically, "to take the greatest care to restrain and severely punish anybody who molests or robs the inhabitants of the country.... If we do not behave with generosity, we will be as much detested as the Spaniards, particularly in New Granada, where there are many important considerations to observe."

The young Daniel O'Leary went with Bolívar's army across the *llanos* and over the Andes, and his description of its march has not been surpassed, in its naturalness and color, by that of any professional writer.[2] Recognizing this, and also in homage to the selflessness with which he and the other legionaries embarked on their sacrifices for the independence of America, we give him the pen.

"The rain had set in with unusual intensity and was falling in torrents. Streams which hardly carried any water in the summer were now flooding the savannas; rivulets which a little earlier had not contained enough water to sate the thirst of the traveler had turned into navigable rivers after bursting their banks. To cross them it was necessary to construct cowhide boats, both to prevent the moisture from damaging the ammunition and to transport those troops who were unable to swim. The troops marched for seven days in water up to their waists, having to camp in the open at places that the water had not covered. The only protection that the soldier had was a miserable blanket, but he did not even use that to cover himself, so great was his anxiety to protect his musket and his ammunition. On June 11, the division reached Tame in the most miserable condition. This was the headquarters of Santander, commander of the vanguard division. The army was afforded some relief by its arrival at this point, for it was possible to add a little salt and a few bananas to the ordinary ration of meat. The soldier needed nothing more to make him forget his troubles and to conjure up enticing visions of success in the campaign which had begun so inauspiciously. The army was composed

---

1. Lecuna, *Crónica razonada...*, ii, p. 308.
2. Captain Richard L. Vowell, another of the British legionaries, also gave an account of the march in his *Campañas y Cruceros*. According to the translator of *Sabanas de Barinas* (Ediciones de 'Cultura Venezolana', Caracas, p. 69), "none of the historians of the period was able to trace such a perfect sketch of the wild natural conditions and obstacles which Bolívar's army was to encounter." However, we prefer O'Leary's description.

entirely of young men who were not greatly affected by the cares of life or its hardships and perils. The President himself was still only thirty-five, and he enjoyed perfect health and surprising physical and mental powers. He was never heard to complain of weariness, not even after arduous work and long marches, during which he often helped to load the mules, unload the canoes, and with other tasks unfitting his high position of first magistrate, but worthy of praise in the fervent patriot and loyal soldier who disregards all human comforts for the sake of a holy cause. When it was a question of the general welfare, no task was too lowly for Bolívar."[1]

O'Leary continues a few pages further on: "From Tame to Pore, the capital of Casanare, the whole route was flooded. Santander says in his account of the campaign that the territory through which the army had to make its first marches was more like a small sea than solid ground. On June 22, obstacles of a different order were encountered. The gigantic Andes, considered impassable in this season, seemed to present an insuperable barrier to the advance of the army. For four days the troops struggled with the difficulties of those rugged paths, if steep precipices deserve such a name. The *llaneros* contemplated the stupendous heights with surprise and fear, and marveled at the very existence of a land so different from their own. As they climbed, their surprise grew more and more intense with each peak that they scaled, because what they had taken for the final summit was simply the start of another and others even higher, from the tops of which they could still see mountains whose peaks seemed to be lost in the ethereal mists of the firmament. Men who were accustomed in the plains to crossing torrential rivers, taming savage horses, and over-coming wild bulls, tigers and crocodiles, were now terrified by the sight of these strange natural conditions. Without hope of overcoming such extraordinary difficulties and with their horses already dead from fatigue, they persuaded themselves that only madmen could keep going at tempera-tures that numbed their senses and froze their bodies. As a result, many of them deserted. The mules that carried the munitions and arms fell under the weight of their burdens; few horses survived the five day march and those of the forward division that died blocked the path and increased the difficulties for the rear guard. It rained incessantly, day and night, and the cold increased as we climbed. The cold water, to which the troops were unaccustomed, gave them diarrhea. An accumulation of inci-dents seemed to be destroying the hopes of Bolívar, who alone remained steadfast amidst hardships so severe that the least of them would have dampened the spirits of someone less great. His presence and his example cheered the troops, as he spoke to them of the glory that awaited them and

---

1. O'Leary, i, pp. 551-2.

of the abundance that reigned in the country they were marching to liberate. The soldiers listened to him with pleasure and redoubled their effort."[1]

The first encounter with the enemy was at Paya, in a rugged defile, where the royalists, although outnumbered, might have detained and even defeated the patriot army. But Santander, who commanded the vanguard, boldly crushed the enemy detachment.

The troops had marched 600 kilometers from Mantecal to reach Pore, weak, hungry and naked, with soldiers having to take the place of the dead mules, and all the units decimated by their unbelievable privations. They reacted, therefore, to their victory at Paya with noisy enthusiasm. Bolívar, who could no longer disguise his intentions, directed a proclamation to the Granadans, informing them of the help that their "Venezuelan brothers" had brought, and calling upon them to throw off the yoke of their oppressors. He repeated his intention to end the war to the death, as he had been doing since 1817, and to receive benevolently those who had been "more the victims than the instruments of tyrants." He concluded "We will hold only the Spanish tyrants responsible, and even they will not perish, except on the field of battle."

However, if the Liberator had been able to look behind him just then, he would have been terrified. Páez had neglected to obtain the indispensible supplies that he was supposed to send, while in Angostura, the capital, a coup d'état was being planned, with even more serious consequences. Before leaving for New Granada, Bolívar had sent General Urdaneta to Margarita with instructions to organize an expedition to attack Caracas, using soldiers from the island and the legionaries arriving from abroad. His intention was to capture the capital or, at least to reduce the royalist threat to his rearguard. But General Arismendi, the political governor of Margarita, and General Francisco Esteban Gómez, refused to accept these plans, and insisted that not one soldier would leave the island. Urdaneta and Soublette vainly exhausted all the means within their authority and the conciliatory tact that distinguished them. In the end, they had to arrest Arismendi and send him to Angostura to account to the government for his conduct. This was the situation in July 1819, when Bolívar found himself at the most difficult stage of his campaign. It was soon to worsen. A group of Congressmen attacked Bolívar on the pretext that he had not consulted Congress about his expedition. Although this attitude was absurd, given that the success of the venture depended upon secrecy, several officers joined the plotters, obliged Zea to resign from the vice-presidency and replaced him with Arismendi. The latter immediately assumed the title of Captain-General, and proceeded on his own initiative to dismiss Ber-

---

1. O'Leary, i, pp. 560-1.

múdez from the command of the eastern army so that he could give it to Mariño. In short, complete military and political anarchy had returned. Bolívar's position could not have been more desperate if those mountains that he had just scaled had crumbled away behind him. It might be said that the war to the death, from which he wanted to spare others, was threatening him behind his back, in a new form but, as always, with the same harsh demand: succeed or die.

Succeed or die. But first the enemy had to be found. O'Leary continues his narrative as follows: "After a few days' rest the army renewed its march on July 2. The royalist detachment which had been beaten at Paya had retreated to Labranza Grande, along a road considered to be the only one passable at that time of year. There was another across the wilderness of Pisba, but it was so broken and uneven that it was hardly used even in summer. The Spaniards considered it impassable and neglected to defend it, and this is precisely why Bolívar chose it. The march from Casanare across the flooded savannas and even the crossing of the Andes, although rugged and vertical, were in every sense easier than the route that the army was about to take. At many points the way was completely blocked by huge boulders and fallen trees, or by washouts caused by the constant rain, which made the ground slippery and dangerous. The soldiers threw away their rations of four days' meat and vegetables and kept only their muskets, for the difficulties of the climb were more than sufficient, even when they were free of their burdens. The few surviving horses died on this journey. The army reached the foot of the Pisba *páramo* late at night, and made camp there. The night was horrible. It was impossible to keep fires going because the constant rain and hail and the icy wind put them out as soon as they were lit. There was no shelter of any kind in the area. Since the troops were almost naked, and most of them were natives of the hot Venezuelan plains, it is easier to imagine than to describe their cruel sufferings. The following day they crossed the *páramo* itself, a bleak and inhospitable desert, devoid of all vegetation because of its height. That day the cold penetrating air proved fatal to many soldiers. Many suddenly collapsed during the march and died within a few minutes. In some cases flagellation successfully resuscitated those who had frozen it seemed to death, and a cavalry colonel was saved in this way. During this day's march my attention was drawn to a group of soldiers who had stopped near the place where I had sat down, overwhelmed by fatigue. Seeing that they were busy, I asked one of them what was happening. He told me that the wife of a soldier of the *Rifles* battalion was in labor. The following morning I saw the same woman with the newborn baby in her arms, and apparently in the best of health, marching along behind the battalion. After the birth she had walked two leagues over one of the worst paths of that rugged terrain. A hundred men would have been sufficient to destroy the patriot army as it crossed that wilderness. During the march it was impossible to keep the soldiers together, because even the officers, let alone the troops, could barely withstand the fatigue of the crossing. That night was more horrible than the previous ones, and, although the camp was more sheltered and the rain fell less frequently, many soldiers perished. As groups of ten or twenty men descended from the *páramo,* the General told them that he hoped the campaign might soon be over, and that they had already conquered the greatest obstacles of the march."[1]

At last, in fact, this was so. Above all, they did not have to rest in an inhospitable place as after Paya. The inexhaustible generosity of the Granadan people awaited them. On July 5, the anniversary of the declaration of independence, the vanguard entered the province of Tunja, after marching for a month and a half. Gneral Anzoátegui commented in the letter to his wife mentioned above: "Only the genius of the Liberator could save us, and save us he did. But he was helped by the patriotism and enthusiasm of the patriots of the province of Tunja, especially the women who, if you can believe it, actually stripped themselves of their clothing to make shirts, pants and jackets for our soldiers, and supplied us with everything that they had in their houses. This was a marvelous resurrection. It restored to us life, valor and faith. . . ."

And Anzoátegui was difficult to please. He was a veteran of the revolution, unselfish, intrepid, skillful and gentlemanly. All loved and admired him. But, despite these qualities and the welcome he received, "he found faults everywhere. One way or another he always found reasons to complain, whether the march was long or short, the weather wet or dry, the road smooth or rough." This was the opinion of O'Leary, who also reported: "Colonel Rook, who commanded a brigade in Anzoátegui's division, had a personality diametrically opposed to that of his commander. Pleased with everyone and everything, and especially with himself, he seemed happy with, rather than indifferent to, the life he was leading. For him the climate of Apure was mild and healthy and superior to any other, until he entered the territory of New Granada, whose climate he naturally considered the best in the world. He had never lived better, he said, than during the Arauca campaign. The soldiers in his brigade were the best in the world, until some of them died. Then, instead of bemoaning the loss, he consoled himself by saying that they deserved to die."

Naturally, the contrast between the two men was made more pointed by the circumstances. When Rook reached headquarters, after having brought his men from Tunja, "he presented himself to the President, whom he found seated on a trunk, with his lunch of roast meat, bread and chocolate on a rough wooden seat in front of him. Rook hurried to congratulate His Excellency on the happy change and notable improvement

---

1. O'Leary, i, pp. 564-5.

in the appearance of the army since he had left it. He gave the most satis-factory answers to all the questions put to him by General Bolívar, and assured him that his unit had not suffered at all on the *páramo*. He stayed to eat alongside His Excellency, who had invited him to share his frugal meal, which Rook apparently insisted consisted of the most appetizing food he had ever tasted. There he was, when General Anzoátegui appeared, looking sad and in a bad mood. 'What news, Anzoátegui?,' asked Bolívar. 'There certainly is news,' Anzoátegui replied, and he immediately asked if His Excellency was aware of the state in which Rook's dragoons had arrived.' 'Yes, I am, for the colonel has just given me the most favorable report, telling me that he suffered no losses at all on the *páramo.'* There followed an explanation, which revealed that a quarter of the English soldiers and two officers had perished on the march."

The mood of the army oscillated between the worries of Anzoátegui and the arrant optimism of Rook, for, despite its pride in its endurance and its first triumphs, it could not close its eyes to its deficiencies. Much of its equipment had been abandoned during the march, and Bolívar hurriedly sent men to collect it. The cavalry, upon which the army relied so much, had lost almost all its horses, and those that had survived were tired and undernourished. Most of the units must have suffered losses similar to Rook's. Despite the assistance provided by the Granadans, the soldiers remained almost naked and unshod. The hospitals were full. The Span-iards, on the other hand, had enjoyed a long, comfortable rest; they were well-clothed and well-fed and had not been defeated in New Granada since Morillo had pacified the country at the beginning of 1816.

Bolívar succeeded in the first encounters thanks, above all, to the skillfulness of his maneuvers, the desperate courage of his troops, and the fear and surprise felt by the royalists in the face of the inconceivable move that they saw their enemies making. But the first battle was terribly bitter and the patriots were on the point of being annihilated. It was fought at a place called Pantano de Vargas on July 25, the anniversary of the founda-tion of Caracas, but also the day of St. James, the warrior patron of Spain. Bolívar had celebrated his thirty-sixth birthday the day before. The patriots, boldly seeking the encounter, feared that Barreiro, the royalist commander, would receive new reinforcements. The Spaniards dominated the heights and Barreiro made skillful use of this superiority, succeeding in disorganizing the republican center by charging it with his best troops while fatal fire fell on them from above. The British legion led by Rook showed extraordinary courage, and twice restored order among the infan-try, but it was in vain. All seemed lost, when the Liberator hurried towards Colonel Juan José Rondón, whose Alto Llano squadron had still not been in action, and cried to him: "Colonel, save the country!" Rondón then charged the royalists squadrons advancing to complete the rout of the patriots, swept them aside, and also destroyed the infantry that came to help them. Two more commanders of the patriot cavalry, Infante and Carvajal, attacked in their turn with equal courage, and the whole royalist army began to hesitate. The republican infantry, for its part, recaptured the heights, after being relieved from the terrible pressure it had suffered, and the battle was decided in favor of the patriots.

The brave, congenial Rook was seriously wounded. O' Leary tells us: "Bathed in blood, he called to a staff officer who was passing to ask if the President was satisfied with his conduct. After expressing his wish to help and console him in such a distressing situation, the officer told him that His Excellency regarded his conduct as heroic. 'He is quite right,' replied Rook with a groan; but he would have given the same reply if the officer had said the opposite. The following day they amputated his arm, and he suffered the operation with his customary good humor, remarking upon the perfection of the hand that he was about to lose for ever. A few days later he died." It is also said that while they were amputating his arm he cheered for his country, and when somebody asked it he was referring to England or Ireland, he replied that his country was the land that was going to give him burial.

The hero of the action, beyond any doubt, was Rondón, who had the glory of deciding it. Bolívar still remembered this a year later, when he wrote to Santander: "Without Rondón. . . . I do not know what would have happened at Vargas."[1] And on July 24, 1820, the eve of the first anniversary of the battle, he repeated to the vice-president in festive tone, "Tomorrow is the day of St. Rondón. . . ."[2]

There is another story, well-known in Venezuela, about Rondón's celebrated success in the battle. It is said that when the situation of the patriots had become desperate, Bolívar exclaimed: "We have not lost yet, because Rondón has not entered the battle!" It was then that he ordered the irresistible lancer to make the charge that snatched victory. According to another version, it was Rondón himself who said this, in response to a desperate appeal from the Liberator. Whatever the exact truth, this stupendous feat has become so well known in Venezuela that the boast is popularly used when anybody finds himself in difficulties and wishes to make clear that he is about to make a decisive effort. Even in games of bowls, dominoes or cards, one frequently hears: "We have not yet lost, because Rondón has not entered the battle!"

The Venezuelan masses, previously inactive and slighted, produced many heroes in this period, but none deserved as much as Rondón to represent

---

1. *Cartas,* ii, p. 149. This recollection disproves Lecuna's contention that "the modern legend that a mere handful of men decided the days is unsound." *Crónica razonada...,* ii, p. 339.
2. *Cartas,* ii, p. 237.

them in history. What does it matter that he began his career with the royalists! What was admirable was that he too abandoned that "brilliant uniform," although a commander, so as to share with his compatriots the harsh privations and the discipline of the republican camp. He joined the forces of General Zaraza in 1816 or 1817 and, as we have seen, Páez entrusted the most daring maneuver to him at Las Queseras del Medio. He saved the army at Pantano de Vargas, and at Boyacá he led the Llano Arriba squadron "with amazing bravery," to quote the official report. He continued to fight for the liberation of Venezuela until he died besieging Puerto Cabello in 1822. There was something ironic and painful, yet plebeian even in the cause of his death: a simple wound in the foot which became infected and led to tetanus. Referring to his death in his *Autobiografía,* Páez gave Rondón the title merely of *"comandante."*[1] This wounding, although involuntary, denial of his rank, and his miserable death, seem to symbolize the misfortunes and injustices that were again about to descend upon the Venezuelan people. For this reason, although this chapter should be dominated by the figure of the Liberator, we have entitled it St. Rondón. Nothing could be more pleasing to Bolívar himself, for although he was inflexible in his insistence on assuming direction and responsibility for the war, when it came to distributing glory and rewards he was always ready to depersonalize his work and associate even his humblest collaborators with it. The complete paragraph of his letter to Santander, quoted above, written to defend Colonel Rangel, reads as follows: "We needed neither Nonato nor Piar, but without Rondón, who is worth more than they, I do not know what would have happened at Vargas. We must be just: without the valor of Piar the Republic would not have won so many victories; without the valor of Nonato and his companions not many patriots would have survived. Right now, despite his defects, Rangel is serving us, and he will soon serve us much more."[2] In deference to this attitude, then, we must include in our glorification of Rondón all the subordinates identified for posterity by Bolívar: men like Nonato Pérez, Aramendi, Infante and Carvajal, who, despite their defects, won many victories for the Republic; those who, like Rondón, gave so much and received so little; the anonymous Granadan women who stripped off their clothing to cover the troops; those soldiers who, as Bolívar told Salom, were like excited children when they were given a ration of bananas. And also those extraordinary foreigners who, like Rook, gave their lives with a smile, or, like O'Leary and Vowell, shared the sufferings of the creoles and recalled them afterwards only so as to exalt the Venezuelan people and their glorious leader.

---

1. *Autobiografía* (Caracas, 1946), p. 223.
2. *Cartas,* ii, p. 149.

Both armies came off badly at Pantano de Vargas, but, whereas Bolívar could repair his losses only with hurriedly recruited volunteers, Barreiro was reinforced by fresh veterans, and it was feared that he had a further considerable force in reserve. The Liberator, therefore, continued his maneuvers in an attempt to force a new confrontation, while trying to ensure that it would take place at a favorable spot.

Finally, on August 7, he managed to intercept Barreiro at the Boyacá bridge. It was already past noon, and the patriots attacked furiously. Santander's division held the heights, while the Liberator and Anzoátegui personally led the troops into battle. According to Lieutenant-Colonel Thomas Charles Wright, of the 'Rifles' battalion, Bolívar reminded "each of the Colombian battalions of something exciting as they advanced into the thick of the firing... General Anzoátegui, commander of the division, behaved in a similar fashion to Bolívar, and from the start of the day until the finish he was always to be seen where the fighting was most intense. For this reason he might with justice call himself the Ney of that battle."[1]

The patriot triumph was complete: 1,600 royalist soldiers, numerous officers, Barreiro himself, and his second-in-command, Jiménez, were made prisoners. All the royalist artillery, arms, standards and ammunition were also captured. Viceroy Sámano fled from Bogotá, and Bolívar occupied the city on 10th. The viceroy's flight was so precipitate that he left in the royal coffers half a million *pesos* in coin and about 100,000 more in gold bars. The army bulletin of the 11th declared: "The liberating army has achieved what was proposed at the beginning of this campaign. After a march lasting 75 days from the town of Mantecal, in the province of Barinas, His Excellency entered the capital of the New Kingdom, having overcome obstacles and difficulties greater than those foreseen when this great operation was decided on, and having destroyed an army three times stronger than that which invaded. It can be said that the liberation of New Granada has infallibly ensured that of all South America."

This was the Liberator's constant thought. Shortly afterwards he wrote to Anzoátegui: "Take much care of the *Guard,* and remember that I have placed all my confidence in it. After we have done our duty to our country, we will march with it to liberate Quito; and who knows if Cuzco will receive the benefit of our arms; and perhaps the Argentine Potosí will be the terminus of our conquests."[2]

He was to accomplish precisely this. But five years of incessant fighting still separated him from his goal.

---

1. Boletín de la Academia Nacional de la Historia, Caracas, no. 79, p. 310.
2. Quoted by J. J. Arocha, *El Sempiterno Regañón* (Caracas, 1957), p. 106.

XXV

"A FORCE
DE FORGER
ON DEVIENT
FORGERON"

As SOON AS HE HAD OCCU-
pied Bogotá, Bolívar began to organize the campaigns that were to be
undertaken in the north and south of the viceroyalty. He proposed in the
north to liberate the Atlantic coast of New Granada, open another front
against Venezuela, and take Maracaibo. To the south his gaze stretched as
far as Lima and the emancipation of the continent.

Of course, his attention was also required by many other problems. His
administrative measures included one which, above all others, was characteristic. He arranged for an abandoned Capuchin convent to be established
as a college and provided with an income, for "orphans, foundlings
and pauper children whom the Republic should support and educate."[1]
He was also worried by what was happening in Venezuela, particularly
the crisis suffered by the civilian government in Angostura, the attitude
of Páez and the conduct of military operations. He was practically isolated from Angostura by distance, the state of the roads in the rainy
season, and the insecurity of communications due to the war itself. It
was ridiculous to issue orders on the basis of information that was three
months out of date, particularly when it would take another three months
for them to reach their destination. After a stay of only a month and
ten days in Bogotá, then, Bolívar left for Angostura, intending to revisit
Páez in Apure on the way.

---

1. O'Leary, *Documentos,* xvi, p. 464.

The Liberator's activity was incredible. He had begun the Apure campaign, during which, according to Anzoátegui, they did not spend "a single day in the same camp," in March 1819. The march on New Granada and the crossing of the Andes had begun in May, and three months of constant marching and fighting had preceded the triumphant entry into Bogotá on August 10. On September 20, he set out for Venezuela, reaching Apure on December 5 and Angostura itself on the 11th. He stayed in the provisional capital until December 24, when he left to supervise operations in the Apure. After visiting Bogotá again—he arrived there on March 5, 1820—he returned to the Venezuelan frontier and was in San Cristóbal by April.

It is almost impossible for us to imagine what it was like going backwards and forwards between Angostura and Bogotá, traveling by mule across an emptiness which was a burning desert in the dry season and an interminable lake in winter. Páez complained that when Bolívar led the army he squandered combat; when he dismounted he had to dispatch his correspondence to the various military commanders, or he dictated his political reflections to some improvised clerk, or personally drew up a draft plan for popular education, or dedicated himself to translating items favorable to the patriot cause from English periodicals.[1] He arrived at Angostura in December 1819 without any baggage, because he had left it behind in his impatience. He told the Toros: "Diego (Ibarra) cannot write to you, for he is still traveling behind with my baggage." He told Santander when he left for the Apure a few days later, "Tomorrow I continue to the Apure, leaving my retinue behind so as to save time."[2] He repeated, in another letter: "The day after tomorrow I shall leave here, though it will be Christmas Eve and a day of great solemnity, but I do not intend to lose a moment, as the army is already on the march for the Apure and Páez is at the mercy of any contingency. The combined army will be immense, but we always lack something and now it will be muskets. However, I except to receive a large quantity of arms at any minute. I must have 10,000 guns in Cundinamarca or I shall go mad. I shall dispatch them before a month is out, in spite of all the world."[3]

Nevertheless, Bolívar must have felt relatively content and very satisfied at this time, for he had just witnessed the fulfillment of one of his most cherished hopes: the union of Venezuela, New Granada and the ancient presidency of Quito into a single state. He wrote to Santander: "The pros-

---

1. This plan for popular education, which we have already discussed, was found among his papers, written in his own hand. With reference to the translation from English, see *Cartas,* ii, p. 201.
2. *Cartas,* ii, p. 125, and xii, p. 151, respectively.
3. *Ibid,* ii, p. 129.

pect afforded by this memorable act is as immense as it is magnificent. Power, prosperity, greatness, stability will be the issue of this happy union." The new nation was called Colombia, the name chosen by Miranda for the great American confederation that he had planned to establish, and its creation was sanctioned by the Congress of Angostura on December 17, 1819. Bolívar's conviction that the union was indestructible became so intense that afterwards he rarely referred separately to Venezuela, New Granada or Quito. Only Colombia was to exist for him. The glory of Colombia, the destiny of Colombia, the services demanded by Colombia, the abnegation of the Colombians, the patriotism of the Colombians; these were the themes that appeared in both his personal letters and his official papers. Even when he referred to the beauty of the landscape, as in his letters to Simón Rodríguez, he was blind to regional peculiarities. It was the magnificence of nature in Colombia that exalted him. He also talked of America as though it were something more concrete than his own Venezuela. Miranda was the only other person to display with equal passion this sort of mystical transport, which turned the invoked vision into reality for them.

Although the intrigues unleashed in Angostura had led some to demand that he be declared a deserter and an outlaw for having embarked on the invasion of Nueva Granada without the permission of Congress, Bolívar's triumphal return quieted all censure. Arismendi hurriedly resigned the command that he had usurped, and the restless whims of those soldiers and politicians who had counted on Bolívar's failing in his bold enterprise also ceased. For his part, Bolívar did not even mention these sad events. In his message to the Congress he confirmed his fidelity, and ceded all responsibility for his success to his companions-in-arms and to the people of New Granada, saying: "It would be far too tedious to describe in detail to the Congress the labors performed by the troops of the army of liberation in accomplishing the task which we had assigned ourselves. The winter on the flooded plains, the frozen peaks of the Andes, the sudden changes of climate, a triple army inured to war and in control of the best military positions in South America —these and many other obstacles we managed to overcome at Paya, Gámeza, Vargas, Boyacá and Popayán, in order to liberate, in less than three months, twelve provinces of New Granada. I commend to the national sovereign body the merit of these great services on the part of my indomitable comrades-in-arms who, with unexampled perseverence, suffered mortal privations, and, with a valor unequaled in the annals of Venezuela, defeated and captured the army of the King. But not alone to the army of liberation do we owe the advantages we have gained. The people of New Granada have proved themselves worthy to be free. Their unfailing co-operation repaired our losses and swelled our ranks. The delirium of an uncontrolled passion is less ardent than the joy felt by New Granada upon recovering her freedom. Those generous people have placed all their possessions and their very lives upon the altars of their country...."

Bolívar's gratitude to the Granadans, who on several occasions provided him with aid for the prodigious leaps of his creative activity, was always sincere and constant. His fiery character and the disconcerting ups and downs of fate often led him to utter bitter or angry statements about the people he found to be unenthusiastic or opposed to his plans. Not even Caracas, which he loved passionately, was spared these momentary outbursts. It was only with the Granadans that he always remained friendly and polite, even in the darkest period, when the imminent dismemberment of Colombia took on the odious appearance of regionalism.

It was in this same period that he began to praise passionately the young Granadan General, Francisco de Paula Santander, to whom he had entrusted command of the vanguard during the crossing of the Andes. After the battle of Boyacá, Bolívar charged Santander with the government of New Granada, giving him the title of vice-president, and, as he left Bogotá for Angostura, he told the Granadans in a proclamation: "I am departing from you, but I am leaving you another Bolívar in Santander."

In February 1820, he told Santander, in an official communication: "After performing the most brilliant services for your country, you have crowned your glory with your moderation, obedience and selflessness. You were summoned by your birth, virtues, bravery and talent to be the first Commander of the Granadan Nation, but you have preferred to be the first subject of Colombia. I, who know more than anybody else what you have the right to hope for, am astonished to see how much you have renounced, thus increasing your right to the gratitude of the nation, a right which already seemed complete. Were you not the first to raise an army to oppose the invasion of Casanare by our powerful enemies? Were you not the first to restore order and wise administration in the free provinces of New Granada? Were you not the first to hurry to perfect her freedom? To open for us the road through the Termópilas de Paya? Were you not the first to spill your blood at Gámeza and to risk your life at Vargas and Boyacá? Have you not justified my choice of you, because of your intelligence, thrift and rectitude, to govern New Granada?"[1]

Were these praises as deserved as those that Bolívar delivered to the people of the viceroyalty? At precisely the same time another Granadan patriot, Francisco Antonio Zea, had declined Bolívar's offer that he serve as the representative of New Granada, on the grounds that he did

---

1. *Cartas,* xi, p. 179.

not deserve such an eminent position. The illustrious Peñalver had written to Bolívar, referring to Zea, ". . . I doubt whether the little old man, who is without experience, would work with probity and skill. . . I know very well that you know him and that the reason for such a poor choice is simply the need to give way to the opinion of the Granadans, so as to strengthen the union and prevent the evils that would arise from discord."[1]

Did the failure of Zea influence the attitude adopted by Bolívar towards Santander? Was it simply a case of substituting one for the other? There would be nothing dishonorable in this, of course, for either the Liberator or Santander. In subsequent years Bolívar often insisted on assigning the principal credit for the civil organization of the republic to Santander, who filled this lofty position ably and with dignity. At the same time, however, the Liberator's desire to find "another Bolívar" for each of the liberated nations arose from a very precise and praiseworthy intention to free them from the anarchy of the *caudillos* and ensure their confederation, which would be very fragile if underwritten by laws alone. The elevation in Venezuela of Páez, and Bolívar's insistence on supporting him even after 1826, when he knew that he could no longer count on the fidelity of the indomitable *llanero,* arose from the same motive. It would have been easy then for Bolívar to promote rivals to Páez, or at least to encourage his existing enemies. He preferred, instead, to reinforce his authority and deliver to him a united, pacified Venezuela. The Venezuelans owed the years of political stability that they afterwards enjoyed to this unselfish design.

Anyway, it is very interesting to observe that, despite those extraordinary eulogies to Santander by Bolívar, the correspondence between them in 1820 provides glimpses here and there of the beginning of the profound differences that were later to separate them.

Certainly, Santander showed himself to be a passionate follower of Bolívar, and wrote to him: "I do not know how to thank you for all that you do and say for me. If, as you say, I have showered favors upon you, I will also say, with greater truth, that you have shown me abundant gratitude. Which are preferable, acts of power or of virtue? Are not the latter better? You have beaten me, then."

Despite this, Santander did not refrain from making frequent "observations," almost all of which were meticulously legalistic, and Bolívar, who was impatient because the responsibility for making progress rested with him, had to remind him, ". . .the best does not always count most. The Christians with their Gospel were beaten by the Turks with their Koran." Occasionally there are signs of dangerous reservations, as

---

1. O'Leary, viii, p. 352.

when Bolívar told Santander: "You like frankness, ingenuous friendship and the truth, and then you take offense when you are copied, like an old coquette who does not want to see her daughter prosper because she will only imitate her. I shall say no more than two little things. How would you like to be told in an official letter: 'I have received the decree, and it does not seem *irregular* to me?' Or to be told in a private letter that one day responsibility will become effective? One does not have to be very subtle to see that this means that it was expected that the decree would be irregular, and that there is no other way to check a person than by invoking the threat of responsibility."

Another letter reveals that the discrepancies between some of the high civil functionaries were even more difficult to smooth out, and that Bolívar, to whom all appealed, felt incapable of resolving them. "I confess to you," with the greatest frankness he told Santander, "that the complaints of the Superior Court of Justice of Cundinamarca have caused me real pain. I do not know whether it is right or not; I would be delighted if it were right so that it could be just, and if I could see the injustice done by Congress, since it is Venezuelan by neither composition nor membership. The members of these two bodies are completely equal to me. Moreover, the discord that is caused by the union I have managed to form makes me suffer the agonies of torture. I will confess something else: the only motive, to call it such, that has led me to propose the creation of Colombia has been the idea of destroying forever the causes of hatred, disagreement and dissolution. What a horrible disappointment if these are to increase!"

Those historians who have stressed Bolívar's authoritarianism, even insisting in many cases that the public institutions created in 1819 with his blessing were no more than a legalistic facade to please the civilians and impress other nations, ignore or deliberately remain silent about this daily struggle that he had to endure, and which, when seen alongside what he had to undertake to make the *caudillos* agree, gives a very different picture of his character. His greatness did not consist of a simplistic exhibition of force. Rather, it was derived from the skill, prudence and constancy with which he was leading that anarchic world towards victory and stability. That he was not prudent by nature is a further reason for us to admire the rigid discipline to which he submitted himself as a statesman. He seemed to apply with inexhaustible energy to both himself and to external affairs a proverb that he quoted in French in one of his letters: *"A force de forger on devient forgeron."*[1]
Sometimes Santander threatened to resign and suggested that he be sent

1. *Cartas,* ii, p. 190.

abroad on a diplomatic mission. But Bolívar hinted to him that he wanted him to replace him as President of the Republic, and he found a way to appease him delicately, telling him: "Respecting your diplomatic mission I can assure you of two things. First, I cannot persuade myself that you really wish to leave your post at this time when you cannot be replaced except by Urdaneta, whom no one can replace in *his* post, and of course I cannot believe that you mean to endanger the Republic. Second, until we have defeated the enemy, and so long as I am in command, I would not think of having you transferred. When peace has been made, that will be another matter. I shall not command then, but I will propose to you that we leave together, though I would prefer lesser company if, thereby, the Republic would gain a leader capable of governing." He repeated to him the following day: "The matter of the resignation is also ruled out, because it has already been discussed three times and, if you make it four, I condemn you to be President of Colombia, which is what I desire and intend."[1]

Another divergence, which Bolívar had to sidestep with much prudence, arose from a bloody deed committed by Santander in a repulsive manner. Immediately after the victory of Boyacá, Bolívar recognized one of the prisoners as Francisco Fernández Vinoni, the officer who had handed over Puerto Cabello to the enemy in 1812, and he had him hanged. But the other royalists were treated with the greatest propriety and kindness, and Bolívar proposed to Viceroy Sámano that they should be exchanged for an equal number of patriot prisoners. Despite this, a few days after Bolívar had left for Venezuela, Santander ordered the execution of the unfortunate General Barreiro and 38 other officers. After being taken to the place of execution, a public square, on foot and with chains around their ankles, the victims were made to kneel and were then shot in the back. The Vice-President himself witnessed the barbarous sacrifice, and when it was over, according to O'Leary, "He addressed a few words not at all appropriate for the occasion, to the populace. Then, preceded by a few musicians, he paraded through the principal streets of the capital, singing the chorus of a song having to do with the act just carried out."

Santander tried in an official communication to justify what had happened, accusing the prisoners of "spreading subversive matter, which not only undermined the spirit of the patriots but also fixed opinion in favor of the king's party. They dedicated themselves to offering protection to the very republican officers who were guarding them." These accusations were indefensible when made against prisoners who had been kept in chains in the midst of a victorious army. Even more lamentable

---

1. For the previous quotations see *Cartas*, ii, pp. 138, 113, 170, 192, 181 and 185, respectively.

was the private letter that Santander sent with the same aim to Bolívar, for, although he insisted that "the action is well covered," he appeared to be strangely apprehensive. He told Bolívar: "It finally became necessary to get rid of Barreiro and his thirty-eight companions. The gossip was driving me mad, the people were cool, and I could hope for nothing, nothing favorable from keeping them imprisoned. The action is well covered; but since you are not eternal (unfortunately for America), and I cannot govern forever, your reply must cover me for all time."[1] Subsequent letters show that Santander persisted in his atrocious attitude. He informed Bolívar on November 10: "That notorious Segovia, who wrote so many infamous things to Barreiro, and two others have fallen into our hands. They will all receive a fitting reward for their iniquities, together with eighteen others whom I have here still consuming our food." On December 3, he reported lightheartedly: "The Spanish Governor of Chocó, Don Juan Aguirre, was arrested and immediately shot. We will be rid of so many devils as a result of Boyacá!" And in September 1820, he offered the opinion, referring not to the Spaniards but to quarreling patriots in Guayana: "I fear only that their example will corrupt us, and unity will turn into disunity and discord. There is no remedy; it is still necessary to hang people without trial or judgement."

Bolívar did not accede to Santander's indelicate request that he should "cover" him, and, although he seemed to believe the accusations against the prisoners, the reticence in his reply was almost sarcastic. He wrote: "I have learned with regret of the perfidious conduct of our prisoners of war, which has obliged you to have them shot at a time when there was pending a negotiation for an exchange, which would have done much honor to the Government of the Republic, because of the applause with which foreign nations greet noble acts of humanity and culture between belligerents. Our enemies in fact will not believe, or at least they will pretend not to, that our severity was an act of forced justice rather than a reprisal or gratuitous vengeance. Be that as it may, I thank you for the zeal and activity with which you have managed to save the Republic by means of this regrettable act. Without doubt our reputation will suffer. In recompense, the applause of our masses, and the new zeal with which they will serve the Republic will be our consolation." In another communication Bolívar indirectly described the deed as "murder," and repeated to Santander that it had damaged the attitude of the public towards him, above all because the offer of exchange had been pending. He concluded: "The other murders in different epochs did not take place in such circumstances, and this is wrong."[2]

1. *Cartas de Santander* (Caracas, 1942), i, p. 82.
2. O'Leary, *Documentos,* xvi, p. 515; *Cartas,* ii, p. 238, respectively.

The truth is that Santander acted degradingly —as he himself revealed elsewhere in his communication— because of the indignation that he still fel⁺ as a result of the recent atrocities committed by the royalists in New Granada. The gravest aspects of his action were that it was suffered by an officer who was not responsible for those atrocities, that it was accompanied by details of excessive cruelty, and that it revived a desire for vengeance which Bolívar and the other patriot commanders now regarded as inopportune and regrettable.

With each day that passed, in fact, it became evident that both creoles and Spaniards disapproved of this barbarous system; but before it disappeared it again manifested itself in a repulsive fashion, particularly in New Granada. When General Morillo left Spain with his pacifying expedition in February 1815, he took with him instructions which were quite mild. Although they were based upon the supposition that the Venezuelans would submit and that "every idea which does not contribute to the maintenance of the fidelity of the vassals" would disappear, they did at least state that "in general, much gentleness is to be shown towards all classes and parties," and they suggested other ways of securing a just settlement.[1] For his part, Bolívar vehemently wanted to bring the war to the death to an end. As soon as he had invaded Margarita, in May 1816, he hurried to inform General Pardo, the Commander of the Spanish forces at Pampatar: " . . . I feel that it is my duty to begin this campaign with a generous act of humanity by sparing the prisoners of the naval forces that have blockaded this island, and by ending on our part the war to the death that dishonors Spain and desolates America." The following month he enthusiastically informed a friend in Haiti: "I believe that the generosity of the conduct that I have proposed with respect to them (the Spaniards) will greatly help me secure the freedom of my country." Similarly, on February 13, 1813, a day after he had crushed Morillo's advance forces on the outskirts of Calabozo, Bolívar wrote to him. "On many occasions, against all justice, our humanity has caused us to suspend the bloody war to the death that the Spaniards wage against us. For the last time I offer to end this horrible calamity and I mark my offer by returning all the prisoners that we captured yesterday on the battlefield."[2] Despite this offer, a few days later Morillo executed all the survivors of a combat, including the young Florencio Tovar who had recently returned from the United States, where his father, Martín Tovar Ponte, had sent him to study. The nuns of the Conception in Caracas interceded for another of these young men, called Portero, whose sister was a member of their order, but Morillo would not even agree to alter the manner of execution, and he was shot in the back.

---

1. Gil Fortoul, *Historia Constitucional de Venezuela* (Caracas, 1930), i, p. 332.
2. *Cartas,* i, p. 228; ix, p. 422; xi, p. 66; ii, p. 3, respectively.

The royalist commanders, unfortunately, still hoped that this "horrible calamity," as Bolívar described the war to the death, would allow them to finish off those creoles who would not accept unconditionally the "paternal government" of Ferdinand VII, who since 1814 had been striving in both Spain and America to send all the liberals to the gallows. When he went on to New Granada in 1815, Morillo left the government of Venezuela in the hands of Salvador Moxó, who without any doubt was the most despicable Spanish official ever to walk the soil of America. As well as being cruel and inept, he was cowardly, a defect that the other Spanish commanders did not possess, greedy, like Monteverde and Cervériz, and, to cap it all, effeminate. His scheme of government for a conquered, exhausted country can be judged from the following instructions, which he sent to Colonel Urreiztieta, the governor of Margarita: "I advise you to set aside all human consideration. All the insurgents, or those who continue with or without arms, those who help or have helped them, and finally all those who have played a part in the crisis in which this island finds itself, are to be shot without fail. There is to be no trial or brief for them, except for a brief verbal discussion among three officers."[1]

Morillo and Morales, the former second-in-command to Boves, embarked on an insane orgy of killing when they reached New Granada. The most eminent and austere patriots—Camilo Torres, García Rovira, Lozano, Torices, Camacho, Gutiérrez, Pombo—most of them civilians, were sent to the gallows. The learned Francisco José Caldas, who had worked with Humboldt, was not even allowed time to finish the important scientific work in which he was occupied before, to quote the official report, "he was shot by firing squad, in the back, and his property was confiscated."[2] In accordance with royalist practice, which in its scorn for "insurgents" refused to observe considerations of simple humanity, a number of women were also sent to the gallows. One of them, Policarpa Salavarrieta, became a symbol of feminine heroism in New Granada. The fiancée of a patriot officer who had been conscripted into the royalist army, she persuaded him to desert and entrusted to him papers for the republican leaders in Casanare. But the unfortunate youth again fell into the hands of the royalists, and both he and Policarpa were sentenced to death. When she contemptuously rejected the offer of a pardon if she would denounce the other plotters,

---

1. Gil Fortoul, *op. cit.,* i, p. 336.
2. Quoted by Ramón Azpúrua in *Biografías de hombres notables de Hispanoamérica* (Caracas, 1887), ii, p. 281. Marcelino Menéndez Pelayo described Caldas as "the immortal Granadan, to whom Spain owes an expiatory monument"; and, in fact, a plaque was erected in the Biblioteca Nacional in Madrid, which reads: "Perpetual pardon of Mother Spain to the memory of the immortal Granadan Don José de Caldas, on the CVII anniversary of his death".

Viceroy Sámano had her executed in the main square of Bogotá. The patriots gave her an anagram of her name for an epitaph: "yace por salvar la patria" (she lies there to save her country). It is easy to imagine the cruelties committed during the military operations. After the battle of Cachirí the royalists killed all the prisoners, and "they say that Colonel Tolrá boasted that he had killed so many Americans that his arm became so swollen that he could not use it for many days."[1]

These, no doubt, were the memories that were tormenting Santander when he ordered the death of Barreiro. Indeed, he said in his report to Bolívar: "...at the same time I saw in these officers the executioners and murderers of our pacific compatriots, the desolators of our precious land, the perpetrators of all the crimes committed in New Granada. I was thinking that these officers had even beheaded our simple soldiers, their prisoners of war, and that they would have unleashed their ferocity upon you, me and my companions, if we had lost the battle of Boyacá."

A slight touch of poetry and love appeared briefly in Bolívar's correspondence in 1820, which on the whole remained tormented in spite of the happy successes that the patriots were beginning to experience. We read in one of his letters to Santander: "How attractive the sentimental Bernardina will be, sighing, reading and talking of the ungrateful Plaza." Two months later he wrote: "Tell Bernardina many things, and that I am tired of writing to her without reply. Tell her that I, too, am single, and that I like her even more than Plaza for I have never been unfaithful to her."[2] The festive tone of these remarks hid a real passion, and this was the only time after he was widowed that Bolívar hinted that he might remarry. Two days after Bolívar entered Bogotá, General Paris noted in his *Diario:* "Bolívar is very popular with the ladies, but he courts only Bernardina Ibáñez."[3] But the beautiful Granadan lady who merited such exceptional attention was already in love with the Venezuelan Colonel Ambrosio Plaza, and she married him soon afterwards. Plaza died at Carabobo the following year, and Bolívar again began to court Bernardina. He wrote to her from Cali in January 1822, addressing the envelope to "the Dainty and more than dainty, beautiful Bernardina. When he referred to her again in 1824, in a letter to Santander, she was "Doña Bernardina," and already out of his life for good. By a strange contrast, her first husband Plaza, was Bolivar's compatriot and intimate friend, while her second, Florentino González, was to make an attempt on his life in 1828.

---

1. O'Leary, i, p. 321.
2. *Cartas,* ii, pp. 194 and 245.
3. Quoted by Alfonso Rumazo González in *Manuela Sánz, la libertadora del Libertador* (Buenos Aires, 1945).

The protest of fidelity that Bolívar made to Bernardina was, of course, a polite lie. In Angostura he had renewed his relationship with the beautiful Josefina Machado, who had been his sweetheart in 1813, and who might also have become his wife for she came from one of the best families of Caracas. But this unfortunate girl was a victim of the misery that the patriot families suffered in exile. After Bolívar's failure at Ocumare in 1816, she had to stay on the island of St. Thomas with her mother, aunt and other ladies, and they suffered from the slander to which poor, abandoned women are exposed. In 1818 Bolívar sent money through his cousin, Leandro Palacios, for their return to Venezuela, and he told Leandro that he would not venture to express an opinion on the gossip circulating about them, "because I could turn out to be unjust or foolish."[1] It is not clear whether the gossip referred to the ladies' political or private affairs. Once they reached Angostura, there was not much opportunity for the romance to blossom, for Bolívar was unable to settle down anywhere because of the demands of the war. There are unconfirmed reports that the loving Josefina tried to follow him to New Granada, but fell ill in Achaguas and died before the end of 1820.

After the victory at Boyacá, military operations within Venezuela were more or less paralyzed, as Bolívar concentrated upon those that he had ordered in the north and south of New Granada. Mariano Montilla was collaborating with him in the north. He had reconciled himself with Bolívar and was to remain a close friend for the rest of his life. Montilla's support was particularly important because of two unfortunate setbacks: the death of Anzoátegui, which occurred suddenly on November 15, 1819 almost in the middle of a celebration to mark his appointment as commander of the northern army, and the renewed illness of General Urdaneta. Apart from the Liberator, Urdaneta was the only strategist to have proved himself in large-scale operations, when he had sole responsibility, and Bolívar had thought of him for the presidency of the Republic. Despite the atrocious suffering caused by his illness, he sometimes rode for many days without sleeping, but it did prevent him from giving all that might have been expected of him in these last years of the emancipation. Bolívar, too, was ill in this period, and he declared that he felt like resting and sleeping, "which for me is a very grave infirmity."

Operations in the south, which were intended to lead to the occupation of Quito and a march on Peru, had been entrusted to the valiant General Manuel Valdés, whom Bolívar described as the most "splendid" man on a battlefield. But Valdés felt uncertain when he saw the tremendous Andean peaks that blocked his path, and Bolívar urged him with the

---

1. *Cartas,* xi, p. 414 and iv, p. 151, respectively.

message: "It must be understood by Valdés that it is a military axiom that where a goat can pass an army can pass." Doubtless, Valdés would not find this principle so axiomatic, although two years later Bolívar applied it in person, in the same area, in order to win the battle of Bomboná.

It was difficult to increase the size of the army operating in Venezuela because of the terrible mortality suffered by the recruits when they moved from the cold highlands of Cundinamarca to the Venezuelan *llanos*. It seems that it was easier for the *llaneros* to adapt to the highlands, although more painful for Bolívar's naked troops. On several occasions he showed his distress at this cruel human sacrifice, and it was partly in the hope of curtailing it that he proposed to liberate the slaves and recruit them for the army. He told Santander. "Every time I am more convinced that they should be liberated, for the unfortunate inhabitants of these provinces are like wax that melts with the heat." The slave-owners were reluctant to sacrifice their "property", but Bolívar warned: "As for the slaves, if the hornets' nest is stirred up the result will be similar to that in Haiti. The greed of the colonists caused that revolution, after the French Republic decreed emancipation and the colonists spurned it. By their recalcitrance and stubbornness they spurred their natural enemies into action.... Our path has been determined. To draw back means weakness and general ruin for all. We must triumph by the road of revolution and no other. The Spaniards will not kill the slaves; they will kill the masters, and then all will be lost."

In a previous letter, he had already made the following sweeping observation: "It is therefore borne out by the maxims of politics and derived from the examples of history that any free government which commits the folly of maintaining slavery is repaid with rebellion and sometimes with collapse, as in Haiti. In effect, the law passed by Congress is wise in all its parts. Is there a more fitting or proper means by which to gain freedom than to fight for it? Is it fair that only free men should die for the liberation of the slaves? Is it not proper that the slaves should acquire their rights on the battlefield, and that their dangerous numbers should be lessened by a process both just and effective? In Venezuela we have seen the free population die and the captive survive. I know not whether or not this is prudent, but I do know that unless we employ the slaves in Cundinamarca they will outlive us again."[1]

The Liberator was anxious to secure maximum administrative efficiency and increasing moderation in political affairs. He even interested himself in the presentation of the official gazette, telling Santander: "The *Gaceta*

---

1. On mortality of recruits, see *Cartas,* ii, p. 189, 212, 248, 256; on incorporation of slaves into the army, *ibid.,* pp. 152, 180, 189.

is very small; there is nothing in it.... Get rid of the hieroglyphs, call it the *Gaceta de Bogotá,* and have the columns filled with the smallest characters available.... The caption *Liberty or Death* can also be removed. All this is too reminiscent of Robespierre and Cristóbal, who are two demons diametrically opposed to the ideas of civilized moderation. Fortune has saved us from the terrible necessity of being terrorists."[1] The Cristóbal to whom he referred was the terrifying Negro leader who had himself crowned Emperor Henry Christophe in Haiti. The allusion was a further indication of the continuing apprehension that the devastating anarchy in Haiti aroused in the creoles.

Another of the Liberator's daily worries was the eternal shortage of money and the difficulty in obtaining arms. The austere Roscio, who would never have done anything indelicate for his own ends in his private life, did not hesitate to advise him from Angostura: "The money arrives very secretly, because if it is publicized it causes many problems. All creditors clamor to be paid from the new receipts. None of the merchants want to extend the Republic credit. All vendors ask to be paid with Santa Fe currency and all foreigners demand it for their salaries. The ministers, agents and administrators, who are diligent and resourceful in their business, become dull and useless when there is coin available, because it makes them willing to evade normal procedure and formality."[2]

Bolívar, for his part, had to pacify Santander, who was alarmed by the constant demands made upon New Granada for the support of the army. When a number of canons protested against a reduction of income from their benefices, Bolívar replied: "When we take half of their rents, we are simply putting them on half-salary, like everybody else." But not even half salary was paid to Bolívar and his subordinates. He wrote on another occasion: "Here we are all on rations of bananas and meat, and it is by God's will that we survive." He informed Santander: "It is pointless to tell you how we live here. For example, Infante obtained a few *reales* from the priest of San Cayetano, and he is supporting me." At times he grew exasperated: "The struggle has left us with nothing more than life, and this is of no value to desperate men."[3]

Bolívar became enthusiastic when he was able to equip an infantry unit in spite of these privations: The "Rifles" were given 1,000 *duros* when they left for Ocaña. There were 524 of them, divinely clothed, equipped and armed. Even the men and the weapons were select."[4] This battalion was one of the bravest in the army, and it played a decisive role in sev-

---

1. *Cartas,* ii, p. 208.
2. Roscio, *Obras,* i, p. XCVI.
3. For these and other relevant quotations, see *Cartas,* ii, p. 121, 124, 142, 164, 168, 172, 173, 179, 281.
4. *Ibid.,* p. 175.

eral battles. The nature of the war is illustrated by the sad fact that from its creation in mid-1818 to its arrival in Quito in June 1822, it consumed 22,000 recruits.[1]

Bolívar could not forget that Morillo's army of veterans, equipped with muskets and artillery sent from Spain, was awaiting him in the center of Venezuela, where the mountainous terrain made the republican cavalry less effective. For this reason he showed extreme caution and an unwillingness to risk a decisive action before he could organize his forces properly. He realized that "discipline is the strength of the enemy troops, just as bravery is that of ours. In a major battle the former is more important than the latter." On many occasions he had seen those imperturbable Spanish foot-soldiers in action, and he recognized the truth of the saying that, even when there were only four of them, they formed a square, shoulder to shoulder, and fought to the death. "The fate of eighteen provinces which are already free is in my hands, and I must not play dice with them," he observed in the same letter.

He communicated his final decision to Santander: "...I have decided to be prudent. I have resolved to adopt the defensive with respect to Venezuela and the offensive in Cundinamarca." And he underlined the following slogan for those charged with the operations: *With audacity in plan, and prudence in execution.*[2]

This new strategy, cautious and thoughtful, based upon careful preparations, was to be his norm in the future; and it reflected the change that had taken place in the overall situation. In previous years he had lacked properly uniformed, equipped and armed soldiers, but now, in 1820, he hoped to be able to make all the army like the "Rifles" battalion. Moreover, victory at Boyacá and successful operations elsewhere in New Granada and Venezuela had given the patriots control of a vast amount of territory, on the basis of which they could consolidate their defense. In both countries the creoles were coming forward in increasing numbers to join the republican armies, and it was now the Spaniards who had good reason to feel confused and worried.

Their most serious cause for concern was the liberal revolution that triumphed in Spain at the beginning of 1820. In the first place, this prevented the dispatch of another expedition destined for the reconquest of America. A further complication was that Ferdinand VII had to accept the restoration of the 1812 constitution, which was to be enforced in America as well as in Spain, and the Spanish government instructed its military commanders to enter into negotiations with the republicans. All despotic regimes start to collapse on all sides as soon as the slightest

---

1. Boletín de la Academia Nacional de la Historia, no. 96, j. 317; O'Leary, *Narración,* ii, p. 123.
2. *Cartas,* ii, pp. 131, 132, 146. See, too, pp. 190, 206, 222, 254 and 275.

crack appears in them. In this case the changes in Spain, and the new policy towards the insurgents that they implied, demoralized the recalcitrant royalists, who were accustomed to regarding the will of the monarch as beyond question, and any concession to new ideas as a crime.

Morillo regarded the order to negotiate with the republicans as a "humiliation," and he angrily pointed out to his government the disorganization that the 1820 revolution would produce in American affairs. The *Memorias* of one of his subordinates, Captain Rafael Sevilla, contain similar testimony.[1]

The Venezuelan Indian, Reyes Vargas, who had betrayed the patriots in 1812 to serve the king, justified his return to the republican ranks in October 1820 with the following proclamation: "The upheavals in our ancient Metropolis have provided me with illuminating lessons on the rights of men. Spain herself has taught me that a king is no more than a subject of the people, and that the people are truly sovereign. When I thought, like my betters, that the king was the legitimate lord of the nation, I risked my life in his defense with pleasure. Now that the immortal Quiroga and Riego have uncovered the inalienable rights of the nation with their liberating arms, I have been able to convince myself that both the Spanish and the American people are entitled to establish a government according to their conscience and their own happiness.... Long live Colombia."[2]

We should not forget that the spread of liberal ideas was a reciprocal process. There was a powerful current flowing from America to Europe. In his prophetic Jamaica Letter of 1815, Bolívar had interpreted the independence of South America as an episode in the world-wide struggle between "conservatives and reformers." Day by day, events were proving the wisdom of his thesis. His interpretation was later accepted unanimously. "If the New World becomes completely republican, the monarchies of the old continent will perish," said Chateaubriand.[3] According to Castelar, the American nations " ... were built upon new social foundations, distinct from and even antagonistic to the social foundations of European monarchy. This new social concept, reacting upon this same Europe that came out to meet it in combat through bellicose Spain and through the political pressure of the Holy Alliance, has now been imposed in both hemispheres."[4] And Unamuno recalled in his *Don Quijote Bolívar:* "Emile Olivier, the Minister of Napoleon III, wrote that in Bolívar's time

---

1. José Domingo Díaz, *Recuerdos sobre la rebelión de Caracas,* p. 239; Andrés Revesz, *Morillo,* p. 148, and Rafael Sevilla, *Memorias,* pp. 260, 263 and 267.
2. Quoted by Gil Fortoul, *Historia Constitucional de Venezuela* (Caracas, 1930), i, p. 400. It is clear that the proclamation was written for Reyes Vargas by somebody more skilled with the pen, but this does not take away its significance.
3. W. P. Cresson, *Diplomatic Portraits,* p. 30.
4. Quoted in the *Revista Bolivariana,* no. 24.

his name circulated in the countries of Europe—including Spain—as a synonym for freedom. With the name of Bolívar on their lips in patriotic songs, the revolutionaries took Paris in 1830."

Bolívar could feel all this coming at the end of 1820, and once again he ventured a number of prophecies which were also soon to be realized. In a letter to William White, he declared: "Though Ferdinand may triumph, he can send no more expeditions, for the expeditionary armies know what to expect. Moreover, there must surely have been great opposition, even among the absolutists, to the idea of sending conscript armies to America. The opinion held by the troops has been clearly shown by their support of the liberals. Even France, I mean the Bourbons, must have trembled as a result of the Spanish revolution and must have condemned Ferdinand's conduct in this matter, as compromising to themselves. I say the same for England, whose concern is more significant. She fears revolution in Europe but welcomes it in America, as the one brings her endless cares, while the other gives her inexhaustible resources.

"North America, in accordance with her business-like conduct of affairs, will avail herself of the opportunity to take the Floridas, to gain our friendship, and to secure a wider field for her commerce. It is a veritable conspiracy of Spain, Europe and America against Ferdinand. He has earned it; but there is no longer any glory in being in so formidable a league against an imbecile tyrant. I, who have always been his enemy, view with disdain this badgering of a ruined and expiring cause. Our resistance was, beyond doubt, very meritorious, when we stood alone, but now it might even be considered treacherous. I am most confident of our resources and prospects . . . !"[1]

Bolívar thought that he was fighting against "a party" rather than Spain. Despite the sarcastic tone of his remarks, one can see in them, with regard to Europe and the United States, the affection for the mother country that survived in the creoles. Even the arrogance with which he sympathized with Ferdinand, in spite of the miseries and uncertainty facing the patriots, was typically Spanish.

---

1. *Cartas,* ii, p. 157. When he referred to the possibility that Ferdinand might triumph, he meant, of course, inside Spain.

XXVI

THESE
MARVELS...

MORILLO TOO, HAD REALIZ-
ed that it was no longer possible to sustain Spain's dominion over
America. It is surprising to find that this arrogant warrior began to think
along these lines in 1815 or 1816 when, after completing the reconquest
of Venezuela and New Granada, he had to admit that it was impossible
to go on from there to undertake the projected pacification of the other
colonies. It was in 1816 in fact that he informed the court that the Venezuelans and the Granadans had to be "smothered with forces," if they
were to be kept in subjection.
His opinion of the creoles was changing rapidly. At first he felt only
anger and contempt for the "insurgents," whose poor dress and apparent
indiscipline made their pretensions even more irritating. Shortly afterwards be began to recognize their bravery, although he still regarded it
more as a proof of their savagery than as a real military virtue. We then
see that some commanders, especially Bolívar, won truly extraordinary
praise from him. Did he finally realize that the poverty and indiscipline
that he had scorned in the creole troops was a legitimate offshoot of
the abnegation with which the Spanish people, too, had struggled for
their independence? Altough he deservedly emerged from this American
war as Marquis de la Puerta and Count of Cartagena, he had to remember
that it was as a humble son of laborers that he had taken up arms—or
perhaps a simple hoe, a long knife or a catapult, rather than arms—against
Napoleon.

By 1820, at any rate, Morillo had no doubt about the excellence of Bolívar's campaigns, and he described the mainland as "military America." He affirmed in a report to the Spanish government: "The *llanos* of Barcelona, Apure and Casanare are all in the hands of the rebels. . . . The fate of Venezuela and New Granada is now certain. . . . These marvels, for such they should be called because of the rapidity with which they were achieved, were the work of Bolívar and a handful of men. . . . If we succumb and lose the mainland, which is military America, the King our lord will never succeed in retaking it, even though he might use thirty thousand men in the attempt. . . ." In this same year Morillo told the Frenchman Roussin: "Give me a hundred thousand *llaneros,* and I will sweep through Europe in the name of the King of Spain."[1]

These sentiments, and the deterioration in his health resulting from the terrible wound received at La Puerta and in general from the hardships suffered in five years of constant fighting, led Morillo to ask to be allowed to retire. He intended to marry and settle down in Spain.

But when he received orders to enter into negotiations with the republicans, Morillo was still prepared to try a final trick to win them over or divide them. He wrote separately to Bolívar, the other military commanders and the government in Angostura, proposing that they accept the Spanish constitution and send deputies to the *Cortes.* But he failed on both counts. Both the Angostura government and the various military commanders replied that Bolívar was the only person authorized to represent them in the negotiations. The Liberator, for his part, told General La Torre, who had announced that he was sending commissioners to him: "If the object of these gentlemen's mission is other than the recognition of the Republic of Colombia, Your Excellency will kindly advise them, on my behalf, that I am resolved neither to receive them, nor to hear any proposal that does not have that principle as its basis."[2]

Bolívar, however, was so confident that a liberal government in Madrid would recognize the right of the Americans to their independence that he had anticipated these negotiations even before they began. He had written to Santander in June 1820: "Congratulations, my dear General! Ferdinand VII has now recognized the courts and the constitution, forced, as he says, by the will of the people. . . It is clear that Ferdinand is going to work through two strange forces; through the general will which, without doubt, is opposed to his aims, and through the absolutists, who will foment civil strife to delay his fall. . . . Who knows whether a plan for negotiation has already reached Angostura? And, although nobody knows,

---

1. Revesz, *op. cit.,* pp. 142 and 140, respectively.
2. *Cartas,* ii, p. 213.

Road which it is believed the Liberator followed in Santa Ana de Trujillo.

I assure you that it has already been decreed in Spain. Make a note of this day and compare the dates to see if I am a good prophet."[1] A first rate prophecy, in fact; but of interest above all because of what it tells us about the Liberator's psychology. He still regarded the war of emancipation more as a civil war between liberals and absolutists than as an international war between Americans and Spaniards; and in spite of the vehemence of his denunciations of Spain, he still had the affectionate credulity which made the creoles listen to any promise reaching them from the mother country.

This attitude on Bolívar's part and Morillo's orders to seek an understanding with the republicans soon led to a radical and, according to all the available documentation, sincere change in the way that they regarded each other, They began to exchange gentlemanly and affectionate greetings, as though they had suddenly realized that the hatred that had separated them had been senseless. Even a bloody episode, which occurred when they embarked upon new negotiations, served to demonstrate this new spirit of mutual admiration. General Rafael Urdaneta describes it as follows in his *Memorias:* "Morillo did not delay his march against Carache, with an army made up of the divisions of La Torre and Tello, infantry and the regiment of *Hussars of Ferdinand VII*. Naturally, he occupied the town, but Colonel Juan Gómez, in retreat, let him know what sort of men he was fighting. When he saw the Spanish army descending the Carache hill, Juan Gómez separated all the men who were unsuitable for his plan because they were ill, crippled, or badly mounted, and ordered them to retire six leagues beyond the village of Santa Ana. He kept 30 men, under the command of Mellao, and advanced with them to meet Morillo before he reached the town. When Morillo saw him, he sent a company of *Hussars* against him, and it was reinforced with another when it failed to frighten him. Gómez began to fall back in good order, and when the Spaniards followed, he turned on them, attacked them with lances, made them retreat and then continued to retire. Morillo was determined to destroy him, and he personally led the whole regiment of *Hussars.* They tried to cut him off, but without success, because the plain of the Carache river is narrow. Gómez faced up to their repeated charges, killing Spaniards, and then retreating again. This went on for a distance of three leagues until, when they reached the foot of the hill called the Higuerote, where the Carache plains end, the Spaniards, who were tired of chasing without success and receiving casualties, gave up the chase. Gómez suffered few losses, and those that he did suffer served to give a good impression of his army. The horse of one of the dragoons was killed in a charge, and the man found himself alone and on foot, but he

---

1.   *Ibid.,* p. 198.

faced up to the Spanish cavalry, bracing his lance and standing on the corpse of his horse. He even killed two of them. When he was surrounded and wounded, he defended himself with the broken shaft of his lance. He would have died if Morillo, who was watching, had not shouted that they should spare that brave man. He was taken with several wounds to the hospital in Carache, and when the negotiations that led to the armistice began a few days later, after Bolívar had sent his aide-de-camp, O'Leary, to Morillo with papers, Morillo spoke of the man with enthusiasm and handed him over to O'Leary so that he could take him to the Liberator. Morillo did not demand an exchange, and he even gave the man money. The Liberator returned eight men from the *Barbastro* regiment."[1]

Bolívar strove to retain the moral ascendancy that circumstances had given him, and he wrote to Morillo: "The Republic of Colombia rejoices to see the dawn of that bright day when freedom will lay its hand of benediction upon unhappy Spain and when our former mother country will follow us in the path of reason."[2] But he also intended to be absolutely firm and loyal with respect to his adversaries, and he told Santander: "To defeat the Spaniards we must be made of steel. It costs us nothing to suspend hostilities *de facto* if it suits our purpose but it may cost us dearly to suspend them *de jure*. The slightest trustfulness may destroy us, and the slightest infraction may dishonor us."[3]

They finally agreed on an armistice for six months, and the treaty was signed on November 25, 1820, in Trujillo, the city where Bolívar had issued the decree of war to the death in 1813. Its aim was to facilitate negotiations for a definitive peace treaty, and it began as follows: "The Governments of Colombia and Spain, being desirous of coming to an understanding over the disputes which exist between both peoples . . . ."

The existence of the Republic, then, was recognized, and Colombia began to negotiate with her former mother country as equal to equal. The Spanish commanders now addressed Bolívar as *President* of the new State, and the republicans saw the disappearance of descriptions like *traitors, rebels, insurgents,* which had been used for them for a decade, and which had made such an impression upon the masses. They had even been used by the sister in the north and by "free England." In several of his letters Bolívar rightly showed his delight and pride at this triumph. For a long time he had regarded as his only the territory that his troops held, and, if he had fallen into the hands of the royalists he would have been hung or shot in the back. Now he was the constitutional representative of a great nation, whose frontiers extended from the mouth of the Orinoco as far as Peru.

---

1. *Memorias del General Rafael Urdaneta* (Caracas, 1888), p. 289.
2. *Cartas,* ii, p. 227.
3. *Ibid.,* p. 233.

The day after the armistice was signed, and in accordance with one of its clauses, another treaty was signed to regularize the war. This agreement, which Bolívar had called "truly holy" when he proposed it to Morillo, again subjected the struggle between the two sides to the principles of humanity and the law of nations. Clause number four, for example, established that: "Soldiers or army dependents, who are captured wounded or ill, whether in hospital or not, will not be made prisoners of war, and they will be free to return to the army to which they belong as soon as they have recovered." Even today we can share the emotion with which Bolívar wrote to Santander: "The treaty which establishes rules for war honors us greatly, for we proposed it."

Both treaties were concluded through plenipotentiaries, but, once they were signed, Morillo proposed a personal meeting and the Liberator accepted with enthusiasm. It took place on the 27th in the village of Santa Ana, halfway between the city of Trujillo, which was occupied by Bolívar, and the town of Carache, which Morillo had taken. Both leaders wrote extraordinarily expressive accounts of the encounter. Morillo wrote the day after: "I have just arrived from the village of Santa Ana where, yesterday, I spent one of the happiest days of my life in the company of Bolívar and several of his staff-officers, whom we embraced with greatest affection. Bolívar and his officers came alone, as a sign of their good faith and friendliness, and I immediately retired a small escort that was accompanying me. Neither you nor anybody else can imagine how interesting this meeting was, or the cordiality and affection that prevailed in it. We were all madly happy, for it seemed like a dream to see ourselves gathered together as Spaniards, brothers and friends. I can tell you that frankness and sincerity governed this reunion. Bolívar was carried away with happiness; we embraced a million times, and we decided to erect a monument to the eternal memory of the start of our reconciliation on the spot where we embraced for the first time."[1]

Bolívar, for his part, wrote to Santander: "From Morillo down, the Spaniards vied with each other in the courtesies that they showed us and in their protestations of friendship. Their praise for our determination and for the valor that has distinguished the Colombians, their repeated toasts to the army of liberation, in short, all the manifestations of their desire for Colombian and Spanish friendship and of deep regret for past tragedies resulting from the strong feelings on either side, and, finally, their outspoken language, which surely came from their hearts, cost me a few tears and inspired in me a warmth of feeling towards more than one of them. There were many courteous and clever toasts, but I was most pleased with those of Colonel Tello and General La Torre. The

---

1. Quoted by Gil Fortoul, *Historia Constitucional de Venezuela* (Caracas, 1930), i, p. 408.

former drank 'to the victories of Boyacá, that brought freedom for Colombia,' and the latter 'to the Colombians and the Spaniards who side by side will march to hell itself, if necessary, against despots and tyrants.' Morillo, among many other exuberant and liberal sentiments, toasted 'the heroes who have died fighting for their country and their country's freedom.' Indeed, it would take a volume to record the toasts that were offered for, as I have indicated, each Spaniard contended for the honor of eulogizing us. We responded to their courtesies in kind, with full measure and due modesty, to their complete satisfaction. General Morillo proposed that a column be erected at the spot where he received me and where we formally embraced, as a monument for all time to commemorate the first day of friendship between Spaniard and Colombian. He has detailed an officer from among his engineers, and I am to appoint another to attend to it. We ourselves began the project by laying the cornerstone. I found that General La Torre pleased me greatly. He refuses to be merely a Spaniard and asserts that he will never depart, regardless of the outcome of the war. He insists that he belongs to Colombia and that the Colombians should accept him as a brother. This declaration, delivered nobly and with great dignity, filled me with admiration. He assured me that he would exert all his influence to terminate the war, for he is resolved never again to draw sword against us. His influence will carry weight, for he expects to remain in command of the army, as it has been announced that General Morillo has received permission to retire."[1]

The Liberator added in the same letter: "Since this meeting, it no longer seems proper to write against these gentlemen in our public prints. I have so proposed and we must comply, especially as it is in keeping with our policy to show that we have not been the irreconcilable enemies of the Spaniards, except when they were ours, and that, at the first sign of peace, we have accepted them as friends.... In printing the agreements, particularly the one on the rules of warfare, some tribute must be paid to the Spanish negotiators, who are excellent men and very human. Brigadier Correa must be singled out, for he is without doubt the best man who treads this earth."

The respect that this Spanish general, Ramón Correa, won from the patriots is impressive. The Liberator fought against him for the first time in 1813, and, although this was the time of greatest acrimony between the two sides because of the recent crimes of Monteverde, Bolívar insistently praised Correa as a soldier and as a gentleman. It was rumored in 1818 that Correa had died at the battle of Cojedes, but when it developed that he was still alive, the *Correo del Orinoco* celebrated

---

1. *Cartas,* ii, pp. 284-6.

the news with the following words: "What grief we would have felt if your noble blood, the blood of a brave, humane, sensitive, just, beneficent, generous man, worthy of fighting for the best cause, had mixed itself on that field of horror with the torrents of poison that were gushing through a thousand wounds of the sons of Morillo."[1] On the occasion of the armistice in 1820, as we have seen, Bolívar called him "the best man who treads this earth." And shortly afterwards he was to choose him as an arbitrator to settle a controversy with the royalists. The truth is that numerous Spanish commanders—Ureña, Cagigal, Miyares, La Torre, for example,—were models of justice and humanity. Others, such as the magnaminous Jalón, embraced the cause of the Republic and gave their lives for it.

There is a very pleasant, popular legend associated with the memory of this meeting between Bolívar and Morillo. It seems that on one of the occasions that the two leaders were together, a young patriot officer turned his back on them without regard for either etiquette or discipline. Morillo, who was rather irritated, exclaimed in a loud voice, "The young man has a handsome back!"

"This is the first time that a Spaniard has seen it," the creole promptly replied.

If the incident did occur, it must have keenly reminded the now taciturn Morillo of his own youth, when as an impetuous junior officer he might well have said something similar to Soult or Ney.

A few days after the Santa Ana meeting, Morillo handed over the government of Venezuela and command of the army to General Miguel de la Torre, and embarked for Spain. Since we have insisted several times on regarding him as having been excessively cruel towards the patriots, it is only just that we here recall his military virtue and his selflessness, which are best described in the eulogy written by his biographer, Rodríguez Villa: "He was loved by his soldiers, for whom he cared more than for himself. A model of heroic bravery and marvelous prudence, and endowed with a herculean physical constitution, he was tireless on the march and in battle. His graceful, arrogant presence encouraged and strengthened his own men, frightened the enemy, and filled all with admiration and respect." The defense which Morillo himself made of his honor in answer to one of his political enemies in Spain was also absolutely truthful: "Fortune made me poor from birth, but she favored me in the career of arms; and, although she made me a general, she did not thereby make me less poor. My poverty was always the basis for my greatest glory, because I perceived luxury and opulence as opposed to the military character, and was always filled with

---

1. *Correo del Orinoco* (Edición facsimilar), 1 August 1818.

Detail of the Monument in Santa Ana de Trujillo, commemorating the Armistice Treaties and the Regularization of the War, 1820.

horror by the depredations of a commander who, for their sake, made himself incapable of inspiring respect."[1] Many attributed the cruelty which Morillo often displayed to the influence of General Pascual Enrile, and Bolívar seemed to share this opinion. O'Leary also takes pleasure in pointing out that, when he took Cartagena, Morillo showed himself to be humane and anxious to relieve the heroic city.

In accordance with the terms of the armistice, the Liberator appointed two plenipotentiaries, José Rafael Revenga, the minister of foreign affairs, and José Tiburcio Echeverría, the governor of Bogotá, to go to Spain to negotiate a peace settlement and the definitive recognition of the Republic. They were told in their instructions that, "since Spain perhaps intends to propose some prince of the house of Bourbon as sovereign of Colombia, you are to protest such a proposition. It is not to be accepted in any circumstances, even though the greatest advantages might be offered. This protest should extend not only to the Bourbons, but also to any other royal house of Europe... Colombia will be independent, sovereign and free of all foreign domination, or it will cease to exist."[2]

Bolívar intended to use the armistice to go in person to Quito, and he was in Bogotá in January 1821. But, despite the fact that the suspension of hostilities applied to all Colombia, he appointed general Antonio José de Sucre to replace Valdés as commander of the expeditionary force for the south, in anticipation of new operations.

In Venezuela, however, an unforeseen occurrence brought about the renewal of the war. On January 28, 1821, the city of Maracaibo, in a royalist occupied zone, rebelled and sought aid from a nearby republican detachment. Without waiting for instructions from the government, the commander of this force, Heras, occupied the city, an act which the Spaniards regarded as a violation of the armistice. At first the Liberator seemed inclined to accept this interpretation. He told La Torre that commander Heras "will be brought to trial for having exceeded his authority." He suggested the appointment of an arbitration commission, over which General Correa should preside, and he invited La Torre to a personal meeting, "a second of Santa Ana day." Above all, Bolívar was worried that a violent reaction from the royalists might again unleash a war to the death, and he pointed out to the Spanish commander: "the greater the reasons for a rupture, the more circumspect should we be in observing treaties and the law of nations, for we are the center of an immense sphere of operations in the New World. At the moment we are the object of the

---

1. Revesz, *op. cit.,* p. 163.
2. Gil Fortoul, *op. cit.,* i, p. 409.

consideration of superior spirits, and we owe honor and good faith to ourselves."[1]

Unfortunately, he was unable to abandon Maracaibo for reasons that he explained to La Torre in another communication: "Since Colombia and the other parts of America at war constitute separate peoples —they cannot be considered part of the Spanish monarchy because Spain's ownership rights in America are only those of force and conquest, and such rights cease to govern when possession is ended— Maracaibo, placed in a similar situation, ceased to be Spanish territory as of January 28. Therefore, in occupying that place, Colombian forces occupied a territory that was beyond the realm of Spanish law, as it was no longer part of Your Excellency's nation. Maracaibo was thus free to choose her form of government or to join the nation best suited to her interests."[2] General Rafael Urdaneta, who as a native of the city not only felt a strong affection for it but also had many supporters there, regarded the assistance given by troops in his division as legitimate. He had already explained to La Torre with considerable logic: "I have been unable to ignore the supplications of the inhabitants of Maracaibo, for if it is licit (within the terms of the armistice) for either side to admit deserters, there is even greater reason to admit a whole people who have risen up unaided and have chosen the protection of our arms."[3]

The truth was that Spanish dominion in Colombia was collapsing on all sides. In the previous October the city of Guayaquil, in the extreme south of the Republic, had declared for independence, and in Venezuela the royalist creole guerrillas were going over to the republican side in ever increasing numbers. General La Torre was aware that all would have to be risked in a decisive battle, and the republican troops, too, were impatient for such a conclusion.

April 28, 1821, was finally set for the renewal of hostilities, and the campaign plans that Bolívar and La Torre would follow had already become clear by this date. La Torre had decided to concentrate his forces in the center of Venezuela, and the Liberator brought together under his personal control the three divisions of his army operating in the south and the west. They were commanded by Páez, Sedeño and Urdaneta, but Urdaneta again fell ill and his command was given to Colonel Ambrosio Plaza. The patriot troops in the east, led by General Bermúdez, were to advance on Caracas, to capture the city if possible, but, if not, to distract the royalist units which were occupying it.

La Torre awaited the Liberator on the Carabobo plain, a hundred kilometers to the west of Caracas, and the battle began on the morning

---

1. *Cartas,* ii, p. 314.
2. *Ibid.,* p. 319.
3. Gil Fortoul, *op. cit.,* i, p. 411.

of June 24. In order to avoid a direct advance onto the field occupied by La Torre where, according to the republican account of the battle, six units of infantry and three of cavalry "gave each other mutual support to deny us access to the plain," Bolívar took his army along a path which came out almost behind the royalists. But this narrow pass obliged the advance units of the republican army to march under enemy fire, and when the *Bravos de Apure* battalion went into action, much larger royalist forces harried it and were on the point of routing it. Fortunately, the *British Battalion,* which was just entering the plain, charged the Spaniards and then resisted resolutely, with its men kneeling on the ground, despite the loss of its commander, the intrepid Colonel Thomas Farrier, and Major Davy, who had taken over the command. They enabled fresh republican forces to reach the battlefield, and victory very soon went to the republicans. The royalist cavalry, with the cruel Morales at is head, escaped. The infantry was made up almost entirely of the best Spanish veterans, but they were demoralized by the flight of Morales and by so many years of useless sacrifice. They either fled or were captured. Only the *Valencey Battalion* formed a square and, despite the keen efforts of the republicans to make it submit, retreated with the courageous discipline characteristic of the Spanish infantry, protecting General La Torre in its center. Its exploit made such an impression upon the people of Venezuela that both the battalion and its commander, Tomás García, are remembered as if they were heroes of the republic, almost on a par with the unforgettable *British Battalion* and its self-denying commanders.

Many Venezuelans, too, made their names legendary on that day. Two of the three divisional commanders died in the battle. General Sedeño, "despairing," Bolívar wrote, that his entire division could not enter the battle because of the nature of the terrain, charged a mass of infantry and, in the attempt, died with a heroism well befitting the end of the noble career of Colombia's bravest of the brave." He added: "The Republic is no less grieved by the death of the most intrepid Colonel Plaza, who with unexampled ardor flung himself upon an enemy battalion to force its surrender." Before Plaza expired, Bolívar reached his side, and the dying man told him: "My General, I die with pleasure on this field of victory, at the most forward position, which Páez did not reach."[1] Another hero, of humbler origin and with the rank only of lieutenant, was also consecrated on that field as a symbol of his anonymous companions. He was a freed slave in Páez's army, known by the name of First Negro, doubtless because he was one of those lancers who used to say during the attack: "In front of me, only the head of my horse."

---

1. *Memorias del Prócer granadino Tomás Cipriano de Mosquera* (Bogotá, 1940), p. 420.

"The Battle of Carabobo," 1821. (Anonymous engraving).

Páez was surprised in the thick of the fighting to see him turn back and approach him, and he inquired: "Are you afraid?" "General, I have come to say good-bye, for I am dead!" the Negro replied, as he and his horse fell at the commander's feet.

Páez fought at Carabobo with his accustomed bravery and skill even though before the battle was over he fell to the ground, suffering from one of the convulsive attacks to which he was subject when he became very excited. It was his division that decided the action, and Bolívar promoted him to commander-in-chief on the very field of battle. General Santiago Mariño, Bolívar's rival since 1813, was also at his side as his chief-of-staff.

The Liberator took great pains to show his generosity towards the vanquished, to such an extent that General La Torre wrote to him from Puerto Cabello, where he had taken refuge with the remnants of his army: "It has come to my notice that Your Excellency has treated with all consideration the individuals of the army under my command who have had the misfortune to become prisoners of war. I express to Your Excellency my due thanks for this act of humanity, which diminishes my concern for the fate of these individuals. . . ."

Other victorious operations very quickly rounded out the Carabobo triumph. Colonel José Pereira, who had held Caracas against Bermúdez with some success, had to surrender at La Guaira on July 3, after a daring attempt to join La Torre at Puerto Cabello. Cumaná, the last Spanish-held city in the east, was taken by Bermúdez in October; and On October 1, the formidable Cartagena, in the north of New Granada, capitulated after a bold attack by land and sea led by General Mariano Montilla and the commander of the patriot naval squadron, José Padilla. By the end of 1821, then, Venezuela and New Granada were already free, except for Puerto Cabello and Coro, where a few bands were still active.

Only one misfortune, although of different type, clouded those days of jubilation: the death in Curaçao on September 25 of Admiral Luis Brión, a native of that island, who had consecrated his considerable wealth to the services of the Republic, and who had fought for it without seeking reward. The Liberator replied to Mr. William Parker, who had communicated the distressing news to him: "It was with great sadness that I received the communication that you kindly sent me with *Señor* Santana. . . the death of His Excellency, Admiral Brión, has filled me with the most profound sorrow. My first companion in the generous enterprise to liberate Colombia no longer exists; but Colombia owes him half his fortune, and will not be ungrateful to an exceptional man who, loving humanity and his new fellow-citizens more than his own wealth, risked all to satisfy his noble sentiments and to sate his thirst for glory. In all the hearts of Colombia the

Admiral will have an altar consecrated to gratitude. I, the leader, will send if I can, to the most remote posterity, eternal monuments to the good that he did for my country and to the loftiness of his magnanimous character."[1] Five days after Carabobo, the Liberator entered Caracas accompanied only by part of his staff and General Páez. The reception given to him by the city, the cradle of the revolution, was delirious. Despite this, and although he was again with friends and relatives who had loved him in his happiest days—as well as near the Avila, the scented groves of the Anauco and the spots on the banks of the Catuche and Guaire where he had studied with Rodríguez and Bello—he remained in the city only as long as was necessary to organize a provisional government for Venezuela. He had been absent for seven years, but did not even take seven days of rest in those places that he loved so much. Bolívar was still obsessed by the idea of the campaign against Quito and Peru, and he considered it essential that he should direct it personally. Some historians and military critics have attributed his reverses in 1816-18 to the affection that he felt for his native city and to his determination to take it at all costs. In 1821, however, he did entirely the opposite. He left Caracas even before he had made all the political and administrative arrangements required for the recently conquered territory, to embark on a campaign which would take him to the extreme south of the continent. But there was no contradiction, or in each case he was motivated not by personal preference but by the extraordinary combativeness that was the key to his triumphs. And by the conviction that the independence of the whole continent would be at risk as long as a single important center of power remained in the hands of the Spaniards.

Bolívar also made a brief visit to Valencia and, on his way back to Caracas he stopped at San Mateo, the most important *hacienda* of his *mayorazgo,* which for over a month in 1814 had been the site of his fights with Boves. After a few more days in Caracas, he finally departed on August 1. In his farewell proclamation he did not forget to help the Spaniards that he was leaving behind with a graceful expression of unity, telling the *caraqueños:* "A final victory has ended the war in Venezuela. There remains only one stronghold to conquer. But peace, which is more glorious than victory, should put us in possession of this fortress and of the hearts of our enemies."[2]

At San Mateo, according to O'Leary, "of the thousand slaves he owned before the revolution, he found only three, and he immediately gave these their liberty." This was more than a romantic touch by Bolívar's Irish aide and biographer. The need to accelerate the abolition of slavery was another of the Liberator's almost obsessive ideas. On July 14, he had

1. *Cartas,* ii, p. 415.
2. O'Leary, *Narración,* ii, p. 98.

written to Congress asking it, in return for the victory of Carabobo, to declare the children of slaves free at birth.[1] He argued: "The resolutions of the General Congress of Colombia respecting the emancipation of the slaves are perfectly in accord with existing laws; but they could have been devised so as to extend their full benefits to those future Colombians who, born in the cradle of cruelty and savagery, are brought into the world only to bow their neck to the yoke. Those children who shall henceforth be born of slaves in Colombia should be free, for these creatures belong only to God and to their parents, and neither God nor their parents wishes them to be unhappy." In these moments of triumph, Bolívar was concerned for those of whom nobody thought: of the Spaniards, whom he did not wish to abandon to the resentment of the victors, and of the slaves, to ask for their freedom. Would it be excessive to see this as a symbol of his character?

The Congress had assembled in Cúcuta on May 6 and, while Bolívar was busy with the Carabobo campaign, it discussed the constitution, which was promulgated on August 30 as the first constitution of Colombia. That of Angostura had been for Venezuela alone.

Although the centralist system triumphed in this new fundamental law over the federal ideas of many of the congressmen, the politicians finally removed the only concession that they had made to the Liberator's ideas: the lifetime senate disappeared, and senators were to serve for eight-year terms. For the offices of president and vice-president of the Republic and for membership in the chamber of representatives, they retained the four-year terms established in 1819. Bogotá was selected as the capital of the Republic, and Bolívar and Santander were elected President and Vice-President, respectively.

Increasingly in these years, the Liberator had been formulating more precisely the idea that had first occurred to him in 1813, of entrusting civil government to a civilian or a general who was also a politician, so that he could be freer to direct the war. It was with this aim that he had insisted since 1819 that Santander, as Vice-President, should control the government, and in a way the congressional decision now legalized this division of authority. One of the three congressional decrees dealing with the matter authorized the President, when on campaign, "to command the arms in person for as long as he considers convenient, with the Vice-President in the capital remaining in charge of the Executive. The President may strengthen the army in the places that he liberates, levy contributions there, admit to the service officers of any rank and entire units of the enemy, confer military ranks and promotions, (seeking the approval of the senate whenever possible), organize the liberated

---

1. O'Leary, *Narración,* i, p. 4 (1952 edition). Lecuna, *Catálogo...*, iii, p. 354.

"The Battle of Carabobo" by Martín Tovar y Tovar.

countries as he wishes, concede prizes and rewards to the towns or individuals that contribute to the success of the campaign, impose punishment on criminals and deserters, etc."[1]

Provisions such as these reconciled, for the time being, the desire for legal regularity, which was guaranteed by the constitution with the need to proceed speedily and efficiently with the prosecution of the war. If this, and the desire for adequate personal authority, had been the Liberator's only problems, he could have felt satisfied.

But, above all, Bolívar was concerned about the fundamental organization of the country. He sought for the Republic not a more-or-less ingenious, transitory arrangement, but a stable, comprehensive political order. He was profoundly disappointed, therefore,with the constitution of Cúcuta, which clearly refused to consider the social basis of our problems and agreed, instead, to cover them up with routine constitutional ideas. It is said that, when he heard the bells ringing to celebrate the constitution, he exclaimed: "They are tolling for Colombia."[2]

Occasionally, the immediate reality that Bolívar had to confront every day made him excessively pessimistic. Soldiers sometimes won a lot of praise from him for their abnegation —as in his letter to Anacleto Clemente— but he wrote to Pedro Gual in May 1821: "You gentlemen cannot form a true picture of the spirit with which our soldiers are imbued. These are not the soldiers you know; these are soldiers you have never known. These are men who have fought long and hard and who, believing that they deserve much, feel thoroughly humiliated and miserable. They are without hope of gathering the fruit of what they have *won by the lance.* They are obstinate, ignorant *llaneros,* who have never regarded themselves as the equal of men who know more or who make a better appearance. I, myself, who have always been at their head, still do not know all their capabilities. I treat them with extreme consideration; and yet this consideration is not enough to inspire in them the confidence and frankness that should exist among comrades and fellow-citizens. You can be sure, Gual, that we are over an abyss, or, rather, over a volcano, that is about to erupt. I fear peace more than war, and, in saying this, I leave it to you to imagine all that I leave unsaid, for it cannot be said. . ."[1]

And what he saw in the field of civil government was no more promising. He told Nariño: "Colombia, governed by the sword of its defenders, is a military camp rather than a body social. Accordingly, abuses, negligence, and lack of any unifying element are the inevitable consequences of those beginnings which, for many reasons, it has not been within my power to

---

1. Gil Fortoul, *op. cit.,* i, p. 431.
2. O'Leary, ii, p. 101 (1883 edition).

counteract. The first reason is that one man cannot, in a very limited time and with scant general knowledge, do it all, either badly or well. Second, I have devoted all my attention to driving out our enemies. Third, there are many considerations that must be kept in mind amidst this amazing chaos of *patriots, godos, self-seekers, whites, pardos, Venezuelans, Cundinamarquises, federalist, republicans, aristocrats,* the *good* and the *bad,* and the swarm of hierarchies which divide each of these groups. So that, friend, I have often had to be unjust as a matter of policy, nor could I be just and not be criticized."[2]

Already, in this letter, one can detect the generous error which finally brought about Bolívar's political downfall: the belief that one man could, in a short time, give organic coherence to those disperse elements of a world in reconstruction. For, although he denied that it was possible, it is clear that he felt obliged to assume the task.

Nevertheless, at the end of 1821, when Bolívar put himself at the head of the expedition he was taking to the south, he left behind him two million square kilometers covered with republican banners. To liberate this territory he had traveled in all directions for ten years.

1. *Cartas,* tomo II, p. 348.
2. *Cartas,* ii, p. 336.

XXVII

TO FEED
ON DANGER . . .

O N OCTOBER 9, 1820, THE
city of Guayaquil, situated in the extreme south of the presidency of
Quito, declared for independence. But it remained isolated from the rest
of Colombia, because both the north of the presidency and the south of
New Granada remained in the hands of the royalists.

An overland expedition from the north was made almost impossible by a
formidable mountain mass, from which flowed rivers impassable for an
army, and the malaria-infested Patía plains region. We have already noted
that the veteran General Manuel Valdés was held up, perplexed, by these
obstacles. But the greatest difficulty for the republicans was that this impregnable natural fortress had in its center the Granadan city of Pasto
which, like all the surrounding region, was rabidly royalist. Stubborn,
fanatical, daring highlanders, the *pastusos* considered support for the king
inseparable from their religious beliefs, and all were ready to offer their
lives as martyrs for this religion, but not without first fighting with marvelous obstinacy to defend it.

General Antonio José de Sucre, who despite his youth, already stood out
among the republicans as a commander of exceptional capacity, had proposed, therefore, to the Colombia government that the liberation of Quito
should be undertaken from the south, using Guayaquil as base. The Pasto
region would thus be left isolated, and it would then be easier to surround
and conquer it.

When this plan had been accepted, Bolívar appointed Sucre to command
the expedition, and he proceeded to sail with some troops to help Guaya-

quil. He reached the city on May 7, 1821, but his campaign was held up by several mishaps, both military and political, with the result that by the end of the year, when Bolívar was finally able to take personal command of the operations from the north, he was still separated from Sucre by all the territory of the presidency of Quito and the Pasto region in the south of New Granada.

At first the Liberator naturally thought of following Sucre's plan and sailing with his forces to Guayaquil rather than endangering the army by taking the Pasto route. But he received news, which later turned out to be inaccurate, that the Pacific was dominated by the Spaniards, and he also recalled that Sucre's expedition, although mounted in the most favorable circumstances, had encountered so many difficulties because of Colombia's scarce naval resources that, after leaving the port of Buenaventura on April 2, it had not reached Guayaquil until May 7. Both land and sea routes, therefore, seemed equally dubious. The Liberator could not leave Sucre isolated any longer at such a distance; if his own army remained inactive the cost to the republic would be great, and there was a danger that its morale might suffer. To crown these difficulties, he was receiving information from Venezuela of a vigorous royalist reaction which was threatening all the country's western coast, and that, due to this and his fear of arrival of Spanish reinforcements, General Soublette, who had been left in charge of military operations, was thinking of withdrawing from Caracas.

Once again as in 1813 and 1814, Bolívar found himself, after so many triumphs, in a situation which obliged him to seek in a daring stroke, a devastating campaign, the solution that could not be entrusted to calculation. He was able until February 1822 to control the impatience with which he habitually reacted to such difficulties, but he finally decided to force an overland passage at all costs.

We are given an idea of the new sacrifices that had to be made by the commentary of O'Leary, who was an eye-witness. He wrote: "I have described on more than one occasion the difficulty of organizing and moving an army in Colombia. But it is necessary, in order to appreciate fully the Liberator's efforts and his military talents, to study these marches and to keep in mind the meager resources of the territory in which they took place. Some battalions had had to march from Valencia to Maracaibo, sail from there to Santa Marta, penetrate inland to Magdalena, travel up the river of the same name in small, uncomfortable craft to the port city of Ocaña, cross the *páramo* of Cachirí, and take the road through Bucaramanga, El Socorro, Chiquinquirá and Bogotá to Popayán, crossing the burning plains of Neiva and the lofty cordillera of the Andes through Guanacas. If it is tiring and laborious to follow on a map the route that I have outlined, imagine the sufferings and fatigue of the troops on this march of more than seven hundred leagues through a sparsely populated land lacking the most essential resources for survival, impoverished by the war, in short a land in almost a primitive state! It is not surprising that some units lost a third of their men, and that when they reached Popayán there were more sick men sent to the hospital than healthy men in the barracks. The benign climate of Popayán is proverbial, but it became infected with the germs of all kinds of diseases, contracted by the troops in their long march through poisonous regions. A great number of veterans of the victorious battles of Boyacá and Carabobo came to a premature end there."

The army was to be organized in Popayán, but new days of interminable marching lay ahead between this city and Pasto, with the inevitable alternatives of swampy, burning plains and icy highlands, rivers that rushed from the heights between precipitous banks, and mountain paths along which a goat could barely pass. Lecuna tells us: "The capital of Cauca, which is celebrated for its culture and for the progress that it has achieved in agriculture, stands in a cool, fertile valley, near the head-waters of the river Cauca, at a height of 1,760 meters above sea level. The road to the south soon crosses a mountain range and then descends to the valley of the Timbío, a tributary of the powerful river Patía, which is fed mainly by the waters of the Mayo, Juanambú and Guáitara rivers, descending to a height of about 500 meters above sea level at Patía. The road then ascends to Mercaderes (1,170 m.) and Berruecos (2,170 m.) until it reaches the spurs of the volcano of Galeras, on the slopes of which stands the city of Pasto at a height of 2,600 meters."[1]

Bolívar had carefully considered all this, and he had explained to Santander, after deciding not to take the sea route: "I have summoned the battalions that are on the march so as to avoid risking them at sea and to prevent us from being divided by accidents that could occur with the enemy navy, which is said to be headed for San Buenaventura. As a result, the expedition will have to cross the infernal Patía region, facing all the difficulties of a hostile, desolate, deadly land. Our cavalry will arrive without horses; all our baggage will be lost; we will be without bread; few cattle will survive the journey; disease will be rife, for the beginning of the rainy season is the worst part of the year. The Juanambú and the Guáitara will present dangerous and difficult obstacles. Desertion, as we already know, will be a constant problem. Bear in mind, too, the advantages of the enemy. They have 4,000 men, which is more than I can get, all well rested and in good positions. In these circumstances, Mourgeon seems bold and active in committing the folly of moving up from Quito, expecting, I suppose, that my army will be large. He has

1.   Lecuna, *Crónica razonada...*, iii, p. 94.

taken with him enough arms and munitions to increase the size of his army, but I cannot strengthen mine, because nobody, not even a simple muleteer, will come from Patía. I calculate that when these obstacles have been surmounted I will find myself on the other side of the Guáitara with half the troops that I set out with, that is, no more than 3,000 men, if we enjoy infinite good fortune, for you should know that this climate and that of Popayán are abominable. The highlanders from the cold region all become ill when they cross the Neiva area, and everybody is deserting in a horrifying fashion. In a word, to end my fine exposition, I will say to you that I am very much afraid that after such great sacrifices and so much disturbance I will not dare to expose the Republic to the risk of an inevitable catastrophe in this region. I see clearly that we are going to fight against the impossible, for I am unable to alter either the nature of this country or that of these weak men."[1]

Bolívar added, a few days later: "I have been awake all night, thinking about the new difficulties that face me and about the new means that the enemy has with which to defend himself. I have now made my calculation, and am certain that I will reach the Juanambú with less than 2,000 men. I am equally certain that the enemy will meet me with more than 4,000. If I wait we will return to the well of recruits to make good our losses, and if I go ahead I will fight a battle more risky than that of Boyacá, and I will fight it out of rage and despair. My greatest hope is based upon the policies that I will pursue to win over the enemy territory and, if possible, even the commanders and troops."[2]

In spite of his claim that he always treated his subordinates with "the greatest consideration," Bolívar also grew impatient with the straits in which he frequently found himself. Santander informed him on January 28 that it was impossible to send any more reinforcements, because the treasury was exhausted and future receipts were already committed. Bolívar replied: "If I had been in Magdalena, the *Tiradores* battalion would have come and Señor Clemente would have reached Maracaibo in time. If I had been in Bogotá, the soldiers would not all have had torn feet, and they would not now be marching to the Juanambú in this state, without sandals. They would have had strings to clean the priming-holes of their muskets, for they cannot do battle without them, and I can assure you that, if I had not been here, they would not have been able to manufacture these strings, nor could they have remade the cartridges, because of a lack of paper, or the bullets, which are of caliber sixteen and seventeen, without a mold. But I have managed to remedy everything. If I had been in Cartagena, Montilla would not have sent

1. *Cartas,* iii,, pp. 8 and 9.
2. *Ibid.,* p. 10.

muskets of one caliber and munitions of another, and, even though I am here, I do not know how to stop the deterioration of an army that is going to ruin. Day and night I do nothing but think and dream about it."[1]

At the same time, however, Bolívar's mind was busy with two projects of a very different nature: The starting of a canal which would connect the Atlantic with the Pacific, and the promotion of the union of all Spanish American countries.

Borrowing the ideas of the priest of Navilla, he thought of basing an inter-oceanic canal upon the rivers Atrato and San Juan, which flow into the Atlantic and the Pacific, respectively. The short strip of land that separated them was suitable for the digging of a connecting channel. The governor of Chocó was told in a communication sent to him on Bolívar's instructions: "I have had the honor to receive in San Pablo Your Excellency's communication of January 25. His Excellency, the Liberator, has instructed me to order you to have the canal laid out across the part of the ithmus than separates the two rivers. It is only three miles wide and the ground is of gravel and soft marl. You are to dig channels towards other spots that are, or are reputed to be, suitable for the canal, and fill them with water. The instruments necessary for the operation are to be obtained from Jamaica, at government expense. His Excellency will be in Chocó in October, and he is resolved to accomplish the important work of joining the two seas. He hopes that when he arrives you will have done all that is ordered above and that, by consulting the experts in the area, you will have obtained precise information and full, detailed, exact reports of what is required for this important work."[2]

The union of the American nations was such a deep-rooted aspiration in Venezuela that it was displayed in the most varied forms from the first days of the revolution: In the projects of Miranda, the creator of the idea, who called his union Colombia or, to be more precise, Colombeia; in the instructions that the revolutionaries of 1810 gave to the commissioners sent to New Granada; in the first constitution of the Republic, which was also the first of Spanish America; in the patriotic songs of the period and particularly in the one that was adopted as Venezuela's national anthem. This idea constantly influenced the Liberator's thought. At times, as in the Jamaica Letter, he dwelt on it to point out the difficulties, but, on other occasions, it seemed more practicable and clearly motivated his proposals. In 1818, for example, he told Juan Martín Pueyredón, the supreme director of the United Provinces of the River Plate: "There should be but one country for all Americans, since we have been perfectly united in every

---

1. *Cartas,* iii, p. 28.
2. O'Leary, *Narración,* ii, p. 126 (1952 edition, Caracas).

other way." And he promised: "Most excellent sir, when the triumph of Venezuela's arms has completed the work of independence, or when more favorable circumstances permit us more frequent communication and closer relations, we, for our part, will hasten with lively interest to establish the American pact which, in forming a political body comprising all our republics, shall present America to the world in an aspect of majesty and grandeur, greater than any that history has recorded. An America thus united, should heaven grant us that devout wish, could truly call herself the queen of nations and the mother of republics."[1]

As soon as he reached Bogotá after his victory at Carabobo, Bolívar followed up this proposal by sending Joaquín Mosquera as plenipotentiary to discuss the appropriate treaties with Peru, Chile and Buenos Aires, and Miguel Santa María went to Mexico with the same mission. The scope of the agreements varied according to political conditions in each of the countries concerned. That concluded with Peru on July 6, 1822, immediately committed both states to reciprocal aid with land and sea forces. Referring to these negotiations, Bolívar told Santander on July 22: "I very much want us to embark on the federation that we have proposed: First, because we have proposed it; second, because it is glorious; third, because it is useful and Europe will see that we are united by sentiment and interest; and finally because our brothers in the south have reason to love us, and we are not disturbed here by jealousies and rivalries." He added, with specific reference to Peru: "I am handling the affairs of Peru with generosity, because rectitude is the best policy."[2]

On May 8, 1822, Bolívar left Popayán to join the army that was already on the march to Pasto. Although it was impossible in this remote region even to obtain paper to remake the cartridges, the patriots were so afraid of crossing the malarial Patía district that the Liberator also had to ensure that the troops took with them "30 loads of brandy with quinine," which was the only known palliative for the terrible disease. But the republican army was invincible. Although its tired, sick, barefoot soldiers had to face the Pasto guerrillas, who were well fed and at home in the mountains that gave them protection, the Liberator forced a crossing of the Juanambú, crossed the Mayo, scaled the heights of the Galeras's volcano and, on April 7, 1822, defeated the royalist commander Basilio García at Bomboná.

The victory was terribly costly for the patriots, because the royalists had waited for them in a most advantageous position, protected on their right by the volcano, on the left by the Guáitara woods, and in front by a deep gorge. They had also felled enormous trees to form a further barrier. The

---

1. *Cartas,* ii, p. 20.
2. *Ibid.,* iii, p. 54.

situation was made worse for the patriots by an early error of General Pedro León Torres. Bolívar had ordered him to occupy the heights that dominated the battlefield before he gave his men their lunch; but Torres misunderstood, and told his men to eat, and while they were doing so the enemy occupied the position. Bolívar angrily ordered: "Hand over your command to Colonel Barreto, who will surely obey the orders that are given to him better than you do." Torres replied: "Liberator, if I am not worthy to serve my country as a general, I will at least serve her as a private soldier," and, taking up a musket, he left to join the front ranks.[1] Immediately the Liberator dismounted, ran to embrace him, and restored him to his command. Soon afterwards Torres was mortally wounded in a head-on attack with the vanguard. Five of the seven Torres brothers, from the Venezuelan city of Carora, had already died for their country; only one was to survive, and he was riddled with wounds.

It was the sacrifice of General Pedro León Torres that decided the battle, for, according to the official report, "while he attacked, General Valdés, showing the bravery and military skill that have always distinguished him, scaled the volcano with the *Rifles* battalion by a route which was really impossible. As they climbed, the troops had to drive in their bayonets to secure a hold and to move forward."

O'Leary tells us: "The Liberator occupied the battlefield, not to celebrate the victory of Bomboná, but to lament the precious blood it had cost. Nightfall prevented the pursuit of the enemy and the pitiful state of the troops made it impossible the following day. The vanguard division lost two thirds of its men, dead and wounded, including almost all its commanders. The *Vencedor* battalion suffered similar carnage. Only the cavalry escaped casualties, because the nature of the terrain prevented it from going into action."[2]

According to Lecuna, the Liberator had intended not to fight a battle but to bypass Pasto and continue his march to the south. Although he completed the first part of the maneuver successfully, he had to attack in desperation, because he was unable to cross the Guáitara river. This interpretation is borne out by the comment of Basilio García that: "Bolívar had already tried to ford the Guáitara, but without success, for it was the rainy season, and I had previously destroyed the Veracruz bridge."[3]

In fact, Bolívar's victory at Bomboná was more important for the impression that it made on the inhabitants of Pasto than for any immediate ad-

---

1. See, with slight variations: Cipriano de Mosquera, *Memoria sobre la vida del General Simón Bolívar* (Bogotá, 1940), p. 441; Lecuna, *Crónica razonada...*, iii, p. 97; Antonio Arráiz, *Culto Bolivariano* (Caracas, 1940), p. 116.
2. O'Leary, ii, p. 130 (1952 edition).
3. Lecuna, *Catálogo...*, ii, p. 152. Basilio García's account was published in Havana in 1822.

vantage that it gave him, for he realized that he had no immediate hope of completely destroying the enemy and he was forced, therefore, to retreat in his turn and to stay on the alert.

Fortunately, Sucre had begun his offensive towards the north, and, after his decisive victory on the slopes of Pichincha on May 24 he occupied Quito. Pasto, therefore, was left isolated, and its commander was obliged to capitulate when Bolívar was again ready to attack him. As on all recent occasions, the Liberator was at pains to act courteously and humanely towards the vanquished. He returned to Colonel Basilio García the sword that he tried to give him at the gates of the city, and he also left him 8,000 pesos that were in the treasury, for the support of those who had surrendered. Bishop Salvador Jiménez, who until then had fanatically encouraged the city's resistance, became a loyal supporter of Bolívar because of this conduct. In 1828, when he could no longer expect anything from the Liberator, he defended him against the calumnies of the loathsome José María Obando.

Bolívar's journey from Pasto to Quito turned into a triumphal march. Everywhere the urban and rural population rushed to acclaim and congratulate him. When he entered the capital on June 15 the bedecked streets and the balconies packed with the beautiful *quiteñas* demonstrated the city's joy. A group of young ladies tried to put a laurel crown on his head, but he gave it to Sucre, saying: "This crown belongs to the victor at Pichincha."

On July 11, 1822, the Liberator arrived at Guayaquil, on Colombia's southern frontier. In the prior 12 months the army under his command had added another million square kilometers to the liberated territory. Moreover, a genial strategist, the young General Antonio José de Sucre, had risen at his side.

Sucre was born in Cumaná, a city in eastern Venezuela, on February 3, 1795. Some of his ancestors were French, others were among the first conquerors of Venezuela, and included one of the founders of Caracas, Francisco Infante, who was also a distant ancestor of the Liberator.[1] In 1810, when he was only fifteen years old, Sucre began to serve in the republican militia. This raises the disturbing question how was it possible for him, having experienced the life of the military camp from such an early age, to develop the stupendous military and political qualities that he was afterwards to show over a long period? It is even more surprising that although he was a witness and a victim of this war of extermination, in which even his own brothers suffered horrible death, his mind was never marred by resentment or bitterness. He was

1. Luis Alberto Sucre, *Bolívar y Sucre unidos por el linaje y por la gloria* (Caracas, 1924). It is almost certain that neither Bolívar nor Sucre was aware of this distant relationship.

a model of unshakable generosity not only towards the Spaniards but also towards those American enemies who eventually tried to kill him. In 1814, at the age of nineteen, he was chief-of-staff in Bermúdez's division. In 1817, when he was a colonel with experience of more than twenty battles and combats, he filled the same position in the Cumaná division, and later in the general army of the east. He was expressly chosen for this last post by the Liberator, who wanted him to use his political tact, his ability and his strength of character to maintain a balance between the eastern *caudillos,* and to advise them on the conduct of the war. Shortly afterwards, Bolívar confided to O'Leary: "He is one of the best officers in the army, since in him are combined the professional experience of Soublette, the generosity of Briceño, the talent of Santander and the energy of Salom. It is surprising that he is unknown and his talents remain unrecognized. I am determined to bring him into the limelight, since I am convinced that one day he will be my rival." Year by year the Liberator was more convinced that he could rely on Sucre as on himself. He said on one occasion: "There is no quality that he lacks to serve the Republic well and to lead the people gracefully," and on another: "Sucre has talent, wisdom, liveliness, zeal and valor." It was with the tenderness of a father that he later rejoiced: "Sucre is the most talented Venezuelan I know. As God gives him a victory he will be my rival in military matters, for he will have done everything from Ecuador as far south as Potosí."

Sucre's movements before the battle of Pichincha, which was fought at a height of 3,500 meters, were a model of military technique, as were those that were to precede the battle of Ayacucho. After both victories Sucre conceded generous terms of surrender to the enemy.

Apart from the extraordinary impact on public opinion in southern Colombia and Peru, where the Spaniards had always been impregnable, the patriot victories at Bomboná and Pichincha cleared their enemies from the vast region between Bogotá and the frontier. But it was not without reason that Bolívar had called himself "the man of difficulties," for he was now confronted by two political problems that were sufficiently serious to put his glory at risk: one had to do with the city of Guayaquil, the other with Peru, which, although it had declared its independence on July 28, 1821, under the protection of the Argentine General José de San Martín, it had to tackle the profound difficulties that resulted from its recently acquired sovereignty. It was also being threatened by royalist forces that had never been beaten.

The position of Guayaquil was as follows. From 1740 it formed part of the presidency of Quito which, in its turn, was dependent upon the viceroyalty of Santa Fe or New Granada. However, it had been temporarily under the jurisdiction of the viceroyalty of Peru on two occasions: in 1805, during the war between Spain and England, when the authorities in Lima were charged with its defense, and in 1810 when, as a result of the revolution of Quito in 1809 and that of Santa Fe in 1810, the Viceroy of Peru took charge of the government of the whole province of Guayaquil. This was not a permanent arrangement. The city, acting on its own initiative, asked the king "to order that the province be joined to the Presidency of Quito, as it used to be," because, among other reasons, "its population and that of its vast province suffers the most burdensome oppression by being joined to this viceroyalty" (Peru). Consequently, a royal *cédula* of June 23, 1819, ordered that the province of Guayaquil should return to the presidency of Quito for everything relative to civil, criminal and financial affairs. It was to remain under the jurisdiction of the Lima government only in military matters.

New alternatives were to jolt public opinion in the disputed city. When Guayaquil declared itself independent in October 1820, it found itself isolated from the rest of Gran Colombia, because the north of the presidency of Quito and all the south of New Granada remained in royalist advocated incorporation into Peru, from which there had arrived, shortly after the October pronouncement, commissioners sent by San Martín to offer his protection; another preferred to keep the city independent; and a third insisted on reunion with Colombia. The governing *junta,* which the city itself set up in 1820, and over which the prestigious poet José Joaquín de Olmedo presided, was inclined towards Peru, while three veteran Venezuelan officers—Luis Urdaneta, León Febres Cordero and Miguel Letamendi—who had led the liberation movement in the city and were engaged in organizing its forces, belonged, naturally, to the Colombian party. San Martín's principal agent in Guayaquil was Tomás Guido. According to the Ecuadorian historian Camilo Destruge, "far from limiting himself to the negotiations with the *junta* that his diplomatic status permitted, he exceeded his authority in an inconsiderate fashion. He was actively engaged in spreading party propaganda, and he intrigued with as much nimbleness as lack of discretion. He introduced rivalries and provoked scandals and even more serious disputes.... And it is clear that, since there were also supporters of union with Colombia, a struggle between parties was bound to follow, with all the enthusiasms and even all the excesses and scandals that appear when such discussions are translated into deeds."[1]

The governing *junta* finally agreed to make an agreement with Tomás Guido whereby it declared itself under the protection of San Martín, although its provisional constitution, and the right to join definitively either Colombia or Peru.

---

1. Quoted by Cristóbal I. Mendoza in *Temas de Historia Americana* (Caracas, 1963), p. 48.

The Colombians were hurt, because this disregarded the historical and judicial link that united Guayaquil with Colombia. But, just as the agreement arose in large measure from a reversal suffered by Luis Urdaneta in his military operations against the royalists, other military accidents—the defeat of the Argentine forces, the flight of Guido, who left the city unprotected, and, later, the arrival of Sucre with the Colombian seaborne forces—re-established the influence of Colombia. Moreover, Sucre, proceeding with the tact and gentlemanliness for which he was renowned, was able to establish friendly relations with the poet Olmedo. He also abstained from trying to pressurize the *junta* in an authoritarian fashion, and dedicated himself to strengthening the local forces, with the sound co-operation of the Colombian contingent. These efforts were rewarded with a new agreement, which replaced that which the *junta* had made with Guido, and under which the province re-accepted the protection of Colombia and authorized the Liberator to represent it "in all negotiations and treaties of alliance, peace and commerce celebrated with friendly, hostile or neutral nations."[1]

Peru was interested in possessing Guayaquil because the splendid port rounded off her northern coastline, and the rich agricultural zone in the interior of the province would provide her with products that she lacked, including wood suitable for building naval ships. To a certain extent, therefore, it was natural for people in Lima to insist that Peru's rights over Guayaquil were well-founded. Moreover, it was because of this dispute that many Peruvians began to bear a grudge against Bolívar, and later against Sucre, who felt obliged to uphold the integrity of Colombia. Peruvian aspirations were also strengthened by the influence of José de la Mar, a native of the province of Cuenca, which was next to Guayaquil. This officer served with the royalists until 1821, when, as commander of the fortress of Callao, he surrendered it to the republicans. La Mar then began to acquire importance in Peru, but since he must have feared that he would be regarded as a foreigner, his strongest desire was to acquire for Peru the southern part of the presidency of Quito. Unfortunately, as we will see, he persisted in this attitude until 1829.

The final factor strengthening the position of the Peruvians was that, when the campaign began, many of the troops with which Sucre had to defend Guayaquil and attack Quito arrived late and in deplorable state as a result of their long journey by land and sea. Sucre began by defeating the royalists at Yaguachi, but shortly afterwards he suffered, near Ambato, the only defeat of his military career. In this situation and since the republican army in Peru contained the former royalist "Numancia" battalion, which had declared for independence and was made up

---

1. Lecuna, *Crónica razonada...*, iii, p. 121.

almost entirely of Venezuelans and Granadans, Sucre repeated his request that it be sent back to Colombia. The battalion's commanders and officers also wanted this, but San Martín refused and sent in its place a brigade formed of raw Peruvian recruits and 110 Argentine veterans under the command of Colonel Andrés de Santa Cruz, a native of Upper Peru. Its arrival strengthened San Martín's influence on the disputed frontier.

Subsequently, Guayaquil never showed any inclination to join Peru, in spite of the innumerable attempts that it made to separate from Quito. This indicates that these vacillations in 1821 were produced simply by the distressing isolation of the city.

Unfortunately, General San Martín, who had been declared Protector of Peru, lost the equanimity that was one of the most frequent signs of his moral greatness. He began by stating the principle that Guayaquil was entitled to decide her own future. This principle can be very wise and just when applied to separate nationalities, but it would cause real chaos if accepted for every city and province in a continent. In America, moreover, the civil strife resulting from such a rule would have provoked instability on the frontiers as great as that within each country, and interminable intrigues and conflicts. Indeed, the subsequent injust dismemberments of Panama and northern Mexico took place when this principle was applied. Colombia could not accept such sophism, and Bolívar declared categorically to the governing *junta* in Guayaquil: "I flatter myself that the Republic of Colombia will have been proclaimed in your capital city prior to my entry. Your Excellency must know that Guayaquil is an integral part of the territory of Colombia. A province has no right to withdraw from a confederation of which it is a part. It would violate the laws of nature and of politics for any buffer state to become a battlefield for two strong states. Furthermore, I believe that Colombia will never permit any American power to hold dominion over her territory."[1] And in the same vein he told the Protector of Peru: "I do not agree with Your Excellency that the wish of a province must be consulted in order to assert its national sovereignty. It is not the parts of a nation but the whole nation that deliberates in freely and lawfully convened general assemblies. The Constitution of Colombia grants Guayaquil most adequate representation and all sections of Colombia, including Caracas the birthplace of liberty, have held themselves sufficiently honored by the full exercise of the sacred right of participating in the nation's councils."[2]

The Venezuelan determination to uphold the doctrine of *uti possidetis* whereby the new states retained their former colonial boundaries, was so sincere that in 1830, when the Granadan province of Casanare pro-

---

1. O'Leary, xix, p. 112.
2. *Cartas,* xi, p. 218.

nounced for union with Venezuela, the Venezuelan Congress refused to admit it, declaring that to violate this principle would set a lamentable example for the rest of America and would cause interminable conflicts in the future.[1]

In fact, San Martín did not respect the principle that he was proclaiming. On numerous occasions he tried to put pressure on Guayaquil to do as he wanted. When the campaign against Quito was about to begin, for example, he asked the city's governing *junta* to replace Sucre with La Mar. Olmedo replied: "The appointment of La Mar to command the division could perhaps produce a result opposite to that which we all propose. If La Mar goes to the division he will not be well received, and there could easily be pitfalls. Sucre, who has often offered him the command with or without sincerity, would take it as disrespect, and we do not know where Colombian resentment might lead. Sucre's commanders and officers think, say and act as he does. Not all the division that has come from Piura (that led by Santa Cruz) is trustworthy, for it is well known that Urdaneta has the support of the part under his command and that he will use it for his own ends, which are different from those of Peru. These reflections and those that result from them have led us to agree to suspend the application of your order until you are able to take a great, effective, powerful step, in the light of this information and the new dangers that we face. (You may know of this from the extraordinary communication that we are sending.) A meeting with you is indispensable. Bolívar has an agent here close to the government of Peru."[2]

The Urdaneta mentioned by Olmedo was the Venezuelan General Luis Urdaneta, who had great influence over the troops and throughout the region because he had been one of the authors of the liberation of Guayaquil. He commanded a battalion in the division of Santa Cruz, and his forces were the first to join those of Sucre. San Martín also wanted to replace Urdaneta with the Argentine Olazábal, who was a major in the same battalion.[3] What was all this leading to, if not to the creation of a situation of force that Bolívar would be unable to check when he reached Guayaquil? The Protector did not even stop here. Exasperated by the firm attitude of Colombia, he proposed a declaration of war to the Peruvian government. Although he finally desisted from such an absurd step, he had no scruples in attempting something else, which although less dangerous for himself, could have been fatal for the Colombians and the *guayaquileños*.

---

1. *Documentos para los Anales de Venezuela* (Caracas, 1889), p. 353. Venezuela pursued the same policy towards similar movements that developed in the Cúcuta region.
2. Camilo Destruge, *Historia de la Revolución de octubre y campaña libertadora de 1820-1822* (Guayaquil, 1920, p. 391). For San Martín's communications, see *Documentos del Archivo de San Martín* (Buenos Aires, 1910), vii, p. 433. Both are quoted by Lecuna in *Crónica razonada*, iii, p. 152.
3. Lecuna, *Crónica razonada...*, iii, p. 159.

He ordered Santa Cruz's division, on campaign with Sucre's army, to return to Guayaquil. But Sucre, who had retained his customary, imperturbable urbanity, adopted the attitude that was to be expected of a commander with his responsibilities. He warned Santa Cruz that he had the right to dispose of the auxiliary troops sent from Peru, "with the same freedom of action as the authorities in Lima had to dispose of the 'Numancia' battalion," and that he was prepared, "no matter what it might cost," to enforce his orders that they should continue to advance with him. He informed San Martín that in order to prevent similar situations in the future he had issued orders for the "Numancia" battalion to join the other Colombian forces without waiting for his permission.

The young, veteran general's action prevented a rupture. The Argentine and Peruvian units, which had apparently been destined to retreat shamefully from the enemy, won deserved glory in the splendid Pichincha campaign.

What was the "great, effective, powerful step" that Olmedo demanded of San Martín? Bolívar was then still in the north, and the Argentine general proposed a personal meeting with him. According to numerous historians, San Martín's real intention was to reach Guayaquil before Bolívar, force the city to accept incorporation into Peru, and thus present the Colombian president with a *fait accompli*.[1] Olmedo's hints seem to bear out this suspicion, especially his cautious remarks that: "A meeting with you is indispensable. Bolívar has an agent here close to the government of Peru." And there is no doubt that San Martín intended to reach Guayaquil before Bolívar and to go on to Quito to meet him. He had written to Bolívar on July 13: "I will leave the port of Callao before the 18th, and, as soon as I land in Guayaquil, I will set out to greet Your Excellency in Quito."[2]

San Martín's plans were thwarted by Bolívar's victory at Bomboná, that of Sucre at Pichincha, the reunión of the two commanders, and Bolívar's prior arrival at Guayaquil. On July 13, 1822, in response to a number of popular demonstrations in Guayaquil in favor of Colombia, Bolívar issued an edict placing the city and the province under the protection of the Republic. On July 31 Guayaquil solemnly declared for incorporation into Colombia. Olmedo himself soon became such an admirer of the Liberator that his *Canto a la Victoria de Junín* has remained one of the most fervent pieces composed to the glory of Bolívar and Colombian arms.

---

1. See in particular the fully documented work of Lecuna, *La cuestión de Guayaquil y la Campaña de Pichincha* and *Crónica razonada...*, iii, pp. 111 and following.
2. O'Leary, xix, p. 335.

San Martín later asked his aide-de-camp, Rufino Guido: "What do you think of the way the Liberator, Simón Bolívar, has tricked us?"[1] And General Bartolomé Mitre, in spite of his efforts to re-arrange the whole history of America in favor of San Martín and to the detriment of Bolívar, reached the following conclusions: "Bolívar's attitude in the Guayaquil affair was more resolute, and it was founded upon a more deliberate military and political plan. Law and might were on his side, even though the majority of the people whom he intended to annex to Colombia at all costs were not.... When these two policies collided, that which was animated with the greatest initial drive was bound to triumph. Since reason and force were also on Bolívar's side, the result was not in doubt."[2] Although Mitre was prepared only to concede that Bolívar "this time perhaps" had observed the principle of *uti possidetis,* he had to admit the importance of having kept it in force for the future relations of the Spanish American republics: "The former Viceroyalty of New Granada, of which the Presidency of Quito was a dependency, had been declared constitutionally an integral part of the Republic of Colombia, in union with the Captaincy General of Venezuela. This declaration had been accepted, with applause and without protest, by the whole American world. If the province of Guayaquil formed part of the political circumscription of Quito, it belonged to Colombia. If, on the contrary, it belonged to the Viceroyalty of Peru, it was Peruvian. This was the *de facto* and the *de jure* question. Force resolved it *de facto,* but the historical legal documents of Colombia show that it is *de jure,* so that in practice and in theory this rule has prevailed for the international relations of the Spanish American republics."[3]

The antagonism between Bolívar and San Martín, which appeared briefly at this time and then immediately disappeared, has been subsequently exaggerated by Argentine historians for two precise purpose: to transfer to San Martín the title of Liberator, which he never used but which Bolívar had had since it was solemnly conferred on him in 1813; and to establish an anachronistic hegemony over the Peruvians through San Martín. It is evident that San Martín can and should be called Liberator, like all the soldiers, commanders and civilian *próceres* who fought for the independence of America. Similarly, Bolívar could be called Protector of Peru and of all the other nations that he freed. But only San Martín deserves the formal title "Protector of Peru," and only

---

1. *La entrevista de Guayaquil,* apuntes atribuidos al general Rufino Guido. In *San Martín en la Historia y en el Bronce* (official edition, Buenos Aires, 1950). Also quoted in Lecuna, *Catálogo...,* iii, p. 593.
2. Mitre, *Historia de San Martín y de la Emancipación Sud-Americana,* iii, pp. 589 and 591.
3. *Ibid.,* iii, p. 593.

Bolívar can be called "the Liberator." The Argentine attempt to exercise influence in Peru by awakening in the Peruvians nostalgia for their vast empire and pretending that Bolívar and Sucre took it away, is now obvious nonsense to anybody with education, so they have tried to strengthen it with another invention, arguing that Bolívar's ambition prevented San Martín from completing the emancipation of America in Peru, and thus condemned this sister country to two more years of war and sacrifice. We will return to this point, because documents and events have been falsified in the attempt to promote this senseless propaganda.

But we leave it for the moment to examine the much more agreeable encounter that fate arranged for the Liberator with the enchanting woman who was to remain with him almost until the hour of his death. She was a twenty-five year old *quiteña* called Manuela Sáenz de Thorne, although she has passed into history without her husband's surname and with the diminutive of her own name by which she was habitually known: Manuelita. She was beautiful, sensual, restless, humorous, and as quick with a welcoming phrase as a biting reply. She boasted that she was "a formidable character, friend of my friends and enemy of my enemies." Her natural talent, which she came to cultivate with considerable zeal, can be seen in the following letter, written years later, in which she rejected her husband's request that she return to him: "My God, man, no, no, no and no again. Why do you make me write against my will? What do you achieve, apart from making me suffer the pain of telling you *no* a thousand times? Sir, you are an excellent, inimitable man, and I will never say anything else about you, but, my friend, to leave you for General Bolívar is something; to leave another husband without your qualities would he nothing.

"And do you believe that, after being the loved one of this general for seven years, with the security of owning his heart, I would prefer to be the wife of the Father, the Son, the Holy Ghost, or the Most Holy Trinity? If I regret anything it is that you did not give me greater cause for leaving you. I am well aware that nothing can unite me with him under the auspices of what you call honor. Do you believe me less honored because he is my lover rather than my husband? Ah! I do not live by the social preoccupations that people invent to torment each other.

"Leave me, my dear Englishman. We will agree to remarry in heaven, but not on earth. Do you regard this as a bad arrangement? Then I must tell you that you were very unhappy. We will live an angelic life in the celestial land, completely spiritual (for as a man you are tiresome). There everything will be in the English style, because the monotonous life is reserved for your nation (in romantic matters, that is, for what people are more skillful in commerce and seafaring?). The English love without pleasure, converse without grace, walk slowly, salute reverently, rise and sit down carefully, joke without laughing. These are divine proprieties, but I am a miserable mortal, who laughs at myself, at you, and at this English seriousness. Things will go badly for me in heaven! As badly as if I were living in England or Constantinople, for I believe that the English are tyrants to their wives, although you were not tyrannical towards me, simply more jealous than a Portuguese. This is not what I want. Do I lack good taste?

"Enough of jest; formally, and without laughing, with all the seriousness, truthfulness and purity of an Englishwoman, I declare that I will not return to you. That you are Anglican while I am an atheist is the strongest religious impediment. The man I love instead is greater and stronger. Do you not see how formally I am reasoning? Your constant friend - *Manuela.*"[1]

Despite her tempestuous character, Manuela was also able to spend a long time reading and dreaming. She sometimes followed the interminable marches of Bolívar through lonely, inhospitable places without feeling bored or weak. She looked after the Liberator's papers in Peru, and she served as his amanuensis on at least one occasion.[2] With unshakeable rectitude she always refused the aid offered by her rich, loving husband, even when she had to live poorly, earning her own keep, after Bolívar's death. Emil Ludwig thinks that Manuelita was "a friend with a superior mind" to the Liberator. We think that she was fitted for this role not only by her grace and ability, but also by a quality that must have brought her particularly close to her glorious lover. To quote O'Leary, "She was the most selfless being I have ever known."

She was the woman who knew to listen to the Liberator's confidences with intelligent attention. She invented flattering pleasantries to soothe him. If he was angry, she calmed him. If he was sad she enlivened him. She could share with him the coarseness of camp life or move in society like a great lady. She used to read to him, particularly at night, and she cared for him when he was ill. She was surprised at his side on the fateful night of September 25, 1828, and she confronted the would-be assassins with the courage and cold blood of the best aide-de-camp.

From its beginning in 1822, the romance between Bolívar and Manuelita had the dual aspect of rash carnal avidity and spiritual sympathy. One of her biographers, Alfonso Rumazo González, tells us: "There was never a passion of two more reckless lovers. Nor was there ever a more profound and moving ardor. Bolívar made his secretary work intensely throughout most of the hours of the day. There were letters and more letters to write:

---

1. O'Leary, *Narración,* iii, p. 377.
2. *Cartas,* iii, p. 262.

to Bogotá, Quito, Lima, Buenos Aires, Guayaquil, Panama, Cali, and everywhere else, for this whole world, which was almost as large as Europe, moved in his brain, rested in his hands, and was completely submissive to his command. Emissaries had to be sent in all directions on numerous secret missions. It was necessary to plan policy, make military plans, find the means to pay for the forthcoming Peruvian campaign, remember all the relatives and friends, resist the enemies, form and supply armies, prepare ships, find arms and ammunition and a thousand other things that his plans made essential. The wearying task could only be tackled by a general who was unaware of fatigue and who forgot nothing. And he had, thereafter, an extraordinary assistant, who taught him to be less trusting, who revealed clearly to him the duplicity of men's minds, and who told him in minute detail about this whirlpool of intrigue, grandeur and misery called Lima, viceregal Lima, whose softness had all but devoured the Protector and his soldiers. She ensured, with more devotion than his secretary, Pérez, that all business was dealt with promptly, she looked after his papers, and she began to live completely with the genius whom she loved with carnal desire and with her mind, all her mind."[1]

Bolívar wrote on one occasion, analyzing his own character: "I feel that the energy of my soul rises and expands, and always matches the magnitude of the danger. My doctor tells me that my mind has to feed on danger for me to retain my judgement, as though God, when he made me, allowed this tempestuous revolution so that I could fulfill my special destiny." When he reached the zenith of his glory and his responsibilities, destiny also provided him with this woman, who, driven by the same vital exuberance, at one and the same time devoured him and multiplied his strength.

---

1. Alfonso Rumazo González, *Manuela Sáenz, la libertadora del Libertador* (Buenos Aires 1945), p. 137.

XXVIII

I DO NOTHING
BUT THINK
AND DREAM

As WE HAVE SEEN, BOLIvar reached Guayaquil before San Martín. He had the pleasure, therefore, of welcoming him to the city, which had already been reincorporated to the territory of Colombia. The Liberator arranged, among other courtesies, for the beautiful *guayaquileña,* Carmen Calderón Garaicoa, to present a laurel crown of enameled gold to the Protector of Peru.[1] In addition to her beauty, Carmen Calderón Garaicoa was famous for the sacrifice that her family had made for the republican cause. Her father, Francisco Calderón, had been shot by the royalists at the beginning of the revolution. Her brother, the young Abdón Calderón, won "special glory" at Pichincha, according to the official account of the battle, for, to quote Sucre, "although he was wounded four times in succession, he never tried to withdraw from the fighting."[2] We will also see later that one of Carmen's aunts, the equally enchanting Joaquina Garaicoa, fell in love with the Liberator and, in his last, sad days, gave the hero moving proof of her loyalty and affection.

Immediately after the first ceremonies that Bolívar had prepared for San Martín and the formal visits that they made to each other, the two liberators had their celebrated meeting which, because of its secrecy, has given rise to so many fantasies.

---

1. Carmen Calderón herself related this to the Chilean historian Vicuña Mackenna. Mentioned by Julio César Chávez, *San Martín y Bolívar en Guayaquil* (Buenos Aires, 1950), p. 140, and Lecuna, *Catálogo...,* iii, p. 286.
2. O'Leary, xix, p. 292.

Our conclusion is that it was completely without importance. First, because the most important, although unstated, purpose of it, the future of Guayaquil, had already been resolved. Second, because the brevity of their discussions, and neither San Martín nor Bolívar sought to prolong them, gave them time only to exchange very general ideas on the numerous problems of America. Third, because neither the Liberator nor the Protector had authority to embark on or conclude any agreement. Fourth, because San Martín was well aware that he was powerless. Peru had reacted against him, and Argentina, divided by factional strife, could offer him nothing. His authority and his prestige had disappeared in both countries.

All this is so certain that the documents provided by the Argentine historians themselves suffice to prove it. We will begin with one of the accounts most hostile to the Liberator, that of General Rufino Guido, taken from the official Argentine edition.

Guido describes events as follows: "The ship sailed on with favorable wind and tide, and it anchored in the port at noon on the following day. Almost immediately two more of General Bolívar's aides arrived to congratulate the general again, and to tell him that the Liberator wished to see him as soon as possible. Since we had been ready to land since we first saw the city, we then went onto the quay. A battalion of infantry was drawn up between this spot and the house in which we were to stay, and it did the general the honors due to his high rank and position. When we entered the house we found at the foot of the staircase the Liberator Bolívar, in a grand uniform and surrounded by his staff. Bolívar advanced towards the general as soon as he saw him and, offering his hand, said "My desire to meet and shake hands with the renowned General San Martín has finally been fulfilled." The general replied, thanking him for such a cordial sentiment, but without accepting the Liberator's praises, and they went up the stairs, followed by everybody else, to a large room which had been prepared for the reception. Presently, the company began to arrive to congratulate General San Martín, and they were followed by the ladies of Guayaquil, whose purpose was the same. This manifestation greatly displeased the Liberator, for it had not been done for him, and his discomfort and jealousy was immediately increased by what followed. When one of the leading ladies who had organized the gathering had finished congratulating the general, and he had replied in full with the majesty and martial bearing that so distinguished him, all was silent. The ladies did not leave, and suddenly a young lady, aged sixteen or eighteen, as pretty as an angel, rose, arms outstretched, and went towards the general, who was in the middle of the room alongside the Liberator. After delivering an address full of enthusiastic praise, she placed an enameled laurel crown on his head. This unexpected demonstration offended the general's natural modesty and, blushing and removing the crown from his head, he told the young lady that he did not deserve it. He said that there were others more deserving than himself, but he was unable to reject such a worthy present, because of the hands that gave it to him and because of the patriotic sentiment that had inspired the gesture. He added that he would keep it forever, as a souvenir of one of his happiest days. After this singular event, the ladies departed. When the Liberator's commanders and officers, and we, the general's two aides-de-camp, had also left, the two generals remained alone for an hour and a half behind locked doors, until the Liberator left for his lodgings, accompanied by his aides, who had been waiting in our rooms along the corridor.

"For those of us who saw it, the notable, and quite notable, thing about the scene with the crown was the different impression that it had on the appearance of these great men. The one who received such a deserved honor was as red as a carmine, while the other, pale and ashen like a corpse, could not hide his indignation at seeing himself less honored and thanked by those great people, who showed their enthusiasm for General San Martín with cheers and acclamations from the moment that he land- ed, and throughout the two days that we remained there. At times the guard of honor at our door had to clear away the enormous crowd that assembled beneath our balcony to see and cheer the general. All this griev- ed General Bolívar, who, because of his proud, overbearing character, could not suffer even an equal, let alone a superior, as General San Martín was.

"But we return to our narrative. After the Liberator left, the general received some visitors, and before dining in the same house, we accom- panied the general to the Liberator's lodgings, where we stayed for half an hour before returning. There were more visitors, including some ladies, during the evening. The following day we returned to the Liberator's house at one in the afternoon, after first arranging our luggage and order- ing that it be taken on board the schooner at eleven o'clock at night. The general had ordered that we should leave that night at the end of the ball to which we were invited. As soon as they were together, the two men locked themselves away until five, when they emerged to sit at a large table prepared for the purpose, with some generals and various commanders of the Colombian army. There were about fifty of us at this sumptuous banquet. The meal was splendid and went on until seven o'clock, with Bolívar at the head of the table and General San Martín on his right. The Liberator began the toasts, standing up with his glass in his hand and inviting us to do the same, as he said: *"To the two greatest men in South America, General San Martín and myself."* General San Martín modest as always, toasted: *"To the prompt end of the war, to the organi- zation of the different Republics of the Continent, and to the health of the*

Liberator." Two or three more toasts were offered by the generals who were present, and we rose from the table. At nine the same evening we went to the ball to which we were invited. The gathering was made brilliant by the number, beauty and elegance of the ladies and the luxury of the salon, which was perfectly lit and decorated. Most of the men present were commanders and officers from the Colombian army and the staff of the Liberator. . . . Our general, who displayed the moderation and decency always possessed by those of good birth even in family gatherings and in the confidence of friendship, was not made more comfortable when he found himself in such a labyrinth. He decided to leave discreetly. He approached me and said: 'Tell Soyer for me that we are going; I cannot stand this bustle.' It was one in the morning when we left the ball without the general bidding farewell to even the Liberator, and nobody noticed our departure. Perhaps they had arranged it this way, so as not to disturb the gaiety of the gathering, for one of his aides took us through a private door and stayed with us until we embarked. Once we were on board the schooner, we weighed anchor and set sail, all glad to be leaving those people who, apart from their deeds and their constancy in the war against the Spaniards, seemed to glory in rudeness and pride. The general arose the next day looking very worried and, as we were strolling on the deck after lunch, he said to me: 'What do you think of the way the Liberator, Simón Bolívar, has tricked us? But I am confident that he will not be able to keep Guayaquil, to add it to Colombia, when the mass of the people want to be annexed to Peru. It will take place voluntarily or by force, as soon as we have finished with the Spaniards who are still in the *sierra*. You have seen the joy and enthusiasm of these people and the victors towards Peru and towards my person.' In fact, these spontaneous demonstrations from all these people so humiliated the Liberator that, from that day, he began to feel jealous of the general. These, then, were the ideas and intentions of our general when we left Guayaquil, and he was so preoccupied with them that the conversation often turned to this same subject. But we reached Callao, and all his plans fell to the ground. The news that he received when we arrived of the revolution against his prime minister, Monteagudo, and, above all, of the connivance of his leading commanders, who should have suppressed it, upset him so much that all of us saw from his face the profound impression that the ingratitude of his principal commanders had made upon his magnaminous and generous heart. Persuaded by this mistake, for such it was, he then thought only of leaving his post to another more fortunate than himself, as Bolívar was, and it was he who had the glory of ending the war in which we were engaged. I say that the general was mistaken to think that he had been betrayed by all his commanders because, with the exception of a few, the others would have sacrificed themselves for him, and they would also have shot the best of their colleagues, if he had ordered it."[1]

The first thing that we notice in this narrative is that Bolívar is referred to on numerous occasions as the *Liberator*. It is the same with the other documents of the period. Why, then, this subsequent Argentine mania to transfer the title to General San Martín?

It is even more interesting to see that San Martín was ready, before the meeting, to embark "that night, at the end of the ball." Why? In addition to his graceful and affectionate reception, which Guido was at pains to attribute solely to the inhabitants of Guayaquil, it seems that he could count on the Peruvian squadron that he had sent to Guayaquil when he had still thought that he could use it to incline the will of the city towards Peru. Why, then, did he suddenly become so peevish and fretful? Obviously, because he had realized that there was nothing for him to do there.

Soon afterwards, according to the same witness, he discovered that he could no longer count either on Peru or on his own forces, "and he then thought only of leaving his post to another more fortunate than himself."

A victim of his own character, overly inclined to self-denial and depression, who was ready to continue the struggle with all the fervor of his temperament, and with the support of the invincible Colombian forces. Bolívar and about to be abandoned by all, San Martín could not work with Bolívar, had grown accustomed in Venezuela to dominating *caudillos* of the stamp of Ribas, Piar, Páez, and Mariño, and to holding doctrinal discussions with men like Santander, Tovar, Palacio Fajardo, Roscio and Urbaneja, who combined talent with the most zealous republican rectitude. He was then so much at the height of his powers that he was capable of promoting his cherished idea for a Spanish American Confederation, and planning how to join the Atlantic and the Pacific by means of the Atrato and San Juan rivers, in the very midst of the difficult Bomboná campaign. Nobody could have been less like the modest general, the blushing San Martín, described for us by Guido. Even before the meeting began, its outcome could be foreseen.

The report of the meeting that Bolívar sent to Santander on July 29, 1822, is completely different from that of Guido, both in form and in the sentiments attributed to the two great participants. But it does confirm the main conclusion that we have reached on the basis of the Argentinian's notes: that, in fact, the two liberators had nothing more than a friendly conversation, which did not even remotely resemble an important discussion about continental problems. Bolívar's letter said the following:

---

1. Narración del General Rufino Guido. Quoted by Lecuna in *Catálogo...*, ii, p. 184.

"My dear general: General San Martín left here the day before yesterday during the night, following a visit of from thirty-six to forty hours. It was, in effect, a visit and nothing more, as we did nothing except exchange compliments, talk and say good-bye. I believe that he came in order to assure himself of our friendship and to make use of it as a defense against his enemies, both at home and abroad. With him went 1,800 Colombian troops in addition to those already received. These will replace his losses, which for the second time, have cost us more than 600 men. Peru will thus have received at least 3,000 reinforcements.

"The Protector assured me of his eternal friendship for Colombia. He promised to intervene in favor of the boundary settlement; not to interfere in the affairs of Guayaquil; and to favor a complete and absolute federation, even if only with Colombia, with Guayaquil as the seat of the congress. He has agreed to send a delegate from Peru to co-operate with us in negotiating with the envoys from Spain. He has also approved Mosquera's mission to Chile and Buenos Aires, recommending that they agree to a federation. He wants our countries to have interchangeable garrisons. In effect, he would have everything work toward union, for without it he knows that there can be neither order nor tranquillity. I would say that he does not want to be king, but neither does he favor democracy. He would like to have some prince brought over from Europe to rule Peru. The latter I believe to be only for form's sake. He said that he would retire to Mendoza, as he was sick of holding the supreme command and of being a target for his enemies.

"He did not mention any special purpose in coming, and he made no demands of Colombia. The troops that went with him had already been detailed for this mission. The one thing that he emphasized was the interchange of garrisons; and, on the personal side, there was no expression of friendship and support that he did not make to me. He impresses me as being very military in character, and he appears to be energetic, quick, and by no means dull. He has the type of correct ideas that would please you; but he did not strike me as being subtle enough to rise to the sublime, whether in the realm of ideas or practical matters. You will soon learn of his character, however, from the report of our conversations that I am sending with Captain Gómez, although it lacks the comments I should have made on each one of his sentences.

"The electoral *junta* of this province today will take up the matter of joining Colombia. I believe that they will vote affirmatively but will claim numerous benefits and privileges. As I hold the executive power in this area, I shall exercise it over the province, allowing the sovereign congress, however, freedom to express its sovereign will, thereby not endangering its sovereign power. This is a case where the division of powers and the scholastic theory that the minority should yield to the majority will be of some

"Bolívar on the Chimborazo" by Tito Salas.

help to me. Our success in harmonizing opinions is due in no small part to the visit of San Martín, who treated the supporters of independence with disdain. This is what I call taking advantage of every turn. This praise is not meant for me but for he who knows when to flatter, even though it be wise. The *Prueba* and the *Venganza* would not be in Peru today but for the policy of San Martín. But more cannot be expected from these simpletons, and so now he places the blame on them.

"Thank God, my dear general, that by great good fortune and with much glory I have achieved some very important things: first, the liberation of the south; second, the unification of Colombia, Guayaquil, Quito, and the other provinces; third, the friendship for Colombia of San Martín and Peru; and fourth, the departure of the allied troops who will earn us glory and gratitude in Peru and those parts. Everyone is grateful, for I have served everyone. We have the respect of all, for I have yielded to no one. The departing Spaniards themselves are filled with respect and gratitude for Colombia. There is now nothing more for me to do, dear friend, except to store away the treasure of my success, concealing it in some secluded spot where no one can take it from me. I simply mean that all remains for me to do is to retire and die. I swear to God that I want nothing else. For the first time in my life I have nothing left to wish for, and I am satisfied with everything. Colonel Lara is in command of those corps which are en route, and general Valdés will follow him —which is all I have to inform you on this occasion. Very affectionately yours—, *Bolívar*."[1]

There also exist two other official reports of the Guayaquil conference, both signed by José Gabriel Pérez, the Liberator's secretary, and sent to the government of Colombia and to General Sucre, who was then intendant of the department of Quito.[2] Essentially, they confirm Bolívar's account, although his is more spontaneous and, since it was written as a private letter, there can be no suspicion that it was embellished for political ends.

Pérez's official report to the government, however, does reveal some concrete points that he identifies as the object of the conversations between the two liberators. Historians have agreed to accept them as such, although Pérez, with almost as much malice as Guido, depicts San Martín "posing vague and unrelated questions regarding military and political matters, not going deeply into any of them, but passing from one to another, mingling the serious and the trivial indiscriminately." He also

---

1. *Cartas,* iii, p. 58.
2. See Lecuna, *Catálogo...,* iii, pp. 186 and 190. The original of the first is in the Archivo del Ministerio de Relaciones Exteriores de Colombia, and that of the second in the Archivo y Museo Central de Quito.

reports: "Having reached the house, the Protector, in asking His Excellency if he was not disgusted with the tangled affairs of Guayaquil, used another coarse and vulgar expression, *pellejerías,* which presumably means trickery."

According to Pérez, the meeting went as follows. On Guayaquil the Protector said that he no longer had any reason to concern himself with it. On the form of government suitable for the American states, San Martín was inclined towards monarchy, and he definitely proposed to offer the crown of Peru to some European prince. Bolívar was completely opposed to this idea, and he stood by the constitutional principles laid down in the Angostura address. On the question of the Spanish American federation, San Martín enthusiastically accepted the ideas of the Liberator and felt "that the government of Chile will have no objection to joining it, but that Buenos Aires cannot join it because of the lack of unity in that country. Above all, nothing was closer to the Protector's heart than the permanent federation of Peru and Colombia, even though no other state should join." The question of boundaries between Peru and Colombia did not cause any disagreement, since neither San Martín nor Bolívar was authorized to resolve it. Pérez added: "Moreover, as the Protector had come merely as a visitor without any object, military or political, and since he did not speak officially even of the troops that Colombia had offered and which he knew were being made ready for departure, His Excellency would have offended, without affording any compensating advantage, if he had shown interest in any then; for the Protector was not at liberty to commit himself in any way." San Martín also approved a proposal made a few days earlier by the Liberator "that the deputies of Colombia, Peru and Chile should be convened at a given point to treat with the Spanish envoys that are coming to Peru for that purpose." They simply exchanged insignificant opinions on other continental matters.

However, despite all this testimony, another interpretation of the meeting made its appearance twenty-two years later, based upon an alleged letter from San Martín to Bolívar, of which neither the original not draft has appeared, but which was published in 1844 by a Frenchman called Lafond.[1] It is because the Argentine historians have striven to inflate and embellish this interpretation that we have had to give such a long, detailed account of what actually happened. The document reads as follows: "Lima, August 29, 1822—Most Excellent Sir, Liberator of Colombia, Simón Bolívar—Dear General: I told you in my last letter, of the 23rd of

---

1. G. Lafond, *Voyages autour du monde et naufrages célebres. Voyages dans les Amériques* (Paris, 1844), ii, p. 136. Reproduced by Bartolomé Mitre in *Historia de San Martín y de la Emancipación Sudamericana,* iv, p. 615; and discussed by Lecuna in *Crónica razonada...,* iii, p. 212.

this month, that I was not able to write to you as fully as I wished, because I had reassumed the supreme command of this republic, for the purpose of removing from it the weak and inept Torre Tagle, and I was thus very busy. I will now make good the omission, not only with the frankness of my character, but also with that demanded by the important interests of America. —The results of our meeting have not been those that you promised for the prompt termination of the war. I regret to say that I am quite convinced either that you did not regard my offer to serve under your orders with my forces as sincere, or that my presence embarrassed you. The reasons that you suggest—that your scrupulousness would never permit you to command me, and that, even if this difficulty could be overcome, the Congress of Colombia would never agree to your leaving the Republic—I must say, General, if you permit me, have not seemed plausible to me. The first contradicts itself. As for the second, I strongly believe that the slightest declaration from you would be unanimously approved by Congress, when it is directed towards ending the war in which we are involved, with your co-operation and that of the army under your command. The high honor of ending it would rebound to your credit as much as to that of the republic over which you preside—Do not deceive yourself, General. The news that you have about the royalist forces is mistaken; they amount in Upper and Lower Peru to 19,000 veterans, who can be assembled in the space of two months. The patriot army, decimated by disease, coul put only 8,500 men, many of them raw recruits, into battle. The division of General Santa Cruz (whose losses, according to what the general writes, have not been made good, despite his complaints) will suffer a considerable loss in its long march overland, and will be of no use in the present campaign. The division of 1,400 Colombians that you are sending will be needed to garrison Callao, and to keep order in Lima. Consequently, without the aid of the army of your command, the operation being prepared through the intermediate ports will not be able to secure the advantages that should be expected, for there will be no powerful forces to distract the attention of the enemy elsewhere. Thus, the struggle will be prolonged indefinitely. I say indefinitely because I am quite convinced that, whatever the vicissitudes of the present war, the independence of America is irrevocable. But I am also convinced that its prolongation will cause the ruin of her peoples, and it is a sacred duty for the men who are entrusted with their destiny to prevent the continuation of such great evils.—Lastly, General, my decision has been taken irrevocably. I have convoked the First Congress of Peru for the 20th of next month, and the day after its installation I will leave for Chile, convinced that my presence is the only obstacle that prevents you from coming to Peru with the army of your command. For me, it would have been the crowning glory to end the war of independence under the orders of a general to whom America owes her freedom. But fate dictates otherwise, and it has to be accepted.—I have no doubt that, when I have left Peru, the government that is established will appeal for the active support of Colombia, and that you will be unable to resist such a just request. I will send, therefore, a note on all the commanders of whose private and military conduct it might be useful for you to have some knowledge. General Arenales will remain in command of the Argentine forces. I am sure that he deserves all consideration from you, because of his honor, courage and experience. —I will say nothing to you about the reunion of Guayaquil with the Republic of Colombia. Permit me, General, to tell you that I believe that it was not for us to decide this important matter. When the war has ended, the respective governments would have settled it, without the difficulties which might now follow for the interests of the new states of South America. General, I have spoken to you with frankness, but the sentiments expressed in this letter will remain buried in the most profound silence. If they were made known, the enemies of our freedom could make use of them to prejudice it, and the intriguers could use them to foment discord. —Commander Delgado, who bears this letter, also has a gun and a pair of pistols for you, as well as the horse that I offered you in Guayaquil. Accept this memorial, General, from the first of your admirers. —With these sentiments, and the wish that you alone will have the glory of ending the war of the independence of South America, I remain your most affectionate servant. - *José de San Martín.*"

The new factor that this letter introduces to reports of the celebrated meeting is San Martín's alleged offer to serve in Peru with the forces that he commanded under the orders of the Liberator. The Argentine commentators have deduced from this that the Protector's extraordinary demonstration of selflessness was frustrated by the excessive ambition of Bolívar, who was responsible, therefore, both for San Martín's withdrawal from public life and for Peru's having to suffer two more years of warfare. The historians of the Bolivarian countries, in their turn, tend to regard the Lafond letter as apocryphal and, in fact, numerous works seem to prove that it is an indefensible invention.[1]

In any case, if this letter is accepted as genuine, it does San Martín very little credit, while it in no way tarnishes the glory of the Liberator. The reason is that San Martín's supposed offer to subordinate himself and his forces to the Liberator could only be regarded, after a most elementary analysis, as either unacceptable nonsense or a very low trick. What right, in effect, did the Protector have, as the person invested with absolute

---

1. Apart from the already mentioned studies by Lecuna, we regard as conclusive the detailed and accurate attitude of Dr. Cristóbal L. Mendoza in a report to the Academia Nacional de la Historia of Venezuela. Published in *Temas de Historia Americana* (Caracas, 1963), p. 34.

political and military power by the Peruvian nation, and as commander of an army which included Argentinians, Chileans and Peruvians, to place all this at the disposal of Bolívar in a simple meeting which did not even have an official character?

What would today's Argentinians, who strive to make San Martín the equal of Bolívar, have to say if their hero had taken office, sincerely and without any embarrassment, at the head of an army of undisciplined troops, as a subordinate of the President of Colombia; and Bolívar, as Commander-in-Chief and with the support of the whole Colombian army, had become the Liberator of Peru? Does it not show a real lack of respect to imagine San Martín receiving from Bolívar the orders that a commander must give to his subordinates? Could San Martín, who until then had exercised supreme power in Peru, become a military subordinate, ready to accept in silence the political direction that Bolívar would give to the State that had been placed under his protection? Was San Martín incapable of foreseeing the dissensions that such a situation would have provoked among the Peruvians and in the army itself?

Bolívar, of course, could have responded to San Martín's offer with one even more generous and prudent, by offering to stand aside and hand over the Colombian contingents to the Protector. But, if San Martín hoped to provoke such a reaction, he was being insincere. Moreover, the enormous disparity between the two sides, as indicated by Lafond —19,000 Spanish veterans against 8,500 patriots, most of them new recruits and many of them Colombians— made it impossible. Reinforcements, no matter how numerous, would be inadequate to deal with either the military situation in Peru or the political intrigues and defections that destroyed San Martín. Rather, it was indispensible to commit all the power and prestige of Colombia to a supreme effort, and this could only be done, despite the initial reservations of the Colombian Congress, under the personal control of Bolívar.

If Peru was so weak and San Martín was incapable of either raising new troops there or obtaining reinforcements from Argentine and Chile, the only proof of genuine selflessness that he could give was to leave Peru, rather than complicate the country's military and political situation by trying to remain as Bolívar's subordinate. This he did in a dignified fashion. Why do the Argentinians strive to regard Lafond's senseless or indecorous invention as authentic, with the sole object of attributing to San Martín selflessness that nobody denies him? And if they admit, on the basis of the testimony of San Martín himself, that he left Peru in such a desperate situation, why do they also toil to regard him as the country's liberator?

When San Martín left Peru, in the month of September, he declared in his farewell proclamation to the Peruvians, and in other public documents, that he was retiring from public life because he was "tired of hearing that he wished to be crowned or to be called tyrant." He also mentioned in the *Instrucciones* left for General Alvarado, "the seriousness of the wrongs that he suffered which did not allow him to retain the command of the army any longer."[1]

On August 25, 1822, a month after the Guayaquil meeting, San Martín had said the same thing in a private letter to O'Higgins, telling him: "You will reprimand me for not finishing the work I have begun. Your attitude is very reasonable, but mine is more so. I am tired of their calling me tyrant, saying that I desire to be king, emperor, and even devil. Another consideration is that my health has deteriorated a lot; the temperature of this country is leading me to the grave. I have sacrificed my youth in the service of the Spaniards and my middle years in that of my country. I believe that I have the right to dispose of my old age."[2]

We thus see San Martín, with the clear mind and steady gait of the veteran, renouncing that which was beyond his grasp. Is it not an injustice to him to argue that he left Peru because Bolívar was unwilling to accept him as his subordinate?

San Martín's aversion to public life was so intense that, although he lived another twenty-eight years, for most of which his country was subjected to anarchy and then to the ferocious tyranny of Rosas, the Argentine liberator never sought to leave the retirement in Europe that he had chosen for himself. Bolívar's concept of his mission was completely different. Apart from being the indefatigable *smith* who for ten years had desperately led three nations in a war of daily combat, and who had finally forged them into the most powerful State in South America, Bolívar always believed that the liberators would face their most arduous task when the armed struggle came to an end. They would then have to organize the countries that they had separated from Spain, and legitimize this separation by creating a political order that would make them respectable and prosperous. He saw the emancipation not as a final objective, but as a point of departure for the social, cultural and moral conquests that had to justify it. It was for this reason that he used to say that he feared peace more than war. He felt that those who had led these nations in their revolution were also responsible for their future.

At the risk of making myself baroque by accumulating quotations on the same theme, I must also use another, which refers to the same sense of responsibility, but seen as a personal problem: "Bolívar knows that he cannot *be* more than he is, but that he can *do* more than he has done,"

1. *Archivo de San Martín*, viii, p. 110.
2. Mitre, *op. cit.*, iii, p. 158. Also quoted by Francisco Rivas Vicuña in *La democracia colombiana y la Conferencia de Guayaquil*, Boletín de la Academia Nacional de la Historia (Caracas), no. 73, p. 136.

said Simón Rodríguez. It is impossible to find a more accurate, penetrating definition of the feelings of a man enslaved to his work. Only a very frivolous or a very petty person could confuse this ideal with the vulgar cupidity usually called ambition.

However, political passions were so extreme at the time, and they have so clouded subsequent historical judgement, that a letter supposedly written by Bolívar to Joaquín Mosquera has passed into history as "the letter of the cleared field." Many historians still use it as though it were authentic, even though Mosquera himself angrily dismissed it as apocryphal and a forgery. In this "document" the following instructions concerning Peru are attributed to the Liberator: "It is necessary to work, because nothing can be established in the country, and the safest method is to divide everyone. Sucre's decision to appoint Torre Tagle, while bringing Riva Agüero and the deputies together, and offering him the aid of the Colombian division so that he can dissolve Congress, is excellent. It is essential that not even an imitation government should exist, and this can be achieved by multiplying the number of leaders and setting them against each other. When I arrive, Peru must be a cleared field, so that I can do there whatever is desirable." As noted, Mosquera himself solemnly repudiated this document in 1852, when he had the following statement published in *El Pasatiempo* of Popayán: "Before giving my opinions, I declare on my word of honor that I did not receive such a letter; that this is the first time I have heard of it and its contents; that I consider it apocryphal and a malicious forgery, and that nobody could authenticate it."[1]

The Liberator waited at the doors of Peru for a year after San Martín's resignation. The main reason was that the Peruvians did not decide to summon him and, when they finally did so, Bolívar had to await the corresponding authorization of the Colombian Congress. We might suppose that this year was one of repose for the hero in the arms of Manuelita, when he could enjoy the hospitality of this part of Ecuador, which was one of the most beautiful regions in the world and one of the most loyal to republicanism and to the person of the Liberator. In fact, it was a year of ceaseless activity and constant worry. A brief survey of the journeys that he had to undertake and of the affairs with which he had to deal in these twelve months will be sufficient to amaze us.

Bolívar was particularly anxious to deal with the organization of the forces to be sent to Peru, to keep an eye upon the dangerous situation there, and to organize the provinces of Loja, Cuenca and Guayaquil, where he expected to remain. On September 1, 1822, just over a month after the Guayaquil meeting, he left for Cuenca. At the beginning of October he moved on to

---

1. Lecuna, *Catálogo...*, i, p. 56.

Loja and returned to Cuenca at the end the month. On December 31 he was in Tulcán, where he congratulated the Congress of Colombia on its installation. It seems that on one of these journeys he climbed Chimborazo and that, shortly afterwards, he wrote the poetic fantasy entitled *My Rapture on Chimborazo*.[1]

He was summoned to the north by another uprising in Pasto, and, after crossing all the territory of modern Ecuador and southern New Granada, he reached the city on January 23. Almost immediately, however, at the end of the month, he had to return to Guayaquil, because the Colombian troops sent to Peru had been returned by the Peruvian government, and they were living in deplorable conditions in the most unhealthy part of the coast. The torrential rains that had begun to fall intensified the sufferings of this semi-abandoned army, and aggravated the diseases that were decimating it. They would also have prevented a less courageous commander than Bolívar from hurrying across hundreds of kilometers of rough trails to join his men. Shortly afterwards Pasto again revolted, and this time its indomitable guerrillas managed to defeat the veteran republican colonel, Juan José Flores, and to seize control of all the surrounding area. They then began to move south, with the hope of taking the city of Quito itself. The Liberator advanced to meet the rebels, and took them by surprise in the city of Ibarra, which they had already captured. He fought in this action with his staff and with an escort of lancers, which had moved forward with the army, and he personally pursued the enemy until they were routed and destroyed. This was on July 17, 1823.

Since the middle of May the Peruvian Congress had been formally summoning for him. Peru was in a desperate situation because of civil dissensions, the treachery of important political and military leaders, and two successive defeats suffered by the patriot forces. Bolívar, who had foreseen all this, was again obliged with his customary haste and anguish, to take the long road from the south of New Granada to the Peruvian frontiers. In Quito he received the third delegation sent by the Peruvians to request that he come to their rescue. The Colombian Congress's permission for him to embark on the campaign arrived on August 2. The same day in Guayaquil he met an aide-de-camp of the Marquis de Torre Tagle, President of Peru, who brought him new appeals for assistance. On the 7th he went on board the brigantine *Chimborazo*. At last

1. The original has not been found, and it is not possible to prove the authenticity of the text from the oldest copies, dated Loja, October 13, 1822. But very reliable critics, including Vicente Lecuna, Angel Grisanti, Pedro Grases and Eduardo Crema in Venezuela—have no doubt that the *Rapture* was written by Bolívar. Lecuna, however, believes that he did not really climb the mountain, while Grisanti not only accepts that he did but also cites many details of the ascent. Other authors regard the *Rapture* as a forgery, written, without much success, in the Bolivarian style.

he was being given the opportunity to realize the goal of his whole military career: To destroy the final remains of Spanish dominion in the very heart of America.

But we would be omitting something even more amazing if we failed to add to this account of what might be called the Liberator's physical activity during this year some consideration of the continental problems that, to use his own phrase, made him "day and night do nothing but think and dream." O'Leary, who accompanied him on this campaign, tells us: "The night before the action at Ibarra, after giving his orders for the following day's advance, he dictated to his clerk one of the best and most eloquent articles that he composed in his life, on the American confederation." We have already seen that on July 6, 1822, before his meeting with San Martín, his plenipotentiaries had celebrated with the Lima government an offensive and defensive treaty of alliance, which made provision for the dispatch of troops from one country to the other when it was necessary. On October 21, 1822, a treaty of union, alliance and confederation was signed with Chile. On March 8 and October 3, 1823, similar agreements, although less comprehensive, were reached with Buenos Aires and Mexico.

At the same time serious news was arriving from Venezuela. General Morillo had pointed out to the court of Madrid that this country was "military America." It was feared, because of this attitude and because of the region's proximity to Spain and to her possessions in the Antilles, that any attempt to reconquer the American continent would be directed initially against Venezuela. Moreover, the Spaniards still held the fortified base of Puerto Cabello, and shortly after the battle of Carabobo, renewed fighting had broken out in the provinces of Coro and Maracaibo. The local republican forces were defeated in several encounters with royalist guerrillas and groups of regulars who had not surrendered, and General Morales—the feared second-in-command of Boves, who had scourged Venezuela since 1814, and whose skill and activity made him seem a Venezuelan *caudillo*—boldly advanced as far as Mérida and Trujillo, after defeating General Carlos Soublette, who had been left in Venezuela to direct the war. The Liberator, then, must have thought very seriously about whether his repeated requests to New Granada and Venezuela for troops to fight in Peru were too bold, and whether his first obligation was not to go in person to the defense of his native land, that "birthplace of the revolution" that he loved so much.

Even before he had dealt with this threat to the very existence of free America, the groups of political theorists and sectarians in Colombia began, unfortunately, to pursue their separate causes. Bolívar had referred to them as an eruption of federalists, unitarians, dictatorials, *pardócratas,* pure republicans, hostile royalists, well-meaning Jacobins like Martín Tovar, and ill-bred intriguers like Rafael Diego Mérida. It was said that they were united only in their intention to destroy the Republic. Even Caracas demanded the revision of the 1821 Constitution, on the pretext that the royalist occupation of the city had prevented it from sending representatives to the Congress that approved it. This argument was untenable, particularly in the mouths of the *caraqueños,* who on April 19, 1810, and on many occasions before and after that date, had claimed to represent the whole of Venezuela and to decide its fate. Bolívar rejected the pretensions of this group and, since the Constitution itself laid down that it could not be altered within ten years of its promulgation, he stated categorically to Vice-President Santander: "This Constitution is inalterable for ten years and, I say, could remain so for an entire generation, for a generation might make itself responsible for its survival.... I declare, for my part, that, bound by an oath to this code, I am not obliged to obey any law that violates and weakens it; that my resolution is to leave Colombia rather than recognize laws that destroy the marvelous work of the Liberating Army."[1]

He was also alarmed at the very same time by news from the other end of the continent, from the Río de la Plata. According to his letter to Bernardo Monteagudo, the government in Buenos Aires had presented "a new plan of confederation which had been received from Lisbon. This plan proposes to convene a congress of plenipotentiaries at Washington for the purpose of organizing an armed confederation against the Holy Alliance, to consist of Spain, Portugal, Greece, the United States, Mexico, Colombia, Haiti, Buenos Aires, Chile and Peru." Bolívar saw the danger in this cunning proposal, and he warned Monteagudo: "After England places herself at the head of such a league, we shall be her humble servants. In making a pact with the strong, the weak assume an eternal obligation. All things considered, we shall have guardians during our youth, masters during our maturity, and freedom in our old age."[2]

Solicited in this way from all parts of the continent, which had still not been liberated and which was now threatened by the tricks of other colonial powers and by the problems of reorganization that were to convulse it for more than a century, Bolívar still thought that the danger in Peru was the most urgent and immediate. He wrote to Santander: "You repeat to me that we should give preference to our own house, before taking care of anybody else's. This does not merit a reply, because the enemy is not another's house but very much our own."

The Peruvians, however, were the most obstinate in refusing to admit the urgency of the aid for which the Liberator was risking his glory and his

---

1. O'Leary, *Narración* (1952 edition), ii, p. 183.
2. *Cartas,* iii, p. 225.

honor. We will examine their reasons later. Some of them were very respectable; others very human or, to be more precise, mistaken and petty. In any case, this year, which might have been one of indolence for Bolívar after all that he had achieved and because of his new romance, or one of wrath and dismay, because of the numerous obstacles that he was still finding all around, was instead, one of extraordinary activity, and it began the culmination of his success.

When he finally embarked for Peru, on August 7, 1823, one of his companions commented: "Today is the anniversary of Boyacá, a good omen for the coming campaign." Perhaps the prophet was his incomparable aide-de-camp and faithful chronicler, O'Leary, by whom we are given the information.

XXIX

TRIUMPH!

ALMOST IMMEDIATELY after the Guayaquil meeting, Bolívar, worried about the fate of Peru, hurriedly offered new contingents of Colombian troops to the Peruvian government. His secretary wrote to it as follows: "Although His Excellency the Protector of Peru, in his interview with the Liberator, did not express any fear respecting the fate of Peru, the Liberator, nevertheless, has since given considerable and deep thought to that country, arriving at numerous conjectures which, although perhaps lacking in fact, have caused him the greatest anxiety. The Liberator has felt it his duty to communicate his fears to the government of Peru and Chile, and also to the government of the Río de la Plata, and to place the services of Colombia at the immediate disposal of Peru.

"As soon as he receives a reply to this note, His Excellency intends to send 4,000 men to Peru in addition to those who have already been sent, assuming that the government of Peru will see fit to accept his offer of these new reinforcements. These troops cannot march immediately because they are not ready, nor have they been requested by His Excellency, the Protector."

Faithful to the Bolivarian proposal that this last campaign against the Spaniards should unite all the nations of South America in brotherhood, Bolívar's secretary went on: "Further, His Excellency, the Liberator, has asked me to inform Your Excellencies of his subsequent plans, should the allied armies not be victorious in the new Peruvian campaign. His Excellency wants the remnants of the allied army, should it suffer a reverse, to retire toward the north in such fashion that it will be able to receive promptly reinforcements of six or eight thousand men, who will immediately leave for Trujillo or a more distant point. Should the rest of the allied army be forced to fall back to the south, His Excellency hopes that the government of Chile will provide it with an equal number of reinforcements, so that by operating in that area the attention of the enemy will be divided, while the Colombian army in the north moves toward Lima, together with companies to be raised in Piura and Trujillo. Regardless of circumstances, it is the Liberator's firm intention to do his utmost to rescue Peru from the Spanish empire. He accordingly ventures to ask, in all sincerity, that the government of Chile follow his example and, by making a similar effort, send six or eight thousand men to southern Peru to operate with the same or, if possible, greater activity than His Excellency hopes to display in the circumstances.

"The Liberator pleads strongly that this government do its best to prevail upon the authorities of the Río de la Plata to prepare an army of at least 4,000 men for dispatch to Cuzco, should the allied army suffer a reverse. Although such an eventuality is remote, we must not view it as such and, instead, considering it to be ever present, we should take every precaution now to wrest victory from the enemy's hands the moment he wins it, and not grant him the time to exploit it and thereby wreck the interests of South America."[1]

As we see, although Bolívar dreamed throughout his military career of leading the victorious republican armies to Lima, he conceived of his ideal as a supreme rendezvous of all the free countries of America in the heart of the continent. No condition or reservation on his part, or that of the Colombian government, tarnished the offers that he made to Peru in 1822.

This attitude, unfortunately, was not appreciated in Lima. It was quite natural, of course, for the Peruvians to aspire to independence by their own efforts, particularly as their experience with the first foreign liberators to enter the country had not been pleasant. The Ecuadorian historian, Alfonso Rumazo González, describes how, shortly after the occupation of Lima by San Martín, and apart from a brief period of military activity provoked by the advance of the Spanish General Canterac towards the capital, "the Protector, excited by his secret adventures (with Rosita Campuzano, who was known as 'la Protectora') and engrossed with issues, seemed to forget that the Iberian army was still intact in the mountains. He busied himself with planning the form of government that would be suitable for a free Peru, and found,

---

1. O'Leary, *Narración,* ii, p. 174 (1952 edition). Also in *Católogo...,* ii, p. 204. Lecuna points out that this plan was published in *Argos,* of Buenos Aires, no. 44, 31 May 1823.

unfortunately, that the best solution would be to impose an American monarch. Who? Why not San Martín himself, who was then at the peak of his success? In order to prepare the ground properly, he had to show signs of energy and radicalism. Decrees were issued against the Spaniards and their families, and there was a certain amount of religious persecution. The Archbishop of Lima, Señor Las Heras, was given a passport to leave Peru within 24 hours, despite his old age (he was 84). The spectators had to be given an intensive impression of royal majesty. His own portrait replaced that of Ferdinand VII in the salons of the viceregal palace. Luxury was extended to all the places visited by the Protector. A state coach, drawn by six horses and with liveried coachmen, took the general from one place to another. The people came out of their houses to see him go by and they admired his showy, new granadier's uniform, with its bright, gold decorations. The royal guard was created.... Celebrations and easy living continued in Lima. The liberating army was everywhere showing signs of decay. In the Lautaro lodge San Martín was referred to by the **nickname of 'King José.'** He shared half a million pesos among his officers so as to further ingratiate himself with them, and each of them received twenty-five thousand. Waste became rife, while commerce stagnated because the war prevented ships from sailing between Spain and America. Misery and discontent spread among the common people. The junior commanders dedicated themselves to intrigue. And, as if this were **not enough to undermine** the emancipation movement, there followed the dispute between the Protector and his valiant assistant Cochrane, without whose support following the blockade of the squadron, it would have been impossible to reach Lima.... Lima was not the only area in which symptoms of decay began to appear. Gangs of robbers sprang up in the countryside, where there was famine...."[1]

The situation grew worse as San Martín and Bolívar moved apart. Beneath the surface, the thorny question of the boundaries between Colombia and Peru became exaggerated. It is not difficult to picture the constant friction between Peruvians, Chileans, Argentinians and Colombians. Personal ambitions and a spirit of intrigue fanned the flames of frequent disputes. Less visible, although more important as a cause of trouble, was the interest of hidden royalists, egoists and cowards in weakening public morale to such an extent that there would be a return to the happy conformity that had apparently given Peru long years of peace and prosperity.

History provides order and distributes responsibilities, when it later reveals the elements that combine at a given moment to make a country

---

1. Alfonso Rumazo González, *Biografía de Manuela Sáenz* (Almendro y Nieto, Buenos Aires), p. 114, 117, 118.

anarchic and break its spirit. But if we consider in good faith the factors that disorganized Peru and those that demoralized its ruling classes and lowered public morale—the latter took the form of conflicting ideas, which were thus more extreme—the truth is that it is impossible to find anybody to blame. It would be even less just to condemn the nation that was the victim of such circumstances. The more it tried to escape from them the more oppressive they seemed, and the less it understood them.

Unfortunately, the bitterness and resentment which the Peruvians legitimately felt towards the foreigners who had tried, without success, to emancipate them, also manifested itself violently against the Liberator and the newly-arrived Colombian troops. His offers were rejected almost scornfully. The long-suffering soldiers, who had been marching from the banks of the Orinoco for weeks and months, putting up with misery, weariness and disease, found only sneers and insults in the public papers of Peru. According to Simón Rodríguez, it was said unjustly, "that when the Colombian soldiers reached Peru, they mutinied because an attempt was made to pay their wages in *money*; that the Commander-in-Chief immediately sent schooners to bring funds from Colombia, that they returned loaded with *yuccas* and that the mutiny turned into *hurrahs*."[1] It was most inappropriate to ridicule these veterans with such an invention. They could claim with pride that, eating only bananas and yuccas, unshod, naked and at times without arms, they had defeated the best royalist troops and liberated three countries.

In fact, they were not given money, for there was no longer any available. The governing *junta* that had succeeded San Martín was not even willing to provide the Colombian troops with what was essential for their subsistence. It hurriedly complied, however, when their commander, Colonel Juan Paz del Castillo, asked for permission to take them back to Colombia.

But the governors were less decisive in bringing order to public administration and in conducting the war against the Spaniards. After the gaiety of the first days, the public treasury was so bare that the government finally had to resort to the issue of paper money. This, in its turn, increased the misery and discontent. An army of 4,000 men, Argentinians and Chileans, under the command of General Rudecindo Alvarado, a brother of one the members of the governing *junta,* was routed by the Spaniards at the battles of Torata and Moquegua, and it lost over three quarters of its men.[2] This disaster led on to another, which in the long term was to prove even worse, when the army forced the government to appoint José de la Riva Agüero President of the Republic. It proved even worse be-

---

1. *Defensa de Bolívar por don Simón Rodríguez* (Caracas, 1915), p. 25.
2. According to O'Leary, 500 men were saved (*Narración*, ii, p. 177); Lecuna says 900 (*Crónica razonada*, iii, p. 241).

cause the inept, conceited Riva Agüero—San Martín called him an evil and contemptible person— was unable to come to an understanding with Congress. He sparked a civil war and ended by making treacherous agreements with the Spaniards.

This state of anarchy made it easy for the active royalist, General Canterac, to enter and sack Lima after threatening to burn the city. At almost the same time, July 1823, an expedition led by Santa Cruz, which had had some success in Upper Peru, was ambushed by the royalists Valdés and Olañeta. After making a hasty retreat, it was scattered. It was then that they summoned Bolívar. General Mariano Portocarrero, the first commissioner sent to him by Riva Agüero, told him: "I finally have the honor to be in the presence of the Liberator of Colombia and Peru." Bolívar replied: "General, tell the government of Peru that the soldiers of Colombia are already hurrying in the ships of the Republic to scatter the clouds that disturb the sun of Peru." He immediately ordered the departure for the viceroyalty of 6,000 troops, that he had ready. Although they were commanded by the hero of Bomboná, General Manuel Valdés—who should not be confused with the royalist General Jerónimo Valdés, the victor at Torata and Moquegua—the Liberator also appointed General Sucre minister plenipotentiary to the Lima government, with the authority to intervene in the conduct of the war when Valdés judged it convenient or when the interests of Peru and Colombia made it necessary for him to do so. However, neither Valdés nor Sucre could do anything in the midst of the disorganization that they found, except to preserve their precious contingent of veterans from disaster. It is sufficient to point out that Santa Cruz, on the eve of his disastrous defeat, refused to accept the assistance of Sucre, who was ready to go to his aid.

A second delegation from the Peruvian president then asked Bolívar to go in person to take charge of the war. The Congress gave a vote of thanks to the Liberator and sent to him, with a third delegation, its decree as well, calling him to Peru.

The poet Olmedo, a member of the Congress who had taken refuge in Lima, spoke to the Liberator on behalf of these commissioners. He began by describing the ruined republic that they were handing over to him: "Sir: The Congress of Peru has desired to entrust a delegation from its heart the honor of renewing its sentiments of consideration and gratitude to Your Excellency, and to reiterate to you its ardent desires that your presence may bring a prompt and glorious end to the evils of the war. The enemy has occupied the capital of the republic. Everywhere, devastation precedes and follows the march of the conceited and cruel Canterac. All his footsteps are covered with blood and ashes...." Doubtless because he was still unable to forget his hostility towards

Colombia at Guayaquil, and that shown towards the Liberator by some Peruvians, Olmedo shrewdly asked Bolívar to disregard these insults, by referring at the end of his discourse to the anger of Achilles. Olmedo told him: "... all eyes, all votes turn naturally to Your Excellency.... Break all the bonds that keep you far from the field of battle. It seems that, after so many centuries, the oracles have again predicted that all these peoples, joined together in a new Asia by their common desire for vengeance, cannot possibly win without Achilles. Give way to the torrent that, perhaps for the last time, will carry you to new glories."

It was not, however, resentment that held back Bolívar, nor even the legitimate desire that posterity should be in no doubt about the summons that they sent him. He replied to Olmedo: "For a long time my heart has impelled me towards Peru, and the most valiant warriors in all America have long done me the honor of calling me to their side. But I have not been able to ignore the duty that has kept me on the shores of Colombia. I have implored the General Congress to permit me to put my sword to the service of my southern brothers. This concession has still not been given me. I fret in this inactivity, when the Colombian troops are amidst dangers and glory, and I am far from them."

The authorization of the Colombian Congress arrived as a fourth Peruvian delegation—sent this time by the Marquis de Torre Tagle, who had replaced Riva Agüero—was making a new appeal to Bolívar to come to their rescue. He finally sailed for Peru on August 7, 1823, and disembarked at Callao on September 1.

The Peruvian Congress had dismissed Riva Agüero, declaring him guilty of high treason. On September 2 it authorized the Liberator to subdue the deposed president. It seemed once again that fate was making fun of the man of difficulties. When he might have thought that his hope for all the free nations of South America coming together in symbolic union to expel the last unvanquished Spaniards was about to be realized, he first had to accept this miserable commission to defeat a rebel. Bolívar had always had a horror of fratricidal strife, because he thought that "blame always falls on the vanquished and the victor."[1] A campaign of Peruvians against Peruvians was to be led by the man who had proclaimed, even amidst the frantic rivalries of Venezuelan and Granadan *caudillismo:* "It is politic in civil wars to be generous, because vengeance grows progressively."[2] He wrote to Santander in 1826: "It is without doubt glorious to serve one's country and to preserve her existence in battle, but it is altogether odious to hold office when one's

---

1. *Cartas,* vi, p. 11.
2. *Ibid.,* i, p. 131.

own fellow-citizens are one's enemies and the people at large appear to be the victims. I have sacrificed everything for my country and her freedom, but I cannot sacrifice the noble role of freeman and the exalted title of Liberator."[1] Olmedo would probably have reminded him of the trials of Hercules and Perseus.

The Riva Agüero faction was dangerous. Although the Spaniards had evacuated Lima, which was again the seat of the legitimate goverment, the ex-president had established himself in the north, near Trujillo, with a force of 3,000 men. He was capable of cutting land communications with Colombia, just at the time that a new rebellion in Pasto was isolating Guayaquil and Quito from distant Bogotá.

Moreover, this scandalous dispute between the Peruvian leaders inevitably encouraged the royalists, whose forces remained intact and victorious in the interior of the country. Their presence aggravated Peru's internal disorganization and made worse the intrigue, violence and slander that civil war often produces. The Colombian commanders were exposed in this situation.

This profound moral decay persisted even after the defeat of the faction, and was combined with other traumas that public morale was to suffer from continuing dissidence. For some Peruvians it still obscures the gratitude that they owe to the Liberator. Bolívar had promised, in his reply to General Portocarrero after being asked to go to Peru: "Colombia will do her duty in Peru. She will send her soldiers as far as Potosí, and these brave men will return to their homes with the sole reward of having helped destroy the last tyrants in the New World. Colombia does not seek a grain of Peruvian territory. Her glory, her happiness and her security depend upon her retaining her own freedom, and in leaving her brothers independent."[2] This promise was scrupulously observed, but it is sad that Bolívar felt obliged to make it, and that today not everibody remembers it.

With the agreement of Congress, Bolívar first tried, as was his custom, to reach an honorable settlement with Riva Agüero, who so far had not openly taken a treasonable course. They began to correspond, and Bolívar promoted an exchange of commissioners. But the Congress itself soon discovered that Riva Agüero was scornful of these attempts to reach an agreement, and that he was in league with Viceroy La Serna, the supreme royalist authority in Peru. Consequently, it categorically ordered Bolívar to move his forces against the outlaw. Fortunately, Colonel Antonio Gutiérrez de la Fuente, the Peruvian commander who was supporting Riva Agüero, was so horrified when he learned of the

---

1. *Ibid.,* v, p. 350.
2. O'Leary, *Narración,* ii, p. 188.

treachery into which he was being drawn by the former president's disloyal pacts, that he agreed with the Liberator on a surrender which included a pardon for him. When Riva Agüero refused to accept the surrender, Gutiérrez arrested him and sent him to Guayaquil, from whence he traveled to Europe. Later, under the pseudonym of Pruvonena, Riva Agüero published *Memorias y Documentos para la Historia de la Independencia del Perú,* a work full of calumnies against San Martín and Bolívar. Unfortunately, some interested writers—including, at the moment, Salvador de Madariaga—refer to these frequently as though they were reliable.

Apart from this revenge, which, although of a personal nature, was important for its effect on public opinion in Peru, Riva Agüero's infamy contributed to the loss of most of the Peruvian forces that had accompanied him and which Bolívar had intended to unite with his own for an attack against the Spaniards. The Liberator found himself then, engaged in four tasks, which had to be dealt with simultaneously with the greatest efficiency. Failure in any one of them could cause complete disaster. He had to urge Torre Tagle and Congress to purify public administration, for the lack of resources for the troops had reached most serious proportions. There was also an urgent need to form a new Peruvian army, give it the consistency of a veteran force, and make the maximum use of Peruvian officers and commanders who showed signs of competence and reliability. In the meantime, he had to speed up the arrival of new Colombian units, a task that involved convincing Santander and the Colombian Congress, who still regarded the enterprise as foolhardy. Finally, he had to hide these desperate circumstances from the Spaniards and hurriedly prepare a base from which, defensively at least, he could contain them.

At the end of 1823 Bolívar described the situation to the Chilean minister in Lima as follows: "Peru is divided into two zones: that in the south belongs to the external war, while that in the north is involved in civil war. Only the sacked and ruined Lima is in the hands of the legitimate government; this government possesses nothing but debts." And he added: "Colombia has sent 7,000 men here at her own expense, apart from seventeen thousand *pesos* that were advanced for the fitting out of our troops. Colombia has 17,000 men under arms, fighting the common enemy in Venezuela and New Granada; and Colombia now is simply a vast desert, but she will do still more for the freedom of her brothers."[1]

It was upon Quito and Guayaquil —the country recently joined to Colombia and in which Bolívar might still fear being regarded as a "foreigner"—that the main burden of these sacrifices had to fall. In one of his letters to General Salom, who was in command of that department,

1. *Cartas,* iii, p. 262.

Bolívar gave him the following orders: Augment the veteran forces with new recruits; train the militia; renew the campaign against Pasto in order to restore communications with Bogotá; send ships to Panama in search of 3,000 men who should have arrived there from northern Venezuela and New Granada; and suspend the payment of all public debts so as to finance this operation. He was also ordered to send to Callao "biscuit made from local flour, rice, pottage and salted meat, to the value of twenty-five thousand *pesos* a month, for the maintenance there of a Colombian garrison."[1] This was tantamount to extending the vast desert of New Granada and Venezuela into these regions that had just joined Colombia.

Of course, he regarded as shameful the idea that he should take anything from Peru for himself, and he informed Santander: "I forgot to tell you that these gentlemen have assigned me a salary of fifty thousand *pesos*. I have told them that I will not accept it, for it is neither just nor noble for me to have a salary in Peru, when the Commander of Colombia can deliver himself from this disgrace with a thousand doubloons to be spent here."[2]

Not even Bolívar's love for Colombia could divert him from his determination to be just and altruistic. He told the Colombian Vice-President in another letter: "Mosquera is here discussing boundaries. I do not intend to take much part, lest the result of the negotiation be attributed to force. In moral affairs, as in politics, there are rules that should not be evaded, and whose violation can prove expensive. A timely protest can destroy the effect of feigned concessions which also increase the grounds for hostility between the parties. We are now benefactors here, and we must not lose this beautiful title even for many square leagues."[3]

Bolívar was worried with greater cause about the effect upon public opinion of the sacrifices that had to be demanded. He explained to Colonel Heres: "I have ordered that the expenditure of public funds be published in the *Gaceta*, for I want there to be the greatest clarity in financial matters so that everybody will be aware of what is happening.... We need to be very cautious and considerate if we are to prevent this nation from becoming entirely royalist *(godo)*. For the same reason we need money to replace the taxes that we cannot and should not impose on these unfortunate men, for here the epoch of independence has been the epoch of crime and plunder. Candidly, the inhabitants have confessed to me that they were treated better by the Spaniards. They will thus return easily and with pleasure to their yoke."[4] He was referring here to the

---

1. *Ibid.,* p. 241.
2. *Ibid.,* iii, p. 273.
3. *Ibid.,* pp. 283-4.
4. *Cartas,* pp. 283-4.

north of Peru, which had been ruined by the Riva Agüero faction, but he also wrote to Salom, with respect to Quito and Guayaquil: "Have all our officials and magistrates treat the people as mildly as possible. But have them beg, ask and cajole the inhabitants into making more and more sacrifices, lest the Spaniards return and they lose everything beyond redemption."[1]

This policy, which Bolívar had not been able to adopt for his own compatriots in the terrible years that had gone before, was not appreciated by the Peruvians. They had always lived in peace and regarded any demand as exorbitant. They also regarded it as odious because it was made, according to them, by a foreigner for the maintenance of foreign troops.

The Liberator's own suffering inspired jokes, as when he wrote on December 8, 1823, "I am writing this letter to you in the midst of the Andes, suffering a mephitic attack that they call *soroche,* in the snow and alongside *vicuñas.* It should arrive frozen, unless a condor carries it off and warms it by the sun." He ended: "In one year either we will have peace and will have won, or the devil will have carried us away."[2] A year and a day later, in fact, his armies triumphed at Ayacucho.

Shortly after his arrival in Peru, Bolívar had also interceded on behalf of the learned Bonpland, who was being held prisoner by the dictator of Paragauy, Dr. Gaspar Rodríguez Francia. The letter that the Liberator sent to this sinister despot proves that the young Bolívar's relations in Paris with Bonpland and Humboldt were steadfast and close. The Liberator was later to invite Bonpland to settle in Colombia, and he retained fond memories of both him and Humboldt. The letter began as follows:

"Most Excellent Sir:

"Since my earliest youth I have had the honor of cultivating the friendship of Mr. Bonpland and Baron von Humboldt, who, with their learning, have done more for America than all the conquistadors.

"I have now learned, to my dismay, that my dear friend Mr. Bonpland has been detained in Paraguay for reasons unknown to me. I suspect that some false reports may have slandered that good and wise man and that the government over which Your Excellency presides has been allowed to be misled concerning this noble gentlemen. Two considerations impel me to plead urgently with Your Excellency for the release of Mr. Bonpland. The first is that he came to America on my behalf, since it was I who invited him to Colombia. After he had decided to undertake his voyage, the events of the war forced him to proceed to Buenos Aires. The second consideration is that this learned man could

1. *Ibid.,* iii, p. 291.
2. *Ibid.,* p. 293.

enlighten my country with his genius, if Your Excellency would graciously allow him to proceed to Colombia, whose government I head by the will of the people."

There was a slight trace of a threat in the Liberator's closing sentence: "I shall await him with the anxiety of a friend and the respect of a pupil, for I would be capable of marching as far as Paraguay only to free this best of men and the most celebrated of travelers."[1] Bolívar repeated these sentiments in a letter to Bonpland's wife, whom he told "If by a wonder of good fortune Mr. Bonpland can emerge from the dungeons of Paraguay, I offer an honorable destination to you and your family, and one which will be useful to the companion of the discoverer of the New World. My satisfaction will then be infinite, for I will rejoin in the womb of my country one of my best friends and a learned man."[2] "Discoverer of the New World" was his apt epithet for Humboldt.

But the situation grew worse daily, and the Liberator was more and more obstructed by all sorts of difficulties. 12,000 men for whom he had asked had not arrived from Colombia and, on the other hand, it seemed that Peru was incapable of maintaining the forces needed for an advance against the Spaniards, no matter where they were raised. Bolívar had asked Mexico, Guatemala, Chile and Buenos Aires for aid —money, arms or men—but, after some early optimism his hopes that they would co-operate evaporated. It already seemed impossible, despite his tact and patience, to avoid disagreements with the other republican commanders, Santa Cruz, Vice-Admiral Guise, Torre Tagle himself, and to contain the plotters and traitors. If the royalist were to attack there was no doubt that they would retake Lima, and it was very possible that they would crush the reduced Colombian contingent and its disorganized allies.

Of course, by the end of 1823 the Liberator had been in Peru for only four months, and it had not been humanly possible for him to secure better results, largely because he had been occupied in overcoming Riva Agüero. This did not reduce his concern, and at times he despaired because of the perspicacity with which he appreciated the complex factors that weakened Peru. He wrote to Heres: "In truth, it is a great task that we have on our hands, amidst an immense range of difficulties, for there reigns a confusion that dismays the most determined. The battlefield is South America. All things are our enemies. Our soldiers are men from all parties and countries, each with its own language, worth, laws and interests. Only the omnipotent finger of Providence can bring

---

1. *Cartas*, iii, p. 264.
2. *Ibid*, iii, p. 266.

order to this chaos, and I will not believe in such a miracle until I see it happen."[1]

He wrote to Sucre in the same tone: "The affair of the war in Peru requires an immense effort and endless resources. It cannot be done without a large body of troops. The means are inadequate for these troops, in my opinion, unless we can gather them together well in advance, with much aptitude and intelligence. We need, above all, to know the country and to calculate what it can provide. Afterwards we will discuss whether its strategy should be offensive or defensive. Then we must collect these resources and employ them. Above all, my dear General, I ask you to help me with all your heart, to produce and execute this plan. There is no-one other than you who can offer me intellectual assistance. On the contrary, there reigns a dislocation of things, men and principles that constantly worries me. At times I lose heart. It is only my love for my country that restores the courage that I lose when I contemplate these obstacles. Problems lessen in one place, only to increase somewhere else. The civil war has ended, but now we have the confusion of this Arica expedition, and nobody knows where it will end. Three ships have reached Callao, Santa and Huanchaco with troops and supplies. The rest will go where God wills. To cap it all we have no money, despite the fine hopes that we had; nor do we have any news of the Panama expedition. We should count on no more than 2,000 of Riva Agüero's men. The country is patriotic but it does not want military service. It is good, but apathetic. It has provisions and beasts of burden, but not much enthusiasm to give them, although they can be taken by force."[2]

But it was civil dissension that most tormented him. He said in a reply to the Peruvian minister of war: "Yesterday's communications have had a disagreeable effect on me. I see from them that the obstacles to the freedom of Peru are multiplying. On one hand, the Chilean expedition is breaking up and even returning home. On the other, we have the sinister ideas of Santa Cruz and his supporters. Guise has similar ideas. The Lima agitators are making progress in Canta and Huarochirí. Herreras's exposition clearly reveals that, strange though it may be, the royalist party predominates in Lima. In short, the overall effect of yesterday's news is horrible. It will be very difficult to overcome this misfortune and strength. Everything threatens ruin in this country. While I advance to the north, the south has collapsed. I am certain that, when I return to the south, this part of the north will experience inevitable upheavals."[3]

---

1. *Cartas* p. 300.
2. *Ibid.,* iii, p. 302.
3. *Cartas,* iii, p. 304.

He ended: "*The government must ask Congress for strong laws against conspirators, whatever party they belong to, and the government must enforce them with unrelenting rigor.* Peru is undermined by her enemies, and only a countermine can save her. I venture to issue orders that I consider necessary. I am not a Peruvian, and everything that I do is attributed to Colombia, and to a hostile intent. . . . I have said before that if the Peruvian government would bear the expense of the hatred that is bound to descend on me because of my strong measures, I would do the rest. As proof of this I have taken charge of this civil war, which has certainly caused much of the hatred and calumny. I had to take charge of it to save this country."[1]

We will see that the government from which he demanded these strong measures against traitors—or at least Torre Tagle and various of his high officials—was itself prepared to cross over to the enemy.

Understandably, the Liberator desperately looked back to Colombia. At such a distance from Bogotá he no longer ventured to order, but he appealed to Santander: "My poor reputation will again be at risk from dangers as great as those already overcome. I ask you as a friend, to send me all the help imaginable."[2] And he insisted to Briceño Méndez, Colombia's minister of war: "Be a nuisance, appeal to, ask, implore the Vice-President and all who have anything to do with the march of the troops to send them quickly, quickly. Insist that they should not sleep, they should not eat, they should not rest, until they see them on their way. If they do otherwise, good-bye Colombia! Good-bye Freedom! How could we lose such precious friends without shedding tears of blood?"[3]

Bolívar's health finally gave in to all the affliction and hardship that he had suffered on the campaign. Since the beginning of operations in the north he had not wanted to return to Lima, out of fear that his presence would aggravate the machinations, disagreements and calumnies that were centered in the capital. Nor was he tempted by the adulation that he would have received there, for which he would perhaps have had to pay by facing up to further slander. He believed, however, that he would have to return when there was no longer any other way to obtain the resources that he needed. In contrast to his advance through the heights where his letters froze, he returned along the hot, desolate road of the coast, "which consists of a sandy desert, 500 leagues long, and with a width varying between seven and fifty miles."[4]

---

1. *Ibid.,* p. 305.
2. *Ibid.,* iii, p. 255.
3. *Cartas,* iii, p. 318.
4. Cornelio Hispano, *El Libro de Oro de Bolívar* (París, 1926). Quoted by Dr. Oscar Beaujon, in his study *El Libertador Enfermo,* Caracas, 1963, p. 36.

Naturally, there occurred that which it was logical to fear. When he reached Pativilca, a small village three days' march from Lima, he collapsed with a high fever. It made him delirious and caused attacks of insanity. Bolívar explained to Santander: "It is a complication of internal irritation, rheumatism, fever, a little trouble with urine, vomiting and stomach-ache. The general effect of all this made me despair, and it still causes me much pain. I cannot exert myself without suffering endlessly. You would not know me, for I am very dilapidated and very old. With a torment like this, I seem senile. From time to time, moreover, I suffer attacks of insanity, even when I am otherwise well. I entirely lose my senses, without suffering the slightest attack of infirmity or pain. Such attacks occur when I cross over the mountain wildernesses of this country with their *soroches*. The coasts are unhealthy and uncomfortable. It is like living in Arabia."[1]

Although Bolívar wrote in this letter that he intended to return to Bogotá leaving Sucre in charge of the army, and that he also intended to abandon public life and leave Colombia, he recovered his normal temperament as soon as he began to recuperate. There reappeared in him the man who saw in these trials his inevitable destiny, his martyrdom and his glory.

While he was ill, Bolívar was visited by Joaquín Mosquera, the Colombian minister to the governments of Peru, Chile and Buenos Aires, who later reported: ". . . I found the Liberator out of danger of dying, but so weak and emaciated that his appearance caused me very severe pain. He was seated on a humble cow-hide seat, leaning against the wall of a small garden, with a white cloth wrapped around his head. His pointed knees and his fleshless legs could be seen through his trousers, his voice was hollow and weak, and he looked like a corpse. I had to make a great effort to hold back my tears, and to prevent him from seeing my distress and my concern for his life.

"You will remember that in this period the six thousand strong Peruvian army had vanished without fighting; that the auxiliary army of Chile had abandoned us by returning to its country; that the only forces that remained consisted of four thousand Colombians and three thousand Peruvians. The Spaniards had a force of twenty thousand men. The Peruvians, divided into factions, had the country in anarchy. All these considerations seemed to me a phalanx of evils to extinguish the existence of the half-dead hero. With a heavy heart, fearing the ruin of our army, I asked him, 'And what do you intend to do now?' His hollow eyes lit up, and he replied, in a firm voice, 'Triumph!' "[2]

---

1. *Cartas,* iv, p. 9.
2. Quoted by Antonio Arraiz, *Culto bolivariano,* p. 107.

The Liberator's physical distress was so severe that when he decided to accompany the departing Mosquera along a stretch of the road, he had to ride "a gentle mule." While Mosquera was waiting for his luggage "at the entrance to the Haarmei desert," Bolívar lay down "on a barracan greatcoat."[1]

During this same interview, he had explained to Mosquera the campaign plan that he would follow: "I have given orders for the raising of a powerful cavalry in Trujillo. I have ordered the manufacture of horseshoes in Cuenca, Guayaquil and Trujillo. I have ordered that all the good horses in the country be taken for military service, and I have seized all the alfalfa fields. As soon as I recover my strength, I will go to Trujillo, If the Spaniards descend from the *sierra,* I will defeat them with the cavalry. If they do not come down, within three months I will climb the mountain and destroy them."

Bolívar had also written to Sucre: "The prospect is horrifying, but I am not afraid, for we are accustomed to seeing the most horrible phantoms, which disappear as we draw near them."[2]

---

1. Oscar Beaujon, *op. cit.,* p. 40.
2. *Cartas,* iii, p. 314.

XXX

PRODUCER OF HAND-WROUGHT REPUBLICS

IN FEBRUARY 1824, BOLIVAR was still in Pativilca. Apart from the weakness caused by his illness, of which he complained in a letter to Sucre, he was suffering from loneliness. He wrote to Heres: "Be good and come.... Morlás has gone and Torres Valdivia does nothing. I am alone with Espinar, attending to Colombia and Peru, to the war and to politics, to the exchequer and the government. There is nobody to advise me on even the most trivial matter, or to remind me if I forget...."[1]

And events were every day more pressing. Although he showed in his correspondence with some of his subordinates that he was confident of defeating the Spaniards if they came north in search of him, he could not even dream of taking the offensive, and his concern was deeper than it seemed. He confessed to O'Leary that the battle of Moquegua and the unfortunate campaign of Santa Cruz had caused the loss of "good squadrons." The Peruvian army in the north had also suffered much as a result of Riva Agüero's treason. He had asked for reinforcements from Colombia, but they had not arrived, and the city of Pasto was rebelling as the Colombian forces withdrew from it, cutting the communications of Peru, Quito and Guayaquil with Bogotá. In January, moreover, he learned that France and the Holy Alliance had restored absolutism in Spain, and that they would probably assist her with the reconquest of America.

---

1. *Cartas,* iv, p. 60.

Bolívar commented to Santander: "The Peruvian *godos* have so far loudly proclaimed that they will not recognize the independence of America, even when the Spanish government recognizes it; all this even before their victories. Moreover, they will know, for we have taken the trouble to publish it, what the Duke of Angouleme said in his proclamation about the submission of America. They will conclude from this profession of French policy that they should continue the war against us with greater zeal. Consequently, we should not expect more than blood and fire from the companions of Canterac, La Serna and Valdés. Consequently we should not expect our freedom except from the 12,000 Colombians that I have requested for Peru, of whom 3,000 should go to Pasto, in order to destroy those Numancian Tartars, who are making themselves almost invincible."[1]

At the same time, he pointed out to the Colombian secretary of foreign affairs: "The Holy Alliance has carried its arms to the walls of Cádiz. The old world now weighs down the new.... It is now feared that King Ferdinand will be able to rid himself of an army that could not and should not have been faithful to him. To do this he will take the step of sending it to America.... France can give him whatever maritime aid he needs."

In view of this, Bolívar suggested "that the executive power take into consideration the critical circumstances that we see threatening us, and invite the British government, through our diplomatic envoy, not only to announce its recognition of the independence of Colombia but also to insist to Spain that she recognize the same independence of all sections of America."[2]

But would these moves be successful? England had cheated them so many times! "Sold for a treaty of commerce," as Miranda had said.

In order to gain time, Bolívar asked President Torre Tagle to request an armistice from the Spaniards, and he suggested that the officer entrusted with this mission should coax them with the suggestion that a suspension of hostilities would disorganize the Colombian army and oblige the Peruvians to reach a settlement with Spain. He stressed in his instructions to Colonel Tomás de Heres, who was to repeat them orally to the president, the need for the greatest dissimulation, even in minute details, and he repeated: "I shall re-state my secret design: to gain, if possible, four to six months' time for the troops from Colombia to arrive, after which everything will be assured. The officer who goes to Jauja must be extremely clever. He should be selected from among all the available officers in the capital. Have him insist that he must see General La Serna himself, *that he has matters of great interest to communicate to him by word of*

---

1. *Cartas,* iv, p. 34.
2. *Ibid.,* p. 38.

"Bolívar, as President of Peru," by José Gil de Castro. (Lima, 1825).

mouth. If he does not succeed in this, then let him inform the commander of the advance guard that, *were the Spaniards to agree to an armistice of eight, ten, or twelve months, the Colombian troops would become demoralized and would eventually leave Peru, as they are not being paid and are suffering a thousand privations; that the government and people of Peru would then have no choice but to seek reconciliation with their brothers, the Spaniards.* Emphasis should be placed on the misery the country is suffering and the insolent bearing of the allies. This officer should say that *the entire population wants peace, even if meant the devil himself were to lead them. He is to say that he would like to remain but cannot do so out of consideration for his relatives, for I would wreak vengeance upon his family.* This man should be selected like a choice sprig of rosemary."[1]

But this ruse, as Bolívar himself called it, had the most unforeseen outcome. President Torre Tagle quite simply went over to the Spaniards with a large part of his official retinue. Bolívar had suggested in his instructions: "Should the officer be questioned as to Tagle's views, or whether or not he has been heard to say anything favoring the Spaniards, he must say *No*, that Tagle is too patriotic to attempt anything, by reason of his previous commitments." But the officer, who had to be chosen like "a choice sprig of rosemary," was no less a person than the minister of war himself, Juan Berindoaga, Count of St. Donás, who served as the secret contact for the treachery, and then followed Torre Tagle. The Liberator had written to Torre Tagle, referring to the plan: "I should like not even the paper itself to know of it, for, if it becomes known, Peru is lost forever."[2] He told Santander, after the betrayal: "The *godos* will allow us time for nothing, since Torre Tagle will tell them of our secret plans to divert them a little until we receive new reinforcements."[3]

Along with Torre Tagle and Berindoaga, there deserted to the royalist camp the Vice-President, Diego de Aliaga, numerous officials, and 337 army officers. Another betrayal had delivered Callao to the royalists. On February 5, the Río de la Plata regiment which was garrisoning the fortress mutinied, imprisoned the governor, General Rudecindo Alvarado, and various loyal officers, persuaded the artillery and other units to join it, and offered everything to the royalists. Its example was soon followed by another Argentine unit, the famous Mounted Grenadiers of the Andes, which overthrew its commanders and joined the traitors. Lecuna tells us: "The Spaniards incorporated more than 1,000 men to their forces

---

1. *Cartas*, iv, p. 17.
2. *Ibid.*, p. 13.
3. Ibid., p. 110.

from the mutinous units, and took as prisoners 105 commanders and officers."[1] Lima, of course, also fell into the hands of the royalists.

As always happens in such cases, Torre Tagle and Berindoaga subsequently tried to justify their conduct by making attacks on and plausible charges against Bolívar. They said, for example, that the Liberator intended to have them shot. In fact, when he first learned of their treachery, he ordered their arrest. The real reason for their behavior is to be found in the manifesto that Torre Tagle provided to excuse it, in which he declared: "Now that I have joined the national army, I will always share its fate. I will never be deceived by the false glitter of chemical ideas, which lead deluded people to their destruction and make the fortune and satisfy the ambition of a few adventurers. All around us we see only ruin and misery. In the course of the war, who other than the so-called defenders of our country have destroyed our fortunes, razed our fields, weakened our customs, oppressed and molested the people? And what has been the fruit of this revolution? What positive benefit has resulted for the country? Nobody has any property or individual security. I detest a system that promises the general good yet fails to reconcile the interests of all the citizens." And, forgetting that he had just been Peru's first magistrate, Torre Tagle concluded: "From the sincere and frank union of Peruvians and Spaniards, all good should be expected; from Bolívar, desolation and death."[2]

Twice, within a few lines, Torre Tagle lamented the material losses of himself and his kind: ". . . have destroyed our fortunes. . . .," "Nobody has any property. . . ." Implicitly, he was asking for a revolution which would not detract from "individual security," and which would "reconcile the interest of all the citizens." He regarded as oppressive and annoying the measures that obviously had to be taken to counteract such ingenuous selfishness. He referred to the people being "oppressed and molested," as if unaware that for more than three centuries the owners of these properties and fortunes, together with the royalists, had wickedly exploited the people.

This language was bound to be incomprehensible to the Venezuelans, Granadans and Ecuadorians. We recall that, since the war began, Bolívar had sacrificed fortune and privileges without even realizing it. Sucre had not only suffered the tremendous hardships of the Venezuelan campaigns from the age of fifteen but had also lost six brothers in atrocious circumstances—one of them lanced in hospital, two shot by the royalists. One of his sisters, moreover, was raped and murdered in her sick-bed.

---

1. *Crónica razonada...*, iii, p. 363.
2. Quoted by Luis Alayza Paz Soldán, *Unanue, San Martín y Bolívar* (Lima, 1934), p. 433.

We have also seen that at the end of 1814 Martín Tovar advised his wife and daughters to hide in the woods, and to support themselves in the Antilles by sewing or making sweets, while he was with the republican army. In 1816 fathers, brothers and husbands left the most refined Venezuelan ladies to play the harp at Negro dances in the Caribbean, while they undertook the reconquest against the recently arrived army of Morillo. The Liberator's own fiancée, Josefina Machado, sacrificed her youth and her love in this hazardous existence. Later, when things had improved, the patriots used all that they extracted from the rich Guayana mission area for the purchase of arms, while they continued to feed themselves on bananas and yuccas and to dress in the motley uniforms captured by the republican privateers. The patriots denied themselves the luxuries of proper shoes and wheat bread so that they could provide them for the recently arrived British troops, or the "foreigners," as they were now called. At Pantano de Vargas and Boyacá, the soldiers who had crossed the mountains fought "dressed as women," to use their embarrassed description because they had nothing to cover their nakedness except the gaudy material that the Granadan women had taken from their own clothing.

After living this life for fourteen years, what scorn the Colombian veterans must have felt for the wails of Torre Tagle about individual security and lost fortunes! But this was what they heard as the basis for all the complaints made against them! And the same attitude is still adopted by some historians, who are almost as ingenuously egoistic as the Marquis de Torre Tagle and the Count de San Donás!

Certainly, Bolívar had to order exactions which must have seemed scandalous to a ruling class accustomed to tranquility and privilege. For example, the Vicar-General of the bishopric of Trujillo was told in an official communication from Bolívar's secretary that, "since there should be no privileged classes when the cause of the people is at stake," the Liberator hoped that the clergy would contribute to the common defense by providing the contributions asked of them.[1] When these warnings proved ineffective, the confiscation of church gold and silver was decreed.[2] What the Peruvians were not aware of was that this money was needed to pay, among others, the English Admiral Martín George Guise, commandant of the Peruvian squadron, who was brave and efficient and who performed invaluable services for the patriots with his ships. He was threatening, however, to return to Chile if he was not paid. Bolívar wrote to him: "I am pleased that Your Excellency has received the twenty thousand pesos that I sent for the squadron, which was ready to sail for Callao to continue

---

1. O'Leary, *Documentos,* xxii, p. 86.
2. Lecuna, *Crónica razonada...,* iii, p. 397.

"Simón Bolívar," by Gil de Castro. (Lima, 1825).

the blockade of the port. This operation is silencing the false rumors that the enemies of Peru were spreading every day about the activities of the squadron commanded by Your Excellency." Nevertheless, the Liberator was not at all confident, and, after offering detailed explanations to the wayward commander, he felt obliged to end his letter with an imperious threat: "I do not doubt that, recognizing the strength of these arguments, Your Excellency will decide not to go to Chile, for this would be seen as a desertion of the cause of Peru with the forces that she has entrusted to you in the most critical circumstances and in the time of her salvation. Thus, if you do decide to adopt this policy, I protest and disapprove, and I hold you responsible for it before Peru, before the whole of America, and before Your Excellency's noble country, England, which has so generously supported the cause Your Excellency has defended with such valor and constancy."[1] How Bolívar must have longed for the magnanimous Brión, who had given Venezuela his entire fortune whithout ever complaining.

The Peruvians were also unaware that Colombia was making similar sacrifices for them. On January 15, 1824, the Liberator had to write to General Bartolomé Salom, governor of the department of Quito: ". . . at the moment the Peruvian exchequer is providing nothing. We will not be able to make any progress unless you send me the recruits, uniforms, helmets, greatcoats, five hundred saddles, *ponchos* or ordinary blankets, and all the other items that I have requested for the army. Otherwise Peru will be irretrievably lost. . . ."[2] He noted in the same letter that "Guayaquil is owed seven hundred thousand *duros*" (apart from what was owed for the numerous similar exactions already made), and only a month later he spoke of imposing a new levy of 25,000 pesos on the city of Quito. Although Colombia, too, was threatened by Spain and the Holy Alliance, she sent about 7,000 muskets to Peru during this campaign.[3]

These constant requests provoked disagreeable incidents in the southern Colombian departments. Bolívar reacted vehemently, telling Santander: "You may offer the most magnificent praises to Sucre and Salom, whom you have sent to the *quiteños,* and who, in truth, are the best men in the world. How ungrateful these people are! We have picked the flower of Venezuela to do them good, and they repay us with calumnies."[4] But this fury was only temporary, for eight days later the Liberator referred enthusiastically to "people as patriotic and as Colombian as those of Quito have been."[5]

1. *Cartas,* iv, p. 140.
2. *Cartas,* iv, p. 23.
3. Lecuna, *Crónica razonada . . .,* iii, p. 391.
4. *Cartas,* iv, p. 10.
5. *Cartas,* p. 23.

The criticisms of Peru in Bolívar's correspondence have frequently been used to turn Peruvians against the Liberator or to support attacks on the country, but it should be realized that these temperamental outbursts are completely without significance. Despite the setbacks that he suffered, Bolívar was just and affectionate in all his objective judgements on Peru. Even when confronted by the treachery of Torre Tagle, he gave Santander an explanation that was almost a justification: "The cause of all this is that these men see their country destroyed without the slightest triumph, and they cannot imagine that it is possible to win with the few resources that I possess. Many have believed the rumor, spread by enemies within the country, that I will abandon them without fighting."[1]

He knew, of course, that the disorganization of government did not reflect a lack of patriotism among the people, and he told Sucre: "Every time that I reflect that we have about 10,000 men, that within four months we will have twice as many, that the country does not lack materials, and that the people, though patriotic, are being lost through lack of government, I first despair then make up my mind to act decisively."[2]

And did he not occasionally show hatred and anger for the Caracas that he loved so passionately? He exclaimed in one of his letters: "How unfortunate is the public servant in Caracas, especially if he is honest."[3] In another letter he described the whites of Quito as "worse than the *caraqueños*, which is no small thing to say."[4]

Above all, it must be remembered that Bolívar was in the position of being solely responsible for *what should be done* to deal with the disasters, problems and misfortunes that were all around him. At the same time he had to answer to those who took it upon themselves to tell him *what should not be done*.

He was restricted by this same condition in his relations with the Colombian Congress and with Vice-President Santander. The politicians in Bogotá were reluctant to send him fresh aid, perhaps because, like the Peruvians, they lacked confidence in the Liberator's ability to triumph; perhaps because they thought that he was leaving Colombia too unprotected; or perhaps because Santander was every day becoming more alienated as a result of his jealousy at the increasing glory of Bolívar and Sucre. For a time Bolívar was able to solve this problem by obtaining supplies from Quito and Guayaquil, where he enjoyed extraordinary powers and could count on loyal friends. But, when the resources of these departments were exhausted, and as new dangers appeared in Peru, he

---

1. *Ibid.,* iv, p. 108.
2. *Ibid.,* p. 69.
3. *Ibid.,* p. 192.
4. *Ibid.,* xi, p. 240.

believed that it was essential for the whole of Colombia to be prepared to sacrifice itself for the final liberation of the continent.

Santander, however, replied phlegmatically on January 6, 1824, that "if Congress provides me with financial support or if I can obtain it from Europe, you will receive aid; if not, not."[1] He added that he would ask Congress for "a law to allow me to send aid, because at the moment I do not have one." The remark was almost sarcastic.

Some time later, on May 1, Santander replied as follows to new exhortations from Bolívar: "I am governing Colombia, not Peru. The laws provided for my direction and for the government of the Republic have nothing to do with Peru, and their nature has not changed because the President of Colombia is commanding an army in a foreign land. I have done too much by sending troops to the south. There was no law to make me act thus, no law subjecting me to your orders, and no law obliging me to send to Peru whatever you might need and request. Either there are laws or there are none. If there are none, why are we deceiving the people with phantoms? If there are laws, we must keep and obey them, even though obedience to them produces harm."[2]

These arguments were too much like those used by the people of Carthage when they refused to help Hannibal in Italy. The scrupulous claim that there were no laws to permit him to come to the aid of his worried commander was an untenable sophistry. Did he really believe that, if he had combined his influence over Congress with Bolívar's prestige and insisted on the importance of this life or death undertaking, the congressmen would have ventured to risk the freedom of America and the very existence of Colombia? The Vice-President was also forgetting his arguments of 1819, when he told the Liberator that "other of our compatriots justly demand the seat of Piar."[3] Just after the reconstruction of the Republic's constitutional government, he had expressed the opinion, referring to what had happened in the Angostura Congress: "There is no remedy; it is still necessary to hang people without trial or judgement."[4]

It is true that the intervention of France and the Holy Alliance in Spain, to restore the absolutism of Ferdinand VII, aroused fears that they would also help with the reconquest of Colombia. But Bolívar explained convincingly to the vice-president: "It seems to me that this fear is unfounded, for nothing can persuade me that France has hostile intentions towards the New World, after she has respected our neutrality in ca-

---

1. *Cartas de Santander* (Caracas, 1942), p. 275. The editor points out that in the original the final "not" is written with larger and darker letters than the other words.
2. *Ibid.,* p. 290.
3. *Ibid.,* p. 99.
4. *Ibid.,* p. 116.

lamitous times when we were truly insignificant. Moreover, the English will adopt our cause on the same day that the French adopt that of Spain; and the superiority of the English over the allies is so great that this would be a triumph. In the meantime, we will not be so senseless as to neglect a clear, immediate danger in order to deal with one that is remote. I assure you that I do not believe that such madness could occur to anybody; for it seems an unpardonable error to me to leave open a door as large as that of the south, when we can close it before the enemy arrives in the north. I am arguing on the assumption that the French are coming. For the same reason we should quickly use all our forces to destroy these Peruvian scoundrels, so that afterwards we can go against the French in the north with all available American forces, willingly and in strength, for strength begets strength and weakness begets weakness.''[1]

In fact, the attitude of England and the proclamation of the Monroe Doctrine removed the danger of a reactionary European intervention in America. But this did not make the people of Bogotá any more willing to take an interest in Peru. It is sufficient to point out that the Congress which Santander intended to ask for "a law to allow me to send aid," although supposed to meet on March 1, was not installed until April 5, and it was the beginning of May before Santander asked it for permission to raise new forces.[2]

On May 6, Bolívar wrote to Santander in a last effort to move him by recalling earlier miracles: "I do not know what to tell you respecting the Peruvian situation. During this year of 1824, it has greatly improved, for I have employed the same energy I used in 1813, heedless of redeemers and complainers. There is no better argument than a *free republic*. The man who can produce one is in a favored position, and I have set myself to be a producer of handwrought republics. This is a full-time job, but a glorious one." He added: "Send the 4,000 men whom Ibarra has gone to seek. The day that you hear they have arrived in Peru, you may turn prophet and exclaim: 'Colombians, not a Spaniard remains on America soil!' "[3]

When this appeal proved fruitless, Bolívar stopped writing to the vice-president for several months. When he next wrote, in November, after the battle of Junín, he repeated that he had not asked him to violate the constitution, and that he could, at least, have sent troops to Guayaquil and the Isthmus."[4]

---

1. *Cartas,* iv, p. 106.
2. Lecuna, *Crónica razonada . . . ,* iii, p. 388.
3. *Cartas,* iv, pp. 149-50.
4. *Cartas,* p. 200.

Bolívar also tried, without success, to obtain troops and supplies from the sister states of Buenos Aires, Chile, Guatemala and Mexico. He appealed on Peru's behalf to O'Higgins, who was in the country.[1] But he obtained nothing. Once again, he was alone.

Fortunately, this painful wrangling did not affect Bolívar's combativeness, nor did it reduce the furious pace with which he had dedicated himself to reorganizing what he had left. On February 4, he wrote from Pativilca to Sucre, who was leading the army: "We retain above all the prestige of the Colombian army. Our glory remains immaculate. I promise you a final result worthy of the greatness of our cause. Impress these ideas deeply upon your soul; profess them as your daily faith and carry them in your heart, so that reluctance cannot weaken or destroy them. Dismiss from your mind any consideration that does not help to strengthen this design. Call to your aid all the thoughts and all the passions that can help to complete it. Your mind is fertile in its expedients, its readiness to co-operate is inexhaustible, your zeal, efficiency and activity are limitless. Employ all this and more to preserve the freedom of America and the honor of Colombia. The design is great and beautiful, and, for this reason, worthy of you."[2]

On February 10, the Peruvian Congress had granted Bolívar dictatorial powers and he, in his turn, appointed Sucre to command the combined army on the 13th. He was able to count on eminent, honest Peruvian patriots for the political and administrative reorganization of the country, including José Sanchez Carrión, whom he appointed minister of commerce, and Hipólito Unanue, who, although he had not sympathized with Bolívar in 1822, worked with him unselfishly in the new circumstances.

Bolívar was still convalescing at Pativilca when he wrote to Sucre, but he made clear his acceptance of his new responsibility with the declaration, "I am going to Trujillo to declare martial law and to place military commanders in the military divisions that I am going to establish. I am determined not to shrink from any means and to commit even my soul to save this country."

During these terrible months, the defeats suffered by the Peruvian forces, the country's spiritual crisis, Torre Tagle's treason, the Liberator's illness and the delay in sending reinforcements from Colombia, put Bolívar on the defensive and in a very serious position. One fortunate circumstance prevented the Spaniards from attacking the embarrassed republicans. It was that they, too, were divided as a result of the triumph of the absolutists in Spain. While General Pedro Antonio de Olañeta was in favor of "an

---

1. *Ibid.*, pp. 28, 97, 100.
2. *Ibid.*, iv, p. 62.

absolutely absolute King," the other commanders, Viceroy La Serna, Canterac, Valdés, were more or less liberal. Olañeta even proclaimed himself independent of the Viceroy, who sent Valdés to Upper Peru in pursuit of him.

This imprudence was attributable to the conceit produced by so many years of triumph in Peru. In Spain they were scornfully referred to as "los Ayacuchos", and the tales invented during the civil war in the peninsula still prevented many Spaniards from appreciating what these men did for their distant government. Bolívar, who saw them at close quarters, certainly knew what to fear from them. He told Santander: "The soldiers of the *godos* march fifteen or twenty leagues a day, and they carry for food a bag of *coca* and another of barley, or boiled or toasted maize. They march on this for weeks and weeks, and their commanders and officers go without sleep to look after the troops. I tell you now that there is not a friend or an enemy who does not talk of the marvels of this Spanish army, and by dint of repeated observation I believe it. They have kept up the war for twelve years, and they have been victorious for twelve years with only minor reverses."[1] He reflected on another occasion that, if he could obtain another 12,000 Colombians, he might be able to sap the minds of these tenacious, these obstinate Spaniards."[2]

Although his eulogy was inspired by despair, he also pointed out, when he realized that none of the royalist groups was prepared to negotiate with the republicans: "Note what Canterac states at the end of his letter. No matter what the outcome, they will always be Spaniards. The attitude of these *godos* has always favored war. Like all Spaniards, they are consistent in maintaining tyranny and injustice, but they do not possess the character to be consistent in supporting liberal principles."[3]

Although Bolívar knew clearly that these hard fighters were the same anywhere, no matter what name they adopted, they knew him only by hearsay. They did not know that he was capable in the space of a few months, alone and unaided, of improvising an army, turning heterogeneous contingents into veterans as they marched, and crossing the dreaded Andean *cordilleras* in search of them. They came to know him on the eve of Junín, when they saw that, although hundreds of leagues from his bases, he dared to cut off their retreat and to decide with cavalry a battle fought at a height of 4,200 meters.

The comparison that we have made between Bolívar and Frederick the Great was never more deserved than during this campaign. He took charge of everything, while Sucre, at the head of the army, defended the mountain passes through which the royalists might come in search of his forces.

---

1. *Cartas,* iv, p. 82.
2. *Ibid.,* p. 63.
3. *Ibid.,* p. 98.

He recommended to General La Mar "indirect, gentle and wise measures" to prevent renewed friction between the Colombian troops and those of Peru. He studied the roads that could be used either for a retreat or to harass the Spaniards. He indicated the places where each unit should be quartered. He ordered the manufacture of uniforms, sabres "and fine lances like those that we use in Venezuela." He gave details of the marches and the other training to be performed by the troops. He provided the design for the horseshoes (and the nails to be used for them) which would protect the hooves of the coastal horses when they were taken to the *sierra.* In one case he even gave the names of the officers who were to command each of the six small boats that were expected from Colombia. He demanded formal reports rather than letters or messages for official matters, because he wanted precision and responsibility in all things.

As chief of state he watched over many matters, from the accounts of the treasury, which had to be impeccable, to the presentation of the *Gaceta* and another periodical, which he criticized like a professional. He was like a simple squadron leader in his concern for the troops. He told Sucre: "Do not allow the horses to be shod with the shoes that have been sent, for the nails are useless. They should continue to dress the shoes until we obtain the good nails, large and small, which I will order of Vizcayan iron. The farriers and smiths should make the shoes perfectly, so that no time is lost." Santander was informed: "Here we have only the lancers who were led by Rondón and the Hussars of Silva. All are in excellent condition. They are capable of routing twice their number but not five times their number, as you can readily imagine, unless, that is, we should repeat our earlier miracles of Maturín, San Mateo and Boyacá." For this reason he watched over these units, even over small details. He considered it a horrible mistake to allow the horses to suffer, and he pointed out: "The animals that have gone to the *sierra* from the coastal valleys suffer much from the climate and the stones. We are looking for means to prevent this problem." He ordered: "Every man will go mounted on a mule, leading his horse by the halter." The problem of horses from areas with sandy soil becoming useless in rocky terrain had arisen in Venezuela in 1818, and Bolívar now stressed in all his instructions to his subordinates: "See that everything possible is done to harden the hooves of the horses from the coast. Burn them with sheets of hot iron and bandage them with rope *(cocuiza),* which you are to get wherever it is available."

O'Leary tells us: "The expedients that were adopted to make good the lack of materials for the manufacture of certain objects will seem unbelievable. In order to make the canteens, for example, he had collected for leagues around all the objects of tin-plate and all the wire cages. There was a nail as he got up from his seat. Examining it immediately, he discovered that it was made of the metal that was needed. A day later there was not a single chair with nails of tin remaining in any house or church in Trujillo."[1]

Bolívar also took pains to move "all the means of the human heart," to use his expression of 1817. The Peruvian town of Lambayeque worked feverishly for the army, and he ordered that it be announced: "The town of Lambayeque is very worthy, and I naturally love it a lot. Tell this to your intendant so that all will know of it."[2]

In reality, Bolívar could count only on this coastal zone in northern Peru. The rest of the country and Upper Peru were occupied by the royalists. As for Colombia, Quito had to keep watch on Pasto in the north, and only Guayaquil and the other southern departments continued to help him. He never knew if the hoped-for reinforcements would arrive from Bogotá and the rest of the country. On one occasion he remarked to Sucre: "They tell me that the Venezuelan soldiers are desperate to join me. The *Guardia* is superb, in excellent condition, and of full complement and strength. May God keep it so."[3]

But the Liberator also busied himself with improving the periodicals available to him, as if he had the whole nation behind him. He told Heres: "Now that there is so little paper for the *Gaceta,* it must have a narrower margin." And he told José Gabriel Pérez in another letter: "I enclose a copy of *El Centinela,* which has been unworthily prepared, so that you can correct it and have it reprinted, with the aim that it should circulate in a decent and correct form. Tear up this damnable newspaper, and make it better. The motto is badly placed. The reply, etc., in capital letters. The punctuation should be corrected; the improprieties removed, everything done again."[4]

This simultaneous impulse that he gave to all his activities was the secret of Bolívar's triumph. The battles were accidents within the vast whole organized by this "producer of hand-wrought republics." We see him becoming a legend between the battles of Boyacá and Ayacucho, a period clearly different from that of 1813-19. The localized, fragmentary war of the earlier period, dominated by guerrillas and indecisive combats, allowed only Bolívar's combativeness and constancy to be appreciated. From 1818 onwards, the character of the war completely changed. The dwindling of the guerrillas, large-scale operations, and the formation of a well-equipped republican infantry permitted Bolívar to reveal his quality as an organizer. He became a river instead of a torrent, increasingly wide and peaceful, irresistible because of the volume of its water rather than violence alone.

---

1. *O'Leary* (Caracas, 1952), i, p. 249.
2. For details of the Liberator's preparations, see *Cartas,* iv, pp. 126-8, 133, 138-40, 144, 146, 149.
3. *Ibid.,* p. 121.
4. *Ibid.,* pp. 139, 146.

He had also found in Sucre the most suitable complement for his character. Although a number of differences which arose in these years could have separated them, we rarely find in history an example of what we might call human nobleness, free of suspicions and meanness, comparable to that presented by the relationship between Bolívar and Sucre during this campaign. Bolívar frequently sent minute instructions and occasionally orders to his subordinate, but he received in exchange observations and advice. Sucre not only organized with unsurpassed ability everything to do with the defense, and then the proposed offensive, but also provided the Liberator with the moral support and security indispensible to him. Bolívar praised him joyfully and, when he called him to his side in 1824, he did so with the following flattering words: "What I now most desire is to meet you here to work out different plans. You should understand them so that you can advise me, and also execute the part that affects you. I have a strong feeling that the war will end, if its outcome conforms to my fervent and well-founded hopes. Because the matter is of the greatest importance, it is indispensible for me to have an adviser like you, who can both think and act. There is no genuine practical science without this combination. Finally, I want nothing so much as to see you arrive quickly."[1] How different is this Bolívar to the authoritarian, violent, "irresistible" man occasionally presented to us by both fools and scoundrels.

Sucre was unable at the time to leave the army to answer this summons, but they continued to consult by means of frequent letters. The Liberator said of one plan that he was sending to Sucre: "You will see that this project coincides with what you suggested to me with both judgement and foresight."[2] The Liberator also displayed genuine affection for Sucre: "Nobody in the world can make up for your absence;" "I have a million things to tell you, but when I sit down to write they escape me;" "I again recommend that you take care, that you do not walk alone, and that you do not take risks."

By June, four months after having been made dictator, Bolívar was ready to take the offensive. To search out the royalists he had to cross the Cordillera Blanca, a formidable mountain mass where the three divisions of the Peruvian Andes come together from the north before continuing southwards in two great chains. The various army units had been stationed by Bolívar and Sucre in positions which made it possible for them to be joined together as the advance took place. Sucre had arranged for stocks of supplies and fuel to be placed along the trails to alleviate the sufferings of the troops. But they had to march through the highest passes

---

1. *Cartas,* iv, p. 63.
2. *Ibid.,* p. 70.

ever used until then by regular armies. The Yanashallahs Pass, for example, which the Liberator used, reaches a height of 5,000 meters. The thin air was asphyxiating, and any excessive or continual effort was fatal. The dreadful mountain sickness, called *soroche* by the natives, caused vertigo, faintness and sometimes attacks of insanity, as Bolívar knew from personal experience. An avalanche or a snow-storm could bury a whole batallion.

In anticipation of these difficulties, Bolívar had suggested to Sucre in January: "Our soldiers must make two marches of ten leagues every week.... We must at the same time see that they are provided with every possible facility and that the convalescing, the weak and the injured are properly cared for, so that they will not become worse. We should also have the men cross the large *cordillera* from time to time to accustom them to *soroche* and to the arid tablelands."[1]

Acting on his own initiative, Sucre had been no less careful than his commander. The English General Miller, who accompanied him, later wrote: "From the beginning of the campaign General Sucre displayed the deepest wisdom in directing the march of the army to Pasco, 200 leagues distant from Cajamarca, across the most rugged terrain of the most mountainous country on earth."[2]

Miller referred as follows to the troops reviewed by the Liberator at the end of the march: "There, surrounded by the spectacle of nature, were assembled men from Caracas, Panama, Quito, Lima, Chile and Buenos Aires; men who had fought on the banks of the Paraná, at Maipó, Boyacá, Carabobo, Pichincha, and at the foot of Chimborazo. In the midst of these valiant American defenders of freedom, there were some foreigners, faithful still to the cause for which so many of their compatriots had perished. Some of them had fought on the banks of the Guadiana and the Rhine, and had been present at the burning of Moscow and the surrender of Paris."[3]

The place where the republicans and royalists faced each other was no less imposing, a majestic, solitary plateau 4,200 meters high, surrounded in the distance by snow-covered peaks, and with the lake of Chinchaycocha or Junín in its midst. The Spaniards, led by General Canterac, went north along the eastern edge of this lake, while Sucre and Bo-
Chinchaycocha, or Junín, in its midst. The Spaniards, led by General Canterac, went north along the eastern edge of this lake, while Sucre and Bo-
of him, intended mainly to learn more about their positions, although a communication to him from Viceroy La Serna shows that his appearance was also intended to frighten the patriots. La Serna wrote: "With such a movement towards the north of Cerro de Pasco, which I believe I sug-

---

1. *Cartas,* iv, p. 49.
2. *Memorias del General Guillermo Miller* (Madrid, 1910), ii, p. 130.
3. *Ibid.,* ii, p. 140.

gested to you some time ago, you will instill fear in the enemy...."[1]
Canterac's surprise, then, must have been extraordinary when he realized that Bolívar, in his turn, was looking for him and that he was forcing the march to cut him off at the southeast of the lake. At the same time Bolívar, too, found himself cut off, because his bases were so far away. But, like Nelson at sea, he often pursued or provoked the enemy when he found himself in difficulties, and succeeded in intimidating them.

Canterac hurriedly tried to retreat, while Bolívar and his cavalry rode ahead of the army to prevent him from escaping. The cavalry got off their mules to mount their horses, which they had been leading by their halters, and galloped to the plain alongside the lake. The royalists then decided to face them, confident that their numerical superiority would prove decisive against an enemy which, after making a forced march, had had to face the difficulties of quickly preparing for battle in open country.

The Liberator had told his men: "Soldiers! The enemies whom you are about to destroy boast fourteen years of triumphs. They will be worthy, therefore, of measuring their arms with ours, which have shone in a thousand combats." In fact, the clash was terrible. The artillery and even the musketeers played no part. Only two pistol shots were heard at the start of the engagement, and they were followed by the furious clatter of swords, sabres and lances in a fierce hand-to-hand encounter. At the outset the republicans were unable to break through, and it seemed that they were dispersing, although this may have been due to their peculiar habit of pretending to flee and then turning around. This disconcerting strategy, which the Venezuelan *llaneros* called *ternejal,* had brought them victory at *Queseras del Medio* and many other places, and the Peruvian royalists were unfamiliar with it. It was five o'clock in the afternoon and the shadows of dusk were beginning to fall on the solemn tableland. Finally, the republicans managed to break through on the left and they penetrated deep into the enemy camp. The fighting then spread all over the Junín plain, as both sides broke into isolated groups of furious lancers. The Argentine General Necochea, who had fought throughout the battle with incomparable bravery and skill, fell to the ground with seven wounds and the royalists seized him. He was soon rescued by Captains Sandoval and Camacaro who, together with Carvajal, Silva and other veteran commanders of the Colombian cavalry, were beginning to get the better of the enemy. The Peruvians fought no less bravely, and one of their units was rewarded by Bolívar with the name of the field where it was victorious. In the future it was called the *Regimiento de Húsares de Junín.*

---

1. Quoted by Lecuna, *Crónica razonada...,* iii, p. 413.

The republican victory was aided by an advantage, at first sight fortuitous, for which Bolívar was responsible. The "fine lances like those that we use in Venezuela," which he had had provided, were three and a half *varas* long, while those of the Spaniards were only two *varas* long. What seems almost unbelievable is that, despite their great length, these weapons were easy to use. General Miller, who wrote a lot of nonsense in an attempt to claim for himself the responsibility for victory at Junín, said of the *llaneros:* "The lances which are used in Colombia are twelve to fourteen feet long, and they have a thick, flexible shaft. The lancers fasten the reins around a knee, in such a way that they can control the horse, and they have two hands free to handle the lance. They generally strike their enemy with such force, especially when they go at a gallop, that they lift him two or three feet out of the saddle."[1]

The royalists were equally surprised by the way in which the *llaneros* dispersed and regrouped, fled in confusion and immediately recharged in compact groups, without revealing at times who was leading them or how he was doing it. It seemed to be a custom born of their excessive individualism and a symptom of indiscipline, but it demanded an extraordinary solidarity and long experience. General Páez and the other *caudillos llaneros* had made in into a strategy that was to be exploited deliberately. The extraordinary and intuitive Páez commented in his *Notas a las Máximas de Napoleón:* "It is essential to teach the cavalry to charge, retire and turn around. As our *llaneros* say, they must be *ternejal* in their charges."[2]

According to the dictionary, *ternejal* means the same as *terne,* that is, persevering, obstinate. But it is clear that the word had a special meaning for the Venezuelan *llaneros.* Their strange maneuver made such an impression upon the Spaniards that, many years later, the royalist General Ferraz confided to Lieutenant Colonel O'Connor that at Ayacucho he was opposed to letting viceroy La Serna's halberdiers pursue the republican lancers, because "the Colombians pretended to disperse so as to draw their opponents towards them; then they waited and lanced them at their pleasure, just as they did on the field of Junín."[3]

After the battle Canterac hurriedly continued his retreat, and halted only when he reached Cuzco. He lost a third of his men, and he left open to Bolívar the roads towards the coast and the entrance to Lima. The moral effect of the victory on the Peruvian people and on the royalists was even more important. Bolívar's ability in a period of four months to organize an army capable of crossing the Cordillera Blanca, to

---

1. *Memorias del General Guillermo Miller* (Madrid, 1910), ii, p. 144.
2. *Notas del General José Antonio Páez a las Máximas de Napoleón* (New York, 1865).
3. Francis Burdett O'Connor, *Recuerdos* (Tarija, 1895). Quoted by Lecuna, *Crónica razonada...*, iii, p. 417.

seek out and defeat those "tenacious, obstinate Spaniards," 200 leagues away from its base, demonstrated that the marvels that were related about the Liberator were more than legends.

There was also a healthy change in the attitude of the politicians in Bogotá. Their spokesman, Santander, wrote to Bolívar: "My pleasure and my jubilation are so much the greater because you have obtained this first victory without the need of reinforcements sent by the government. I want this to be the forerunner of absolute independence of the whole of Peru, secured solely by your efforts."[1]

The army, of course, was keen and full of enthusiasm. Bolívar promised in a proclamation: "Peruvians! The campaign that must complete your freedom has begun under the most favorable auspices. General Canterac's army received a mortal blow at Junín, losing a third of its manpower and all its confidence.... Peruvians! Soon we will visit the cradle of the Peruvian empire and the Temple of the Sun. On the first day of its freedom Cuzco will be happier and more glorious than under the golden rule of its Incas."[2] Without doubt, he had been dreaming of this proclamation for eleven years.

The battle of Junín was fought on August 6, 1824. The following day was the anniversary of Boyacá and the first anniversary of Bolívar's departure from the coasts of Colombia to fulfill his promises to Peru.

---

1. Santander, *Cartas* (Caracas, 1942), p. 311.
2. *Proclamas y discursos del Libertador* (Caracas, 1939), p. 290.

TO HER
LIBERATOR
SIMON BOLIVAR

B OLIVAR'S OPTIMISTIC AF-
fection for Sucre and the brotherly loyalty with which the latter responded might suggest that there were never any differences between them.
Nothing could be further from the truth. Sucre was proud, very attached
to his own convictions, and unshakeable on matters of principle and
honor. Naturally, they disagreed relatively frequently and, precisely at this
time of absolute co-operation in other spheres, the two leaders had to
overcome personal differences that might have been serious.

The first of these incidents occurred in circumstances that were very
painful for Bolívar. Recently arrived in Peru, he found himself obliged
to take sides in the dispute between Congress and Riva Agüero, instead
of being able to lead all the nations of America, symbolically at least,
in the hoped for campaign against the royalists. Later, when Riva Agüero
opted for treason, the Liberator had to compromise his prestige and
the arms of Colombia in the miserable task of bringing him to submission.
This represented a terrible test for Bolívar, for in his own country he had
always considered it humiliating to be a factional leader.

The Liberator explained the situation frankly to Sucre: "I have lost
patience with Riva Agüero. While he was conspiring at the head of a
faction of the Peruvian army, I abstained from using force against him;
but I have just learned that he is plotting with La Serna. As long as he
supported a Peruvian revolution, I could appeal to him in good faith,
but now that he is dealing with the Viceroy we must draw our swords
to subdue him. I want you to march to Haraz for this purpose." Sucre

replied, cuttingly: "You may not count on me for this; we have come to help the Peruvians, and we should not involve ourselves with their domestic affairs."[1] In vain Bolívar explained the objective reasons for his hard attitude, and stressed his own tribulations. Sucre agreed only to go with him, but without playing any role in the operation. Nevertheless, when the Liberator later wrote a *Resumen sucinto de la vida del General Sucre,* he nobly explained as follows the reasons for Sucre's refusal: "At that time General Sucre provided brilliant testimony of his generous character. Riva Agüero had slandered him atrociously, regarding him as the author of the decrees of the Congress, the agent of the Liberator's ambition, and the instrument of his ruin. Despite this, Sucre earnestly and passionately asked the Liberator not to use him in the campaign against Riva Agüero, even as a simple private. He would go only as a spectator, not as commander of the combined army. His resistance was absolute. He said that in no circumstances would it be fitting for the auxiliaries to intervene in the struggle, and that his own intervention was infinitely less permissible, for he was regarded as a personal enemy of Riva Agüero, and as his rival. It was said that the Liberator acceded to the vehement requests of General Sucre with infinite regret. He took personal command of the army until General La Fuente nobly decided to stifle his Commander's treachery and save his country from civil war by arresting Riva Agüero and his accomplices. General Sucre then reassumed command of the army."[2]

The second dispute between Bolívar and Sucre began a few days later. Offended by "the memorial or report of the secretary of war (of Colombia) to Congress, in which the government has described me to the people of my country as an incapable and incompetent commander," Sucre refused to accept the command of the Colombian troops in Peru. He added in a letter to Bolívar: "If I accepted active service at the head of soldiers who have always deserved victory while still suffering this humiliation, my compatriots and you yourself would consider me a general prepared to tolerate it all in order to retain his uniform and his post."[3] The Liberator, who had nothing to do with these extravagant opinions of the Colombian minister of war, replied to Sucre: "I have seen everything, and I have tried to make amends to you. I will do still more to persuade you that I have not offended you, not even remotely, and that, if I have, I am ready to give you full satisfac-

1. Larrazábal, *Vida de Bolívar,* ii, p. 217. This was reported by Joaquín Mosquera, whom the Liberator asked to persuade Sucre.
2. Bolívar, *Resumen sucinto de la vida del General Sucre,* in O'Leary, *Correspondencia,* i, p. 13.
3. O'Leary, *Cartas del Libertador,* i, p. 98.

tion, because I am just and because I love you very cordially in spite of everything."[1]

The third and most serious of these disagreements occurred in August 1824. A large number of troops had been left behind during the forced march in search of the Spaniards, some forming a rear guard and others in hospitals. Bolívar considered it indispensible to entrust the reorganization of these men to a commander of the highest ability, and he gave the commission to Sucre. Sucre's task, in fact, was to be identical to that performed by Bolívar between February and June when Sucre was with the vanguard preparing to cross the Cordillera Blanca. Sucre, however, felt humiliated, and he wrote to the Liberator: "I have been removed from the head of the army to execute a commission usually entrusted to, at most, an adjutant general, and sent to the rear guard at a time when we are marching against the enemy. Consequently I have been informed publicly that I am held to be incapable of active operations, and my companions have been authorized to regard me as an imbecile or as an unnecessary person. I believe, sir, that I will not be accused of conceit or ambition for using this language. Having refused with all my heart the leading position of Peru, which was once offered to me by the national authority, it seems that I have the right to demand of my compatriots that they understand that I seek only a little public respect. But this indifference of the fates does not separate me from the respect that I owe to my present position, nor does it authorize me to debase its decorum."[2]

Although he concluded by asking the Liberator to decide what should happen, Sucre made it clear that he wanted to leave the army. There was a certain ring of sarcasm in his closing comment: "For, as I have told you on other occasions, I can and wish to be a simple private individual in Colombia, a good citizen, now that fortune has not given me the protection I need to be a good soldier."

Bolívar's reply was one of the most attractive manifestations of the greatness of his character. He began merrily, using an expression from Rousseau, by telling Sucre, "this is the only thing that you have done in your life without talent." He went on: "I believe that you have completely lost your judgement if you think that I could offend you. I am full of sadness at your sadness, but I do not have the slightest regret for having offended you. The commission that I have given to you was one that I wanted to undertake; but thinking that you would execute it better than I, due to your immense activity, I conferred it on you more as a sign of preference than of humiliation. You know that I do not lie, and you also know that the elevation of my spirit is never degraded by deceit. You should, therefore, believe me." He went on to make a number of similar remarks, and

---

1. *Cartas,* iii, p. 281.
2. O'Leary, *Correspondencia,* i, p. 173.

then added: "If you wish to know whether your presence with the rear guard was necessary, take a look at our treasury, our munitions, our provisions, our hospitals, and the Zulia column; all dispersed and lost in a hostile country, incapable of surviving and moving. . . . If it is dishonorable to save the army of Colombia, I do not understand either the words or the ideas." He ended: "These delicacies, these rumors of the common people, are unworthy of you. Glory is in being great and in being useful.... If you wish to come to put yourself at the head of the army, I will go behind, and you will march ahead, so that everyone can see *that I do not reject for myself the task that I have given to you.*"[1]

Bolívar's letter was written on September 4, 1824, and a few days later, in fact, he left Sucre in charge of the army and went to the coast to receive the reinforcements expected from Colombia, and to attend to various governmental matters. However, he was always so attentive to the state and situation of the troops that one of his letters, containing instructions for Sucre, bore the heading, after the date, "At five o'clock in the morning."[2]

On October 24, he received news that could have been a mortal blow to his enterprise. He was informed from Bogotá that, by a law voted on July 28, followed by a decree of August 2, the Colombian government had taken away the extraordinary powers which he had been given to direct the war in the south. They also deprived him of the command of the auxiliary forces in Peru and of his authority to grant military promotions during the campaign.

These senseless decisions had been taken before the victory at Junín, and it is evident that, if this had not surprised the politicians in Bogotá shortly afterwards, they would also have ordered the withdrawal of the Colombian army front Peru. For what was the position of the army without Bolívar, who was both President of Colombia and Dictator of Peru? How right the Liberator had been to accelerate his bold operations!

The worst of it was that the Chamber of Representatives in Bogotá even discussed whether the Liberator "had ceased to be President for accepting the dictatorship without the permission of Congress," to quote from Santander's letter to Bolívar. Although the vice-president expressed regret for this and assured Bolívar that he had not opposed the law "to show them that the question of extraordinary powers was a matter of no importance to us," there is no doubt that he aggravated the intrigue in an extraordinary fashion by asking Congress "if the rank and posts granted by the Liberator in the army of Colombia would have validity here."[3]

---

1. *Cartas,* iv, p. 179. The underlining is Bolívar's.
2. *Cartas,* iv, p. 181.
3. *Cartas de Santander* (Caracas, 1942), i, p. 305. See, too, O'Leary, *Narración,* ", p. 278 and following.

Bolívar was alarmed at the possibly disastrous effect that all this might have on the army, and he earnestly recommended Sucre to exercise the greatest prudence in the face of the reaction that could be expected. But Sucre himself led all the Colombian forces in drawing up an address to the Liberator, in which, although they were discreet about the law itself, they showed their exasperation at "the atrocious insult of the executive power in asking Congress if the offices which Your Excellency has given to the army should be recognized in Colombia, as if we had renounced our country." They also expressed their desire to return to Colombia, saying: "After fourteen years, in which the enemies were driven out of Ecuador and we fulfilled our oaths to Colombia by making the Republic whole in its territory, the army was invited to join the Peruvian campaign. Your Excellency sent it, and then, with constitutional authorization, came to command it in accordance with a solemn request that had been made to you. If this army owed a debt of obedience to the government in the Peruvian war due to existing treaties, the obligations of Your Excellency are much more sacred, particularly since February, when, with the normal order of things in this country completely disrupted, Your Excellency offered to share its misfortunes or lead it to victory. . . . If you were to leave us halfway through the race, for no human reason, we would have the right to beg Your Excellency to return us to our country. There, close to the government, close to the authorities of the Republic, we would immediately benefit from the kindness of the laws; the army would soon receive its rewards, and the extraordinary powers that Your Excellency used to reward it would be unnecessary." This severe but justified irony contained a threat that should have been foreseen by the comfortable legislators, "the tired men of Bogotá," as Sucre described them in a letter.

Bolívar, however, obeyed the orders of the Colombian government, handed over full military control to Sucre, and agreed to send him frequent advice and suggestions.

It was clear to all that a definitive conclusion was drawing near. The Spanish army was not only much larger than that of the republicans but also possessed those infantrymen who undertook unbelievable marches on only a bag of grain and a few leaves of *coca*. The strategy of Viceroy La Serna and of Canterac consisted, then, of tiring and confusing the patriots by means of speedy, prolonged maneuvers in an attempt to surprise them in some hopeless position. Sucre counted on the enthusiasm and the confidence displayed by his forces, and he ardently wanted a decisive battle. The Liberator, for his part, suggested: "Since, unlike the enemy, we are unable to run away, let us maintain ourselves with prudence and circumspection. In the end he must come to a halt, and then we shall fight him."[1]

---

1. *Cartas,* iv, p. 214.

Bolívar later described these operations as follows: "General Sucre displayed all the superior talents that have led him to win the most brilliant campaign of all those that form the glory of the sons of the New World. The march of the combined army from the province of Cochabamba to Huamanga is a notable operation, comparable perhaps to the greatest in military history. Our army was half the size of that of the enemy, which also possessed infinite material advantages over ours. We saw ourselves forced to march in single file over cliffs, ravines, rivers, peaks, abysses, always in the presence of a hostile, larger army."[1]

Twice, during these prolonged maneuvers, the royalists took the republican army by surprise, and on December 3 they inflicted serious casualties on it while it was marching through the gorge of Corpahuaico—or Collpahuaico—and captured part of its artillery and munitions. But, as Sucre himself said, this momentary calamity amounted to the freeing of Peru, for it led the Spaniards to decide to accept battle.

It was fought on December 9, 1824, at Ayacucho, on a field crowned by the heights of Cundurcunca, where the royalists had taken up positions. The republican victory was overwhelming, and the victor was restricted only by his generosity when he conceded a capitulation to the vanquished, after Viceroy La Serna had been wounded and captured. Sucre's official report stated: "Our spoils already consisted of more than a thousand prisoners, including sixty commanders and officers, fourteen pieces of artillery, two thousand five hundred muskets, and many other articles of war. The enemy was in flight and cut off in all directions, when General Canterac, commander-in-chief of the Spanish army, accompanied by General La Mar, presented himself to me to seek a surrender. Although the position of the enemy could reduce it to an unconditional surrender, I thought it worthy of American generosity to concede some honors to the vanquished, who had triumphed in Peru for fourteen years.

"In consequence, at this moment the liberating army has in its power Lieutenant Generals La Serna and Canterac, Marshals Valdés, Carratalá, Monet and Villalobos, Brigadier Generals Bedoya, Ferraz, Camba, Somocursio, Cacho, Atero, Landázuri, Vigil, Pardo and Tur, together with sixteen colonels, sixty-eight lieutenant colonels, four hundred and eighty-four majors and officers, more than two thousand soldiers as prisoners, and all the military funds, munitions and other supplies that they possessed. There were one thousand eight hundred dead and seven hundred wounded in the battle of Ayacucho, victims of Spanish obstinancy and temerity."

This rebuke for the tenacious, stubborn Spaniards sounds like praise. But when these commanders returned to the Metropolis their political enemies succeeded in having them contemptuously called "the Ayacuchos," as if

---

1. In the summary of the life of Sucre, mentioned previously.

their surrender there could obscure the indomitable spirit with which they had prolonged Spanish dominion for fourteen years. What is even more curious is that even some modern Spanish writers have tried, with the same narrow or hostile attitude, to perpetuate the defaming mistake. The truth is that the Peruvian campaign was not won at Junín or Ayacucho, although both actions were brilliant. It was won in those short months in which Bolívar reconstructed the temperament of the Peruvian nation and formed the invincible army with which he ventured across the Cordillera Blanca.

The whole emancipation movement had the same character. It could not fail because it represented an idea converted into a collective aim which could not be destroyed. It was the direct fruit, not so much of bravery and skill in battle, but more of the organizing ability of its greatest *caudillo,* and of his faith and enthusiasm. The Liberator then displayed as on no other occasion the best qualities of his character: foresight, activity, experience, the ability to make the fullest use of human resources, the quiet energy of the reflective man, and the imagination and courage with which he had fought the Admirable Campaign eleven years earlier. If, in 1819, a commander of the capacity of Morillo advised his king from Venezuela that the republicans could be overcome only by "smothering them" with much larger forces and described as "marvels" what he had seen Bolívar do, how could the Spaniards fighting in Peru in 1824, almost deserted by their own forces, be expected to alter the course of the war?

It should be remembered that when Bolívar left Venezuela in 1821 to begin the part of his work which was to culminate in Ayacucho, he left behind veterans like Urdaneta, Páez, Montilla and Monagas, whom he might have considered irreplaceable. He was to raise to the highest positions men like Sucre, Córdova, Salom, Lara, Heres, La Mar, Flores, Miller, O'Connor and Silva, seeing infallibly from the beginning the tasks and the duties for which they were suited. In Peru he openly ignored those who were corrupt or inept and surrounded himself with valuable assistants such as Sánchez Carrión and Unanue. He rescued the country's officer corps, which had been wasted by incompetent commanders, recognized the reserves of patriotism and combativeness of the Peruvian people, and turned raw recruits into veterans and humble artisans into self-denying suppliers of the army. It was all this that made victory inevitable. The only way in which fate rewarded Bolívar beyond what he could anticipate was in giving him Sucre, his spiritual son, who, for the first time, allowed the tireless warrior some rest.

These remarks about the character of the Liberator and the war of emancipation are also directed to those American writers for whom our independence is solely a military adventure. Its true significance, and it is this that still makes it worthy of historical analysis, is that it revealed the fundamental virtues of our peoples—tenacity, patience, selflessness, spiritual discipline and faith—which perhaps could be called together again by another great voice. We can certainly admire the fourteen charges at Mucuritas and the lances of Junín, but it is in the collective spirit and in Bolívar's wisdom in using it that we find permanent values, far superior to these happy accidents.

Even after Ayacucho, the misery that had always accompanied the republican army did not leave it. Three days after the battle, Sucre wrote to the Liberator: "We lack medicines and everything for the wounded, who altogether number more than a thousand. . . . All the units need uniforms. . . . The officers are unclothed, for all of us, from myself down, have had our baggage stolen by the people of Huanta."[1]

But the dream of these combatants throughout their long suffering had been to enter Cuzco as liberators, and before the end of the year, on December 30, Sucre informed Bolívar with obvious emotion: "I finally write to you from Cuzco in 1824, and I can now say that there are no longer any enemies in Peru. Your offer to these people to end the war this year has been fulfilled, and it is one of my greatest satisfactions. I make you a present of the standard that Pizarro brought to Cuzco three hundred years ago. It is one of the things that has been thrown away, but it has the merit of being the conqueror of Peru."[2]

Only two Spanish commanders remained under arms: General Olañeta, who had stayed in Upper Peru as a dissident absolutist and who was not included in the Ayacucho surrender, and General José Ramón Rodil, who rejected the agreement and withstood the republican siege of Callao until 1826. The siege of the fortress was conducted by General Bartolomé Salom, the veteran who ten years earlier had agreed to serve as a subordinate with the 250-strong Los Cayos expedition, and it was he who accepted the surrender of this last Spanish bastion in America.

With all Peru free, the Liberator hurried to convene the Congress, which met on February 10, 1825, exactly a year after it had given him dictatorial powers. History provides only a few examples of a man achieving such splendid results within such a short time of being invested by a nation with supreme authority. Peru's misfortunes had been at their height in February 1824, with all the territory occupied by Spanish forces, the treasury ruined, the best units in the army destroyed, the people demoralized, and the country's leaders desperate or uncontrollable. The Liberator himself had been so ill that, as we saw, he was not even able to ride a docile mule. A year later two splendid victories had put the sym-

---

1. *Cartas de Sucre*. O'Leary, *Correspondencia,* i, p. 200.
2. *Ibid.,* p. 209.

bolic standard of Pizarro in the hands of the republicans. In both actions the Peruvian army, admirably reorganized, had matched the bravery, efficiency and discipline of the veterans who had been perfecting themselves in Venezuela and New Granada since 1810. Peru was now free, not only because her vast territory had been reconquered, but also because patriotism, enthusiasm and confidence had been restored among all classes of society.

Naturally, the displays of pleasure and of gratefulness to the Liberator were delirious. Congress asked him to continue to exercise supreme authority for a further year. It offered him a million pesos for himself, and an equal sum for the army. It decreed that he be given the honor of perpetual president, with the title Father and Savior of Peru. The city of Trujillo was renamed Bolívar. Sucre received from the Peruvians the title Grand Marshal of Ayacucho, and Bolívar, for his part, ceded to him in a way the greatest glory for the emancipation of America, when he declared in a proclamation that Sucre had won "the most glorious victory of all those obtained by the arms of the New World."

The Liberator refused the million *pesos* offered to him by Peru, because "I have never been willing to accept a reward of this sort from my own country." The Congress left the money at his disposal, so that he could use it for "works for the benefit of the fortunate nation, whose birth he saw, and for others in the Republic of Colombia which His Excellency chooses," but he did not accept the offer even on these terms. Of all the honors provided by Peru, the most moving for him was, without doubt, the medal which its representatives ordered to be struck with the inscription: "To her Liberator Simón Bolívar." The title that Caracas had given to Bolívar eleven years earlier, the insignia of obligation and glory that he regarded as superior to a crown, was thereby extended as far as the frontiers of Chile.

Despite these celebrations, Bolívar stayed in Lima for only four months. In April 1825 he left on a tour of inspection of the southern departments, to see conditions there for himself and to continue the work of administrative reorganization with which he had been engaged since his arrival in Peru.

Bolívar considered the tremendous inequality between social classes as one of the most serious problems in Peru. He had stated in 1815, in the Jamaica Letter, that this would profoundly hamper Peru's republican reorganization. Now that he could see it at close quarters, it seemed even more alarming and unjust. We have already discussed the measures that he ordered in Trujillo for the protection of slaves who wished to change their master. But, like the unfortunate Negroes, the Indians suffered horrible oppression. Sucre was more discreet in his judgements, but he, too, reported a startling situation in Upper Peru in 1826, which without doubt was identical to what Bolívar saw every day. Sucre told him: "With respect to the parish priests, I can inform you that they are unhappy with the order that no Indian should be forcibly obliged to hold a *fiesta,* and that only those who voluntarily want them should pay. You cannot imagine the infamous means that the priests use to make the Indians pay for these *fiestas.* In one case they took away the prettiest daughter of one poor man, who could not pay the fifty or hundred *pesos* for his *fiesta,* to sell her for the use of the first person to pay.... I am convinced that they will be satisfied only if we leave them their immunities, all the riches of the country, and I even believe that we will have to give them the government itself to make them happy."[1]

Of course, if this was permitted for the priests, it is easy to imagine what was done by the large property owners and the authorities; even the *caciques* themselves indulged in the most outrageous exploitation of their Indian brothers, instead of taking pity on them. In reality, Negroes, Indians, *mestizos* and the general mass of the people found themselves at the bottom of a profound, spiral hierarchy that seemed to reach down to hell.

On March 8, 1824, in Trujillo, Bolívar had decreed the division of land among the Indians and the abolition of the *cacicazgos.* On July 4, 1825, he amplified these measures and declared the Indians perpetually exempt from any kind of obligatory personal service.[2] O'Leary tells us: "*Mita* work, which had been prohibited since the previous year, was not the only burden beneath which the miserable Indian groaned. He was oppressed by innumerable injustices, any one of which would have been enough to crush him. The magistrate, the priest, the farmer, the miner, the artisan, each and all of them were his oppressors, obliging him to fulfill the most onerous and fraudulent agreements. Such servitude made life a curse for the Indian; even the consolations of religion were sold at the price of gold. But the Liberator put his authority to the defense of the Indians, issuing decrees to eradicate such abuses and prohibiting, under the most severe penalties, their employment in any work without a freely-agreed contract. He ordered all citizens to share equally in the performance of public works, which until then had been imposed only on the Indians, and he prohibited the further use of force to make them work."[3]

How enthusiastically the Liberator took these measures! It was only in Peru and Mexico that the two principal ethnic components of society both possessed an ancestry of greatness and culture. The defective social

---

1. *Cartas de Sucre.* O'Leary, *Correspondencia,* i, p. 384.
2. Lecuna, *Catálogo...,* iii, pp. 363 and 370.
3. O'Leary, *Narración,* ii, p. 352 (1952 edition).

organization produced by the conquest—which even perverted the ministers of God—had also changed this most fortunate inheritance into a curse for both races, with the whites benumbed by opulence and the Indians by misery. But would it not still be possible to begin to bring them together in a fruitful union? At least, Bolívar would not fail to point out to future generations this abandoned, rich vein of spiritual gold.

When we consider these generous measures taken by the Liberator, we are given pause by the heart-rending realization that they were to provoke so much hidden hatred and sly resentment against him amongst those who were accustomed to using their privileges remorselessly. Many of these evil attitudes still prevail in the judgements of those who are the heirs—at times they themselves do not realize this—of this iniquitous tradition. The forsaken, whom he also wished to liberate, still do not have a voice to speak for them.

Naturally, the development of popular education, which was to be accessible to all, became one of the Liberator's daily preoccupations, just as it had been in Colombia. He founded a university in the city of Trujillo, which he had declared the provisional capital of Peru before the Junín campaign. He instructed the Council of Government, which he invested with authority when he began his journey to the south, to send "ten youths to England, with the commissioners or separately, so that they can be instructed there in European languages, public law, political economy and other subjects necessary for the formation of the man of State." He decreed the establishment of a normal school, according to the system of Lancaster, in the capital of each department. He founded various colleges for secondary education—for both boys and girls—using former Jesuit buildings for some of them, and in all cases, carefully providing them with rents for their maintenance.[1]

But he was particularly interested in primary and technical education to improve the social and economic conditions of the common people, and in the protection of the most neglected—women, orphans and old people—and those who had never had the opportunity to learn a trade to support themselves.

Bolívar hoped to be able to secure the valuable assistance of Simón Rodríguez for this task. As we saw in one of the early chapters of this biography, he had insistently asked Santander to send his extraordinary teacher to him, in December 1823 and May 1824, as soon as he learned of his arrival in Bogotá. While he was ill at Pativilca, he wrote to Don Simón that extraordinary letter in which he told him: "You molded

---

1. *Decretos del Libertador* (Caracas, 1961), i, pp. 300, 323, 354, 417, 420. See |too O'Leary, *Narración*, i, pp. 318, 344, 354.

my heart for liberty, justice, greatness and beauty." Despite these displays of affection, Rodríguez had not hurried to join him, partly because of his understandable fear that he would be regarded as a parasite at the side of his omnipotent disciple, and partly because he was becoming increasingly intractable and unstable. When he finally reached Lima, O'Leary commented: "I saw the humble pedagogue dismount at the entrance to the dictatorial palace, to be greeted, not by the brusque rebuff of the sentry, which he perhaps expected, but by the affection of his friend, with due respect for his experience and their old friendship. Bolívar embraced him with brotherly affection, and treated him with a kindliness which showed that prosperity had not been able to corrupt the goodness of his heart."

Rodríguez's own account of the plan that they proposed to follow shows that their relationship, like the Liberator's effort to create educational institutions, was not entirely sentimental. Rodríguez declared, some years later: "He issued a decree for the gathering together of children of both sexes... not in *alms-houses* to spin for the State, not it *convents* to pray for their benefactors, not in *prisons* to purge the wretchedness and vices of their parents, not in *orphanages,* where they spend their time learning servility so that they will be bought by those who seek faithful servants or innocent wives, but in *comfortable, clean houses,* with rooms fitted out as workshops, supplied with instruments and directed by good teachers. The boys had to learn three principal trades: *Building, Carpentry* and *Smithery,* because the most essential things are made with earth, wood and iron, and because the operations of the secondary mechanical arts require a knowledge of these skills. The girls learned skills suited to their sex and to their strength. Consequently many tasks which men usurp from women were taken away from them. All had to be decently housed, clothed, fed and cured, and they received moral, social and religious instruction. In addition to the teachers of the different trades, they had agents to look after their persons and watch over their conduct, and a Director who drew up the plan of operations and had it enforced. The parents of the children gathered there were given employment if they were capable of it; and if they were invalids they were supported at the expense of their children. This avoided the necessity of creating a house for the idle poor, and it gave the children a practical lesson on one of their main obligations. Both the pupils and their parents enjoyed their liberty—the children were not made to become monks and their parents were not imprisoned. They were busy during the day, and at night they returned to their homes, unless they wished to remain. The intention, contrary to what was believed, was not to fill the country with wretched or competing artisans, but to instruct and accustom them to work so as to make them useful men, who could be given land and aid in beginning to work it . . . it was *to colonize the country with its own inhabitants.* Instruction and work was given to the women so that they would not be forced into prostitution, or to marry simply to ensure their subsistence."[1]

In order to fully appreciate the scope of this plan at the time, we should remember that in Europe there existed for the children of the common people only those *alms-houses, convents, prisons* and *orphanages* that angered Bolívar and Don Simón; and that until the beginning of this century women, without employment and enslaved by prejudice, grew up terrified by the dilemma of openly prostituting themselves or accepting a discreet form of prostitution in marriage. The stupendous synthesis of the project —*to colonize the country with its own inhabitants*— anticipated one of the most serious problems that immigration later caused for Spanish America: the possibility that the new arrivals would displace or overcome the creoles, victims of their lack of preparation and of defective social customs. The fear made the immigrant, who should have served as an example for us, into something frightful, and it has aroused odious xenophobia. At the same time, it occasionally gives the foreigner an exaggerated idea of his superiority, and in some countries it has held back the benefits that should arise from his presence. To begin by *colonizing the country with its own inhabitants* articulates in the happiest and most just form the benefits of education and immigration, and it would help both processes to disseminate reciprocal benefits.

The Liberator issued numerous decrees of another sort, dealing with the improvement of public administration and the judicial system, economic affairs, roads, etc. Some, such as that proposing the protection, breeding and domestication of *vicuñas* for the benefit of the people, had a very modern flavor. But these decrees merit hardly a mention when we compare their social significance with that of those already discussed. However, one of his recommendations to the Council of Government is worth quoting, for it shows his unshakeable determination to defend America against any hostile power. He ordered: "If any European power in addition to Spain declares war against any of the American states formerly held by Spain, or if there are reasonable fears of a rupture, the Council of Government will take such precautions as it deems convenient against the subjects of the power or powers that declare war, expelling those whom it suspects. It will take whatever measures it considers necessary to strengthen the sea and land forces of the Republic

---

1. Simón Rodríguez, 'El Libertador del mediodía de América y sus compañeros de armas defendidos por un amigo de la causa social' (Arequipa, 1830). Rodríguez was referring to the arrangements for Bolivia, but the plans for Peru and Colombia were the same. Rodríguez had just established a 'Casa de Industria Pública', on the same pattern, in Bogotá.

and to prepare to send reinforcements to the threatened states, observing on this matter the law of Congress concerning assistance to the new governments and most particularly to Colombia, whose forces are in this territory and which has made so many sacrifices for the freedom of Peru."[1]

During his tour of the southern departments, this work was frequently interrupted by the friendly receptions that he received everywhere. Some of these ceremonies were humble and moving, such as those improvised by the people who came to the roads or to small villages to see him pass. Others, like those arranged by the authorities in Arequipa and Cuzco, were magnificent.

O'Leary tells us that in Arequipa "the municipality and a large gathering of citizens went many leagues out of the city to welcome him, taking him a magnificent horse with a splendid harness. The stirrups, the bit, the breastplate and the saddletrappings were of solid gold. As he drew near to the city, a great number of people from all the surrounding villages crowded the road, blocking his path."

Bolívar, for his part, improvised one of his most beautiful speeches in this city. Greeting the students of Arequipa and through them the women of Peru, he showed how much his imagination was carried away in these lands of such extraordinary memories, when he declared: "Daughters of the sun! You are now as free as you are beautiful! You possess a country illuminated by the arms of the liberating army! Your fathers and your brothers are free! Your husbands will be free and in freedom you will give the world the fruits of your love."[2]

Cuzco was no less splendid. O'Leary tells us: "The fronts of the houses were adorned with rich tapestries and gold and silver ornaments, and the triumphal arches in the streets displayed the same rich trappings, attractively arranged. From the windows and balconies there fell a rain of flowers and laurel crowns, thrown by the precious hands of the beauties as the party passed, and handfuls of coins and medals were thrown to the cheering crowd. As in Arequipa, the municipal authorities gave him a horse with gold trappings, and the keys of the city presented to him were of the same metal. After attending a solemn *Te Deum,* sung in the cathedral, he went to the municipal building, where the city's leading ladies were waiting for him with a civic crown of gold covered with diamonds and pearls. Although he could not refuse to accept these costly gifts without offending those who offered them, I am certain that he did not keep any of them for himself. He distributed them among his staff officers and some of the army commanders, and even among

---

1. O'Leary, Narración, ii, p. 357.
2. *Proclamas y discursos del Libertador* (Caracas, 1939), p. 311.

the soldiers, giving preference to those who had most distinguished themselves during the campaign. I had the honor of receiving the keys of the city as a gift from him."[1]

But, without doubt, more than all these honors, the best reward of fate for the Liberator was that in this region, center of the Inca civilization, he had been able to complete the program which for him was the soul of the continental revolution. A decree that he issued in Cuzco on July 4, 1825, began as follows: "Considering, first, that equality between all citizens is the basis of the Constitution of the Republic;" and, after other considerations, it ordered: "First, that no individual of the State shall directly or indirectly demand personal service of the indigenous Peruvians without first agreeing to the payment for the work in a free contract. Second, the prefects of the departments, intendants, governors, judges, ecclesiastical prelates, priests and their assistants, landowners, and owners of mines and *obrajes* are forbidden to employ the natives against their will in *faenas, séptimas, mitas, pongueajes,* and other customary forms of personal service. Third, that for public works of common utility which the government might order, every citizen is to contribute in proportion to his means and faculties, and the whole burden should not be borne by the natives, as has been the case until now. Fourth, the public authorities, acting through the *alcaldes* or the local municipalities, will arrange for the provision of animals, supplies and other items for the troops or for any other purpose without burdening the natives more than the other citizens. Fifth, the wages of the workers in mines, *obrajes* and on estates are to be paid at the agreed rate in ready money, and they are not to be made to accept goods against their will or at inflated prices."[2]

Each of the phrases in this decree indirectly tells of the three centuries of exploitation and suffering that had weighed down the Peruvian people. But these measures, combined with those that Bolívar had announced on education in order to make effective the declared equality, were above all the moral justification of independence and of all the sacrifices that it had demanded. For a century, dreams, meditations and punishments had been combining powerfully in this great historical movement: the apostleship and the sufferings of Miranda, the executions of Tupac Amaru, the *Comuneros* of Socorro and José María España, the rigorous thinking of Manuel Gual, and the blood of the *quiteños* of 1809. To achieve independence, Venezuela and New Granada were turned into deserts by a fourteen-year long war. Quito, Guayaquil and Peru had to suffer constant exactions, when the Liberator was obliged to equip and feed an army under the gaze of 20,000 Spanish veterans.

---

1. O'Leary, *Narración,* ii, p. 351.
2. *Decretos del Libertador* (Caracas, 1961), i, p. 407.

If the proclamation of independence of a country should consist of a declaration of principles which justify it, we might as well say that the measures announced by Bolívar after Ayacucho, in accordance with a coherent doctrine of popular redemption, constitute an Act of American Independence much more important than all the documents with this title produced by the different countries. And they also radically changed the position of the Liberator in history. We must see him no longer as simply the leader of a successful military venture. He was the guide to the goals of justice and dignity without which the emancipation was meaningless. This was his ultimate reality: Bolívar was above all a social reformer, who had to mount the horse of the *conquistadores* simply because of the need to make his ideals triumph.

This was not an *a posteriori* addition. We turn once more to the testimony of Simón Rodríguez: "Bolívar, unlike the general public, saw dependence on Spain not in terms of ignominy or shame, but as an obstacle to the development of society in his country." It is this that gives permanent significance to his life and his teachings.

XXXII

TO COLONIZE
THE COUNTRY WITH
ITS OWN
INHABITANTS

Abrir

A FTER AYACUCHO, SUCRE
continued the campaign against the royalist detachments still under arms
in the south of Peru. He was also obliged to deal with General Olañeta, in Upper Peru, who was a danger not only to the newly liberated
country but also to the provinces of the Río de la Plata.

The Grand Marshal felt, of course, that these operations would be hardly
more than a military parade, after the resounding victory that he had
just won; and, in fact, the royalist units, which were without a unified
command and were demoralized, were surrendering as Sucre advanced
against them. Olañeta was more tenacious, and he intended to resist
even after he had been forced back to the frontier with Argentina. But
he lost his life in an unsuccessful attempt to subdue one of his own
subordinates who had pronounced against him.

The great Venezuelan strategist hesitated because of a different, more
serious problem of political law. For many years Upper Peru had been
a dependency of the viceroyalty of Lima, but from 1778 it belonged to
that of the Río de la Plata. Both states, therefore, could make claims
for jurisdiction, which were equally legitimate and equally debatable,
and Sucre, for his part, felt a repugnance at exercising a purely military
authority in this vast territory which, logically, aspired to a different
political order. These aspirations were supported by a number of arguments, but one in particular carried much moral weight. Two of Upper
Peru's most important cities, Chuquisaca and La Paz, had anticipated
the separatist movement of the Spanish American capital in 1810, and

La Paz had deposed the Spanish authorities, on its own initiative and with only its own resources, in July 1809. Although this movement was crushed in a bloody fashion by the royalists, it had given the city the prestige of being the first-born of freedom. Upper Peru displayed its patriotism on a number of other occasions, too, with the result that expectations were high when the time came to decide its future. Sucre later explained: "All my embarrassment had ceased, and I had decided to control Upper Peru with a military government, but this is not really a government, and I am not going to present military laws to the first sons of the revolution as the benefits that they expected from our victory."[1]

Guided, then, as always, by this pressing need for spiritual neatness, Sucre decided to call a meeting of representatives of the whole country and, by a decree of February 9, 1825, he announced the object of the assembly as the establishment of a "provisional system of government" for these provinces. Moreover, he stated categorically: "First, that the sole object of the liberating army in crossing the Desaguadero was to redeem the provinces of Upper Peru from Spanish oppression and to leave them in possession of their rights. Second, that it is not for the liberating army to interfere in the internal affairs of these people."[2]

The Liberator, however, did not approve of Sucre's decision, and he pointed out to him with sound arguments that the summoning of an assembly was in itself an act of sovereignty that could offend both Lima and Buenos Aires.

But what other solution was there? If they relied on the *uti possidetis* in force in 1810, the principle which Colombia had repeatedly proclaimed and in virtue of which she justified her rights to Guayaquil, they had to treat Upper Peru as a dependency of the viceroyalty of Buenos Aires. But this would create a most difficult situation. First, because it would mean openly taking up a position contrary to the interests of Peru. Second, because the other provinces of the viceroyalty of the Río de la Plata had declared themselves autonomous, and had their own deliberative bodies, thus suggesting that Upper Peru had even more right to call its own assembly. Third, because when Sucre issued his decree Olañeta was still a serious danger to the two neighboring countries, and Buenos Aires, faced with this lack of unity, had no hope of overcoming him. Fourth, because the provinces of Upper Peru were decidedly opposed to union with the Argentinians. Sucre told Bolívar: "From now on I warn you that neither you nor anybody else

---

1. Vicente Lecuna, *Documentos referentes a la creación de Bolivia* (Caracas, 1924), i, p. 285, memorial of Sucre to the General Assembly of the Departments of Upper Perú, 6 August 1825.
2. Quoted by O'Leary, *Narración,* ii, p. 366.

can join them voluntarily to Buenos Aires, for there is a horrible aversion to this connection. If you have the idea of joining them, you can tell Buenos Aires to send a strong army to enforce the union, because otherwise it will be difficult."[1] The other solution—to consider the area as Peruvian territory—would have been openly brutal, it would have immediately given the liberating army the character of a conquering force, and it would have overthrown the *uti possidetis,* which provided the only possibility of legitimate international peace among the South American nations.

Bolívar, then, had to accept Sucre's opinion, and on May 16, 1825, in Arequipa, he issued another decree which ratified that of February 9 about the meeting of the assembly.

He must have been greatly helped in taking this decision by information from Sucre that General Juan Antonio Alvarez de Arenales, who had been commissioned by the government of Buenos Aires to negotiate with the departments of Upper Peru, had been instructed to allow the provinces to decide their own fate. Sucre added: "Yesterday General Arenales came to my house. I told him that I had decided to suspend the gathering of the assembly until you arrived, or until I received replies from Buenos Aires, but he replied that in his opinion all delay was an evil, for increasingly in every town people were becoming more and more convinced that the meeting of the assembly was the only way of saving the provinces."[2] Following this, the Congress of Buenos Aires declared in a decree: "Although the four provinces of Upper Peru have always belonged to this State, it is the will of the General Constituent Congress that they be entirely free to decide their future according to what they believe best suits their interests and their happiness."[3]

Peru, which was more reluctant to renounce its claims, had replied to an inquiry from Bolívar in the following terms: "First, the combined army should continue to march against the enemy until, in the opinion of the Liberator, it has completely removed the danger that the freedom of Peru migh' again be invaded or disturbed; and in the liberated provinces it should provisionally establish a government best adapted to their circumstances. Second, the enterprise will be the responsibility of the Republic of Peru until the situation mentioned in the previous article arises. Third, if, when the demarcation has been made according to the constitutional provision and the Upper Provinces are separated from this Republic, the government to which they belong will indemnify Peru for the costs incurred in emancipating them."[4]

1. *Ibid.,* p. 373.
2. *Ibid.,* p. 375.
3. Lecuna, *Documentos referentes a la Creación de Bolivia,* i, p. 202.
4. Paz Soldán, *Historia del Perú Independiente,* ii, p. 3.

In short, the situation was one which was impossible to resolve to the satisfaction of all parties. Subsequently history has made it abundantly clear that neither Peru nor Argentina would have gained anything in wealth, stability or happiness if they had kept control of Upper Peru. On the contrary, the geographical extent of the area, its desire for its own government, and the distance that separated its cities from those of Lima and Buenos Aires, would always have caused hatred and turbulence if it had been joined to either of these states.

Nevertheless, resentment was still felt at the policies of Sucre and Bolívar, and it was with reason that the Liberator pointed out in a letter to Sucre: "Yesterday, upon my arrival here, I received your two letters, dated the 27th at Chuquisaca, together with an official communication from General Arenales, in which he tells me that his government has ordered him to make it possible for these provinces to determine their own interests and government. This representation on the part of General Arenales has impelled me to issue the accompanying decree, to be executed and put into effect immediately. You will note therein that I seek to reconcile whatever is reconcilable between opposing extremes and interests. I do not think that those who claim Upper Peru can possibly reproach me in any fashion, for, on the one hand, I cite the decree of the Peruvian Congress and, on the other, I recognize the expressed will of the government of Buenos Aires. Naturally, I leave Upper Peru the right of expressing her own wishes freely. Nevertheless, I am convinced that everyone will be displeased, for I have done nothing more than palliate, or rather neutralize, the different measures that each party could hope to adopt. Among contending groups, the judgements that result from equity are the ones that please the least, since they give satisfaction to neither party."[1]

Bolívar was so conscious of the delicacy of the situation that he was not prepared to go to Upper Peru while its representatives were deliberating, and he advised Sucre: "The meeting place of the assembly must be cleared of troops of the liberation army within a radius of twenty leagues. No soldier is to remain within the area so defined. A civilian judge must govern the area, and you, of course, will remain as far away as possible."

The whole of Upper Peru was happy and enthusiastic at such happy auguries. The unfortunate disputes and the personalist intrigues that had marred Bolívar's arrival in Peru were not to be found here, and all greeted the liberators with a combination of genuine gratitude and jubilation. The assembly of deputies which was installed in Chuquisaca on July 10 declared that it was trusting in "the protecting hand of the father of all Peru, the savior of the peoples, the first-born son of the New World, the immortal Bolívar." It proclaimed the independence of

---

1. O'Leary, *Narración,* ii, p. 376.

Upper Peru on August 6, the anniversary of Junín, and ordered that the new state should be called the Republic of Bolívar; this was shortly changed to Bolivia.

A commission of the assembly carried these messages of affection to Bolívar, who was still in Peru, and it was then that he decided to visit the country that bore his name. In one of the frontier towns, José Domingo Choquehuanca, a *mestizo* of Inca origin, who enjoyed the rare distintion of having obtained his doctorate, greeted him with words that have become memorable: "Nothing done before your time can compare with what you have done, and there would need to be a world to liberate for anybody to be able to imitate you. You have founded three republics, which, in the enormous development that awaits them, will carry your greatness farther than that of any other man. Your fame will grow as time passes with the lapse of the centuries, just as shadows grow as the sun sets."

All the towns bedecked themselves to receive him, and they competed with each other in festivities and praises. In La Paz he was presented with a civic crown of gold and diamonds, but Bolívar handed it to Sucre, saying: "This reward belongs to the victor, and that is why I am giving it to the hero of Ayacucho."[1] Several cities had commemorative medals struck in honor of the two liberators, and fine presents awaited them in all of them.

Bolívar's triumphal tour extended as far as Potosí, which since 1814 had been the declared terminus of his dreams of glory and freedom. But, although he perhaps mentioned it occasionally as a distant symbol, he never thought that in reality, in concrete form, he would end his campaigns in this city and climb the mountain which represented fabulous riches and power to the whole world.

O'Leary, who went with him, tells us: "Shortly after his arrival the Liberator, accompanied by General Sucre, the prefect of the department, the plenipotentiaries from La Plata, and his staff, visited the lofty mountain after which the city is named. The climb is steep, almost perpendicular, and mules can be ridden only two-thirds of the way up. The rest of the way must be climbed on foot, and the going is anything but easy because of the rugged terrain and the difficulty of breathing. . . . On that famous peak the Liberator unfurled the flags of Colombia,

---

1. O'Leary, *Narración*, ii, p. 384. Lecuna, *Crónica razonada...*, iii, p. 502, confirms O'Leary's account, but in the same vol., pp. 493 and 643, mentions another crown, given to Bolívar in Cuzco, which he kept for Sucre, and which the Grand Marshal gave to the National Museum of Bogotá, where it is called the Crown of Cuzco. Angel Grisanti, for his part, says in his *Vida ejemplar del Gran Mariscal de Ayacucho* (Caracas, 1952) that the garland offered to Bolívar in La Paz was given by him to Sucre, and by the Grand Marshal to the Granadan general José María Córdova.

Peru and La Plata.... That notable day on which he climbed the celebrated peak of the gigantic Andes, whose grandeur was rivaled by his own when he reached the pinnacle of fame, must certainly have been the happiest day in Bolívar's life."[1]

Moreover, the representatives of Buenos Aires who accompanied him had brought with them a tempting proposition. The government of La Plata was involved in a serious conflict with Brazil, which had invaded the Banda Oriental, now the republic of Uruguay, with the intention of incorporating it to the empire; and, as Brazilian troops had also invaded the province of Chiquitos, which belonged to Bolivia, the Argentinians came to propose joint action against the aggressors, directed by the Liberator himself. The proposition was dazzling. Bolívar could put himself at the head of the republican troops of South America to punish this first usurpation of frontiers on the part of the imperial regime, perhaps proclaim a republic in Brazil, and return in triumph to Venezuela along the Atlantic coast of the vast, redeemed continent.

Fortunately, the Liberator was able to control himself. This personal glory would have been won at the cost of new sacrifices for the exhausted people, and serious complications with several European powers could be expected. He was more attracted by his old idea of invading Paraguay to overthrow the dark despotism of Dr. Francia and free the learned Bonpland; but he renounced this idea, too, when the Argentine commissioners reacted unfavorably to it.

Meanwhile, he was confronted by the more urgent, difficult task of giving the revolution, which until then had triumphed only on the battlefields, a transcendental significance, the scope for the salvation of the people. Bolívar had always thought along these lines, and he noted at the time: "Every revolution has three stages: war, reform and organization. The first was the affair of the soldiers. We dealt with the second in Cúcuta and Bogotá. I would like this stage to be the one where we organize ourselves."[2] For Bolívar, then, the military victory and the juridical reconstruction of the state achieved in Cúcuta and Bogotá were only transitory stages in the real revolution, which had to consist of a reorganization of society.

We have already seen that the merciless exploitation suffered by the common people aroused the indignation of both Sucre and Bolívar. Together they tackled the task of remedying the situation, devoting to it as much time as could be spared from the celebrations arranged for them. Apart from numerous urgent dispositions about roads, judicial organization, selection of administrative personnel, exchequer affairs, exploitation of the mines, reforestation of desert or devastated areas, etc., the Liberator

---

1. *Narración,* ii, p. 388.
2. Vicente Lecuna (ed.), *Papeles de Bolívar.* Fragmentos autógrafos (Caracas, 1917).

and Sucre did all they could to extend to Bolivia the measures announced in Peru to free the natives and provide them with their own land, to suppress the abuses that practically reduced them to slavery, and to improve, if only by a little, their most miserable situation. We have already discussed the proposals to extend education and incorporate it into a wide plan for social reform.

The collaboration between Bolívar and Sucre was based not only upon their spiritual affinity but also on their official positions, for the Chuquisaca Assembly had decided that the Liberator was to exercise supreme authority as long as he remained in the country and that when he left, his powers would pass to Sucre. The transfer of authority took place when the Liberator decided, early in 1826, to return to Peru.

The representatives of Bolivia had also asked the Liberator to draw up the constitution of the new republic. He immediately applied himself to the task with such enthusiasm that, although he did not reach Lima until February 1826, he was able to submit his plans with supporting arguments to the Bolivians in May. The lifetime president reappeared in this draft as the supreme representative of the state and the center of equilibrium among its different powers, "for in non-hierarchical systems, more than in others, a fixed point is needed about which leaders and citizens, men and affairs can revolve." But the president would not enjoy complete power, as Bolívar explained: "He is deprived of all patronage. He can appoint neither governors, nor judges, nor ecclesiastical dignitaries of any kind. This limitation of powers has never before been imposed in any constituted government. One check after another has thus been placed upon the authority of the head of government, who will in every way find that the people are ruled directly by those who exercise the significant functions of society. The priests will rule in matters of conscience, the judges in matters involving property, honor and life, and the magistrates in all major public acts. As they owe their position, their distinction and their fortune to the people alone, the President cannot hope to entangle them in his personal ambitions. If to this is added the natural growth of opposition which a democratic government experiences throughout the course of its administration, there is reason to believe that, under this form of government, usurpation of the popular sovereignty is less likely to occur than under any other."

The Liberator, then, built his constitutional organization upon the representative bodies, which, in practice, would control public life, and the judicial body, which, endowed with "an absolute independence," would provide the real defense for the rights of the citizen. There were to be four main representative bodies. To begin with, each province would have an electoral college, elected directly by the citizens, to represent "their needs and interests and serve as a forum from which to denounce any infractions of the laws or abuses by the magistrates." These colleges, which together composed the electoral body, also had the right to propose candidates for almost all public positions, including those of judge, prefect, *corregidor,* priest and curate. The legislative body consisted of three houses: one of tribunes, elected for four years, another of senators, who were to serve for eight years; and a third chamber of censors, appointed for life to exercise—like the Moral Power proposed at Angostura—"a political and moral power not unlike that of the Areopagus of Athens and the Censors of Rome."

But we regard as more important than the formal organization of the state, Bolívar's customary intention to make himself a social reformer. His vehement arguments in favor of the abolition of slavery in Bolivia and the need to commit the country to real equality for all citizens cannot be omitted: "Legislators," he exclaimed, "slavery is the negation of all law, and any law which should perpetuate it would be most sacrilegious! What justification can there be for its perpetuation? Examine this crime from every aspect and tell me if there is a single Bolivian so depraved as to wish to sanctify by law this shameless violation of human dignity. One man owned by another! A man reduced to a chattel! An image of God coupled to the yoke like a beast! Where are the legal claims of the enslavers of men? . . . . To transmit, to prolong, to perpetuate crime mixed with torture would be a most detestable outrage. To establish a principle of ownership based upon a heinous dereliction cannot be conceived unless the very elements of law and right are distorted and all our concepts of men's obligations perverted beyond recognition. No one can violate the sacred doctrine of equality. And can slavery exist where equality reigns supreme? Such contradictions impugn our sense of reason even more than our sense of justice. We would be better entitled madmen than tyrants."

The boldness of these declarations can only be appreciated fully if we remember that in North America, which was considered a model of democracy, the abolition of slavery was declared more than thirty years later, and even then it caused a bitter war. In the countries addressed by the Liberator, moreover, time-honored customs of government had consolidated a hierarchy so rigid that all the inferior social classes were hardly distinguished from the slaves. And Bolívar was fully aware that these innovations would arouse the hatred of the most powerful. He wrote to Santander: "Those who are intolerant and those who love slavery will read my dissertation with horror, but I was obliged to speak in this manner, because I think I am in the right and because good policy, in this instance, is backed by truth."[1]

---

1. *Cartas,* v, p. 323.

At this same time Bolívar was also involved with another project: the assembly in Panama of representatives of all the Spanish American countries, so as to gradually achieve, through successive meetings, continental unity. The idea came from Miranda, and it had become so rooted in Venezuela that one of the first patriotic songs of the revolution, which later became the national anthem, assumed that it had already been achieved: "Joined by knots which heaven fashioned, the whole of America exists as a nation," sang the revolutionaries there. But Bolívar, more than anyone else, had fought insistently for its triumph, especially in 1815, 1818, 1821 and 1823, as we have seen. Finally, on December 7, 1824, two days before Ayacucho, and in spite of his worries about the campaign, he asked the other American governments to proceed to the nomination of their plenipotentiaries, telling them: "It seems that, if the whole world should have to choose its capital, the Isthmus of Panama, located as it is in the center of the globe, with Asia on one side and Africa and Europe on the other, would be the site chosen for this grand design. The Isthmus of Panama has been offered for this purpose in the existing treaties by the Colombian government. The Isthmus is equidistant from the extremities of the continent, and for this reason it ought to be the provisional location for the first meeting of the confederates." However, in order to understand the importance that Bolívar attributed to this initiative, we must refer not only to his words on this occasion, but also to the sum of his reflections on the future of Spanish America and its need for organization. Taking this Bolivarian doctrine, revealed in numerous letters and documents, into account, we can summarize as follows the objectives that he assigned to the meeting of delegates at Panama: First, permanent peace among the American nations and mutual respect for frontiers, and the settlement of differences by friendly discussion or compulsory arbitration; second, joint defense against any external aggression; third, the stabilization of republicanism in all the states; fourth, periodic or permanent consultation among all the states to resolve their common problems and to advance the social reforms of the revolution.

The *Papeles de Bolívar* contain a draft of Bolívar's views on the Congress of Panama in which he defined its aims as follows: "1. The New World would consist of independent nations, bound together by a common set of laws which would govern their foreign relations and afford them a right to survival through a general and permanent congress. 2. The existence of these new states would receive fresh guarantees. 3. England and Spain would make peace and the Holy Alliance would grant recognition to these infant nations. 4. Domestic control would be preserved intact among the states, and within each of them. 5. No one of them would be weaker than another, nor would any be stonger. 6. A perfect balance would be established by this truly new order of things. 7. The power of all would come to the aid of any one state which might suffer at the hands of a foreign enemy or from internal anarchic factions. 8. Differences of origin and color would lose their influence and power. 9. America would have nothing more to fear from that tremendous monster who has devoured the island of Santo Domingo nor would she have cause to fear the numerical preponderance of the aborigines. 10. In short, a social reform would be achieved under the blessed auspices of freedom and peace."[1]

The need to obtain the support of Great Britain against the Holy Alliance and the black reaction that had made itself master of Europe, led Bolívar to stress that the project be placed under the protection of England. He was perhaps also motivated by his desire to use the example of British political institutions to neutralize the widespread tendency of the Spanish Americans to imitate North American federalism, which Bolívar was prepared to accept as the bond of union among the confederated countries, but not for their internal constitutions.

The assembly finally met in Panama on June 22, 1826, with representatives from only Mexico, Central America, Colombia and Peru. England sent an observer; the United States and Brazil promised to attend but, for different reasons, they failed to do so; Bolivia, which was not even independent when the summonses were issued, later delegated the appointment of its delegates to the Liberator, but it did so too late; Chile and Argentina were, to quote Bolívar, "in a lamentable state, almost without government." At any rate the plenipotentiaries who did attend represented the largest and most powerful Spanish American nations, and the treaty that they signed on July 15, 1826, was of extraordinary doctrinal significance, compared with what international law had known previously.

The main points of the agreement are summed up as follows by the eminent commentator, Dr. José Gil Fortoul: "...a league and perpetual confederation was established for the common support, defensive or offensive, of the sovereignty and independence of the allied powers against all foreign domination. Every two years in peacetime, and annually in wartime, each state would send two plenipotentiaries to a general assembly for the following purposes: to negotiate and conclude all treaties, conventions and other acts that would produce the best reciprocal relations among the confederates; to contribute to the maintenance of peace and friendships by serving as a point of contact in the face of common danger; as a faithful interpreter of the treaties and conventions concluded in the same assembly when any doubt about their

---

1. This document was first published by Dr. Vicente Lecuna in Washington in 1916; he later included it in *Papeles de Bolívar* (Caracas, 1917), p. 237. and in *Crónica razonada...*, iii, p. 526.

meaning arose, and as a conciliator in their disputes and differences; to arrange conciliation and mediation between the allied powers, and with one or more powers outside the confederation, if they were at war or were threatening a rupture; and 'during war between the contracting parties and one or more powers outside the confederation, to arrange and conclude all those treaties of alliance, compacts, subsidies and contingents necessary to accelerate its termination.' No one party could make alliances with another power without first consulting the others. Whenever they were unable to settle amicably their present or future differences, they would submit them to the judgement of the assembly, but its decision would not be binding unless the disputing parties had previously agreed that it should be. Nor could any of the confederates declare war or order an act of reprisal against another, without first submitting its case, with documentation, to the conciliatory decision of the assembly. In order for a confederate to declare war or embark on hostilities against a foreign power, it should first seek the good offices and mediation of its allies. In no case could the confederation join itself with the enemy of one of the allied powers. A state that declared war or opened hostilities without having sought mediation, or which refused to accept the decisions of the Confederation if it had submitted the case to it, would be expelled. The other American states could join the confederation within a year of the ratification of the treaty if they accepted all its provisions. The confederates also bound themselves to co-operate in the complete abolition of the slave trade, and to declare ships bringing them from Africa pirates. Each state would retain its sovereign army for its foreign relations with the other powers, insofar as it was not opposed to the spirit and letter of the treaty. Special agreements, also signed on July 15, stipulated that each state had to raise and maintain an army of 60,000 infantry and cavalry, and a fleet of twenty-eight ships, for defense against Spain. And on the same date Congress agreed to move to the town of Tacubaya, near Mexico City, to continue there its deliberations. It proved impossible to do this."[1]

Although the internal problems of their republican reorganization were to prevent the countries from developing these principles, their doctrinal importance honors Spanish America, which gave the world an exceptional example. Inter-American relations have gradually gravitated to them, as to a superior moral model. In view of this it should be regarded simply as an accident that the aims of the great assembly were not realized immediately. The words with which the Liberator stressed its permanent significance, in his letter of convocation of December 7, 1824, have turned out to have represented a prophecy rather than a dream: "A hundred centuries hence,

---

1. José Gil Fortoul, *Historia Constitucional de Venezuela* (Caracas, 1930), i, p. 546.

posterity, searching for the origin of our public law and recalling the compacts that solidified its destiny, will point with respect to the protocols of the Isthmus. In them will be found the plan of the first alliances that will have marked the beginning of our relations with the universe."

In one of his letters to Pedro Gual, the Colombian representative at the Panama Congress, the Liberator discussed a further project, to which he returned several times and which, although it was not realized, merits some discussion. He wanted a military alliance among Colombia, Mexico and Guatemala for the purpose of liberating Cuba and Puerto Rico; but he was determined that, if assistance was not forthcoming, Colombia alone would undertake the expedition. He told Gual: "I also think that the army (of the proposed allies) should have at least 20,000 men, and the squadron should be at least equal to that of the Spaniards in America, always with the ostensible idea of taking Havana and Puerto Rico; but he was determined that, if assistance were not forthcoming, providing men, we must put up with it, so as not to find ourselves alone in the struggle; for ultimately Colombia alone will have to fight."[1]

It was also in this period that Bolívar produced his essay on public education, which was discussed in the early chapters of this book. He thought about education so intensely that he indicated the best methods of teaching reading and writing, explained to what point good manners should be insisted on, and recommended that games and recreation be permitted, for they were "as necessary as food for children."[2]

A similar document was the undated set of instructions sent by Bolívar to the director of a North American college, in which he discussed the method to be followed for the education of his nephew, Fernando. It contained very original pedagogic suggestions, and Bolívar even expressed an opinion on dancing, "which is the poetry of movement." But it is interesting, above all, because it reminds us that when he was a youth, Bolívar took an interest in the education of his other nephew, Anacleto, and he now took charge of that of Fernando, even to the point of thinking and writing about what he considered most convenient for his spiritual training.

Even though such important duties and the worry that they caused must have kept Bolívar's mind in constant tension—not to mention the burden of the everyday responsibilities of a man in his position—his political adversaries had set about the sad task of declaring that he had abandoned himself to a life of pleasure in his villa at La Magdalena, near Lima. It was said that he was insatiable as far as women were concerned.

---

1. *Cartas,* vi, p. 54.
2. *Papeles de Bolívar,* p. 301.

Of course, these legends should be set within the atmosphere of the period, so that we neither attach too much importance to them nor indignantly reject them as dishonorable calumnies. Models that provoked imitation were reaching America from Europe. Even if we ignore the adventures that Byron undertook with satanic vanity, and those that Chateaubriand unctuously exalted with the aid of his Christian spirit, those of a number· of politicians and soldiers, in particular Nelson, echoed around the world. There were some examples in which the indiscretions attributed to Manuelita Sáenz and Bolívar were mirrored: the case, for example, of the Duchess of Devonshire, the friend of Pitt's rival, Charles James Fox, who in England had organized military parades dressed as a soldier.[1] It is most likely, then, that these examples were influential in a dual sense: either in dispelling the scruples that Bolívar might have felt in copying them, or in encouraging his detractors to invent things that did not really occur.

We should also remember that until recently *donjuanismo* was regarded as a sign of superior virility, and almost every important figure was adorned with it. The Venezuelans themselves had no desire to be backward in this with respect to Bolívar, and we have already seen how they insisted on versifying adventures as trivial as that with Fanny du Villars. But we believe it worthwhile to clarify the situation, for distortion in either direction could misrepresent completely the character of the subject. As far as we are concerned, it seems that in Lima, as in Paris, the truth is to be found somewhere in the middle. There is no doubt that by nature Bolívar, like Miranda and even like the long suffering Andrés Bello, possessed an exaggerated sexual appetite. At the same time, all the evidence shows that, like his two eminent compatriots, he never allowed this inclination to interfere with the superior goals that he had marked out for himself. We have seen that during the Venezuelan campaigns he spent only a few days in the cities, because of his constant zeal to get back to the military camps, either to continue military operations or to care for his troops and watch over his subordinates. Love could not detain him even in Angostura where he had Josefina Machado, or in Bogotá, where he courted Bernardina Ibáñez. When he reached Peru he left Lima and established himself in the north, at times in places like Pativilca, where he lived alone and without any creature comforts. He declared repeatedly in letters written at this time that he did not want to return to city life "to lose time and patience." With the exception of his forced exile in Jamaica, his longest stay in a city from the end of 1813 was in Lima, where he spent four months between December 1824 and April 1825 and seven months in 1826, February to

---

1.   Jacques Chastenet, *William Pitt* (Buenos Aires, 1945), p. 41.

September, when he was involved with the wearying tasks described above. There is absolutely no doubt that such a life does not show an inclination towards pleasure or vanity.

The final point is that in Peru the constant company of Manuelita, who looked after his archives, sometimes acted as his amanuensis and, as his lover, noisily watched over him, allowed Bolívar only brief, clandestine flirtations. But those who invent these legends about him are discredited above all by their exaggeration. The Peruvian genre writer, Ricardo Palma, even invented roguish anecdotes—as in the very well known *Las tres etcéteras del Libertador*—in which, in order to make the supposed adventures of the hero amusing, he did not hesitate to depict his compatriots as solicitous purveyors, who awaited Bolívar in even the most distant towns to offer him women. Similarly, there are tales about the exorbitant sums of money that he spent on perfumes and at his table.

Simón Rodríguez commented, arrogantly and rightly: "What Peruvian does not know that Bolívar was born in abundance and that he renounced it for the life of a soldier? A man who is used to eating off a drum with his officers does not travel to be given *splendid banquets.* Bolívar did not come to Peru *to eat well.* What will Europe say when it reads, in a *political essay,* remarks about soups? When it sees a man moved to pity by the presence of a table?"[1] Despite these criticisms, Rodríguez also acknowledged that "the Peruvians are liberal with their attentions. Accustomed to make displays at every opportunity, they are held back by neither inconvenience nor cost; they spend extraordinary sums, when they feel the obligation, for persons less important than Bolívar; their generosity does them honor. . . ."

Bolívar, who had refused to accept a salary in Peru and the million *pesos* granted to him after Ayacucho, wrote to Santander in October 1825 about some payments that he had ordered him to make: "It was not right for the President of Colombia to be in the pay of Peru. If there is any difficulty about these monies, have them charged to my back pay. The amount involved is not more than sixteen thousand *pesos,* a small sum not worth troubling even to refuse. I told the Peruvian authorities that my government would pay it and, therefore, I would not accept the fifty thousand *pesos* which they offered me."[2]

Another kind of opposition, truly respectable, also grew in Peru. It was natural for the country, once independent, to want to dedicate itself to determining its own future. Many Peruvians must have felt uncomfortable in the presence of these foreign liberators, some out of vanity or petty

---

1. *Defensa* (Caracas, 1916), p. 85.
2. *Cartas,* v, p. 156.

BOLIVAR.

The Liberator. Small charcoal drawing on cardboard, made in Bogotá by the Colombian artist José María Espinosa in 1828. The drawing has the following legend at the bottom: "Bolívar, portrayed on the 1st of August 1828 by José María Espinosa." The original belongs to the Vargas Lorenzana family.

33

resentment, but the majority, without doubt, because of justified nationalist sentiment. And, of course, there was increasing opposition in the top circles to Bolívar's political ideas.

The situation was complicated by the Liberator's desire to have the constitution which he had drafted for Bolivia adopted in Peru, too, and his plans extended to the union of the two countries and their subsequent confederation with Colombia. The Peruvian electoral colleges, in fact, accepted the constitution, but everything augured that such vast plans would soon provoke sharp disagreements. Sucre himself, whom people regarded as Bolívar's political heir, but who, for his part, thought only of returning to Colombia, declared: "For my part I will confess sincerely that I do not support the Bolivian Constitution. It gives the government stability on paper, while in practice it takes from it the means of making itself respected. If the President has neither the strength nor the force to support himself, his rights will mean nothing and there will be frequent upheavals."[1] Unfortunately, not even this sufficed to prove to his enemies, and to those of Bolívar, that they did not aspire to the tyranny that their opponents seemed to fear.

It was from Venezuela, however, that the first warning of the coming political disorder reached Bolívar. Many problems afflicted the Liberator's devastated country. There was such misery that, according to the testimony of a foreign officer, captains from the army of emancipation were seen begging in the streets of Caracas. The hazards of the long war had kept the best elements of the population in a sort of constant nomadic state, which, together with the misery, had encouraged ignorance and anarchic habits of improvidence and abuse. The splendid collective blossoming which led to independence had been directed by a cultured bourgeoisie sufficiently close to the common people, which, because of these fortunate circumstances, had displayed the best public virtues: patriotism, altruism, social solidarity, balanced political ideas, industry and constancy, respect for legality, and, at the same time, sufficient independence of judgement to be healthily revolutionary. But this bourgeoisie, which has been mistakenly described as an aristocracy or an oligarchy, disappeared almost completely, and its survivors were scattered and confused.

As frequently happens in times of general discontent, the Venezuelans, and particularly the *caraqueños,* accused the Bogotá government of doing nothing to remedy their difficulties. The tendency towards separatism, which had been present since 1821, grew stronger every day.

Moreover, the republic was threatened by another danger, which, although apparently superficial, was no less serious, namely the rivalry between

---

1. *Documentos referentes a la creación de Bolivia,* ii, p. 607.

civilians and soldiers. Some of the military leaders had been made arrogant by their triumphs, but many of the civilians acted out of petulance. Entrenched on the municipal councils and other deliberative bodies, and using and abusing the freedom of the press, they began to spread the hateful and fearful slogan "to liberate ourselves from the liberators." Many of these presumed champions of *civicism* were mere intriguers, of the lowest moral calibre, such as Rafael Diego Mérida, *el Malo,* or former royalists or sons of royalists, who were trying to clamber back to the top or settle old scores.

On top of all this, General Páez, who years later, when he was more educated, was to become an admirable President of the Republic, was still too immature for the top-ranking position that circumstances had brought him. He had been involved personally in excesses which deserved severe censure, but he was so exasperated by this civilian opposition —which, we repeat, he later tolerated with admirable patience when it deserved it less—that he described the antagonism between soldiers and civilians to the Liberator with such violence that we find ourselves doubting even those of his complaints that were justified.

In a letter dated Caracas, October 1, 1825, and which Bolívar received in Lima in March 1826, Páez told him: "Dear General: You cannot imagine the havoc caused in this country by intrigue. I have to confess that Morillo spoke the truth at Santa Ana, when he told you *'that he had done the republic a favor in killing the lawyers.'* We have to accuse ourselves of the sin of having left Morillo's work unfinished, for not having done the same with those who ended up on our side. We did the opposite, putting the Republic in their hands, and they have fashioned it in the Spanish manner, for even the best of them knows nothing else. They are in open war against an army to which they owe all their being, and whose headquarters established the congresses with which they, as a corporation, had absolutely nothing to do. The soldiers acted with the good faith that is found only in their noble profession."[1]

Páez added that men "who anywhere else, where there is public morality, would occupy the most inferior position... control the elections as they wish and choose the first magistrate of the Republic." He concluded: "The valiant men who have made this Republic are already being denied that which the laws grant to the lowest classes in the state. In Caracas, as in Puerto Cabello, the vote of the army was disputed in the parochial elections; in Valencia and Maracaibo it was obstructed by the same cunning means. I could have resorted to force, but I did not wish to give the intriguers a further argument, for all this springs from partiality, and it should be cured once and for all by another means. The attorneys are

---

1. *Cartas,* v, p. 242.

trying to reduce us to the condition of slaves, and this cannot be tolerated, because of our honor and, even more important, the security of the country, which has still not reached an understanding with its outside enemies. Our army will soon be destroyed unless we deal promptly with its legitimate grievances, and I am certain that, in the event of war, the lawyers and the merchants would take to flight, as always, or would compromise with the enemy, while the poor soldiers would suffer further casualties in order to again provide employment and riches for these who at the moment are oppressing them."

Unfortunately, the remedy proposed by Páez was equally senseless. He told Bolívar: "The situation in this country is very similar to that found in France when the Great Napoleon was in Egypt, and he was summoned by the first men of the revolution, who were convinced that a government which had fallen into the hands of the vilest rabble was not the one that could save the nation. You are in a position to say what this celebrated man said on that occasion: the intriguers are going to lose the fatherland, we are going to save it." As if to leave no doubt about what he was suggesting, Páez added: "This country, with its small population, has nothing more than the remnants of a Spanish colony; consequently, it is without any of the qualities needed for the creation of a republic."

Bolívar reacted by categorically reaffirming his republican principles. He told Páez: "It seems to me that you have not judged the men and the events with sufficient impartiality. Colombia is not France, nor am I Napoleon. In France they think deeply, and their wisdom is deeper still. The population is homogeneous, and war had brought her to the brink of the precipice. No republic was as great as France, which throughout history had always been a kingdom. The republican government, discredited, had become the object of nearly universal execration. The monsters who ruled France were both cruel and incompetent. Napoleon was great and unique, but highly ambitious. Here we have none of this. I am not, nor do I care to be, a Napoleon. I do not wish to imitate Caesar either, and even less Iturbide. I regard these examples as unworthy of the glory that I have achieved. The title of Liberator is superior to any that human pride has ever sought. It cannot, therefore, be degraded."

Bolívar rejected the pessimism of Páez, stressing: "The Republic has raised the country to heights of glory and prosperity, endowing it with laws and freedom. No Colombian leader is a Robespierre or a Marat. The danger was over when hope began to appear. Accordingly, nothing justifies the course that you propose. Republics surround Colombia on all sides, and Colombia has never been a kingdom. By its elevation as by its splendor, a throne would inspire terror. Equality would end, and the men of color would lose their rights to a new aristocracy."[1]

---

1. *Cartas*, v, p. 240.

With the same intention of protecting himself against any temptation, Bolívar again invoked the title of Liberator in a letter to Santander. He told him on September 19, 1826, "Liberator or dead is my old motto. To be the Liberator means more than everything else; and for this reason I will not degrade myself before a throne."[1]

Shortly after he received the letter from Páez worse news arrived from Venezuela. Already, on several occasions, frequent recruiting for the army had led to manifestations of discontent and friction between the different authorities. In December 1825, after the publication by Páez of a new proclamation on conscription, the inhabitants of Caracas refused to obey the call of the authorities. This irritated Páez, who issued orders to the regular troops to round up all the men they could find in the streets of the capital, with the result, to quote Gil Fortoul, "that the city gave the appearance of a market being sacked." It is only fair to point out that the proclamation published by Páez arose from a decree of the Bogotá government, and that the General had been reluctant to make new levies of troops against general opinion. Despite this, and although the conscription was finally accomplished without further disturbance, both the intendant of the department of Venezuela, General Juan Escalona, and the municipality of Caracas, brought charges against Páez, the former in a report to the executive in Bogotá, and the latter before the Chamber of Representatives. The Chamber, in turn, took the accusation to the Senate, which, after agreeing to consider it, suspended Páez from his post of commandant-general of the department and summoned him to Bogotá to appear before "the Commission of the Senate appointed to put the case in legal form."

But after a number of incidences, which we will look at later, Páez refused to obey. The immediate danger was that Venezuela, led by this frightening *caudillo,* would definitively remove itself from the Colombian union. For the time being, his disrespect for Congress disturbed the juridical structure of the nation, while also provoking deep consideration of how difficult it would be to punish him.

Bolívar decided, therefore, to return to Caracas. On September 1, he entrusted the government of Peru to General Santa Cruz and the Council of Ministers, and on the 3rd he sailed from Callao for Guayaquil. But he did not arrive in Bogotá until November 14, and it was the beginning of December 1826 before he reached the frontier with Venezuela.

---

1. *Cartas,* vi, p. 75.

XXXIII

HE KNOWS
THAT HE *CANNOT BE*
MORE THAN HE *IS;*
BUT HE ALSO KNOWS
THAT HE CAN *DO* MORE
THAN HE *HAS DONE*

S ANCHEZ CARRION USED TO say in Peru that Bolívar was like the caduceus of Mercury, surrounded by friendly serpents, but that all would leave him when he no longer had the caduceus.

In Colombia, on the other hand, the violence of passions was such that a man as respectful of legal forms and of such moral severity as Sucre, wrote to the Liberator after Ayacucho: "Every day I am more convinced that we need to keep this army keen and ready to restore order in Colombia, should she be disturbed by parties."[1]

And Bolívar, with the insuperable plasticity of his style, pointed out in a letter to Santander: "Nothing persuades me that we can rid ourselves of the prodigious number of difficulties that face us. It is as if we were miraculously suspended upon a point of fortuitous equilibrium, as when two powerful waves meet at a given point and remain still, supporting one another, in a calm which seems real, although instantaneous."

Such was the situation when the unwise decision of Congress to summon Páez to Bogotá to be judged unleashed the conflict among the anarchic elements that writhed beneath this social reality. The fact that Páez had been obeying repeated orders from the government when he embarked on the conscription was overlooked, as was the fact that his first attempts to organize it without violence had been scoffed at by the inhabitants of Caracas. The Executive in Bogotá made the congressional decision worse

---

1. O'Leary, *Narración,* ii, p. 305 (1952 edition).

with an inexplicable provocation, for, when Páez indicated in the first instance that he was willing to give up the military command of Venezuela to go to Bogotá, Vice-President Santander named as his substitute General Juan de Escalona, the man who had accused him and who, motivated by personal resentment, even informed the government of the slanderous rumor that "General Páez had ordered that those who fled should be shot, and that houses should be searched if necessary."

Santander, moreover, had always shown an excessive zeal to insist on his prerogatives when dealing with the military leaders. It was believed in Venezuela that this susceptibility grew out of all proportion when the soldiers were Venezuelans. It was also known that he was particularly hostile towards Páez for a number of special reasons, and that, although he pretended to be impartial, he was anxious to deal him a mortal blow. Any doubt was dispelled when Santander's spokesman in Congress, Francisco Soto, immediately and with the greatest vehemence assumed the role of accuser of the *llanero* leader.

These circumstances seemed particularly ominous in light of a case involving the retired Venezuelan Colonel, Leonardo Infante. Although a man of color and totally unschooled, Infante had reached high rank as a result of his extraordinary bravery and his constant services to his country. Condemned to forced inaction because of his war wounds, he unleashed his resentment in frequent assaults on the inhabitants of the district of Bogotá in which he resided, and he had thus made himself hated. When a junior officer, called Francisco Perdomo, was found murdered, Infante was accused of the crime, and a council of war sentenced him to death. But the case had clearly been handled with bias and, when an appeal was made to a court-martial, a deadlock was reached. O'Leary tells us: "Two members of this tribunal were in favor of death, two for his release, and the fifth for a prison sentence of ten years. According to the military regulations, this was already sufficient to free him from the sentence of death; but despite this, it was argued that the court should not base its decision upon this code, even though the accused was a soldier, as were two members of this high tribunal. The court declared itself divided, and the co-judge appointed to reconcile its members voted for death. Even then, there was still not the absolute majority of votes required by the ordinance or by the ordinary penal legislation. To overcome this difficulty, a law prescribing only a relative majority was cited, and capital punishment was then imposed."[1]

The odiousness of the affair was underlined by two pathetic events. The first was that at the moment of death Infante protested: "*Señores*, I committed many crimes during the war, and I am now going to pay

---

1. O'Leary *Narración* (1952 edition), ii, p. 560.

for them, but, as for the death of Perdomo, I declare in front of all of you that I had no part in it, and that I die innocent." The second occurred as a contrast to this moving declaration, when Santander appeared on horseback at the place of execution and, in front of the corpse, delivered a speech to the troops. He had done the same in 1819, when General Barreiro was executed.

However, the repercussions of this unfortunate event did not end there, for Dr. Miguel Peña, also a Venezuelan and President of the High Court of Justice, who heard Infante's appeal against his sentence, refused to sign it, for he considered it unjust. After being impeached before the Senate, and suspended from his post, he returned to Venezuela and was there in 1826, alongside Páez, encouraging, naturally, his distrust and his fears.

It was clear to Páez that both Congress and the Executive in Bogotá were hostile to him, and he was afraid of suffering the same fate as Infante. A personal enemy, moreover, would remain as supreme authority in Venezuela, for Bolívar was still absent and had not yet announced his intention to return. Páez decided, therefore, not to obey the summons from the Senate. However, the methods that he, or his advisers, thought it necessary to adopt to give a decent appearance to this disobedience led to excesses much more serious than those committed previously.

An attempt was made to give the impression that the Venezuelans were opposed to Páez's departure by encouraging the municipalities to issue "pronouncements" to this effect. In Valencia, which was where Páez had most prestige, the council, in its first meeting on April 27, deplored his dismissal, but also acknowledged the need "to obey the laws and the established institutions." The effect of this was to drive the rebels to all sorts of intrigue, alarming rumors and violence in an attempt to fulfill their purpose, even to the point of assassinating three unfortunate men who had absolutely nothing to do with the affair and throwing their corpses at the door of the *ayuntamiento* of Valencia. At the same time, General Mariño tried to intimidate Caracas by announcing that he required lodgings and rations for a force of 3,000 troops that he was bringing to the city. Because of the alarm produced by such developments, and with public opinion divided as it was, both cities finally acquiesced, and their representatives entrusted civil and military command of the department to Páez.

The Venezuelans called these events of 1826 *La Cosiata*, which is slang for something obscure and ambiguous, dangerous and rather dishonest. It seemed, in fact, that everything was to be like this, for in his oath to the municipality of Valencia Páez promised to respect the established laws, but "on condition that the orders of the Government of Bogotá are not to be obeyed."

Even the constitution that the Liberator had written for Bolivia caused discord. Bolívar had sent it to various friends and politicians in Quito, New Granada and Venezuela, seeking their opinions on it, and almost all of them now related it to what had happened. His supporters argued that the collapse of the constitutional structure made it possible to adopt it immediately, while his adversaries also stressed this possibility in order to depict it as a threat to the established order.

One of the envoys sent by Bolívar with the constitution was O'Leary, who was to continue on to Venezuela and report on the situation there. But even the cautious Irishman lost his head in the midst of all the intrigue and had the hair-brained idea of leading a coup against Páez in Caracas and taking him to Bogotá by force. Bolívar was furious with him and for some time afterwards banished him from his side. However, the future historian showed, with this exception, that he had a very good grasp of the situation, and he informed the Liberator: "I must say that in truth everybody has been wanting reforms for months, but at the moment they are not so anxious for them, for nobody wants civilization to come from the Apure, or the new code to be written with the point of Páez's lance."[1]

The situation was so unstable that it was impossible to find any firm ground on which to step. At first Santander seemed to attach little importance to it, and he confined himself to telling Bolívar, who was still in Peru, in the postscript to a letter: "Yesterday the Senate admitted the accusation introduced against Páez by the Chamber of Representatives because of insignificant deeds committed by him in Caracas in connection with the organization of the militia. I am very worried by this affair."[2]

But he began to reveal a very different state of mind as new developments both inflamed him against Páez and increasingly revealed how difficult it would be to overcome him. He ended by making the following strange suggestion to Bolívar: "With respect to your return, let me give you my opinion. You should not return to the Government, for this Government, surrounded by so many laws, with its hands tied and involved in a thousand difficulties, would expose you to many quarrels and earn you enemies. . . . Supposing, then, that you should not return to discharge the Government, this should give you full authority, such as you had in the South, to go with an army to Venezuela to settle all this."[3]

Santander was thus ceding to Bolívar the control of a civil war in which the resentment of the soldiers and the separatist tendencies displayed in Caracas since 1821 had immediately been lined up behind Páez, and he

---

1. O'Leary, *Narración* (Caracas, 1883), iii, pp. 66 and 68.
2. *Cartas de Santander* (Caracas, 1942), ii, p. 184.
3. *Ibid.*, ii, p. 258.

was doing it to free him from quarrels and enemies! A further point, overlooked by Santander, was that Morales was still threatening Venezuela from Havana. Indeed, Bolívar had written to Páez from Lima: "I learned at almost the same time that Morales in Havana was ready to lead an expedition of 14,000 men to the mainland, and that, in these circumstances, you have been summoned to the capital to be tried. In this state of affairs everything has to be feared: anarchy and war, war and anarchy. I am very worried about what you should do in such an exceptional situation. If you go, Morales will be encouraged to attack, and we will be inviting him to lay waste our beloved native land. If you do not observe the order of Congress, anarchy, which is worse than war, will be introduced. The legislators said when they called you: *the republic will die before the principles;* they do not realize that the principles will be buried with the republic."[1]

Santander himself had written to Bolívar about the danger of this Spanish invasion: "In Madrid they have hurried to organize the expedition against Colombia, since learning of Páez's rebellion. Morillo, who had returned to Spain from Paris, after being purified, has been called to take command of the expedition, and he will take Morales as his second-incommand."[2]

Without doubt, the Liberator was meditating on all these things during his long journey from Peru to the Venezuelan frontier, although he made clear what his attitude would be as soon as he stepped onto Colombian soil at Guayaquil. Addressing himself to all Colombians without distinction, he told them in a proclamation: "Colombians... I again offer you my services, the services of a brother. I have not wanted to know who has done wrong; I have never forgotten that you are my blood-brothers and my companions in arms. I bring a kiss for all of you, and two arms to clasp you to my breast. You will enter it as far as my heart, Granadans and Venezuelans, just and unjust, all the members of the army of liberation, all the citizens of the great republic."

"There is only one person at fault in your conflict; I am he. I have not come in time. Two friendly republics, daughters of our victories, held me back, entranced by their immense gratitude and their immortal rewards. I present myself as the victim of your sacrifice. Aim your blows at me; I will enjoy them if they dispel your malevolence.

"Colombians, I am treading the soil of the fatherland. Therefore, let us have an end to the scandal of your abuses, the crime of your disunity. There will be no more Venezuela, no more Cundinamarca. I am Colombian and we will all be Colombians, or the deserts left by anarchy will be covered by death."[3]

---

1. *Cartas,* v, p. 284.
2. Santander, *Cartas,* ii, p. 290.
3. *Proclamas y discursos del Libertador* (Caracas, 1939), p. 340.

The Liberator continued in correspondence with Páez, including in his letters both warnings which occasionally became reproaches and expressions of friendship and consideration. But, when he learned that plans were being formed in Caracas and Valencia to separate Venezuela from the Colombian union and that slanderous rumors were being spread about himself, he wrote rudely to the *caudillo* from the *llanos:* "I cannot but be surprised that these extraordinary events should have occurred after Guzmán arrived at your general headquarters, and that my name was used to promote the most infamous intrigues. You know perfectly well that Guzmán came to Lima only to propose to me in your name, the destruction of the Republic after the manner of Bonaparte, as you yourself have said in your letter, the original of which is in my possession. Through Colonel Ibarra and Urbaneja, you offered me a crown, which I was duty bound to refuse. General Mariño, as well as Carabaño, Rivas and several other gentlemen of this type, wrote to me to the same effect, urging me to become a sovereign prince. Everyone in Peru and Colombia knows this. It is stupidity, therefore, to attribute this diabolical plan to me, since I scorned it as a fevered concoction born of the contemptible ambition of certain hangers-on.... I want no throne, no presidency, nothing. Hence, I seek only tranquility for Venezuela so that I may resign my office. But first we must assure the future of our country without bloodshed and battle. This is my most earnest and sincere desire. I offer myself as a victim for this sacrifice; but I will not allow anybody to make himself sovereign in our nation. You have no right to do so, nor I, nor any part of the people; consequently, everything that is done will be null and the constitution to be issued on January 15 for the Department of Venezuela will have no more value than if it had been issued by a hamlet, for, with respect to the entire nation, any single part is nothing."[1]

Adopting a more personal tone, rarely seen in his correspondence, he told Páez in another letter: "The nation has manifested but one unanimous wish: *reforms and Bolívar.* No one has challenged me, no one has replaced me.... Do not presume to disgrace Caracas by making her appear to be the patron of infamy and the mockery of ingratitude itself. Does not everyone in Venezuela owe everything to me, and are not even you indebted to me for life itself? But for my services, the perils I faced, and the victories that I won by dint of perseverance and hardships without number, the Apure would be a wasteland, the tomb of heroic dead."[2]

Páez had authority only in the Department of Venezuela. The other departments of what had been and would again become the Republic of

---

1. *Cartas,* vi, p. 117.
2. *Cartas,* vi, p. 133.

Venezuela were under different authorities. On December 19, 1826, from Maracaibo, Bolívar decreed that they should all come under his direct control, announcing: "From this day the Departments of Maturín, Venezuela, Orinoco and Zulia are under my immediate orders.... As soon as the competent authorities receive this decree, they will cease to obey any supreme authority that is not mine."[1] And he took the wise precaution of moving several army units to the center of Venezuela.

This skillful and energetic policy finally bore fruit. The turbulent lost heart or took fright. Commanders very close to Páez, such as Carabaño, again tried to ingratiate themselves with the Liberator. An entire army unit, which was garrisoning Caracas, left the city for the east to join General Bermúdez, who had remained loyal. The fortified city of Puerto Cabello pronounced against Páez and proclaimed its support for Bolívar. Bolívar, for his part, did all he could to help Páez to submit peacefully. He offered to summon a general assembly to discuss the "reforms" that Venezuela was seeking, and he explained to Páez from Puerto Cabello on the day that he disembarked there, December 31, 1826, "Since my authority is not recognized in the territory that you command, I have had to bring with me a force sufficient to make myself respected."[2]

With the same authoritative but cordial tone, he insisted in a letter written to Páez a day later: "I think that you are mad when you do not wish to come to see me and fear that I will receive you badly. General, do you really believe that I will be less generous with you, who has always been my friend, than with my own enemies? Do not think such a thing. I shall give your face a hard slap by going myself to embrace you. Morillo set out to meet me with a column, and I went alone, because treachery is too vile to enter the heart of a great man."[3]

Bolívar decreed on the same day that nobody could be prosecuted for deeds, speeches or opinions relating to what had happened. He confirmed Páez in the office of Supreme Commander of Venezuela. He again promised that a great national convention would be summoned and he repeated that he himself should be immediately recognized and obeyed as President of the Republic. Páez agreed on this. He and Bolívar embraced on the Valencia road, as the Liberator had proposed, and they entered Caracas together on January 12, in the midst of easily-imagined festivities and veneration.

In Valencia, however, on the 4th, there had occurred an incident that was typical. During a banquet offered to the Liberator by Páez, Colonel Escuté, a former royalist now among Páez's courtiers, failed to show respect to a

---

1. *Decretos del Libertador* (Caracas, 1961), ii, p. 67.
2. *Cartas,* vi, p. 139.
3. *Cartas,* vi, p. 141.

priest traveling with Bolívar. Bolívar rebuked him: "*Señor* Escuté, your hands are still stained with American blood, and you dare to insult my chaplain, to show discourtesy to me, the President of Colombia. Do you think that I do not remember that you commanded a company of royalist infantry at Semen? . . . . Are you aware that here there is no other authority, no other power, than mine, that I am like the sun among my lieutenants, and that if they shine it is with the light that I lend them."

Caracas was unable to offer the Liberator the sumptuous receptions provided by the cities of Peru and Bolivia. The ruins of the earthquake of 1812 still scarred much of the city, and the general misery was such that even the beautiful Belén Aristeguieta, friend and relative of Bolívar, Sucre and the Toros, did not possess clothes suitable to present herself in public, and she told Bolívar "I do not even have a light to see by." But this harsh reality was hidden to an extent by the spontaneous enthusiasm displayed by everybody. The cries of the people in support of Bolívar, Páez, and the restored harmony between them, revealed the rejoicing of the old patriots, and that of the young people, who were perhaps seeing the most glorious of the *caraqueños* for the first time.

Crowns of palm leaves or baskets of flowers were offered to the Liberator as the most popular signs of this unanimous affection, and a delegation of beautiful girls presented him with bandoliers, adorned with mottos referring to his virtues and those of the army that had secured the freedom of the continent. The Liberator distributed them among his companions, keeping for himself only the one that said *Constancy*. The one bearing the word *Generosity* was dedicated to the city of Caracas.

Of course, the families that still possessed some wealth organized banquets or excursions to the beautiful surroundings of the city in his honor. Two of the latter particularly pleased the Liberator: one to Bello Monte, on the banks of the Guaire and the Valle rivers, and another to the so-called Casa de Anauco, near the banks of that stream, in the middle of a delightful, scented grove on the slopes of the Avila. Bolívar had always dreamed of living in this house which belonged to his relatives, the Toros, and he frequently spoke of this possibility, which seemed to calm his spirit, in his letters from Bogotá or Lima.

However, the Liberator removed himself from this attractive, loving friendship, just as he had left behind the pomp and pleasures offered to him at the other end of the continent, in order to dedicate himself stubbornly to the administrative reorganization of the country and to the improvement of public education.

He had to begin, of course, by enforcing strict economies, which were bound to offend many. But the Liberator was inflexible, even with his companions in arms, with whom he sympathized in their difficulties. He had decreed in Bogotá on November 24 that all generals, colonels and other officers not on active service "are regarded as on temporary leave, without any salary, until circumstances alter, and without the right to appeal against this."[1] Páez himself was treated like everybody else, and we are obliged to copy a communication to him to show the energy and impartiality that was proposed. It read as follows: "To His Excellency General José A. Páez, Supreme Commander, etc. Sir: The Treasury of this Department has enquired if the peremptory period of eight days fixed for collections should also apply to Your Excellency, who owes the Public Exchequer the sum of 8,871 *pesos* and 7 *reales,* for excess salaries received. The Liberator offered to ask Your Excellency personally to pay this debt, and I am writing on his instructions for this purpose. Your Excellency is well aware of how important it is for the magistrates to set an example. I remain with all respect Your Excellency's very obedient servant. Secretary of State and General of the Liberator, *J. R. Revenga.* Caracas, January 25, 1827."[2]

All his other measures were directed towards this same goal, the creation of maximum regularity and efficiency in public administration. Years later, when the fury of the demagogues and the resentful was again unleashed against him, one of them proposed an amnesty for all who had been convicted of contraband or defrauding the state, on the grounds that they had also been victims of the Liberator's tyranny. Fortunately, this senseless suggestion was rejected.

As always, Bolívar again took an interest in the fate of the slaves, with the aim of studying for himself what had been the results of the law of manumission passed by Congress in 1821. Revenga officially informed the intendant: "The Liberator, keenly interested in the fate of that unfortunate part of humanity that still suffers the burden of slavery, and anxious to alleviate their lot by all the legal means at his disposal, has ordered me to ask you for a general list of the slaves emancipated each year in this Department since the publication of the Law sanctioned in Cúcuta on July 19, 1821."[3]

But, above all, he wanted to give a new stimulus to public education. To help him with this task he had at his side Dr. José Rafael Revenga, the stupendous economist and diplomat, who had returned to Colombia from London with a cargo of educational equipment, bought at his own expense for the foundation of a free normal school.

Through Revenga, Bolívar made contact with another Venezuelan of the same moral and intellectual calibre, who was also absorbed with identical aims, Dr. José María Vargas. Since the closing days of the colonial regime, Vargas had been noted for his patriotism, his philanthropy and

---

1. *Decretos del Libertador,* ii, p. 59.
2. *Revista de la Sociedad Bolivariana de Venezuela,* no. 3, Caracas, 1939, p. 247.
3. *Ibid.,* p. 248.

his devotion to the cause of popular education. It is believed that he undertook a translation of the *Social Contract,* but it has unfortunately been lost. Expelled from the country after the collapse of the first republic, he studied medicine in Edinburgh with the intention of using his knowledge for the benefit of his compatriots and to reform medical studies at the University of Caracas. Medicine was so backward in Venezuela, and its practitioners were held in such low esteem, that doctors did not have access to the rectorship of the university. Its statutes not only ordered that this high office should alternate between an ecclesiastic and a layman but also that those who had only the title of Doctor of Medicine were not eligible for election.

The Liberator decreed the abolition of these archaic restrictions and, shortly afterwards, he also revoked the racial and religious discrimination that until then had restricted access to high scientific office and even to the simple profession of lawyer.[1] Among others, no less a person than the erudite, aggressive Juan Germán Roscio had had to fight a long case to overcome these restrictions. He succeeded even though he was only a *mestizo* (the son of a white man and a woman with Indian blood) without any trace of Negro or *mulatto* ancestry or any history of religious unorthodoxy, for these latter "blemishes," even if only inherited from remote ancestors, constituted insuperable obstacles.

The changes concerning the rectorship introduced by the Liberator made possible the election of Vargas to the office. The task imposed upon him was titanic, for he was obliged not only to fill personally several chairs of medicine, which were vacant because of the lack of suitable men and of money to bring professors from abroad, but also to take charge of the teaching of odontolgy and ophthalmology, which were even more backward, and chemistry, botany and mineralogy which were almost unknown in the country. Fortunately, Vargas, conscious of all Venezuela's needs, had prepared himself for the task, and his amazing scholarship brought about a complete transformation in the ancient house of learning entrusted to him.

There survive a number of succinct lines from Revenga to Vargas, inviting him to an intimate meal with himself and the Liberator. It refreshes our minds to picture these three men, momentarily isolated from the bitter political reality around them, deliberating in their improvised symposium about their plans to ensure an undreamed of future for their country. The most attractive aspect is that, although one was a soldier, another an academic, and the third an economist and diplomat, they were most concerned about popular education.

---

1. *Decretos del Libertador,* ii, pp. 86 and 276, respectively.

Even in Peru and Bolivia, in the midst of the celebrations that his enemies so held against him, Bolívar had been concerned about the lamentable
state of education in Venezuela. In 1810, as we have seen, under Miranda's influence, he began to consider the so-called "Lancasterian method," which seemed to be the only way of educating the people with
the scarce resources in teachers and money that the country possessed.
Soon after Carabobo, Lancaster arrived in Venezuela to teach his system,
but the municipality of Caracas gave him a hostile reception, and he
immediately stumbled against the ever-present and insurmountable problem of lack of resources. Bolívar then took the pedagogue under his
protection. He wrote to him from Lima to encourage him in his work,
he rebuked the *ayuntamiento* of Caracas in another letter for its hostility, and he offered him 20,000 *pesos* from the million placed at his disposal
by the Peruvian government. When the Peruvian government was later
unable to discharge the debt thus incurred, Bolívar ordered that when
the Aroa mines—the last of his family properties—were sold, Lancaster should be paid 22,000 *pesos,* which represented the sum of the
debt and interest charges.

But the depth of interest that these men took in popular education is most
clearly demonstrated by the controversy that the Lancasterian system
provoked among them. Bolívar and Revenga placed great hopes in it.
Later, Vargas and Cagigal, the founder of mathematical studies in Venezuela, were also inclined to adopt it. Simón Rodríguez, however, attacked
it vehemently, comparing it to certain soups served in hospitals, which
filled the stomach without giving nourishment. On the point which most
interested Bolívar, Rodríguez was later to write: "The leaders of the
people persuade themselves that they will achieve nothing if they do not
instruct. Many people disagree with this, arguing that the government is
not a teacher and that it takes centuries to mold a people. Neither view is
correct. The government should be a teacher. Five years, at the most, are all
that are needed to provide a people for each Republic. But, in order to
achieve this, it is necessary to do more than found Lancasterian schools."
Andrés Bello took up a position in the middle. He believed that the Lancasterian method could be used profitably for primary instruction, but not
for secondary and further education. These differences of opinion are easily
explained. Bolívar, Revenga, Vargas and Cagigal believed above all that
"mutual instruction", upon which the method was based, would allow
economies in teachers and money. Simón Rodríguez refused to accept
this imposition of circumstances. Andrés Bello reduced it to its just proportions. In England itself, the system gained many supporters and
was adopted in 95 schools, with more than 30,000 pupils.

But these moments of optimistic work, of great projects for the
future; were to be the last that fate was to allow Bolívar. The

collapse of all his political creation was soon about to begin, this time for good.

The first blow was the mutiny in Lima of the third Colombian auxiliary division, organized by its chief of staff, a Granadan officer called José Bustamante, who, after skillfully imprisoning his superior officers, took his troops to southern Colombia. When they reached Guayaquil the mutineers named as civil and military commander General La Mar who, as we have seen, was in favor of transferring these provinces to Peru. It seemed, then, that their mutiny was being compounded by treason against their own country. However, since they had tried to justify their attitude with the claim that they were defending liberal principles against the Bolivian constitution, Santander jubilantly praised their scandalous pronouncement. In a private letter to Bustamante he spoke of "the feelings of jubilation expressed by the people at the sight of the fidelity and loyalty shown by the soldiers of this division." In an official note, which General Soublette agreed to sign as Minister of War, the government in Bogotá unreservedly gave its approval to the mutiny.

This last step of course, provoked a reaction of stupor and horror in the other army units and among conscientious, patriotic citizens. Sucre wrote to Santander from Bolivia: "The support that the ministerial papers from Bogotá give to the conduct of Bustamante in Lima shows how much progress the party spirit is making. Already these eulogists will be humiliated under the weight of their shame, knowing that there was nothing noble in the proceedings of this bad Colombian. General La Mar's note of May 12 to General Flores shows that the intention of these mutineers was to remove the departments of the South from Colombia and join them to Peru, in exchange for a little money offered to Bustamante and his accomplices." Sucre added, with all the weight of his unquestioned moral authority: "The note of the Secretary of War to Bustamante, approving of the insurrection, is Colombia's death sentence. No more discipline, no more troops, no more defenders of our country. The glory of the army of liberation will be followed by brigandage and dissolution."[1]

Santander, however, was unwilling to retreat. Blinded with indignation and wrath because of Bolívar's failure to "punish" Páez, he planned to destroy Colombia and to use every means at his disposal against the prestige of the Liberator, which he was incapable of checking. He had already told Bolívar in a haughty manner: "I want us to be what we are, or nothing. If there is neither moral nor physical force to restrain the troublemakers and support the present system, as the Constitution provides, the union must be dissolved into the independent states of Venezuela,

---

1. O'Leary, *Cartas,* i, p. 611.

New Granada and the South." He added, in a subsequent letter: "Otherwise, and if the right to accelerate the convocation of a Great Convention to reform the institutions is insisted upon, I inform you, here and now, that there is no Colombian Union, and that an attempt will be made to re-establish the republic of New Granada of 1815. Men of influence think in these terms, and I am of the opinion that it is better to be alone than in bad company."[1]

Páez, unfortunately, was pulling at the other end of the blanket, having made the same decision. Although Santander had begun by describing Páez's activities in Venezuela as "insignificant deeds," he later thought that he should be executed. He wrote to Bolívar on October 15, 1826, apparently offering a concession: "There are ways of saving him from the gallows without compromising the laws, or the honor of the government and yourself."[2]

It is still difficult to judge these confused events impartially; perhaps things that did not come to light or that did not happen were more important than those that did. But there can be no doubt that it would not only have been rash to run the risk of a civil war, as well as destroying Venezuela's military spirit while Spain was still threatening her, by taking Páez to Bogotá by force, but also iniquitous to hand over the glorious *caudillo llanero* to a group of politicians, who, despite calling themselves civilians, still exhibited violent passions. And were not these politicians of Bogotá who were now offering Bolívar extraordinary powers to lead a war against Páez, the very same men who had taken them from him before they learned about the victory of Junín, putting the Colombian army and the emancipation of America itself in mortal danger?

The truth is that Bolívar was confronted not only by the inflamed antagonism between Páez and Santander but also by an anticipation of the century and a half of sad trials that America had to suffer. All the bitterness and frustration that he could see in the future was already weighing upon his heart.

When news of Bustamante's mutiny reached Bogotá at the beginning of March 1827, the Liberator's enemies organized public celebrations, fired rockets, rang bells and held musical parades in the streets. Santander took part in the festivities and, shortly afterwards, promoted the traitor to the rank of colonel.

One of the most fiery agitators, Vicente Azuero, had drafted a *memorial,* as part of an intense press campaign against the Bolivian constitution and the Liberator's Caesarist proposals. This began before Bolívar and Santander had moved so far apart, while the Vice-President was still

---

1. Santander, *Cartas* (Caracas, 1942), p. 307.
2. *Ibid.,* ii, p. 299.

offering to support the Liberator's constitutional project. Thereafter, however, he surreptitiously encouraged Azuero's campaign, and finally decided to sign the document himself. The eminent Granadan historian Liévano Aguirre tells us: "In this way Azuero's famous memorial, now signed by Santander himself and by the majority of the members of government, was presented to the public, and the Vice-President, using official funds, bought a large part of the edition to distribute it in the country through administrative channels."[1]

In order to accelerate this campaign against the Liberator, Santander hurried to recall Congress, in which he enjoyed a majority since its election had been controlled by himself as Vice-President encharged with executive authority. Bolívar, for his part, threatened to appeal to the electoral colleges to authorize the summoning of the great national convention that he had promised. The weakness of Bolívar's position was that the constitution, according to his own dispositions, could not be altered before 1831. The fragility in Santander's attitude sprang from the frankly subversive activities in which he had been engaged. Bolívar could justify his plan to summon the constituent convention by arguing that the rebellion of Páez and the amnesty that he had been obliged to concede to him, had, in practice, destroyed the constitution. Santander, for his part, claimed that his conduct, including support for Bustamante, had been inspired solely by the need to defend the law and freedom. The rupture between them, of course, had become permanent, and everywhere it was rapidly defined as a rift between Granadans and Venezuelans. Even today the people of New Granada, that is, Colombia, tend to regard Venezuela as militarist and inclined towards personalism, while the Venezuelans claim that the supposed fondness of the Granadans for the laws is simply an artifice to allow them to frame them according to the interests of an oppressive oligarchy, and to interpret them according to their traditional passions and hatreds. These attitudes are the sad consequences of the antagonism that was then unleashed.

Santander arranged for Congress to meet in Tunja at the beginning of May, 1827. In June, Bolívar, who was still working in Caracas on his decree on public instruction and on the organization of the university, announced his intention to return to Bogotá. In his journey from Lima he had ridden 1,346 leagues in four months, inspired by the hope of reducing party strife and then turning to the improvement of conditions for the people of Venezuela. Now, six short months after his arrival, he had to depart again, leaving his work on administration and public education entrusted to the doubtful interest of Páez, and increasingly aware of the difficult future awaiting the Colombian union.

---

1. Indalecio Liévano Aguirre, *Bolívar* (Editorial 'El Liberal', Bogotá), p. 453.

On July 5, Bolívar left La Guaira for Cartagena, but it was September before he reached Bogotá. In the meantime, there were further serious developments, all of them exploited by Santander for the purpose of accelerating the dissolution of Colombia, an outcome which Dr. Vicente Azuero proposed, frankly and openly, in *El Conductor* of Bogotá on July 19.

The results of Bustamante's infamy were not confined to Colombia. In reality, this wretch had been bought by the oligarchic groups in Peru, and when, as they hoped, his treachery led to the withdrawal of Colombian troops from their country, they managed also to promote a reaction there against the Liberator and to take power themselves. But their aims did not stop there. Anxious to revenge themselves on Bolívar and Sucre for the social reforms they had promoted, and needing at the same time to make the populace forget them, they attempted for both ends to deceive public opinion with two proposals which could easily be turned into a "national cause": the incorporation into Peru of Guayaquil in the north and Bolivia in the south-east. But the creation of this vast empire would never have brought the Peruvian people even a scrap of happiness.

In an attempt to secure the first of these aims, they appointed to the presidency of Peru, General José de la Mar, who had been striving for years for the annexation of the provinces where he had been born. In order to upset Sucre, and to pave the way for Peruvian penetration of Bolivia, they dedicated themselves, again using money, to encouraging conspiracies and pronouncements in the neighboring country. They were successful, unfortunately, on both fronts. With respect to Guayaquil the antagonism between Colombia and Peru was exacerbated, until it soon culminated in a fratricidal war between them; and in Bolivia, Sucre, who had never wanted the presidency and who continued to fill the office only to please the Bolivians themselves and the Liberator, had to face intrigues and mutinies, which finally persuaded him to resign for good and return to Colombia.

Bolívar had written to Sucre a few months earlier: "It will be said that I have liberated the New World, but it will not be said that I perfected the stability and the happiness of any of the nations that compose it. You, my dear friend, are more fortunate than I."[1] The Liberator now had to abandon this last hope, too. He was confined to Colombia, increasingly involved in regionalist strife, and his dreams of continental politics would not return to him except, like the eagle of Prometheus, to eat away his entrails.

The Colombian Congress, as we have seen, was dominated by Santander and his party. On March 2, 1828, nevertheless, it decided to summon the

---

1. *Cartas,* vi, p. 203.

convention planned by Bolívar, which was intended to modify the constitution before the date laid down in the document itself. Why this change of attitude? Did it not amount to support for the idea of constitutional revision, which had been regarded as an attack on existing institutions when it was professed by Bolívar and Páez? Evidently. But the point is that Santander was now confident of being able to use this parliamentary debate to further his new plans; not, as Bolívar had intended, to consolidate Colombia, but to destroy it.

To achieve this it was sufficient for him to use in the convention the same methods that had made him master of Congress. An additional advantage was that, in his new role of standard-bearer for the "reforms" and for the division of Colombia, he secured the support of many Venezuelans who detested the union with New Granada, and who were ready to sacrifice their personal adhesion to Bolívar for this feeling. The tricks to which Santander resorted to secure his aim can be illustrated by the following example. When preparations for the Congress were being made, one of those elected to it took ill in Tunja and was unable to travel to Bogotá. Santander decided, therefore, that the Congress should meet in Tunja, rather than in the capital, so that he would not lose this vote. He was determined to dominate the convention by adopting astute measures of this sort. Liévano Aguirre tells us: "He did not even forget to arrange lodgings along the highways for his friends and any other persons who wanted to support his cause."

At the same time he directed an underground press campaign against the Liberator, which was so violent and unscrupulous that it seems impossible that a man of such privileged talent could have been involved in it. He wrote on March 10 to one of his experts, Juan Madiedo: ". . . I enclose a sheet printed in Lima, which tells us a thousand things about our hero. Although there may be some difficulty about publishing extracts, it is always advantageous to circulate such information in the clubs of the patriots, so that they know about the great deeds of our Liberator or Enslaver. Lastly, I send the reprimand which Soto has written about the infamous, unconstitutional, absurd decree of the Liberator President, in which he declares himself in charge of government for Venezuela and leaves Bogotá to his degraded ministers. This is the most absurd and arbitrary step that Bolívar has taken, and we must reveal to the people and to the world the absurdities and arbitrariness of this man, who says that he governs in accordance with the law and that he loves the rights of the people. Add whatever you wish to print and publish it as an editorial, for our only concern is for the public good."[1]

---

1. *Cartas de Santander,* p. 138.

With such antecedents, it was not surprising that even before the formal installation of the convention, the first deputies to arrive in Ocaña, which was where they were to meet, gave displays of sectarianism very similar to those that had followed the Bustamante affair. General José Padilla, a colored Granadan officer who, like Infante, had won high rank because of his oustanding and constant services to his country, and who until then was highly thought of by the Liberator, led a mutiny at Cartagena on March 1, 1828. Naturally, Bolívar ordered that he be prosecuted under the laws against conspiracy, but the deputies in Ocaña, who had formed themselves into the preparatory commission for the assembly, led by Francisco Soto, agreed "to inform General Padilla of the appreciation with which his feelings with respect to the Great Convention have been received."[1]

A contemporary description of Padilla, written by a Frenchman who knew him, is very interesting. We are told: "Having risen from being a simple pilot to the rank of Admiral of the Republic, Padilla always displayed a jealousy of the pre-eminence of the whites. Irritated by a number of real or imagined insults, and probably in complicity with other enemies of the government, he tried to rouse the Negro and mulatto population to rebellion. . . . The inhabitants and the foreigners lived in consternation for the space of three days, but, thanks to the vigorous measures taken by the commandant-general, the revolutionary plan failed. The conspirators scattered. Padilla hurried to place himself under the protection of the Ocaña Convention, in which the influence of Santander still predominated. . . . During my stay in Cartagena I often spent the evenings in Admiral Padilla's house. He was a giant of a man, a demagogue like Danton, strong and one-eyed like Polyphemus, and so full of hate for the European race that it sometimes showed through his meticulous courtesy and his ostentatious hospitality. When, mounted on a spirited mule, he stood out with his broad chest among the staff of the fortress, the artist's brush could have worked well on his Homeric face, contrasting it with that of Bolívar, which was impregnated with pensive melancholy, weakened by anxiety and watching, and as pale as that of the First Consul."[2]

Once again a foreigner thus describes for us Bolívar's melancholy, which his compatriots did not seem to notice. If only they had known that while they were indulging in their suicidal strife, he was most anxious about the lack of moral authority in an assembly corrupted by such excesses! In a letter to Páez he observed: ". . . the laws the convention adopts will cause powerful repercussions, for, as soon as a new

---

1. Quoted by Lecuna, in *Catálogo. . .*, iii, p. 381.
2. P.D. Martin-Maillefer, *Los novios de Caracas* (Caracas, 1954), p. 91.

institution lacks full legality, its opponents are apt to believe themselves authorized and entitled to destroy it, while people of honor show little interest, or they may even consider such plans for destroying it justifiable. Only law or the sanction of many generations can protect a government. Lacking these foundations, it is exposed to endless friction and quarrels, whereupon annihilation follows, because sheer fatigue permits that which is least desired to ensue. No other institution is so cruel and costly!"[1]

But the Liberator's pessimism was far outstripped by reality. Soto and Azuero, Santander's spokesmen, submitted to the assembly a project for a federal constitution, which, in addition to the inherent weakness of this system, contained several features carefully designed to destroy the central power. In short, they were seeking not the immediate dissolution of Colombia, but something which was even more attractive, its disintegration in the hands of Bolívar. As Santander had anticipated, this project was approved not only by a majority of the Granadans, but also by a number of the Venezuelans, because it fitted in with their separatist tendencies.

The deputies inspired by Bolívar who wanted to save the Colombian union, had presented another constitutional project, and, when they realized that they were in a minority, they proposed that the Liberator be called to address the convention. The suggestion was reasonable, since Santander, although Vice-President, was a member of the assembly and participated in all its deliberations. Why not hear Bolívar, if only once? The supporters of Santander, however, cried out against the proposal, claiming that the presence of the "tyrant" in the nearby town of Bucaramanga was already a sufficient threat to their deliberations. Moreover, Santander himself, laying aside this coarse invective, submitted a different argument, more in keeping with his character. He began by recalling the Liberator's great services and the admiration that all men owed him, but concluded that this very prestige made his presence something to be feared. He pointed out agitatedly that he personally had approached Bolívar full of anger and distrust but, after listening to him, had completely given in to his charm.

Finding, therefore, that all avenues were closed to them, Bolívar's supporters abandoned the assembly and left it without a quorum. But, as a result of this struggle, the Republic was almost without government and its laws had lost their prestige. What was going to happen?

It was already the beginning of June 1828. For the last two months Bolívar had been in Bucaramanga, where one of his circle, Colonel Luis Perú de Lacroix, edited the *Diario* bearing the name of the city, which

---

1. *Cartas,* vii, p. 215.

we have cited on a number of occasions. But the Liberator did not want to wait there for the deputies who had left the assembly. When he learned what had happened he left for the capital and, on reaching Socorro, was informed that a popular demonstration in Bogotá had proclaimed him Dictator. This initiative was soon imitated by the country's most important cities.

This was in no way a triumph for the Liberator. He realized from the beginning that it meant more responsibility, but less power, because his apparently limitless authority would always be checked by the obstacle of the illegitimacy that he considered so damaging to the decisions of the convention. During the war he had frequently accepted or demanded absolute authority; but now where could the irresistible *forgeron* strike without his hammer hitting a compatriot? If he had not wanted to be a Napoleon, he had wanted even less to be a Sulla. The parallel suggested itself to him so insistently that we find it in different forms in three of his letters. He had written in June 1826: "To save my country I have had to be a Brutus, but to restrain her in civil war I should have to be a Sulla. This role does not suit me; I should, instead, prefer to lose everything, including life itself."[1] He repeated, in August of the same year: "I do not believe that Colombia can be saved with the Bolivian Constitution, a federation or an empire. I can already see Africa coming to take control of America, and all the infernal hordes establishing themselves in our country. If I wanted to imitate Sulla, I could perhaps delay somewhat our collapse, but, after having played Nero to the Spaniards, I have had enough bloodshed."[2] And in June 1827 he wrote to Sir Robert Wilson, who had sent him his son to serve as his aide-de-camp: "I want to leave everything. I prefer to abandon my hopes rather than be taken for a tyrant, or even appear suspicious. My impetuous passion, my greatest hope, is to bear the name of lover of freedom. The role of Brutus is my madness; that of Sulla, even though he saved the Roman constitution, is detestable to me."[3]

With every day that passed his proud boast of being a "producer of hand-wrought republics" seemed more distant. His clay, his wheel and his pattern had been lost during the unexpected tempest, and even the skilled hand of the craftsman no longer possessed the patience and perseverance of former days. He was tormented with excessive frequency by introspection and doubt. "I am not studying the Convention, but the whole Republic and the character of the human race," he wrote, like a lonely Hamlet, lost among meaningless events and desolate caviling.

---

1. *Cartas*, v, p. 350.
2. *Ibid.*, vi, p. 47.
3. *Ibid*, vi, p. 311.

We can see how much he suffered from a detail which, although it might appear trivial, is in fact, very significant. During the six months that he stayed in Caracas, no woman interested him. He left no memory or legend of any encounter in the city that he loved most. He was aged only forty-four, and Manuelita was not with him. In Lima—if what was said there can be believed—he had avidly enjoyed romances and pleasures after Ayacucho. Why this sudden ascetiscism in Caracas?

It might be said that a jealous Jupiter was snatching from his hands the crowns of palm leaves and flowers brought to him by the maidens of Caracas, and was condemning him to go round and round in the fiery wheel of Ixion. His friends, and those who still believed that it was possible to reconstruct Colombia, were urging him to continue the struggle, and they believed that they could encourage him with the reproach that could most wound his pride: that to refuse was to desert. But the perplexed Bolívar replied, "If I desert, I do badly; If I stay, I do worse."

At the same time he was perhaps stirred from the depths of his consciousness by the synthesis with which Simón Rodríguez explained the nature of his ambition: Bolívar knows that he cannot *be* more than he *is;* but he also know that he can *do* more than he *has done.*" He was about to sacrifice the last remaining months of his life in the pursuit of this chimera.

XXXIV

IT IS THIS
THAT HOLDS ME BACK
AND MAKES ME DOUBT

Bolivar's aversion to "Machiavellism", which we discussed when dealing with his youth, led him to a cutting decision when he became convinced that Santander was playing a double game. He asked him to stop writing to him, because he no longer regarded him as his friend. The Vice-President replied on April 27, 1827, "... I will suffer this latest blow with the serenity inspired by innocence.... My desires will always be for your health and prosperity; my heart will always love you with gratitude; my hand will never write a line that might do you harm. Even if you ignore me for the rest of your life, and do not regard me as your friend, I will always be a friend, filled with feelings of profound respect and just consideration."[1]

However, we have already seen something of the aggression with which Santander directed the press campaign against the Liberator. The letter to Madiedo, from which we quoted previously, also testified to his encouragement for Padilla. He reported: "General Padilla has written two enchanting letters to me, offering always to support liberal institutions and the reforms of the Convention. Referring to an alarming military petition which was being circulated in Lima, he tells me that he has not only refused to sign it, but also will prevent any individual under his orders from signing it, and that he will support the Convention with his sword and his influence. This is very laudable. Refer to Padilla in

---

1. *Cartas de Santander,* iii, p. 125.

your papers with dignity and justice, depicting him as the best prop of the cause of freedom and the most vigorous defender and supporter of the decrees of the Convention. Today I am writing to him in admiring fashion."

Santander personally explained this peculiar strategy to Azuero, telling him quite openly: "In my profession one avoids fighting a pitched battle against a powerful, well placed enemy, when there is hope of destroying him by means of guerrillas, raids, ambushes, and similar tactics."[1]

O'Leary, who was present at the time, tells us: "At this time there were formed secret societies called *Circles,* whose principal object was to undermine the reputation of the Liberator and sow among the different classes in Colombia the distrust that was later to yield such bitter fruit. The main *Circle* was in Bogotá, and it consisted of twelve individuals, each of them the leader of a subsidiary *Circle.* These, in turn, had twelve members each, and beneath them others were formed in the provinces, corresponding with the central body in Bogotá. By means of this organization, of which the principal leaders were Santander, Soto and Azuero, the country was kept in a state of agitation, and hatred of the Liberator was aroused by making him appear as the enemy of the people and the promoter of libertine schemes."[2]

All this occurred before Bolívar assumed dictatorial powers. The argument that he had violated the laws, by conceding amnesty to Páez and promising a national assembly to study the reforms demanded by Venezuela, was untenable, given that Congress itself convoked the convention and Santander came forward as the standard-bearer of the reform program.

What, then, drove the Vice-President to adopt this angry, imprudent attitude?

Almost all historians suppose that it was the hartred that he felt for Páez, and his anger at Bolívar's failure to punish him. Bolívar himself seems to have believed this, and he wrote much later, in November 1830, that the struggle between Santander and Páez "has ruined everything for us".[3] So far I have tended to follow this interpretation, for it is the one which fits in best with the events we have examined. But that a man so much in control of himself as Santander was to become increasingly intransigent, instead of mellowing with time, indicates that we must seek a less accidental motive for his behavior.

Other writers have preferred to attribute the break between Bolívar and Santander to the Bolivian constitution, which, according to some, was

---

1. Liévano Aguirre, *op. cit.,* p. 468.
2. From prologue of Mgr. Nicolás E. Navarro to O'Leary (Caracas, 1952), p. XVI.
3. *Cartas,* ix, p. 389. See too p. 353.

unacceptable to the Vice-President because it clashed with his liberal principles and, according to others, because it meant the promotion of Sucre to the vice-presidency of the great Confederation of Colombia, Peru and Bolivia, and the relegation of Santander. But we find that precisely at the time when these two ideas—a new constitution on the Bolivarian model and the confederation of the three states—formed a single project, Santander, far from disapproving, promised to do all he could to win them support. On December 3, 1826, he wrote to General Santa Cruz, President of the Council of Government of Peru: "I have talked at length with the Liberator about the plan for a Confederation between Bolivia, Peru and Colombia. Before, I was not in favor of it, more because I did not know the plan in detail than for any other reason. This project, like most, presents difficulties and disadvantages, which it will be difficult, although not impossible, to overcome. But its advantages and merits can compensate these in such a way as to allow us to pick the fruit of the sacrifices that our respective countries have made for liberty and independence. I am still not so convinced of the need for the Confederation that I can be accused of presenting only its advantages or replying to the objections to it; but I can assure you that the general idea does not displease me. If Bolivia and Peru are held back from putting it into effect by a lack of co-operation from Colombia, I promise for my part to do everything in my power to make it popular and to accomplish it."[1]

Even if we do not attach much importance to these promises from Santander, or admit that they are outweighed by his declarations against the Bolivian Constitution, there remains a most important point. When the Ocaña convention met, neither Bolívar nor his friends still thought in terms of this constitution, as the constitutional project that they submitted to it proves.

Santander's increasingly extreme opposition to Bolívar has to be explained, then, by a human motive. After acting as President of the Republic for so many years while Bolívar was at war, Santander was now unable to accept the subordinate role to which he was relegated with the return of the Liberator. It was for this reason that he tried at first to attach little importance to "the insignificant actions" that led to his accusation against Páez, so as to prevent Bolívar from returning from Peru. When Bolívar's return became inevitable after Santander himself had been forced to request it by the impossibility of overcoming Páez, the same motive led him to propose to the Liberator the strange suggestion that he should fight a civil war in Venezuela, while he remained in Bogotá as constitutional Vice-President, with his Congress and his journalists.

---

1. *Cartas de Santander,* iii, p. 11.

Naturally, he must have been very disappointed when he learned that the Liberator was returning to New Granada with Venezuela at peace. Although Bolívar was not to insist on his plan for a great confederation, and although Sucre, who was loved and respected by politicians and soldiers from Venezuela to Potosí, was not to return to relegate Santander to the third place that he feared so much, his future at the side of the Liberator wsa inevitably uncertain. Sentiments such as these can grom day by day in the mind of a politician and can be inflamed by every little detail of public life.

There is a strong possibility that Santander was influenced by all of the motives that we have been analyzing, either simultaneously or in succession. We also believe that he sincerely came to see himself as the representative of liberal principles. In almost all men, the concept of justice is stronger than that of legality, and they feel that if a thing is unjust it cannot be legal. But jurists soon grow accustomed to the idea that everything that can be defended by law is just, and politicians come to regard as "justifiable" all the means that they are able to employ to secure the triumph of their cause, as long as appearances are kept up. This professional deformity was always to be seen very clearly in Santander, who was both a jurist and a politician. As long as he could find a law or a good argument to explain his conduct, he felt satisfied no matter what he had done. After the execution of Barreiro, the only request that he made was that Bolívar should "cover" him with his approval. During the Peruvian campaign, he refused to share the Liberator's anguish for the fate of the country and that of the Colombian army, because he had still not obtained "a law to allow aid to be sent." When the Bogotá Congress dismissed Bolívar from command of the army, he did not veto this law, which could have caused complete disaster, but impassively told the Liberator that he wanted to show in this way that the Executive did not mind whether or not it had extraordinary powers. Immediately afterwards, he made the situation worse by asking this same Congress if promotions granted during the campaign would be valid in Colombia; "as if we had ceased to be Colombians," those veterans who were giving their lives at such a great distance from their country commented bitterly. The new Incorruptible replied, showing once again his fondness for institutions: But why not? Was not this consultation strictly legal? Similarly, in 1826, when faced by the disobedience of Páez, Santander was concerned not with the horrors of civil war in Venezuela or the danger from Spain, about which he himself had written to the Liberator, but with the need for Bolívar to automatically jump at Páez, soldier against soldier. In the cases of Bustamante and Padilla he was unable to invoke a law, but his mind was at ease and his tongue arrogant, because, he would claim, they were defending a "good cause." The argument of the politician.

By 1828 it could not be said that Bolívar's presidencial authority had been extensive or oppressive, since he had exercised it for only a few months, in the intervals between his campaigns. The most that his enemies could attribute to him were "libertine schemes." In the Bogotá newspapers, however, excuses for "tyrannicide" had already appeared, while in the "clubs of the patriots," to which Santander referred in his letter to Madiedo, the following lines of Vargas Tejada were already being recited:

> *If we take from Bolívar his first letter*
> *and that with which he ends,*
> *we have "Oliva", the symbol of peace.*
> *This means that we must cut off*
> *the head and the feet of the Tyrant*
> *if we wish to enjoy a lasting peace.*

While the Ocaña convention was still in session, the Liberator received information that he was to be assassinated, but, as always in these cases, he did not believe it. Perú de Lacroix noted: "Although he is well aware of the wickedness of Santander and his companions, he could not believe that they would sink to such a scheme."[1] Another conspiracy with the same aim was organized, to take effect on August 10, during a great masked ball celebrating the anniversary of Bolívar's entry into Bogotá after the victory of Boyacá. It was foiled by a desperate maneuver by Manuelita Sáenz, who turned up at the celebration disheveled, dirty, and acting strangely; this enraged the Liberator and made him leave the ball early.[2]

The plot, then, was under way when Bolívar became dictator as a result of the dissolution of the assembly and the Bogotá pronouncement. One of the leading conspirators, Dr. Florentino González—the husband of the beautiful Bernardina Ibáñez, who had been wooed by the Liberator—reported in a *Narración* published many years later: "Our object was to destroy this regime, arresting the persons of Bolívar and his ministers, overcoming any resistance that we might meet from groups of the armed forces, and immediately putting at the head of the govern-

---

1. Mgr. Nicolás E. Navarro (ed.), *Diario de Bucaramanga* (Caracas, 1935), p. 170.
2. This is the interpretation given by Rumazo González in the biography cited above. A slightly different account, published in Bogotá in April 1853 by Marcelo Tenorio, is in the Blanco y Azpúrua collection, vol. xiii, p. 68.

ment the constitutional leader of the country (Santander), who would decide the fate of the usurpers."[1]

Bolívar was so unprepared that on September 21, 1828, accompanied by only two friends, he went for a walk to the village of Soacha near Bogotá. Another of the plotters, the Venezuelan Pedro Carujo, who had four assassins with him, wanted to make use of this opportunity to put the diabolical plan into effect. It seems that they desisted due to the intervention of Santander, and those involved then set a new date, September 28. But on the afternoon of the 25th, after the arrest of a certain Captain Benedicto Triana, who was also party to the plan, for publicly uttering threats, they all believed that they had been discovered, and they decided to attempt the assassination that very night. They counted on the co-operation of a number of soldiers, including the chief-of-staff of the garrison and, according to González, "We resolved to face all dangers, take by force the *Vargas* and *Granaderos* barracks and the palace of the Dictator, and to seize his person, dead or alive, according to what was possible, in the midst of the fight during which we proposed to enter. We did not flatter ourselves that we would triumph, even though the news of the death of Bolívar, we knew, would cause an impression of terror among our opponents. It was decided at this supreme moment that in this respect it was impossible to conform to the original plan."

The assault on the presidential palace began at midnight. After killing a sentry and a corporal who offered resistance, the attackers subdued the rest of the guard, which suspected nothing. Lieutenant Andrés Ibarra, the only aide of the Liberator sleeping there, came out to face them, almost naked, and they wounded him with a sabre, "believing that he was Bolívar," according to González. But, as they arrived at the bedroom of the Liberator himself, uttering cries and threats, "there came out to meet us a beautiful lady, with a sword in her hand, who, with admirable presence of mind and very courteously, asked us what we wanted."

The lady was Manuelita Sáenz, whom Bolívar had called to his side that night because he felt ill. As usual she cared for him and read to him until she saw that he was sleeping. When she heard the first noises of the attack she awoke the Liberator, helped him to dress, and managed to persuade him to jump to the street though a window that the assassins had overlooked. She later told O'Leary: "I went out to meet them in order to give him time to get away, but I did not have time to see him jump or to close the window. As soon as they saw me, they seized hold of me and asked, 'Where is Bolívar?' I said that he was in the Council, which was the first thing that occurred to me. They carefully searched the

---

1. González's narrative, which, naturally, is quoted in all histories of the event, is in Azpúrua, vol. xiii, p. 84.

first room, passed on to the second and, seeing the open window, exclaimed: 'He fled; he has saved himself.' "[1]

The plotters killed Colonel Ferguson, another of the aides, who, although ill and not in the palace, hurried to it to do his duty. They attacked the artillery barracks to free Padilla, and in the process killed Colonel José Bolívar, who was a Venezuelan, but not related to the Liberator.

Bolívar, meanwhile, took refuge under a bridge, while his cook, whom he had met by chance as he hurled himself out the window, went to find out what was happening in the barracks. The barracks had remained loyal, and the indignation aroused in the army and among the people by the news of the outrage very quickly intimidated the plotters. Angry crowds paraded through the streets, cheering the Liberator and demanding death for the assassins. General Santander had to take refuge in the house of General Urdaneta, the Minister of War, because from the first moment everybody had identified him as the intellectual author of the crime.

The Liberator's first impulse was to pardon all the conspirators, and he wanted to prohibit the summoning of Manuelita to identify those who had entered the palace, announcing: "I declare that this lady will never be the instrument of death or the accuser of wretches." He told Sucre a month after the incident, "I am crushing the abortive conspiracy. Every accomplice will be punished in one fashion or another. Santander is the leader, but he is also the most fortunate, for my generosity protects him."[2]

The conspirators were tried according to the law, and fourteen of them were condemned to death. They included five anonymous soldiers and, of the leaders, General Padilla. Florentino González, Pedro Carujo and others of those who were most to blame received only prison sentences and, for a variety of reasons, they were soon at liberty. Bolívar commuted Santander's sentence of death to banishment, and, before the year was out, those who had fled or hidden were pardoned. Bolívar informed O'Leary: "We are prosecuting the conspirators, and the sentences are being executed more or less rigorously, according to what the situation and their offenses demand. But my heart is broken with pain because of this black ingratitude. My sadness will be eternal, and the blood of the guilty aggravates my sorrow. I am devoured by their torments and my own."[3]

This scrupulous preoccupation with morality, which tormented the Liberator, was reflected in all his decisions. He was obsessed by the idea that his adversaries had arrogated to themselves the principles of freedom and justice which he had always invoked, and he did not dare

1. Manuela Sáenz to O'Leary, 10 August 1850, in *Narración,* iii, p. 370.
2. *Cartas,* viii, p. 98.
3. *Cartas,* viii, p. 93.

take any decision, except after mortal doubts. Increasingly, he contradicted or confused his friends, or he grew exasperated when they advised
him to act with his accustomed energy. During the last three years of his
life, all his actions revealed this ceaseless anguish, and it is for this reason
that we have said that it was then—at the time of his failure as
a politician—that he reached the peak of his personal greatness. His sadness
was of a fine spiritual quality as he bore the burden of an apparently
omnipotent authority, which, in reality, he dared not use. He understood
his tragedy very clearly, but the lucidity of his analysis did not help him
escape from it. In a letter to Urdaneta he had commented as follows: "I
should go to destroy this evil. The latter would be tyranny, and the former
cannot be called weakness, because I do not suffer from it. I am convinced
that if I fight I will triumph and save the country, and you know that I
am not afraid of combat. But why should I fight against the will of the
good men who call themselves free and moderate? They will reply to this
that I did not consult these same good, free men before destroying the
Spaniards, and that I scorned the opinion of the people; but the Spaniards
were called tyrants, absolutists, slaves, while those who are now at the
helm use the pompous names of republicans, liberals, citizens. It is this
that holds me back and makes me doubt."[1]

"It is this that holds me back and makes me doubt": an excellent proof
for posterity that these principles of public morality were more sincere
in Bolívar than in his enemies. He was held back by neither Páez nor
Santander, but by this invisible stockade that he himself erected.

At times he tried in vain to identify his present situation with that of
his best days, but, even in these moments, the optimistic invocation ended
in the Hamlet-like dilemma that was paralyzing him. He wrote: "When
I hear talk of bravery and daring I feel my whole being restored; I am
reborn, as it were, for my country and for glory. How happy we should
be if wisdom could be guided by strength! Then I could promise the
impossible; then Colombia and the rest of America could be saved. Consequently, let all our friends adopt this sentiment, and I shall banish from
my lips forever all unworthy talk of danger and fear. Let them command
me to uproot anarchy, and not even the memory of it shall remain. When
the law authorizes me to act, I find nothing impossible."[2]

This sadness that robbed him of sleep and the serious damage caused to
his precarious health by the hours spent in the open on the fatal night, had
reduced Bolívar to a pitiful state. The diplomatic representative of France
saw him as follows: "We arrived at the villa and were received by
Doña Manuela Sáenz. She told us that even though the hero was very

---

1. *Cartas,* vii, p. 260.
2. *Ibid.,* p. 280.

ill, she would announce our visit. A few moments later there appeared a man with a very long, yellow face and a miserable expression, wearing a cotton cap and wrapped in his dressing-gown with his legs swimming in wide flannel trousers. He replied to our first words concerning his health, showing us his emaciated arms: 'Ah! I have been reduced to this state not by the laws of nature but by the grief that gnaws at my heart. My fellow-citizens, who were unable to stab me to death, are now trying to assassinate me morally with their ingratitude and calumnies. When I cease to exist, these demagogues will devour each other, like wolves, and the edifice that I constructed with superhuman efforts wil crumble away in the fire of revolutions.' "[1]

Despite his debility, Bolívar could still find strength for one of the great projects that had always aroused his enthusiasm. In December 1828 he commissioned Revenga, who was then Minister of Finance, to realize his idea of paying off the Colombian public debt with Venezuelan tobacco. The Republic's obligations were such that international markets were on the point of regarding it as insolvent. Throughout the previous century Europe had kept a close watch upon these nations with the hope that, if they failed to "fulfill their obligations," the great powers would be able to make them into lands of conquest once again, claiming the right to commit the greatest outrages. But Bolívar and Revenga hoped that, if they could increase the cultivation of tobacco in Venezuela and improve the collection of the revenue that it produced, Colombia would be able to repay not only interest charges but also the debt itself. Revenga, then, went to Venezuela for this purpose, and he achieved marvellous results in only a few months. He busied himself with everything, from the method of packing the tobacco and the state of the roads along which it had to be transported to finding new overseas markets for it and ships to carry it. This task was sufficient to test the strength of even the most industrious official, but Revenga also followed his usual practice of sending the Liberator reports about each part of the country that he visited, with information on the state of public education, buildings that might be used for the foundation of schools and colleges, rents that could be assigned to them, and so on.[2]

Bolívar, meanwhile, had to attend to a most unpleasant task at the opposite end of the Republic, where, on February 1, 1829, the President of Peru, General La Mar, had seized control of Guayaquil after mounting an invasion. Resistance was organized by the veteran General Juan José Flores, the Venezuelan whose ability and services had raised him from humble origins to this high rank, and who was later to become Pres-

---

1. Liévano Aguirre, *op. cit.*, p. 486.
2. 'La Hacienda Pública de Venezuela en 1828-1830. Misión de José Rafael Revenga como Ministro de Hacienda'. Edición del Banco Central de Venezuela, Caracas, 1953.

ident of Ecuador. But Bolívar soon found himself obliged to inform Flores that he was unable to send him even a cent or a soldier, such were the demands being made on him from all sides.

Fortunately, Sucre had returned, after establishing what should be regarded as a memorable precedent for the future relations of the Spanish American states during his last days in Bolivia. He had repeatedly made it clear to the Bolivians that he would be unable to remain with them, because he did not want to renounce his Venezuelan nationality. But, when he found himself surrounded by conspirators and assassins, after an attempt on his life in Chuquisaca, his first concern was that Colombian auxiliary forces should not come to his aid, because the task was one for the Bolivians themselves, and he rightly trusted in their loyalty and affection for him. And at the same time he rejected the crafty intervention of General Gamarra who, on the pretext of assisting him, had invaded the country with Peruvian troops. Sucre wrote to him: "Since the 18th I have known that you and your troops would help me in a conflict if I summoned them. But I was very careful not to take this step, for the greatest of public calamities is to have foreign troops interfering in a country's disputes, and it would have been a fatal example to set. I was so circumspect and cautious in this that I warned the Ministers, in the very midst of our difficulties, that they were not to summon for any motive even one of the few remaining Colombian soldiers in La Paz, and that they were to do no more than inform General Urdinínea of what had happened, enclosing the decree appointing him President of the Council of Ministers, so that he might take whatever measures he judged opportune, as a Bolivian and as the man responsible for the administration. . . . Without asking anybody for assistance, I have been rescued from the hands of the assassins by the soldiers and the people of Bolivia. All the Provinces took arms against the rebels as soon as they heard the news. Perhaps you will have been aware of the enthusiasm of Potosí, Chichas, Cinti, Porco, Chayanta, etc., where more than six thousand inhabitants enlisted to march against the rebels. I have received a wound, but I have also received testimony of the most cordial affection from these people. . . . In March last year, when I was in La Paz, I received many letters from Peru, from respectable persons and many authorities, asking me to come. Although I had four thousand veteran troops there, and Peru had no forces with which to oppose me, and although I had suffered personal insults, I was very careful not to set a precedent for foreigners interfering in the domestic affairs of a country. . . In short, my esteemed General, I thank you for showing your gratitude for my services to Peru, by coming with your army to place yourself between me and my assassins, and I hope that to complete this display of appreciation you will return to Peru. I would rather die a thousand deaths than be responsible for introducing to America the ominous idea that might is right. Let no American nation set the abominable example of intervention, far less of hellish invasions. Tomorrow Colombia, stronger than Peru, and with more right, would intervene in Peruvian affairs; and, when Europe saw that our international law consisted of power and bayonets, she would not hesitate in providing us with rules and deciding our fate. Think how fatal is the lesson that you have given. I would have preferred not to receive the favor that you offer me; I would have preferred to be the victim of dissensions in Bolivia before having seen the rights and the independence of an American nation trampled under foot."[1]

It is easy to imagine the delight with which Bolívar learned that Sucre was once again in Colombia. He immediately appointed him to command all the southern provinces, where he knew that he was adored, and put under his orders the army organized by Flores to expel La Mar. As always he found a fine, paternal tribute for his subordinate, telling him: "I have vested in you the very being of Simón Bolívar. Yes, my dear Sucre, you are one with me, except for the goodness of your heart and the fate that is mine."[2]

As the Liberator had hoped, Sucre completely defeated the invaders on February 27 at Portete de Tarqui. As he had done after Pichincha and Ayacucho, this Bayard of American history granted an honorable surrender to the defeated, limiting his demands to the return of the provinces they had invaded. He stated in the official report: "I wanted to show that our justice was the same after the battle as before it. "Within a few days, however, the haughty La Mar ignored this treaty and refused to hand over Guayaquil. Bolívar then decided to assume personal control of the operations, and once again, disregarding his feeble state, he made the long trip from Bogotá to Quito, via Pasto. In Quito he announced in a proclamation: "We will retake Guayaquil only to enable us to comply with the preliminaries of peace concluded with Peru. We will not fire a shot, even to defend ourselves, without first having endured every suffering and having insisted in vain upon our undeniable rights. We will do more; once the Peruvians and the rebels have been expelled from Guayaquil, we will ask the vanquished for peace. This will be our revenge."[3] Fortunately, the Peruvians themselves removed La Mar from office and then expelled him from the country. Peace was restored between the two sister-states.

1. Blanco y Azpúrua, *Documentos para la historia de la vida pública del Libertador*, xii, p. 426.
2. *Cartas,* viii, p. 100.
3. *Proclamas y discursos del Libertador,* p. 392.

The Liberator was then faced by the tempting possibility of returning to Peru where public opinion rapidly swung back in his favor, and Congress was preparing to do him homage.[1] Would it be possible to try again to create the great confederation, to give political stability to the five countries he had freed, and to consolidate in South America a powerful state which could make Europe and the United States of North America respect it? The idea was dazzling, but Bolívar now knew that it was no more than a mirage. Before he had set out on this last campaign, Briceño Méndez, the intendant of the Department, had written to him from Venezuela: "If your presence is needed in the south, it will also be the ruin of the Republic. You will go, and it will probably follow you a long way; but you must understand that you cannot even look behind you. I am taking measures for my personal safety before your departure is announced, for it will be the alarm bell for all parties. If you have the good fortune of our arms triumphing in Popayán or Peru without need of your personal presence, it may be that we can live peacefully; but if you go, it is goody-bye forever, whether or not you win. This is my opinion and that of all your friends."[2] With the same hope that Bolívar would dedicate himself exclusively to the land of his birth, Revenga told the President of the Council of Ministers: "The people groan and only their trust in the Liberator consoles them. It is already being published, and it is repeated as a refrain, that only the hope that the Liberator will correct the evils they are suffering encourages them to continue to endure them."[3]

Yes, they were calling him from all parts, but no longer to undertake a great work, simply to correct the innumerable evils and errors that were dividing the Republic. It was as though fate was using a sarcastic double to humiliate him with what had previously exalted him.

Moreover, another conflict had broken out. General Córdova, whom Bolívar and Sucre had so regaled for his brilliant contribution to the victory at Ayacucho, and who was still in the government in July as Minister of Marine, rose against the Liberator in September and occupied the province of Antioquia. Until then he had been a passionate supporter of Bolívar's authority, implacable in his hostility towards those involved in the conspiracy of September 25. His adventure did not last very long. After refusing a proffered pardon, he confronted with extraordinary bravery General O'Leary, who had been sent to subdue him, and was mortally wounded during his defeat at El Santuario on October 17.

Córdova's attitude towards the *setembristas* had been so hard that, according to one historian, "before he mounted the gallows, Colonel Guerra

---

1. *Cartas,* ix, pp. 184 and 187.
2. Gil Fortoul, *op. cit.,* i, p. 623.
3. Revenga, *op. cit.,* p. 158.

exclaimed: 'It is not the Liberator who is shooting me; it is Córdova who is killing me!' "[1] Although this accusation cannot be accepted, since Guerra, who had played an active role in the conspiracy when he was chief-of-staff in Bogotá, was legally subject to a mandatory death sentence, Dr. Florentino González, in his narrative, also accused Córdova of having (on a previous occasion) publicly threatened those who opposed the dictatorship.[2]

How, then, do we explain this sudden change in Córdova? Although in his letter to Páez, inviting him to rebel with him, he spoke only of Bolívar's "tyranny" and of a constitutional project which was being planned, but which, according to him, was no different from the Bolivian constitution, which he supported, almost all historians relate his new attitude to the rumor which soon afterwards spread throughout Colombia of Bolívar's intention to crown himself.[3]

This alarming news arose, unfortunately, from a mad plan conceived, while the Liberator was in the south, by the Council of Ministers and other individuals "of experience and influence," to quote Restrepo, who was an eye-witness to what occurred. According to his account, the plan was "to adopt in principle constitutional monarchy in Colombia. As long as Bolívar survived he was to govern with the title of Liberator President, but he was to be succeeded by a foreign prince, who would become the first king, with the throne to be inherited by his descendants."

Bolívar first heard of this plan at the end of 1828, and on December 14 he wrote to Estanislao Vergara, the Minister of Foreign Affairs: "I can tell you that, since this is a difficult, thorny, risky affair a precipitous decision could, in my opinion, endanger the government of Colombia. It must be the product of circumstances. A circumspect, even passive policy is preferable to what we have here. A government in a precarious, unstable position cannot have wide aims."[4] Two days later, as if to dispel any doubt about his personal opinion, he stated categorically: "One hears nothing except that I am a tyrant in my country and that I aspire only to erect an imperial throne on the debris of the freedom of Colombia. Although my friends, that is, all wise men, laugh at these calumnies, they multiply among the innocent, unwary common people; they thrive in the shade of the deaf party in the convention; and when we least expect them these fictions appear clothed with a colossal character to make themselves masters of public opinion. The English papers, those of the United States, and who knows what others, talk for the same reason of

1. J.D. Monsalve, *Estudios sobre el Libertador,* p. 238. Quoted by Rumazo González in his biography of Manuela Sáenz, p. 250.
2. Blanco y Azpúrua, xiii, p. 66.
3. O'Leary, vii, p. 414.
4. *Cartas,* viii, p. 153.

a monarchy. It is, then, of prime importance to refute these false, completely false, rumors, give the lie to the impostors with the acrimony, precision and energy that they deserve, disabuse the whole nation and promise that next year it will see its representatives gathered together with an abundance of freedom and guarantees such as I never enjoyed."[1] On December 24, he convoked a congress which was to assemble on January 2, 1830, the one which was rightly called the *Admirable Congress.*[2]

The Council of Ministers, however, continued to sound out the opinion of a number of foreign diplomatic representatives towards its project, and on July 6, 1829, when the Liberator was at Camp Buijó, opposite Guayaquil, his secretary, José D. Espinar, sent a truly confusing communication to the same Minister of Foreign Affairs. The document reflected a bitter pessimism, based upon a keen analysis of what was happening in America; but, although its conclusions seemed to be similar to Bolívar's ideas on the need for England to protect the compromised independence of South America, it exaggerated them to the point of distorting them. Its most expressive part read as follows: "What means are available to enable us to save ourselves from the almost universal trembling which has overthrown empires, buried republics and made whole nations disappear? How are we to free America from the anarchy that devours her and the European colonization that menaces her? A general Congress of States was called, and its work was ignored by the nations most interested in its agreements. A partial federation of three sovereign states was proposed, and the slander and scandal rose to the heavens. In short, America needs a governor, whose mediation, protection or influence emanate from a powerful nation of the old continent, and with sufficient power to employ force and make the voice of duty heard, if ever his policies are ignored or insufficient; the rest is merely a question of name.

"His Excellency is conversant with the difficulties that prevent Colombia from imploring the favor of Europe or any nation for herself and for the other American states, and because of the rivalry that would be aroused among the European powers if one of them (it would not be Spain) exercised an influence over America. But, since she owes England two hundred million *pesos,* Spain, without doubt, is the nation most interested in preventing the destruction and enslavement of America. But if this interest is isolated, or not applied or exercised, it will not protect America from being recolonized by Spain or another continental nation. This would mean the end of the revolution and the fruit of twenty years of sacrifice.

---

1. *Cartas,* viii, p. 168.
2. *Decretos del Libertador,* iii, p. 300.

"His Excellency has not even the most remote personal interest in this affair, apart from that of Colombia, apart from that of America. Do not take his word for it; study the matter. Call it what you will, as long as the result conforms to his wishes that America should place herself under the custody or protection, the mediation or influence, of one or more powerful states, which would save her from the destruction to which she is being taken by the inherent anarchy in her system and by the colonial regime that is menacing her. Did not England spontaneously offer to mediate between Brazil and the Río de la Plata? Did she not intervene with force between Turkey and Greece? Let us search, then, *Señor* Minister, for a raft to cling to or let us resign ourselves to shipwreck in the vast abundance of evils that flood unhappy America."[1]

Did these statements really reflect the Liberator's thoughts? If they did, did they represent his real political intentions, or simply a transitory state of depression, caused with some justification by the circumstances in which he found himself?

Seven days later, in any case, on July 13, Bolívar wrote directly to Vergara, and he not only pointed out the dangers of the monarchical plan with exceptional clear-sightedness but also explained the reasons for his apparent hesitation, as if to dispel any slight hope the authors of the scheme might have. He told Vergara: "So far I have said yes, yes to everything that you gentlemen have suggested without venturing to express my true opinion, fearing that my letters might be intercepted and turned against the government or used to discredit the Council in the eyes of the masses. My views are of long standing and I therefore consider them to have been carefully thought out. First, I cannot continue to be the head of the government forever and, when I leave, the country will be broken up by civil war and frightful disorder of every kind. Second, to avert the horrible disasters that will surely come to pass before another ten years have elapsed, it is to be preferred that the country be legally divided and enjoy peace and harmony. Third, if the people's representatives in Congress feel that such a settlement would be favorably received by the people, let them effect it openly and deliberately and, at the same time, issue a declaration concerning mutual rights and interests. Fourth, if the representatives are of the opinion that they are not sufficiently empowered to take such an important step, they might ask for a ruling of the electoral colleges of Colombia, in order that the latter can voice their opinions and desires and provide Colombia with a government in conformity with them. Fifth, if none of these measures can be adopted because the Congress opposes them, no other alternative should be entertained but that of a government with life tenure, as in

---

1. *Cartas,* ix, p. 11.

the case of Bolivia, and a hereditary senate, such as I proposed in Guayana. This is the most that we can do for the stability of the government, a stability which, as regards Venezuela and New Granada, I consider to be illusory, since antipathies exist in both countries that cannot be overcome. On this point the Páez and the Santander factions are in complete agreement, although others in the country have different opinions about it.

"The idea of a foreign monarchy taking over the reins of government from me, however promising of results, is impractical for a thousand reasons: First, no foreign prince would accept the legacy of an anarchic principality that offers no security. Second, the national debt and the poverty of the country cannot provide the means with which to maintain a prince and his court, however penuriously. Third, the lower classes would become alarmed, fearing the effects of aristocracy and inequality. Fourth, neither the generals nor those who lust after power could bear to see themselves barred from supreme authority. I have said nothing of the obstacles that Europe might put in the way, as it is conceivable that, given a rare combination of favorable circumstances, none might arise.

"As for myself, you may well believe that I am weary of serving and disgusted with the acts of ingratitude and the crimes that are daily committed against me. You have seen how the great convention confronted me with the alternatives of either abandoning the country to its fate or saving it at my own expense. The article of which you speak, the most favorable that has been written on my behalf, states simply that my *usurpation of power is a fortunate thing and for the public good.* I, an usurper? I usurp power? My friend, this is horrible. I cannot tolerate the thought. It arouses within me such horror that I should prefer Colombia's ruin to having this epithet attached to my name. You say that later it will not be the same. I retort that, as our country will tolerate neither freedom nor slavery, a thousand revolutions will produce a thousand usurpations. This is fact, my friend, and, however viewed, the events of 1828 have sealed my fate. . . .

"A country that depends on the life of one man runs a risk as great as if its future were daily staked upon the cast of dice. And if that man has suffered greatly for twenty years, has many enemies who would gladly destroy him, is weary of public office and thoroughly loathes it, then the problem of maintaining such a state becomes infinitely greater. Such is the situation, my dear friend, I give you my word. I do not want to deceive you gentlemen, nor to be my own undoing. *I cannot go on,* and my heart reminds me of this a hundred times a day. Put yourself in my place and you will understand. If you will carefully analyze your own position, you will surely see that what I say is true. We must both reach a decision—you, yours, and I, mine. Through such a policy all of us will benefit, at least to some extent."[1]

He reiterated to General Urdaneta on the same date: "There is nobody available for the project of the monarchy, for I do not want the crown, nor do I want any European prince to mount a royal scaffold; should I ever forget what I told Bolivia, I have Iturbide at my side to remind me of it every day. If you do not want to leave Colombia, go to Caracas and help Páez reunite Venezuelan opinions. If you wish to leave the country, I will offer you half of what I have; you can count on this. It is better to live quietly than on the throne of the universe. Convince yourself of this, and you will leave me free to work as I wish and as it suits me. Understand that your difficulties are like heavy chains for me. Rid yourself of them, I repeat, and we will be freer than ever before. I never want to return to Bogotá, and, even if I say the opposite, this is what I really intend. I will not attempt to hide it from you, for it would be wrong of me. We have triumphed, my dear General, and this is the precise moment at which we must abandon everything, so that it might never be said that we were forced to go. I have appointed Córdoba Secretary of Marine. If necessary, I too will go to Venezuela to help my friends rebuild the country. Páez can become an excellent leader if we all help. You are authorized to inform Montilla of my opinion."[2]

And on September 13, 1829, he insisted in a letter to O'Leary: "Let us suppose that the constituent congress to be assembled in January will be wise enough to undertake successful legislative reforms. What might these be? Consider the size of Colombia, her population, the prevailing spirit, the trend of opinions today, the continent in which she is located, the bordering states, and the widespread resistance to the establishment of a stable order. We thus face a chain of fearsome threats that we cannot ignore. The size of our territory demands one of two entirely different types of government, both of them extremely unfavorable to the country's welfare: royal authority or general confederation are the only forms suitable for the ruling of this far-flung territory. I cannot even conceive the possibility of establishing a kingdom in a country which is essentially democratic. The lower and most numerous classes claim their prerogatives, to which they have an incontestable right. Equality before the law is indispensable where physical inequality exists, in order that the injustices of nature can, in some measure, be corrected. Moreover, who would be king in Colombia? No one, as I see it. No foreign prince would accept a throne surrounded by dangers and misery. The generals would be compelled, at least, to submit to someone else and to renounce forever

---

1. *Cartas,* ix, p. 20.
2. *Ibid.,* p. 25.

the supreme authority. The people, frightened by this innovation, would consider themselves sacrificed to the numerous consequences they would foresee in the structure and foundations of a monarchy. The agitators would rouse the people with deceitful arguments, and their persuasiveness would be irresistible, for everything conspires to make this specter of tyranny appear odious; its very name strikes terror. The poverty of the country does not permit the establishment of an expensive government favoring every abuse of luxury and dissipation. The new nobility, indispensable in a monarchy, would stem from the people as a whole, and so it would have all the envy of one group and all the arrogance of the other. No one would patiently endure such an aristocracy, steeped in poverty and ignorance and animated by ridiculous pretensions.... Let us speak no more, then, of this chimera."[1]

We have been careful to give the dates of each document, because they indicate that whenever there was any doubt in Bolívar's mind, he immediately dispelled it, and that his convictions, which were opposed to the creation of a monarchy in America, remained firm throughout these months. When he expressed them they were always supported by detailed explanations.

Those responsible for the confusion over this wretched affair were the writers who vehemently criticized Bolívar, occasionally attributing to him ideas that were not his. Some even hoped in this way to force him to give his support to their schemes. It is surprising to see, for example, that a soldier of the rectitude of Diego Ibarra, who had had the responsibility of serving as the Liberator's first aide-de-camp, did not shrink from asking Urdaneta to send a favorable report on the project in Bolívar's name, *whether genuine or not,* for the purpose of gaining support for it in Venezuela. He wrote to Urdaneta from Caracas on October 14, 1829: "General Páez says that he will clear the way for nothing until he receives a final answer from the Liberator, and he also says that he fears that this will not go well, despite his offer to follow Don Simón to the grave. I have told him that he should not expect anything final from General Bolívar.... This is the way things are here, and it would thus be very good if Pepe were to return promptly, bringing a favorable reply from Don Simón, whether genuine or not, so as to get rid of this difficulty which is the one which makes itself most apparent. The man would then have no excuse, and he would have to pronounce for or against."[2]

The unhappy year 1829 thus came to an end, with Bolívar still determined that Congress should meet on January 2 to enable him to resign his command. He again repeated on December 6 in a letter to Guzmán:

---

1. *Cartas,* ix, p. 123.
2. O'Leary, xi, p. 401.

"The nation can choose any system it wants. The people have been invited in a thousand ways to make known their will, and this should be the only guide for Congress in its deliberations. But persuade yourself, and let everybody else be persuaded, that I will not be the king of Colombia, even if extraordinary events occur, nor will I put myself in a position whereby posterity would rightly take away the title of Liberator, which my fellow-citizens gave me and which flatters all my ambition."[1] He was still in Popayán, because of his desire to stay away from Bogotá, lest it be said that he had come to exert pressure on the deputies to the Congress, who were beginning to arrive. He returned to the capital on January 15, 1830, and on the 20th, he submitted his resignation to this assembly.

In the last paragraph of his message he declared, melancholy and optimistic at the same time: "Fellow-citizens, I am ashamed to say it, but independence is the sole benefit we have gained, at the sacrifice of all others. Yet independence, under your sovereign auspices, opens the gates to the recovery of these others, in all the splendor of glory and liberty."[2]

---

1. *Cartas,* ix, p. 210.
2. *Proclamas y discursos del Libertador,* p. 398.

XXXV

TAKE MY LUGGAGE
ON BOARD
THE FRIGATE

O N THE DAY OF HIS RESIG-
nation, Bolívar declared in a proclamation to the Colombians: "Today I
have ceased to lead you," and he decided to relinquish his authority
without waiting for Congress to elect a new President. He sought the
advice of Congress on a substitute, since Dr. Castillo y Rada, President
of the Council of Ministers, who was legally entitled to take over his
duties, was also a congressman. However, the assembly refused to have
anything to do with the decision, declaring that it lay outside its
jurisdiction. The Liberator then named General Domingo Caicedo by
decree as President of the Council and, on March 1, 1830, he made him
President of the Republic.

Congress rightly feared that once Bolívar's resignation was declared final,
the dissolution of Colombia, which was already apparent on all sides,
would be accelerated. Since the previous year, Venezuela had make known
her desire to break away, and the former presidency of Quito was disposed
to do the same. Congress sent a commission, over which Sucre presided,
to the Venezuelan frontier to discuss her problems in a friendly fashion
with delegates whom Páez had been asked to appoint, but it was in vain.
The movement which was underway in Venezuela had taken on a bitter,
personalist character, and conciliation was no longer possible. Moreover,
it was no longer directed solely towards the organization of the country as
an independent republic, to which, of course, it was entitled. Anxious to
consolidate his own authority and always afraid of his inability to resist the

prestige of the Liberator, should he decide to reduce him by force, Páez had hurried to fortify himself with all those who might aid him in his designs: discontented soldiers, such as Mariño and Arismendi; former royalists, or sons of royalists, who, because of their grudges or the desire to regain their pre-eminence, were ardently in favor of change; demagogues, who are always present on such occasions and —why not?— some men of good faith and little foresight, such as the unchangeable Martín Tovar.

The deliberations on the frontier, then, were doomed to fail. Once again Sucre, with the rectitude that was always manifest in him as supreme elegance of spirit, gave a lecture on public morality, proposing: "Since some soldiers have had the misfortune to trample on the laws, by abusing their power and influence, and others are under suspicion of trying to change the forms of government, it should be prohibited for a period of at least four years for any commander-in-chief, or any other generals who have held high office in the Republic between 1820 and 1830, to be president or vice-president of Colombia, or president or vice-president of any of the states, should the confederation of the three great districts be established. High office should be understood as the position of president, vice-president, ministers of state and superior commander."

As we can see, Sucre's proposal excluded Bolívar and himself from all participation in government and, with respect to the Liberator, had the moral value of making it possible to discuss "suspicion of trying to change the forms of government." But, since Páez and his leading followers were also excluded, the Venezuelan commissioners rejected it. A revealing sign of the unscrupulousness being provoked by their passions was that they even informed their government that "the bad faith" of the delegates from Bogotá was what had prevented a "friendly and fruitful understanding."

The means resorted to in an attempt to give Venezuela's "pronouncement" against the Liberator the appearance of a national plebiscite were equally repulsive. According to instructions sent by one of Páez's allies to his other agents in the provinces, "there is not even time to scratch one's head in this Secretaryship, for we are working day and night and even until dawn, to send the correspondence and the commissioners bound for Oriente, Apure, Occidente, Maracaibo and the fifth hell. The General (Páez) and Don Carlos (Soublette) want them all to have detailed instructions to enable them to cut any knot they encounter. They also must take the pronouncements, written here, to be made by municipalities, the village committees, and every idol; for it is desired that all, all, all their minutes be sent in, without any corner being missed, demanding three things: nothing of union with the Granadans; the General as commander of Venezuela; and down with Don Simón. Everybody must ask for this, or be treated as an enemy; and then. . . ."[1]

The original document itself leaves the threat at the end of the paragraph suspended in this way. What happened in the town of Escuque is a good example of the way in which this intimidation worked in practice. In February 1830, Francisco A. Labastida protested on behalf of the inhabitants about the conduct of the district's military commander, reporting: "Even the popular assemblies have been playthings for his insolence. He has tried to make the citizens sign, not what they have really said and agreed in their meetings, but some papers that he wrote in his fashion in his house. Those who were unwilling to obey were threatened with his terrors. And can this be freedom, Excellency? Could a town speak freely when, as it was meeting, it saw a squadron of cavalry and a company of fusileers drawn up in the square? If the papers which *Señor* Segarra wanted us to sign had contained just, well-founded complaints to back up our pronouncement, it would have been right for him to insist, but it did not seem right to us to want us to subscribe to a multitude of insults, injuries and insolences against General Bolívar, for we believed that we could disregard his authority and treat it with decorum."[2] Similarly, numerous unpublished documents in the National Archives of Caracas show how espionage was organized against private individuals, and how the violation of correspondence was handled.[3]

The Liberator, naturally, knew little or nothing of this endless trickery, and the reaction against him that he could see wherever he looked was all the more painful because it seemed inexplicable. He wrote to O'Leary: "I cannot live beneath the burden of the ignominy that oppresses me, nor can Colombia be well served by a desperate man, for whom they have broken all stimuli of the spirit, and whose hopes they have destroyed forever."[4] Another letter, written on January 4, 1830 to Castillo Rada suggests that he even thought of suicide. Bolívar told him, "I assure you, my dear friend, that I have never suffered as much as now, when I am seeking, almost with eagerness, a moment of desperation in order to end a life which is my opprobrium."[5]

For three years the combined activities of Páez and Santander had been employed against him and his works: wooing malcontents to create enemies for him; intrigues and rumors to discredit him, threats to move cowards; demagogy and moral intimidation to make honorable

1. Blanco y Azpúrua, xiii, p. 706.
2. Archivo Nacional, Caracas, Sección 'Secretaría del Interior y Justicia', v, f. 421.
3. *Ibid,* i and v, ff. 48 and 269.
4. *Cartas,* ix, p. 92.
5. *Cartas,* ix, p. 227.

men and even the Liberator himself hesitate. At the same time, what was he offered by his friends and those who wanted to save Colombia? They offered him nothing; they made demands. They demanded a solution for so many evils which nobody, no matter who, was capable of providing. With increasing frequency, and foolishly, they demanded that he again make himself the irresistible hero of former days. But, whom was he to fight?

None of his correspondence of this period reveals wide-ranging ideas. He was lost amidst a vast sadness and small cares, such as Baudelaire was to describe. Politics forced him into a daily improvisation of immediate solutions. Only once, in a letter to O'Leary, did he return to the idea, first formed in 1813, of separating political government from the military command, so as to entrust the former to a magistrate who would be responsible for the legal order and that of liberty, while he, retaining only military authority and circumstancial functions, dedicated himself to preserving peace and constitutionalism. He told O'Leary: "The truth is that if they wish to restrain me too much they will make me more despondent than I am. Here is an idea for you to fuss about and consider thoroughly: would it not be better for Colombia and me, and even more for public opinion, if a president were appointed and I remained as a simple commander-in-chief? I would fuss about the goverment like a bull around a field full of cows. I would defend it with all my strength and that of the Republic. This government would be stronger than mine, because it would have, in addition to my own strength, that intrinsic to government and that of the person who served it. General administration would always be complete and finished without need of legitimacy or authority. The government would be strong on its own account and because of the support that I would give it. It would have unity, stability and continuity. Unlike me, it would not see itself obliged to take enormous leaps, leaving immense spaces behind. Instead of having an unbalanced administration which upsets everything else, as constantly happens to me, it would form a plan of action which it would enforce without variations and without placing it in different hands, as happens now with everything painted in different colors and in an extravagant manner. I would tour the Departments; I would prevent disorders; I would go on campaign without having to abandon the government. All my attention would then be dedicated to the army and to the use of armed force. My mobility would be admirable to enable me to go quickly and opportunely wherever necessity or danger called me. All insurrections and unexpected attacks would be avoided, and the government would be seated on a chair enjoying complete tranquillity and confidence that I would appear everywhere, like a wall, behind which public order and domestic peace would be preserved. Administration would proceed without obstacles; the citizens would relax, enjoying the rule of law; and my reputation would regain the sparkle that it has lost. It would bring Colombia many gains, and I would have glory, freedom and happiness. If this policy is not adopted, they will either lose me or they will lose Colombia; and in either case we lose everything."[1]

This idea, which, like many others of Bolívar, was subsequently discredited by crude imitations, was perhaps the only system which might have ensured temporary freedom and stability for Colombia, while, in accordance with his plans for social reforms and popular education, more extensive foundations were being prepared for a stable constitutional reorganization.

This project must have been surrounded in his mind by flattering reflections. During the war the most important contribution of Venezuela, Colombia, all America, had been, not the combativeness and skill of the soldiers, not the abnegation and moral bravery with which they suffered weariness and privations, but the capacity for organization, the tenacity and the discipline with which they fought, step by step, against misfortune and forlornness on the road to victory. All the elements that compose what might be called political understanding in men and nations—solidarity, patience and perseverance, intuition of what is convenient and possible in every case, moderation of character to prevent abandonment to whims and improvisation—were the secret of the American triumph during the fourteen-year long contest. Had all these virtues died? Would it not still be possible to reanimate them for the task of consolidating the independence and making it fruitful? The plan that had seemed so coherent and feasible in Peru—education in work for all, and hope based upon the ownership of property... the colonization of the country with its own inhabitants, according to the maxims of Simón Rodríguez—would perhaps need no more than five or ten years, under a sound administration, and it could provide these improvised republics with a new people.

But it was too late. A plan of this sort was the last thing that the *caudillos* and the regional politicians who now held effective power wanted. And, although the Liberator was only aware from time to time of his physical weakness, the truth is, and his friends and subordinates saw it, that he was unable to offer the country those ten or five years. Even one year was beyond him. His body had been so weakened by the ravages of the September night, the long journey to and from Guayaquil, and the constant state of anxiety in which he lived, that his friends were horrified when they saw him again in Bogotá. General Joaquín Posada Gutiérrez

---

1. *Cartas,* ix, p. 91.

narrates in his *Memorias:* "When Bolívar appeared, I saw tears being shed. He was pale, drawn, and his eyes, so brilliant and expressive in his good days, were already dull; his deep voice was hardly audible; all this, and the gauntness of his face announced, arousing a vehement sympathy, the forthcoming dissolution of his body."

In the end he broke the last bonds with which the appeals of his friends and his own dreams were martyring him. "I desire no more than my *furlough* or my *freedom,* like the soldiers or the slaves," he had written to José Angel Alamo. On April 27, 1830, in a message to Congress, he ratified his resignation from the Presidency of the Republic.

In the same document he announced his decision to emigrate, so that his name could not be used as a pretext for new disturbances: "You can be certain that the good of the country demands of me the sacrifice of separating myself forever from the country that gave me life, lest my presence in Colombia should be an impediment to the happiness of my fellow-citizens."[1]

The southern provinces, which already considered themselves separated from Colombia in practice, and which were to constitute the Republic of Ecuador, had invited him to live there. They told him in a representation signed in Quito on March 27, 1830, and headed by the name of General Flores: ". . . we address ourselves to Your Excellency, begging you to select for your residence this land which adores Your Excellency and admires your virtues. Come to live in our hearts, and receive the homage of gratitude and respect due to the Genius of America, the Liberator of a world."[2] Sucre, who was already back in from Colombia in practice, and which were to constitute the Republic is about to break up; and in whichever part I find myself they will try to make me their *caudillo,* to lead them in rebellion; neither my dignity nor my position allows me to make myself a leader of factions."[3]

But he had no money to support himself decently abroad. His sizeable fortune had been consumed by the war and the constant grants and pensions he had ordered against it in favor of relatives, friends and comrades-in-arms. One of the Liberator's bitterest detractors, the adventurer H. L. Ducoudray Holstein, wrote as follows about his indifference to money: "I must, however, do him justice by declaring that he was never miserly, for he was generous and he cared little or not at all about money. I often saw him empty his purse and give his last doubloon to any officer who asked for something on account of his salary. As they parted, I always heard Bolívar say, laughing: '*Le pauvre diable!* His need is greater than mine, and this misery of gold has no

---

1. *Proclamas y discursos del Libertador* (Caracas, 1939), p. 404.
2. Blanco y Azpúrua, xiv, p. 163.
3. Quoted by José Ignacio Méndez in *El ocaso de Bolívar* (Bogotá, 1951), p. 38.

value for me; I have given him all I had."[1] The Liberator's correspondence also shows that he twice offered half his fortune to Urdaneta, when, during the sad years of 1828 to 1830, he suggested that they both retire from public life. His generosity to Fernando Peñalver in 1821 seems like an attractive invention, but it, too, is authenticated by his letters. They were both still suffering from the privations which were typical of this period. We recall, for example, that in May 1820 Bolívar wrote: "Infante obtained a few *reales* from the priest of San Cayetano, and he is supporting me."[2] A year later, in May 1821, they were still living in this state of penury when Bolívar wrote to Peñalver: "My dear friend, last night I received your letter brought to me by Anacleto. It was with great distress that I learned of your extreme misery; since I do not have even a *maravedí* to give you, I am enclosing an order for my servant, who has my belongings, to give them to you, so that you might sell them. Among them there should be some silverware, which, whatever happens, will sell quickly."[3]

Numerous similar examples could be cited, and it might be said that he became absolutely indifferent towards money, just as he did to every sort of comfort and ostentation. In December 1829, he told José Angel Alamo, "I regret that you and other friends are worrying yourselves about promoting this business for me; and I regret even more that anybody should fear to go to court against me. This is a cruel plot against my honor. Abandon my defense, then, and let the enemy and the judge take my property. . . . Do nothing more in the affair. I will die as I was born, naked. You have money and will provide me with the means to eat when I have none."[4]

He was referring to some copper mines—all that remained of the family patrimony—which he was trying to sell. He was prevented from doing so by litigation, which was encouraged by the hostility and the political motives of his enemies in Venezuela.

Moreover, he was still responsible for the 22,000 *pesos* offered to Lancaster for his attempt to establish popular education in Caracas. On April 28, 1830, he instructed his legal |representative: "Messrs. Powles and Co. are demanding what I owe them for that promissory note of Mr. Lancaster, of which you are aware, and I want you to arrange payment as soon as the first money is received. If the mines are not sold, Mr. Powles is to receive the rent from them until his twenty-two thousand *pesos* are paid. . . . Please inform him of this at that house so as to calm his worries about this sum."[5] Thus Bolívar was faithful to the last

---

1. Antonio Arráiz, *op. cit.,* p. 65.
2. *Cartas,* ii, p. 172.
3. *Ibid.,* p. 349.
4. *Cartas,* ix, p. 221.
5. *Cartas,* ix , p. 260.

moment and to the last piece of money to the project that had so attracted him; these instructions were issued the day after his final resignation.

In the end he had to put up for sale his jewels and horses to finance his journey, and his own silverware yielded 2,500 *pesos* when sold by weight to the mint. On May 8 he left Bogotá for Cartagena. Four days earlier Congress had elected Joaquín Mosquera President of the Republic, and General Domingo Caicedo Vice-President.

On the eve of his departure, Bolívar had occasion to witness a sad example of the anarchy he was leaving behind him. A battalion and a squadron of cavalry, composed mainly of Venezuelans, mutinied and demanded money and supplies to enable them to return to Venezuela. The government had to agree to their demands, and the two units paraded through the streets of Bogotá, with drums beating and flags flying, as though they were celebrating one of their former glorious campaigns rather than a mass desertion.

However, these veteran mutineers were not entirely unjustified in their action. In Spanish America the soldiers are frequently accused of inclination to violence and sectarianism, but the politicians, in turn, fall into these same excesses, which destroy the foundations of social harmony and create a collective state of mind propitious for any anarchic adventure. And this is just what happened then. As soon as the Liberator had removed himself from power, the demagogues wanted to hurl themselves against him, his friends and supporters, the soldiers, and the Venezuelans who remained in Granadan territory. Strife is inevitable when those who are threatened are not only numerous but also little inclined to turn the other cheek.

In the midst of the imprecise and extensive malaise which this caused, the approaching hostility even reached Manuelita Sáenz. The supporters of Santander hated her, and they especially threw in her face the fact that she had shot Santander in effigy in a grotesque parody which she carefully organized in her house. They overlooked of course, that at the same time Vargas Tejada was reciting in conspiratorial circles, amidst shouts and acclamation, the verses in which he proposed to cut off the "tyrant's" head and feet.

During the trial of the *setembristas,* Manuela lied to save the lives of some of them, and she interceded for others, hiding them or helping them in other ways. When she told O'Leary of this twenty years after the Liberator's death, in the letter already cited, she had the delicacy to attribute the merit for her attitude to him. She reported: "When the General (Bolívar) left Bogotá for I know not where, he told me: 'General Padilla is about to arrive as a prisoner. I encharge you with visiting him in prison, consoling him, and serving him in anything that occurs to you.' This I did. *Señor* General Obando, whom may God preserve for many years, said in Lima that despite my bad qualities I had behaved very generously, to which I replied that this virtue was not mine, but the Liberator's, who had given me so many and such repeated lessons in clemency towards the eulogist himself. This is quite certain: you know of it. Thus, the fact that so many escaped death was due to the Liberator. It is sufficient to tell you that I had in my house persons who were being sought, and that the Liberator was aware of it. He advised General Gaitán to leave a certain place because it was already known. When I rode into a house I saw Dr. Merizalde, and I said to the owner: 'If I had come like this with somebody else, instead of my servant, they would have seen Dr. Merizalde. Tell him to be more careful.' It was perhaps because of this that Merizalde made me a close friend after the Librator's death. I could tell you an infinite number of things of this sort, but I omit them for the sake of brevity, assuring you that in the beginning I was no more than the instrument of the magnanimity of the great Bolívar."[1]

She provided testimony of this charitable influence in a letter to the Liberator. In this case she interceded for other individuals, and she wrote to Bolívar, in the style she was accustomed to using with him, which was both affectionate and proud: "You know that I have never pleaded with you except for deserters and those condemned to death; if you have pardoned them, I have thanked you in my heart without making a fuss; if you have not pardoned them, I have excused and tolerated you without complaining. I am well aware of how much I can do for a friend, and I will certainly not compromise the man whom I most adore."

But they did not pardon her for having saved the Liberator on the fatal night, and they also wanted to wound him through her. For this reason they insisted on claiming that she had numerous lovers. It is not difficult, unfortunately, to imagine that in accordance with her aggressive independence of mind, Manuela would have occasionally drawn a distinction between the passionate spiritual fidelity which she always retained tor the Liberator, and physical fidelity, which perhaps had no importance for her. But it also seems probable that the same strength of character would not have permitted the passivity necessary for her to give herself to other men without love. If she had accepted another, it is likely she would have done so exclusively and completely. Moreover, there is a further argument, which on one occasion we heard from the penetrating critic Enrique Planchart, and which seems decisive. After Bolívar's death these tales about Manuelita's lasciviousness were never repeated. Is not this sufficient proof that they were invented only to wound the Liberator?

Manuela was so proud to be Bolívar's lover, and so self denying when he was ill, spiritually destroyed and proscribed, as in those splendid

---

1. O'Leary, iii, p. 375.

months in Lima. She was aged only thirty-three when her hero died; she was left poor, and she was persecuted furiously. Her former husband wanted to help her, but she refused all assistance. She ended her days working for a living in an obscure Peruvian village, but even then, when reduced to a state of extreme forlornness, she defended the memory of her lost love with the same firmness and enthusiasm as always. Why not ask ourselves passionately, then, why this free, beautiful, ardent and desired woman had sufficient strength to resist the summons that must have assailed her from all sides?

What Manuela said at the time to her persecutors in a public handbill seems to be an anticipated reply to this question: "They may call my exaltation a crime, they may condemn me; they slake their thirst, then, but they have not been able to make me despair. My tranquillity rests upon the repose of my conscience, and not upon the malice of my enemies, or that of the enemies of His Excellency the Liberator. If not even the withdrawal of this gentleman from public affairs has been enough to appease their anger, and they have taken me for a coward, I tell them that they can do everything, they can treacherously dispose of my existence, but they cannot make me retreat even an inch in my respect, friendship and gratitude for General Bolívar; and those who regard this as a crime are simply revealing the poverty of their minds and the firmness of my nature."[1]

The new President, Joaquín Mosquera, belonged to a family which Bolívar so loved and honored that he came to be regarded almost as a brother by the Liberator. Despite this, he had appointed the spiteful Dr. Vicente Azuero to the Ministry of the Interior, and this naturally, emboldened the Liberator's enemies. For her part, Manuela dedicated herself to provoking them with tricks, which they took as signs of a conspiracy. One of the placards that she had posted at the street corners said simply: "Long live Bolívar, founder of the Republic," but Azuero explained it as follows: "A Negro had posted subversive, incendiary lampoons on the house situated in the diagonal of the Cathedral tower and on the church of San Francisco; this Negro was one of the servants of Manuela Sáenz, who had sent a *zambita* to treat the soldiers who were on guard at the Palace of the Most Excellent Vice-President of Colombia, General Domingo Caicedo, with a bottle of beer, a plate of sweet loaves, cheroots, a silver *peso* and a jar of chilli sauce."[2] On another occasion Manuela discovered that a number of firework castles, including an offensive image of herself and the Liberator, were to be burned in the main square. She immediately gave a lance each to two

---

1. Alfonso Rumazo González, *Manuela Sáenz*, p. 271.
2. *Ibid.,* p. 272.

Drawing of Bolívar in 1830, by the painter José María Espinosa.

of her slave-women, and took another herself, and the three women destroyed the object, after chasing away its guardians.

News of some of these things must have reached the ears of the Liberator, for he hurried to write to her while on the road: "My love: I want to tell you that I am very well but full of sadness at your affliction and that which I suffer because of our separation. My love, I love you very much, but I will love you more if now, more than ever, you retain good judgment. Take care with what you do; if not, you will lose both of us if you lose yourself. I am your most faithful lover. *Bolívar*."[1]

Some historians think that another of his letters to her, which does not bear a date, must have been written shortly afterwards. He told her: "The ice of my years melts with your kindness and graces. Your love revives a life that is expiring. I cannot be without you, I cannot willingly deprive myself of my Manuela. I do not have your will to stop myself from seeing you; an immense distance hardly suffices. I see you, although I am far from you. Come, come, come immediately." He signed it: Yours in spirit."[2]

This strange idyll at the edge of the grave was complicated, as if the Liberator were still in his prime, by another letter, in which Joaquina Garaicoa, *la Gloriosa*, told him from Guayaquil: *"Mi Glorioso:* I am beside myself when I reflect that you have already left Colombia; but the latest news confirms it. Even you, who knows my enthusiasm and all that you mean to me, cannot realize how much I grieve. I tried to show you by saying all I could when I sent a letter by the overland mail, as soon as I saw your last message; but it is all to no avail. There are no words capable of transmitting what I feel for my *Liberator, the Father of Colombia*. In the midst of the oppression we suffer from the burden of this misfortune, I comfort myself with the thought that I always have you in my heart; that there I see you, I talk to you, I embrace you, I admire you and, finally, I please myself with the confidence that everywhere you are the man who is admired throughout the world; and you will be much more admired with this last flourish of selflessness, which will startle ambitious men and seal the lips of your baseless, unjust enemies. If until now I have cared for and loved Delicacy *(Fineza)* as a token of you, and because of her own graces, I will esteem her more every day, and I will always see her as your Delicacy. She will be my best companion, and she will always remain in my fondest and sweetest recollections. Please accept the consideration of my mother and of each person in this her house, the unlimited respect of the priest, and the most

---

1. *Cartas,* ix, p. 265.
2. *Cartas,* vii, p. 377.

cordial love of your unchanging admirer, who has the glory of signing with the great names which you yourself gave her in your generosity. Gloriosa, Simona Joaquina Trinidad... y Bolívar."[1]

If the Liberator was comforted by these proofs of the love of Manuela and Joaquina, the moments of peace or satisfaction that he was able to enjoy were soon interrupted by an atrocious peace of news. On July 1, 1830, when he had already reached Cartagena, he learned that Sucre had been assassinated on June 4 in the Berruecos Mountains, near Pasto. "Good God! The blood of Abel has been spilled!" was all he managed to say, and he then remained silent, absorbed in inexpressible grief.

Bolívar had written to Sucre for the last time on May 26, when he told him, "I shall forget you only when those who love glory forget Pichincha and Ayacucho." In the *Diario de Bucaramanga,* too, there is a phrase of the Liberator which, although contained in a report put together with little skill by Perú de Lacroix, seems to be an advance epitaph for his unequaled companion: "... his mind is great and strong; he knows how to persuade and lead men; he knows how to judge them...."

Sucre had been so upright and humanitarian that he had not even wanted to be harsh with the royalists during the period of the war to the death. In Peru, for the first time, he condemned to death a Spanish officer called Echeverría, but he soon reprieved him. However, his order for clemency came too late, and Echeverría was executed. Sucre felt obliged to justify himself, and he did so as follows: "... in the course of our terrible, disastrous war, in which three of my brothers have been shot in cold blood, Echeverría is the first Spaniard I have condemned to death out of twenty-eight generals and one thousand three hundred Spanish officers whom I have had at my disposal from Pichincha to Potosí." His conduct towards his personal enemies is illustrated by the case of Valentín Matos, an officer who tried to assassinate him in Bolivia. He was tried and condemned to death, but Sucre commuted the sentence to deportation, and he gave him 200 *pesos* of his own money for his traveling expenses. The first anniversary of the creation of the Republic was celebrated shortly afterwards, and Sucre decreed: "the criminal Valentín Matos, condemned to death and now suffering the punishment of exile, to which his sentence was commuted, for the premeditated assassination of my person, is now exempt from all punishment for this offense...."[2]

Sucre's assassination was ordered by one of the sinister leaders from Pasto, General José María Obando, a former royalist, whose most recent crime had been to rebel in connivance with the Peruvians when they invaded Colombia. The leader of the outlaws who actually committed the

---

1. Lecuna, *Catálogo...,* iii, p. 285.
2. Gil Fortoul, *op. cit.,* i, p. 475.

crime, a certain Apolinar Morillo, a Venezuelan, insisted on Obando's complicity until the moment of mounting the gallows, and his leading accomplices told the same story. But, as Obando was already identified with the circles in New Granada which were beginning to call themselves "liberal", and later became their leader, he was able to get his followers to cover up the evidence against him.

This process also involved the covering up of something else, which, although less easily proved, is true and is supported by important testimony: that Obando, in his turn, received instructions for the assassination from one of the "liberal" circles in Bogotá. Even the house near the cathedral in which the criminal decision was taken is known, and, years later, one of those who attended the secret meeting reported: "... that he was the first to leave the house and, when he reached the door, he saw General Sucre, with his arms folded, walking on the porch of the Cathedral; that this made a deep impression on him, for, moments before, they had decreed his death, and it was as if a ghost was appearing before him...."[1] Moreover, these fanatics had publicly announced their crime, and had even identified the person to commit it. On June 1, they said in *El Demócrata,* one of their newspapers, referring to Sucre's departure for the south: "It may be that Obando will do with Sucre what we failed to do with Bolívar; because of our failure the government is branded as weak, and we, and the government itself, lack security."

Bolívar, of course, immediately understood their motives. On the day that he received the fatal news, he wrote to General Flores: "The immaculate Sucre has been unable to escape from the ambushes of these monsters. I do not know what cause this General has given for them to make an attempt on his life, when he has been more liberal and more generous than all the heroes in the annals of fate, and when he was too strict even with the friends who did not entirely share his ideas. I think that the purpose of this crime was to deprive the country of a successor to me...."[2]

Within a few days the Liberator suffered another mortal blow. With Venezuela definitively separated from the Colombian union, a constituent Congress had met in Valencia. Under pressure from those individuals who were being incited by Páez to disgrace Bolívar's name by all available means, it declared that fresh negotiations could begin with New Granada and Quito, "but Venezuela," the President of the Valencia Congress told the President of Colombia, "which has been taught to be prudent by a series of evils of every sort, which sees the origin of them in General Simón Bolívar, and which still trembles when she contemplates the risk she

1. Carlos Héctor Larrazábal, *Sucre, figura continental* (Buenos Aires, 1950), p. 289.
2. *Cartas,* ix, p. 279.

ran of becoming his patrimony forever, insists that the proposed settlements will not take place as long as the Liberator remains in the territory of Colombia."[1] The spite reflected in these charges was sufficient of course, to discredit them, for there is absolutely no doubt that the Venezuelans should have been the last to complain of despotism on the part of the Liberator. From 1813 to 1821 he was in Venezuela only to fight in the most difficult conditions, and in almost deserted areas; he left for the south immediately after Carabobo; and after he returned in 1827, Venezuela remained practically independent of the central government, except for the six-month long period during which he remained in Caracas, dedicating himself to the fruitful administrative work which has been described above.

But the worst aspect of this disgraceful affair was that it provided Dr. Vicente Azuero with the vile satisfaction of informing the Liberator of this insult from his native land. He wrote: "The Most Excellent President of the Republic, embarrassed by the contents of the said communication, and in doubt about the decision he should take, has finally resolved that a copy be sent to Your Excellency. I have the honor of fulfilling this resolution, taken so that you might be informed of this remarkable circumstance, because of the influence you might have on the nation's happiness, and because of its consequences for the glory of Your Excellency."[2]

Mosquera's government had absolutely no need to pass on these thoughtless declarations of the Valencia Congress to Bolívar, who was then a mere private individual, on his way abroad. And what was the meaning of these ambiguous phrases: "in doubt about the decision he should take . . . because of the influence you might have on the nation's happiness?" Did they mean that Mosquera had thought of expelling the Liberator? Was he asking him to accelerate his departure, so that such an order might be avoided? This was how Bolívar took it, and he commented in one of his letters: "To be implicitly thrown out of Colombia by my best friend, whom I would have chosen for a brother. . . I had nothing to write to *Señor* Mosquera, and my greatest moderation has consisted of not having replied to him."[3]

But the intemperance of demagogues in government is no less blind than that of tyrants and, like them, they seem to grow more passionate with each outrage that is committed. One of the measures that occurred to Mosquera's government was to discharge a unit of Venezuelan troops, but only after removing them from the capital, so as to isolate them. Naturally, these veterans feared that they were to be dispersed defenseless

---

1. Blanco y Azpúrua, xiv, p. 294.
2. Blanco y Azpúrua, xiv, p. 295.
3. *Cartas,* ix, p. 343.

and without resources, a long way from their native land and at the mercy of the hostility between Granadans and Venezuelans, which was daily becoming more intense. They decided, therefore, to mutiny, and, after defeating the forces of the government, they overthrew it.

Unfortunately for Bolívar, they immediately pronounced in his favor, and at the beginning of September, by means of a document signed in Bogotá, they summoned him to exercise supreme authority; in the meantime it was entrusted to General Rafael Urdaneta. As always, his friends and supporters pestered him to return to public life.

The Liberator reacted violently. On September 10, 1830, he wrote to General Briceño Méndez: "You gentlemen press me strongly to return as a member of a faction and put myself at the head of some rebels; at least this is the meaning of a very long letter from *Señor* Aranda. I have read this letter, and it has certainly filled me with disgust, instead of encouraging me to commit a criminal act. Are they still not content with having cost me the support of the public with their advice at Ocaña and their infamous acts and monarchical projects, without also wanting to deprive me of my personal honor by dragging me down to the level of an enemy of the country? Aranda says that I am ungrateful towards my friends and weak, and he even accuses me of cowardice. You are well aware that mine is the only energetic character to be found in Colombia, for this is the only title I have to lead all the others, and you also know that my dislike for command has been as sincere as my whole character. They demand that I sacrifice my name as an honored citizen, solely in order to take four emigrés back to their homes. Well, I will not do it, and I swear to you that I will never return to take command, in order to avoid being ungrateful to my friends or cowardly with my enemies."[1]

He was already in Cartagena, and he added, in the same letter: "Here they have wanted to declare me a general in the army, in imitation of a document from Socorro and a proclamation by Justo Briceño. There is no point in adding that I did not accept such impertinence."

But the habit of command and, above all, his anxiety not to abandon Urdaneta, who had assumed such difficult responsibilities, led him to give advice to this general, to declare vaguely that he would serve as "a citizen and soldier," and to promise Urdaneta that he would help with "the restoration of order, the reconciliation of our enemy brothers, and the recuperation of national integrity." He even offered in the same letter to return to the capital "to reiterate my solemn promises to obey the laws and the constituted authorities, until constitutional elections provide us with the benefits of a legislative body and new magistrates chosen by the votes of the nation."[2]

---

1. *Cartas,* ix, p. 303.
2. *Ibid.,* p. 312.

Bolívar, by Tenerani. 1831 (courtesy of Alfredo Boulton).

Almost immediately, however, Bolívar recovered his customary lucidity and with it his repugnance at being regarded as the leader of a faction. On September 25th he wrote to Vergara: "You tell me that you will soon leave the ministry because you must attend to your family, and then you demand that I march to Bogotá to perfect a usurpation which the extraordinary gazette has announced without disguising in even a comma the nature of the outrage. No, my friend, I cannot go, nor am I obliged to, for nobody should be forced to act against his conscience and the laws. I have not contributed in the slightest to this reaction, nor have I promised anybody that I would. If I pick the fruit of this insurrection, I will assume all responsibility for it. Believe me, I have never looked kindly on insurrections; and recently I have deplored even that which we organized against the Spaniards."

And on October 16 he ratified to Urdaneta: "Understand that history has always shown that in all civil wars victory goes to the most ferocious or the most energetic, depending on the choice of words. The only recourse left open to your faction is to choose between leaving the country or getting rid of your enemies, for their return would be frightful. It is to avoid being involved in this cruel choice that I have not dared to take part in this reaction, for I am convinced that our authority and our lives can be preserved only at the cost of the blood of our opponents, and this sacrifice will not bring peace or happiness, much less honor."[1]

His health, moreover, was failing relentlessly and continually. Just as images are mixed up and confused in the mind of a feverish man —in fact, this was probably what happened— so in his letters written then anguish and sadness were pushed aside by contradictory fragments of unrealizable projects. On September 20, he wrote to Briceño Méndez from Cartagena: "You gentlemen will see my proclamation. Although it seems that I am offering a lot, I am offering nothing, except to serve as a soldier. I have not wanted to accept the command which the proceedings conferred upon me, because I do not want to be taken for the leader of rebels and the military nominee of victors. I have offered to serve the government, because I cannot excuse myself during such dangers. If they give me an army, I shall accept it, and, if they send me to Venezuela, I shall go.... I cannot live among assassins and factious men; I cannot be honored amidst such rabble, and I cannot enjoy repose amid anxiety. They ask me for sacrifices such as they demand of no-one else, and they do so so that all can do what they want. Here, my friend, there is no justice. Consequently, I must take the part of justice by myself. I am old, ill, tired, disillusioned, harassed, slandered and badly paid. I ask for nothing more in compensation than

---

1. *Cartas,* ix, p. 336.

repose and the conservation of my honor; unfortunately, this is what I am unable to obtain."[1]

He wrote to Urdaneta from Turbaco on October 2: "I have come here from Cartagena, rather ill with attacks of nerves, bile and rheumatism. The state of my nature is unbelievable. It is almost exhausted and I no longer expect to recover completely anywhere or in any way. Only a climate such as that of Ocaña can bring me some comfort, for the hot region kills me, and I am not well where it is cold...."[2] Fourteen days later he had to declare from Soledad: "...my nerves are suffering extraordinarily from this great heat, to such an extent that, although I can stir myself and walk around the house with much pain, I am unable to climb the stairs because of what I suffer.... All this, my dear General, makes it impossible for me to offer to return to the government or, rather, to fulfill my promise to the people to aid them with all my strength, for I have none to use and no hopes of regaining it."[3]

He had no doctors, but, at the same time, he did not want any and he refused to take any medicine. He proposed, in accordance with the ideas of the period and with his own character, to take exercise in order to fight the weakness that he felt, and he announced his intention of "sailing for a few days at sea to remove my bilious humors and clean my stomach by means of sea-sickness."

The damage that these desperate measures would cause to his worn-out body can be imagined. He observed on November 6: "My illness is getting worse, and I am so weak that this very day I suffered a dreadful fall; I fell down without knowing how, and I was half-dead."[4]

He found Soledad too damp, and went on to Barranquilla. A Granadan patriot in this city kept a diary for four days of what he saw Bolívar do and heard him say, and he noted one detail which seems to be a bitter allegory. When the Liberator received him, "he came down the stairs helped by Captain Iturbide, his aide-de-camp."[5] This Captain Iturbide was the son of Agustín I of Mexico; what sarcasm from fate! The Irish patriot O'Connell had sent his son to the Liberator "so that he can serve under your orders, admiring and imitating your example." Sir Robert Wilson, a veteran of all the European wars of his time, did the same; a nephew of Kosciusko and a son of Murat also shared this aspiration, and the former declared, on presenting himself to Bolívar: "I have crossed the circle of the globe, exalted by the glories of

1. *Cartas,* ix, p. 321.
2. *Ibid.,* p. 328.
3. *Ibid.,* p. 334.
4. *Cartas,* ix, p. 369.
5. José Vallarino Jiménez, *Diario de Barranquilla cuando estuve cerca del Libertador,* Boletín de la Academia Nacional de la Historia, Caracas, n° 104, p. 262.

the hero of the New World, in order to have the honor of serving you."[1] And yet, when he descended this staircase, which seemed symbolic, he had only the son of the failed emperor of Mexico to help him. Similarly, he had been admired by Byron, Lafayette, the family of Washington, and Bernadotte, and, as Unamuno tells us, "the revolutionaries of 1830 took Paris with the name of Bolívar on their lips, in patriotic songs." But at this time only the libels that his enemies spread were reaching Bolívar, and he exclaimed, already destroyed: "my affliction knows no bounds, for calumny is choking me, like the serpents of Laocoon."[2]

As he had planned, Bolívar went by sea to Santa Marta, arriving on the night of December 1. There he met a French doctor, Alejandro Próspero Reverend, who dedicated himself to caring for him, and, from the first day, kept a diary in which he noted the progress of the illness.[3] In the first entry he noted: "His Excellency reached this city of Santa Marta at half past seven in the evening, having come from Sabanilla in the national brigantine *Manuel*. He was brought ashore in a sedan chair, because of his inability to walk, and I found him to be in the following state: body very weak and emaciated; a look of affliction and constant mental restlessness; the voice hoarse, and a deep cough with viscous greenish sputum. The pulse even but slow. Digestion painful. The patient's countenance frequently suggested mortal suffering. Finally it seemed to me that His Excellency's illness was most serious, and my first opinion was that his lungs were damaged."

This diagnosis was confirmed the following day by Dr. N. Night, surgeon on the U.S. navy schooner *Grampus,* which happened to be in port. Both doctors agreed on the treatment to be given, but there was no improvement. On the 3rd Reverend noted: "He sleeps for only two or three hours at the beginning of the night, and, with brief interludes of delirium, he lies awake the rest of the time." He was suffering, in addition, from hiccups, nausea and chest pains.

However, on the 6th he moved to the country-house of San Pedro Alejandrino, on the outskirts of the city, and there was an extraordinary improvement. The note for this day reports: "He arrived quite happy with the journey, which he said had done him good, because they brought him in a landau." The house belonged to Joaquín de Mier, a Spaniard, who had already presented him with beer, wine and vegetables for his table when he was in Barranquilla, and who now provided him with noble hospitality in this refuge.

1. Arráiz, *op. cit.,* p. 214. For the son of Murat see *Cartas,* ix, p. 60, where he thanks "the nephew of the great Napoleon and the son of the world's first soldier" for this offer.
2. *Cartas,* ix, p. 246.
3. Blanco y Azpúrua, xiv, p. 464.

According to a tradition recorded by the historian Salgado Gómez, "*Señor Mier, who was traveling with the patient to his country house, stopped the coach at the entrance to his house in Santa Marta to say good-bye to his wife, Señora Rovira. As they came out, the lady said to him in French,*" "Wait a moment, and we will bring in the Liberator to converse with him." "Impossible," replied her husband, "Can't you see the state he is in? He cannot take a step." And the Liberator, sitting up in the coach with difficulty, interrupted in the purist French, "*Madame, I still have the strength to go to kiss your hands!*"[1]

The patient maintained his improvement on the 7th, and it was recorded in the diary: "His Excellency spent a good night and a contented day, greatly praising the change of climate." With his indomitable will, which did not capitulate even in this situation, Bolívar had continued his political correspondence, and he wrote at least two letters, which have survived, on the 7th. In one of them, which was quite long, he told Urdaneta: "Eight Venezuelan commanders have arrived here, among them Generals Infante, Silva and Portocarrero."[2]

The following day, however, he suffered a sudden, serious relapse. The hiccups, the insomnia and the delirium returned. Reverend noted: "The patient was hiding his sufferings, for when he was alone he groaned somewhat."

Surprisingly, there was no woman with the Liberator in his last days. Not even a servant is mentioned. But the comrades-in-arms who surrounded him included Generals José María Carreño, the glorious cripple who fought alongside him from 1813, José Laurencio Silva, the veteran of Carabobo, Junín and Ayacucho, and Mariano Montilla, who had again become his close friend. It was Montilla who assumed the sad responsibility of asking the doctor for a firm opinion about the Liberator's condition. Reverend tells us that, when Montilla heard that there was no hope of saving him, "he slapped himself hard on the forehead, causing a loud noise, and at the same time his eyes were overflowing with tears."

At Montilla's initiative, the Bishop, José María Esteves, came from Santa Marta, and informed the Liberator that he was in danger of dying. It was December 10. The following day Bolívar, aged but 47, received the sacraments and he signed his will, a farewell proclamation to the Colombians, and the last of his letters.

Had the Liberator returned to the religious beliefs of his youth? We have found only one indication that really seems to suggest convincingly that he had. In a letter to Montilla on November 13, he referred to his

---

1. Reproduced by Antonio Arráiz, *op. cit.,* p. 224.
2. *Cartas,* ix, p. 405.

health and to his plans to restore it, and he added in brackets: "if God wishes to grant us this favor."[1] Even the apparent insignificance of the remark makes it more meaningful and spontaneous. We have no hesitation in affirming that, since the far-off days in which he spoke of his prayers for the release of his uncle Esteban, he did not show this humility before the divine will in any other letter or family confidence.

In his will he ordered that his remains be laid to rest in the city of Caracas, and he left to its university two works from Napoleon's library, which General Wilson had presented to him: Rousseau's *Social Contract* and Montecuculi's *The Art of War.* In one of his last letters he had already left the people of Caracas the testimony of his pardon and his love. He declared, referring to the attacks made on him in his native city: "I will say, however, that I do not hate them, that I am very far from feeling the desire for revenge, and that my heart has already forgiven them, for they are my beloved compatriots and, above all, *caraqueños. . . ."*[2]

In another clause of his will, Bolívar ordered "that the papers in the keeping of Mr. Pavageau be burned." In his recollections Dr. Reverend made the following comment on this request: "Of the papers which the Liberator ordered to be burned by testamentary disposition, one, the only one which Mr. Pavageau kept for himself, was shown to me. It was an *acta* or representation of various subjects, whose signatures I remember very clearly and which would perhaps be recognized by contemporaries of the period if they were alive, in which they proposed to the Liberator that he be crowned. Bolívar rejected this proposal in these terms: 'To accept a crown would be to tarnish my glory; rather, I prefer the precious title of 'first citizen of Colombia.' I affirm, as a man of honor, that I saw these words stamped on this document, which was not published to comply with the orders of the Liberator, and also to avoid compromising the signatures of the authors of the proposal."[3]

From the 12th the Liberator's condition steadily worsened. He repeatedly became delirious, and during one of these attacks, imagining that he was with his soldiers, he ordered: "Let's go! Let's go! ...these people do not want us in this land... Come, boys! ...take my luggage on board the frigate."

On December 17, at midday, Reverend, who, as always, was at his side, realized that his last moments were drawing near. He tells us: "I sat at the head of the bed, holding the Liberator's hand in mine; he no longer

---

1. *Cartas,* ix, p. 384.
2. *Cartas,* ix, p. 264.
3. Blanco y Azpúrua, xiv, p. 479.

San Pedro Alejandrino Country House. Santa Marta, Colombia.

spoke, except in a confused way. His features displayed a perfect serenity, and his noble face showed no signs of pain or suffering. When I saw that his breathing had become stertorous, that his shaky pulse was almost imperceptible, and that death was imminent, I went to the door of the room and announced to the generals, aides and others who made up Bolívar's retinue: 'Gentlemen, if you wish to witness the last moments and the last breath of the Liberator, it is now time.' The bed of the illustrious patient was immediately surrounded, and a few minutes later Simón Bolívar breathed his last breath. . . ." Dr. Reverend, who cared for the Liberator with such solicitude, who at times personally carried him from his hammock to his bed, and who was unwilling to accept payment for these attentions, also took charge of the dressing of the corpse. He describes an episode which occurred then, and which has sometimes been distorted: "Among the different items of clothing that they brought, I found a shirt which I was about to put on him, when I noticed that it was torn. I was unable to contain my wrath and, pulling at the shirt, I exclaimed: 'Bolívar, even as a corpse, did not see torn clothing; if there is no other, I am going to send for one of mine'. It was then that they brought me a shirt belonging to General Laurencio Silva."

The Liberator's last letter, written on December 11, asked General Justo Briceño to reconcile himself with Urdaneta and help him to maintain the Colombian union. In his last proclamation he made the same appeal to all the Colombians, telling them:

"Colombians:

"You have witnessed my efforts to establish liberty where tyranny once reigned. I have labored unselfishly, sacrificing my fortune and my peace of mind. When I became convinced that you distrusted my motives, I resigned my command. My enemies have played upon your credulity and destroyed what I hold most sacred, my reputation and my love of liberty. I have been the victim of my persecutors, who have brought me to the brink of the grave. I forgive them.

"As I depart from your midst, my love for you tells me that I should make known my last wishes. I aspire to no other glory than the consolidation of Colombia. You must all work for the supreme good of the Union: the people, by obeying the present government in order to rid themselves of anarchy; the ministers, from their sanctuary, by addressing their supplications to heaven; and the military, by using the sword to defend the guarantees of organized society.

"Colombians! My last wishes are for the happiness of our native land. If my death will help to end party strife and to consolidate the Union, I shall go to my grave in peace.

"Hacienda de San Pedro, in Santa Marta, December 10, 1830. The 20th (year)."

"SIMON BOLIVAR"

He was not heeded, and even the name of Colombia was to disappear, for it was the middle of the century before New Granada adopted it for herself.

However, the essence of his work was saved: the freedom of America, which had to be the point of departure for the attainment of all the other benefits, as he explained to the Colombian Congress. The social reforms to which he aspired as the objective and justification of independence could not be secured by the will of a single man; they had to be entrusted to future generations. Since beginning to think about them as an adolescent at Simón Rodríguez's side, he had to admit that the thought that was a lesson for him in perseverance and moral courage must also be applied to the life of a nation: The road to perfection is built of advantageous modifications.

SUPPOSED LETTERS FROM BOLIVAR TO FANNY DU VILLARS
(Appendix to Chapter VIII)

FOR A LONG TIME IT WAS BELIEVED THAT THESE letters were absolutely reliable, and they caught the imagination of not a few writers. They explained the fact that they were addressed to somebody called Teresa, rather than Fanny, with the suggestion that Bolívar, either voluntarily or in a lyric rapture, was trying to personalize his lost wife in his Paris lover. Blanco Fombona tells us: "Bolívar takes away this woman's name and calls her by that of his dead wife." Ludwig invented the theory that "he called her Teresa to obtain forgiveness from the ghost of his dead wife." The error extends even to Madariaga, who preferred to imagine that Bolívar idealized Fanny "to the point of seeing her as reincarnation of his dead wife."

In our opinion, contrary to that of these writers, this "poetic" transposition of feelings would have been rather indelicate and disagreeable, for both the dead wife and the live lover. In any case, despite what was believed, thanks to a series of errors that would take too long to explain, there is now no doubt that these letters were not for Fanny. The Venezuelan historian Marcos Falcón Briceño has been able to establish that the true recipient was a French lady called Teresa Laisney, the wife of the Peruvian Colonel Mariano de Tristán. He also shows that nobody has seen the originals, and that the source for them was their publication in the Paris newspaper *Le Voleur* on July 31, 1838, by the socialist writer Flora Tristán, the daughter of Mariano and Teresa.[1]

---

1. Marcos Falcón Briceño, *Teresa, la confidente de Bolívar. Historia de unas cartas de juventud del Libertador* (Caracas, 1955).

We will give the text of both letters, as translated by Dr. Falcón Briceño (into Spanish) from the newspaper, the original of which he reproduces in facsimile. We will then analyze the errors that they contain, although the reader, too, will notice many of them as he goes along, in accordance with what is known with absolute certainty about Bolívar's youth.

We should point out first that opinions about the authenticity of these letters are divided as follows. Some writers, although only a few, consider them reliable. Others think that they were based upon fragments of letters actually written by Bolívar, but with alterations and interpolations which, naturally, cannot be isolated with accuracy. Some historians, such as Carlos Pereira, regard them as not only false but also ridiculous. We wish to reveal a fourth interpretation. Perhaps Bolívar did write the first of these letters and part of the second, but with the intention of beginning, with Teresa's collaboration, one of the novels in epistolary form that were then very fashionable, rather than, as has been supposed, narrating real events. We reach this conclusion because, although everything narrated in these letters is false and must have been incredible to both Bolívar and Teresa, they do contain the Christian name and the surname of Simón Rodríguez, evidence of Bolívar's affection for him, and other details which would be unlikely to appear in completely apocryphal letters. We should not be alarmed that the style sometimes descends to unappealing verbosity, when we bear in mind that as a youth Napoleon, too, tried to write fiction, and that in his *Memorias de Ultra-tumba* Chateaubriand described the future emperor's prose as declamatory. This tendency later grew worse and reached extravagant proportions; even Victor Hugo was greatly affected by it.

Our final point is that, although these were regarded as love letters when it was thought that they were for Fanny, there is not a single expression in them that permits us to see them in this light. We are even obliged to think that it would be very improper for a lover to confess to the object of his affections that he feels bored after spending three weeks in Paris, that the present is "a complete void" for him, and that as soon as he satisfies a desire it changes into an object of disgust. The first letter reads as follows:

"Dear Madam and friend:

"You are right. If you want to know anything about me you must write to me; in this way you will oblige me to reply to you, and this will be a pleasant task. I use the word task, because anything that obliges me to concentrate on the same theme, even if only for ten minutes, tires my head, and obliges me to lay down my pen or cut short the conversation to take air at the window.

Monument to the Liberator, Caracas. Drawing by Alejandro Sánchez Felipe.
"Simón Bolívar, Liberator of Venezuela, New Granada, Ecuador and Peru, and
Founder of Bolivia."

"You say you would give a lot to know who was able to transform the poor, young Bolívar of Bilbao, so modest, so studious, so thrifty, into the back-biting, lazy, prodigal Bolívar of the Rue Vivienne. Oh!, Teresa, imprudent woman, to whom, nevertheless, I can deny nothing, because she cried with me in my days of grief, why do you want to learn this secret? When you understand the enigma, you will no longer believe in virtue. . . .

"Ah: How awful it is not to believe in virtue. Who has transformed me? Alas! A single *word,* a magic word which the learned Rodríguez should never have uttered. Listen, if you want to know what it is.

"You remember how sad I was when I left you to join Rodríguez in Vienna. I expected much of the company of my friend, the companion of my childhood, the confidant of all my likes and sorrows, the mentor whose advice and consolation have always had such a hold over me. Alas! In these circumstances his friendship was sterile. Rodríguez has loved only the sciences. My tears moved him because he is sincerely fond of me, but he does not understand them. I found him busy in a laboratory belonging to a German gentleman, in which Rodríguez was to give a public demonstration of physics and chemistry. I saw him for barely an hour a day. When I met him, he promptly told me, 'My friend, enjoy yourself, meet young people your own age, go to see the show. In short, you must amuse yourself and this is the only way in which you can be cured.' I understood then that this man, the wisest, the most virtuous, the most extraordinary man one could meet, lacked something. I soon fell into such a serious consumptive state that the doctors declared that I was going to die. This was what he wanted. One night, when I was very ill, Rodríguez awakened me with my doctor; they were talking together in German. I did not undestand a word of what they were saying, but I knew from their tone and appearance that their conversation was very animated. The doctor left, after having given me a careful examination. I was fully conscious and, although very weak, still capable of carrying on a conversation. Rodríguez sat down near me. He spoke to me with this affectionate kindness that he always showed me in all the serious circumstances of my life; he told me gently that he wanted me to die and leave him half-way along the road. He made me understand that there existed in a man's life something else besides love, and that I could be very happy dedicating myself to science or giving myself up to ambition. You know the persuasive charm with which this man speaks; although he utters the most absurd sophisms, one thinks that he is right. He convinced me, as he always does, that he cares. When he saw I was a little better, he left me, but the following day he addressed similar exhortations to me. The following night, with my imagination exalted by all the fine, great things that I might do, whether for the sciences or the liberty of nations, I told him: 'Yes, without any doubt, I feel that I could take up the brilliant career that you present to me, but for this I would need to be rich: without the means of execution, nothing is achieved; and, far from being rich, I am poor and I am ill and dejected. Ah, Rodríguez, I prefer to die!' And I extended my hand to him to ask him to let me die in peace. There was a sudden change in Rodríguez's expression. For a moment, he hesitated, like a man who is uncertain of the decision he should make. Suddenly, raising his eyes and his hands to heaven, he exclaimed, in an inspired voice: 'He is saved!' He drew near me, took my hands, clasped them in his own trembling and sweaty ones and said to me, in a voice that I did not recognize: 'So, my friend, if you were rich, you would consent to live? Speak! Answer me, answer me!' I was undecided; I did not know what this meant; I replied: 'Yes.' 'Ah!' he exclaimed, 'gold is of some use, then? Well, Simón Bolívar, you are rich. At present you have *four million*....' I will not attempt to describe for you, my dear Teresa, the impression made on me by these words, at present you have four million! Despite the richness of our Spanish tongue, it is incapable, like all others, of explaining such emotions. Men experience them on few occasions: their words correspond to the ordinary sensations of this world; those that I felt were superhuman; I marvel that my being was able to stand them.

"I pause, the memory that I have just evoked is overwhelming me. Oh, how far are riches from providing the enjoyment for which they make us hope!... I am bathed in perspiration and more tired than after my long walks with Rodríguez. I am going to bathe. I will go to look for you after dinner to go to the Théatre *Français*. I impose on you the condition that you will ask me nothing about this letter, and I promise to continue it after the performance. - *Simón Bolívar*."

"Rodríguez had not lied to me: I really had four million. This capricious man, whose own affairs are in disorder, who owed money to everybody and paid nobody, and who is often reduced to being without bare essentials, this man has handled the fortune left to me by my father with both skill and integrity, and he has increased it by a third. He has spent only twenty-eight thousand francs on me during the eight years that I have been under his guardianship. Certainly, he has had to be very careful with it. To tell the truth, the way he made me travel was very economical. The only debts he has paid are those that I contracted with my tailors. As for my instruction, this did not involve any expense, since he was my teacher in all subjects.

"Rodríguez intended to instill in me intellectual passions, which would proudly overcome and enslave those of the senses. Frightened by the sway over me of my first love, and by the feelings of sorrow that led me to the gates of the tomb, he flattered himself that my former dedication to the sciences would develop, for I had the means to make discoveries, if I made celebrity the sole idea of my thoughts. Alas! The wise Rodríguez is deceiving himself; he was judging me by himself. I had just reached the age of twenty-one, and he was no longer able to hide my fortune from me, although he would have informed me of it gradually, and of this I am certain, if circumstances had not obliged him to do so at a stroke. I had not wanted riches; they presented themselves to me without my seeking them, and without being prepared to resist their seduction. I abandoned myself to them completely. We are the playthings of fortune; it is to this great deity, the only one that I recognize, that we must attribute our vices and our virtues. If she had not put an immense fortune in the path, the only object of my thoughts, the only object of my life would have been to achieve glory as a zealous servant of the sciences, an enthusiast for freedom. Pleasures have enslaved me only in a superficial way. The rapture was short-lived, for it came very close to loathing. You say that I am more inclined to pomp than to pleasures. I agree with this, because it seems to me that pomp has a false air of glory.

"Rodríguez did not approve of the use that I made of my fortune; it seemed to him that it was better to spend it on laboratory instruments and chemical experiments; this is why he does not stop condemning the disbursements that he calls follies or frivolities. Thenceforth, I venture to confess, thenceforth his reproaches bothered me, and I was obliged to leave Vienna to escape from them. I went to London, where I spent a hundred and fifty thousand francs in three months. I then went to Madrid, where I kept up the ostentation of a prince. I did the same in Lisbon. In short, I displayed the greatest luxury everywhere, and I squandered gold at the mere appearance of pleasures, but, in the midst of these pleasures, I remained indifferent.

"Bored with the great cities I have visited, I return to Paris with the hope of finding what I have not discovered anywhere, a *way of life that suits me*. But, Teresa, I am not a man like all the rest, and Paris is not the place that can bring an end to the restless uncertainty that torments me. I arrived here only three weeks ago and I am bored.

"See here, dear friend, all that I had to tell you about the past; the present does not exist for me, it is a complete void, in which I am unable to form a single desire that leaves any impression on my memory. It will be the desert of my life. As soon as I have a slight caprice, I satisfy it instantly, and what I believe to be a desire is only an object of disgust when I possess it. Will my life perhaps be re-animated by the continuous changes that are the fruit of chance? I do not know; but if this does happen, I will again sink into the consumptive state from which Rodríguez had rescued me when he informed me of my four million. However, do not think that my head is bursting with vain conjectures about the future.

Only madmen occupy themselves with these chimerical combinations. We can submit to calculation only the things whose data is known to us; then, as in mathematics, the decision can be reached in an exact way.

"What will you think of me? Reply with frankness. It will not reform me. I think that there are few men who are corrigible, but, since it is always useful to know oneself and to know what can be expected of oneself, I will consider myself happy when chance presents me with a friend who can serve me as a mirror.

"Goodbye, I will go to dine with you tomorrow. - *Simón Bolívar.*"

As we see immediately, the whole letter centers around two incorrect facts: that Simón Rodríguez was Bolívar's guardian, and that the ward was ignorant of his fortune until Rodríguez, seeing him on the point of dying, revealed it to him in this novelistic fashion. Therefore, there is not a single line of historical information that escapes from this fundamental falsity, which makes the whole narrative void. Rodríguez was not Bolívar's guardian; he was not allowed to be, because this duty was always entrusted to close relatives who replaced the parents in caring for the minor and conserving his property. And, as far as his fortune is concerned, Bolívar was aware of it from when he was solemnly taken, as a very young child, by judicial officials, to take material possession of the *mayorazgo* that he had inherited. Moreover, we know that this picture of desperate profligacy which the letter paints, and which is one of the things which has most excited some writers, is false. On the contrary, Bolívar had founded agricultural establishments in Venezuela and, as the correspondence from Cádiz to his agent, which we quoted, makes clear, he asked for very detailed information about them.

Even as a literary fantasy —in accordance with our suggested interpretation— the fiction that Bolívar was ignorant of his fortune introduces in the letter contradictions that can hardly be excused, even on the grounds that the author was a very young, unskilled writer. If he was unaware of his fortune, how had he been able to marry and how had he been able to travel to Vienna? How could Rodríguez advise him, before he had disclosed his riches to him, to meet with young people of his own age and to go to shows?

We have already pointed out in the text that it is an untenable fantasy to attribute to Bolívar a life of extravagant spending; and there are other unlikely details that Teresa herself would not have failed to notice. If the author believed in nothing and wanted to think of nothing, how is it that he considers himself "a zealous servant of the sciences, an enthusiast for freedom"? And how is it possible that the mere discovery of his fortune would have destroyed this zeal and enthusiasm? Had he not said a few paragraphs earlier that it was his poverty that prevented him from taking up the brilliant careers suggested to him by Rodríguez?

Our theory that Bolívar was simply attempting to produce a novelistic fiction, and that it would be unreasonable to demand of him at this first attempt the skill and the care of an experienced writer, allows us to excuse these incongruencies. On the other hand, the interruption of the letter in the middle, on the pretext of showing it to Teresa at the theatre, so that she could then return it and allow him to finish it, strongly inclines us to suppose that the supposed correspondence formed part of a fiction agreed between them.

There is another detail, which has escaped the critics, which conflicts with our interpretation. In the fourth paragraph of the letter, where Rodríguez is mentioned twice, the original French version says "*don* Rodríguez", and not simply Rodríguez, as in Falcón Briceño's translation, or *señor* Rodríguez, as in other translations.[1] In both Spain and Venezuela "*don*" is used with the Christian name, not the surname; Bolívar, therefore, could not have written *don* Rodríguez, and we must deduce from this that the letter was falsified by somebody who was ignorant of the correct usage of "*don*" in Spanish. The other possibilities are that Bolívar wrote "*Don* Rodríguez" in an attempt to imitate French fashion, or that, although he wrote "Rodríguez or *"Señor Rodríguez,"* Flora translated it as *"Don* Rodríguez."

The second letter, which lacks the color of the first is even further removed from reality. It reads as follows:

"Dear Madam and friend:

"I have not written to you since leaving Paris. Ah!, what could I have told you? I have nothing to report that might interest you. Always the same way of life, always the same weariness! I am going to seek another form of existence; I am tired of Europe and its old societies. I am returning to America: what shall I do there? I do not know. You know that with me everything is spontaneous, that I never make plans. The life of the savage is enchanting for me, and I will probably build a hut in the middle of the beautiful forests of Venezuela. There I will be able to pull the branches from the trees when I want, without fear of being grumbled at, as happened with you when I had the misfortune to pick some leaves from your orange trees. Ah!, Teresa, happy are those who believe in a better world, for this one is very barren.

"It would have been very nice for me to embrace the Colonel before leaving. I am not writing to him. Ha!, what could I tell him that he does

---

1. "Vous vous rapellez l'état de tristesse dans lequel j'étais tombé lorsque je vous quittai pour aller rejoindre don Rodríguez a Vienne... Don Rodríguez n'a jamais éprouvé d'amour que pour les sciences", etc. From the facsimile reproduction included by Falcón Briceño in the work already cited.

The Tenerani Monument and the cinerary urn, work of the sculptor Chicharro Gamo, in the National Pantheon. Caracas, Venezuela.

not know already? He would treat me as a madman if I told him that life is sad, he who does not have enough time to admire the clouds above his head, the leaves stirring in the breeze, the rain falling in the brook, and the plants that grow on its banks! Happy mortal. He has no need to enliven his life by taking part in the dramas of men. For him nature is full of movement and variety. As for me, nature seems as monotonous as the man who torments her. I am going to return to see other men, another nature. The memories of my childhood will lend it an enchantment that will vanish when I have seen them again; but the great emperor has just invaded Spain and I want to be a witness of the welcome that this event will receive in America. Tell Mariano that I will always love him, and that I will make the long journey from Caracas to Peru, even if only to give news of him to his family; tell him that I will embrace his brother, *Don* Pío, with as much affection as be could do it himself. Going by all that he has told us, this *Don* Pío must be a very friendly man.

"Good-bye *(Adiós),* dear Teresa, or, rather, to nothing... for, as you know, I do not have the happiness of believing in life in the other world. - *Simón Bolívar.*"

It could occur only to a person absolutely ignorant of want America was that a creole would return there to lead "the life of the savage."

Humboldt saw something very different, even outside Caracas, and Bolívar knew him very well. He wrote: "Almost all the families whose friendship we had cultivated in Caracas, the Ustárizes, the Tovars, the Toros, were gathered together in the beautiful Aragua valleys. As owners of the richest plantations, they competed amongst themselves to make our stay agreeable. Before probing into the jungles of the Orinoco, we enjoyed once again all the advantages of an advanced civilization."[1]

It was even more extravagant for Bolívar to promise another Spanish American —who was familiar with the geography of the New World— that he would go from Venezuela to Peru to take news of Mariano to his family. We can state, without any exaggeration, that, before the Liberator's fabulous campaigns destroyed the image that everybody had of the enormous distances between these countries and of the natural barriers that separated them, nobody ever thought of going by land from Caracas to Lima. Perhaps nobody has done it since the Independence, even in a car!

The inconsistencies in the details of this letter are no less irritating; in the barriers that separated them, nobody ever thought of going by land second that nature seems as monotonous as the man, etc., etc.

Finally, the most serious inconsistency: according to the brief historical narrative which Flora Tristán published with these letters, Bolívar sent

---

1   Humboldt, *Viaje...,* iii, p. 75.

the second to Teresa from Cádiz in 1807. It is known, however, that Bolívar left Europe at the end of 1806, and from Hamburg, not Cádiz. Moreover, the letter says that Napoleon had just invaded Spain, but this was something that occurred only when Bolívar was back in Venezuela.

Thus, even if one accepts the interpretation that I suggest, at least this part —or all the second letter— should be regarded as having been invented many years after the events to which it refers. The other anachronisms and contradictions lose their importance if we regard the letters as part of a novelistic invention; that they are undated, for example, can be explained by this theory. But there is no explanation that accounts for Bolívar referring in Europe to an event that had still not occurred. I repeat that I have been led to suggest this hypothesis only by the references in the first letter to Simón Rodríguez and the bonds of affection between him and Bolívar, and the use of his surname, for we cannot imagine that Flora Tristán obtained this information from a third person. But for this peculiarity, we would regard both letters as completely apocryphal.

If we move from the analysis of the letters to that of the historical account that Flora Tristán published with them, we could go on forever pointing out absurdities. She introduced Rodríguez as a young foreigner who lived in Caracas at the end of the eighteenth century, and described him and Bolívar's father as "two scholars." The supposed guardianship of Simón over the son of his friend was a product of their close intimacy. Referring later to the relationship in Paris between the Tristáns and Bolívar, she says that they did not see him for two years, from when he was twenty-one until he was twenty-three, and that they found, when they met again, that he had grown four inches, and that he was displaying side whiskers and a beautiful black moustache; previously, she said, he had been a beardless youth. Naturally, these physiological anomalies simply stimulated Flora to invent others, and she added: "The moral transformation was no less complete; she was not to see again the silent, modest melancholy man, who used to occupy himself with nothing but science and manual work."

Likewise, Flora Tristán included in her publication another letter, sent to her father, and attributed to Bolívar, in which he told Colonel Tristán, "I have loved you for six years with the most genuine friendship, and I profess the most profound respect for the nobility of your character and the sincerity of your opinions." This seems to indicate, at least according to Flora Tristán, that Bolívar's letters to Teresa should not be considered love letters and evidence of a comfortable *"ménage à trois,"* as some historians have claimed. And if we abandon the idea that they were sent to Fanny du Villars, there is nothing in them to suggest that they were love letters.

But this letter which is attributed to Bolívar also introduces another inexplicable anachronism to the affair. If this friendship had already lasted six years, the letter must have been written in 1805 or a later year, since he made his first voyage to Europe in 1799. In it, however, Bolívar referred to Napoleon as First Consul, he had been emperor since 1804, and he tried to persuade Colonel Tristán that liberty could not survive in France, when, in fact, this had been indisputable for some years.

The cock-and-bull stories introduced to history by these inventions of Flora Tristán, by those that Fanny thought up, and by those that a number of Spanish Americans hurriedly gathered together in Paris shortly after the Liberator's death —when, as a result of the 1830 revolution, his remembrance was more fashionable— are so numerous, that here we stumble against another tangle. According to this last letter that we are discussing, a violent scene was created in Bolívar's own house in Paris— during a reception that he arranged, and to which high officials in the French government came as guests— as a result of charges made against the "First Consul" by the host himself. Flora tells us that thereafter Bolívar was classified as a *Jacobin,* and all French society shunned him. Bolívar reached Paris in May 1804, and Napoleon was proclaimed Emperor on the 18th of that month. The Venezuelan had not had time, therefore, to begin entertaining and uttering invectives about the "First Consul." According to O'Leary, whose informant was Fanny, it was in her house that Bolívar engaged in these quarrels; thus, Fanny and Teresa Laisney again become involved in another plot of extravagances and anachronisms.

As we have pointed out, a whole volume could be written about these fabulous stories without exhausting criticisms that can be made of them. Although we imagine that the reader already has sufficient material to form his own judgement on such historical sources, we must still mention another invention of Flora Tristán, which some historians have incorporated into their judgements on the Liberator, even basing on it theories about the nature of his genius generally. According to the supposed recollections of the Tristáns, Bolívar, when he visited them, "was unable to avoid breaking everything within his reach: branches of trees, shoots in the vineyard, flowers, fruit, etc. . . . The house, too, was not safe from his destructive mania; he tore the fringes from the curtains, wrenched the binding from books that were on the table with his teeth, and upset the hearth with the tongs; in a word, he could not stay for ten minutes without breaking or destroying something." The bias resulting from seeing Bolívar from his youth as the future Liberator is clearly seen in these inventions, for it is easy to believe that, when a man has acquired universal fame, he is celebrated for these excesses. But if in this period Bolívar was to Colonel Tristán only "the poor little Bolívar"—ac-

The Pantheon of Heroes, by Arturo Michelena.

cording to Flora this is what her father used to call him—it is not clear why such misbehavior was tolerated by him.

Flora gives details of even more compromising excesses. She tells us: "Round the corner from the Rue Richelieu my mother was almost run over by the spirited horses of a magnificent coach, which turned the corner at full speed. She pressed herself against the wall to save herself, but what a surprise she had when she saw the coach suddenly come to a halt, and the individual who was traveling in it, quickly opened the door, threw himself towards my mother and took her in his arms, squeezing her as though he wanted to asphyxiate her! 'It is I, it is I. Do you not recognize me, then? Ah!, so much the better; this proves to me that I am changed!' And this man, or, rather, this madman, carried my mother to the coach, made my father get in, and gave orders to return to the hotel. 'Well, Colonel, here is your poor little Bolívar. He has grown at last, his beard has appeared, and he looks better, don't you think?' "

Apart from this preoccupation of Bolívar with his beard, when he was already more than twenty, had married and been widowed, and was maintaining such a way of life in Paris, it is also quite ridiculous to suggest that Colonel Tristán would allow himself or his wife to be treated like this. Nor can we imagine how Flora could reconcile this behavior with the "profound respect" that, according to her, Bolívar showed for her father. Moreover, according to her narrative, this was the first meeting of Bolívar with the Tristáns in 1804. Previously he had dealt with them only in Bilbao, during his first voyage. Can it be accepted that such a casual friendship would drive him, and give him the right, to such displays?

It is said that on one occasion it was decided to clean the rain-tree of Güere, in Venezuela, of the parasites that covered it, and it was found that this foreign vegetation piling up on the giant of the Aragua fields weighed more than 5,000 pounds. Something similar occurs when we try to clear away from Bolívar the inventions that we find adhering to his history at every step. And if the reader complains about having to bear part of this useless weight, we will say that he is right to do so, but that it is inevitable. Many of these falsehoods have been copied without scrutiny by well-read historians; others have exaggerated them out of poor taste, and some have even used them as data for their interpretations of the hero.

* * *

Since the above was written, we have received from Paris, as a gift from the distinguished writer G.F. Pardo de Leygonier, a book entitled *Flora Tristan. —Morceaux choisis précedés de La Geste Romantique de Flora*

Tristan— contée par Lucien Scheler pour le centenaire de 1848. —La Bibliothèque Française. Paris, 1947." We see in this volume that Flora went to Arequipa, Peru shortly after 1830, that is, when Simón Rodríguez was still in this city or had just left it. It is very possible, then, that while she was there Flora obtained the information about the relation between Bolívar and Rodríguez, which, in an adulterated form, figure in these letters; and this further inclines us to regard them as apocryphal. A further point is that Flora exalts the fantasy of the commentator to such an extent that he has no hesitation in presenting Mariano Tristán as a descendant of... Montezuma. Such a leap, from Peru to Mexico, shows that Flora would also believe to be possible the journey from Caracas to Peru, which, according to one of these letters, Bolívar told Mariano he would undertake in order to greet his family.